Guide Library

Hillwood Museum
Washington, D.C.

MERCHANTS AND

ENTREPRENEURS IN

IMPERIAL RUSSIA

MERCHANTS AND

ENTREPRENEURS IN

IMPERIAL RUSSIA

ALFRED J. RIEBER

UNIVERSITY OF NORTH CAROLINA PRESS

CHAPEL HILL

© 1982 The University of North Carolina Press

All rights reserved

Manufactured in the United States of America

Library of Congress Cataloging in Publication Data

Rieber, Alfred J
  Merchants and entrepreneurs in Imperial Russia.

  Bibliography: p.
  Includes index.
  1. Merchants—Russia—History. 2. Capitalists and
financiers—Russia—History. 3. Russia—Social conditions. I. Title.
HF3624.R53 338'.04'0947 80-28554
ISBN 0-8078-1481-4 AACR1
ISBN 0-8078-4305-9 (pbk.)
95 94 93 92 91 6 5 4 3 2

TO EDI

AND TO THE MEMORY OF

VIKTOR STOLIN (1935–1971)

CONTENTS

TABLES AND FIGURES

ILLUSTRATIONS

ABBREVIATIONS

BE   F. A. Brokgauz and I. A. Efron, eds. *Entsiklopedicheskii slovar'* [Encyclopedic dictionary].

EPR   *Ekonomicheskoe polozhenie Rossii nakanune velikoi oktiabr'skoi sotsialisticheskoi revoliutsii: Dokumenty i materialy* [The economic situation of Russia on the eve of the Great October Socialist Revolution: Documents and materials].

FBON   Fundamental'naia biblioteka obshchestvennykh nauk [The Main Library of the Social Sciences].

IMV–PK   *Izvestiia Moskovskogo voenno-promyshlennogo komiteta* [The proceedings of the Moscow War Industries Committee].

IZ   *Istoricheskie zapiski* [Historical notes].

ORBL   Otdel rukopisei biblioteka im. Lenina [Manuscript Division, Lenin Library, Moscow].

PSZRI   *Polnoe sobranie zakonov Rossiiskoi imperii* [The complete collection of the laws of the Russian Empire].

PT   *Promyshlennost' i torgovlia* [Trade and industry].

PVP   *Pervaia vseobshchaia perepis'* [The first general census].

PVT–PS   *Pervyi vserossiiskii torgovo-promyshlennyi s'ezd v Moskve* [The First All-Russian Trade and Industry Congress in Moscow].

PSKZh   Postoiatel'naia soveshchatel'naia kontora zheleznozavodchikov [Permanent Advisory Office of the Metallurgical Industry].

RA   *Russkii arkhiv* [Russian archive].

RBS	*Russkii biograficheskii slovar'* [Russian biographical dictionary].
REO	*Russkoe ekonomicheskoe obozrenie* [The Russia economic review].
RS	*Russkaia starina* [Russian antiquities].
RV	Russkii vestnik [The Russian messenger].
SGIR	S'ezd gornopromyshlennikov iuga Rossii [Congress of the Southern Coal and Steel Producers of Russia].
SIRIO	*Sbornik imperatorskogo russkogo istoricheskogo obshchestva* [Collection of the Imperial Russian Historical Society].
SZRI	*Svod zakonov rossiiskoi imperii* [Collected laws of the Russian Empire].
TIVEO	*Trudy imperatorskogo volnogo eknomicheskogo Obshchestva* [Proceedings of the Imperial Free Economic Society].
TOSRPT	*Trudy Obshchestva dlia sodeistviia russkoi promyshlennosti i torgovli* [Proceedings of the Society for the Encouragement of Russian Industry and Trade].
TsGAOR	Tsentral'nyi gosudarstvennyi arkhiv oktiabr'skoi revoliutsii [Central State Archive of the October Revolution, Moscow].
TsGIA	Tsentral'nyi gosudarstvennyi istoricheskii arkhiv [Central State Historical Archive, Leningrad].
VP	*Vestnik promyshlennosti* [Messenger of industry].
ZHOS	*Zhurnal osobogo soveshchaniia dlia obsuzhdeniia i ob'edineniia meropriatii po oborone gosudarstva* [The minutes of the Special Council for the Discussion and Coordination of Measures for the Defense of the State].
ZIRTO	*Zapiski imperatorskogo russkogo tekhnologicheskogo Obshchestva* [Transactions of the Imperial Russian Technological Society].
ZOSRPT	*Zhurnal godogo obshchego sobraniia Obshchestva dlia sodeistviia russkoi promyshlennosti i torgovli* [Journal of the Annual General Session of the Society for the Encouragement of Russian Industry and Trade.].

Citations to Soviet Archival Collections

The most commonly used form of archival citation in this book
is as follows: The name of the archive or its abbreviation, "f." (*fond*,
collection), "op." (*opis*, inventory), "d." (*delo*, item), and "pp." (for *list*,
sheet numbered on one side only). In the ORBL the form is somewhat
different; "fond" is followed by "carton" (box) and "no." (number
of item).

ACKNOWLEDGMENTS

        This book began modestly enough as several chapters in a planned study "Politics and Industrialization in Imperial Russia." In the course of writing I discovered that a preliminary full-length work dealing with the character and evolution of Russian merchants and industrialists was necessary before I could proceed with the original plan. Thus, my intellectual and personal debts extend back well before this present book was conceived. My research has been generously supported by the International Research and Exchanges Board, which made possible three visits to the Soviet Union in 1966, 1970, and 1973 under the auspices of the American Council of Learned Societies and the Academy of Sciences of the USSR. A senior fellowship from the National Endowment for the Humanities enabled me to devote an entire year to writing. The University of Pennsylvania supplemented these grants whenever necessary and permitted me to take several scholarly leaves in order to carry on the research and complete the writing.

    For allowing me access to archival sources I am grateful to the Central State Archival Administration in Moscow and particularly to its director, M. Ia. Kapran. The staffs of the individual Soviet archives were helpful in locating scattered materials. My special thanks are due to the director and staff of the Manuscript Division of the Lenin Library for their unfailing kindnesses and scholarly assistance. Among the many other libraries that furnished me with valuable materials and bibliographical help I should like to mention the Slavic Library of Helsinki University, Bibliothèque nationale, Bibliothèque de l'institut d'études slaves, Bibliothèque slave, Leningrad Public Library (Saltykov-Shchedrin), Fundamental'naia biblioteka obshchestvennykh nauk (Moscow), New York Public Library, Library of Congress, University of Illinois Library at Champaign-Urbana, Columbia

University Libraries, and the Van Pelt Library of the University of Pennsylvania.

Among many colleagues in Moscow and Leningrad who assisted me in a variety of ways, I wish to thank personally, V. I. Bovykin, E. A. Dudzinskaia, A. A. Fursenko, P. G. Ryndziunskii, K. F. Shatsillo, P. A. Zaionchkovskii, and I. L. Znachko-Iavorskii.

At various stages the manuscript in part or as a whole was read by William Blackwell, Muriel Joffe, Walter Pintner, Alexander V. Riasanovsky, S. Frederick Starr, Alexander Yanov, and Michael Zuckerman, and I benefited from their criticism and encouragement. My special thanks are due to Leopold Haimson, Moshe Lewin, and Marc Raeff for their thorough and penetrating readings which helped me greatly to improve the manuscript in its final stage. My research assistants, Muriel Joffe and Nancy Pollack, worked thoughtfully and energetically on my behalf. The editors of the *Jahrbücher für Geschichte Osteuropas* kindly gave their permission to republish in expanded form a two-part article, "The Moscow Entrepreneurial Group: The Emergence of a New Form in Autocratic Politics," *Jahrbücher für Geschichte Osteuropas* 25 (1977), no. 1, pp. 1–20, and no. 2, pp. 174–99, as chapters 4 and 5.

I am also grateful to Lewis Bateman, executive editor of the University of North Carolina Press, for his interest in this work and to David Perry, editor, for his careful editorial assistance.

The dedication of this book expresses in an altogether inadequate way my happiest and my saddest appreciations. To my wife, Edith Finton Rieber, who has shared both the joys and the frustrations of our Russian adventures, kept my perspective broad and tolerant, and opened the rich world of Russian musical life to me, I remain eternally grateful. And to my great friend Viktor Stolin, who represented for us the best in that life, this is a final tribute.

INTRODUCTION

The social history of Imperial Russia is still largely terra incognita. In its present state it resembles an aerial photograph in which individual features of the landscape are blurred and compressed into deceptively large and uniform blocs representing socioeconomic classes. Even the most reliable surveys of that terrain consider only those groups at the ends of the social scale—the nobility and the peasantry—and leave the remainder largely undefined. Because historians attribute enormous importance to the middle classes as the makers of modern European history, they recognize this omission as a serious obstacle to an understanding of a number of crucial issues in Russian history, ranging from industrialization to the collapse of the empire. Yet, ironically, the very manner of stating the problem has contributed to its neglect. To ask, as historians have, whether a bourgeoisie was absent or present in Russian history is to limit severely the dimensions of social inquiry. For whatever the answer, the result has been to ignore alternative forms of social evolution within capitalist economic systems. To put it another way, a preoccupation with general models of social change derived from West European experience and fed by domestic political conflicts in late-Imperial Russia has long obscured the real dimensions of Russia's social structure.

This book suggests a different approach. It seeks to avoid the dangers of what Robert Nisbet calls the "metaphor of development," which portrays social change as though it were a linear movement in a single direction.[1] Instead it accepts the existence of a variety of social identities and groupings as a legitimate subject for historical inquiry without assuming a necessary or uniform pattern of internal change or response to external stimuli. In other words this study deals with the history of intermediate social structures that exist in the theoreti-

1. Nisbet, *Social Change*.

cal space between caste and class. Specific meanings of the terms *caste* and *class* vary in different cultural contexts. But in the most general sense used here they represent the two most extreme forms of social organization: one closed, rigid, hereditary; the other open, mobile, and socioeconomic in character. As this book will argue, the Russian merchantry neither evolved along a series of clearly marked stages from caste to class, passing through such intermediate forms as estates, nor failed to evolve at all, remaining immured in its primordial caste. Rather, it acquired over the course of several centuries features of different forms of social organization and oscillated between the various forms. Yet throughout this process of change the merchants managed to retain some of their traditional values and patterns of behavior. Consequently, there are very great difficulties in providing satisfactory definitions of what they were at any one time, let alone throughout the entire, irregular course of their history. The problem of this study, therefore, is to avoid confusion without eliminating complexity.

One approach would sketch in the broad outlines of social change that defined the place of the merchantry in Russian society. Two distinct but connected processes were involved. The first was the activity of the state in defining and ordering social organization in Russia. The second was the reaction of the merchantry, which often confounded the expectations of government. Like other large, well-defined social groups in Russia, the merchantry possessed an inner life of its own not easily penetrated by even the most zealous bureaucrats. The dynamic interplay between the two processes breaks through the narrative from time to time. But a summary of the main points here may help to resolve at the outset the recurrent problem of definition and terminology.

Throughout most of the imperial period Russia bore a close resemblance to a classical hierarchical society. That is to say, from the mid-seventeenth to the second half of the nineteenth century the stratification of Russian society was largely determined by reference to a single principle—that of state service.[2] Even as the legal foundations of this principle were eroded first by the nobility in the eighteenth and then for the rest of society in the nineteenth century, the institutional and psychological residue of the system retained considerable social force. The foundations of the hierarchical society were laid down in Muscovite Russia, where after a half century of social turmoil and war the state, supported by strong elements of its military servitors, imposed a highly rigid social system. In the Collection of Laws (*Ulozhenie*) of 1649 the state administration partitioned society into

2. Cf. Dumont, *Homo hierarchicus*, p. 92.

three closed, hereditary categories—service, urban (including mer-chants), and peasants—and assigned each specific duties and obli-gations. The apparent simplicity and uniformity of the system was deceptive. In fact, each category contained a great variety of social groups complete with their own legal distinctions, economic advan-tages, and ranks. Whole groups of ranks together with the privileges attached to them were made hereditary in the service category and among the merchantry. Moreover, movement between the three large social categories was virtually impossible, and upward mobility even within the ranks of the service category and merchantry was limited. It seems appropriate, then, to regard this rigidly stratified society as "castelike," even though it lacked an explicit religious sanction and was not, strictly speaking, endogamous.[3]

Over the following two centuries the external structure of this hier-archical society remained largely intact, although several important internal changes took place. Peter completed the shift, already well underway in the seventeenth century, from birth to service as the principle upon which the system operated. He also sought to spread the fiscal and military burden more evenly among all elements of the population. The object of making service general and uniform was to create a new political idea—the state—which could fuse the discrete, fragmented social units of Muscovy into a unified mass of subjects organized around service classes.

Peter's reforms suffered in the long run from the same short-comings that hampered all subsequent attempts to impose an official social organization on the merchantry. On the one hand the merchant was not guaranteed hereditary status or a monopoly over commerce and industry. On the other hand, he was not freed from the obliga-tions and restrictions that weakened his competitive position in the marketplace. As a result the merchantry was more vulnerable to loss of status and wealth than any other service class. It quickly became the most unstable social group in the empire. The fluctuations in its numbers and the loss of its potential leaders to the nobility deprived it of the social cohesion and political consciousness necessary for its further development into a full-fledged estate.

A second important set of institutional changes occurred under Catherine II, who strengthened the corporate, self-administrative or-

3. In using the word *caste* I have been guided by the more flexible definitions provided by Alfred Kroeber in "Caste," *Encyclopedia of Social Science*, 3:254–56, and applied by Mörner, *Race Mixture*, pp. 53–54. Dumont is more categorical (*Homo hierarchicus*, p. 269). In the Russian setting most recently Richard Hellie has gone so far as to use the expression *closed caste* to define the social structure of mid-seventeenth-century Mus-covy (*Enserfment*, pp. 240, 375). See also Smirnov, *Posadskie*, 1:256–57, 399–400, 447.

gans of the nobility and the merchantry. By confirming the emancipation of the nobility from service and seeking to loosen the bonds of the merchantry, she intended to create citizens out of subjects whose participation in public life would be inspired by enlightened self-interest instead of duties and obligations. The urban charter of 1775 and the charter of the nobility in 1785 crowned this system. Historians of the late nineteenth century describe this process as the formation of an estate (*soslovie*) system in Russia.[4]

With respect to the merchantry at least there are several difficulties with this definition which repeat those encountered in defining the emergence of a bourgeois class in Russia in the twentieth century. In the first place, eighteenth-century sources refer to the merchantry as *zvanie* (a calling or occupation) but not as soslovie. Second, and more important, it is doubtful whether an estate system identical to that of Western Europe ever existed in Russia. Even after Catherine's charters the nobility and the merchantry lacked the autonomous, self-governing, representative institutions and the juridical rights that enabled them to govern jointly with the ruler as the estates did in Western and Central Europe during much of the early-modern period. One major problem in Russia was that absolutism preceded the granting of corporate privileges to the nobility and merchantry. Another was that throughout the eighteenth century the parallel growth of bureaucratic absolutism checked and in some cases reversed the trend toward granting merchants greater control over their internal affairs. Whenever it came to a test of strength, the merchantry proved incapable of defending itself as a corporate group against the bureaucracy's arbitrary encroachments on its privileges and membership. In other words the merchantry had acquired some of the external forms of a West European estate without shedding all the attributes of a service class in a hierarchical society. Nevertheless, in the absence of any other generally recognized term, the word *soslovie* may be used to describe the social situation of the merchantry after 1785, as long as it is taken to connote an intermediate social form possessing a legal identity and collective privileges but no inviolate corporate rights. In other words soslovie as "estate" has a very special meaning within the Russian setting.

Rather than answer the needs of the people, this hybrid system of autocracy resting upon sosloviia served the purposes of the state. As long as it remained flexible, the rulers had no compelling reason to replace it. Throughout the late eighteenth century and the first half

4. For example, Kliuchevskii, *Istoriia soslovii*, especially pp. 200–225; Kizevetter, *Posadskaia obshchina*; Ditiatin, *Ustroistvo*; and Korf, *Dvorianstvo*.

of the nineteenth century the system proved resilient. Under the powerful pressures of an expanding economy, foreign wars, and external cultural influences, it bent but did not break. Until the disaster of the Crimean War the autocrats remained convinced that it was the most effective and expedient means of mobilizing the enormous fiscal and human resources necessary to convert a huge, poor, agrarian country into a great European power.

Yet for the merchantry this was a period of sharp decline in its guild membership and wealth and of transformation in its social composition. The constant fear of loss of security and status reinforced the merchant's conservative social attitudes and cautious economic activity. His inner life centered on the patriarchal family, the family firm, and the guilds. Great Russian merchants felt steadily more threatened by vigorous competitors among ethnic and foreign merchants along the periphery. At the same time, there was a massive influx of emancipated trading peasants into the guilds. The revival of economic activity that they brought with them was balanced by the servile and xenophobic mentality of the newcomers. With the partial, if notable, exception of the Old Believer merchants, the new guild members wholeheartedly embraced the traditional values of the merchant soslovie.

The great reforms and the expansion of capitalism in the second half of the nineteenth century broke down many of the administrative and legal barriers separating the merchantry from the rest of society. Yet in the Collection of Laws of 1892, published shortly after the "all-class principle" was introduced into the institutions of public life, the government restored the division of the population into four sosloviia: nobility, clergy, townspeople, and rural inhabitants. The legal definition of the term remained obscure, particularly as it was applied to the townspeople, who were subdivided into four status groups (*sostoianie*): honored citizen, merchant, lower middle class (*meshchane*), and artisan (*tsekhovyi*). Membership in the merchant guilds was now open to anyone who paid a guild tax. In the eyes of the legal scholars the merchantry had ceased to be a soslovie. Yet merchants continued to employ the term to identify themselves as a social group. They also retained their internal soslovie organization. As if to add to the confusion the government practically ignored the definition of townspeople as a soslovie for fiscal and administrative purposes. It preferred to use the subdivisions into sostoianiia as the basis for taxation, census taking, and separate curia for local government elections. In this system the merchantry continued to enjoy certain privileges and status under law. In other words, the government continued to treat the merchantry as a distinctive legally defined social group—as soslovie—even though it was no longer hereditary and had lost all of its service obligations.

However indistinct the modified soslovie system appeared, it exercised a powerful influence on social life in Russia up to the revolution of March 1917, especially among the merchantry, the nobility, and the peasantry.[5] Over the centuries there had been an accumulation of laws and custom based upon the same hierarchy of social strata that was sanctioned anew by the Collection of Laws in 1892. Remaining in force, this legislation reenforced the shadowy legal existence of the soslovie at the turn of the twentieth century. More important perhaps, many traditional social distinctions rooted in the sosloviia lived on in the daily activities and outlook of a very large part of the population.

Because sosloviia continued to provide a strong sense of social identity, they cast a long shadow over the emergence of a middle class in Russia. To be sure, the term *class*, like *caste* and *estate*, is only an approximation of social reality. Middle class here refers to the owners of the main means of production, the creators of the dominant social values and aspirations, and the leaders in the drive for control of political power—the triad of the classical bourgeoisie in nineteenth-century Europe.[6] In Russia the autocrats and most of the bureaucracy feared and opposed the development of precisely this kind of dynamic, cohesive, and politically conscious social organization. For them the modified form of the soslovie system in the postreform period gradually assumed greater importance as a bulwark against social and political change than as a means of mobilizing the country's fiscal and human resources, a task for which it was increasingly ill suited in the twentieth century.

This book argues that in the twentieth century the remnants of a hierarchical society combined with the social conservatism of the merchantry to prevent the amalgamation of those social elements which constituted the bourgeoisie in Western and Central Europe. In Russia these propertied and politically moderate groups included the

5. The great prerevolutionary legal scholar N. M. Korkunov argued that the soslovie principle had no deep roots in Russian history and that its presence in government legislation contradicted the realities of social life. Insofar as he means estate law in the Western European sense I agree with him. But the peculiar variety of soslovie law introduced in Russia during the eighteenth century had a very profound effect upon the merchantry's concept of self-identity. Cf. Korkunov, *Russkoe pravo*, 1:274–76.

6. See for example, Daumard, *La Bourgeoisie parisienne*, especially pp. 643–47; Jean Lhomme, *La Grande Bourgeoisie*, pp. 42–52 and throughout; *La Question de la "bourgeoisie,"* especially the article by A. Derosier, "Le 'Semanario patriotico' et son idéologie de classe (1808–1812)," and discussion, pp. 15–46.

free professions, especially engineers and lawyers, well-off peasants (kulaks), and the shopkeepers, artisans, and shop assistants in the meshchanstvo. Most important of all, there were the new industrialists—called here "entrepreneurs"—who sought to break out of the traditional merchant pattern of economic timidity, social inertia, and political indifference by creating regional interest groups. With the exception of Moscow, which was a special case, the entrepreneurs were not even members of the merchant guilds. They represented a new, dynamic social force. Yet the fact that they were regionally based and ethnically distinctive also prevented them from becoming the core of a national bourgeoisie.

The first dramatic test of the strength of the old social forms and attitudes confronted with the transforming power of a revolutionary situation came in 1905. The propertied elements, who appeared to have so much in common, were confronted by a succession of rapid changes: the elections to the duma, the creation of national parties and lobbying organizations, the Stolypin reforms, the renewed industrial surge after 1910, and finally World War I all delivered a series of hammer blows to the decaying system of sosloviia. No social group remained immune to the combined effects. There were signs of political awakening among the merchantry as well as among their potential allies. Proposals multiplied for new political organizations and new economic combinations. Commercial and industrial interests became bolder in their demands on the government. Yet throughout this feverish decade of change runs another tale of mutual suspicion between merchantry and intelligentsia and between industrial interests of one region and those of another. This tale features abortive alliances, sterile agreements, and failed hopes. The soslovie system was crumbling away, but socially cohesive and politically unified classes were not emerging to take its place. A discussion of the social disintegration and political impotence of the middle ranks of Imperial Russian society on the eve of war and revolution brings the book to its climax.

The tripartite organization of the book seeks to address the issues in topical fashion. Part 1 treats the external structures and internal social forces responsible for the evolution of the merchantry from Peter the Great to the twentieth century. Part 2 traces the rise of the entrepreneurial interest groups and their relationship to both the merchantry and the state. Part 3 examines the problem of social cohesion and political participation of the merchantry, entrepreneurs, and certain other social groups in the intermediate ground between nobility and peasantry. The conclusion attempts to redefine the social characteristics of the middle range of Russian society and to consider the implications for the stability of the old regime and the fate of its successor, the Provisional Government.

The difficulties of undertaking such a study are immediately apparent. Not only has the merchantry been neglected or treated in confusing conceptual terms, but sources of information on its members are limited, scattered, and elusive. The intellectual poverty of the merchantry as a whole explains the dearth of letters, diaries, memoirs, and expository material originating from the merchants themselves. Beyond this there is the deep but unstated bias of Russian (and Soviet) bureaucrats and intellectuals against the merchantry, which shows up most harmfully in the skimpy information collected about it in major reference works, especially encyclopedias and collective biographies, as well as in statistical compilations and the reports of government commissions.

The few local studies impose limitations of a different order. For political reasons, in part, these studies have emphasized integration and homogeneity at the expense of regional peculiarities. Monographs on individual firms are even more scarce, and they too concentrate almost exclusively on economic growth and give short shrift to social and organizational questions. In light of these lacunae, this book cannot claim to be a definitive study of the merchantry. It will serve its purpose well if it succeeds in rescuing the merchantry from historical obscurity and in opening a new debate on the nature of social change in Imperial Russia.

PART 1

THE EVOLUTION OF

THE MERCHANTRY

CHAPTER 1

STATE PATERNALISM

AND SOCIAL STAGNATION

In reshaping Russia's social institutions, Peter the Great left the merchants suspended between the two worlds of Old Muscovy and the new service state. They were caught in the contradictions of a policy which attempted to combine hierarchy and mobility into a single system. For it was Peter's cherished aim to promote the supreme power of the state and at the same time to encourage and reward individual initiative. His method of introducing greater mobility into the decaying Muscovite social hierarchy was to substitute service for birth as the basis of rank. Yet for fiscal and military purposes he bound most of the population including the merchantry to their communities (*obshchestvo*) through joint responsibility for taxes. As a result the Russian merchantry stood awkwardly poised between opportunity and bondage. One foot was placed on a rung of the Table of Ranks, which led to upward mobility. The other was stuck fast in the legal and fiscal obligations of the urban community (*posadskoe obshchestvo*).[1]

The Merchantry in the Service State

The most innovative aspect of Peter's reforms was to establish what amounted to three service classes—the noble, the clerical, and the urban.[2] Although the new service classes were hereditary, their ranks

1. Kizevetter, *Posadskaia*, pp. 2–12. An earlier work dealing mainly with the juridical status of the merchantry is Ditiatin, *Ustroistvo*. For a useful recent survey of the literature on the urban classes of Muscovite Russia which stresses the absence of a communal tradition, see Langer, "Medieval Russian Town," and Miller, "State and City," in Hamm, *City*, pp. 11–52.
2. The idea of enlarging the definition of service group beyond the nobility to include the clergy and at least the upper part of the urban community is not universally ac-

were not. Individuals could not only move up the ranks through meritorious service but could also transfer under certain conditions from one class to another. In the urban service class the merchants shouldered the heaviest administrative duties but also enjoyed easiest access to upward mobility. They performed both fiscal (*kazennye*) and civil (*grazhdanskie*) obligations as tax collectors, inspectors of manufactured goods, and census takers. Their most important service task, however, was to administer the new town administration (*Magistrat*), which Peter inaugurated in the waning years of his reign. It should be emphasized again that these reforms did not create autonomous self-governing urban communities in Russia. But the wealthy merchants (so-called *pervostateiny* because of their top rank on the tax rolls) were accorded a prominent place alongside appointed government officials in administering local public services, staffing courts, and apportioning fiscal responsibilities.

In the context of the hierarchical service state as a whole, the merchants' main function was to preserve the integrity of urban communities. In other words they were to protect the commercial privileges and taxpaying capabilities of the towns. No one outside a community was allowed to trade in a town, and no one could enroll in a community without declaring a personal worth of five hundred rubles (three hundred for St. Petersburg). It was expected that the new merchant administrators would be more zealous than appointees of the crown in enforcing restrictions against peasants who competed with the urban traders by bringing cheaper goods into a town from their villages or by moving into a town to escape the fiscal and recruiting obligations attached to their rural communities (*sel'skoe obshchestvo*) without assuming similar burdens in the urban community. It was also assumed that the merchant administrators were the most interested party in preventing the flight of their own urban population. Any loss in taxpayers would have to be made up by reapportioning taxes among the remaining inhabitants including the merchants themselves. These reforms turned the merchants into their own jailers. Because the merchant administrators were fearful of losing the biggest taxpayers, they were reluctant to issue their fellow merchants passports that did not contain a terminal date for return.[3]

Onerous as these obligations were, they had the advantage of being

---

cepted. But recent interpretations of these groups give solid grounds for the acceptance of the idea. For the clergy see Freeze, *Russian Levites*, pp. 16–17. For the town as a service concept see Hittle, *Service City*, pp. 9–16 and 82–90.

3. *PSZRI*, 1st ser., December 1724, no day, no. 4624; Kizevetter, *Posadskaia*, pp. 12–16, 170–74.

attached to the Table of Ranks. They opened the way to promotion by merit. For the more prosperous merchants who occupied the most responsible fiscal posts, opportunities for promotion to high rank and rise in status to personal and even hereditary nobility were abundant. Moreover, Peter was eager to reward individual entrepreneurs who contributed to the general welfare with high rank and noble status. Thus, while allowing the old, closed, privileged merchant corporations to wither away, Peter encouraged individual entrepreneurs from whatever social background to give proof of their talents and earn their way into the upper ranks of Russian society.

However, Peter's insistence that the merchantry remain an organic part of the urban community weakened its newfound identity as a service class in a socially mobile society. This meant, among other things, sharing the burden of obligations and taxes (*tiaglo*), including the despised poll tax, with the lower orders of the population (*podlye liudi*). Why Peter did this is something of a mystery. Perhaps it was simply for fiscal and administrative reasons. If so, the cost in social terms was very high. In the eyes of the nobility, the merchantry bore the stigma of belonging to the bonded part of the population. The rest of the urban masses regarded merchants as exploiters who paid up the tax arrears in order to keep the entire town population dependent upon them.

Once having imposed a unified administrative and social structure upon the towns, Peter weakened it by dividing the merchants into two guilds (*gil'dy*) based on occupation and by creating an entirely different set of guilds for the artisans (*tsekhy*). The effect, once again, was to preserve in slightly different form the old Muscovite social distinctions in rank among merchants and between them and the urban masses. The primary loyalties of the merchants and artisans were naturally to their guilds, which defined the most important of their obligations and privileges, rather than to the town administration or the urban service class as a whole.

The economic position of the merchantry in Peter's system was also weighed down with unresolved anomalies from the Muscovite past. Putting the finishing touches to his service state in the last years of his reign, Peter assigned the merchantry the task of performing the main commercial and manufacturing functions in the empire.[4] Clearly, he

---

4. The basic legislation defining merchant functions and obligations in *PSZRI*, 1st ser., 3 December 1723, no. 4378. Merchants (as well as nobles) were permitted to purchase populated villages "on condition that the villages remain permanently attached to the factories" (ibid., 18 January 1721, no. 3711). Individuals of any group were permitted to establish factories and engage in trade in a town, but only if enrolled in the town population. No restrictions were placed, however, on trade in the villages or in the

expected the merchants as faithful servants of the state to match the boldness and success of his armed forces. In fact, they had already displayed remarkable vigor in supplying capital and entrepreneurial skill for his mini-industrialization of Russia. But he hesitated to give them a complete and legal monopoly over trade and industry. This course of action had been urged upon him by Ivan Pososhkov, Russia's first and most famous merchant-publicist, who feared that the commercial competition of other groups in Russian society would sap the very energies that Peter sought to release.[5]

Peter had no desire to reestablish the hegemony of a small merchant elite like the old privileged Muscovite merchants (*gosti*), whom he was just in the final stages of eliminating. He refused to grant a monopoly of trade to the merchants, but he also refused to exempt them from joint responsibility and give them freedom of movement. So the merchantry, or at least its wealthiest and most energetic section, gained neither the security of its Muscovite predecessors nor freedom from its collective tax obligations, which tied it to an urban community and hampered it from competing with domestic and foreign rivals for control over a national market.

Peter's eagerness to transfer state properties and manufactures into private hands was also balanced by a desire to retain control over a large and profitable sector of the economy. The state operated the salt, alcohol, and potash monopolies, owned mines and metallurgical and cloth factories supplying the armed forces, and exploited enormous tracts of arable and timber lands. As it had in Muscovite times, the state remained the single largest entrepreneur in the country. Despite the special character of its productive activities, the state sector continued to be a competitor of the merchantry and an obstacle to further expansion of private capitalism right down to the end of the empire.

Even the private sector was not allowed to develop without close government supervision. The commercial and manufacturing colleges established by Peter awarded monopolies to individuals or companies to produce or sell certain specific goods. Though Peter intended that all citizens would be permitted to compete for these privileges, in fact only the merchantry and the nobility received monopolies. Thus, the colleges kept alive the Muscovite tradition of pro-

---

countryside (ibid., September 1723, no. 4312). Clearly, one of the main aims of this legislation was to transform the monopolistic but conservative position of the old merchant elite (gosti) into a competitive progressive commercial class. See Samuel Baron, "Fate of the gosti," pp. 488–512, and Lappo-Danilevskii, "Russkie," pp. 314–22, 325, 345–48, 365.

5. Pososhkov, *Kniga*, pp. 192–216.

tecting a highly restricted commercial and manufacturing community and reenforcing the dominant position of the big merchants. At the same time the bureaucrats in these colleges retained for themselves wide discretionary powers of intervention in the activities of the private enterprises that had received privileges from them. This paved the way for unpredictable and arbitrary interference at every level of the productive process. It also frequently led to collusion between the wealthier merchants and government officials at the expense of the impoverished lower orders of the population. Finally, by creating two separate colleges for commerce and manufacturing, Peter unintentionally introduced another disruptive element into the economic life of the merchantry. Each college granted a different set of privileges to their clients, and in accord with Peter's preferences manufacturing merchants benefited more than trading merchants. This was another case, like that of the guilds, in which Peter's arbitrary division of the population along functional lines—either by service, wealth, or occupation—violated the delicate and complex web of social realities.

Undoubtedly, Peter's aims in all these reforms were to preserve the wealth of the state, foster private initiative, and distribute the tiaglo burden fairly while reserving the power of the state to mediate jurisdictional disputes among the service classes. But the results were mixed. Peter's greatest successes were registered in the economic growth of the country. The older historiographical view that his forced industrialization had shallow roots and withered after his death has been thoroughly revised. Moreover, it is now also clear that the merchantry provided the bulk of the capital for this industrialization within the favorable conditions created by the state.[6] In economic terms the first half of the eighteenth century represented a second phase of the golden age of the merchantry begun in the second half of the previous century. But it is also true that in social terms the long-range effect on Russian society in general was divisive. On the merchantry in particular it was debilitating as well. An enormous gulf continued to exist between the upper stratum and the mass of the urban population, which was itself fragmented. The opportunities for arbitrary interference by state officials and the absence of social cohesion blocked the emergence of a unified and politically active urban citizenry.

To be sure, the institutional restraints were not by themselves insurmountable obstacles to the evolution of the merchantry toward a soslovie enjoying strong corporate rights. After all, Peter also bound

6. For a useful summary of important contributions of the Soviet literature on this question see Kahan, "Economic Activity and Policy," pp. 63–71. See also Portal, L'Oural, p. 167 and throughout.

the nobility to an oppressive burden of lifelong service to the state. Yet within sixty years of his death the nobility was emancipated from its obligations and was granted legal recognition of its corporate privileges. The Charter of the Nobility in 1785 symbolized the nobility's political and cultural transformation in response to the changing needs of the government for trained military and administrative personnel.

By contrast the merchantry did not make a similar bid for emancipation. The Town Charter of 1775 granted the merchants the form but not the reality of corporate rights. Neither did the merchantry undergo a major cultural or political transformation during the eighteenth century despite its active participation in the general economic development of the expanding empire. The explanation of this comparatively retarded social evolution must be sought not only in the persistence of state paternalism but also within the collective mentality and behavior of the merchants themselves.

By the end of Peter's reign the sum of his institutional reforms set four distinct limitations upon the further political and social development of the merchantry: (1) a close, constant, and often petty supervision of the merchants' economic activities by the state bureaucracy; (2) a heavy burden of fiscal and civic obligations which separated the towns from the countryside and sharply divided the town population along lines of wealth and status; (3) a form of elective urban "self-government" which obediently performed services for the central government and in so doing clashed with the appointed representatives of the central government in the provinces; and (4) a lack of any direct access to the policymaking organs of the autocracy by the merchants acting either as individuals or as a corporate body. These basic features of the merchantry's public life remained unchanged until the 1870s despite the urban reforms of Catherine II and the guild reforms of Nicholas I, which some historians have misinterpreted as important landmarks in the evolution of the merchant soslovie toward a genuine bourgeoisie.

The Economic Condition of the Merchantry

From Peter to Catherine the state regulation of trade and industry entangled the merchants in a web of bureaucratic rules and litigation without protecting them from sudden and unpredictable changes in the government's economic policies. Direct administrative interference reached a high point in the reign of Anna Ivanovna when a literal application of existing rules would have virtually abolished manufacturing in Russia.[7] At the same time, the most important central organ for controlling industry, the Manufacturing College, was undergoing a series of radical transformations. Originally established in 1724 to grant approval and privileges to every new industrial enterprise, it was abolished soon after in 1727. Reestablished that same year, it was fused with the commerce and mining (Berg) colleges in 1731, separated out again in 1741, and finally put to rest in 1779. These fits and starts were not simply caprices of the bureaucratic mentality. The problem also stemmed from the growing rivalry between merchant-manufacturers and merchant-traders, which, to be sure, Peter had done so much to initiate in his crude effort to force the movement of capital from commerce into industry. In the shadow of each administrative reshuffle stood real economic interests. Running parallel to the rise and fall of the Manufacturing College was the expansion or limitation of the manufacturers' rights to buy villages of serfs and to be exempted from fiscal and service burdens.[8] Thus the principle of unlimited state intervention in industry clashed with economic realities, and the merchants were caught in the middle.

During the same period the disparities of status and wealth within the merchantry grew enormously as the result of another arbitrary decision of the state to alter the institutional structure of society. For reasons that are not altogether clear but may be guessed, the government under Catherine I created a third guild, thereby more than doubling the number of merchants. Presumably, the need for fresh sources of tax revenue inspired the move, but the original decree has been lost and there is no certainty even about its declared purpose. In any event, the legal redefinition of thousands of podlye liudi living in the towns scarcely enhanced the status of the merchantry or strengthened its corporate identity. If the government expected that once the townspeople were called merchants they would begin to act like them, it was sadly mistaken. More than a generation after this ill-advised decree, the large majority remained merchants in name only. In the late 1760s a survey conducted by the Academy of Sciences revealed an extraordinary picture of socioeconomic diversity and widespread poverty among the merchants of what became known as the central industrial region. In those towns that contained virtually no artisans or factories at all in Moscow, Vladimir, Iaroslavl, Riazan, Tula, and Kaluga provinces, as they were subsequently reorganized, the merchants depended heavily upon the peasants to supply them with agricultural goods—hemp, grain, horned cattle, mead, and wax—and handicrafts —wheels, barrels, wooden utensils, bast, and pottery. The mass of the

7. Baburin, Ocherki, pp. 136–37.
8. Ibid., pp. 89–90, 120–25, 131–35, 139–41, 143–47, 296–307.

third-guild merchants scratched out a living at the level of the peasants. For the most part they cultivated their own gardens and sold the produce, primarily onions and garlic, along with the other goods, to the peasants either in the town-market stalls or in nearby country-village fairs. This low level of economic activity characterized the commercial life of most medium sized towns including Koshira, Ruza, Dmitrov, Klim, Volokolamsk, Shuia, Maloiaroslavets, Pronsk, Peremyshl, Vorotynsk, Meshchovsk, Likhvin, Odoev, Bogoroditsk, Kropiva, and Aleksin.[9] The few artisan-merchants who subsisted in towns like Bezhetsk or Kulin were smiths who made primitive tools —scythes, sickles, and other "petty products"—for sale.[10]

In some larger towns merchants loaded the hemp and grain on barges destined for St. Petersburg, but this constituted the only wholesale trade in Kolomna, Borovsk, and Vereia, where very few individuals were involved—in Vereia, for example, "several" out of 1,870 registered merchants. The rest in most of these smaller places gave up all pretense of trading for themselves and either toiled in the fields as manual laborers (*chernaia rabota*) or hired themselves out as shop assistants to merchants in the main commercial centers of St. Petersburg and Riga.[11] Even in towns in which a cloth factory or bleaching plant or two belonged to a merchant, as in Sapozhok, Rostov, or Serpeisk, "the merchants for the most part ploughed the land and the rest traded but little."[12]

Merchants living along the old trading routes profited from the wholesale trade, but this was not sufficient to stimulate manufactures or even a vigorous artisan life in towns like Mozhaisk, Kolomna, Pereiaslavl-Zaleskii, and Suzdal. Here too, then, most of the third-guild merchants were "very poor" and could hardly be distinguished from trading peasants in their mode of living.[13] Normally, the presence of several factories or more than a handful of artisan-merchants in a town was a reliable sign of a more vigorous commercial life. For example, the two leather factories in Vladimir making Russian leather (*yuft*) and the blacksmith and tailor shops gave a more varied and lively appearance to the trading stalls in town, where the peasants came to buy red calico, silk, paper, and garden vegetables in exchange for their own handmade wooden utensils, pottery, and flax. Once a week the merchants visited the country fairs on the outskirts. Al-

9. Bakmeister, *Topograficheskiia*, vol. 1, pt. 1, pp. 11, 29, 34, 40–41, 91; pt. 2, pp. 154, 177; pt. 3, pp. 199, 201, 202, 210, 229, 232, 243. Dmitrov offers one of the few cases of an exact breakdown of the merchantry by guilds: first, 8; second, 82; third, 371.

10. Ibid., pt. 3, pp. 280, 284.

11. Ibid., pt. 1, pp. 4–5, 84–85, 86–87.

12. Ibid., pt. 2, pp. 110–11, 181; pt. 3, p. 196.

13. Ibid., pt. 1, pp. 4–5, 16; pt. 2, pp. 99, 140.

though perhaps different in detail, the pattern of impoverishment was the same in Vladimir, where the majority of merchants worked "on the ploughlands or in the gardens."[14] In Gorokhovets, Uglich, and Murom leather manufacturing enabled a few well-to-do merchants to trade with St. Petersburg. Gorokhovets in particular had a large artisan population, including bell makers and silversmiths as well as the usual blacksmiths, tailors, boot makers, and shirtmakers, but even they "had little work" and were forced to seek supplementary employment in "manual field labor."[15] Uglich also boasted three paper factories and held two big regional fairs, yet "the merchantry was extremely poor."[16] In Kaluga and Pereiaslavl-Riazanskii a vigorous artisan population contributed to a lively trade with the peasantry in cloth and metal products. Kaluga merchants owned several sailcloth factories and a paper factory and traded with St. Petersburg, Siberia, and the Ukraine, while Pereiaslavl-Riazanskii attracted merchants from all over Vladimir province. But the beneficiaries were the pervostateiny merchants; the third-guild merchants of these towns and others were no different from others in the central industrial region.[17]

Outside of Moscow the only two towns in the region that could boast a vigorous and distinctive urban culture were Iaroslavl and Tula. Iaroslavl had almost six thousand merchants, some of whom were moderately wealthy, though here too "most suffered from poverty." The well-to-do merchants owned leather factories and traded overseas. Artisan life was strong and varied, at least in relation to the rest of the towns, and included sixteen silversmiths, twenty-three coppersmiths, seven pewter makers, twenty-three hosierers, nineteen hatmakers, nine joiners, twenty-one butchers, and nineteen bakers of various sorts. An unusual number of factories were located within the city—two cloth, three silk, three hat, three red lead, and a bleaching plant. Merchants in the suburbs specialized in the nail and iron trade, while the poorer merchants dealt in timber and wood. Tula, of course, owed its prosperity to the huge state armament works. Its "wealthier merchants for the most part conducted their business by absenting themselves in various towns" throughout the empire, whereas the lesser merchants served as their shop assistants. A skilled and numerous artisan population was famous for its military equipment, as well as furniture, tableware, and precision instruments.[18]

The overall picture of the provincial merchantry was a bleak one.

14. Ibid., pt. 2, pp. 120–24.
15. Ibid., pp. 125–26.
16. Ibid., pt. 3, p. 269.
17. Ibid., pt. 2, pp. 162–69, 187.
18. Ibid., pt. 3, pp. 219–23; pt. 4, pp. 292–304.

With few exceptions the trading pattern was the reverse of that in Western Europe. In Russia the merchants in the small and medium-sized towns sold agricultural produce in the countryside—mainly food products—while the peasants brought their handicrafts to sell in the towns. This reverse flow contributed to the blurring of the boundaries between town and country and deprived urban dwellers of what one Russian historian later called "the productive self-education" of urban life in the West.[19] The pre-Petrine tradition that manufacturing and trade were carried on independent of rank or membership in social category persisted and continued to weaken the internal cohesion of the urban community in general and the merchantry in particular.

A secondary effect of the reverse flow was that artisans and peasants alike made handicrafts for the petty trader to market, rather than "on order." Together with the absence of apprenticeship and guild regulation of quality, this tended to lower the standards of workmanship.[20] In trading these mediocre goods in the countryside the petty merchants of the third guild had no interest in building up a solid and well-satisfied clientele, the kind of clientele that would certainly be necessary in a fixed place of business such as a store or shop in town. What they hoped for was a quick sale to a customer whom they would never see again. This bazaar mentality was reflected both in the low level of commercial honesty and in the shoddy quality of many goods. Because the mass of the urban petty traders enjoyed the legal and social status of merchant, the good name of the merchantry as a whole suffered. As the next chapter will make clear, it was precisely this lowly stratum of the merchantry that aroused the contempt and anger of the nobility, whose peasants were often its victims. Moreover, the pervostateiny merchants had few interests in common with the mass of the merchantry, many of whom did not trade and some of whom were their low-paid employees. The state's arbitrary redefinition of the merchantry had an opposite effect from the one intended. Instead of strengthening the commercial and manufacturing population it succeeded in discrediting it and heaping new burdens upon what was already a fragile urban structure.

Merchantry and the Soslovie System

Catherine the Great's tax and local-government reforms in the 1770s and 1780s sought to resolve the contradictions inherited from Peter

19. Korsak, *O formakh*, p. 109.
20. Ibid., pp. 123–25.

and his successors. Their two chief aims were to transform the merchantry into a genuine full-fledged soslovie and to create "all-class" municipal governments. The first aim was achieved by overhauling the loose, customary organization of the merchant guilds, converting them into rigid and legally binding hierarchies and granting them new rights based upon precise distinctions of status and wealth. A kind of rough equivalence now emerged between the rights and the obligations of the guilds. The government shifted the basis for taxation of the merchantry from their person to their capital. By this device the state increased its revenues and the merchantry improved its social status. Even though the merchants did not gain the much-coveted tax-free privileges of the nobility and clergy, they were exempt from the despised head tax, which the rest of the population continued to pay. The first two guilds enjoyed much broader commercial rights than did the third. In return they had to shoulder the main fiscal and administrative duties in the towns. But as it did in Muscovite Russia, the state entrusted the most responsible positions to the pervostateiny merchants, who easily turned these obligations to their own advantage by squeezing the population and bargaining with state officials. The first two guilds also won the treasured right of exemption from military service, but no merchant was freed from the obnoxious obligation to quarter troops.

Catherine's second aim proved more elusive. In order to enrich and enliven the cultural and intellectual life of the towns, she sought to fill important posts in the urban administrations with nobles and members of the newly emerging professional community (raznochintsy). Her hopes were quickly disappointed. The elected town dumas were simply overwhelmed by the mass of obligations that the government inflicted upon them. The functional distinction between the interests of the municipalities as a whole and those of the separate parts of the urban soslovie disappeared in the jumble of administrative, judicial, and police regulations accumulated by different departments of the bureaucracy over the previous half century. The nobles saw little sense in assuming additional service obligations at a time when they were just settling into their new roles as provincial administrators. Besides they were loath to work on the same footing as the merchants, whom they affected to despise.

Consequently, the separation of the "self government" of the towns from the administration of the merchant guilds became a legal fiction. The merchants were left to man both sets of offices, and much overlapping and confusion resulted. By sharpening the distinctions in wealth and status among the three guilds, the reforms drove a deeper wedge between the pervostateiny merchants and their lesser colleagues. Utilizing their control of the municipal courts, the wealthier and stronger merchants capitalized on the chaotic situation to interfere even more arbitrarily in the affairs of the rest of the urban population. Meanwhile, the majority of the townsmen were reorganized into a separate soslovie, the *meshchanstvo*, where they were more sharply differentiated from the merchantry. Moreover, they remained saddled with the socially humiliating burdens of the head tax and recruitment.[21] Rather than create a free, united urban citizenry, Catherine's reforms reintroduced many of the divisive social distinctions of Muscovite Russia.

Though the merchants enjoyed higher status in their brand new soslovie, they were not protected against the imposition of new obligations, some of which were illegally imposed upon them by the Petersburg bureaucracy. During the Napoleonic Wars, for example, it proved simpler for the central government to increase taxes on merchant capital than to raise the head tax on the impoverished peasants or the meshchanstvo. In the first two decades of the nineteenth century the tax rate on merchant capital continued its relentless rise. At the same time, merchants were engaged in a constant struggle with local authorities, who made extortionary demands upon them for money and service well beyond the limitations of the law. Service in town governments once again became so onerous for the merchants that on the eve of elections to administrative posts the leading candidates often distributed heavy bribes or changed their residence in order to avoid being chosen.[22] Meanwhile, the elective bodies themselves were gradually stripped of their administrative responsibilities,

21. On Catherine's reforms a succinct and reliable account is Klokman, *Sotsial'no-ekonomicheskaia istoriia*, pp. 90–91, 100, 110–12, 119–22. It corrects Kizevetter's optimistic bias on the creation of an urban bourgeoisie, but does not replace the older work in many other respects. For the merchants' administration of their estate, see Storozhev, *Istoriia*, vol. 5, pt. 3, pp. 41, 87, and 114. This is an exhaustive treatment of the period 1785–1801. For the first half of the nineteenth century see Ditiatin, *Ustroistvo*, 2:215–17 and throughout. See also Lincoln, "Russian State," pp. 531–39, which uses fresh archival material.
22. TsGAOR, f. 672 (Nicholas I), op. 1, d. 272, "Zapiska Moskovskogo gorodskogo golovy Kumanina 'zamechanie po nekotorye stat'i dopolnitel'nogo postanovleniia ob ustroistve gil'di i o torgovle prochikh sostoianii" (no date given but no earlier than July 1826). Kumanin noted that "in the course of the past three years in election to several judicial posts the designated number of places were not filled with the result that it was not possible for [the court] to function properly" (ibid., p. 8). Merchants showed much ingenuity in evading their duties. For example in Kursk province they attempted to avoid service by becoming church wardens until the government put a stop to the practice (*PSZRI*, 1st ser., 6 February 1817, no. 26661). See also Vishniakov, *Svedeniia*, 2:93–95, and Naidenov, *Vospominaniia*, pt. 1, p. 57.

which were transferred to ad hoc committees under the control of the central bureaucracy.[23] As an agency of urban public welfare, the town duma lost all significance. Reduced mainly to keeping accounts, it became a vestigial appendage of the central bureaucracy. The traditional pattern of relations between merchants and officials reasserted itself. Petersburg took away with one hand what it gave with the other. It was to require the passage of a whole century before Catherine's dreams of urban self-government could even come close to being realized.

Throughout the first half of the nineteenth century the civic status of the merchantry changed very little except to deteriorate. Under Alexander I a reorganization of the central bureaucracy simplified the procedures for merchants wishing to submit petitions. This involved a few administrative adjustments in the structure of the merchant soslovie, but hardly affected the merchants' influence on decisions concerning their interests. The guild merchants of each town sitting as a body (*kupecheskoe obshchestvo*) or through their elected representatives (*sobranie vybornykh*) could petition the Ministry of Finance as well as local officials, but only after prior approval by the chief administrator of the province. This procedure created few difficulties under the enlightened administration of a governor-general like D. V. Golitsyn in Moscow. But under petty tyrants like his notorious successor, Count A. A. Zakrevskii, the new procedure became a nightmare of humiliation and delays for the merchants. On the periphery of the empire most officials were especially impatient with or contemptuous of Great Russian merchants. They regarded them as overly cautious and inefficient in comparison with the vigorous foreign entrepreneurs who often sustained the economic vitality of their regions.

Even the form of the petitions and the language of the correspondence between merchants and officials was stamped with a patriarchal character which emphasized the submissive and passive nature of the relationship. The government frequently requested information from the merchant societies, only to ignore it in the most disdainful way. For example, in response to an inquiry by the Ministry of Finance, merchant societies toiled for months to prepare an analysis on the reasons for the decline of their capital during the first two decades of the nineteenth century. Once submitted, however, the report lay

---

23. Ditiatin, *Ustroistvo*, 2:229–30, 234–35; Ryndziunskii, *Gorodskoe*, pp. 42, 45–51. Under Nicholas the merchants were also brushed aside when they protested the drafting of reform legislation that aimed at strengthening the relative position of both the bureaucrats and the nobility in the municipal government of St. Petersburg. See Lincoln, "Miliutin," pp. 55–68.

shelved in the ministry's archives for fourteen years. When officials renewed their long-forgotten request, the merchants dutifully presented another copy of the same report without a word of reproach.[24]

The government refused to grant the merchants permanent representation in the central administrative organs until the reign of Nicholas I, despite the obvious advantages of consulting them on economic matters.[25] When in 1828 the manufacturing and commercial councils were created under the Ministry of Finance, the high officials who drafted the legislation made certain that the merchants' role would be suitably modest. It may be exaggerated to dismiss the councils as "still-born children," in the words of the Soviet historian I. F. Gindin, but it is certainly correct to discount them as effective representatives of merchant interests.[26] While the merchants gained this precarious foothold in the central bureaucracy, the creaky edifice of their town governments began to crumble under the pressure of Nicholas's arbitrary administration, leaving the merchants practically helpless before provincial authorities.[27]

Meanwhile, the legal and political isolation of the merchant soslovie was reinforced by the Digest of Laws (*Svod Zakonov*), published in 1835 in an attempt to regularize and systematize the mass of legislation that had accumulated haphazardly over almost two centuries. The basic character permeating all nine volumes was a sharp differentiation of the population along soslovie lines. Article after article echoed the last previous collection of laws, the ulozhenie of 1649,

24. For a complete account of the unsuccessful petitions of 1805, 1807, and 1809 see Storozhev, *Istoriia*, vol. 2, pt. 1, pp. 25–29, 40, 51, 120–22. In one case, the petition of 29 June 1809, the merchants were sharply rebuked by the Department of the Moscow Magistrate for having invoked their own normative standards for guild membership against the legal statutes. For the report of 1823, ibid., p. 334; for the request of 1840, ibid., pp. 290–328. The guild reform of 1824 actually was contrary to the spirit of the merchant report, though it was by no means entirely favorable to noble interests either. For a balanced evaluation see Pintner, *Economic Policy*, pp. 57–61, 63–64.

25. Paul I introduced merchant representatives into the manufacturing and commercial councils, but they were quickly eliminated from these positions after his assassination. For details and the argument that Paul conducted a "bourgeois policy" see the controversial but always stimulating work of Klochkov, *Ocherki*, pp. 344–77. On the purges see Zlotnikov, *Kontinental'naia*, pp. 88–89 and 61 ff., who in general follows Klochkov without citing him.

26. Gindin, "Russkaia burzhuaziia," pp. 61–64. This view is supported by most authorities, for example, Pintner, *Economic Policy*, pp. 53–55, and Blackwell, *Beginnings*, pp. 153–54. For the opposite view see Tugan-Baranovskii. *Russian Factory*, pp. 142–45, and Kniapina, *Politika*, pp. 206–10. The controversy is explained in part by the fact that only four manuscript volumes of the annual records of the Manufacturing Council in Moscow before 1857 have survived: FBON, "Zhurnal zasedaniia manufakturnogo soveta; Moskovskoe otdeleniia," 1829, 1833, 1843, and 1846.

27. Naidenov, *Vospominaniia*, 2:4–6.

which had imposed on Russia a castelike social structure. One by one the escape hatches opened by Peter were closed down. To be sure, the extent of the reaction was obscured because the rights and obligations of the various soslovie were scattered throughout the collection. When added together, they had the general effect of insulating the merchantry from the rest of the population in all but trading relations. Over the entire range of administration, from taxation, military service, and the right of movement to commercial-industrial law and soslovie organization, the merchantry was sealed off from the nobility and clergy above it and meshchanstvo and the peasantry below it.[28] Thus, on the eve of the great reforms that were destined to undermine, if not topple, the eighteenth-century soslovie structure, the separate and distinctive character of the merchant soslovie received its most complete legal expression. Paradoxically, as the following chapter will show, this rigid structure was imposed upon a society that was undergoing an unprecedented economic expansion and cultural flowering and upon a merchantry that was passing through a social transformation of the same magnitude.

Political Inertia among Merchants

The merchants reacted cautiously to this ruthless subordination of their evolution and political development to the fiscal and administrative imperatives of the state. One wonders how broadly they perceived their own interests and what vision they held of the good society. As their problems mounted, they appeared incapable of devising new forms of collective action outside official channels.

The merchants harbored few illusions about the difficulty and persistence of the problems facing them. Bitter experience had taught them that, with the exception of a handful of the wealthiest, they had little to gain from state service. It required frequent and costly interruptions of their commercial activities, but did not compensate them with an adequate defense for their privileges against the encroachment of the bureaucracy and the nobility. Their plight emerged most clearly in their petitions (*nakazy*) to the Legislative Commission in 1767, which represented the most comprehensive survey of their attitudes in the eighteenth century. At the top of their list of grievances

28. These distinctions can be found in the following sections of the *SZRI*, edition of 1832 (St. Petersburg, 1835): vol. 4, "Ustavy o povinnostiakh"; vol. 5, "Ustav o priamykh nalogakh"; vol. 9 "Zakony o sostoianiiakh"; vol. 10, "Polozhenie o kazennykh podriadakh i postavkakh"; vol. 11, "Ustav kreditnyi," "Ustav torgovyi," and "Ustav o promyshlennosti."

they placed economic competition from the nobles and the peasantry. They followed this with strong complaints against their obligations to collect taxes for the state, to serve for unspecified terms in the town administrations, to quarter troops, and to provide recruits for the army. They expressed indignation over the insults that they suffered at the hands of the nobility and the raznochintsy, and they bemoaned the attacks on their judicial privileges by the provincial authorities, mainly the chancellery of the governor (*voevoda*).[29]

Implicit in all these petitions was the merchants' desire to gain greater control over their lives in order to conduct their trade more vigorously and profitably. The average merchant could not be expected suddenly to drop his business affairs and set out on a long, exhausting tax-collecting junket in the district surrounding his town or throughout his entire province. Neither could he afford to turn over his horses and carts, which were constantly engaged in moving goods, to the postal authorities or to a regiment which happened to pass along the highroad or to camp in the vicinity. His commercial activities were seriously disrupted if his sons, often his most trusted assistants, were drafted into the army. In court cases held in a provin-

29. My analysis of the merchant petitions from all thirty-eight towns of Moscow province and for the smaller urban centers in Smolensk and Nizhegorod (Nizhnyi Novgorod) and Siberian provinces reveals a fairly clear pattern. The frequency of repetition of the same complaint of request is tabulated below. In the case of the main complaint concerning competition on the part of nobility, peasants, and occasionally raznochintsy and clergy, it must be noted that there were at least two and more often five or six variations on the theme in almost every one of the petitions. I have counted these only once in each case. *SIRIO* (1894), 93:83–584; Moscow (1911), 134:3–58, 59–116, 283–367. The most complete and detailed analysis of the merchant petitions and their implications is now Knabe, *Struktur.* See especially pp. 287–90 for a convenient summary.

	Moscow (n=38)	Smolensk (n=4)	Nizhgorod (n=7)	Sibir' (n=10)
Reduce or eliminate nobility, peasantry, and other competitors in trade and industry	38	4	6	8
Purchase domestic serfs	31	2	5	5
Place police under town authorities and have trials involving merchants held only in the courts of the merchant soslovie	24	3	3	6
Lighten service obligations	23	4	6	10
Purchase exemption from military service	22	0	4	0
Free merchants from obligation to collect state taxes	20	3	6	8

cial capital far from his place of business, he was forced to engage in lengthy and costly written proceedings rather than give informal oral testimony in the sympathetic atmosphere of the merchant courts in his hometown. Because the merchant had no right to refuse election as burgomaster or ratman, he could be returned to office over an indefinite period while his business died a slow death. He could not serve both the government and his trade. He needed to become master of his own destiny.

Yet even this formidable list of grievances did not inspire the merchants to propose a comprehensive program of reforms. Their humble requests reflected a narrow soslovie mentality. They sought primarily to weaken their commercial rivals, to win the right to own household serfs, to reduce their service obligations, and to obtain honorific rewards rather than to eliminate restraints on trade and industry, to abolish serfdom, or to create genuine self-government in the towns.[30]

There was one crucial distinction between the merchantry and the nobility, which also fiercely defended its material interests in its own list of grievances. The merchantry continued to perceive the state as the sole guarantor of its well-being. It made no effort to secure for itself an independent juridical position in society like that of the Russian nobility or the estates in Central and Western Europe.

Only the nakaz of Moscow struck a note of civic concern that transcended special interests. Urgent requests for what we would now call improvement of the environment, ranging from fire prevention, sanitation, pure water supply, and preservation of woodlands to better public health facilities, alternated with the defense of merchant rights against foreigners. But as subsequent events were to prove, this heightened awareness of urban problems must be attributed to the active participation of the town nobles in the drafting committee (including thirteen princes and two counts) and not to any especially progressive views on the part of the Moscow merchants.[31] Two generations after the passage of Catherine's urban reforms the merchant remained astonishingly indifferent to public welfare in the towns. He displayed little of his vaunted business acumen in managing muncipal budgets. In the 1840s a majority of towns could not furnish any information whatsoever on the fiscal and tax structures that provided the income for public services. Modest sums collected in a casual

30. "Proekt zakonov o pravakh sredniago roda gosudarstvennykh zhitelei," *SIRIO* (1882), 36:202–21. In Moscow province only one town, Nerekhta, out of thirty-eight requested merchant membership in the College of Manufacturing and Trade (ibid. [1894], 93:515).

31. Ibid. (1894), 93:120–24, 133.

manner were squandered, leaving vital services like fire fighting in a uniformly deplorable condition.[32]

Even when economic interests were directly at stake, the merchants were hesitant to take collective action. When impelled to do so, they were cautious lest they offend the authorities. Merchant representatives were invited by the government on several occasions in the second half of the eighteenth century to participate in discussions on tax and tariff revision, but they made no effort to draft a collective proposal.[33] Finally, in 1801, the merchant delegates elected by their soslovie organizations to serve in the Commercial College submitted jointly with noble manufacturers a project for tariff reform that strongly argued the case for higher duties on exports and imports. The government first paid them no attention and then abruptly expelled them from the Commercial College. The expulsion decree concluded on a characteristically disdainful note: their presence was "not only unsuccessful in furthering the interests of commerce but by distracting them from their business and occupation is in effect ruinous for the merchantry itself."[34] Subsequently, during the Napoleonic Wars, the commercial interests of the merchants were subordinated to the requirements of power politics in the international arena.[35] The economic effects upon the merchantry were devastating. Yet the merchants passively accepted both their elimination from the central bureaucracy and the tariff revisions that discriminated against them.

Only much later, during the preliminary discussions preceding the tariff revisions of 1850, did merchants actually take the initiative in drafting alternative proposals to those of the Ministry of Finance. By this time, it must be remembered, the merchants had shifted the bulk of their capital out of commerce into industry, gradually replacing the nobility as the leading manufacturers in the central provinces. Still they did not coordinate their efforts through the Moscow Exchange Committee or any of their soslovie organizations. Instead, representa-

32. Ditiatin, *Ustroistvo*, 2:272–73, 278–79.

33. Rubinshtein, "Ulozhennaia komissiia," pp. 208–51, attempts to prove on the basis of individual merchant petitions and merchant representation on the commission to draft a new law code that the merchantry actually played an active role in the political life of the country. However, his own evidence, as well as that of others he cites, shows that the merchants were acting as individuals, that they were mainly first-guild merchants, and that they followed the initiative and leadership of the nobility, especially the rival factions of the Vorontsovs and the Shuvalovs. See also S. M. Solov'ev, *Istoriia*, 23:765, and Bartenev, *Arkhiva*, 3:308 ff.

34. *PSZRI*, 1st ser., 16 March 1801, no. 19792. Significantly, the government did not express any concern over the far more onerous duties that it had imposed upon the merchantry in the field of local government.

35. Zlotnikov, *Kontinental'naia*, pp. 88 ff; Lodyzhenskii, *Istoriia*, pp. 157–63.

tives of different industries—textiles, iron, and chemical—submitted separate petitions which pitted the merchants against one another to the disgust of officials in the ministry. It was left to the few remaining big noble entrepreneurs, like Sergei Mal'tsov, to take the lead in defending the interests of industry as a whole.[36]

In part this display of merchant inertia may be attributed to the absence of any effective commercial organizations outside the institutional framework of the autocracy. In Russia, unlike in Western Europe, the government, and not the merchantry, took the initiative in creating the first commercial exchange (*birzha*). Peter the Great adopted the autonomous organization of the London and Amsterdam exchanges as the model for organizing the St. Petersburg Exchange in 1703, but he soon tired of the sluggish and unsystematic response of his merchants and ordered the exchange subordinated to the Commercial College.

Its subsequent history over the succeeding century consisted in large part of the government's efforts to instill a sense of order, regularity, and responsibility into the activities of the merchants dealing on the exchange. The government quickly discovered that brokers were necessary to handle its own large-scale exchange operations, as well as to serve as intermediaries between merchants who did not know (and therefore did not trust) one another. But, as in most other cases of government regulation of private activities, laws governing the exchange acted mainly to forbid rather than to facilitate; thus the bans on fighting, spreading unfounded rumors, engaging in political discussions, and trading in paper securities were periodically introduced and frequently repeated.

The merchantry found ways to ignore or circumvent most of these prohibitions, despite the threat of large fines. A small point that proved highly contentious, however, was the establishment of the daily working hours of the exchange. Russian brokers customarily preferred to trade in the late afternoon, whereas foreigners preferred the early morning. This momentous issue was finally resolved only by the Senate, which judiciously compromised on the hours from noon to two o'clock.[37] While this was a relatively unimportant issue, it was symptomatic of larger and more serious problems.

Aside from the restraints imposed by government regulation, the St. Petersburg merchantry had to contend with the foreign merchant, who was both a direct competitor and a necessary adjunct to commercial success. Throughout the eighteenth century Russian merchants

36. Kniapina, *Politika*, pp. 135–38. For a full account of Mal'tsov's remarkable entrepreneurial activities see *Sergei Ivanovich Mal'tsov*, especially pp. 2–10.
37. Timofeev, *Istoriia*, pp. 4–5, 12–15, 30–36, 48–49.

involved in public affairs walked a fine line in their struggle to prevent foreigners from dominating the commercial life of the port without discouraging them from trading there. Their efforts met with indifferent success. The great surge in foreign trade, which reached its peak in 1825 when the capital handled 70 percent of the empire's imports and 50 percent of its exports, irretrievably linked the Russian merchants in St. Petersburg to the foreigners. At the same time they relied increasingly on government subsidies and contracts to avoid falling under the complete control of the foreigners. This double dependence remained a permanent feature of merchant life in St. Petersburg even after heavy industry and banking became the city's main form of economic activity at the end of the nineteenth century. It also had a lasting and paradoxical effect upon the role of the St. Petersburg merchantry in the life of the empire. Constant contact with the gosti inspired the Russian merchants to cooperate with them in seeking to free them both from petty government regulations and in establishing in 1832 a largely self-administering exchange committee.[38] But this initial step toward obtaining recognition as an autonomous corporate social body was bought at great cost and proved self-limiting. By identifying their aspirations with those of the foreign merchants, they forfeited the political leadership of the Russian merchantry as a whole. Flourishing in an international milieu artificially created by Peter, they perceived their economic and social interests in a way quite different from that of Russian merchants in the interior. This had the effect not only of cutting them off from the rest of the merchantry but also of checking any further demands for corporate rights, which would jeopardize their profitable relationships with both the foreigners and the government. Thus, their cosmopolitan outlook notwithstanding, the St. Petersburg merchants failed to emerge as the champions of a strongly self-conscious Russian bourgeoisie. On the contrary, they nourished a passivity toward authority equal to that displayed by their provincial brethren in Moscow.

It took the rest of Russia more than a century to introduce commercial exchanges—in Kremenchug (1834), Moscow (1839), Rybinsk (1842), and Odessa and Nizhnyi Novgorod (1848). In Moscow the process was prolonged and painful. The first public organization of the Moscow merchantry was the Moscow Merchants' Club, founded in 1786 by a foreigner, mainly for charitable purposes. Its statutes forbade the discussion of religion or politics on penalty of expulsion. Plans to build an exchange were formulated a few years later, but Moscow merchants preferred to gather in their own homes or warehouses or in the streets and courtyards along the Il'inka. There they

38. Ibid., pp. 70–73, 110, 154–57.

conducted business in much the same way as the kulak or the jobber in the countryside, that is, without the services of a broker. In the early 1830s a small group of Moscow wholesale merchants who were leaders in the rapidly expanding trade in tea and cotton petitioned the sympathetic governor-general, D. V. Golitsyn, for permission to construct a commercial exchange building in Moscow. They intended it to house both the Moscow Exchange Society, made up of all merchants dealing on the exchange, and the executive exchange committee, of which they were the leading members. The building would then serve as the central place for the social as well as the business activities of the exchange members. In 1839, four years after the tsar's approval of their plans, the exchange opened its doors amidst the high hopes of its founders that henceforth modern business methods would prevail. To their great dismay, a majority of the merchants refused to use the hall and continued to hold their meetings in the bazaar (*gostinyi dvor*). In vain the exchange committee appealed to the chief of police to forbid these gatherings and to put pressure on the shop owners in the bazaar to conform to the new regulations. Finally, in 1860 the merchants agreed to transfer their business dealings into the exchange.[39] The history of the Rybinsk Exchange was almost identical.[40]

By any criteria the merchantry must be ranked as the most passive and submissive soslovie in Russian society. In the hundred years preceding the Crimean War there was only one recorded case of outright resistance on the part of the merchants to official state policy. In 1754, dissatisfied with the newly created Merchant Bank in St. Petersburg, the merchants organized a boycott until the Governing Senate met some of their demands for revising the statutes. Compare this behavior to that of any other soslovie during the same period. The submissive attitude of the merchants stands in striking contrast to the violent, if sporadic, outbreaks of the nobility, peasantry, and artisan-workers against the arbitrary power of the autocracy. Even the village clergy participated in and occasionally led peasant uprisings in the 1830s. Although suffering under a long history of frustrations on issues ranging from inadequate credit facilities to discriminatory tariffs, the merchants continued to shrink from any form of collective action.[41]

39. *Moskovskoe kupecheskoe sobranie*, p. 15; Naidenov, *Moskovskaia*, pp. 12–16. Golitsyn's efforts in 1825 to establish a society of manufacturing and industry in Moscow collapsed as the result of merchant indifference (Kniapina, *Politika*, pp. 247–48).
40. Meshcherskii, *Ocherki*, pp. 209–10.
41. S. M. Solov'ev, *Istoriia*, 23:793. Solov'ev's exhaustive investigation of the Senate archives reveals that there was considerable friction and rivalry among the merchants themselves leading, on occasion, to violence and court suits (for example, ibid. 24:1081, 1481–87).

The Merchants' Way of Life

The reluctance of the merchantry to promote social and political change cannot be attributed solely to the inhibiting influence of the government. Nor can it be explained as a consequence of economic stagnation, for the growth and expansion of commerce and industry in Russia throughout the eighteenth century has been clearly established. The merchants' unwillingness to alter traditional patterns of behavior under favorable economic conditions suggests that beneath the maze of legal and bureaucratic restraints lay an even tougher layer of resistance to social and political change. At this deeper level of cultural values and social structure, the essential characteristics of merchant life were patriarchal authority, religious piety, and insecurity of status. In combination the three elements paralyzed independent action and retarded the development of a political consciousness.

Although the merchants perceived that many of their difficulties could be traced to the government's policy, their patriarchal attitudes toward legitimate authority discouraged them from organizing against it. In merchant families child rearing, religious and educational practices, and business mores centered on the father, who commanded almost complete obedience. The family was the school, and the father was the teacher of both ethical norms and practical lessons. Well into the nineteenth century the traditional pre-Petrine values were instilled in generation after generation by what V. O. Kliuchevskii so aptly called the development of an "automatic conscience." Firmly rooted in the principles of the *Domostroi*, especially chapter sixty-four, "An Epistle and a Chastisement from Father to Son," attributed to the priest Sylvester, child rearing emphasized rules of behavior rather than theoretical knowledge. "Christian living" pervaded the three basic spheres of human activity—moral duties, civil duties, and domestic duties—providing under almost all circumstances clear guidelines to the activities of the mind, the will, and the feelings.[42]

Success in maintaining the old forms depended upon raising children at home, sealing them off from the outside world in the tightly knit, isolated life of the family, and preserving the formal, highly stylized etiquette that hindered social intercourse with anyone outside the narrow circle of relations. In this atmosphere, so vividly portrayed in merchant memoirs, the business was safe. Whatever specialized knowledge the merchant possessed about his trade he passed on to his son. To be sure, it was important to be literate, to master the fundamentals of arithmetic, to draw up bills of exchange, and perhaps even

42. Kliuchevskii, "Dva vospitaniia," pp. 231–33, 228–30, 243.

to read a few "good books." After all, respect for the well-read, God-fearing man had many precedents in Old Russian culture. But the practical lessons of buying and selling took precedence over book learning, for "knowledge nourishes badly." Outside observers came to similar conclusions, but deplored the lack of a broad commercial education for merchants' sons which placed them at the mercy of foreign competitors who easily excluded them from foreign trade.[43]

Even the meager available data on the social composition of Russian schools confirm the impressions left by merchant memoirs. The enrollments of merchants' children in the secondary and higher schools in the years 1838, 1844, and 1855 represented 6.8, 7.4, and 7.5 percent of the total. By all accounts these figures are astonishingly low. No comparable figures exist on the percentage of merchants in the total population, but merchants made up about 5 percent of the population in the towns (where most schools were located) during this twenty-year period.[44] This meant that the proportion of merchants' children in secondary and higher schools barely exceeded their share of the urban population even though the overwhelming majority of that population was composed of the lower classes (meshchanstvo, peasants, and soldiers), whose access to these schools was severely limited by their low cultural and material standard of living. The proportionately higher percentages of nobility, clergy, and raznochintsy who attended these schools dramatically exposes the relative indifference of the merchants to formal education.

What particularly worried the merchants about schooling was that excessive or indiscriminate reading might spawn pretensions to high culture that could find no outlet in merchant society and would certainly lead to efforts to escape from it. Once removed from their parents and exposed to the harsh environment of church or secular schools, the merchants reasoned, their sons would lose the emotional component of their instruction and training. Thus, obedience and filial piety would rest on the uncertain foundation of punishment;[45]

43. Semenov, *Izuchenie*, 3:231–39, 242–43; Androssov, *Statisticheskaia*, pp. 171–72.

44. Kamosko, "Izmeneniia," p. 204; Rashin, *Naselenie*, p. 119; Kliuchevskii, "Dva vospitaniia," pp. 227–28.

45. Vishniakov, *Svedeniia*, pt. 2, pp. 35, 158. It was still true a generation later when Meshcherskii toured the central provinces observing the merchantry: "Of education in a gymnasium or commercial school, there can be no question" (*Ocherki*, p. 57). With increased opportunities for secular education in the 1850s a small number of merchants' sons left their soslovie but in the absence of any accurate figures only certain outstanding individuals can be identified including Anton and Nikolai Rubinshtein (born 1829 and 1835, respectively), musicians and founders of the St. Petersburg and Moscow conservatories, respectively; A. I. Kirpichnikov (born 1845), literary historian; I. F. Balandin (born 1834), physician; A. I. Selivanov (born 1835), ethnographer and librarian,

new allegiances would be formed and new aspirations cherished; and the family as the basic economic unit would be doomed. As long as the father maintained a monopoly over the son's education, he could protect the sanctity of the family firm—the main defense against loss or ruin with its inevitable consequence of decline in social status. Thus, he was apt to resist innovation, no matter how efficient and profitable, if it threatened to weaken the primary loyalty to the family. In his memoirs, N. K. Krestovnikov recalled that his grandfather selected a site for a spinning factory in 1849 in order to be near "the family nest" and the workers whom he knew personally, despite the insufficient woodland for fuel and lack of good roads in the area. When the family opened a tallow factory after the Crimean War, even the workers were relatives.[46]

For many merchants the family meant not just blood relatives and relatives by marriage but also dependent people. These began to play an increasingly important role as a few of the wealthiest merchants yielded to the temptation to give their sons a formal education in order to allow them to compete with foreigners in the export trade or even to move into the nobility. When the better-educated scion of the merchant began, predictably, to "take on airs," abandon commerce, and desert his soslovie, the head of the household relied more and more on the faithful "servitor" in his shop to carry on the business. An orphan or the child of an impoverished family, he would have been brought into the household and the shop as a ward and errand boy, slowly making his way up by dint of hard work, total subservience, and complete honesty to become a clerk or assistant. Then, frequently, the merchant would command either during his lifetime or in his will that his daughter marry the tried and tested young man, thus rewarding business acumen and submission to patriarchal authority with adoption into the family.[47] In these cases, social origin

---

and N. P. Lanin (born 1832), publicist; and S. P. Botkin (born 1834), brother of V. P. Botkin, physician and close friend of T. N. Granovskii.

46. N. Krestovnikov, *Semeinaia*, 1:39–40. See also Chetverikov, *Bezvozvratno*, pp. 102–4.

47. While developing an important point in one of his most famous trial cases, the jurist A. F. Koni referred to this practice as a "common" one, especially in merchant families whose sons were educated beyond their station. Koni, *Izbrannye*, pp. 343–44, dealing with the affairs of testament of the estate of the merchant Kozma Beliaev. Koni knew whereof he spoke, since he was the grandson of a merchant who had allowed his son to enter the professional world, *RBS*, 9:104. In his will, M. Z. Tret'iakov, the father of the famous Moscow merchant patrons, left his sons all his property, but expressed the wish (which filial piety made a command) that they take as their partner his former shop assistant and marry their younger sister to him. This was done as he wished, and the fortunate young man, V. D. Konshin, later became one of Russia's richest and most enterprising merchants (Botkina, *Tret'iakov*, pp. 17, 19). The theme of the wealthy

meant little to the merchant in comparison with the advantages of having personally supervised the teaching and training of someone whose utter dependence on him was in many ways greater than that of his own son.

The reluctance to employ new business techniques was also rooted in the close identification of firm, family, and membership in the merchant guilds. Subscription in the guilds was not individual but collective. By declaring its common capital all members of the family shared equally in the privileges and the obligations of whichever guild its stated wealth entitled it to belong to.[48] This regulation not only reinforced the authority of the father but strengthened the interdependency among other members of the family as well. Long after double bookkeeping was introduced into Russia in 1780, merchant account books made no distinction between personal and business expenses. Although promissory notes were first made legal in 1729, they were used primarily in banking operations rather than for commercial purposes because merchants opposed the practice of discounting notes.[49] They had learned from harsh experience that they could not always expect their customers to settle accounts at the conclusion of the Nizhnyi market (especially if they were non-Russians), so they could have little faith in an impersonal system of credit.[50] Trust in anyone outside the family was bound to be misplaced. The lesson was clear enough from the histories of trading companies in the eighteenth century. Most were short-lived because of the clashes between merchant and noble members and family feuds among the participating merchants.[51]

The rampant suspicion of the merchants toward outsiders confounded public officials and private citizens who sought to gather information on their commercial activities. While traveling in 1854 through the market towns of southern Russia collecting information for a book, Ivan Aksakov soon discovered that the merchants' secre-

---

merchant's daughter being forced to marry the shop assistant turns up in Ostrovskii's play *Your drink, my hangover* (1856).

48. Storozhev, *Istoriia*, pt. 3, 70.

49. "Iz vospominanii Lamanskogo," p. 340; Levin, *Aktsionernye*, 1:8–10; Akademiia nauk, *Istoriia Moskvy*, 3:313. On the other hand, the government forbade peasants from binding themselves to the merchants by promissory notes, presumably because the nobility did not favor the idea of their serfs becoming legally indebted to the merchants (*PSZRI*, 1st ser., 14 February 1761, no. 11204). For the highly critical attitude of foreign merchants toward their Russian colleagues' primitive business practices see Kirchner, *Commercial Relations*, p. 18.

50. Vishniakov, *Svedeniia*, pt. 2, p. 75.

51. Polianskii, *Pervonachal'noe*, pp. 108–12; Lappo-Danilevskii, "Russkie," vol. 321, pt. 2, pp. 424–25.

tiveness prevented them from acquiring the insights necessary to their taking full advantage of prevailing market conditions. Confronted with conflicting answers on the most fundamental questions, he began "to lose respect for the much vaunted Russian common sense; yes and truly each one has his own pet notion, so that if I talk to ten merchants a day, I do not know from lack of information whom to believe."[52] Prince Meshcherskii discovered that the merchants' suspicion of outside influences extended to almost every sphere of life. In the 1830s wealthy merchants at the big river port of Torzhok petitioned against the construction of the St. Petersburg–Moscow railroad despite the obvious benefits that would accrue to them from it. A generation later the majority of the Volga grain merchants refused to use the railroads. The same merchants also spurned any veterinary assistance in combating the terrible anthrax epidemics that ravaged their herds of horses.[53]

Before the Crimean War joint-stock companies for commercial or industrial purposes aroused little interest among merchants. Of the forty-one joint-stock companies founded between 1799 and 1836, half had nothing directly to do with trade or manufacturing (they dealt with insurance and noncommercial transportation), and most of the rest were devoted to agricultural occupations, suggesting that their founders were nobles. Three-quarters of these companies were located in St. Petersburg and Odessa, where foreign entrepreneurs predominated. Yet these were the decades when Russian merchants were transferring their capital from commerce to manufacturing, a shift which some would argue ought to have brought about a significant change in attitudes as well. Before the emancipation the situation improved only slightly with the introduction in 1836 of a comprehensive law on joint-stock companies. The government shared responsibility for this state of affairs by drafting vague and confusing legislation which it subsequently ignored or violated. Nicholas's powerful finance minister, E. F. Kankrin, openly opposed stock companies as encouraging dangerous speculation. But even when the merchants were offered extensive privileges, they were reluctant to form large-scale stock companies that would have to compete with foreigners. Until the Crimean War other forms of corporate capital outside the family were even rarer.[54]

52. *Aksakov v ego pis'makh*, 3:93, 12 October 1854. Meshcherskii found the same thing to be true in the mid-1860s in the Moscow region (*Ocherki*, pp. 58–59, 296–97).
53. Meshcherskii, *Ocherki*, pp. 56, 208–9.
54. Shepelev, *Aktsionernye*, pp. 30–33. The standard work on joint-stock companies in Russia remains Kaminka, *Aktsionernye*. On bureaucratic discussions leading to the passage of the principal legislation on joint-stock companies in the nineteenth century see Shepelev, "Iz istorii," pp. 168–96. The merchants were conspicuous by their absence at

One incident reveals the extremes to which a merchant might go to maintain his family as an economic unit. On his death bed, P. M. Vishniakov extracted an oath from all the members of his extended family to live in one house and conduct his business affairs as a group for a period of six years after his death.[55] The ties between family ideology and business practice cushioned the shock of economic change and enabled the merchantry to resist the introduction of new forms of business organization. Merchants felt no compelling need to demand from the state the economic and social reforms that were an integral part of capitalist development elsewhere in Europe.

Attitudes toward authority within the family were transferred automatically into public life. In society, as in the home, life was governed by "mysterious and arbitrary acts from above." Outside the family the prevailing code of behavior was that of Solomon: "The wise see misfortune and seek cover; the naive march forward and are punished." Children were taught that "it was necessary to be afraid, to be quiet, to hold one's tongue as if one knew nothing." In the long run God's will would triumph. When secular literature penetrated merchant households, it normally came in the form of defenders of absolutism like Karamzin, Derzhavin, Lomonosov, and Boussuet (in Russian translation) against the poisonous ideas of "Voltairians, Aetheists, Masons and Martinists."[56] The first plebian journalists to emerge from a merchant milieu, N. A. Polevoi, I. P. Pesotskii, and M. P. Pogodin, the editors of *Moskovskii telegraf* (1825–34), *Ekonom* (1841–53), and *Moskvitianin* (1841–56), sought to show how the loyal and obedient conduct of the merchants furthered the economic power of the autocratic state.[57] The only area in Russian public life in which

all stages in this preparatory work. On other forms of corporate organization see Bunge, *Znachenie*, especially pp. 12–15.

55. Vishniakov, *Svedeniia*, pt. 3, p. 8.

56. An exceptionally well-educated merchant like G. P. Kamenev, a product of the best pension in Kazan, was likely to become an object of suspicion among merchants within his own soslovie. "He is a hopeless case," remarked the father of one of his friends. "Though he is our brother merchant, his head has been filled with Voltairism, [vol'terianstvo]" (Zaklund, *Kamenev*, pp. 15–16, 91). For similar reactions see Vishniakov, *Svedeniia*, pt. 2, pp. 32, 35, 40, 158, and Polevoi, *Zapiski*, pt. 1, p. 5. To be sure, books of the Bible and other ecclesiastical works were standard fare for any literate merchant. But well into the second quarter of the nineteenth century, interest in secular literature was largely restricted to merchant families who owned and operated bookstores in the two capitals.

57. See, for example, Polevoi, "O vospitanii voobshche i osobenno kuptsov," *Moskovskii telegraf*, no. 19 (September 1829); "O vystavke rossiiskikh manufaktur," ibid., no. 6 (March 1829); "Smes," ibid., no. 18 (September 1828); and "O kupechestve," *Moskvitianin*, no. 5 (1842); M. Pogodin, "Peter velikii," ibid., no. 1 (1841); idem, "Krest'ianin Ivan Pososhkov, gosudarstvennyi muzh vremen Petra Velikogo," ibid., no. 3 (1842); A.

the merchantry made a significant voluntary contribution was in the charities, where service to the throne and Christian living found a happy union. Even here the state set limits upon the range of choices. Merchants were required to obtain imperial approval for the establishment of any new charitable organization and were forbidden to support any outside their own soslovie. The main beneficiaries of merchant giving were the institutions that exemplified Christian virtues —hospitals, shelters for the poor, orphanages, and the church.[58] Donations to educational institutions lagged behind; these were largely restricted to the establishment of the Moscow Commercial School and the Moscow Practical Academy at the beginning of the nineteenth century.

In the family, the firm, the church, and the school, the merchantry clung much more tenaciously to the older forms of Russian life than did the nobles, petty officials, and professional cadres emerging from the raznochintsy. Among those groups Western forms of child rearing were beginning to break down the traditional patterns of authority. Exposure to Western books and to higher education at the universities or the technical institutes opened new intellectual vistas for a small but influential number of cultural leaders drawn from these same sources. Before mid-century there were, to be sure, a few notable exceptions to the bleak picture of merchant isolation, such as the Botkin brothers, who were friends of the radical critic Vissarion Belinskii and the liberal historian T. N. Granovskii, or the Plavil'shchikov family, which owned a bookstore in St. Petersburg.[59] But the unavoidable conclusion is that the overwhelming majority of the merchantry, including the bulk of the pervostateiny, were cut off from the intellectual currents and social contacts that might have enriched their meager larder of ideas and supplied them with alternative explanations of their place in the social and political order.

The merchants' way of life resembled that of the meshchanstvo and the peasantry at the other end of the social scale, with their patriarchal

---

Roslavskii, "Sravneniia Rossii v statisticheskom otnoshenii s drugimi pervoklasnymi evropeiskimi derzhavami," ibid., no. 5 (1844); "O manufakturnoi promyshlennosti Rossii v otnosheniiakh ei k obshchei proizvoditel'nosti i k bytu nizshikh klassov naroda," ibid., no. 2 (1845). A good survey of Polevoi's views on industrialization can be found in Tatarinov, Zhurnal, especially pp. 16–18. Polevoi and Pesotskii were merchants' sons, and Pogodin was the son of an emancipated serf who had gained his business experience as steward on the Stroganov estates.

58. Storozhev, Istoriia, vol. 2, pt. 1, pp. 35–50.

59. Belinskii, Sochinenie, 9:514–17 and 11:179–80. The Plavil'shchikov brothers, Vasili, Aleksei, and Peter Alekseevich, became respectively, a bibliophile, a writer, and an actor. Vasili was one of the largest book dealers and publishers in St. Petersburg in the 1820s (RBS, 14:1–6).

attitudes, religious piety, and social isolation. The crucial difference was that the merchant had more of a stake in preserving the status quo. His ownership of property, his hard-won but shaky "social honor" (*chest'*), his petty office holding made him far more cautious than the lower orders of the population in challenging state authority, even during periods of deep social and economic crisis.

Social Instability and Status Anxiety

Insecurity of status was another characteristic of the merchantry which warped its social role in the urban community. The merchantry had become by the early nineteenth century the most internally unstable of all the sosloviia. What distinguished it from every other soslovie was that economic factors alone determined membership. Any free citizen could petition to enroll in one of the three merchant guilds. It was only necessary to declare that he possessed a specific sum of capital, fixed by law but varying in size over the period 1775–1863, and to be approved by the elected representatives of the merchant estate. A heavy financial loss, a large fine, or even a sharp tax increase could wipe out a merchant's capital and drop him precipitously into a lower guild or into the meshchanstvo.[60] Heavy penalties accompanied loss of status. Economically, each guild enjoyed advantages denied the lower guilds and the meshchanstvo and trading peasantry. More important, however, were the social privileges that the merchants shared with the nobility and clergy. All merchants were exempt from military service, and those of the first two guilds had immunity from corporal punishment as well. To spare their sons from serving in the army—a living death in Nicholaen Russia—an entire stratum of "fictional" third-guild merchants came into existence. Falsely declaring more capital than they possessed, small tradesmen with sons eligible for military service struggled for years to pay guild taxes. When their sons passed the age limit, they lapsed back into the meshchanstvo, in many cases without ever having been able to trade at the level to which they were entitled by virtue of their membership in the guilds. According to an independent survey by the Imperial Geographic Society in the late 1840s, merchants clung so desperately to their precarious status that they were willing to sell property in order to pay guild taxes on capital that they did not possess.[61] For the merchantry downward mobility was a constant and

60. TsGAOR, f. 672 (Nicholas I), op. 1, d. 272, "Zapiska," p. 4; Naidenov, *Vospominaniia*, pt. 2, p. 6; Vishniakov, *Svedeniia*, pt. 2, pp. 83, 93–95.
61. Ditiatin, *Ustroistvo*, 2:328–30; ORBL, f. 332 (Chizhov), carton 78, no. 27, Geo-

far-greater hazard than it was for any other soslovie. Much evidence suggests that the turnover was significant, and the fear of losing status was persistent and deep seated.

The attrition rate was high even in the metallurgical field, where the government lavished subsidies on enterprising merchants. In European Russia during the eighteenth century thirty-nine out of forty-seven wealthy merchant families lost control of the enterprises that they had founded. In the Urals five out of seven families maintained their holdings, but even here the vast Demidov enterprises declined in size and output.[62]

The merchants were particularly vulnerable to the destructive impact of wars and natural calamities, from which they found it painfully difficult to recover. In the wake of the Napoleonic Wars and the subsequent economic dislocation, their numbers and wealth fell sharply, as shown in table 1.1.[63] This precipitous decline continued into the next decade as a result of three government policies. During these years taxes were quadrupled for the merchants. In 1819 a relatively moderate tariff was introduced, reducing the rates and allowing a flood of foreign imports. In the early 1820s trading peasants paying quitrent (*obrok*) were permitted to compete with merchants on highly favorable terms.[64] By 1824 the guild population fell under fifty thousand, representing a loss of almost two-thirds of the population of 1808. During the same period merchant capital shrank from over twenty million to just over thirteen million rubles. The decline was fairly uniform in all regions of the empire. Although Moscow province was not hit hardest, its merchant population was halved between 1808 and 1824, and its capital decreased by one-third.

The sudden recovery after 1824 reflected the impact of the guild reform, which allowed trading peasants to enroll in the merchant guilds. But within five years another drastic decline was registered when the cotton industry went through a crisis of overproduction. Throughout most of the 1840s the recovery was slow, and it was by no

graficheskoe obshchestvo, Komissiia dlia issledovaniia vnutrenei torgovli (po sredstve, pozhertvovanie Petersburgskim kupechestvom), "Kratkii ocherk sostoianiia vnutrennei torgovli i prichin ee upadka," n.d. (after 1849).

62. Pavlenko, *Istoriia*, pp. 161, 214–15.

63. The sources for merchants enrolled in guilds in European Russia are Kabuzan, *Narodonaselenie*, p. 134, for the period 1808–30; Kniapina, *Politika*, p. 102, for 1840; and ORBL, f. 332, no. 27, p. 2 for 1847. The source for merchants enrolled in guilds by areas and provinces is Ryndziunskii, *Gorodskoe*, table 9, pp. 98–103, which does not tabulate the totals for all provinces, and table 28, p. 297.

64. For taxes see Ryndziunskii, *Gorodskoe*, p. 42; for the tariff see Lodyzhenskii, *Istoriia*, pp. 182–89; for the trading peasants see Ryndziunskii, "Gorodskoe naselenie," p. 308, and below, chapter 2.

means complete in the center and the Black Earth regions on the eve of the Crimean War. As there was no massive ennoblement of the merchants at any time during this period, it can only be assumed that in the large majority of cases either merchants left the guilds voluntarily to escape taxes or they were forced by business failures to enter the lower orders of the urban population.[65]

These dramatic losses demonstrated on a massive scale the ever-present danger that faced the individual merchant throughout the eighteenth and early-nineteenth centuries. Intimidated by the state and riddled with status anxieties, he was incapable of joining with others to check the erosion of the entire soslovie. Even if he cast off his reverence for the state, he could ill afford to take the further risk of jeopardizing his own social standing and that of his family by diverting his energies away from his enterprise into the uncharted waters of public life. Therefore, it was safer and more profitable in the short run to compete more vigorously against his fellow merchants. In that competition he might hope to amass sufficient capital to secure him against all but the greatest catastrophes.

Still, even the wealthiest merchant might acknowledge that the only means of obtaining absolute security for his family was to enter the hereditary nobility. There, status if not wealth could never be lost short of lèse majesté. In the meantime, he could only petition the government to keep his competitors at bay lest they destroy him. Thus, instead of challenging state policies that lay at the source of their parlous condition, the merchants devised alternative and inadequate solutions to their dilemma. Their obsessive drive for security led them in two directions: either into a struggle within their soslovie for wealth and higher status or toward an upward flight out of their soslovie into the nobility. As it turned out, both these responses further weakened the merchantry and increased its dependence upon the state at a time when the nobility and peasantry were striving to emancipate themselves.

Long before Catherine's reforms a small oligarchy of big merchants emerged as the dominant force in the towns. Using their wealth, status, and official positions in the town administrations they exploited the less affluent guild members and lorded over the rest of the town

65. A recent study by Smetanin discounts the economic importance of this drastic decline by arguing that most of the losses came from the impoverished third guild. No doubt this was true but it neither explains the great loss of merchant capital nor changes the impression of a soslovie in decline. Moreover, Smetanin himself observes that in Perm, the one province he has studied on the basis of archival sources, the upper ranks of the merchantry between 1789 and 1848 were completely decimated ("Formirovanie," pp. 158, 163).

TABLE 1.1. *Merchants Enrolled in the Guilds*

A. European Russia

1808	1816	1818	1820	1822	1824
150,475	84,388	73,850	67,343	59,269	49,460

B. Areas and Provinces

	1800	1808	1816	1824
Central				
Moscow	14,016	14,646	12,179	7,198
Nizhegorod	2,891	3,375	1,444	930
Black Earth				
Orel	8,167	11,238	5,913	3,163
West and Southwest				
Vitebsk	1,282	1,769	690	165
Volynia	975	527	214	214
Ural				
Viatka	878	1,325	926	744
South and Southeast				
Orenburg	1,964	2,003	1,305	529

populations. Under Elizabeth they even sought to revive the title and privileges of the old gosti. The tax system, based on joint responsibility and graduated rates, enabled the rich merchants to reduce the town populations to economic dependence on them. Although the rich were in a small minority in the town assemblies, which apportioned the taxes, the smaller merchants and artisans were too intimidated and debt ridden to organize resistance. No wonder, then, that the big merchants' only form of political action was to smash the opposition of their rivals, and often their heads as well, to secure control of the top offices in the town administrations.[66] The most famous case in the eighteenth century was that of Grigorii Ochapov, president of the town council of Arkhangelsk, who tyrannized the merchants with the help of his accomplices, Anton Bardin, a first-guild merchant, and a former shop assistant. Ochapov had his rivals beaten, publically hu-

66. Kizevetter, *Posadskaia*, pp. 132, 610–13; Golikova, "Rostovshchichestvo," pp. 242–91; S. M. Solov'ev, *Istoriia*, 24:1465–66; Naidenov, *Vospominaniia*, 2:7–8, who shows that by the end of the nineteenth century there were more gentle forms of persuasion to achieve the same ends.

1825	1826	1830	1840	1847
77,494	71,638	72,715	35,947	40,993

1827	1854
9,084	17,292
937	1,647
4,000	7,548
598	1,682
910	4,103
956	2,061
733	3,141

miliated, and put in irons for years before his victims organized to replace him.[67]

Inadequate laws on usury and the shortage of credit in Russia also played into the hands of the wealthy merchants. Because they enjoyed a high credit rating from the state, they were able to borrow large sums from the few existing government lending institutions and loan money to needy merchants at exorbitant interest rates—never less than 30 percent.[68] Their enormous profits from these operations explain their long and successful opposition to the establishment of popular credit facilities in Russia.

If some wealthy merchants chose to protect their interests and defend their status through terror and extortion, many more preferred the more genteel method of ennoblement. In either case the natural leaders of the merchantry abdicated their responsibilities to the urban community and further undermined the structure of their own soslovie. Originally, three ways were open to the merchants seeking

67. Krestinin, *Kratkaia*, pp. 16–26.
68. Borovoi, *Kredit*, pp. 86, 126.

entry into the nobility: by imperial favor, normally in return for some outstanding public service to the state; by promotion in rank (*chin*), for those merchants who served as town officials or tax collectors; and by imperial decoration (*orden*) of the first class. Merchants sought honors, decorations, promotions, and the right to own serfs not as ends in themselves but as the means to obtain security of status that only a patent of nobility could guarantee. Even after the government prohibited the majority of newly ennobled merchant industrialists from buying serfs, the merchants continued their pursuit of noble status, thus demonstrating their real motives.[69]

Education became another vehicle for ascending the social scale. The statistician Androssov was astounded to note that the Moscow Commercial School and the Practical Academy advertised that their graduates could enter state service, which was normally closed to merchants' sons. What the "semi-literate merchants" desperately needed, in his eyes, was to raise the technical and cultural level of commerce. Instead, they used the schools that they had endowed to promote access to the Table of Ranks at a level at which personal ennoblement became a real possibility.[70]

The merchantry pressed so hard, in fact, that the nobility stiffened its resistance. At the turn of the nineteenth century the government found it necessary to declare again that merchants could not become nobles simply by achieving a certain rank. Only service in the specific civil and military offices designated in the Table of Ranks could bring about an automatic promotion into the noble soslovie. All other cases had to be approved by the emperor himself. Although the pill was sweetened for some individual merchants by confirming their special privileges to buy land and peasants, the law solemnly affirmed that these privileges could not be transmitted to their descendents; "in this way the rights secured eternally to the nobility and their descendents are preserved inviolate."[71]

A generation later the government became so deeply concerned over the exodus of wealthy merchants from their soslovie that it created a new social rank—honored citizen—to meet the craving for status. The measure closed down the path to ennoblement through obtaining a decoration and made it more difficult through promotion. But it offered a limited number of merchants hereditary exemption from military service, corporal punishment, and the head tax.[72] It is difficult to say whether or not this stemmed the tide. There are a

69. *PSZRI*, 1st ser., 29 March 1762, no. 11490.
70. Androssov, *Statisticheskaia*, p. 128.
71. *PSZRI*, lst ser., 18 October 1804, no. 21481.
72. Ibid., 2nd ser., 10 April 1832, no. 5284. Pintner shows that the proposal fell far

sufficient number of well-known individual cases to suggest that whatever the reduction in numbers, some of the wealthiest families continued to seek and gain ennoblement. Alexander III's minister of state domains, M. N. Ostrovskii, was an ennobled merchant's son. Two great railroad barons, Samuel Poliakov, a converted Jew, and P. I. Gubonin achieved the rank of third class with the title general as a reward for educational and charitable donations. Others gave important collections to the Academy of Sciences like A. A. Titov in Russian history and A. A. Bakhrushin in theater arts.[73] P. I. Shchukin, who also received a patent of nobility for donating his great collection of paintings to the state, revealed in his memoirs that the sources of his social aspirations were his mother, who was a Botkin, and his father, who had already acquired all the tastes and habits of a noble in the mid-nineteenth century.[74]

In addition to providing security noble status also translated social prestige into concrete economic advantages. In metallurgy and the farming out of the state vodka tax the close relationship between private enterprise and government placed the ennobled industrialist in a more favorable position relative to that of the socially inferior merchant in dealing with state bureaucrats, who were themselves noble. The most striking case here is that of the legendary Tula blacksmith Nikita Demidov, who rose to become one of the greatest iron and coal magnates in Russia under Peter the Great. Even before he was ennobled in 1720, Demidov was not afraid to tangle with imperial officials ranking as high as a voevoda. But after he became a noble, it was far easier and less costly for him to take on a man of such stature as the famous historian V. N. Tatishchev, who was the head of all the state mining enterprises.[75] It is not surprising, then, to discover that at the end of the eighteenth century the leaders in the metallurgical industry were ennobled merchants who owned 66.2 percent of the enterprises and produced 53 percent of the copper and 67.8 percent of the pig iron. These included the Demidovs, Iakovlevs, Batashovs, Stroganovs, Krasil'nikovs, Osokins, and Mosolovs. At least a dozen big vodka tax farming merchants were ennobled, including such distinguished families as the Khlebnikovs, Kishins, Loginovs, Baryshnikovs, Lukins, Meshchaninovs, and Zubkovs.[76]

---

short of the more ambitious plans of Kankrin in the 1820s to create a stable middle class (*Economic Policy*, pp. 63–66).

73. Zaionchkovskii, *Rossiiskoe*, pp. 116–17; Buryshkin, *Moskva*, p. 323.

74. Shchukin, *Vospominaniia*, 1:3–12, 2:20–6.

75. B. B. Kafengauz, *Istoriia*, 1:142–44, 163–66.

76. Pavlenko, "Odvorianivanie," pp. 84–85. The merchants' zealous pursuit of noble rank was already an established theme in eighteenth-century satirical comedies (Welsh, "Satirical Themes," p. 407).

By the end of the nineteenth century all but one of the great merchant families who played a leading role at the time of Peter the Great had moved out of their estate, having been either raised to the nobility, which appears most probable given their wealth and high status to begin with, or dropped into the lower orders; presumably, a certain few families died out. Among the old merchant families absorbed into the nobility, most of them from the first guild originally, were the Orlovs, Dubyshkins, Titovs, Panteleevs, Fadeevs, Kalustrovs, Popovs, Zabylins, Iartsovs, and Chulkovs.[77] Even in Siberia, where the nobility had no local roots, the big merchants scrambled for hereditary ennoblement.[78]

Disparaged by the legendary merchant tax farmer V. A. Kokorev as "the sickness of rank-mania [*chinobesie*]," this upward surge also infected sons of merchants who had become personally ennobled. No longer content to sit in warehouses or to haggle in bazaars, they sought to pursue more genteel professions. In the eyes of Kokorev this "desertion from the ranks of the merchants' soslovie" sapped the vitality of the oldest and most trustworthy business firms and wiped out the good will, lines of credit, and knowledge of local conditions which had been acquired so painstakingly over the years.[79] Strongly echoing this lament, the minister of finance under Nicholas I, Count E. F. Kankrin, shrewdly observed that the constant striving of the most capable and energetic merchants to achieve noble status was a very regrettable but understandable reaction to the precariousness of their social position.[80] What Kokorev and Kankrin were reluctant to admit was that the striving for ennoblement also sharpened and transformed the naturally competitive economic relations among merchants into a bitter social struggle with victory going to those who could invoke the authority of the state on their side. The circle was full drawn: the insecurity of the merchants not only sapped their will to organize and impelled them whenever possible to abandon their soslovie but also forced them into greater reliance upon the state.

This dependence was tested in the late eighteenth and early nineteenth centuries by the subversive power of a capitalist transformation of Russia. Merchants shifted from commerce, with its passive turnover of capital, to industry with its dynamic investment capital, as the markets expanded and the hiring of free labor grew rapidly. Under similar circumstances at an earlier period, the commercial and indus-

77. Chulkov, "Moskovskoe," pp. 490–91, 501–2.
78. Gromyko, "K kharakteristike," p. 70.
79. Kokorev, *Ekonomicheskie*, pp. 140–41, 192–96. See also the memorandum of O. L. Sveshnikov to N. S. Mordvinov dated 1823 in Bilbasov, *Arkhiv*, 6:427–30, 435.
80. Pintner, *Economic Policy*, p. 64.

trial leaders of Western Europe had sought to break down the administrative and social constraints that blocked their drive for greater profits and economic power. A comparable response by Russian merchants was seriously hampered by the peculiarities of the soslovie system. Peter the Great's weak successors allowed a succession of economic competitors to challenge the merchants' control over trade and industry without freeing the merchants from their obligations to the state so that they could compete on equal terms.

To be sure, the merchants themselves did little to rise to the challenge. In their patriarchal fashion it was easier for them to perceive these alien social groups, rather than the state or their own inertia, as constituting the main threat to their preeminent position in commerce and manufacturing. Moreover, unless the merchantry could hold on to its natural leaders, who were themselves tempted by new openings for upward mobility, and generate a political consciousness, it would be forced to continue to appeal to an unresponsive state for protection. Hostile feelings toward social outsiders would feed the merchants' growing sense of isolation. Under these circumstances, the merchant soslovie could easily adopt the mentality of a besieged camp.

CHAPTER 2

THE ENCIRCLEMENT OF

THE MERCHANTRY

From 1750 to 1850 three groups of economic competitors assaulted the weak defenses of the merchantry—noble industrialists, trading peasants, and foreign capitalists. Their ascendance was the result both of the slow growth of capitalism within the country and the rapid expansion of the imperial frontiers. New market conditions and the costs of westernization transformed subsistence agriculture, stimulated a money economy, and opened the way for enterprising nobles and their serfs to launch careers in commerce and manufacturing. At the same time, the state manipulated tariffs, taxation, and monopolies to nourish its most valuable service class—the nobility—often at the expense of merchant interests. The expansion of serfdom into newly acquired territories, which took place throughout the eighteenth century, also discriminated against the economic interests of the merchants, especially after 1762, when they were expressly forbidden to purchase serfs; it slowed the growth of a free labor force, artificially restricted the domestic market, and placed the peasant trader under the protection of the powerful landlord. Following territorial annexations the state generously granted special privileges to foreign capitalists in the areas of manufacturing and transit trade, which stimulated economic activities in western and southern borderlands. The merchants found it difficult to compete with noble industrialists because of their legal and financial obligations and their conservative commercial attitudes cultivated under a different set of expectations about the exclusive character of their socioeconomic role. The merchantry had not been created to fight off a ring of competitors aided and abetted by its own government. The functional rationale of Peter's service state crumbled into ruins around the embattled merchants.

Meanwhile, in the geographic center of the country the Great Russian merchantry was also surrounded by another competitor brought under the flag by military conquest. These were merchants from different ethnic groups—Poles, Germans, Jews, Greeks, Armenians, and Tatars—who were enrolled in the guilds but remained culturally unassimilated. In their competition with the Great Russians they enjoyed easy access to Western and Asiatic trade, close ties with European capitalists, and special concessions from the Imperial Russian government, which was eager to secure their talents and loyalties. It is no wonder then that the Great Russian merchants perceived themselves as engaged in a prolonged and relentless struggle against alien social elements supported by powerful officials in both the central and provincial bureaucracies. That the threat was also real and dangerous emerges clearly from a review of the prolonged rivalry between the Russian merchants and their formidable rivals.

Noble Industrialists

Emerging as the first major competitors of the merchantry in the second half of the eighteenth century, the noble industrialists built up a commanding position in the three basic sectors of manufacturing— distillation of spirits, iron, and wool. During the reigns of Elizabeth and Catherine, through the influence at court of such favorites as the Shuvalovs and the Vorontsovs, the nobility obtained the exclusive rights to own serfs, to produce alcohol and salt, to raise tobacco, to manufacture tallow, to export grain, and to trade with Khiva, Bukhara, and Persia. By contracting with merchants for the sale and distribution of alcohol, noble families such as the Saltykovs, Apraksins, Viazemskiis, Odoevskiis, Gagarins, and Petrovo-Solovevs amassed great fortunes.[1] Once again through court politics, the nobility was able to obtain the bulk of government contracts for iron and coarse wool for use by the armed forces. At the end of the century the nobility owned factories producing 88 percent of the pig iron, 85 percent of the copper, and 46 percent of the cloth in the empire. Because the burgeoning manufacturing activities of the great noble families matched the military and financial interests of the state, they were brought under the protective umbrella of the tariffs of 1755, 1766, and 1782.[2] In the long, seesaw struggle for control over the labor force, the nobility persuaded the government as early as 1762 to

1. Iakovtsevskii, *Kupecheskii*, pp. 155–60; Karnovich, *Zamechatel'nye*, p. 45; Pokrovskii, *Vneshnaia*, pp. 78, 114–16.
2. Pavlenko, "Odvorianivanie," p. 84; idem, *Istoriia*, p. 455. To be sure the largest share in this production was supplied by ennobled merchants, but they were nobles nonetheless. Pokrovskii, *Vneshnaia*, pp. 98, 114–16.

forbid all non-noble manufacturers from buying peasants with or without land. But the merchants persisted in violating the ban, and it had to be restated in the strongest possible terms in 1804.[3]

Under the banner of free trade the nobility steadily whittled away the influence of the Manufacturing College. Responding to the demands of the nobles, the government eliminated many privileges for individuals engaged in manufacturing, thus terminating most monopolies and opening the way for anyone to establish factories in most branches of the economy. The immediate beneficiaries were nobles and their peasants. Discriminatory taxes further strengthened the nobles' position at the expense of the merchant-manufacturers. Prominent nobles like the publicist Prince M. M. Shcherbatov and the vice-president of the Manufacturing College, Sukin, pressed for stricter limitations on the rights of the merchant-manufacturers in order to prevent "the blurring of sosloviia."[4] The climax came in 1779 with the abolition of the Manufacturing College. Deprived of support from the state the merchants were squeezed out of heavy industry. During the following half century they became identified more exclusively with trading than at any other time in the modern period. Only after the Napoleonic Wars did the merchantry begin to reverse this trend. Yet as late as 1825 the overwhelming majority of labor employed in the metallurgical and textile industries belonged to the nobility either as manorial or possessional serfs. Against Peter's intentions the merchant soslovie acquired a proscriptive occupational role to match its narrowly defined legal and administrative character. The division of labor between the two sosloviia—the nobility in industry and the merchant in commerce—led to competition rather than cooperation, prevented the development of a firm political alliance between them, and blocked the creation of a unified capitalist class.[5] The reverberations of this struggle continued long after the economic relations between the two sosloviia changed.

Their economic rivalry fueled a lasting social antagonism. Not that the nobility harbored any deep-seated cultural hostility toward making money through direct involvement in business enterprise. Quite

3. *PSZRI*, 1st ser., 29 March 1762, no. 11880; ibid., 18 October 1804, no. 21481.
4. Baburin, *Ocherki*, pp. 160–61.
5. Pavlenko, "Iz istorii," pp. 328–44, makes clear, in spite of its title, the distinction between the aspirations of the traders, who were mostly merchants, and the industrialists, who were mainly nobles or ennobled merchants. The industrialists wanted the right to attach peasants to mines and factories in labor-short areas like the Urals. The merchants only wanted a few household serfs to mind their stores and warehouses. Even later, when the merchants went into the textile industry, they could hire labor in the overpopulated central regions and did not need possessional serfs. Similarly, the industrialists wanted the establishment of state banks while the merchants did not.

the contrary, nobles sought and won in 1824 the right to enroll in the merchant guilds. But they took a disdainful attitude toward "trade," as opposed to "manufacture," that was characteristic of nobilities elsewhere in Europe. Moreover, their membership in the guilds in no way weakened their primary attachment to their noble rank. They would never accept the epithet "kuptsy." Perhaps more important the nobles prided themselves on an altogether different view of business practices and the uses of money. It was all too easy for the nobility to transfer to its industrial enterprises the same wasteful, extravagant, and inefficient practices that characterized the exploitation of its landed estates, where bonded labor made a shambles of cost accounting. The cultural outlook of the nobility placed a much higher value on consumption of profits, often at a staggering rate, than on reinvestment. Thus, while the nobles were engaged in the same pursuit of gain as the merchants, their style of life became vastly different. At great cost they acquired the veneer of Western culture.[6] They regarded the bearded, slow-moving merchant dressed in his traditional Muscovite costume with bemused or contemptuous eyes. They frequently attributed the commercial successes of the merchants to sharp practices in discounting promissory notes, cheating manorial peasants in the grain trade, and violating the law of 1762 that forbade merchants from acquiring any landed estates.[7] At the Legislative Commission under Catherine, Shcherbatov's remarks fairly characterized the nobility's high-tory views that the factory workers employed by Moscow merchants lived under "debased conditions" and that the merchants themselves were uncouth and unenterprising.[8] The economic dependence of many spendthrift nobles on merchant usurers for money to support their European living standards helped sharpen this resentment.[9]

In the eighteenth century the nobility took full advantage of its social prestige to harass and humiliate the merchantry. According to petitions to the Legislative Commission, merchants in the provincial towns were exposed to constant abuse and often vicious beatings at the hands of nobles. The seriousness of their plight can be best judged

6. Confino, *Domaines*, pp. 130, 141, and throughout; Kahan, "Cost of 'Westernization,'" pp. 40–60.
7. *SIRIO* (1889), 68:349–50, 491, 495, 516–17, 518–20, 543, 568–69, 613; ibid. (1911), 134:400 ff.
8. S. M. Solov'ev, *Istoriia*, 17:368, 371; Baburin, *Ocherki*, pp. 157, 160–61.
9. Bolotov, *Zapiski*, 4:967. Bolotov's account of his frequent visits to merchants' homes carefully balanced his disapproval of the merchants' sharp practices and "peddling of alcohol" with his praise for their Old Russian values of hospitality and even stimulating conversation, especially among booksellers (ibid., 3:672, 691–92, 821–25, 941, 1028–29; ibid., 4:413, 416, 427, 431, 459, 888–90).

by the merchantry's poignant request that in cases of serious bodily harm, such as the loss of sight or a maimed limb resulting from such beatings, the payment of a fine by the guilty party was not enough— even if such a verdict could be extracted from the noble-controlled voevoda's court; they demanded quite literally "an eye for an eye and a tooth for a tooth."[10]

The nobility was not averse to crippling its competitors by political means as well. In 1754, Lieutenant General Baron Sivers, the court marshall himself—and the owner of a paper and box factory—attempted to ruin the merchant Ol'khin, who was engaged in the same business, by obtaining a state order forbidding him to expand his plant. When Ol'khin resisted the pressures, Sivers demanded personal satisfaction from the poor man and took the case to the Senate, the highest judicial body in the empire.[11] These were no penny-ante games between nobles and merchants.

As far as the nobles were concerned, at least until Catherine's urban reforms in 1785, the merchants were hardly distinguishable from the peasants on their estates. The merchants were, after all, part of the tax-paying population (*podatnoe naselenie*), a distinctive legal category which relegated them in the eyes of the nobles to the lower half of humanity. In the provinces, moreover, most of the merchants, as we have seen, actually lived at the same economic level as the trading peasants and in certain cases, as we shall see, even possessed less wealth and displayed less commercial enterprise than their peasant competitors. For most nobles this was all the evidence they needed to despise the merchants.

Scattered evidence from the nineteenth century reveals the persistence of the nobility's social snobbery. Noble industrialists were opposed to serving with merchants on joint committees such as that proposed by the minister of finance in 1823 to prevent illicit trade.[12] One of the most notorious cases of social antagonism was the reign of terror that Moscow Governor-General A. A. Zakrevskii unleashed against the city merchants, squeezing money out of them for "public projects," threatening them with their own workers, and insulting them coarsely when they hesitated to comply with his outrageous demands. Of petty-noble origin, Zakrevskii was a boor compared to

10. *SIRIO* (1894), 93:183 (Borovsk), 219 (Libin), 236 (Gzhatsk), 248 (Vereia), 306 (Aleksin), 454 (Koshira), 469 (Kashin), 531 (Bui), 569 (Uglich); ibid. (1911), 134:400 (Irkutsk).
11. S. M. Solov'ev, *Istoriia*, 24:1128. For other incidents see Bernadskii, "Ocherki," pp. 76, 91–93.
12. Storozhev, *Istoriia*, vol. 2, pt. 1, p. 186.
13. Naidenov, *Vospominaniia*, pt. 1, pp. 88–102.

other governor-generals like Shuvalov and Golitsyn, but even these natural aristocrats maintained a superior paternalistic attitude toward the merchants.[13] Long after the emancipation condescending views toward the merchantry prevailed among high officials of noble origin, including members of the imperial family. A particular object of derision was the merchant whose fortune had been made from vodka tax farming. "Pot house sages," Minister of the Interior P. A. Valuev called them. "Liquor dealers' Jew trick," the normally enlightened Grand Duke Konstantin Nikolaevich said, referring to a perfectly legal entrepreneurial effort by a Christian merchant. Even the tsar, Alexander II, shared these opinions.[14]

As the tastemakers of society, the nobility legitimated and spread these derogatory attitudes until the merchants became highly sensitive and openly defensive about their social role. In 1861 a highly respected political economist who was sympathetic to the merchantry concluded that "insulting a merchant, just so long as it did not lead to blows, went unnoticed by the eyes and ears of public opinion."[15] In sum, although the merchants and noble industrialists were engaged in similar kinds of capitalist enterprise, they were deeply divided by the legal obligations imposed on them as hereditary soslovie and by the social attitudes engendered by the westernization of the nobility.

Trading Peasants

The rise of the trading peasant as a competitor of the merchant was directly related to the costs of westernization. The upper nobility aspired to a new and expensive level of culture, and the government needed greater revenues to finance the conquest and administration of new territories. To meet their expenses the big landlords shifted the obligations of their serfs from labor services to payments in kind or cash, and the government encouraged its state peasants to follow suit. Together they released thousands of peasants for work in nonagricultural sectors of the economy. In perhaps the best-known case, the

14. Valuev, *Dnevnik*, 2:263, entry 14 April 1868; TsGAOR, f. 722, op. 1, d. 94, "Dnevnik Vel. Kn. Konstantin Nikolaevich," entry 8 April 1868; ibid., f. 677 (Alexander III), op. 1, d. 669, Alexander II to Alexander Alexandrovich, 9 August 1868. The triumphs of even the most public-spirited merchants were spoiled by aristocratic disdain, as when the count chamberlain, Count Adlerberg, tried to dissuade the merchant owners of the Moscow-Kursk railroad from accepting the invitation of the empress to accompany her during a trip on their own line. "I don't know, it seems there is no room on the train," he said, "furrowing his eyebrows" (ORBL, f. 332, T. S. Morozov to F. V. Chizhov, 1 September 1871).

15. (I. K. Babst) "Obozrenie," *VP*, no. 10 (1861): 13.

serfs of Count Sheremetev in the village of Ivanovo transformed the town into the "Russian Manchester" and then with their profits bought their freedom.[16] The largest number of "departures" (*otkhod*) were registered in the central industrial and central agricultural provinces, but the phenomenon was empire-wide. The movement reached massive proportions in the early nineteenth century; in the single year 1826 over 574,000 passports were issued to private serfs and state peasants to allow them to seek work away from the ploughlands.[17] To be sure, at any one time the overwhelming majority of these peasants were not employed in commerce but rather in small workshops and factories. For example, less than 10 percent of the more than 60,000 hired serfs in Iaroslavl province on the eve of the emancipation engaged in trade or ran a shop.[18] But their activities were so wide ranging and successful that they cut deeply into the merchantry's profits and thus helped undermine its social stability.

The trading peasant often began his career as a shopkeeper, artisan, or petty contractor in the employ of a merchant-*skupshchik*, that is, a buyer of semifinished or finished goods who served as the middleman between the peasant handicrafts and the market. Once he had accumulated some capital the peasant might strike out on his own as a skupshchik and frequently double as a usurer. To needy peasants, especially in remote areas, he would be willing to extend credit and lend money, grain, or raw materials at extremely high short-term rates — 15 percent a month![19] Gradually, he would work up to wholesale trading and then might purchase shops or factories employing whole villages. In Moscow province, most of the successful trading peasants made their mark in textiles, but others moved into furniture, clock making, and scientific and musical instruments. In Vladimir province, trading peasants captured the metal-working industry in the early nineteenth century and penetrated into the dye, glue, and starch industries as well as furs. In the manufacturing center of Pavlov, in Nizhnyi Novgorod province, the local metal artisans were all peasants working for a Moscow merchant until the end of the eighteenth century, when well-to-do trading peasants took over his role. Along the middle Volga the trading peasants bought and sold grain, tallow, soap, and leather, established their own factories, and elimi-

16. Portal, "Origines," pp. 35–60. For a useful summary of the literature on the serf entrepreneur see Blackwell, *Beginnings*,, pp. 205–11.

17. Druzhinin, *Gosudarstvennye*, 1:74.

18. Fedorov, *Pomeshchich'ie*, p. 210.

19. Korsak, *O formakh*, pp. 144–45, 248–50. See also the graphic official descriptions in Zablotskii-Desiatovskii, *Graf Kiselev*, 4:285–90. This is part of the author's report entitled "O krepostnom sostoianii v Rossii," dated 1841.

nated the Moscow merchants from competition. In Iaroslavl and Kostroma provinces, the peasant dominated the timber and wood-working industries. By the turn of the century, then, the traditional dependent relationship of the trading peasant on the merchant was undergoing a significant change. As the merchants found it difficult to establish new manufacturing enterprises because of the prohibition on their purchasing serfs, they relied more heavily upon local peasant manufacturers to supply them with goods.[20] But here in the villages they encountered a determined rival who benefited from his anomalous position in society and enjoyed the protection of the nobility and the state bureaucracy.

Well into the nineteenth century the trading peasant had no legal rights and was completely at the mercy of his owner, yet he enjoyed several advantages over the merchant. He was immune from bankruptcy penalties and exempt from commercial taxes and service obligations. Operating with practically no overhead, not restricted to trading in a single district unless so specified by his landlord, and indifferent to his business reputation, he was occasionally able to overcome the technical and organizational superiority of his merchant competitor. But the merchant could more than hold his own as long as the legal privileges attached to his soslovie remained intact. When they began to come under attack from the nobility in the second half of the eighteenth century, the merchant was forced on the defensive.

The first major setback for the merchants in this struggle had come much earlier, in 1755, when, on the initiative of Count Peter Shuvalov, Russia abolished its internal tolls. One stroke of the pen destroyed the virtual monopoly of the local merchants over retail trade in the towns and exposed them to ruinous competition from trading peasants in the surrounding countryside.[21] After this, whenever the nobles found it impossible to put through new laws favoring the trading peasant, they blithely helped their serfs circumvent the old ones. Illegal manufacturing and trading by landlords and their peasants became so widespread in Russia under Catherine II that the merchants singled out this issue in their petitions to the Legislative Commission in 1767 as the single greatest threat to their economic security and well-being.

Throughout this obscure and clandestine struggle, the bureaucracy took a vacillating position. In the eyes of the increasingly professionalized financial bureaucracy it was necessary to preserve the commercial vitality and taxpaying ability of the urban guild merchants. At the same time, it was not always clear to them how best to increase the

20. Fedorov, *Pomeshchich'ie*, pp. 97–109, 118 ff., 125 ff., 136–37, 143; Vartanov, "Kupechestvo," pp. 177–80.
21. Volkov, "Tamozhennaia," pp. 151–52.

revenues of the state—whether to side with one soslovie or another in this conflict. After all, the trading peasants had also proven their ability to move goods over long distances at competitive prices and contributed to the economic awakening of the countryside. Even when the Petersburg officials saw their duty clearly, they often lacked sufficient trained personnel to enforce the law at the local level. This meant turning over the difficult task to the elected representatives of the town administration, who were themselves merchants and no match for the powerful provincial voevodas appointed from the ranks of the higher nobility.[22] The government ended up fostering a contradictory policy. On the one hand, it forbade trading peasants from enrolling in the urban society, in order to prevent the loss of taxpayers and recruits from the countryside. On the other hand, it allowed those same peasants to engage in trade that was legally restricted to those who were enrolled in the urban society, in order to encourage economic growth and tax revenues. Once again the merchants were the victims of the government's compromises.

Catherine, at least, held the line against further legal encroachments on the merchants' privileges; but once she passed from the scene the assault was renewed. In 1798 and 1799 the government granted trading peasants equal rights with merchants in the retail trade of foodstuffs in St. Petersburg and Moscow. During the Napoleonic Wars the peasants obtained a series of concessions, including the rights to engage in petty trade, to establish a great variety of commercial establishments in the two capitals, and to conduct retail trade not only in their own provinces but throughout the empire.[23] At the same time the legal rights of the peasants to own and inherit immovable property further strengthened the peasants' competitive position vis-à-vis the merchants. The collective impact of these measures was devastating for the merchants. By the end of the Napoleonic Wars, the number of textile enterprises operated by trading peasants was increasing at a more rapid rate than the number owned by either nobles or merchants.[24] A decade later the Moscow Merchant Society complained that unless the activities of the peasant industrialists were

22. *SIRIO* (1894), 93:183, 219, 236, 248, 306; ibid. (1885), 43:204–10. These bureaucrats perceived the plight of the merchants correctly as part of the general confusion in social roles caused by the erosion, but not the elimination, of traditional soslovie boundaries. Their solution was a vague policy of free trade and equal obligations for all entrepreneurs. This symptom of Russia's social malaise was diagnosed early enough, but no real cure was found to the end of the empire.

23. *PSZRI*, 1st ser., 10 January 1799, no. 18814. For additional legislation favoring trading peasants see Iakovtsevskii, *Kupecheskii*, pp. 164–68.

24. Isaev, *Rol'*, p. 105.

checked, they "would destroy the merchant class in Russia."[25] These appeals fell on deaf ears because of the government's desperate need to stimulate trade and industry, raise tax revenues, and replenish the terrible losses suffered by the merchant guilds as a result of high taxes, the war, and the country's destructive tariff policies. The guild reform of 1824 culminated the long process that raised the trading peasant to a level of economic quality with the merchantry. In a stunning concession this legislation granted the private serfs and state peasants the same commercial and industrial rights as the merchantry simply upon payment of a turnover or store tax and application for a license. Merchants retained their personal rights, but this was little consolation for the final loss of their privileged economic position in Russian society.[26]

At the same time the trading peasants took advantage of new opportunities to achieve social, as well as economic, equality with the merchants through the process of redemption, which began to be widely used in the 1820s and reached its peak in the 1850s. In order to buy his freedom, a privately owned trading peasant had to engage in prolonged, humiliating negotiations with his noble landlord. Often he had to surrender half his capital and all his immovable property, and then had to lease his old properties back from the landlord and promise to employ his other peasants. Apparently for the trading peasants no price was too high. The legendary sums paid by the trading-peasant founders of great industrial dynasties, like the Morozovs, Kondratovs, and Garelins, to the great landowners, like the Sheremetevs and Iusupovs, testified to the vitality of capitalism in the Russian countryside. As for the nobles, their insatiable appetite for cash impelled them, against their better judgement in some cases, to sacrifice their own best interests. In the 1840s, nobles actually began initiating the redemption process for their serfs.[27] Among state trading peasants the process of self-emancipation was greatly facilitated by government legislation that gradually eliminated most of the restrictions on transferring into the urban community by the 1820s and 1830s. Whatever their original status, the wealthier free peasants hastened to enroll in the merchant guilds. The consequences for the social and economic evolution of the merchantry can scarcely be exaggerated, though they have been generally ignored.

From 1820 to 1860 the urban merchantry in the Great Russian center of the empire was not only encircled by noble industrialists and their enterprising serfs in the countryside but it was literally engulfed

25. Storozhev, *Istoriia*, vol. 2, pt. 1, p. 302.
26. *PSZRI*, 1st ser., 14 November 1824, no. 30115.
27. Fedorov, *Pomeshchich'ie*, pp. 191–92.

by a massive influx of trading peasants into its guilds. There are no exact and comprehensive statistics to chart this transformation, but scattered data are highly suggestive of the general trend. Moreover, this surge of free peasants into the towns took place at the very time when the old guild population of the merchantry was declining drastically in the wake of the Napoleonic Wars, increased taxes, and the liberal tariff policies of the state. From 1827 to 1840, the merchant population decreased from approximately 70,000 to just under 36,000. Meanwhile, in the decade 1830–39, over 27,000 freedmen (*volnootpushcheniki*), most of whom were trading peasants, left the countryside to take up residence in the towns. The total number of these who enrolled in the guilds is not known, but in the three years between 1834 and 1836, over 2,500 state trading peasants alone transferred into the merchantry.[28] Statistics on trading licenses provide further evidence of the social transformation within the merchant soslovie. During the critical years 1830 to 1834 the number of licenses issued to trading peasants fell precipitously from seven to two thousand—the only four-year period between 1825 and 1854 when any decline at all was registered. In the four years that followed, from 1834 to 1839, the number of licenses issued to merchants rose sharply from about 28,000 to 34,000, representing the largest four-year increase in that soslovie over the same thirty years.[29] Only a small proportion of the newcomers could have come from the meshchanstvo, for no specific or general cause could explain a sudden influx into the merchantry from that source. The shift of approximately the same number of licenses from one soslovie to the other, coming immediately after the guild reform of 1824, indicates that the trading peasants were beginning to pour into the guilds. As economic competition drove thousands of old merchant families to the wall and into the lower orders of the urban population, thousands more of trading peasants replaced them. The process went on at an accelerating rate. By the mid-1850s, the merchant population soared to over 175,000, and there can be no doubt that the overwhelming majority of these had struggled up from storekeeper or artisan to skupshchik and wholesale trader, having amassed enough capital in the process to buy their freedom and having saved enough surplus to establish their own enterprises. Then they crowned their success with the title lost by their defeated rivals.

The major economic consequences of the rise of the trading peasantry were, first, to stimulate certain sectors of the country's industrial life, like textiles, where the land-owning nobility had no further inter-

28. Druzhinin, *Gosudarstvennye*, 1:76.
29. Ryndziunskii, *Gorodskoe*, pp. 376, 378.

est in laying out big capital investments for machinery, and, second, to reestablish members of the merchantry as the owners of the major industrial enterprises in the Great Russian center. In their pursuit of profits the new guild members from the trading peasantry behaved more like genuine merchants than had most of the old "fictional" third guild, who were rapidly falling back into the meshchanstvo under the dual pressures of state taxes and peasant competition. The decline of the guild population, then, represented a clearing out of the poorer merchants and their replacement by a richer element.[30] The social consequences of this process, however, proved to be less favorable for the merchant soslovie. For in the half century between the guild reform of 1824 and the town statute of 1870, Russian urban society was re-peasantized. Instead of the merchantry having slowly evolved out of the free urban artisan population in imitation of the West, as Peter had wished and anticipated, it had drawn its strength from the servile rural population.

On the eve of the emancipation, the great majority of merchants had close personal and family ties to the villages. They were deeply marked by the customs and beliefs of the bonded peasantry. In many respects they shared with the old merchantry similar beliefs, patriarchal family traditions, and submissive attitudes toward authority. But there were important shades of difference. With the exception of the sectarians, their faith was more syncretic, alloyed with pagan superstition. The supremacy of the oldest males in the family probably rested more on fear and coercion and less on recognized moral authority. Similarly, their attitudes toward state officials must surely have been more complex, a blend of external subservience and deep-seated suspicion and hostility. And they naturally retained mixed feelings toward their former lords, who had owned them, exploited them, and then driven hard bargains for their freedom. Moreover, there can be little doubt that the cultural level of their families fell far below that of the old first-guild merchant families. With few exceptions they were less literate, coarser in manner, and innocent of any Western influences. Theirs had been a harsh and even brutal struggle to climb out of the ranks of their impoverished brethren. They paid for their successes with personal suffering in a milieu of the most primitive capitalist accumulation. Besides possessing a shrewd business sense they had to know how "to save oneself and one's pals" (*spasti sebia i prisnykh*), in the marvelously apt phrase of M. E. Saltykov-Shchedrin, whose keen satires exposed the underside of the peasant huckster's life.[31]

30. Smetanin, "Formirovanie," pp. 153–58.
31. See Saltykov-Shchedrin, *Melochi Zhizni, 1846–87,* in *Sochineniia,* vol. 16, bk. 2, es-

In effect, their economic activities imposed a second bondage upon their fellow serfs. Masses of handicraft workers were completely dependent on the peasant skupshchik, contractor, or meat and fish jobber (*prasol*, a term also used locally to mean a cheat) and also permanently in debt to them as was the case in Iaroslavl province.[32] In many ways this bondage resembled the conditions that had originally led to the enserfment of the peasantry by the Muscovite service nobility; now it was happening again from within the peasantry. The survivors went on to constitute the bulk of the merchantry in the postreform decades.

It was not a pleasant legacy. Just at the time when some old merchant families were beginning to emerge from their domestic isolation and seek a more cultivated public life, raw elements from the villages inundated their soslovie. These newcomers resembled nothing so much as their remote forebears, who also had emerged from the peasantry a century earlier. This process was repeated again after the emancipation. Its general effects on the merchantry were to lower its cultural tone, to delay the Westernization of its education, to disrupt the introduction of modern business practices, and to stunt its participation in public life. Finally, this increase in the peasant element in the merchant soslovie could scarcely have raised the status of the merchantry in the eyes of the rest of society. The social evolution of the merchantry toward a bourgeoisie sustained a serious setback, even as its economic power burgeoned.

Ethnic Encirclement

By the end of the eighteenth century, competition from Jewish, German, Polish, Ukrainian, Greek, Armenian, and Tatar merchants, often in alliance with foreigners, had become as threatening to the merchantry as that of the trading peasantry. The problem resulted from the government's strategy of winning over the elites of the newly conquered territories by granting them a wide variety of economic concessions. Peter's centralizing policies made exceptions for Tatars on the Volga, Germans in the Baltic provinces, and Ukrainians in the Hetmanate, who were allowed to retain their traditional commercial privileges.

Up to 1755 Russian merchants vainly petitioned the government to

---

pecially the two nonfiction essays "Khoziaistvennyi muzhichok," pp. 45–51, and "Miroedy," pp. 77–85, which though dealing with a later period brilliantly capture all "the tricks of the trade."

32. Zablotskii-Desiatovskii, *Graf Kiselev*, 4:288.

abolish the internal tariff frontier, which, by separating the central provinces from the Ukraine and the Don Military District, enabled foreigners to import goods into the empire. Extremely low duties virtually guaranteed a monopoly of trade in the Hetmanate to Ukrainian merchants and the Cossack leadership class (*starshyna*). When the tariff was abolished, so too were all internal tolls. This proved a mixed blessing for the Russian merchants, as we have seen. In the coal-rich Don area the Cossack landowners defended their exclusive privileges over the subsoil for another century, blocked the movement of outside capital into the area, and delayed the large-scale exploitation of the pits and mines until the 1880s.[33]

After the great surge of imperial expansion under Catherine the Great, Russian merchants faced an even more formidable array of competitors in the Polish and Jewish merchants to the west and Greeks and Armenians along the entire littoral of the Black Sea. Neither the government nor its new subjects wished to jeopardize their well-established and profitable commercial relations with countries to the west and south. Although foreigners were legally forbidden to trade in the interior provinces, they were able to take advantage of their contacts with the ethnic minorities to compete successfully with Russians in the port cities of St. Petersburg, Riga, and Odessa and also to penetrate the heart of Russia—Moscow itself.[34] Even in Arkhangelsk, one of the few ports where there was no ethnic minority, foreigners were so strong that they forced the local Russian merchants, against their will, to help smuggle imported goods into internal markets as far away as Moscow.[35]

Everywhere their activities were encouraged or at least tolerated by ambitious governor-generals who perceived the economic advantages of furthering close cooperation between foreign and local merchants

33. For the internal tariff see Volkov, "Tamozhennaia," pp. 145–47; on Cossack privileges over the subsoil see Khlostov, *Don*, pp. 126–27, 131.
34. In petitions to the Legislative Commission of 1767, Russian merchants requested that foreigners, especially Greeks and Asians, be prevented from trading outside frontier towns and ports. The complaints were submitted by the merchantry of Moscow itself and four towns on its approaches to the west and south, Aleksin, Tula, and Zaraisk in Moscow province and Smolensk (*SIRIO* [1894], 93:104, 128, 130, 311, 437; ibid. [1911], 134:64–65). In Moscow itself the Russian merchantry found itself "encircled" when, from the mid-eighteenth century, arcades (*passazhy*) of luxury shops (*magaziny*) established by foreigners catering to the Russian nobility began to surround the old-fashioned trade rows of the Kitai Gorod. Despite the rivalry the Russian merchants stubbornly resisted efforts to dismantle their crowded quarters until 1886 when the rows were torn down and replaced with arcades, as they exist today. See Gohstand, "Shaping of Moscow," in Hamm, *City*, pp. 173–78.
35. Ogorodnikova, *Ocherk*, p. 231.

in the regions that they administered. Hetman K. G. Razumovskii in the Ukraine, Governor-General Karl Sivers in the Baltic provinces, and G. A. Potemkin in New Russia defended and expanded the activities of Ukrainian, German, Greek, and Armenian merchants.[36]

The division of the commercial groups in Russia along cultural-territorial lines revived dormant regionalism and seriously impaired the development of a single all-Russian capitalist class. Although the political implications of this situation became clear only after the Crimean War, the groundwork was laid in the late eighteenth and early nineteenth centuries for an explosive alliance between the economic interests of the Moscow-based merchants and Great Russian chauvinism.

The northwest anchor of this ethnic encirclement was St. Petersburg, where ethnic minorities, foreigners, and their descendants dominated the economic life of the city from its earliest days. At the turn of the nineteenth century the export-import trade was controlled by German and English concerns. As late as 1860, 70 percent of the workers in machine-producing factories were employed by English or Scottish firms like Baird and Wilson. The St. Petersburg Statistical Committee attributed the ownership of almost one-half of all enterprises classified as *fabriki* or *zavody* (mills and factories) to foreigners living in the capital. Even after the emancipation of the serfs entrepreneurs of foreign origin continued to own and operate the largest textile and paper factories in the city. In size and productivity these enterprises ranked among the largest in the empire.[37]

Immediately to the south in the Baltic provinces, the Russian merchants faced a formidable coalition of local German merchants, their Petersburg allies, and foreign concerns. In Tallin the town govern-

---

36. For Potemkin see Raeff, "Prince Potemkin," pp. 1–51. For Sivers see D. Ilovaiskii, "Novgorodskaia," vol. 55, pp. 5–47, 628–84, and vol. 56, pp. 153–215. For Razumovskii see Kohut, "Abolition," chap. 4.

37. *Fabriki v 1863*, p. 8. Timiriazev, *Statisticheskii atlas*, 1:2, 3, 4, 13, 16, 22, 25, 27, gives the following data on textile factories in the capital:

Type	Owner	Value of Production in Rubles (in millions)	Rank in Empire
Cotton spinning	Shtiglits	3,350	2
Cotton fabric	Sampson	1,252	2
Linen fabric	Shtiglits	705	1
Wool spinning	Turpen	153	4
Wool fabric	Thornton	500	5
Cloth	Berman	957	3
	Shtiglits	800	4
Rope and cord	Got	807	1

ment was entirely in the hands of the German merchants, and this facilitated close relations with foreign firms in St. Petersburg like Gerdau, Liuddert, Momma, and Shtiglits, which supplied the capital for the development of local trade and industry. Although in the 1840s the majority of merchants trading at the great market in Tartu were from St. Petersburg, by 1852 local merchants from Riga and Tallin predominated. The Moscow group trailed far behind.[38] In Riga the situation was more complex and the stakes were higher. Second only to St. Petersburg in foreign trade turnover, the port witnessed a continuous three-way rivalry between the large English import-export firms, which in the 1840s controlled half the export trade, the local German merchants, who lost ground steadily during the first half of the nineteenth century in their efforts to retain their medieval privileges, and a much smaller group of Latvian and Russian merchants, who like many of their German rivals were forced to accept a role as commission agents for the foreign enterprises that dominated the wholesale trade. The small textile industry, which employed more than 50 percent of the workers in Riga, was owned and operated by German families.[39]

Over a fifty-year period, in a steady stream of petitions, the embattled Russian merchants accused the German elite in the Baltic provinces of discriminating against them in civil and commercial affairs, but they gained no satisfaction from St. Petersburg. However, they won the sympathy of Slavophils like Iuri Samarin and Ivan Aksakov and, later on, the powerful support of M. N. Katkov, who helped transform their cause from a local quarrel into a national campaign.[40]

38. Vassor and Nann, *Istoriia Estonskoi*, 1:791, 800, 807, 808. See also Karma, "Ocherk," pp. 150–86. These otherwise valuable works do not make clear that the transition from traditional (or feudal) to modern capitalist economic behavior was not accompanied by a shift in the ethnic composition of the business class, which remained predominantly German.

39. Ryndziunskii, *Gorodskoe*, pp. 288–89.

40. *SIRIO* (1885), 43:609–15, reprints a petition dated 1767 to Catherine II from the Moscow merchant Ivan Klimov protesting discrimination of the Reval (German) meshchanstvo against Russian merchants. In petitions to the Legislative Commission the merchants of Viazma and Smolensk accused the Riga merchants of interfering with their shipments and creating difficulties for external trade (ibid. [1911], 134:64–65, 95). In 1792 two Russian merchants from Narva petitioned the Senate, protesting that the non-Russian-dominated magistracy forbade them to trade with foreign merchants on the basis of legislation dating back to Swedish control of the town (*PSZRI*, 1st ser., 12 September 1782, no. 15510). Merchant petitions in the period 1796–1840 are summarized in Samarin, *Sochineniia*, "Pis'ma iz Rigi i istoriia Rigi," 7:16–105. Ivan Aksakov's articles on this issue in *Den'*, *Moskva*, and *Rus'* from 1862 to 1885 were reprinted in his *Sochineniia*, "Pribaltiiskii vopros . . . ," 6:3–167. See also Katkov, *Sobranie*, especially 5 October 1879, 8 April 1880, 22 March and 6 July 1887.

Thus, the growth of capitalist enterprises destroyed medieval trading corporations and tied the area to the all-Russian market without destroying the cultural differences, especially language, customs, and even dress, that distinguished the dominant German from the competing Russian merchants. On the contrary, these distinctions became the basis for an even more intense rivalry between the two groups.

In the western and southwestern provinces carved out of the old Polish territories, Russian merchants saw themselves outnumbered and outmaneuvered by Jewish mercantile interests, who were apparently aided and abetted by the imperial government. Economic necessity, combined with the policies of enlightened bureaucrats like G. R. Derzhavin and M. M. Speranskii, provided the Jewish population with a special statute in 1804 which improved their civil status and their commercial position. With the outbreak of the war against France the army's urgent need for uniforms and boots further prompted the government to remove temporarily the last remaining travel restrictions on Jewish merchants engaged in the manufacture and trade of wool cloth and leather goods.[41] The immediate reaction of the Kiev magistrat was to protest that this legislation would undermine the city's merchant guilds. The reimposition of certain anti-Jewish restrictions following Speranskii's fall did not relieve the pressure on the Russian merchants from illegal Jewish trading. In a petition of 1814 the Russian merchants of Polotsk complained that "their agents had long suffered commercial losses from the activities of meshchane, mainly Jewish, who bought up bread, shipped it by wooden barges to Riga," Vilna, and Moscow, and "transport[ed] no small amount of various products which they do not have a right to trade." The Jewish meshchane were also accused of accepting contracts restricted exclusively for second-guild merchants and of controlling the vodka tax farming of the entire city of Polotsk. The merchants bewailed the failure of the government to put a stop to these illegal practices despite its repeated promises to do so. A similar protest was addressed to the minister from "the merchantry of the Christian faith in Vilna."[42]

In the struggle for commercial supremacy in the region, the government intervened for the most part only erratically and arbitrarily, but it strictly adhered to one aspect of its restrictive policy—that which forbade Jews from trading in the countryside. In the Ukraine, particularly, where big landowners were also high government officials, like Rumiantsev and Vorontsov, and thus susceptible to pressure from the local nobility, this policy aimed at protecting the landlords' peas-

41. *PSZRI*, 1st ser., 9 December 1804, no. 21547; ibid., 29 December 1808, no. 23424.
42. Shugurov, "Istoriia evreev," pt. 2, pp. 95–96. For the Vilna petition and the reply of the Senate see *PSZRI*, 1st ser., 17 August 1814, no. 25639.

ants against economic competition from the Jewish population. Consequently, Jews gradually drifted out of the villages and into the towns and cities. They began their entrepreneurial careers as impoverished peddlars, small storekeepers, tavern owners, and money lenders, and by the 1830s they formed a majority of both the well-to-do merchants and the increasingly impoverished meshchanstvo in the Pale of Settlement.[43]

In the Ukrainian provinces, Jewish merchants emerged from a complex three-way struggle among Polish, Ukrainian, and Russian cloth merchants to become the overwhelmingly predominant ethnic group in the guilds. Following the repression of the Polish Revolt in 1832, Russian merchants, encouraged by their government's discriminatory tariff policy against the rebels, steadily forced out their Polish competitors from the southwest provinces. Ivan Aksakov was the first to notice that this Great Russian surge also brought the Ukrainian merchants under its control.[44] However, in the meantime, Jewish traders were able, with the help of state subsidies, to buy up large woolen cloth enterprises from the declining Polish nobility, especially in old Volynia. By the 1830s Jewish merchants controlled 30 percent of the textile industry of the Ukraine. Meanwhile, a number of enterprising families like the Brodskys, Zaitsevs, Halperins, and Balakhovskys moved into the emerging sugar-beet industry, of which by 1872, 25 percent was reported to be in Jewish hands.[45] According to Aksakov, by mid-century almost all the trade in foreign goods passing along the overland routes from the West was handled by Russian and Austrian Jews.[46] The traditional picture of the Jewish trader as lumpenproletariat has long since given way to a more balanced view of his major contribution to the capitalist development of the Ukraine. But the Jewish advantage in wealth over other merchants residing in the region, as shown in the statistical compilations in table 2.1, was truly staggering.[47]

What is particularly striking in the table is the heavy preponderance of Jews in the wealthy first and second guilds. Ironically, the policies of the Russian government, which were aimed at integrating the

43. Salo Baron, *Russian Jews*, emphasizes the impoverishment of the masses, but the table on p. 85 based on a manuscript source in Kiev confirms the preponderance of Jews in the merchant guilds of the Pale. Cf. table below. See also Blackwell, *Beginnings*, pp. 74–75 and 229–37, for a good summary of Jewish entrepreneurs in Russia.

44. Aksakov, *Sochineniia*, 6:24–25. For a thorough analysis of the complexities of the struggles see Ogloblin, *Ocherki*, pp. 28–52.

45. Iuditskii, "Evreiskaia," pp. 116–21; Salo Baron, *Russian Jews*, p. 91.

46. Aksakov, *Sochineniia*, 6:59.

47. Calculations based on figures in Keppen, *Deviataia*, pp. 182–86. I am grateful to P. G. Ryndzuinskii for pointing out to me the importance of this source.

TABLE 2.1. *Jewish and Christian Merchants in 1851*

Province	Jews by Guild			Christians by Guild			Total Guild Merchants
	1	2	3	1	2	3	
Bessarabia	19	129	1,410	59	122	1,058	2,800
Vilna	24	10	353	9	5	347	748
Vitebsk	52	18	607	5	23	1,069	1,774
Volynia	25	117	3,498	2	0	136	3,778
Grodo	34	12	567	5	0	19	637
Ekaterinoslav	11	7	958	19	64	2,946	4,018
Kiev	24	145	5,741	28	81	789	6,836
Kovno	16	24	588	3	2	200	833
Kurland	9	22	1,128	29	49	414	1,652
Minsk	55	64	1,007	0	1	166	1,301
Mogilev	20	39	1,150	5	17	362	1,593
Podolia	7	125	5,747	0	4	244	6,127
Poltava	6	22	1,353	4	30	1,107	2,522
Chernigov	59	15	2,766	0	85	693	3,634

Ukraine economically as well as politically and increasing Russian, as against foreign, influence, had the unexpected result of transforming the Jews into the richest merchants in the cities of the Ukraine. Yet by still another ironic twist the Russian merchants did not regard this development as altogether unacceptable. In fact, in exerting joint pressure against the Poles and Ukrainians, Jews and Russians more often than not collaborated rather than competed with one another. The Russians were mainly absentee owners of industrial enterprises amounting to almost 45 percent of the total in the Ukraine, and they frequently hired Jewish managers. Russian merchants engaged in commerce traveled down from the north during the great annual fairs and frequently discovered that Jewish merchants were their best

Percentage of Jews by Guild			Percentage of Jews in All Three Guilds
1	2	3	
24	51	57	55.6
73	75	50	51
91	44	36	38
93	100	94	96
92	100	97	96
37	10	25	24
46	64	88	86
84	92	75	75
24	31	73	70
100	99	86	87
80	70	76	76
00	97	96	96
60	42	55	55
00	15	80	81

customers, buying from the wholesalers and spreading out into the countryside to retail their purchases to the local populations. The arrangement was so mutually profitable that the Russians even protected the illegal trading at the Kharkov fair, where Jews were forbidden to appear.[48] While it is true that the Jewish- and Russian-owned textile firms sometimes competed for the same markets, this

48. Aksakov, *Sochineniia*, 6:38–39, 51, 58. It is a curious irony of historiography that Ukrainian historians writing in the Soviet Union under the influence of Pokrovskii's school portrayed this dual pressure exclusively in anti-Russian—that is, anti-imperialist—terms. Possibly this was to eradicate any trace of incipient anti-Semitism. See, for example, Slabchenko, *Orhanizatsiya*, 2:146–50, 228, and Ogloblin, *Ocherki*, pp. 44–45.

rivalry could not offset the mutual advantages of cooperation. The decisive factor in preserving this working alliance was, undoubtedly, that the political hegemony of the Russians in the Ukrainian towns could not be challenged by the Jews. Even though this group included the overwhelming majority of guild merchants, they were not enfranchised. Thus, once the Russian carpetbaggers had wrested control of the Kiev city administration from the Ukrainians, they had no need to worry about sharing power with the Jews.

What the Russian merchants were willing to tolerate in the far-distant Ukraine they were not ready to accept on their own doorstep in Moscow. As early as the end of the eighteenth century Russians in the Moscow Merchant Society tried to prevent qualified Jews from enrolling and protested to the mayor of Moscow that Jews were trading illegally in the city. Although they insisted that they did not consider Jewish traders "very dangerous competitors," they repeated their strong protests in their big collective petitions of 1823 and 1840.[49] The Russian merchants in Moscow were incensed by the success of the Jewish merchants in importing foreign goods into the city, buying the manufactures of Moscow factories, and then sending them to the provinces of the Jewish Pale or even exporting them to Austria "without any relationship with the Moscow merchants to the clear detriment of the latter." That the value of the goods sent out of Moscow alone amounted to almost twenty-seven million rubles demonstrates that this was no petty annoyance. Moreover, the merchants coupled their complaint with a petition requesting a series of harsh restrictive measures to be imposed on Jewish merchants: reducing the duration of their legal visits to Moscow from six months to one month; placing them under strict police surveillance; forbidding them to trade themselves, to run a store, or to bring their wives and children with them; and confining them to live in two designated buildings. The government gave its approval to all but the last point. But it did oblige all Jews in Moscow "to live exclusively in one place."[50] Thus, the Moscow merchants initiated the creation of a ghetto in Moscow under close police supervision. Subsequently, this led to illegal harassment and the persecution of the entire Jewish merchant community in the city.

When in 1859 the imperial government permitted Jewish merchants in the first guild to live and trade outside the Pale of Settlement, Russian merchants found themselves directly challenged on their home ground in diverse fields, such as railroad construction,

49. Storozhev, *Istoriia*, vol. 2, pt. 1, pp. 8–9, 160–62, 194, 446–80.
50. Shugurov, "Istoriia evreev," pt. 1, pp. 163–67; Marek, "K istorii evreev," pp. 73–75; Pipes, "Catherine II," pp. 14–17.

military contracting, and banking.[51] At the same time, Russian merchants, especially those in Moscow who were shifting from trading to manufacturing, discovered the advantages of using Jewish merchants as middlemen and retailers in the western provinces. Clearly, then, the merchants acted on conflicting impulses in their relations with the Jews, and it is no easy matter to sort these out. Just how deeply the ethnic and religious feelings of the Russian merchants toward the Jews ran may be observed in their behavior during the pogroms that broke out in 1881 following the assassination of Alexander II. The official records, subsequently published in Soviet Russia, give no indication that any Russian merchants either encouraged or participated in anti-Jewish violence in the Pale, while there is a good deal of evidence that masses of Russian and Ukrainian meshchane and peasants and, in the Ukraine, a few nobles were involved.[52] Yet, it may be argued that this is not so much proof of the merchants' benevolent or even neutral attitude toward the Jews as an expression of their traditional dislike of public disorder, their subservience to authority, their inertness. Two subsequent incidents occurring within the space of a few years may, however, provide a clearer definition of the admittedly ambivalent character of the merchantry's anti-Semitism.

In 1888 the board of governors of the Nizhnyi Novgorod fair, composed mainly of Moscow merchants, instituted a set of rules imposing new restrictions on Jewish merchants trading there. In response to the complaints of the Jewish merchants, the governor of the province, N. M. Baranov, admitted that the board was fully within its rights, but reassured them that the officials would be very tolerant in enforcing the measures directed against the Jews.[53] By contrast, five years later leading representatives of the merchantry in Moscow raised their voices against the deportation of twenty thousand Jewish artisans, skilled workers, and shopkeepers as part of a savagely repressive policy inaugurated by the new governor-general of the city, Grand Duke Sergei Aleksandrovich. It was not so much the brutality that upset the Moscow merchants as the devastating effects on the local economy, including the complete ruin of the million-ruble silk

51. Among the best known of these were A. M. Varshavskii, who helped supply the Russian armies in 1877–78, the great railroad entrepreneurs I. S. Bliokh, Baron L. Kronenberg, and S. S. and Ia. S. Poliakov, and the Petersburg bankers E. G. and G. O. Gintsburg (Witte, *Vospominaniia*, 1:116–18, 121–24; Sliozberg, *Baron Gintsburg*, pp. 29–44).

52. Krasnyi-Admoni, *Materialy*, 2:325–27, 344, 942, and throughout.

53. Vermel, "Expulsion," pp. 10–11. I am grateful to Lawrence Schofer for bringing this item to my attention and translating it. The Russian original, S. S. Vermel', *Moskovskoe izgnanie (1891–1892 gg.)*, privately printed in 1924, was not available to me.

industry in the Bogorodskii district.[54] The government ignored the petition and throughout the rest of the decade stepped up its persecution of Jews.

In both cases the merchants acted consistently in accord with their economic interests, though their attitudes were not altogether free of religious and cultural hostility. As was so often the case in questions of ethnic tension the government's position conflicted with that of the merchants. Yet, in the 1890s it was no longer the difference in economic perspective that divided them, but the government's slide toward an uncompromising Great Russian chauvinism. By that time the merchantry was in no position to oppose the irrational application of a policy that it had done so much to encourage in the first place.

In the early decades of the nineteenth century, the most formidable challenge to the economic well-being of the Moscow merchants arose in the Kingdom of Poland, where fiscal reform and a brief industrial spurt threatened for a time to convert that region into the foremost industrial center of the empire. Under the hard-driving and imaginative leadership of Prince F.-S. Drutskii-Liubetskii, the minister of finance of the Kingdom of Poland from 1821 to 1831, the first comprehensive plan was undertaken for the economic development of a region of the Russian Empire. Seeking to balance the budget as his first step, Drutskii-Liubetskii ran roughshod over the privileges of nobles and burghers alike, collecting debts dating back to prepartition times, establishing a state vodka monopoly, reforming the tax system, and selling off the national lands. With the surplus income, supplemented after 1829 by a large foreign loan, he built up a capital reserve and created a fund for launching the kingdom into a small industrial revolution. By offering loans and subsidies he encouraged foreign investment, leading to the establishment of the famous Girard works, a bold and successful attempt to form a large, up-to-date flax-spinning enterprise in Poland at a time when, outside of England, the industry was still in its infancy. A few years later Drutskii-Liubetskii petitioned Nicholas I for various trading privileges to allow the surplus production of Polish cloth to be sold throughout the empire, and in a dramatic personal appearance before the Committee of Ministers he faced down his rival Kankrin, the Russian finance minister, and defended the superiority of Polish cloth over the Russian.[55] Because of the creation of a free-trade area in the kingdom by a decision of the Great Powers at the Congress of Vienna, Polish and Jewish textile manufacturers enjoyed great advantages over their Russian rivals in

54. Gol'dovskii, "Evrei," pp. 155–56.
55. *RBS*, 6:697–701; Przhetslavskii, "Drutskoi-Liubetskii," pp. 631–40; Missalowa, *Studia*, pp. 70–74, 83–95.

importing machinery and raw materials from Prussia and the Hapsburg Monarchy, and they now took advantage of the tariff concessions that Drutskii-Liubetskii had won for them in his negotiations to penetrate the Russian market.

Throughout the 1820s and 1830s the Moscow merchants protested vigorously and repeatedly to the government that the duty-free importation of woolen yarn into the kingdom enabled Polish factories to produce an inexpensive cloth which undersold the equivalent Russian product not only in Moscow itself but also in the Persian trade and at Kiakhta on the Chinese frontier.[56] For once, Russian merchant protests elicited some sympathy from the government, but it did not help them very much. Even the tariff revision of 1832, which in general reflected a punitive attitude toward the rebellious Poles by setting new limitations on the export of manufactured cloth from the kingdom into Russia, did not give real relief. The following year the Moscow merchants complained to Nicholas in person that the advantages enjoyed by the Polish textile factories was causing great difficulties for the manufacturers of broadcloth in Moscow.[57]

Textiles was only one aspect of Drutskii-Liubetskii's plan which aroused the antagonism of Moscow merchants and Petersburg bureaucrats: the rise in coal production and the growth of the kingdom's financial power were equally unsettling consequences of his policies. Perceiving the need for a more vigorous management of Poland's languishing mines, Drutskii-Liubetskii had their independent administration transferred to his ministry, and under his personal direction the mines of Dombrowa began their spectacular development, which soon carried them to first place in the empire, a position they maintained until 1889.[58] But Drutskii-Liubetskii's crowning achievement was the founding of the Polish State Bank in 1828, more than thirty years before a comparable institution was established for the Russian Empire as a whole. Although he managed it for only three years, his policies attracted a group of rising Polish and converted Jewish entrepreneurs who succeeded him as its leaders and implemented his plans

56. Rosa Luxemburg found over eighteen hundred petitions from Russian merchants complaining about Polish manufacturing competition in 1826 alone (Luxemburg, *Industrial Development*, p. 120). For one such see Voblyi, *Ocherki*, pp. 317, 330–34, 337–40, 343–45, and appendix 2, "Proshenie moskovskikh sukhonnykh fabrikantov, podannoe po Vysochaishee imia, 13 marta 1831, g.," pp. 404–5. Voblyi denied that the Poles received all the commercial advantages in their relations with St. Petersburg and sought to blame the Jews, in some strong anti-Semitic passages, for much of the Polish-Russian hostility (ibid., pp. 340–42).

57. Rybnikov, "Rossiiskoe kupechestvo," pp. 563.

58. Luxemburg, *Industrial Development*, p. 110.

for using the bank as the catalyst for creating a metallurgical industry and financing railroads in the kingdom. This was an industrial investment bank the likes of which the rest of the empire would not see until the 1890s.

At the head of the group stood Henryk Lubienski, the scion of an influential noble family and vice-president of the Bank of Poland for the Mining Administration; Peter Steinkeller, a Jewish manufacturer of machine tools, with interests in salt, coal mining, and the newest English technology; and Maurycy Konyar (Koniar), a converted Jewish merchant-financier who had made his money in snuff, moved to St. Petersburg, and enjoyed the confidence of the Russian administration in Warsaw after the uprising. Within their orbit were a number of Jewish bankers, like S. A. Fraenkel and Leopold Kronenberg, who also maintained good connections with big Berlin and Vienna banking houses like Epstein, Magnus, and Steiner. The Polish State Bank was one of the very few institutions of the kingdom that retained a degree of autonomy after the Organic Statute of 1833 replaced the constitution. Lubienski used his official position and friendship with Steinkeller and later Koniar to channel the bank's investments through private hands into the coal, zinc, and iron mines and to undertake the construction of the first railroad company in the kingdom, linking Warsaw with Vienna by way of the mining and metallurgy enterprises of the southwest.[59] While Polish engineers working for the bank drafted the technical plans, Lubienski and Steinkeller endorsed a method of financing the line, which had just been devised in France, that combined private capital with a state guarantee of 4 percent return on capital, a scheme adopted by St. Petersburg only much later after the Crimean War as the basis for the construction of Russia's main trunk lines. To appreciate the farsightedness of the Polish merchants, it should be recalled that the Warsaw-Vienna line was the first private railroad company backed by a government guarantee established in Europe.[60]

Despite these promising beginnings, Lubienski and the bank ran into financial trouble. Their difficulties stemmed as much from the opposition of the Russian authorities and the complaints of the Russian merchants as from the shortage of capital in the European money market. To mollify the suspicious Russian bureaucrats in Field Marshal Paskevich's administration in Warsaw, Lubienski had stressed the strategic and commercial importance of linking Warsaw to Vienna and freeing Poland from economic dependence on Prussia and the

59. Jedlicki, *Nieudana*, pp. 64–73; Rutkowski, *Historia*, 2:27–28.
60. Kislinskii, *Nasha*, 1:20–21; Hilchen, *Historia*, pp. 20–34, 67–75.

Baltic ports.[61] But the Russian bureaucracy, which on this issue hardly needed the prompting it got from the Moscow merchants, distrusted the bank's policy of merging private capital with its own enterprises, especially as this was leading to a virtual monopoly of the bank over the mining, metallurgical, textile, and nascent railroad industries. Responding in a series of obscure maneuvers, the bank leased most of the smelting industry to Konyar, whom Paskevich trusted, but under conditions that retained some indirect control by the bank. Next the reaction against the bank's activities spread to the Ukraine, where Governor-General Bibikov petitioned for liquidation of its Berdichev branch, which he saw as a stronghold of "the Polish element" in his region. Engaged in a full-fledged war against its Russian opponents, the bank faltered as its ventures slipped into the red, and it was forced to turn the railroad over to the government in Warsaw and submit to a thoroughgoing purge of its directors.[62] The first spurt of Polish industrialization had been checked, but only temporarily. The basic capital accumulation for Polish industry had been achieved and its relations with Western Europe consolidated. It required an entire generation of slow growth, interrupted by still another revolt in 1863, before a massive flow of foreign investment would revive the sluggish textile and metallurgical industries of Poland and once again transform them into vigorous competitors with the Russian merchants.

The period from 1850 to 1870 was a prelude to a second industrial spurt, this one more solidly based than the first. Following the abolition of the tariff frontier between the kingdom and the rest of the empire in 1851, a gradual commercial recovery began. The military demands of the Crimean War provided another impetus, and the construction of railroads linking Poland to the main urban center of the empire in the 1860s and early 1870s opened up an inexhaustible mass market and spurred the conversion of Polish textiles to mechanical looms and spindles. Foreign capital, primarily German, flowed into the hands of resident foreign capitalists like Ludwig Geyer, a Saxon, and Karol Scheibler, a Belgian. Another Russian tariff revision in 1877 encouraged Polish textile manufacturers to advance their mechanization. In the decade 1877–86 they increased the number of spindles by 134 percent, as compared to an increase of 45 percent in Moscow over the same period. The spectacular growth of the city of Lodz may be judged by the tenfold increase in its production of cloth and cheap yarn, which competed with Moscow and led directly to the

61. Shcherbatov, *Kniaz' Paskevich*, 5:191–92.
62. Edlitskii, "Gosudarstvennaia promyshlennost'," pp. 291–94. In the period 1835–38 more than half the currency brought by bankers to the Kievan fairs belonged to the Bank of Poland (Borovoi, *Kredit*, p. 219).

great battle of the 1870s and 1880s for control over the entire Russian market.[63]

At the same time a renewed influx of French technical personnel, accompanied by small but strategically placed capital investments, began to modernize and expand the Huta-Bankova works near Dombrowa into one of the great steel-producing complexes in the empire.[64] Meanwhile, in fifteen short years the vast pine forest around Sosnowieca underwent a startling transformation into a vast coal-mining area. Polish coal producers adapted so swiftly to the coal crisis after 1884 that in a few years they had conquered all the important markets in Russia—Petersburg, Moscow, Odessa, and even southern Russia. During the same period Warsaw became the center of a technological revolution in sugar refining, and with the help of a new tax system and a de facto export subsidy the Poles quadrupled their production of sugar from 1870 to 1890. As early as 1860 Russian merchants were already bemoaning the severe losses inflicted upon them by the flood of duty-free refined sugar imported from the rest of the empire.[65]

The sum total of this remarkable economic activity was that by the mid-1880s the former Kingdom of Poland, where only slightly more than 7 percent of the total population of the country lived, was producing one-quarter of the steel, two-fifths of the coal, one-fifth of the sugar, and just under one-fifth of the value of all textiles in the Russian Empire. On top of this, 50 percent of all products made in Poland were sold in Russia.[66] As this conquest of the Russian market occurred in the midst of a rising tide of Great Russian nationalism, the public reaction it engendered among Russian merchants, as might have been expected, made their protests of the 1820s seem mild by comparison.

On the eve of the great industrial spurt in Russia, the Jews and the Poles together continued to dominate the economic life of the western borderlands. Their numerical superiority among the urban propertied elements was so great that the imperial government delayed putting into effect the new town statutes of 1870 until special legislation was passed to prevent their control over the zemstvos and the dumas

63. Luxemburg, *Industrial Development*, pp. 91–95; Missalowa, *Studia*, pp. 147–64; Brandt, *Inostrannye kapitaly*, pt. 3, pp. 22–23, 25–29; Shuster, "Ekonomicheskaia bor'ba," pp. 188–234. See below, chapter 5, for a fuller discussion of the conflict.

64. McKay, *Pioneers*, pp. 337–46.

65. ORBL, f. 332, no. 38, "Proshenie ot russkikh kuptsov v sviazi s besposhlinoi perevozkoi pol' skogo rafinada," 26 November 1860. The memo was sent to Minister of Finance A. P. Kniazhevich.

66. Luxemburg, *Industrial Development*, pp. 113–15.

in the northwestern and southwestern provinces.[67] Although the statistics in tables 2.2 and 2.3, compiled by the Ministry of the Interior, do not break down the urban population by soslovie or guilds, they strongly suggest the overwhelming preponderance of Jewish and Polish merchants in both the small and large towns of the western borderlands.[68]

Turning east along the southern rim of the empire, Russian merchants encountered discriminatory policies in the rapidly growing emporium of Odessa. In 1817, on the advice of the first French governors, Richelieu and Langeron, the tsarist government established a free port in order to encourage foreign trade. Over the following three decades foreign merchants virtually took over the commercial life of the town. Following the Crimean War the biggest Odessa merchants remained Greeks and Italians, followed by a small number of Germans, Russians, and Jews in that order. Inferior in numbers, the Russians also lagged behind their competitors in business organization. They rarely entered the Odessa Exchange, which was established in 1807, thirty-two years before the Moscow merchants organized one. They almost never traded under their own names in the great cities of Europe. Their sluggishness dulled Russian enterprise far beyond the port itself because Odessa served as the principal money and credit market for all the other ports of the Black Sea, the Sea of Azov, and in part for Moscow itself.[69] Throughout the coastal area the Greeks and the "Asians living in Russia," as official documents defined the Armenians, Crimean Tatars, and Karaimy sect (Jews), ignored the geographical limitations written into their trade licenses, moved out of the port cities of the Black Sea, and penetrated into the interior of the country where they aroused the indignation of the Russian merchants.[70]

67. Ministerstvo vnutrennykh del, Khoziaistvennyi department, *Materialy*, 5:142–46. In the northwestern provinces property qualifications were actually lowered in order to increase the number of Russian Orthodox voters. In the southwest the statutes were changed to restrict the total number of Jewish and Polish members of each town council to no more than one third.

68. Ibid., pp. 79, 81, 82–102, 103.

69. A. A. Skal'kovskii, *Zapiski*, pp. 108–9, 120–21. A similar situation prevailed in steamboat and banking enterprises (ibid., pp. 114–15, 125–30). However, for the problem of interpreting statistical material on the number of foreign and Russian merchants see Ryndziunskii, *Gorodskoe*, p. 351.

70. TsGAOR, f. 672 (Nicholas I), op. 1, d. 277 , "Osnovanie dlia proekta o torguiushchikh sosloviakh s otmenoi vsekh nyneshnikh platezhei i zatrudenie po gil'diem," n.d., but no earlier than 1827, pp. 5–6. In part the problem stemmed from the illegal connivance of the magistrats in Odessa, Feodosia, and Taganrog in enrolling non-Russian merchants in their towns without proof of their having residence or trading

TABLE 2.2. *Numbers of Jews and Catholics (Poles) in Towns of the Northwestern Provinces*

Province	Catholics	Jews	Total Population	Percentage of Catholics and Jews
Grodo	29,737	65,734	115,201	82.87
Vitebsk	9,157	54,313	98,184	64.65
Vilna	31,164	45,110	90,243	84.52
Kovno	17,562	51,905	73,677	94.29
Mogilev	3,717	47,201	90,376	56.34
Total	92,337	264,263	476,681	76.24

Granting a privileged position to foreigners, especially Greeks, in Odessa was only part of the Russian government's general policy to win support among the Christian population of the Ottoman Empire by extending protection to those engaged in the Asiatic trade. In the Transcaucasus similar considerations led the government to grant tariff reductions on foreign imports and to eliminate all duties on goods passing through Georgia in transit from the Black Sea port of Redut Kali to the Persian frontier. As in the Kingdom of Poland and along the northern shores of the Black Sea, the government employed economic weapons to strengthen its political control over recently acquired territories of strategic importance. Once again the burden of this policy fell heavily on the Moscow merchants. After visiting Tiflis and Baku in the 1820s, they complained that "the competition of foreign goods had undermined the market for Russian manufactures in the Transcaucasus and even in Persia" at the very time when Asiatic Turkey and Persia had become their best customers outside the empire. In 1831 the government finally responded to the merchants' petition and abolished the transit rights. By this time English commercial interests were so firmly entrenched in the area that for the next twenty years the Russians were unable to increase substantially the value of their trade in the Transcaucasus.[71]

In the Caucasus, as in other peripheral areas of the empire, the

---

houses and thus enabling them to obtain passports for trade in other towns and provinces of the empire and not pay commercial duties (*PSZRI*, 2nd ser., 19 May 1825, no. 32273).

71. Rozhkova, *Ekonomicheskie*, pp. 49, 51; Fadeev, *Rossiia*, pp. 56–58.

TABLE 2.3. *Numbers of Jewish Merchants and Petty Traders (Meshchane) in the Small Towns (Mestechki) of the Northwestern and Southwestern Provinces*

	Jews	Christians	Percentage of Jews
Northwestern Provinces			
Grodno	47,593	4,210	91.87
Vitebsk	16,889	2,321	87.92
Vilna	35,179	2,552	93.24
Kovno	86,063	7,328	92.15
Mogilev	56,349	2,371	95.96
Minsk	46,673	14,451	76.36
Southwestern Provinces			
Volynia	116,318	14,052	89.22
Kiev	129,622	8,929	93.56
Podolsk	116,610	7,072	94.28

Russian merchants gained little sympathy from the highest officials. Three successive viceroys, Prince M. S. Vorontsov, Prince A. I. Baria-tinskii, and Grand Duke Mikhail Nikolaevich, blamed the Russian merchants for waiting cautiously at the Nizhnyi fair for the local Caucasian merchants to come to them instead of moving energetically into the newly pacified regions. Gradually, they restored many of the old transit privileges to foreign merchants and obtained further re-ductions in the tariff. As late as 1868, Grand Duke Mikhail attempted to delay applying the comprehensive imperial tariff revision of that year to the Caucasus. Russian merchant organizations lodged a strong protest to the Ministry of Finance, claiming that the influx of foreign goods "steadily alienates the area from Russian industry despite the great losses of Russian blood and treasure in acquiring it."[72] Thus were the voices of Great Russian nationalism raised against the cosmo-politan policies of the tsar's own brother.

Local Armenian merchants took advantage of the faltering Russian merchantry to profit from the reestablished transit trade. Due largely to their efforts the export of locally produced goods increased ten fold from 1821 to 1864. The Russians closed down their own trade organizations in the 1850s, and the Armenians took over most of the

72. FBON, "Zhurnal zasedaniia manufakturnogo-kommercheskogo soveta," 2 and 28 November 1868, no pagination.

government contracts as well. Vorontsov rewarded the enterprising Armenian merchants of Tiflis by granting them the rank of honored citizen, thus confirming their leading commercial position in the Transcaucasus.[73]

On the southeastern and eastern fringes of the empire the Russian merchants encountered fewer problems, but their position was by no means secure. Throughout the eighteenth century the Russian government sought to consolidate its recently occupied territories along the Black Sea, Azov, and Caspian coasts by settling Armenian colonists and granting them extensive commercial and tax privileges. Thus encouraged, the Armenian merchants in Astrakhan helped to introduce weaving and silk manufacturing into Russia. They soon became the dominant group in these industries and extended their operations to Moscow, St. Petersburg, and the Kingdom of Poland. By the early nineteenth century the big Moscow textile merchant-manufacturers gained ascendancy over their smaller competitors to the south. But they still complained to the government that the Armenians were fierce rivals in foreign commerce because they, like the Greeks, benefited from the official policy of special treatment for peoples of the borderlands engaged in the Asiatic trade.[74] Once again local officials saw the matter differently: "The indolence of our merchantry and their indifference to improving the means of water transportation is incomprehensible," wrote a naval officer surveying the eastern shores of the Caspian. "By a strange stubborn resistance to innovation and despite the rebukes of the government and their personal losses, and occasional ruin, the merchantry clings unshakably to its age-old customs."[75]

On the Volga, and all along the thinly populated steppe frontiers of Western Siberia and Central Asia, Russian merchants struggled to hold their own against Tatar, Bashkir, and other local ethnic groups whose knowledge of the area and its languages and customs gave them formidable, often decisive, advantages. Once again the indigenous peoples also benefited from the benevolent attitude of the state. As it did in the western provinces, Catherine the Great's policy of religious toleration had important commercial implications. Extensive

73. Suny, "Russian Rule," pp. 53–78.
74. *SIRIO* (1911), 134:141, 148–49; Liubomirov, *Ocherki*, pp. 100–102, 632–59, 577–78; Gregorian, "Impact of Russia," especially pp. 172–75; Storozhev, *Istoriia*, vol. 2, pt. 1, pp. 352–53.
75. TsGAOR, f. 1639, op. 1, d. 53, "Kaspiiskie putia soobshcheniia i ukrepleniia po vostochnom beregu Kaspiiskogo moria," 1856, p. 33. The report by P. Stepanov to General S. A. Khrulev concluded, "It is still strange that the Russian merchants indolently hand over to foreigners such a vast branch of the commerce of Russia with Northern Persia and the Caucasus."

privileges granted to Muslim merchants enabled the Tatar merchant colonies to spread their influence all along the expanding imperial frontiers.

The alliance of religious zeal and enterprising trade made them powerful instruments of Islamization in Central Asia and Siberia.[76] By mid-century in the old Tatar city of Kazan Muslim merchants still represented 27 percent of the first guild, 31 percent of the second, and 35 percent of the third, for a total of 34 percent of the merchant population. Smaller numbers of them, mainly third guild, also remained active in Samara (12 percent) and Penza (11 percent). In Orenburg to the southeast throughout most of the eighteenth century Russian merchants appealed for the government's assistance to prevent trading by "many godless [i.e., Muslim] hucksters and peasants [who] came and drove down the price of goods."[77] Up until the 1840s all Russian trade with the khanates was in the hands of Central Asian merchants. Gradually, a small number of big Orenburg merchants took advantage of greater support from local Russian bureaucrats to increase their share of the steppe trade. Yet, as table 2.4 shows, while the Russians formed the overwhelming majority of wealthy merchants, the majority of the third-guild merchants remained Muslim.[78]

In the most far-flung reaches of the empire—the Amur region— Russian merchants from Siberian towns met stiff competition from local Cossacks, peasants, native tribes (inorodtsy), and Americans, who, like foreigners elsewhere on the periphery of the empire, took advantage of Governor-General N. N. Murav'ev's policy of granting them special privileges to monopolize the wholesale trade. In 1859, St. Petersburg responded to the merchants' warning that the Americans were penetrating deep into Eastern Siberia by banning navigation to foreign vessels beyond a point three hundred versts from the mouth of the Amur, but it refused to abolish the right of free trade along the entire river. Murav'ev continued to champion the interests of foreign merchants and even forwarded their complaints against arbitrary treatment by local officials to the tsar himself.[79] Throughout the decade of the 1860s Russian merchants in Irkutsk and Moscow criticized proposals that emanated from the Ministry of Finance and the governor-general of Eastern Siberia and aimed at converting the en-

76. Bennigsen, "Muslims," p. 142.
77. Apollova, "Kazakhstan," p. 780. See also Klochkov, Ocherki, p. 366.
78. Calculated from figures in Keppen, Deviataia, pp. 182–86. In addition, the great mass of petty traders who did not hire assistants were non-Russians, mainly Tatar and Bashkir peasants (Rozhkova, Ekonomicheskie, pp. 128–35).
79. Kabanov, Amurskii, pp. 218–19; TsGAOR, f. 722, op. 1, d. 482, "Pis'mo Kuptsa Liudarfa general-gubernatoru vostochnoi Sibiry Murav'evu, N. N.," 4 November 1860.

TABLE 2.4. *Muslim and Christian Merchants in the Volga-Ural Region in 1851*

Province	Christians by Guild			Muslims by Guild			Total	Muslims, Percentage, by Guild			Muslims, Percentage, All Guilds
	1	2	3	1	2	3		1	2	3	
Penza	1	39	1,399	0	0	189	1,628	0	0	11.8	11.6
Samara	0	27	5,057	0	0	608	5,692	0	0	12	12
Viatka	15	101	1,843	1	0	122	2,084	.6	0	.6	.6
Kazan	24	90	1,341	9	40	713	2,216	27	31	35	34
Orenburg	12	43	1,259	0	6	1,746	3,066	0	12	58	57
Tobolsk	27	60	747	3	7	77	922	9	9	12	9

tire province into a free-trade area. Their arguments concluded with the now-familiar xenophobic refrain that agreement to such a proposal would mean that "half of all Siberia with a population of more than one million would be turned into a tributary of the foreigners."[80] In Russia trade and industry followed the flag only grudgingly.

The Great Russian Merchantry

It is only too clear that Russian merchants had not kept pace with the march of empire. As table 2.5 shows, geographically they remained bunched in the provinces of old Muscovy; in 1851 over 75 percent of the Great Russian merchants lived within the boundaries of pre-Petrine Russia, and almost all of these were concentrated in the European provinces. Comparable statistics for the entire population of the empire show that 63 percent lived within the European core of Muscovy, with another 4.6 percent in the Siberian provinces.[81]

By failing to break out of its isolated, inland position, the merchantry allowed foreigners to dominate the export-import trade as they had before Peter the Great opened a window to the West. Unable to prevent the penetration of foreign merchants into their city and their guilds, the Moscow merchants warned the government that foreigners were undermining Russia's trade balance and fiscal stability. They insisted that the foreigners become Russian citizens, settle in the towns, and assume their appropriate service and financial obligations. Originally stated in the petitions of the Legislative Commission, these complaints were renewed in 1805, 1810, 1823, and 1840,[82] but it was all to no avail. According to statistics compiled by G. P. Nebolsin in 1847, foreign merchants controlled 90 percent of Russia's imports and 97 percent of its exports out of a total of 200 million rubles.[83]

During the following fifteen years many factors conspired to keep constant the proportion of the export-import trade in foreign hands. While the Russian merchantry continued to suffer from high internal transportation costs and poor credit facilities, foreigners enjoyed cheaper rates on ocean-going ships and financial assistance from

80. FBON, "Zhurnal zasedaniia Manufakturnogo soveta," 13 February 1869.
81. Calculated on the basis of statistics in Keppen, *Deviataia*, pp. 182–86, and Rashin, *Naselenie*, pp. 28–29, 68, 74.
82. *SIRIO* (1894), 93:104 (Tula), 130 (Moscow); Storozhev, *Istoriia*, 2:37, 127, 200, 480.
83. Nebolsin, *Statisticheskoe*, 2:460–64. No wonder that distraught merchants complained to high government officials that "there is scarcely another country in the whole world where foreigners could enjoy such a comfortable living at the expense of native citizens as in Russia" (memorandum of anonymous merchant to Admiral N. S. Mordvinov, dated 1823, *Arkhiv Mordvinovykh*, 6:368).

TABLE 2.5. *Concentration of Great Russian Merchantry in the Empire in 1851*

A. Merchantry

Geographical Area	Number of Great Russian (Christian) Male Merchants	Percentage of Total Male Merchants
Provinces of Old Muscovy		
European	108,475	75.5
Siberian	1,475	1.1
Total	109,932	76.6

B. Population as a Whole

Geographical Area	Population	Percentage of Total Population
Provinces of Old Muscovy		
European	37,646,400	63
Siberian, estimated	2,759,168	4.6
Total	40,405,568	67.6
All European provinces	52,864,500	
Siberian provinces	2,759,168	
Caucasian provinces (1863)	4,157,900	
Total	59,781,568	

branch offices of their own banks in Russian ports. The Crimean War had wreaked havoc with the small Russian merchant marine, and the losses were not quickly restored. Although after the war Russia had begun to construct a railroad network, it was not until 1863 that a trunk line linked the grain-surplus-producing provinces with a seaport. Assuming that the percentage of foreign trade in the hands of foreigners remained approximately the same, the foreigners' share of Russia's external trade in 1863 would have been over 270 million rubles. If this figure is compared with the total value of all goods traded at domestic fairs, which was only 243 million rubles in 1863, the preponderant role of the foreign merchants in the entire commercial life of the country becomes startlingly clear. It may be argued that internal trade was also carried out in retail stores and town bazaars, for which there are no reliable data. But the fairs continued to play an enormously important role in wholesale trade well into the 1880s. Moreover, the cooperation between foreign and non-Russian merchants on the periphery cut deeply into the share of domestic trade and industry controlled by Russian merchants. In the struggle over the internal market, fairs located in provinces where the non-Russian merchantry predominated accounted for over one-third of the turnover value of the empire as a whole, that is, 66 million rubles.[84] Thus, in large-scale operations with rapid turnover of capital the foreign merchants retained or even increased their long-standing domination over their Russian counterparts.

There were other signs of slippage from the center to the periphery. Although Central Russia continued to dominate the textile industry, its commanding position in the early nineteenth century had been whittled down by mid-century. In 1814, 99 percent of the workers and enterprises in the industry were concentrated around Moscow. In 1859, the figures had fallen to 75 percent of the workers and only about 54 percent of the enterprises.[85] In the same period the sugar-refining industry also shifted, but even more rapidly, away from the center to the periphery; between 1842 and 1856–57 the value of granulated sugar produced in the Ukraine rose from 45 percent to almost 80 percent of the total.[86] On the eve of the Crimean War manufacturing industries located in the central industrial provinces produced goods worth 58.5 percent of the total value in the empire, while the peripheral provinces where non-Russian merchants predominated accounted for 33.7 percent. These figures do not, however, include the Kingdom of Poland or the Grand Duchy of Finland where there were an insignificant number of Russian merchants and which in 1860, for example, supplied 10 percent of the iron and steel produced in the empire.[87]

Non-Russian merchants not only reaped commercial and investment advantages from their close and constant contact with foreigners in the ports and frontier towns but also benefited from easy access to Western technology and know-how. This explains in large measure how they were able to compete with the growing industrial power of the Russian merchants that followed the emancipation of the serfs and the development of new internal credit facilities. Despite its edge in gross production, the center yielded to the periphery in the area of

---

84. Calculated from figures in Khromov, *Ekonomicheskoe*, pp. 472–73, 480–81.
85. Calculated from figures in Livshits, *Razmeshchenie*, pp. 95, 131–33.
86. Ministerstvo finansov, Departament manufactur i vnutrennei torgovli, *Obzor*, 2:462, 469.
87. Calculated from figures in Khromov, *Ekonomicheskoe*, pp. 480–81, and Kniapkina, *Politika*, p. 99.

labor productivity, a clear indication of the latter's technical superiority. As late as 1854, Central Russia required 66.5 percent of the empire's labor force to produce 58.5 percent of the total value of industrial goods, while on the periphery only 22.6 percent of the workers accounted for 33.7 percent.

The aggregate figures suggesting the technological superiority of the periphery over Moscow are borne out by comparative figures within particular industries, as for example in the machine-construction industry (see table 2.6).[88] In agricultural machinery by 1861, firms owned by non-Russians (Schumann, Menstel) or nobility (Potemkin) in the south overtook those in the center in both the number of enterprises (forty-one as against thirty-seven in the center) and also in the introduction of steam-driven machinery.[89] A similar advantage was held by the sugar producers of the Ukraine, who in 1856 owned 76 percent of the steam engines producing 80 percent of the sugar in Russia.[90]

Textiles was one sector of the economy where the central provinces forged dramatically ahead of the rest of the country, with important results for the social structure and outlook of the Great Russian merchantry. By the mid-nineteenth century Petersburg was gradually losing the big lead in cotton spinning which it had long enjoyed because of the dependence of the Russian textile industry on the importation of cotton from overseas. At the same time, the weaving enterprises and printed-cloth manufacturers concentrated in the Moscow and Vladimir provinces surpassed spinning in quality and level of technology. Two concurrent economic changes accelerated these trends. First, the trading peasants were moving into manufacturing based upon the old handicrafts, seeking out a mass market in the countryside and amassing sufficient cash not only to purchase their freedom but also to invest in capital improvements. Second, in 1842 the English lifted their ban on exporting machinery, and the peasant manufactures could be converted to larger-scale factory production.[91] This helped revitalize the merchant guilds by adding fresh blood and new capital. A distinctive regional economic system was emerging in the center. Because the cotton textile industry became so profitable, it

88. Livshits, *Razmeshchenie*, pp. 106–7; Kozmin, *Ocherki*, p. 140.
89. Iasman, "Vozniknovenie," pp. 54–55. Other major firms in Russia also bore foreign names, including Wilson, Rikhter, and Fal'k.
90. For sugar production see Voblyi, *Opyt'*, 1:176–79. It is noteworthy that until the mid-1850s machinery was sold to Ukrainian producers by foreigners at the Kiev fair. When Count Bobrinskoi and other Ukrainian entrepreneurs built a machine factory at Kharkov, they became the chief suppliers for the sugar factories (ibid., p. 173).
91. Livshits, *Razmeshchenie*, pp. 90–104; Portal, "Industriels," pp. 6–18.

TABLE 2.6. *Productivity in the Machine-Construction Industry*

Place	Year	Number of Workers	Total Value Goods	Average per Worker
Moscow	1860	880	382,000	434
Riga	1864	289	163,900	567
St. Petersburg	1860	5,335	6,217,000	1,165

dominated the regional manufacturing of the center well into the twentieth century. But this economic boom had its social and political disadvantages as well.

The proven success of the trading peasant in cotton textiles tended to discourage all but the most enterprising of them from seeking new investment opportunities or entering foreign trade, particularly as these were the province of the nobility, foreigners, or merchants from ethnic minorities on the periphery. They sought rather to secure the protection of their markets by the state against competition from the outside. This reaction was economically rational, though it led to social particularism by reinforcing the specific regional character of the Great Russian merchantry and separating its economic interests from the rest of the empire. The Russian merchants faced an unhappy choice. If they continued to rely upon the state to defend them against foreign domination, they would perpetuate their political subservience to the imperial bureaucracy. Conversely, if they sought to break free of state tutelage, they risked becoming economically dependent on foreign capitalists in the fashion of the comprador societies of China and the Ottoman Empire.

By mid-century it was still premature to regard the merchantry as the core of a rising capitalist class. Far from heading in a single direction, they were being buffeted by crosscurrents. There were signs of economic vitality: a steady increase in the guild population in the 1850s and an even stronger movement of commercial capital into industry based on hired labor. Moreover, in the textile industry of the central industrial provinces a veritable technological revolution was under way. But the nobility still clung to its control over the crucial, if decaying, sectors of mining and metallurgy, and it monopolized the profitable agricultural industries—distilling, timber, wool, and especially sugar refining. The machine industry was almost exclusively in the hands of foreigners. It was scarcely possible to speak of a national market in manufacturing goods. Railroads were in their infancy. The labor supply still depended upon the fluctuating needs of serf-owning

landlords. An alliance of foreigners and non-Russian merchants dominated the regional economies along the periphery.

There were also signs of social renewal, but here too the picture was
mixed. A small number of individual merchants among the second or
third generation of families enrolled in the guilds since the eighteenth
century were beginning to adopt Western European influences, edu-
cating their sons, sending them abroad, establishing branches of their
family firms in other towns, and joining the newly established exchanges. But all too often the result was a loss of their identity as
merchants, through either their own ennoblement or the entrance of
their sons into the professions. A second, stronger, and more ominous
trend was the influx of trading peasants into the merchant soslovie.
The trading peasant's economic successes were a tribute to his natural
shrewdness, energy, and skill in organization and management. But it
was also a sobering commentary on the practical necessity for ruthless
and unscrupulous commercial behavior in order to rise to the top in
the vicious social system that was serfdom. The very fact that the majority of new capitalists in the mid-nineteenth century were products
of a servile system rather than its most dedicated opponents boded ill
for the future social and political evolution of the merchantry.

It was no easy matter for the trading peasant to change his ways
once he had achieved his higher status. Moreover, he was no less
eager than the old established merchant to defend his hard-won privileges and rights against the rest of the trading peasants who were
pressing him from below. In his social outlook and attitudes toward
authority he did not differ significantly from members of the old
merchantry. Coming from the village milieu, he was predisposed to
accept rather than challenge the patriarchal, politically submissive,
and xenophobic values of his newly adopted estate. In a word, he
reinforced the social and political conservatism of the merchantry at
the very time when economic and institutional pressures for change
building both inside and outside the merchant soslovie.

The trickle of nobles who entered the merchant guilds after 1824
were also former competitors of the old merchantry. But, unlike the
trading peasants, they did not renounce their former status and rank.
With few exceptions they gave their primary allegiance to the nobility
rather than transfer it to what they regarded as an inferior soslovie.
They did not provide political leadership for or influence the intellectual and cultural life of the merchants. Rather, they remained aloof
and contemptuous. Similarly, the newly conquered subjects from ethnic minorities who enrolled in the merchant guilds remained socially
and culturally distinct from the Great Russian merchantry. The latter
were perfectly willing to treat them as intermediaries and middlemen

but never as equals. Thus, the social composition and economic power of the guild merchants changed greatly, while their social values and legal condition remained the same. This foreshadowed the opening up of horizontal and vertical cleavages within the merchantry in the second half of the nineteenth century.

At this point in its internal evolution the merchant soslovie was shaken from the outside by a succession of rapid changes which invaded every corner of Russian society. The great reforms of the 1860s and 1870s bestowed upon the merchants many of the benefits that free citizens enjoyed in Western Europe, but they also deeply eroded the fragile stability and unity of their insular community. The construction of a railroad network in the 1870s and 1880s and the great industrial spurt of the 1890s opened up fresh opportunities for investment, profits, and political influence, but threatened to increase bureaucratic interference, labor disturbances, and the economic power of foreign capitalists and their allies among the non-Russian merchants, all at the expense of the Great Russian merchantry.

CHAPTER 3

THE PERSISTENCE

OF TRADITION

In the second half of the nineteenth century the merchantry lost many of its castelike features under the dual impact of institutional reforms and industrialization. As it shed its legal and administrative shell, it acquired more of the characteristics of a social class. But its evolution took some unpredictable turns, and the transformation remained incomplete. Once again the state strongly influenced events. First, it carefully limited the nature and the pace of social change, primarily through its conservative emancipation policies. Second, it allowed a full generation to elapse between the emancipation and the great industrial spurt. During this time large reserves of newly freed labor remained dammed up in the villages, and institutional obstacles blocked the operation of free-market forces elsewhere in the country. To be sure, industrialization had never been uppermost in the minds of the tsar and his officials, who planned and implemented the reforms. What had concerned them most were the military strength and fiscal stability of the empire. These aims continued to preoccupy them in the postreform period. In the crucial case of railroads, for example, strategic and commercial considerations overshadowed all others in designing the first network. Similarly, in banking and credit policy the government cautiously promoted improvements in agriculture and trade, adhered to a firm monetary policy, reduced tariffs, and opposed any form of speculative activity, including state-backed industrial loans, uniform joint-stock-company laws, and a modern stock market.[1]

At the same time the government set strict limits on the activities of private organizations. Governor-generals were given the authority to close down societies and clubs that displayed "anything opposed to the state order, public security, and morality." Organizations were

1. For a more detailed analysis of this view see Rieber, "Alexander II" and "Formation."

expressly forbidden to discuss any topics not directly connected with "the aims for which they had been established."[2] Although this legislation was not directed against any one social group, it effectively prevented the creation of a broadly based organization representing the interests of trade and industry as a whole, as well as thwarted overt political action by the intelligentsia.

In its official rationale in the 1860s and 1870s, the government proposed to avoid the disruptive effects of both rapid economic growth and massive demographic shifts by strictly controlling the pace of its modest structural reforms. By so doing, it hoped to give existing social groups time to absorb the initial shock of institutional changes handed down from above. Thus, when it became appropriate to industrialize, Russia could avoid the widespread social dislocation and political disorders that had shaken Western Europe at a comparable stage in its development.

There were many reasons why these policies should have met with a sympathetic response from the merchantry as a whole and the Great Russians in particular. The idea of a unique, Russian path to industrialization and national greatness exercised a powerful attraction for them. If successful, it would muffle the class struggle, guarantee high rates of profit, and allay status anxieties. But the merchantry could no longer be counted upon to react collectively. The partial dismantling of the soslovie system and the influx of new social elements into the merchantry promised unpredictable consequences.

The great difficulty in writing the history of the merchantry in this period is the need to portray simultaneously two distinctive but intertwined social processes: stagnation and innovation. The musician can run contrasting melodic lines along parallel staffs, but the historian must choose between two unsatisfactory methods. He can alternate the two themes within a chronological narrative, pulling the reader back and forth between one and the other, or he can treat them separately, carrying the reader over the same ground twice. I have risked repetition in order to avoid confusion.

The bulk of the merchantry responded sluggishly to the new structural changes, preferring to trust to the old ways to insulate themselves against the effects of social and economic disruption. But small numbers of merchants in the central industrial provinces broke with traditional behavior. They were drawn in part from the new social elements like the déclassé nobles and sectarian peasants, mainly Old Believers. Their innovative economic activities and participation in local politics opened fresh vistas for the merchantry as a whole. At the

2. *PSZRI*, 2nd ser., 22 July 1866, no. 43501; ibid., 27 March 1867, no. 44402.

same time, a different kind of business leader began to appear on the periphery—the industrial manager. Having no connection at all with the old merchantry, he was instrumental in promoting the economic transformation of his region. The interaction between these contradictory social forces etched the peculiar profile of Russia's social history during the great industrial spurt at the end of the century. The following chapter emphasizes the traditional elements that characterized the mass of the merchantry. Part 2 analyzes the innovative elements—the entrepreneurial groups.

Impact of the Great Reforms

The great reforms of the sixties and seventies gradually lowered the barriers that had divided the Russian population into hereditary sosloviia, but they did not abolish completely all the legal distinctions that continued to prevent the formation within Russia of social classes and the emergence of a national citizenry, at least as these were known in Western and Central Europe. As regards the merchantry, the soslovie principle was deeply eroded by the introduction of the "all-class principle" into the judicial reforms (1864) and more indirectly by the abolition of the legal restrictions on trade (1863–65) and of the head tax (1883–85). Gone were the days when merchants could enjoy the privileges of having civil cases tried in their own courts, of being excused from military service, and of being exempted from a head tax. They also lost their dominant, indeed, exclusive, position in the administration of the towns, which at least had conferred rewards and status on the pervostateiny merchants. Henceforth they had to compete with other social groups in town elections or else surrender a valuable defense of their economic interests. The structure of the merchant soslovie underwent a transformation. Its hereditary character virtually disappeared, and the link between economic function and social status was broken. Widespread though these changes appeared, they remained selective and left the social landscape strewn with anachronisms.

The judicial reform of 1864 made one concession to the particularist sentiments of the merchants by retaining commercial courts with sole jurisdiction over all commercial disputes in the main urban centers of St. Petersburg, Moscow, Odessa, Warsaw, Arkhangelsk, Tagenrog, and Kerch. Unlike their counterparts in the rest of Europe, these courts had a purely soslovie character and their judicial procedures were regulated by a special commercial statute. In other localities the regular circuit courts tried commercial cases, but procedures were to be based on the commercial statute so long as both liti-gants were merchants.[3] However small a crack in the all-class system of law this might have appeared to the outsider, it meant a great deal to the merchants.

Throughout the empire for half a century they displayed remark-able solidarity in defending the commercial courts in the face of repeated attempts to dismantle them. In 1866 in an early show of im-pressive strength the Moscow Exchange Committee rallied exchange committees and merchant societies in all the major cities and flooded the government with petitions. On another occasion the mere appear-ance of a newspaper report predicting abolition roused the Warsaw Exchange Committee in the name of "an alarmed merchantry" to submit an impassioned plea to the minister of finance. In cities where commercial courts did not exist, like Riga, Libau, Lodz, Rostov, and Kiev, exchange committees constantly requested their establishment. The first all-Russian congress of representatives of Russian exchange committees, meeting in 1904, appealed for the extension of commer-cial courts to all the big cities. In the eyes of the merchantry the great value of these courts lay in the commercial expertise of their staffs, the informality of their settings, their reputation for quick justice, and their responsiveness to "the variety of local economic conditions."[4] Their importance was further enhanced by the fact that in Russia there was no clear-cut distinction between the jurisdiction of the com-mercial and civil codes. Eminent jurists even disagreed as to whether commercial affairs could be defined by any objective criteria at all.[5] In a legal system where the boundaries of commercial law were ill de-fined and even less understood by the merchants, custom was bound to play a crucial role in court settlements, and the commercial courts recognized this fully. The merchantry's position on its place in the legal system had changed hardly at all since its petitions of the Legis-lative Commission of 1767 laid down the arguments that they were still using at the turn of the twentieth century. The social implications of all this were clear enough: the merchants still considered them-selves in some important ways fundamentally different from the rest of society.

Yet another soslovie survival from an even more remote past was

3. Nisselovich, *Obshchedostupnye*, 1:54–56; B. Shein, "Kommercheskie sudy," *BE*, 30: 858–61.
4. Evg. Liubovich, "Kommercheskii sud," *PT*, no. 5 (1 March 1910):281–84.
5. For example, Tsitovich, *Uchebnik*, maintained that there were no objective commer-cial transactions in Russian law, whereas Shershenevich, *Kurs*, perceived signs of an ob-jective difference not in the peculiarities of their juridical nature but in the purpose that each of them served.

buried in the ancient division of the population into two fiscal categories. Even though the head tax had been abolished, the legal distinctions between those who had paid it (*podatnoe naselenie*) and those who had been exempt (*nepodatnoe naselenie*) continued in other forms. A mass of legislation which had originally been based upon the existence of these two groups remained on the books, some of it dating back to pre-Petrine times. The most onerous of the so-called "natural obligations" required former members of the "taxable population" to continue to perform a variety of labor and supply services, even though the tax upon which that category had been based no longer existed. Consequently, after 1885 an individual living outside the city who left the merchant soslovie for the meshchanstvo or peasantry crossed an invisible but real line between the old nontaxable and taxable categories and suddenly found himself saddled with a host of heavy, socially demeaning obligations.[6]

In reforming its economic legislation the government retained some of the substance and much of the spirit of the Nicholaen system. The laws of 1863 and 1865 pointed in two directions, revealing the profound ambivalence of the bureaucracy toward the place of commerce and industry in Russian society. Clearly, one aim was to invigorate the economy by permitting "any Russian citizen or foreigner of either sex irrespective of social status (sostoianie)" to purchase a certificate enabling him to engage in trade or manufacturing. But another, more obscure purpose lurked in the exceptions and restrictions on this right. First, the lower ranks of the bureaucracy were prohibited from obtaining these certificates, a leftover from the old fear that commerce corrupts. Second, Jewish merchants were not permitted to enroll in guilds outside the Pale, except in certain specific categories or ranks. Finally, in order to conduct wholesale or retail trade in shops or construct a mill or factory it was still necessary to enroll in a merchant guild. The certificate by itself, then, only permitted the bearer to engage in petty trade and manufacturing. However, a meshchanin or nobleman who bought a certificate and enrolled in a guild had the right to retain his former rank and status or to abandon them in exchange for merchant status.[7] Like so many pieces of legislation

6. N. I. Lazarevskii, "Soslovie," *BE*, 30:912–13. The distinction was particularly important with respect to the so-called natural obligations, the corvée, and obligations to provide food, fodder, and shelter for soldiers and prisoners being transported to Siberia. Long in existence, they were regulated only in 1851 and were enforced even after the emancipation (*SZRI*, 4 (1899): "O natural'nykh zemskikh povinnostiakh voobshche," articles 261–88, and "O povinnosti dorozhnoi," articles 289–95).

7. *PSZRI*, 2nd ser., 1 January 1863, no. 39118; ibid., 9 February 1865, no. 41779. For a useful analysis of this legislation, especially as it pertained to Jewish merchants, see G.

concerning commerce and industry, this one appeared designed to compromise opposing interests and principles. Once again, as they had been in Peter's day, elements of hierarchy and mobility were mixed. The merchantry was a distinctive social and legal group, but some people could enter it under certain conditions.

Wealth remained the main criteria for entry into the merchantry. Inscription in the first guild required a declared capital of at least 15,000 rubles and in the second between 5,000 and 7,000 rubles; the third guild was abolished in 1865. The cost of the certificates also varied according to guild membership. The first-guild merchant paid 500 rubles annually for his, which permitted him to enter the wholesale trade and obtain government contracts without restrictions. A certificate for the second guild cost from 400 to 120 rubles a year, depending upon the location of the business, and it limited trading to retail operations and government contracts of up to 30,000 rubles. In addition, merchants were obliged to purchase a permit for each establishment they owned; these ranged from 20 to 55 rubles for the first guild and from 10 to 35 for the second guild. Thus the merchants found their persons and their enterprises inextricably bound together as a taxable unit. At the same time the merchantry was more sharply distinguished in rights and status from the mass of small traders, who, under the new law, were pushed into the meshchanstvo unless they could demonstrate their financial ability to move up into the second guild.[8]

Under the new system the merchants retained important social privileges, including freedom from corporal punishment, freedom of movement—that is, a passport without a time limit—exemption from military service (until 1874), and the right to perform outstanding public services, which could lead to promotion in rank or a decoration (*orden*) and honorary citizenship, though rarely ennoblement after 1892. Following the prereform tradition, the government continued to regulate the social position of the merchantry, as well as other sosloviia, through minutely detailed laws. Merchants of the first guild were eligible after twelve years tenure in their guild for the rank of commercial or manufacturing councillor. Only those holding these ranks were eligible in turn for higher decorations which conferred the right to wear a uniform and spurs in public and the right of male merchants to be received at court. These honors meant enormous prestige and influence within the merchant soslovie and also opened

---

Vol'tke, "Pravo torgovli i promyshlennosti v Rossii v istoricheskom razvitii (XIX vek)," *REO*, no. 8 (August 1901): 47–51.

8. V. Iaretskii, "Promyshlennyi nalog," *BE*, 59:417–18.

the door to intimate social contact with the higher nobility and officials, which could be of considerable value to the merchant in his
business dealings as well as his social life.[9] More than a mere residue
of the traditional soslovie system, these signal marks of honor and
status represented a perpetuation of the rigid social hierarchy that
extended back to pre-Petrine times.

There were other more subtle indications that the old ways were
not being jettisoned in favor of an open capitalist society based upon
individual initiative. The authority of the male head of the merchant
family was confirmed by the provision that the purchase of a certificate and guild membership secured the same soslovie privileges for
all members of the family, including wife, sons, sons' children (if their
father did not trade under his own name), and unmarried sisters.
After the merchant's death his widows and daughters could still enjoy
these privileges but they could not engage in trade.[10] Thus the integrity of the extended patriarchal family stood unchallenged even
though the merchant soslovie was no longer a closed hereditary
corporation.

Finally, legal restrictions remained to block certain social groups
from enrolling in the merchant soslovie, if not from engaging in
trade. Up until 1893 the law excluded nobles in state service, clergy,
honored citizens, and soldiers of the lower ranks. For individuals
enrolled in a category of the formerly taxable population to transfer
into the merchantry, prior approval was required from the social
organization (obshchestvo) in which he was a member. This regulation remained in force even after the abolition of the head tax in the
1880s ended joint responsibility for taxes which had originally justified the sanction on departure by the rest of the taxpaying unit.[11]

The functional identification of the merchant soslovie with large-
scale trade and industry rapidly broke down under pressure from two
sources: a revival of status consciousness among the nobility and an
expanding economy. At the social level, the nobility once again stiffened its resistance to the promotion of increasing numbers of wealthy
merchants into its soslovie. To placate them and at the same time to
satisfy the merchants' "rank mania," the government resuscitated the
institution of honorary citizenship first established under Catherine

9. *SZRI*, 9(1899): articles 548, 551, 552, 556; ibid., 14(1903): "Ustav o pasportakh," article 39; *PSZRI*, 3rd ser., 9 July 1892, no. 8845. A fine analysis of the role of ranks and
decorations in the Russian bureaucracy and its implications for the rest of society is
Bennett, "Chiny," pp. 162–89.

10. *SZRI*, 9 (1899): articles 532, 537, 540; ibid., 5 (1914) "Ustav o priamykh nalogakh,"
articles 455–57, 471, 474.

11. Ibid., 9 (1899): "Zakony o sostoianiiakh," articles 534, 535, 537, 540, 545.

and unsuccessfully revived by Nicholas I. The reorganization of the merchant soslovie in 1863 and, much later, the new regulations of 1892 opened the floodgates to status seekers who were eager to assume the title, though by the latter date it had primarily an honorific meaning and did not give the merchant any new privileges. It is impossible to determine exactly how many rank-conscious merchants took advantage of this opportunity to scramble up another notch in the social hierarchy, but the available evidence suggests that they numbered in the thousands.[12]

In 1898 the passage of a new industrial tax law gave a clear economic character to the social division within the ranks of trade and industry. To increase revenue from the under-taxed industrial sector of the economy, the government shifted the tax base from the individual to the enterprise and made it possible for the first time to tax the large-scale industries that had sprung up in the 1890s at something like their true economic value. But it also broke the last direct connection between the merchant soslovie and big capitalist industry. The new business certificate replacing the old guild or merchant certificate was purchased not by the individual merchant, on the basis of his wealth and the number of his establishments, but by the enterprise, according to its size and locality. In addition the government imposed a flat-rate tax on net profit for each industrial and commercial company. Payment of these taxes did not confer membership in the merchant soslovie; that was obtainable only by purchasing a separate merchant's soslovie certificate at a nominal fee, fifty rubles for the first guild and twenty for the second (raised to seventy-five and thirty, respectively, in 1907).[13] For the merchant himself this meant a change in degree rather than kind. The new situation did not seriously affect the internal structure of the merchant's soslovie or his traditional pattern of behavior. In fact, of all the soslovie in the em-

---

12. *PSZRI*, 3rd ser., 9 July 1892, no. 8845. Nifontov, "Formirovanie," p. 244, gives the following figures:

	1852	1871	1882	1897
Merchants	13,943	29,222	22,916	19,491
Honored citizens	1,682	7,117	9,223	21,603

The two big increases followed the great reforms and the regulations of 1892, and the increase from 1882 to 1897 among the honored citizens is more than three times the decline in the number of merchants while almost just the reverse is true of the period 1871 to 1882.

13. *SZRI*, 5 (1893): "Ustav o priamykh nalogakh," articles 228, 224; ibid., 9 (1899): articles 532, 533, and appendix to article 533 following 1906 edition; ibid., 5 (1893): "Polozhenie o kazennykh postavkakh i podriadakh," article 265.

pire his remained the only one solely dependent upon economic factors. A sharp decline in the amount of his capital or his failure to purchase a merchant's certificate in any one year would result in the automatic exclusion of him and his family from the soslovie, no matter how successfully he had previously conducted his affairs. To be sure, after 1898 he had to pay less for his privileges than for his right to trade at a certain level. But the threat of loss of status hovered over him and exposed him more than it did others to the vicissitudes of rapid change at a time when Russia was passing through the most tumultuous period in its prerevolutionary history.

What the new tax system and easier access to honorary citizenship did change was the social makeup of the group that comprised the big industrialists. It foreshadowed the emergence of a new category of capitalists who were not necessarily members of the merchant soslovie, who presumably would be less constricted by the traditional life-style of that soslovie, and who would seek different forms of organization to defend their interests. The reappearance of the eighteenth-century dichotomy between commercial and industrial activities introduced another social cleavage which raised further barriers to the consolidation of a middle class.

It may appear that the economic legislation and economic growth of the postreform period most affected the merchantry by changing its social composition. By the beginning of the twentieth century the "old merchant families," those enrolled in the first guild before 1861, no longer constituted a majority. As early as 1873 in Moscow over 50 percent of the first guild had entered after the emancipation of the serfs. Only 17 percent belonged to the eighteenth-century families. Many of the newcomers poured into the city from the provinces. In the last four decades of the century the capital inscribed in the Moscow guilds increased a modest 15 percent, but the portion of the total that originated outside the city jumped from 16 to almost 44 percent.[14] The old families also steadily lost their leading position in capital registered in both the first and second guilds. Their share declined by a third, while that of the trading peasants and meshchane more than doubled (see table 3.1).[15]

But it would be misleading to conclude that this data signified the end of the old merchants' dominance and the fusion of disparate social elements into a new, powerful, and unified bourgeois class. In the first place, the bulk of the newcomers in the guilds were in no position to challenge the old leadership. A profile of them reveals that

14. Gavlin, "Rol'," pp. 340–44.
15. Adapted from Gavlin, "Sotsial'nyi sostav," pp. 168–70.

TABLE 3.1. *Units of Capital Registered in Merchant Guilds (by percentage)*

Social Group	1870	1898
Merchants and honored citizens	74.4	47.5
Trading peasants	9.4	21.7
Meshchane	4.6	10.4
Nobles, officers	1.7	2.8
Intelligentsia	0.7	2.5
Foreigners	5.9	7.4
Joint-stock companies and partnerships	0.6	5.3
Other	2.7	2.4

about half were trading peasants, almost three-quarters came from the central industrial (about one-half) and the central agricultural (about one-quarter) provinces, and all but a handful enrolled in the second guild. Taken together with data on units of capital registered, it is clear that a substantial percentage of the remainder were from the meshchanstvo. This kind of influx into the guilds from below had been taking place since the 1830s and had not appreciably changed the merchants' outlook or their social role. Moreover, inscribed capital did not mean real amounts of cash invested but rather the taxable unit established by law for entry into the guilds. Thus, the declining share of old merchant capital did not necessarily mean a shift in real wealth away from the old merchants. Since the bulk of the newcomers inscribed in the second guild, the contrary seems more likely.

The provincials simply were in no position to match the old merchant elite in wealth, status, cultural awareness, or political influence. Since they were drawn from the same regional, ethnic, and patriarchal peasant backgrounds as the founders of the old families, there was no compelling reason why they should have tried. Located at the bottom of the soslovie hierarchy, in a much more precarious economic situation than the old elite, they were far more disposed to defer to the established figures and strive to amass more capital.

As for the nobility, neither their status and education nor their interests inclined them to play an active role in the guilds.[16] For the most part, in fact, they were rentiers rather than active participants in the industrial process and had little reason to mix with the old merchants on any account. As one of the most prominent leaders of the

16. Ibid., pp. 175, 183. Gavlin points out that there was a small group of engineers represented among the noble industrialists and these were clearly active managers of enterprises.

old merchantry later recalled, the nobles continued to refer to a merchant with the derogatory diminutive "kupchik" and had nothing to do with them.[17] The conspicuous absence of close social and political relations between the Moscow merchants and nobles enrolled in the same guilds is a striking phenomenon which will surface again and again in the last section of this book.

The changing social composition of the guilds leaves one practical problem for the historian, however. It increases the difficulty of making clear social distinctions among the capitalists in Russia after 1898. Henceforth in this narrative, at least, the term merchant may be taken to mean a member of a guild whose social origin can be traced to the old (pre-1861) merchantry or else whose social loyalty had shifted from his previous status to that of the merchantry. It must be assumed that the majority of those in this latter category came out of the peasantry and meshchanstvo rather than the nobility or the intelligentsia. In other words those who saw guild membership as the sign of higher status identified with the old guild population; those who did not did not. In brief, for the purposes of analysis, it is necessary to make a distinction between joining a guild, which actually says very little about social identity, loyalty, and aspirations, and accepting the traditional social role of the merchantry.

The merchant's view of himself was formed as much by the organization of his soslovie as by the privileges attached to it. The reconstruction of 1863 reduced bureaucratic interference and increased self-regulation, but did not entirely abolish the burden of service obligations. For the following thirty years, soslovie organizations shared responsibility for collecting taxes on trade and industry as well as local taxes, for issuing merchants' certificates, and for furnishing the government with a mass of information on the present state of commerce and industry. In Moscow the reorganized merchants' board (*kupecheskaia uprava*) remained saddled with a host of petty administrative duties, including "the maintenance of order and tranquility" within the merchant soslovie. The revised statutes obliged the assembly of electors (sobranie vybornykh) to elect at least seventy-eight of its number to perform special duties, including guild elders, commercial police serving from two to four years, and, in addition, an undesignated number of notaries, brokers, and tax collectors.[18] In the wake of the emancipation of the serfs, the decision to retain elements of the old Muscovite administration psychologically reinforced the tradi-

17. Riabushinskii, "Kupechestvo," p. 175.
18. Storozhev, *Istoriia*, vol. 5, pt. 1, appendix, "Instruktsiia sobraniam vybornykh," pp. 81–102, and "Instruktsiia moskovskoi kupecheskoi uprave," pp. 67–81.

tional social conservatism and political inertia among the merchantry and ill prepared them for further social evolution.

Most of these obligations were only lifted in the town reform of 1870, which was adopted in Moscow only three years later. But the merchants' society (kupecheskoe obshchestvo) conserved its eighteenth-century structure and remained as the corporate regulatory body for the guilds, even though it lost many of its old functions to the new town administration (see figure 3.1). The importance attached to the merchant society by bureaucrats and merchants alike may be gauged from the fact that of all the soslovie organizations it alone was represented as such on a number of government departments, including the commercial courts and the tax boards.[19] Therefore, the argument that the reforms of the 1860s transformed the merchant society into something like a professional organization by abolishing its hereditary, corporate nature ignores two special qualities of the merchant's society: its unimpaired internal structure and its performance of distinctive functions within the central bureaucracy. The comparison is also misleading because in Russia the organizations of the free professions, which only began in the 1860s, resembled rather more the old soslovie organizations than their counterparts in the rest of Europe.[20]

During this period of institutional and economic change the merchant soslovie as a whole preserved a hard structural residue and a more subtle psychological awareness of its distinctive social role. But its other dimension, its strongly marked ethno-territorial character, was hard pressed to survive the pressures of a burgeoning industrialization which stimulated social mobility and internal migration. As we have seen, a rapid turnover continued unabated in the ranks of the Great Russian merchantry during the immediate postreform period. But this movement was largely confined to the regional boundaries of the center. Indeed, wherever social mobility affected the social composition of the merchantry, it was intraregional and left no mark on the ethnic geography of the merchantry. The territorial blocs of non-Russian merchants stood intact on the periphery of the empire surrounding the Great Russian core.

As shown in table 3.2, in 1897 the Great Russian merchants remained a distinct minority within their own soslovie along the western and southern periphery of the empire, in the Baltic region (but not

19. *SZRI*, 5 (1914): "Ustav o priamykh nalogakh," articles 406, 408, 422; ibid., 9 (1903): "Ustav sudoproizvodstva torgovogo," articles 1, 2, 7, 10, 42–48; Naidenov, *Vospominaniia*, 2:45–46.

20. A revealing comparison may be made between the structure and functions of the kupecheskoe obshchestvo, based on Storozhev, *Istoriia*, vol. 2, and the soslovie organization of the Russian bar in Tager, "Soslovnaia," pp. 58–114.

FIGURE 3.1. *Merchant Soslovie Organization*

kupecheskoe obshchestvo
(merchant-society: after 1863, two guilds)

sobranie vybornykh
(the assembly of electors)

kupecheskaia starshina
(merchant elder)

kupecheskaia uprava
(merchants' board)

St. Petersburg), Bielorussia, the former Kingdom of Poland, Little Russia, New Russia, New Russia and the Don, and the Caucasus. In Central Asia they had achieved equality with the native merchants. Only in Siberia did they command an overwhelming majority of the regional merchantry. It is not possible to make more than a rough comparison between the census of 1897 and the revision of 1851, because ethnic identity in the former was based on language, whereas in the latter it was religion. Nevertheless, what emerges in even the crudest terms is the persistence of an ethnic-regional pattern set by military conquest in the late eighteenth and early nineteenth centuries and barely affected in the west and south by seventy-five to one hundred years of Russian control. That the preponderance of the non-Russian merchants continued precisely in those regions of the country where foreign capital penetrated most readily suggests the enormous potential for conflict between the center and the periphery during the period of the empire's greatest industrial expansion and nationalist resurgence.[21]

Merchants and Local Government

The merchant soslovie survived heavy social and economic pressures, but competitive electoral politics provided a different kind of test. The zemstvo reform of 1864 pitted the provincial merchants against

21. *PVP*, 2:150, 3:226, 4:162–63, 5:254–55, 8:248–49, 11:288, 12:228, 13:206, 14:258, 16:258, 17:208, 19:210, 21:208, 22:222, 23:250, 32:256, 33:286, 37:232, 41:274, 48:308, 49:114, 51:286, 52:204, 53:136, 54:160, 55:236, 56:230, 57:162, 59:166, 60:198, 61:150, 62:190, 63:164, 64:192, 65:238, 66:272, 67:132, 68:210, 69:264, 70:104, 71:164, 72:58, 73:166, 74:162, 75:154, 76:192, 78:22, 79:222.

TABLE 3.2. *The Great Russian Merchantry: An Ethnic Profile in 1897*

Region and Province	Great Russian Merchants	Total Merchant Population	Percentage Great Russian
Petersburg and Baltic			
St. Petersburgskaia	14,000	17,411	85
Estlandskaia	106	626	17
Kurlandskaia	80	996	8
Liflandskaia	932	4,953	18
West and Bielorussia			
Vilenskaia	540	2,630	21
Vitebskaia	661	5,236	13
Kovenskaia	137	2,420	6
Grodenskaia	454	3,401	13
Minskaia	440	3,519	12
Mogilevskaia	295	3,496	8
Volynskaia	385	3,883	10
The Kingdom of Poland			
Varshavskaia	521	4,666	11
Kalishskaia	21	513	4
Keletskaia	6	54	10
Lomzhinskaia	39	289	13
Liublinskaia	55	512	11
Plotskaia	7	73	10
Petrokovskaia	137	2,387	6
Sedletskaia	23	393	6
Suvalskaia	14	382	4
Radomskaia	11	308	4
Little Russia, New Russia, and the Don			
Bessarabskaia	625	3,492	18
Kievskaia	3,035	11,934	25
Chernigovskaia	1,565	6,364	25
Poltavskaia	1,027	7,774	13
Ekaterinoslavskaia	2,554	7,898	32
Kharkovskaia	3,965	6,177	64
Khersonskaia	5,631	12,303	45
Chernomorskaia	110	231	47
Tavrichskaia	2,680	7,732	35
Don Military Oblast	2,166	3,779	58

TABLE 3.2. *(Continued)*

Region and Province	Great Russian Merchants	Total Merchant Population	Percentage Great Russian
Caucasus			
Bakinskaia	369	3,040	12
Daghestanskaia	84	602	14
Elizavetopolskaia	15	1,019	1
Karskaia	9	241	3
Kubanskaia	1,776	2,865	62
Stavropolskaia	810	1,073	75
Kutaisskaia	80	2,457	43
Terskaia	948	2,066	46
Tiflisskaia	308	3,947	8
Erivanskaia	7	1,014	<1
Central Asia			
Akmolinskaia obl.	621	1,107	58
Samarkandskaia obl.	74	153	48
Semipalatinskaia	452	1,033	40
Semirechenskaia	309	749	41
Syr Dar'inskaia	328	661	50
Turgaiskaia	48	65	74
Ural'skaia	264	304	86
Ferganskaia	53	121	45
Siberia			
Amurskaia	929	965	96
Eniseiskaia	771	975	79
Zabaikalskaia	765	1,285	60
Irkutskaia	980	1,450	67
Primorskaia	447	521	85
Tobolskaia	1,229	1,352	90
Tomskaia	1,756	2,232	78
Iakutskaia	165	182	90

the nobility, their traditional soslovie rival for economic control of the countryside. Although the town statutes of 1870 was the third major urban reform of the empire, it was the first to expose the merchants to the temptations of party and ideology, which could dissolve traditional loyalties to soslovie in a genuine all-class electoral system.

During the first two decades of the zemstvos' existence, the merchantry was the beneficiary of a voting system that combined property qualifications and soslovie membership. It steadily increased its relative weight in the first curia of electors and in delegates to the district assemblies, especially in the central industrial provinces. But the percentage increase in merchant representatives fell well below that of eligible merchant voters, a sure sign of political timidity or deference to the nobility. In the second curia the merchants and other urban groups actually lost ground to the nobles and officials. During the same period the merchants managed to enlarge their representation in district zemstvos throughout the empire only by an insignificant 4 percent.[22]

However modest these gains, they were suddenly jeopardized by certain proposals submitted to the Kakhanov Commission, which met in the Ministry of the Interior from 1882 to 1883 to draft new zemstvo legislation. In one of them, prepared by A. D. Pazukhin, who enjoyed the powerful patronage of Katkov and Prince Meshcherskii, the soslovie system was to be resurrected and the merchantry virtually excluded from the first curia, all for the express purpose of guaranteeing landed gentry predominance in the zemstvos.[23] The interests of the merchantry vanished completely in the flurry of counterproposals and the ensuing bureaucratic infighting. Faced with an unexpectedly strong frondeur sentiment among elements of the nobility, the bureaucracy split over the question whether to recast the zemstvos in the image of the old soslovie system or to perfect the "all-class principle" of election.[24] Yet whatever their ideological positions, the main protagonists displayed in equal measure either hostility or indifference to the merchantry. Characteristically, the merchants themselves hardly raised their voices in the debate, except to complain about unfair

22. Zakharova, *Zemskaia*, pp. 14–15, 22.

23. Pazukhin had touched off the entire controversy in the first place when he submitted a memo that through intermediaries reached Alexander III (TsGAOR, f. 722 [Alexander III], op. 1, no., 617, "Sovremennoe sostoianie Rossii i soslovnyi vopros"). In this draft, dated by archivists "1881–2?" Pazukhin virtually ignored the merchantry except to deplore the decline in influence of the merchant "old timers," pp. 18–19. (The use of the term *starozhiltsy*, normally employed to designate long-time peasant residents of communes, speaks volumes for Pazukhin's social views.) The memo and Pazukhin were picked up by Katkov, who published a revised version in *RV*, January 1884, and again in a separate pamphlet in 1886. The internal history of the incident is still unclear, but it appears that the main target of Pazukhin and, more importantly, of Katkov and Meshcherskii was the urban intelligentsia and that the merchantry, considered as a negligible political factor by both sides, was simply caught in the middle.

24. The most detailed account of the noble revival is now the important study by Iu. B. Solov'ev, *Samoderzhavie*, especially pp. 165 ff. See also Zaionchkovskii, *Rossiiskoe*, chaps. 4 and 8; Anfimov, *Krupnoe*; and Yaney, *Systematization*, pp. 346–51, 364–76.

treatment. At issue were two questions, at least, which directly touched the vital interests of the merchants—the zemstvo election law and the zemstvos' power of taxation. That the merchants showed greater concern over loss of votes is not surprising; that they ignored the connection between the two says little for their political awareness.

The compromise law that finally emerged in June 1890 gave greater prominence to sosloviia in the zemstvo electoral law and further reduced the participation of corporate industrial enterprises in the suffrage. The practical result was to reverse a trend of twenty years toward growing urban participation in zemstvos (see table 3.3).[25] Surely the main victims of this decline were the merchants, for they were the largest and presumably the wealthiest owners of manufacturing enterprises, at least in the central provinces, whereas the noble, peasant, and meshchane industrialists ranked far below them.[26]

The decline in the merchants' influence within the zemstvos coincided with a crisis over the tax system that led to a further deterioration of relations between the urban and landed sosloviia. The revenue powers of the zemstvos had been left vague by the local government reforms of 1864. The landed nobility immediately perceived the great advantage of raising additional income by taxing commercial and industrial certificates. When the Ministry of Finance intervened to protect the merchantry, the controversy rapidly heated up. In a prophetic warning a Slavophil sympathizer with the merchants, A. I. Koshelev, pointed out the serious consequences of basing the zemstvo tax structure on the traditional distinctions between sosloviia. Such a policy could only divide the propertied elements. Much fairer, in his eyes, was a progressive tax on all capital. This was, he argued, the only equitable and efficient means of raising fresh revenues from hitherto untaxed commercial and industrial properties while assuring active merchant participation in zemstvo activities. The merchants would be certain to take an interest in local government if they understood that

25. Zakharova, *Zemskaia*, pp. 152–53. The figures changed very little after this. In 1908, for example, the percentage figures for delegates elected to district zemstvos were as follows: nobility and officials, 57.1; merchants and other sostoianiia of the urban soslovie, 13.3 (*PT*, 1 June 1908, no. 11, p. 654).
26. The figures for Moscow in 1887 are:

Size of Firm	Owners in Percentage			
	Merchant	Nobility	Peasantry	Meshchanstvo
Less than six workers	34.9	62.4	62.2	63.7
More than sixteen workers	41.8	13.3	5.4	4.9

Adapted from L. M. Ivanov, "O soslovno-klassovoi," p. 339.

TABLE 3.3. *Representation in the Zemstvos*

	1883–86		1890	
	Number of Delegates	Percentage of Whole	Number of Delegates	Percentage of Whole
District Zemstvos				
Nobles and officials	5595	42.4	5647	55.2
Merchants and urban soslovie	2223	16.9	1415	13.8
Provincial Zemstvos				
Nobles and officials	1862	81.5	1448	89.5
Merchants and urban soslovie	255	11.2	141	8.7

it was their money that was being spent.[27] His advice was ignored, and as he predicted, the latent conflict over the relative proportions of tax revenue raised from commerce and land flared up in aggravated form two decades later. At a formative stage in the liberation movement, which bore the hopes for Russian liberalism, the quarrel hampered a rapprochement between town dumas and rural zemstvos.

In the meantime, during the 1870s the majority of provincial zemstvos endorsed a shift from the head tax to an income tax as the main fiscal basis for the national budget. This was simply another device to extract revenue from the untaxed commercial and industrial properties and to relieve the peasantry (and indirectly the landlord as well) from the crushing fiscal burden that had held back an economic revival of the countryside ever since the emancipation. But the government delayed abolishing the head tax until 1887. Even then, characteristically, it hesitated to introduce an all-class revenue system and continued to base tax collecting on the outmoded sosloviia. As the bureaucrats grappled indecisively over tax reform, resentment continued to build within the zemstvos against the privileged economic position of trade and industry: that is to say, the landed gentry attacked high protective tariffs, which increased the cost of agricultural

27. Koshelev, *Golos*, 1:11.

machinery, and deplored the virtual absence of any taxes on industrial properties and commercial profits. In the early nineties, the progressive income tax won adherents among the landowners, who perceived that their share of the tax burden would be reduced and their heavy indebtedness would spare them from the higher rates.[28]

The growing antagonism between nobles and merchants over who should pay for public services in the countryside became particularly acute following the zemstvo counterreform and the famine of 1891–92. At this point, moderate elements in both camps sought a historic compromise. D. N. Shipov, subsequently a leader of the zemstvo wing of the liberation movement, made a dramatic bid to negotiate the differences with K. V. Rukavishnikov, the mayor of Moscow, a wealthy patron of charities and a leader of the liberal, innovative wing of the merchants in the town duma. But when conservative merchants raised objections, the discussions broke down amidst mutual recriminations over the unilateral action of the Moscow provincial zemstvo in raising the rates on urban properties.[29] Thus, the potential for a political coalition among those groups in both urban and landed sosloviia who considered themselves "progressives" evaporated.

This and other quarrels were signs of a renewed suspicion between nobles and merchants, which peaked at the end of the century. The subsidized press of the merchants denounced the landowners as "social autonomists" and "Jacobins," who milked the towns for all they were worth and blamed the government for everything that went wrong.[30] Self-styled conservatives among the nobility, both in and out of service, cherished the hoary myth that their soslovie alone embodied the higher interests of the state, by virtue of its attachment to the land and its "noble spirit." In a mood of exalted desperation they convinced the government to slam shut the door of nobility in the face of aspiring raznochintsy and merchantry by imposing the most rigid restrictions in over a century on access to their soslovie.[31] The last gasp of this dying tradition was their unsuccessful attempt to

28. Veselovskii, *Istoriia*, 2:154–61, 170–71.

29. Shipov, *Vospominaniia*, pp. 28, 539–44; Astrov, *Vospominaniia*, pp. 273–74. (Astrov was secretary of the Moscow duma.) Admittedly, this controversy had strong overtones of town versus countryside, irrespective of soslovie loyalties.

30. See especially the articles by A. I. Elishev, "Vnutrennee obozrenie," *Russkoe obozrenie*, September 1896, pp. 445–58; ibid., March 1897, pp. 525–35; ibid., May 1897, pp. 477–86; ibid., February 1898, pp. 986–88.

31. *PSZRI*, 3rd ser., 28 May 1900, no. 18681. The ukaz reduced the opportunities for ennoblement by means of obtaining certain orders and stipulated that an aspiring merchant hold land in the province where the inscription was made and receive approval by a vote of two-thirds of the provincial noble assembly. The restrictions on orders were particularly damaging to the aspirations of the merchantry.

recapture for themselves a monopoly of state service.[32] There is no way to calculate the precise effect of this renewed rivalry between the nobility and the merchantry, but it is important to bear in mind that the controversy was couched in the words and sentiments of sosloviia. The language itself encouraged the belief in the minds of the nobles that it was not economic power but half-mythical emblems of land and blood that distinguished social groups among Russian citizens. As will become clear, some merchants were perfectly willing to reply in much the same spirit with their own set of symbols rooted in another powerful but no less mythical tradition.

The reforms of the town administrations in the 1860s and 1870s offered the merchantry its best opportunity to assume a leading role in the embryonic political life of the empire. Still, the challenge was slow in developing. The bureaucrats were divided over the degree of self-government that should be entrusted to the towns. In 1862, with characteristic caution, they limited their first step to drafting a new statute for Moscow. Throughout the document two opposing princi-ples of citizenship—the all-class and the soslovie—warred with one another, as they had since Catherine's abortive reform of 1785. The unwieldy administrative structure was based on separate assemblies elected by each soslovie sitting separately. Even though delegates to all five sosloviia jointly elected a mayor and sat together on occasion to consider questions of general order, they continued to behave like discrete social units. The exclusion from the town government of the intellectual and professional groups deprived the organization of the catalyst needed to fuse the rigid sosloviia. Their absence fully justifies the opinion of the leading authority on Moscow's urban life that the statute of 1862 was in fact a retreat from the broader principles of town citizenship first enunciated by Catherine almost a hundred years earlier.[33]

The town statutes of 1870 introduced throughout the empire (ex-cept for the western provinces, the former Kingdom of Poland, and Central Asia) appeared to shift the basis for voting from soslovie to property qualifications. But in fact the peculiar definition of property smuggled back the soslovie principle in a curiously restrictive way. Possession of immovable property, purchase of commercial licenses, and payment of commercial and industrial taxes enfranchised the landowners, merchants, lower middle class (meshchanstvo), artisans (remeslenoe naselenie), and trading peasants, but excluded professors, teachers, doctors, journalists, and others, even though many were personal or hereditary nobles. As far as the merchants were con-

32. Iu. B. Solov'ev, *Samoderzhavie*, pp. 282–95, 310–14, 370–72.
33. Shchepkin, *Obshchestvennoe*, pt. 1, p. 86.

cerned, little had changed. If anything, their position was stronger vis à vis the nobility, who lost some leading personalities. The merchants continued to elect the same people, who continued to regard themselves as representatives of their soslovie.

On the other hand, the municipal reform finally emancipated the merchantry from its tiaglo burden. To be more precise, it shifted that burden from the merchant soslovie to the municipality as a whole. Quartering of troops and maintaining a police force and the justices of the peace were made obligatory duties of the town government. Henceforth, salaried employees hired by the town council and chosen from any soslovie of the urban population performed the various functions—police, charitable, health, and fiscal—that had for so long weighed heavily on the merchantry. The town duma had legislative power over a wide range of activities. The role of the central and local bureaucracy was reduced to "surveillance" over the activities of the elected officials to make certain that there were no violations of the law. In contrast to earlier practice, the illegalities were now very carefully defined. Thus, the opportunities for arbitrary bureaucratic interference were substantially reduced, if not altogether eliminated.[34]

At first the merchants showed a reluctance to take command of the new town governments. In 1862, in Moscow, where for the first time in Russian history merchant and noble representatives faced one another in a direct electoral contest for mayor, the merchants enjoyed a majority of votes in the new duma. What they lacked was confidence in their own abilities. Although the merchant delegates nominated candidates from their own ranks, a significant number of them defected in the balloting, permitting the election of the nobility's mayoralty candidate, Prince Shcherbatov. Pogodin summed up the prevailing attitude when he declared that for all his promerchant feelings, he believed that only a noble candidate could meet the need for "political maturity, education, and firmness in dealing with the state bureaucracy."[35] For the moment at least, the nobility shared these perceptions.

The subsequent reelection of Prince Shcherbatov in 1867 and the election of Prince Cherkassky in 1869 (to fill out the unexpired term of Shcherbatov, who retired) proved to be a disappointment for the liberal Slavophil nobility, who sought to make the Moscow duma a sounding board for their political pronouncements. Cherkassky

34. Ibid., pp. 90–95. For a recent lucid summary comparing the structure of city governments in the nineteenth century see Hanchett, "Tsarist Regulation," in Hamm, City, pp. 91–113.
35. Pogodin, Sochineniia, 3:378–79.

and Ivan Aksakov did manage to stampede the duma into passing unanimously the famous declaration of 1870 that advocated genuine self-government and final trust in the people by the tsar. But the demonstration was ignored in St. Petersburg and found no echo in the country. The merchants quickly realized the error of their ways and until 1905 avoided becoming involved in this kind of political demonstration. Henceforth, the "constitutional" voices were heard only in the provincial zemstvos, where the landowning nobility asserted its leadership. In the towns, politics revolved around the conflict between the sosloviia over the construction of public works. Relations with the central government took on the familiar form of humble petitions of loyalty to the throne.

In the seventies and eighties the Moscow merchants had several opportunities to consolidate their numerical superiority in the duma and to assume the leadership of urban reform. With two notable exceptions, they failed, as they had in the past, to form lasting alliances with those groups at both ends of the social spectrum that were necessary for their political ascendancy—the nobility for its technical and administrative skills and the meshchanstvo for its mass support. When the merchants finally elected one of their own, I. A. Liamin, as mayor in 1871, the poor man was forced, almost immediately thereafter, to resign by the governor, P. P. Durnovo. The incident reawakened in the minds of the nobles doubts about the ability of merchants to succeed in public life.[36] Six more years were to pass before another merchant became mayor.

By that time the representation of the nobility, who formed the bulk of the urban intelligentsia, was diminished by the adoption in Moscow in 1873 of town statutes that disenfranchised those who did not own landed property in the city. Even fewer survived the so-called slaughter of the intelligentsia in the election of 1879–80, which marked the emergence of the artisans and shopkeepers as a real political force. Popularly known as the *tekintsy,* after the fierce Turkomen tribesmen, the meshchane stoked the antiintellectual fires, while the merchantry looked on passively, unable to harness these fractious elements for their own ends. The steady decline of the intelligentsia in the duma was only briefly interrupted by the election of Boris Chicherin as mayor; but this ended predictably in a clash with the central administration that scared off the merchants again. When the

36. Nikitenko, *Dnevnik,* 3:271–72, is the most graphic description of the incident. The editor misread the original manuscript, however, and incorrectly identified the mayor as N. A. Lanin. See also p. 525.

nobility attempted to recoup its fortunes by promoting an electoral reform linking suffrage to a tax on dwellings, the majority of merchants refused to support them.[37]

While it is true that the nobles could be blamed for sacrificing urban reform to empty political gestures, the merchantry lacked the excuse of a higher cause to justify its dismal record. In almost every area of public service—lighting, sewage, water supply, public housing for indigents, and municipal slaughterhouses—the time between proposal of an issue on the floor of the duma and final approval was fifteen to twenty years.[38] Again and again the merchant majority voted down proposals to raise revenues by means of public loans or higher taxes on industrial and commercial properties, both of which it regarded as inimical to its interests. At the same time the merchants stubbornly insisted upon consulting foreign specialists before they would even agree to consider the construction of public works. Aside from serving as a delaying tactic, their position exhibited the same contempt for the Russian technical intelligentsia as that that had long pervaded hiring practices in their own factories.[39]

As the Moscow municipal government slipped back into the hands of the merchantry, an archaic style of administration still practiced by the governing boards of the merchant soslovie quietly settled over the duma as well. "Bureaucratic red tape [*formalizm i kantsel arizm*] only dragged things along to the point of absurdity, and ruled out any personal responsibility and initiative," wrote I. N. Mamontov, a dissenting voice among the merchant deputies. Most of them viewed their own elected leadership with suspicion. The duma and the executive board confronted one another like "two bitter enemies," paralyzing one another, spreading apathy among the public at large, and breeding contempt among the Petersburg bureaucrats.[40]

It was one thing to assert belligerently their identity as members of the merchant soslovie and to rebuff the nobility as their social superiors. This was as far as what some called "the younger generation"

---

37. Chicherin, *Vospominaniia*, pp. 176–81, 184; Naidenov, *Vospominaniia*, 2:34–35; Golitsyn, "Moskva," pp. 147, 151; Gurko, *Nashi vybory*, pp. 8–10, 23, 34–35. Petersburg editor V. L. Dolinskii argued that "the faith of people in the noble soslovie did not exist in Russia among the masses" as "a natural consequence of the unfavorably established historical conditions in Russia [that is, serfdom]," and that "in the towns, especially the large ones like Moscow, they had always been and were now more like guests than hosts" (*V zashchitu*, pp. 1, 8–10). Dolinskii's optimism in the "enlightened Moscow merchantry" turned out to be misplaced.

38. Veselovskii, "Gorodskoe khoziaistvo," Akademiia nauk, *Istoriia Moskvy*, 4:528–30, 532–33, 536–37, 539, 542.

39. Chicherin, *Vospominaniia*, pp. 195, 197, 201.

40. Mamontov, *Programma*, pp. 9–10.

of merchants was prepared to go in raising the level of its political consciousness. It was quite another thing to break out of their self-imposed social isolation and join hands with public-spirited elements among the nobility and the urban intelligentsia to create and administer a genuine urban community. The beginnings of a real change in the merchantry's role in urban affairs came in the late seventies. The election of Sergei Tret'iakov and Nikolai Alekseev as mayors gave the merchants a decade of energetic champions of urban development in Moscow. But they were representatives of the small group of innovators. For all their accomplishments, to be reviewed in the next chapter, their example did not survive them.

Even this belated flurry of activity failed to overcome the deepening hostility of the Ministry of the Interior, which condemned the merchants for managing or mismanaging the city in its own selfish interests. In the wake of the zemstvo counterreform, V. K. Pleve and I. N. Durnovo drafted legislation that sharply limited suffrage, eliminated all the commercial industrial electors outside the first-guild merchants, and strengthened the hand of the appointed bureaucrats from the ministry to intervene in urban affairs.[41] In this way town administration returned to much the same condition as that which had prevailed under Nicholas I: the big merchants had nominal control, but they were completely dominated by the central bureaucracy. The merchants had been given their chance, and they had frittered it away.

Professional Organizations

The final test of the Russian merchantry's political consciousness centers on membership in professional organizations. In the period from the emancipation to the revolution in 1905, two representative types of groups existed outside the soslovie organization—one was quasi-governmental and the other was autonomous. The manufacturing and commercial councils and committees, which had been created under Nicholas I to serve as permanent links between the bureaucracy and the merchant soslovie, continued to operate under supervision of the Ministry of Finance. In 1872, after the urban reforms, the Ministry of Finance ordered a mild reorganization, but did not change the basic purpose of the councils. Thus, while the government allowed for a broader definition of the merchants' administrative role, it kept a tight rein on their commercial freedom. In a purely bureaucratic change the separate councils for commerce and industry in Moscow

41. Zaionchkovskii, *Rossiiskoe*, pp. 412–14, 420–27.

and St. Petersburg were merged into a single Council of Trade and Manufacturing. Both councils were authorized to discuss at the request of the minister of finance, specific questions ranging from approval of patents and inventions to the effect of new factories upon the health and welfare of the urban population. The council was still appointed by the minister, however, and the meetings were chaired by a deputy minister.[42]

The one significant change that was introduced could not have been appreciated by the Moscow merchants. On the recommendation of the Society for the Encouragement of Industry and Trade, membership on the councils was expanded to include individual factory owners, traders outside the guilds, and technical specialists, whatever their soslovie affiliations. This innovation seriously challenged the dominant position that the merchants had held in the Moscow section of the old manufacturing and commercial councils. Previously, the merchants had wielded great power over potential competitors, including foreign capitalists, by exercising their rights to recommend for or against the introduction of new technology (especially steam engines) into factories, to investigate industrial accidents, and to adjudicate complaints of patent infringement and breaches of contract. Over the years they strove for and achieved a more nearly equal status with the bureaucrats on the council.[43] The "democratization" of the council in 1872 opened the way for the penetration into their stronghold of the technical intelligentsia whom the merchants had always held at arms length.

The second part of the reform created committees of trade and manufacturing in other ports and major cities for much the same purpose. Their establishment proceeded sluggishly in Archangelsk (1873), Tikhvin, Tver, Odessa and Rostov (1875), Ivanovo-Vosnesensk (1879), and Belostok (1893). In characteristically unsystematic fashion, the ministry permitted the older type of manufacturing committee which had been established in Warsaw and Lublin in 1871 to continue to exist, rather than go to the trouble of reorganizing it.[44]

In three ways, then, the Ministry of Finance reimposed its control over the merchantry in general and the Moscow merchants in particular: by diluting the membership of two councils with technical specialists, by setting limits to the agenda, and by preserving the regional character of the councils as opposed to an empire-wide organization.

42. *SZRI*, 11, pt. 2 (1893): "Ustav o promyshlennosti," articles 11, 12.
43. This conclusion is based on a reading of FBON "Zhurnaly" for the years 1858, 1864, 1868, and 1869.
44. *SZRI*, 11, pt. 2 (1887): "Ustav o promyshlennosti," articles 14–27.

Thus, in both the soslovie and the quasi-bureaucratic organizations the merchants continued to serve the state in time-honored fashion.

The first autonomous organizations of the merchants were formed after the big tariff fight of 1867. The organized reaction of the Moscow merchantry in particular had convinced the government of the need to impose fixed rules and institutional constraints upon this unexpected and spontaneous manifestation before it had a chance to coalesce into a real social movement. Eager to discourage the appearance of an all-Russian organization of trade and industry, the Ministry of Finance selected petitions from the merchantry as the basis for drafting separate exchange statutes for each individual town or city over the five-year period 1870–75. It was an extraordinary display of the government's reluctance to introduce a uniform and systematic structure into the commercial life of the empire. The one notable exception to the government's policy of treating each exchange differently was, as might be expected, restrictive. The ministry insisted upon strict and uniform regulations on the buying and selling of securities, particularly in those areas where speculation might be anticipated. Dealing in futures was illegal before 1893, and trading was confined to locally incorporated joint-stock companies. The complex and delicate web of credit relationships that enabled other European businessmen to move capital rapidly and efficiently on a nationwide scale was altogether missing on the Russian exchanges.[45] It was a poor environment in which to cultivate a spirit of enterprise.

A comparison of the exchange statutes reveals significant differences among them in defining the membership aims and relations of the exchange committees with the local authorities, as well as a lack of clarity on several subsidiary questions.[46] Regional considerations loomed large both in the formal organization and in the actual functioning of the exchanges, especially in St. Petersburg, Moscow, Warsaw, and Kiev. St. Petersburg was the first to propose reforms and the last to have its statute approved. Finally, in 1875 the ministry accepted a set of "temporary regulations," which subsequently became permanent by default. For the first time they clarified the difference between the exchange society and its elective committee, outlined the

45. Shepelev, *Aktsionernye*, p. 150; *ZIRTO* (1871), no. 1, "Protokoly i stenograficheskii otchet zasedaniia shestogo otdeleniia pervogo vserossiiskogo s'ezda fabrikantov, zavodchikov i lits interesuiushchikhsia otechestvennoiu promyshlennostiu," especially pp. 8, 11, 26, 70–71. For other differences between West European and Russian exchange rules see the article "Birzhevye operatsii" in *BE*, 6:889–90.

46. Lur'e *Organizatsiia*, pp. 49–59; Novitskii, *Sbornik*, pp. 146–51 (Moscow), 159–62 (Saratov), 163–66 (Revel), 171–74 (Warsaw), which make clear the greater role of the governor-generals in the affairs of the exchanges of the periphery than of the center.

duties of the committee, and gave it full control over its internal affairs. But, unlike that of all but a handful of exchanges, the Petersburg committee's membership was restricted to first-guild merchants, thus effectively reducing its social role.

The committee's subsequent attempts to strengthen its position were halted abruptly in the 1890s when the Ministry of Finance refused to allow brokers to form their own elective council and then rejected the committee's proposal to enlarge its membership and concentrate disciplinary authority in its own hands. In 1900 the ministry introduced a new statue for the securities section of the exchange that tightened the already stringent controls over buying and selling to the absurd point of requiring a thick partition to be constructed between the securities and commodities markets on the floor of the exchange. The virtual exclusion of industrial representatives and the predominance of foreign over domestic commercial interests contributed to the ineffectiveness of the exchange as a potential center for exercising merchant influence over the government.[47] Harassed by the petty supervision of the bureaucrats and disinterested in larger economic questions, the St. Petersburg Exchange did not aspire to the social or political role of its more active counterparts in Kiev and Moscow until 1905.

The Kiev Exchange Committee owed its existence and early vigor to the inspiration and initiative of N. Kh. Bunge, long before he became minister of finance. As a professor at the university and manager of the local branch of the State Commercial Bank in the mid-1860s, Bunge overcame Russian merchant opposition to found an exchange and raise a building. From the outset the exchange escaped the double burden of state paternalism and merchant apathy and operated in an atmosphere of social harmony among traders and industrialists of varied estate and ethnic origin. No single ethnic group predominated among Russian, Ukrainian, Polish, Jewish, and German members of the committee, although Jews continued to maintain their overwhelming preponderance among guild merchants in the province. As early as 1871 the committee ended all restrictions on the right of first-guild merchants to act as brokers. Even more startling

---

47. Timofeev, *Istoriia*, pp. 252–59, 269–80. Although the presidents of the exchange committees were normally Russian, for example, A. Ia. Prokhorov (1893–97) and A. Ia. Prozorov (1897–1906), well over half the seventy-eight electors in 1903 had non-Russian names—German, Jewish, French, or British (ibid., appendix 7, pp. 21–23). Taken by themselves these names signify little in determining attitudes, but in the context of the overseas orientation of commerce they underline the difficulties that faced any effort to lead the exchange beyond its preoccupation with the activities of the port.

for the time was the committee's decision to honor the Jewish Sabbath by transferring one of its bi-weekly sessions from Saturday to Friday.

No visible friction existed either between merchants and noble members or between commercial, agricultural, and industrial interests on the exchange. The overarching importance of the area's sugar-beet industry ensured the cooperation of all elements in growing, refining, and marketing operations.[48] The committee also enjoyed cordial relations with the Kiev intellectual community, the local branch of the Russian Technological Society, the university, and the Agricultural Society. Their mutual cooperation flowered in the Kiev Polytechnical Institute. On the initiative of the enormously wealthy Jewish sugar-beet industrialist Lazar I. Brodsky and his brother Lev, a conference of Kiev university professors, engineers, and representatives of industry launched a campaign to found the institute. Half the original capital was contributed by the governor-general and the other half was raised by Brodskii and N. A. Tereshchenko, a Ukrainian sugar magnate, patron of the arts, and future minister in the provisional government.[49]

Under the powerful influence of the sugar manufacturers the Kiev Exchange Committee concentrated its lobbying on freight rates and production norms for sugar. In 1892, during the first revision of freight rates on sugar, the Ministry of Finance agreed to set a differential rate for sugar; favorable revisions followed. A whole series of exclusively beneficial rates was introduced for the shipment of refined sugar to the Russian market and of raw sugar to factories in Tula and Moscow province.[50] When the manufacturers' own efforts to regulate the production of sugar collapsed in the crisis of 1894–95, they petitioned the government to impose obligatory norms for the industry. With the help of Bunge, who first chaired the sugar conference, and of Sergei Witte himself, who supported its recommendations, they obtained a very advantageous arrangement which set domestic quotas, subsidized cheap exports through a system of rebates on the excise tax, and stabilized high profits, all at the expense of

48. *Dvadtsatiletie kievskoi birzhi*, pp. i–iii, vii, xxvi.
49. A. Abragamson, "Kievskii politekhnicheskii institut imperatora Aleksandra II-go," *Inzhener* 22, no. 10 (1898): 404–8.
50. *Materialy po peresmotru tarifov*, pp. 27–33. In the 1920s Soviet Ukrainian historians, following Pokrovskii's line that the empire was a prison of nationalities, argued that differential rates plus the excise tax and the sugar norms discriminated against the Ukraine and favored Russian producers, but the main burden of discrimination fell on all consumers, Ukrainian and Russian alike, while the producers flourished. Cf. S. Ostapenko, "Kapitalizm," pp. 195–98.

artifically supported domestic prices, which were passed on to the consumer.[51]

In many ways, then, the Kiev Exchange Committee played much the same role in the southwest as the Moscow Exchange Committee played in the center. Because of the harmonious blend of social groups and productive forces, the region offered a tempting model of economic development. It was not surprising, therefore, that this environment produced the three ministers of finance, Bunge, Vyshnegradskii, and Witte, who led the empire into the great industrial spurt at the end of the nineteenth century. From their experience in the region they brought to government a new outlook, tempered by a balance between theoretical knowledge, an appreciation for technical education, and practical business experience. Their ambitious drive to knit together the disparate social and regional strands of Russian economic life in order to launch a full-scale industrialization of the empire was inspired by the example of the south.[52]

In Moscow the shock waves of the tariff fight roused the guild merchants to demand recognition of the exchange society as a juridical person. In 1870 the government approved the new statutes, which in their broad definition of duties and precision of language strongly implied a more prominent role for Moscow than for any of the other exchanges. Under the strong leadership of T. S. Morozov, again one of the small group of innovators, the society's membership rose during the seventies from one thousand to fifteen hundred, suggesting

51. The clearest brief explanation of the system may be found in the article by A. Svirshevskii, "Sveklosakharnaia normirovka," in *BE*, 57:26–30. A more extended treatment is Levin, *Nasha sakharnaia*. As a result of these reforms sugar production in the Ukraine more than doubled between 1890 and 1914, making it second only to Germany by 1909–11 (Ostapenko, "Kapitalizm," p. 199).

52. The relations of Witte with the intellectual and business groups in the Kiev region has scarcely been explored. Aside from tantalizing hints scattered in his memoirs see the even more suggestive comments in Sliozberg, *Dela*, 1:82–83, who shows Witte's ties with a small group of Jewish intelligentsia in Poltava and Kiev, including B. F. Brandt, and also with a clique of professors at Kiev University, including A. Ia. Antonovich, who became Witte's deputy minister of finance from 1893 to 1896, D. I. Pikhno, editor of *Kievlianin* and later member of the State Council, who broke with Witte over the revolution of 1905, and P. P. Tsitovich, a well-known writer on economic problems (Witte, *Vospominaniia*, 1:167–69, 173–74; ibid., 2:88–89. Witte was also closely connected to the Kiev section of the Russian Technological Society and contributed to its journal (e.g., S. Iu. Witte, "Printsipy zheleznodorozhnykh tarifov," *Inzhener* 3, no. 2 [1883]: 53–63, and no. 3 [1883]: 109–18; idem, "Popovodu mneniia Leon Say o zheleznodorozhnykh tarifakh," ibid., no. 1 [1883]: 9–13). One of Witte's earliest patrons, Count V. A. Bobrinskoi, acting minister of transportation, came from the Kiev family of big sugar industrialists. For a broad picture of the interaction between various social and ethnic groups from the technical intelligentsia and business world of the southwest see Mel'nik, *Promyshlennyi*, especially, pp. 21, 41–43.

that here indeed was an organization capable of representing the economic interests of the Great Russian merchantry in the entire central industrial region.[53] But the familiar combination of bureaucratic manipulation and merchant indifference to matters outside their immediate interests steadily eroded the strength of the society. Its membership declined to around five hundred by the end of the century. Long before that, especially after Morozov's term as president expired in 1877, caution had become the watchword. The leadership of the executive committee fell into the hands of N. A. Naidenov.

Although he claimed to be one of the progressive leaders of the "younger generation" who challenged the patriarchal old merchants, Naidenov was more concerned with appearance than substance. Dressed in frock coat and top hat, he sat at the "German," and not the "Russian," table at restaurants and adopted the manners and poise of the cultivated gentleman. Naidenov and his ilk easily passed the test of what a modern businessman should be, at least in the eyes of the Petersburg bureaucrats. This self-styled "younger generation" was in fact much like an earlier generation of Russian gentry who aped European fashions in the eighteenth century.[54] Naidenov nourished particular disdain for "the old-fashioned" Old Believer merchants, but they were often more "modern" than he was in their enterprise and vision. To weaken his liberal opponents and ingratiate himself with the authorities, Naidenov went so far as to throw his weight against Rukavishnikov, the innovators' candidate in the mayoralty election of 1897, and supported the successful candidate of the aristocratic and bureaucratic elements in the city, Prince V. M. Golitsyn, the former governor of Moscow.[55] In the town duma, Naidenov and his son were frequently to be found among the opponents of public works and sanitary regulations that might have imposed new burdens upon the merchantry.[56] An accurate assessment of his real allegiances was made by Boris Chicherin, who, as mayor of Moscow, had ample opportunity to make a judgment: "For him [Naidenov] the interest of the merchant soslovie was higher than that of the city and his personal importance was highest of all."[57] In retrospect Naidenov's claim that

53. Naidenov, *Moskovskaia*, pp. 25, 59, and 75–86, for a complete membership list. See also idem, *Vospominaniia*, 2:91–97.
54. Naidenov, *Vospominaniia*, 2:7–8, 91–93; Shchukin, "Iz vospominanii," p. 99.
55. Astrov, *Vospominaniia*, pp. 250–51.
56. See, for example, *Zhurnaly Moskovskoi dumy*, "Zhurnal za 1898," appendix, pp. 18–21. Naidenov was also one of the most patriarchal of the leading merchants in his views toward the labor question (Ianzhul, "Iz vospominanii," pp. 92, 95). On his resistance to sanitary inspection of dairies see Astrov, *Vospominaniia*, p. 267.
57. Chicherin, *Vospominaniia*, p. 180.

under his leadership the Exchange Association had become "an independent public institution" must be discounted as a grandiloquent exaggeration. In the final analysis the bureaucrats continued to decide when and under what conditions the government would consult the merchants.

This was why the minister of finance, M. K. Reitern, was perfectly willing to work together with the association. He had no desire to repeat the unpleasant history of the tariff fight. Whether or not he really feared direct pressure from the merchants, a permanent rift with them could only benefit his enemies in the bureaucracy and jeopardize the credit standing of the government abroad. When in 1870 he visited the new Moscow Exchange building, he promised the assembled merchants that "as long as he was minister not a single [government] measure 'would fall like snow on their heads.'" The merchants had easy access to his office in St. Petersburg and their petitions met a sympathetic, if not always positive, response from the director of trade and industry.[58] True to his word, Reitern saw to it that the association was represented on most of the important commissions, including the Valuev Commission, appointed in 1874 to examine the unresolved and controversial question of labor legislation, even though he knew full well that over the previous thirty years the merchants had consistently opposed any government regulation in the field.[59]

When issues touching the merchantry's interests became matters of public knowledge, the Moscow Exchange Committee discussed them at its regular sessions, but it reacted to specific problems, rather than articulate a general economic policy. Once having defined a position, it followed the well-worn channels of communication with the government through petitions and gave up the idea of appealing to a broader public through the press or in open meetings, a process that had briefly characterized the history of its formative years. For the bulk of the merchantry it was more important to conserve cordial relations with the Ministry of Finance than to adopt an independent and controversial posture. So, to the extent that the association served as yet another conduit of influence and information, it can be viewed as a

58. Naidenov, *Vospominaniia*, 2:142, 147, 153–54.
59. On the other hand Reitern may well have viewed the merchants as temporary allies in blocking Valuev's alleged attempt to bring all Russian industry under the control of the minister of state domains, which he then was. From all the available evidence it appears that bureaucratic rivalries rather than merchant opposition were responsible for another delay of eight years before any labor legislation was approved by the State Council (Valuev, *Dnevnik*, 2:507–8; TsGAOR, f. 722, op. 1, d. 110, "Dnevnik Konstantina Nikolaevicha," pp. 4, 48, 49, 54, 57, 58, 67).

distinct improvement for the merchants over previous arrangements between them and the state. It did not, however, alter the fundamental relationship between the Great Russian merchantry and the state.

Business Practices

The persistence of traditional attitudes among bureaucrats and merchants toward business organization and techniques may be traced to their common interest in preserving a stable society. Both favored Russia's economic growth, but neither thought it desirable or necessary that the country pass through what they perceived to have been the inferno of the early years of industrialization in Western Europe. Thus, the government remained reluctant to allow the full play of free-market forces, while the merchantry was unwilling to confront the risks of competition.

The government's policy emerges most clearly in its tactic of delaying the institutional changes that would have benefited the vigorous expansion of the business community. The first of these postponements came over the question of creating a separate ministry of trade and industry. As early as the mid-1870s the small group of merchant-innovators proposed detaching the Department of Trade and Industry from the Ministry of Finance and transforming it into "a defender of industrial and commercial interests intervening on their behalf at the highest levels of government."[60] This was exactly what the Ministry of Finance did not want a government agency to become. Not until 1905 did the Ministry of Finance reluctantly turn over the regulation of business activities to the Ministry of Trade and Industry. Even this renunciation was more formal than real. The new ministry neither achieved independence from Finance nor became the protector of business that its earliest proponents had envisaged.

An even more astonishing record of delays and evasion marked the history of reforms in joint-stock legislation. Beginning in 1859, with the first draft law, a half century of fitful effort was required to bring about any significant changes in the law of 1836. The new legislation was already out of date when it finally went into effect in 1901. For a long time the minister of finance, Reitern, was the chief culprit, choosing to negotiate separately with a different group of entrepreneurs for each new company. But his successors Bunge and Vyshnegradskii

60. ORBL, f. 332, carton 78, no. 29, "Proekt uchrezhdeniia ministerstva torgovli i promyshlennosti," n.d. [1875–76?], with penciled corrections by Prince V. Cherkassky. The original draft appears to have been written by Chizhov. In any case it exudes an attitude which is at once fiercely antibureaucratic and patronizing of noble industrialists.

displayed little more energy in pressing for general legislation that would lay down a systematic procedure for the establishment of joint-stock companies. Conspicuous by its indifference to the lengthy delays, the merchantry made no visible effort to advocate reform in this area. Over this long period the only concrete results were to limit the rights of Jews, Poles, and foreigners (mainly Germans) to set up and manage joint-stock companies in the empire.[61] The discriminatory laws began to appear after 1881 when the government began to share with the Great Russian merchants the fear of ethnic encirclement in the western borderlands.

The government's endorsement of Great Russian nationalism did not, however, match that of the merchants in all respects. The official discrimination toward certain ethnic groups—Jews, Poles, and certain foreigners, like the Germans—was largely political. Economic considerations prevented the adoption of more xenophobic exclusion policies. As Vyshnegradskii explained with bureaucratic prolixity, "In the presence of the weak development here of private enterprise and the indecisiveness with which our indigenous capitalists take up anything new that is not well rooted and therefore is fraught with unavoidable risks and will not guarantee a certain profitable return to the entrepreneurs, the attraction of foreign capital to Russia represents one of the necessary conditions for the development of national industry by introducing improvements in various branches of industry and furthering the spread among the laboring population of useful technical knowledge, without which many aspects of industrial production would remain unavailable to us and the poorest classes of the population would be deprived of the means of putting their labor to good use."[62] Ironically for the merchantry, by the end of the century foreign joint-stock companies in Russia (mainly Belgian, French, and English) enjoyed more favorable conditions than those owned by Russian citizens. The Russian merchants appeared to have broken the encirclement only to have the enemy admitted into their camp.

If the bureaucrats harbored traditional views about the merchant's lack of enterprise, the merchantry gave them little reason to change their minds. Sheltered behind state tariffs and supported by state subsidies, the great majority of the merchantry felt no pressing need to alter its business practices. In general, throughout the nineteenth century the introduction of new machinery into industry, especially textiles, required little adjustment in the behavior or attitudes of capitalists. The burden of change fell on workers. Thus, it was not sur-

61. Shepelev, *Aktsionernye*, pp. 111–21.
62. Ibid., p. 127.

prising that in the 1880s the Moscow merchantry found it easier to undertake a technological transformation of the textile industry than to introduce new organizational and marketing techniques.[63]

Government officials found it necessary again and again to remind the merchantry of its legal obligation to keep commercial books. Even the pervostateiny merchants did not understand the reasons for doing so. In one case the Ministry of Finance was astounded to learn that a wealthy merchant who handled hundreds of thousands of rubles on the exchange did not know how much he had borrowed from his current operations because he kept no books at all.[64]

Russian merchants clung to their preference for selling their products at fairs and markets right down to the end of the nineteenth century. In 1900 well over a third of all cotton goods produced by the Moscow industrialists was sold at the Nizhnyi fair, and this during its decline as an emporium for central Russia.[65] Consequently, the factory owners tied their production to long-term projections and were unable to react to rapid shifts in market conditions. This state of affairs also spawned a large number of petty traders and intermediaries who proved to be inefficient and expensive appendages of the wholesale merchants' organization. The more astute merchants like N. K. Krestovnikov of Kazan perceived that the government was partly to blame. Commercial law was hopelessly vague and outmoded. By restricting the juridical rights of brokers and commercial travelers, the statute on trade made it risky for wholesalers to develop the network of warehouses and local agents. As a result, according to Krestovnikov, "most of Russia's export trade was handled by brokerage offices in the hands of Jews and Greeks who are not regulated by Russian law and [consequently] can victimize Russian traders."[66] In publicizing these shortcomings, Krestovnikov tried to arouse the merchants to work for reform of the law, but his words fell on deaf ears. The bulk of the Moscow merchants had no desire to abandon their annual trips to the fairs or to hand over the buying and selling of goods to a stranger, whatever his knowledge and skills.

The business activities of the Moscow banks were also strictly delimited by the merchants' cultural frontiers of family, soslovie, and region. The founders, major shareholders, and administrators of the Moscow Merchants' Bank, the Moscow Merchants' Society of Mutual

63. For an economic analysis of structural changes within the industry see Gately, "Textile Industry."
64. Nisselovich, *Obshchedostupnye*, pp. 5–8.
65. Semeniuk, "Bor'ba," pp. 102–3.
66. Krestovnikov, "O neobkhodimosti," pp. 4, 6–7, 14. This was a report to the Moscow section of the Society for the Encouragement of Russian Trade and Industry.

Credit, and the Moscow Discount Bank were almost exclusively merchants. Organized as partnerships (*tovarishchestvo na paiakh*) rather than joint-stock companies, these banks retained their familial, patriarchal character beyond 1900, when many large families, even including such innovators as the Morozovs, Khludovs, Liamins, Lepeshkins, and Krestovnikovs, still held controlling interest. The banks' operations were commercial, discounting bills of exchange and lending for commercial rather than industrial investments. No efforts were made to establish provincial branches, and the borrowers were mainly Moscow merchants.[67] Because of the structural peculiarities of the dominant regional industry, namely textiles, the Moscow merchantry did not require the large-scale injections of capital from the State Bank that other industrial areas needed, and this, too, helped protect the strong local position of the merchant banks.[68] A small but revealing peculiarity of these banks was the "tithe" of 10 percent which they paid annually to merchant charities, a condition written into the statutes of the Mutual Credit Bank, for example, by its founders.[69] The peculiar social foundations of the Moscow banks marked them off sharply from the Petersburg banks, which by virtue of their international ties, broad social base, provincial branches, and industrial operations were far more advantageously placed to play a lead role in the industrialization of the empire.[70]

Slow to enter into monopolistic agreements, the merchantry of the central provinces lagged behind those on the periphery in embracing the most advanced forms of capitalist organization. Moscow factories did not participate in the first significant monopoly in Russian industry—the Union of Rail Manufacturers—until 1892, a decade after its formation. In the metal-working industry the first lasting monopolistic agreement in 1886 was organized by a group of recent German immigrants to Russia who copied similar arrangements of factory owners in Germany. Even the language of the agreement itself was German. Almost all the participating firms were located on the periphery, in Odessa, Riga, Vilna, Warsaw, St. Petersburg, and even in the Kingdom of Poland. The sole Moscow participant was the Association of the Moscow Metal Factory of Jules Goujon (Guzhon). Although the agreement was short-lived, it led to others that involved mainly Petersburg and Baltic firms.[71]

67. Gindin, "Moskovskie banki," pp. 39–52.
68. Gindin, *Gosudarstvennyi bank*, pp. 322–27.
69. *Ocherk deiatel'nosti*, pp. 29–31.
70. Gindin, *Russkie kommercheskie banki*, pp. 48–52, 302–5; idem, "Moskovskie banki," pp. 213–16. For a contemporary critique along the same lines see Krestovnikov, *Posrednicheskie*, pp. 1–72.
71. L. B. Kafengauz, *Sindikaty*, pp. 32, 54–60.

After the economic crisis at the turn of the century, the industrialists of the south took the initiative and supplied the overwhelming preponderance of participating enterprises for what were to become the most famous monopolies. With its central office originally in Kharkov, Prodamet grouped all the metallurgical concerns of the south and included the big Briansk complex in the center only for some products. Prodarud was founded in 1908 exclusively by southern ore-mining enterprises.[72]

The great struggle over an oil monopoly in the Transcaucasus was fought out among three groups, local Armenian and Azerbaijani, foreign, and Petersburg capitalists, particularly L. E. Nobel. Moscow's single big participant was the textile merchant S. N. Shibaev, an Old Believer friend of T. S. Morozov.

The earliest monopolistic agreements in the building industry were drawn up in 1890 among brick makers in the Warsaw area. An abortive agreement among cement plants in 1899 included foreign firms like Filmans, the Franco-Russian, and Landsgaf in the Novorossiisk area. Only in the glass industry were Moscow firms involved with those of St. Petersburg.[73]

In textiles, which dominated the central industrial region, monopolistic agreements followed behind those in other industries. This was by no means a uniquely Russian phenomenon. Structural factors, especially the high degree of specialization in the industry, accounted for the lag. Still, even the big Moscow wholesale houses responded slowly to the crisis in the cotton industry at the turn of the century and allowed the Lodz group to take the initiative in price fixing, first on cotton fabrics and later on textiles. Lodz also proposed to form an export association, but the central region demurred. When, in 1909, the Moscow textile magnates finally launched their own Russian Export Association, they did not have much success.[74]

To be sure the bulk of heavy industry most susceptible to cartelization was on the periphery. Still, the Moscow merchants displayed great reluctance to invest either as individuals or through the medium of their banks in the most advanced forms of capitalist enterprise in the empire. Before adopting new business methods and techniques to improve their competitive position and their relative economic power, the Russian merchants preferred, as in the past, to appeal for government protection against their more enterprising ethnic and foreign

72. Ibid., pp. 80–88, 89–91. The strongly regional character of the monopolies is deemphasized in the very large Soviet literature on the subject. See, for example, Bovykin, *Zarazhdenie*, pp. 133, 136, 152–55.
73. Bovykin, *Zarozhdenie*, pp. 177, 181–83, gives the evidence, but does not reach the same conclusion.
74. Laverychev, *Monopolisticheskii*, pp. 62 ff., 73–74, 77 ff., 84.

rivals. Erecting tariff walls and abolishing free ports and transit rights remained the merchantry's first and main line of defense.

During the decade of steady movement toward protectionism in Russia from 1882 to 1891, the Moscow merchants stood in the forefront of the demands for higher duties on all imports for use in manufacturing, from raw materials to finished goods. Consequently, they came into conflict repeatedly with most of the enterprises on the periphery, which relied upon close commercial or industrial relations with the outside world.

The debate over the duties on coal that raged throughout the 1880s ranged the Moscow merchants with the Donets coal-mining interests on one side against the exchange committees of St. Petersburg, Reval, Riga, Libau, Kiev, and Odessa, supported by local committees on trade and industry and, in the case of Odessa, even by the governor-general. On the surface the Moscow position seemed straightforward enough. Because of the city's central geographical location and the construction of the southern railroad, coal originating in the Donets cost no more than foreign coal imported through the Baltic ports. Thus, higher duties on seaborne coal would not damage Moscow's industrial interests. But neither could it enhance them. The small number of Moscow railroad entrepreneurs, led by one of the merchant-innovators, Savva Mamontov, the president of the Donets coal railroad line, argued that higher duties would widen the market for Donets coal and increase the revenue of the railroads.[75] But the official stand taken by the Moscow Council of Trade and Industry and the Moscow Exchange Committee placed the issue in a broader context, asserting that "the coal business ought to constitute one of the chief sources of wealth of Russia and be developed not only where it has already been established but in other areas of the Empire."[76] Strengthening ties between Moscow and the south had always been a dream of a small number of local patriots. But the reasoning behind the stand taken by the more traditional merchants was rooted in their antagonism toward all industry on the periphery, whether directly competitive, like textiles, or not. The higher the costs imposed upon those industries, the greater the chance that the Moscow merchants could compete with them without altering their traditional business culture or increasing the risks of failure.

In the metal and metallurgical industry the separation of interests between the center and the periphery was not quite so clear-cut. The Moscow Exchange Committee and the Moscow Council of Trade and

75. Sobolev, *Tamozhennaia*, pp. 508–14, 518–25.
76. TsGIA, f. 1152, op. 10, d. 203, p. 18.

Industry favored higher duties on pig iron and some semifinished iron products, but individual metal factory owners in the city opposed them. A closer look at the controversy reveals, however, that the owners were German or Jewish (Heckman, Nabgoltz, and Schmidt, with Dobrov the exception) and that after 1880 they were eliminated from participating in the negotiations with the government bureaucrats over the tariff.[77] By 1884 the opposing camps on iron duties virtually duplicated those on coal; the Moscow organizations were joined by those of Ivanovo-Vosnesensk, Nizhnyi-Novgorod, Kharkov, and Kiev marshaled against the organizations of St. Petersburg, Odessa, the Baltic littoral, and the Kingdom of Poland. The alliance of the center and south argued that higher duties could help Russian iron foundries and the coal industry, while they would have an unfavorable effect only on the finishing industries in the port cities and other factories that relied solely on foreign materials and therefore did not deserve government support. This last could only refer to the foreign firms in Moscow. Once again, however, while endorsing the immediate imposition of a protective tariff, the Moscow merchants sounded the patriotic note peculiar to them in these debates: the higher duty was necessary "in view of the fact that it was acknowledged by the mine owners of southern Russia as the very least measure [which could be taken] to encourage the national [*otechestvennyi*] iron industry and also because only with such a tariff could Ural pig iron . . . be in a position to compete in Moscow with the English."[78] This tendency to identify Moscow with the national interest had a certain rhetorical and even dissimulating character, but beneath it lay strong feelings which grew with every tariff controversy.

In 1891 the first general tariff reform since 1868 marked a triumph of protectionism. Yet for the most part even these high rates fell short of the demands of the Moscow merchants, which were openly prohibitive. Moscow sought not merely to support industries in existence but also to encourage the creation of new ones far from the pernicious influence of the periphery. Their philosophy was summed up by Krestovnikov, representing the Moscow Exchange Committee. Commenting on the need for higher duties on sulphur, he said: "Low duties for fiscal purposes merely places a tax on an industry and does not lead to our producing sulphur; if a higher tax is levied then, even if in the short run this measure raises the cost of the material, the extra payment will be repaid by the production of sulphur in Russia." The representatives of the Moscow organization held this position

77. Sobolev, *Tamozhennaia*, pp. 551–57.
78. TsGIA, f. 1152, op. 10, d. 203, p. 218.

consistently throughout the negotiations. They argued, for example, that a high duty should be placed on alum even though it was extremely difficult to supply the Kingdom of Poland with Russian alum because in the long run this would stimulate new manufactures in Russia "and then Russian alum [would] drive out the foreign product from that area."[79] This position was the exact reverse of that held for so long by the Ministry of Finance and its protégés on the western and southern periphery.

Occasionally, an individual factory owner in Moscow of foreign extraction submitted a separate petition for higher duties on certain items such as glass beads or faience, which would not be supported by the Moscow organizations. Once in a while, individual industrialists on the periphery supported the prohibitive rates proposed by the center: Rosenblum of Warsaw endorsed a 100-percent increase in the tariffs on machinery. But these were exceptions. In the overwhelming number of cases it was Moscow versus the periphery, the merchants versus the nobles. On coal and coke Odessa opposed them; on coke it was Warsaw; on agricultural machinery it was the Ukrainian, Baltic, and even Moscow landed nobles (the Moscow Agricultural Society) against the Moscow merchant organizations.[80] Meanwhile, the Moscow merchants pursued the search for new markets in the Middle East and Far East by petitioning the government to plug the last free-trade loopholes on the imperial frontiers. The long struggle to close the free ports of Siberia appeared to be won in 1890 when the government finally acceded to the petitions of the Moscow Exchange Committee to the extent that it published a list of prohibited imports, including, as might have been expected, cotton textiles. Within three years the goods famine in Siberia forced the government to reverse its stand. The growing traffic on the Trans-Siberian railroad gradually enabled the Moscow merchants to make adequate supplies available and bring about the closing of the last free port in the Russian Far East in 1897.[81]

Similarly, the construction of the Transcaucasian railroad removed the last obstacle to shutting down the free transit of foreign goods across the Caucasus. Yet even after 1883 most of the Moscow textile trade with Persia passed through the hands of the agents of Persian merchants buying at Russian fairs and Tatar or Caucasian traders who knew local conditions better than Russian merchants. One of the few exceptions was Pavel Tret'iakov's partner and son-in-law, V. D. Konshin, who tried on several occasions in the 1880s to establish

79. Sobolev, *Tamozhennaia*, pp. 719, 750.
80. Ibid., pp. 759–60, 764–65, 775, 784.
81. Semeniuk, "Bor'ba," pp. 121–23.

direct trade links with Persia, going so far as to organize a large exhibition of Russian goods in Teheran. He attributed his failure to the conservatism and narrow-mindedness of his fellow merchants, who displayed "an utter lack of responsiveness to any new affair unless it is encouraged by special privileges from the government or is fully guaranteed besides offering comparatively large profits." The merchantry continued to protest that the Persian tariff system created the obstacles to trade, while the Department of Trade and Industry of the Ministry of Finance echoed Konshin's diatribe by criticizing the Russian merchants for failing to take into account the needs and tastes of the Persian consumer.[82]

Nor was the situation any better in the Near East, even when local conditions were extremely favorable for the penetration of Russian goods. Following the Bosnian crisis of 1907, for example, the irate Ottoman government boycotted Austrian and Greek products, clearing the way for a Russian takeover of the Turkish textile market. The Russian merchants limited their response to sending a few traveling salesmen who were largely ignorant of foreign trade and did not inspire confidence. Again in 1911 during the Libyan War the Russian merchants let slip another golden opportunity. In normal times they were simply no match for the superbly organized West Europeans, with their networks of agents and warehouses throughout the Ottoman Empire.[83]

The ineptness of the merchantry infuriated officials in the Ministry of Finance. From time to time they let fly a burst of public criticism against the disorderly condition of Russian commercial life featuring the "flashy merchant," "the skinner," and the "bankrupt merchant," three choice types with their "special ethic" of business which had "long been discredited in the Western European order of things." Because the Near East had been tutored in such matters by the West, it was no longer willing to tolerate such practices as the Russians brought with them. And even the honest Russian merchant, according to the officials, thought nothing of substituting one quality grade for another that he might not have in stock.[84]

82. Ibid., pp. 127–28; Shuster, "Ekonomicheskaia," pp. 205–6.
83. Even the big St. Petersburg firms like the Russian-American Rubber Company and Provodnik preferred to market their manufactures through Viennese trading houses rather than entrust their overseas commercial operations to Russian merchants (Kassis, *Polozhenie*, pp. 13, 22–26).
84. *Torgovo-promyshlennaia gazeta*, 2 February 1911, no. 26. Articles in a similar vein can be found in the following issues of the same periodical: 6 August 1910, no. 177; 3 September 1910, no. 199; 18 September 1910, no. 210; 26 September 1910, no. 217; 21 October 1910, no. 237. Another familiar refrain in the ministry's litany of criticism was its praise for the more enterprising and self-reliant merchants of the southern ports, as

The government was equally concerned over the disorganized and dishonest business practices prevailing in the grain export trade, an area of vital importance to the economic well-being of the empire. After the emancipation a mass of newly liberated peasants had taken over the internal grain trade, undercutting the big commercial houses. Strong regional differences in marketing and sorting destroyed uniform standards. By 1891 more than 40 percent of grain for export contained higher levels of impurities than was acceptable on the international market. The big merchants and the commercial exchanges cooperated with the government to simplify and enforce the classification of grain, but they could not prevail against the army of small merchants, skupshchiki, and kulaks who continued to mix grades and adulterate the grain.[85]

Home, School, and Factory

In its social relationships the Russian merchantry clung tenaciously throughout the late nineteenth century to its hierarchical paternalistic view of the universe. Although the social obligations of the merchant soslovie were reduced by the great reforms and outmoded by an expanding economy, they had long since become internalized as behavioral norms and could not be shed so easily as the kaftan. This is easier to demonstrate in the broader arena of public affairs than in the closed world of the merchants' family nest. One major problem is the difficulty of penetrating the inner life of the merchant family. Reminiscences, which are scarce in earlier periods, become even rarer for the end of the century. Not surprisingly, those which exist were written by those who emancipated themselves from the old ways. While their portraits of the tradition from which they freed themselves are vivid and typical of the merchant milieu, their successful strivings toward a new life may be much less characteristic of what occurred among their contemporaries, for memoirists like the Vishniakovs, Krestovnikovs, and Shchukins achieved a level of political and cultural awareness and business acumen that set them apart from the mass of the merchantry. Yet one piece of evidence emerges from these atypical sources which confirms the persistence of the patriarchal condition—the terrible fate of women in merchant families.

compared to those in Moscow (ibid., 20 October 1910, no. 236). On the other hand, from 1894 to 1906 cotton manufacturers tripled their exports mainly to the Far East. Yet this still amounted to only 5.3 percent of their production (Joffe, "Cotton," chap. 5).

85. Kitanina, *Khlebnaia*, pp. 60–74.

This situation prevailed well into the 1890s even for those who had achieved a measure of culture.

The social isolation of the merchant family also imposed hardships on the younger generation. According to one contemporary, because merchants "almost never appeared in public places" outside their own places of business and a few restaurants, it was difficult for young people to meet at all. This situation fostered a whole class of match-makers in Moscow society and promoted the primitive custom among well-to-do merchants of parading their daughters, painted up like dolls and dressed to the nines, in open coaches along the crowded paths of the Sokolniki Park on Sunday afternoons in search of eligible bachelors.[86]

In the absence of first-hand evidence, it is tempting to turn to the rich literary heritage of the period for additional insights into merchant life. But here the danger of selectivity is compounded by the ideological predispositions of the writers. As Donald Fanger has shown so graphically for the peasantry, the writers' search for a con-cept that captured the essential character of a social class led to a bewildering profusion of typical peasants, who are incompatible with one another.[87] Although the merchant was not as "mute, inexpressive and minimally individualized" as the peasant, the perception of his true image through the looking glass of Russian literature remains problematic.

For example, Ostrovskii's gloomy picture of the merchant ruling his "kingdom of darkness" enraged the merchantry in the 1850s, but also sparked a controversy among contemporary critics over the larger social meaning of his work.[88] In the works of Leskov, Chekhov, and Gorky the life of the merchant took on more subtle and varied hues, but the ambivalence remained. In Leskov's merchant household a ceremonial, strict, even puritanical atmosphere prevailed, softened only by a kind of material comfort that can only be described as "coziness." In Gorky's strong hands the merchant emerged as an ener-getic, often violent, and ruthless entrepreneur whose moral sensibili-ties suffered under the weight of his twin urges to transform the

86. B. B. Kafengauz, "Kupecheskie," pp. 126–27. Belousov, *Ushedshaia*, pp. 113–20. The author was the son of an artisan recalling his earlier life in the Moscow of the 1870s and 1880s.

87. Fanger, "Peasant," pp. 231–62.

88. See above, chapter 4. A brilliant analysis of Ostrovskii's work as a source of social history is Patouillet, *Ostrovskii*, a work which has few equals of its kind in Russian literary criticism. For a conventional survey of the radical critics' views on Ostrovskii see *A. N. Ostrovskii v kritike*.

world and fill his own pockets. Chekhov gave us both sides. In *Three Years* (1895) he condemned the tyrannical merchant-patriarch Laptev, whose son was educated well enough to understand but not to free himself from his enslavement to the insensible world of business. By 1903, in the *The Cherry Orchard*, Chekhov had come to sympathize with the decent, hard-working merchant Lopukhin, who appeared to be on the verge of inheriting a new Russia.[89] The difference between these archetypal merchants may have been based upon the historical evolution of their estate from the 1880s to the turn of the century, or at least on Chekhov's perception of such an evolution, but a satisfactory confirmation of this would require going beyond these brilliant but impressionistic treatments. Even though they were grounded in a close knowledge of the commercial milieu, they were pervaded by the authors' hopes and fears for the future of their country. For this reason alone they cannot serve by themselves as a guide to the social history of the Russian merchantry. Before dismissing them entirely, however, it is essential to point out that despite their differences these authors share a central vision of merchant family life. Whatever the changes they observed in the merchant's ethics, they all agreed implicitly that the authority structure within the merchant family remained rock solid.

Outside the family the merchantry expressed its strongest social interests in charities, education, and the labor question. In all three they revealed the underlying nature of their relationship with the social strata both above and below them.

The merchants contributed both individually and collectively to charities, but in each case their purpose was slightly different. As individuals they sought to enhance their status and achieve higher rank; as a collective they sought to strengthen the prestige of their soslovie. This is not to deny the moral imperative that in either case may have inspired their desire to help the poor, the sick, and the lonely, but merely to explain the apportionment of their charitable gifts. Although the statistics are incomplete and do not indicate the total contribution made by each soslovie, it is possible to suggest a few trends by concentrating on an analysis of charities in Moscow prov-

89. See especially N. Leskov, "Chertogon," and "Grabezh" in *Izbrannoe*; idem, *Zhizn'*, pp. 118–24, for Leskov's commercial experiences. The best introduction to Chekhov's views on the merchantry is Bruford, *Chekhov*, pp. 178–85. See also Chekhov, *Sochineniia*, vol. 12, letter to K. Stanislavskii, 30 October 1903, in which Chekhov characterized Lopukhin in a revealing phrase: "Lopukhin is, it is true, a merchant, but an honest fellow in every way, he ought to behave quite decently and intelligently without any pettiness or trickery."

ince, where the Great Russian merchantry was most actively involved. At the turn of the century Moscow easily held first place among the provinces of the empire in the number of charitable institutions and the sum of annual expenditures (8,877,152 rubles, or about 17 percent of total expenditures in all provinces). The merchant society, representing the collective conscience of the soslovie, gave a relatively small portion, 305,267 rubles, or a little over 3 percent of total expenditures in all provinces. Based on a small but representative sample of the institutions receiving aid from this source, it is clear that the main beneficiaries were orphans, widows of the merchantry and those who served them, such as shop assistants, and graduates of the commercial schools.[90] Here, the soslovie continued to serve as the corporate surrogate for the disrupted merchant family.

A different form of collective giving in which the merchants participated was the charitable contribution of the town administrations, which amounted to over a million and a half rubles, or 17 percent of the total charitable contributions. This sum represented a continuation in voluntary form of the prereform merchant obligations to support public charities in the towns. Although in this case the beneficiaries were mainly the lower orders of the urban population, the public character of the donation presumably compensated the merchant electors, who were playing their traditional role as defenders of the unfortunate.

Still, it appears that by far the largest portion of merchant contributions to charity was made by individuals to specific societies or institutions. Because there is no identification of individual donors by name or soslovie, it is impossible to tell for certain what share of the remaining 80 percent of charitable expenditures may be assigned to the merchants. However, given their great wealth, traditional attachment to and reputation for charitable activities, and the opportunities for personal reward and advancement connected with them, it is a safe assumption that it was significant, surely half and perhaps more. The particular attraction to the merchantry of contributing to such prestigious institutions as the Imperial Philanthropic Society and the Department of the Institutions of Empress Maria of His Imperial Majesty's Chancellery was to rub shoulders with the aristocracy and obtain honors and the coveted title of honored citizen. Even though the institution of honored citizenship offered fewer privileges than it had in the past, it was more eagerly pursued after the great reforms than before. While the number of guild merchants in Moscow prov-

90. *Blagotvoritel'nost'*, 1:xlv, lxxii, 56–130.

ince declined between 1871 and 1897 from 29,222 to 19,491, the number of honored citizens increased from 7,117 to 21,603.[91] Confronted with greater obstacles to promotion to noble status, the socially ambitious merchant looked to honored citizenship as a partial substitute for personal ennoblement. Postreform honored citizenship represented a substantial rise in status compared with that which the rank had entailed in prereform days because it was no longer reserved solely for the merchantry. As it had been in the past, the most reliable road to honorary citizenship, either personal or hereditary, was by achieving a certain rank or earning certain medals or decorations. For merchants individual charitable activity was one of the most accessible paths to these honors. To an extent, therefore, the disproportion between individual and collective donations may be attributed to the magnitude of the rewards available. Like service in the reformed town administrations, charity remained, as it had always been, a means of both defending the merchant soslovie and promoting the status of its most ambitious individual members. In a rigidly hierarchical society in which corporate and individual identities were still largely defined in legal terms, status meant both privileges and prestige, and the merchant scrambled after these by whatever means available.

Similarly, the merchants perceived education as a means for their children to improve their status, not to broaden their intellectual horizons or even obtain practical knowledge about the business world. This explains the apparent contradiction between the two prevailing trends in the education of merchant children at the end of the nineteenth century—indifference toward formal schooling in commerce or any other practical activity and admiration for secondary and higher education in those bastions of classicism, the gymnasia and the universities.

In 1895 no less an authority than Krestovnikov deplored Russia's backwardness in commercial schooling compared to Central and Western Europe. Throughout the empire he counted only 7 commercial schools with 2,930 students, in addition to several commercial sections of *real* schools, where, he noted, the lack of trained teachers kept both theoretical and practical knowledge at a low level. In contrast, Germany boasted 193 elementary, 6 intermediate, and 52 higher commercial schools with 24,309 students, while the Austro-Hungarian Empire maintained 86 elementary, 25 intermediate, and 22 higher schools with 23,186 students. Western Europe had fewer elementary and intermediate schools, but in France a wide network of special day or night classes for those with a general secondary education enrolled

91. Nifontov, "Formirovanie," p. 244.

over 8,600 students. Moreover, he added, the higher schools in France and Belgium were among the very best in the world.[92]

Moscow contained 3 of the 7 commercial schools, but of these the Moscow Commercial School was the only one that had earned a solid reputation among the merchantry. Yet it graduated, on the average, only 25 to 27 students annually. Most of these were orphans of merchants and meshchane rather than the sons of successful merchants.[93] This was hardly surprising because the Moscow schools were only intermediate and prepared students for low-status jobs like bookkeeper, clerk, and salesperson. As late as 1905, the Riga Polytechnical Institute was the only commercial institution of higher learning in the Russian Empire, and as might be expected, hardly any Moscow merchants' sons were included in its student body. Consequently, merchants' sons who intended to follow in their fathers' footsteps continued as before to acquire their knowledge of the business from their fathers. Yet, "what was needed," one critic of the system pointed out, "[was] people with broad horizons, bold initiative, with good specialized knowledge as only higher schools can provide." Otherwise, Russian merchants could "never hope to compete with foreigners who control foreign trade and transportation." Equating the state of commercial education with that of business organization, perceptive contemporaries expressed concern over the "insufficient social initiative" in the central provinces as compared to the Western borderlands and the need to reverse the ratio so that "the center can exercise its influence over the periphery."[94]

In an effort to rectify the situation the government introduced new legislation in 1896 which encouraged private initiative and strengthened the role of representative councils administering the schools. At first the response was sluggish, but after the turn of the century the number of intermediate commercial schools jumped dramatically from 12 to 191 in 1905 with 32,316 students.[95] None of the new schools was a higher institution like the Riga Polytechnic, and the merchants perceived little advantage in sending their sons, to say nothing of their daughters, to school with the children of meshchane and trading peasants. By 1914 the school population in the higher

92. Krestovnikov, *Znachenie*, pp. 2–4.
93. *Spisok vospitannikov*, throughout.
94. S. Grigor'ev, "Kommercheskoe obrazovanie v Rossii i ego nuzhdy," *REO*, no. 8 (1898): 39, 41; ibid., no. 9, pp. 16–17, 30–31; see also M. A. Tolpygun, "Neobkhodimost' vyshikh tekhnicheskikh shkolov Rossii," *REO*, no. 1 (1898): 135–36, for the view that technical education is essential for administering large-scale enterprises and overcoming the merchants' reputation for inertia.
95. "Kommercheskoe obrazovanie," *BE*, supplement 2 (1905), pp. 935–36.

technical institutions still stood below 10,000, and the merchants supplied under 16 percent of the students—and this in the area that should have attracted them more than any other. In absolute figures there were twice as many meshchane, a quarter more peasants, and almost as many children of personal nobles and officials enrolled as there were children of merchants.[96]

Increasingly, the merchants enrolled their children in gymnasia, which served as stepping stones to the universities or, for the girls, to an advantageous marriage. The children of merchants constituted about one-tenth of the gymnasia population, a considerable improvement over the figure of 7.5 percent for secondary and higher schools at mid-century. The merchants were even willing to send their sons in the same proportion of the *real* schools, which conserved a reputation as a better preparation for practical life. But they shied away from enrolling their children in the elementary urban schools, where they would have had to mix with the lower orders of the population.[97]

If the merchants persisted in meekly submitting to political authority and deferring to their social superiors while striving to emulate them, they displayed toward the lower orders a haughty, contemptuous, and authoritarian attitude. There was nothing new in this, but the growth of a factory working-class population transformed the relationship from a closed family quarrel into open social conflict.

It is easy to dismiss the patriarchal attitude of the Russian merchantry toward the workers as nothing but a reflection of economic exploitation and the Moscow merchantry's stubborn opposition to abolishing night work and child labor as only a function of the abun-

96. Ministerstvo narodnogo prosveshcheniia, *Otchet za 1912*, appendix, p. 27. The exact figures are:

Merchants and honored citizens	1474
Meshchane	2981
Peasants	1878
Personal nobles and officials	1370
Others	1639
Total	9343

97. Ibid., appendix, pp. 28–29, 178–79, 220–21. The exact figures are:

	Boys Gymnasia	Girls Gymnasia	*Real* Schools	Urban	Artisan
Merchants	14,749	29,707	7,621	3,898	249
Total	142,935	303,690	79,971	162,858	17,945

It should be noted that the figures for merchants include children of honored citizens, who did not, by any means, all come from the merchant soslovie.

dance of cheap labor in the central provinces.[98] To be sure, these assertions contain much truth. In the prolonged debate within the empire over the introduction of factory legislation, the Moscow merchants found themselves, once again, at odds with the merchants and technical specialists in St. Petersburg, Riga, and Lodz. They complained that the periphery had easier access to foreign materials and new machinery and could therefore afford to appear "philanthropic." But the opposition of the Moscow factory owners to changes in working conditions was neither absolute nor uniform. From the 1860s to the 1880s they displayed a willingness to compromise, albeit grudgingly and under pressure, on a range of issues. Not surprisingly, the leaders of moderation in the Moscow Manufacturing Council were innovators like Krestovnikov, Chetverikov, and Nikolai Alekseev.[99]

The one issue on which all the Moscow merchants closed ranks in obdurate resistance was the intervention of bureaucrats in the relations between owner and worker. That they clung to this position with amazing persistence emerges clearly from their responses over two decades to proposed legislation to create factory inspectors. In 1863 the Moscow section of the Manufacturing Council criticized the first draft of the report of the Commission Established to Examine the Factory and Artisan Statutes (the Shtakel'berg Commission) on four counts, three of which dealt directly with the degree of the owner's control over the life of the worker. In particular, the Moscow section warned that "interference" by inspectors could "destroy all the bonds between employers and workers, serve as a pretext for abuses, and increase the number of complaints."[100] Twenty-four years later the Moscow section of the Society for the Encouragement of Russian Industry and Trade repeated the argument in more sophisticated form by extolling the organic ties between employers engaged in mental labor and workers engaged in physical labor toward the same end. The inspectors, the section argued, would disrupt this delicate organism and pit the two naturally complementary elements against one another.[101]

The attitudes so passionately embraced by the Moscow merchants

98. Cf. Tugan-Baranovsky, *Russian Factory*, pp. 322–23.
99. Balabanov, *Ocherki*, 2:336 ,378, 380–83.
100. Zelnik, *Labor*, p. 155.
101. "Ekonomicheskie zametki," *Russkoe obozrenie*, April 1893, pp. 1089–91. The remainder of this long polemic consists of a point-by-point refutation of the government's proposed legislation. The sustained attack against bureaucratic interference in the "calm natural" flow of labor-management relations was continued in ibid., September 1893, pp. 514–23, which even took to task the Moscow section of the Society for the Aid of Commerce and Industry for failing to petition more strongly in its own interests.

—that child labor was good for the worker's family, that severe fines and punishment for minor infractions were the only means of disciplining the basically lazy and drunken male worker, that the factory could be a happy extended family under the stern but loving owner— were shared by capitalists in Western Europe during the early stages of industrialization. They persisted beyond that point in central Russia. The preponderance of the textile industry over all others fostered this illusion, but the cultural outlook of the Moscow merchants nourished it far beyond its normal life expectancy. Blinded by their adherence to their own unchanging ideals of social life, the merchants eagerly embraced the seductive myth propagated by the Slavophils that the Russian worker really was intrinsically different from his Western counterpart and should be kept that way.

The Morozov textile strike in 1885 shattered this myth in the minds of many public officials and led to the law of the following year that imposed regulations on the factory owners and established the inspectorate system. But the Moscow owners were unreconstructed. Ignoring the early warning of the Nevsky strike in 1870, they attributed the Morozov strike to outside agitators. Incapable of putting these events in a new focus they fell back, as they had always done, on the self-defeating policy of clinging to the government as their sole means of defense, even as they openly attacked the notion of bureaucratic interference and sought to discredit the most conscientious inspectors and buy off the others.[102]

Meanwhile, the workers increasingly took matters into their own hands; they began forming illegal organizations and gradually accepted a larger role for the intelligentsia in defending their rights. Although starting later than the merchants in their search for a group identity, the workers soon displayed a greater degree of cohesion and a greater willingness to break out of their isolation from the rest of society.[103] The old organizational forms of soslovie and artels and attitudes of submission disintegrated before mass urban migration and the imposition of new work patterns in the large factories. The rapidity of this transformation contrasted dramatically with the slow pace of change among the merchantry.

By the end of the nineteenth century the powerful combination of industrial development and social reform had moved the Russian Empire farther along the road to becoming a single national market and invoking a common citizenship than ever before. Fearing the disruptive effects of this transformation, the Russian merchantry identified its security, status, and profits with the integrity of the patri-

102. Ianzhul, "Iz vospominanii," 142:95–97.
103. Cf. Haimson, "Social Stability," pp. 619–42.

archal family, the merchant soslovie, the Moscow region, and, above all, the autocracy in its Great Russian manifestation. To dismiss these attitudes simply as irrational or backward would be to ignore the peculiar historical circumstances that determined this view of its interests. Submissive to authority and intellectually stagnant, the merchants feared a loss of its precarious social status and encirclement, both of which continued to threaten, though in somewhat altered but no less compelling form, up to the end of the empire. Moreover, in aggregate economic terms there was some justification for their behavior. By the end of the nineteenth century, they controlled four-fifths of the industry in the central industrial region and reaped enormous profits from it. But the struggle to reach these heights had been long and costly and was by no means finished.

Their success in abolishing the transit trade, erecting protective tariff walls, and discriminating in other ways against their competitors on the periphery—in a word, their economic gains—was not duplicated in other spheres of life. Outside the Moscow duma they still deferred to the nobility in social matters and in local government. Their penetration of the bureaucratic structure was offset by the bureaucratic penetration of their factories. While they clung to traditional attitudes toward authority, their workers challenged the patriarchal order. Although the merchants were largely unaware of it, they now faced two cruel choices: either they would have to defend an authoritarian bureaucratic state that increasingly encroached upon their control over their factories or they would have to join the attack upon that order at the expense of surrendering the privileges and economic benefits that the state had guaranteed to them.

PART 2

THE RISE OF THE

ENTREPRENEURS

CHAPTER 4

THE MOSCOW

ENTREPRENEURIAL GROUP:

A QUEST FOR IDENTITY

It would be wrong to conclude from the failure of the merchantry to become the core of a Russian bourgeoisie that indigenous Russian capitalists made no significant contribution to the great industrial spurt, the cultural renaissance, and the political awakening of the empire in the early years of the twentieth century. But those who stepped boldly into the mainstream of modern Russian life had no choice but to break with the traditional merchant mentality and behavior.

Difficult to identify, these pathbreakers came from various social backgrounds and included peasants, nobles, and merchants. Their number was too small and their origins too disparate to constitute a class; in their collective economic power and political influence, they cannot be dismissed merely as a collection of outstanding individuals. Yet it is in just such terms that historians have misrepresented their role in Russian society, either equating them with a rising bourgeoisie or else ignoring them as a minor aberration that had little impact on the larger questions of capital formation and industrial enterprise. If one is predisposed to admit only certain types of social evolution, then no other explanations fit. In this case, however, the evidence contradicts such an explanation. Thus, the task here is not to uncover proof of the presence or absence of a bourgeoisie but to explain how social change could take place in a system characterized by an expanding capitalist economy and a stable autocracy resting upon a social hierarchy of decaying sosloviia.

The Interest Group Defined

The following discussion suggests that Russian capitalists made an important contribution to Russia's industrialization through strong regional interest groups that disposed of sufficient capital, managerial skills, and vision to influence, if not determine, the evolution of Imperial Russian society. Such interest groups were an alternative way of organizing public life in a time of rapid economic change in a hierarchical society still dominated by a politically authoritarian regime and socially conservative sosloviia. Their appearance was spontaneous and initially informal. Only later, when the government relaxed restrictions, did they take the form of representative organizations with official statutes. They were not confined to the world of commerce and industry, but it was there that they displayed their greatest influence. For reasons which will become clear I have chosen to call them *entrepreneurial interest groups*. Moscow, St. Petersburg, and the south were the three regions where they were most fully developed.

Before proceeding to unravel their origins and activities a few definitional clarifications are in order, particularly because this purports to be a pioneering effort to introduce entrepreneurial interest groups as a mode of analyzing Russian social change in the second half of the nineteenth century. The first term, *entrepreneurial*, must be used with caution, since it has become increasingly charged with metahistorical significance. It is not intended here as a means of supplying the missing ingredient in general theories of economic growth. Whatever the merits of such theories as applied to other societies, in the case of Russia, as Alexander Gerschenkron and others have shown, foreign capital and the state bureaucracy were perfectly capable of providing the leadership and organizational skills necessary for an advanced stage of industrialization. Indeed, a debate over the nature of an entrepreneurial class in Russia suffers from the same methodological weaknesses as the quest for a bourgeoisie: it becomes, in the apt phrase of one critic, tantamount to "hunting the heffalump."[1] This does not mean, however, that the term must be banished from the historian's vocabulary, especially if it can be clearly defined and carefully applied within a specific temporal, social, and institutional setting. To be specific, then, the term *entrepreneur*, as used here, identifies a social type emerging in Imperial Russia in the decades from 1840 to

1. Peter Kilby, "Hunting the Heffalump," in *Entrepreneurship*, pp. 1–43. The remainder of the essays in this collection are extremely suggestive and were helpful in formulating my own views. For Gerschenkron's criticism of the "role set theory" as employed in economic history see his "Social Attitudes, Entrepreneurship and Economic Development," in *Economic Backwardness*, pp. 52–71.

1860 who was engaged in large-scale private economic activity yet was distinguished in a variety of ways from both the capitalist, who was merely an owner of the means of production, and the bourgeois, who would have been a member of a numerous, politically conscious, and nationally organized class striving for a share in or control over political power. To move beyond this preliminary introduction requires a more elaborate historical analysis of his origins and development.

The second term, *interest group*, means a small number of men, ranging from a dozen or so activists to a hundred associates, who organize to defend specific economic and political goals. In Russia their interrelationships were marked by four distinctive features: (1) a common social role; (2) a value system consistent with that role; (3) a political program that fused that role and those values into a broader ideology; and (4) a network of formal and informal means of communication, association, and interaction along a broad spectrum of public life.

The third and last definitional term identifies the region; thus, the Moscow, St. Petersburg, and southern entrepreneurial groups represent three distinctive areas of economic specialization and ethnic and cultural identity. One final word of caution—it should be kept in mind that none of these interest groups identified themselves as they are designated here. Thus, it becomes all the more of a challenge for the historian to reconstruct their regional character, social origins, and organizational activities.

To begin with the Moscow entrepreneurial group, its geographical location should be understood in its broadest sense. The city became the base for the entrepreneurial group's operations and the symbolic center of its ideology. The Moscow entrepreneurs' business activities spread throughout the central industrial region and upper Volga, especially in the provinces of Kostroma and Nizhnyi Novgorod. The Moscow entrepreneurs were the most important group of indigenous capitalists who owed their wealth and influence to their own efforts. Unlike their competitors in other economic regions, St. Petersburg, the south, and also Poland, they did not depend upon foreign capital and state orders to build their economic power. The Moscow group accumulated its capital from internal trade, a local textile industry, and vodka tax farming. The combination of their Great Russian ethnic stock and the almost exclusively indigenous character of their economic life supplied them with a rationalization of and a justification for their separateness and their mission. They became the center of a powerful economic nationalism which carried strong political overtones.

The Moscow entrepreneurial group was a complex mix of individuals drawn from three social strata—Old Believer peasants moving into the guilds from below, noble industrialists trickling into the guilds from above, and long-established merchant families tracing their guild membership back into the eighteenth century. That they were exceptional personalities cannot be denied. They combined great energy with daring entrepreneurial skill and a willingness to defy the conventions of their social milieu. The Old Believer peasants broke with conservative communal traditions to become industrial leaders and public spokesmen for the merchantry as a whole. The nobles entered fully into the business world of the merchantry in the face of formidable social disapproval. The old merchant families had already survived the high attrition rate that devastated their soslovie, yet they undertook risky new ventures that could easily have jeopardized their assured place in the social order. Beyond these personal traits they were linked at a deeper level by a common set of ethical norms drawn from different aspects of Old Russian culture. In the late 1850s, under the shadow of the emancipation of the serfs, their cooperation blossomed into a determined effort to free the merchantry from its service bondage to the state, to infuse it with a new sense of its own worth, and to smash once and for all the danger of encirclement.

During the first three decades of the nineteenth century, several little-noticed and apparently disconnected social changes prefigured the emergence of Russia's first entrepreneurial interest group. Eddies of social mobility swirled beneath the main current of rigid social stratification. Noble industrialists began to enter the merchant guilds in small numbers for the first time following the guild reform of 1824. Before then the merchants had refused to admit them unless they gave up their noble status. Understandably, they were reluctant to do this. The reform allowed only those who were not in state service to enroll in the first guild. By withholding trading privileges from those who did not enroll, the law clearly aimed at pumping new blood into the anemic guild population.[2] Although the measure fell far short of official expectations and failed to check the long decline in the merchant population, the nobles who joined the guilds, though small in number, turned out to be energetic individuals determined to arouse the merchantry from its intellectual torpor and break with established commercial habits. Unlike the noble industrialists in the eighteenth century, these men displayed those qualities that have come

2. *PSZRI*, 1st ser., 14 November 1824, no. 30115. See also Ryndziunskii, "Gil'deiskaia," pp. 110–39, which does not, however, mention new rights for the nobility. By 1850 (the tenth census) the number of nobles enrolled in guilds was still very small, as the following statistics indicate: first guild, 31 (out of 3,488 total); second guild, 65 (out of 10,197 total); third guild, 314 (out of 160,682 total) (Keppen, *Deviataia*, pp. 182–86).

to be associated with the modern entrepreneurial spirit—rational organization, technical innovation, and willingness to take risks. Judging from a few outstanding examples like the Shipovs, Mal'tsovs, Koshelevs, Odoevskys, and Chizhovs, they also combined an impressive grasp of technical knowledge with direct management of their enterprises. Uncorrupted by state service and yet enjoying high status, they strongly opposed the interference of government agencies in running the economy and refused to be intimidated by officials.

Although it may appear paradoxical, these admirers of the technical and scientific achievements of Western Europe were more attracted by the cultural values of the Slavophils than by those of the Westernizers. Actually, the Westernizers, with the notable exceptions of Alexander Herzen and Dmitri Pisarev, were largely indifferent to questions of economic development, preferring instead to emphasize the legal-constitutional and social dimensions of Russia's backwardness.[3] By contrast, those intellectuals who did not belong to the Westernizer camp and who shared an attraction to Slavophil ideas believed deeply in achieving economic self-sufficiency and discovering a Russian path to industrialization. Besides the Slavophils themselves they included many members of the Lovers of Wisdom Society, which continued to be active in Russian society into the 1860s, like the statistician and economist V. P. Androssov and Prince V. F. Odoevsky, and also certain individuals like M. P. Pogodin, who had been associated with the Official Nationalists. Rejecting both the mechanistic and the biogenetic models of science, they favored the morphological approach developed in Russia by figures like Karl von Baer, the embryologist, and M. G. Pavlov, the biologist and agronomist. Above all, they insisted on the necessity of overcoming the gap between speculative thought and practical economic activity and of placing science in the form of technology at the service of the nation.[4]

Among the Slavophils, Aleksei Khomiakov's researches brought him close to a discovery of the caloric theory of heat, yielded some

3. Cf. Alexander Gerschenkron's stimulating essay, "Economic Development in Russian Intellectual History of the Nineteenth Century," *Economic Backwardness*, pp. 152–87, which argues that, in general, the Russian intelligentsia were unwilling to accept industrialization, although he does make distinctions that in the case of the Slavophils helped stimulate me to pursue and deepen the exceptions.

4. The major sources for the line of argument sketched above are Gaisonovich, *Vol'f*, especially pp. 483 ff.; Baer, *Aftobiografiia*, pp. 182–83, 199; Gasking, *Investigations* (but cf. also Meyer, *Human Generation*, chap. 6); Mikulinskii, *Razvitiia*, pp. 81–124; Sakulin, *Odoevskii*, vol. 1, pt. 2, pp. 89–99; and V. Androssov, "Zamechaniia na pribavlenie k stat'e o filosofii, *Vestnik Evropy*, no. 6 (1823): 85–92, and idem, "Proizvodimost' i zhivye sily," *Moskovskii nabliudatel'*, no. 1, pt. 1 (1835):36. The problem is a complex one which I hope to treat in a separate work.

useful inventions, and turned him into a champion of railroad construction. Alexander Koshelev applied scientific agriculture and capitalist methods to his estates and, together with Fedor Chizhov, threw himself into railroad construction. In general, the Slavophils envisaged the railroad as a network of arteries radiating from "the heart of Russia"—Moscow—and bringing to the borderlands the vital transforming substance of Great Russian culture. In their eyes the higher aim of manufacturing was to make available for the common people cheap and durable labor-saving devices, rather than produce luxury goods for an indolent noble soslovie.[5]

The next logical step for this group was to recognize and accept the Russian merchantry as the social group best suited by virtue of its wealth, occupation, and cultural predilections to become their main allies in the economic transformation of the country. But logic may well have quailed at the vast social gap still separating the cultivated industrialist noble of Slavophil leanings from the rough-hewn, quasi-literate merchantry.

The first to seek new ties with the merchantry was the editor of *Moskvitianin*, M. P. Pogodin, who in the tradition of N. A. Polevoi strove to rehabilitate the merchantry and give it a more prominent place in Russian public life.[6] It was not simply coincidence, then, that the great playwright of the merchant milieu, A. N. Ostrovskii, chose to publish his early work in Pogodin's journal. Nor was it surprising that the younger generation of critics on the staff of *Moskvitianin*, like Appolon Grigor'ev and E. N. Edel'son, known as "the young editors" or, more accurately, as adherents of the nativist movement called *pochvennichestvo* (enthusiasts of the soil), mined Ostrovskii's plays for those rich, if hidden, veins of pure Russian culture that glittered deep below the coarse surface of the merchantry's daily life. In outlining the main tasks of their criticism, Grigor'ev wrote to Koshelev that the only guarantee of Russia's future lay with the popular masses and by this he meant not simply the peasantry but "also the merchantry who conserve the faith, morals, and language of our fathers" with its good and bad sides.[7]

5. Khomiakov, "Pis'mo v Peterburg po povodu zheleznoi dorogi," *Sochineniia*, 3:105–18; Christoff, *Khomyakov*, pp. 141–49; Rieber, "Formation," pp. 386–87. See also Dudzinskaia, "Burzhuaznye," pp. 49–64; Genkin, "Obshchestvenno-politicheskaia," pp. 75–76, 98.
6. See, for example, "O kupechestve," *Moskvitianin*, no. 5 (1842): 97–100; M. N. Pogodin, "Moskovskie izvestiia M.I. Krasheninnikov," ibid., no. 1 (1851): 38–65; idem, "Fizinomiia Nizhegorodskoi iarmaki," ibid., no. 4, pt. 2 (1851): 223–63.
7. Kniazhin, *Grigor'ev*, p. 151 (dated 25 March 1856). For Grigor'ev's idealized portrait of the merchants in Ostrovskii see his review in Grigor'ev, *Sochineniia*, 1:117, 473.

Ivan Aksakov also uncovered redeeming features in the brutal external behavior of the *samodur*, the self-willed merchant patriarch like the legendary Kit Kitych, who for the radical critics was the epitome of traditional, tyrannical Russia, "The Kingdom of Darkness," as Nikolai Dobroliubov called it. In a letter to Turgenev in 1853 about the merchant in Ostrovskii's play *Stick to Your Own Sleigh (Ne v svoi sani ne sadis')*, Aksakov wrote: "The moral dignity of man, hidden until now behind the ludicrous external appearance and poor education of the merchant, emerges here on the stage in contrast to the representatives of the other sosloviia who display nothing ludicrous—all of their behavior *comme il faut* and quite respectable—but who on the other hand turn out not to have any moral dignity."[8]

Here, then, in summary form, is a neglected theme of Russian intellectual history. Individual cultural leaders representing a broad spectrum of political belief but united in their struggle to counterbalance harmful Western influences strove to define a comprehensive set of social values which were unmistakably Russian yet rested upon a more solid, potentially more dynamic, and more productive social base than the peasantry. What they envisaged was an aroused merchantry freed of its inertia but uncorrupted by the base materialism of the West—in short, an entrepreneurial, capitalist class that would not be a bourgeoisie. Their task was to set a stamp of legitimacy on the heretofore ambiguous social role of the Russian merchant, to locate entrepreneurship in a community of true believers, and to offer the déclassé nobility newly enrolled in the guilds the intellectual leadership of Russia's economic development along national lines. Their success depended upon the receptivity of the merchants to a vague appeal still in the process of being formulated. As it turned out, the most fertile seed bed for these plantings was in the Old Believer communities of the central industrial provinces where successful trading peasants were buying their freedom and entering the merchant soslovie.

Cultural Foundations: Old Believers and Slavophils

The impact on Russian economic life of the great church schism of the seventeenth century is widely acknowledged and much debated, but still inadequately understood. Gerschenkron has rightly stressed that the social organization rather than the religious values of the schismatics (Old Believers or Old Ritualists) provided the stimulus for

8. Barsukov, *Zhizn'*, 12:286–87 (dated 14 March 1853).

their entrepreneurial activities. Their "defensive reaction against intolerance" took the form of a strong work ethic. Their unusually high rate of literacy may be attributed to their veneration of the holy word and to the constant shortage of priests among them. Their accumulation of capital served to preserve and enlarge their communities in the face of a hostile state authority.[9] To these should be added their dispersal along the perimeter of the empire, which deprived them of plowlands and imposed a commercial-manufacturing pattern upon their economic life.

The movement of the thriving Old Believer communities back from the northern and eastern frontiers to the economic heartland of the central provinces began under Catherine II's policy of official toleration. They settled in the manufacturing towns of Vladimir and Kostroma provinces, in the Starodub district of Chernigov province, in St. Petersburg, where they engaged in the wholesale trade, and, above all, in Moscow, where they organized two communities around the Rogozhskii and Preobrazhenskii cemeteries and enrolled in the meshchanstvo and the merchants guilds.

The reconstruction of Moscow following the French occupation and the fire of 1812 offered fresh opportunities for provincials to establish new enterprises and stimulated a second wave of Old Believer migration. This time they came from the villages of the central industrial region, where small numbers of the most enterprising Old Believer peasant serfs had amassed sufficient wealth as hired laborers to buy their freedom and set themselves up in business. Textiles and vodka tax farming provided most of their capital. Old Believers Rogozhin and Morozov introduced the first Jacquard loom and built the first cotton-spinning mill with imported English machinery in Russia. Old Believer millionaire V. A. Kokorev drafted a reorganization of the entire liquor revenue system, which was subsequently adopted by the state.[10]

Despite their visible material success the Old Believers at first firmly resisted acculturation and social integration. Then, late in the reign of Alexander, official policy took a sinister turn. Rising pressures to convert and police harassment produced serious tensions within the communities. A new phase opened in the long history of the Old Believers' accommodation to persecution by the state.

In the long run compromises with the state left their mark on the

9. Gerschenkron, *Europe*, pp. 34–37, which is critical of Max Weber's attempt to apply the Puritan ethic to the Old Belief. Cf. Blackwell, *Beginnings*, pp. 212–29, which accepts a modified version of the Weberian analysis.

10. Shul'tse-Gevernits, *Krupnoe*, pp. 34–35; K. A. Skal'kovskii, *Nashi gosudarstvennye*, pp. 165–66.

economic life of the Old Believers and on their attitudes toward state authority. From the outset the state regarded the Old Belief as a form of permanent rebellion. For a long time it took little account of the doctrinal differences that separated sectarians who accepted the need for their own church hierarchy (*popovtsy*) and those who rejected it (*bezpopovtsy*). For over a century official state policy wavered between cruel repression and passive hostility. Meanwhile, the widely dispersed Old Believer communities of both tendencies continued to subdivide into smaller sects. What they all shared, however, was a refusal to accept the state as a legitimate authority. This often took the form of internal resistance but at times it meant open revolt. At the end of the eighteenth century, under the influence of Catherine's more tolerant views, the Orthodox Church sought to reintegrate the schismatics and, together with a few Old Believer clerics, worked out a compromise called *edinoverie* (united faith), by which the formal recognition of the authority of the church hierarchy would be exchanged for the right to retain books from the pre-Nikon period and to perform the old sacramental rituals.[11]

At first, the reconciliation had little effect, but with Nicholas I's decision to crack down on the so-called pernicious sects—that is, those which did not recognize a priesthood or the sacraments—the movement to conversion gained momentum, particularly among the large Theodosian sect of bezpopovtsy clustered around the Preobrazhenskii Cemetery in Moscow. Economic differentiation had already weakened its internal cohesion and led to a split in 1816 between the traditional egalitarian-communal majority and renegades who sought to modify the old customs in order to accommodate the spirit of capitalist enterprise. Gradually, the well-to-do minority, including the famous Guchkov family, permitted marriage and the hereditary transfer of individual private property and tolerated the hierarchical owner-worker relationship of the factory system, which was anathema to the more communally oriented Theodesians. It was now an easy step to join the edinoverie, and Nicholas's police pressures made it even easier to accept. In the thirties and forties many of the big merchant families, including the Guchkovs and the Khludovs, who supplied members to the Moscow entrepreneurial group found the edinoverie a comfortable halfway house to orthodoxy where they could reconcile their conscience with their need to run their business free of harassment. Crossovers from the Old Belief reached an annual

11. "Rech' po novomu rassuzhdenii o nuzhdakh edinovertsev proiznesennaia professorom L.F. Nil'skim 4-dekabria 1873 goda v zasedannii S-Peterburgskogo otdela obshchestva liubitelei dukhovnogo prosveshcheniia," *Khristianskoe chtenie*, no. 1 (1874): 40–48; ibid., no. 2 (1874):219–29.

peak of over 15,000 in 1854, largely in response to the government's decree that no Old Believers would be permitted to enroll in the merchant guilds after 1 January 1855.[12]

Paradoxically, the merchants in the less pernicious sects offered greater resistance to the pressures for conversion. To restore their so-called impoverished clergy the popovtsy community of Rogozhskii—120,000 strong—acknowledged the episcopal authority of the Old Believer church in Belaia Krinitsa in Bukovina across the Habsburg frontier and thus assured themselves of a steady source of properly ordained priests from their own faith.[13] Once again, as in the case of the Preobrazhenskii community, the leaders in the formation of the "Belokrinitskii persuasion" were the big merchant families like the Riabushinskiis and the Sirotkins, who were to occupy prominent places in the second generation of the Moscow entrepreneurial group.

Thus, as Old Believer families became more successful and wealthier, they found themselves confronted with the choice of compromising on matters of faith or facing economic ruin. In the provinces it was possible to go underground or feign submission, but for those living under direct police surveillance in Moscow evasion was out of the question. There were honorable precedents among the Old Believers for accommodating their religious beliefs to economic and political realities. As early as the first decade of the eighteenth century, the Old Believer community at Vyg supplied Peter the Great with iron in return for a degree of autonomy, thus saving "the essential features of its life by making an agreement with the infidel state."[14] To be sure, the regime of Nicholas I demanded more than this; yet even as the merchants worked out their torturous compromises and ex-

12. Ryndziunskii, "Staroobriadcheskaia," pp. 190–91, 210–11, 217–18, 242; Andreev, *Raskol*, pp. 153, 163–64, 211, 219, 225; Nikolskii, *Istoriia*, pp. 296–97; Bonch-Bruevich, "Sektanstvo i staroobriadchestvo v pervoi polovine XIX v.," *Sochineniia*, 1:266–68, also gives a periodic breakdown of conversions from 1828 to 1855 which came to the following totals: to Orthodoxy, 177,051, and to edinoverie, 164,604. The exact number of Old Believer merchants in these totals is difficult to ascertain. According to official figures of the Ministry of the Interior in 1858 in Moscow, there were 424 males of priestless and priestist sects enrolled in merchant guilds. This was only a slight increase over figures for 1850, 1854, and 1855 (Storozhev, *Istoriia*, vol. 5, pt. 2, pp. 203, 220, 232). On the other hand, these official registers are not reliable because they were used as a basis for inheritance settlements unfavorable to the priestless, whose marriages were not recognized. Other official reports emphasize the existance of "select" Old Believers who dominated such towns as Galich and had important ties with cohorts in Moscow, Nizhnyi Novgorod, Vologda, and Arkhangelsk (Kelsiev, *Sbornik*, 2:24–25).

13. Melnikov, "Sapelkina," pp. 186–94, gives a vivid picture of an Old Believer in the Rogozhskii community whose decision to join the edinoverie brought down on him the wrath of the entire community.

14. Crummey, *Old Believers*, pp. 69–70.

pressed their formal obedience, they conserved an attitude toward authority that marked them off from the rest of Russian society. Although the Old Believers cherished the patriarchal values embedded in the Domostroi, they did not automatically transfer their veneration of the pater families to the little father tsar (*batiushka*). On the contrary, for them political authority was at best alien and corrupt, even if legitimate. At its worst it was a physical manifestation of the Antichrist. The theological justification, then, for their patriotic outlook lay in a revised version of the Third Rome Doctrine, which proclaimed that the saints of the Russian church and the Russian people as a whole, not the tsar and his government, were the true bearers of the true faith.[15] Unlike the bulk of the merchantry they were morally armed to resist interference by the bureaucracy and the police. Even when their tightly knit society in Moscow began to crack under pressure, they did not abandon their ethical norms and cultural identity but rather transferred them from the decaying religious communities to the Great Russian people. It was here that they found common ground with the Slavophils.

At the same time the Slavophils, Khomiakov and Aksakov in particular, recognized and admired the religious vigor and cultural purity of the Old Believers, perceiving in them a link with the peasant masses and an ally against the bureaucratic state.[16] What they sought above all was to obtain freedom of conscience for the Old Believers and to persuade the Orthodox Church hierarchy to abandon its policy of coercion and engage the Old Believers in a spiritual dialogue that would show them the errors of their ways. Although the Slavophils did not fully appreciate the depth of the Old Believers' religious feelings, which extended far beyond questions of ritual, they stood for religious tolerance and helped prepare the way for practical cooperation between Slavophil entrepreneurs like Chizhov, Koshelev, and Aksakov and Old Believer merchants like the Morozovs, Soldatenkov, and Kokorev.[17]

The Old Believer and Slavophil entrepreneurs were linked to a few long-established merchant families by a cluster of shared attitudes toward the myths and realities of Old Russian culture. Moscow represented the symbolic and physical center of their work and life. Their suspicion of foreigners and of the Westernized bureaucracy made

15. Zenkovsky, "Denisov Brothers," pp. 49–66. See also Cherniavsky, "Old Believers," pp. 1–39.
16. Aksakov, Sochineniia, 4:34–43, 44–45, 103–10. These were editorials in *Den'* (18 September and 16 October 1865) and *Moskva* (2 August 1868).
17. Riabushinskii, Staroobriadchestvo, p. 78; Aksakov, Sochineniia, 4:180, editorial in *Rus'* (26 September 1881).

St. Petersburg the natural focus of their enmity. By the end of the eighteenth century the rivalry between "official" Petersburg and "plebeian" Moscow was already well established, but two dramatic events in the early nineteenth century intensified and broadened these keenly felt differences. When Napoleon invaded Russia in 1812, the Moscow merchant society volunteered to pay one half of the extraordinary war levy imposed by the government on Moscow province. In addition, individual merchant families contributed over 1.7 million rubles in cash and kind to the war effort. During the burning of Moscow many of the noble families and government officials abandoned the city, some never to return, while most of the merchants remained behind.[18] This demographic shift in the relative weight of the two sosloviia became a permanent feature of the population of the city and strengthened the merchants' patriotic image of themselves. In sharp contrast the appointment of Count Zakrevskii as governor-general brought little more than humiliation and heavy financial burdens to the merchants, but his menacing presence deepened their hostility toward aristocratic officials from St. Petersburg who lorded over them in the heart of their own city.

The Old Believers and the merchants in Moscow were neighbors, inhabiting adjoining districts in the southeastern and southern sections of the city. Ever since their return to Moscow in the last quarter of the eighteenth century, the Old Believers had clustered around the Rogozhskii Cemetery, where they had constructed their chapel, charitable institutions—including orphanages and refugees—school, library, archive, and several large houses belonging to wealthy Old Believer merchants.[19] Across the Moscow River on the western edge of the three Rogozhskii districts lay the six districts composing the Zamoskvorechie or "south side," where the majority of Orthodox merchants dwelled on quiet tree-lined streets surrounding their churches, cultural and benevolent societies, warehouses, and outdoor markets. For both groups, however, the center of trade was the Kitai Gorod. Here in the 1840s sprawled the trade rows composed of permanent shops and roofed-over passageways housing about two thousand establishments. The physical form of these crowded, unattractive, and unheated shops contrasted sharply with the elegant trading arcades of the capital and even of the more fashionable streets in Moscow, such as Kuznetskii Most, where German and French retail merchants established shops catering to the nobles who lived in the west end of the city. Russian merchants in Moscow clung to their conservative ways until the 1880s, when the government finally insisted, against the

18. Tartakovskii, "Naselenie," pp. 356–79; Storozhev, *Voina*, pp. 59, 98.
19. N. I. Subbotin, "Epizod iz istorii Moskovskogo rogozhskogo kladbishcha."

spirited opposition of the proprietors, that the crumbling trade rows be demolished and replaced by arcades.[20]

Socially and culturally, the Old Believers and the Russian merchantry had more in common with one another than they had with any other group in imperial society. In the first place both were fiercely attached to the social norms of the Domostroi, which, moreover, the Slavophils idealized even if they did not emulate. The Old Believers' religious fervor and the charitable assistance that they extended to poor members of their faith without any hope of rewards from the government aroused the admiration of merchants and Slavophils because this spirit contrasted so clearly with the spiritual poverty and social inertia of the official church, and especially of the provincial clergy. Among merchants in Moscow and the central industrial provinces the religious distinctions that the official church struggled to maintain between Orthodoxy, the edinoverie, the Old Believers, and the sectarians were often blurred to the point of becoming meaningless. In Moscow, following the decree forbidding Old Believers to enroll in the guilds after the beginning of 1855, the government discovered that the edinoverie clergy were handing out conversion certificates without ever having baptized the recipients. Kostroma province was renowned for the production and distribution of icons of the Old Believer type, with their "byzantine style," yet the overwhelming majority of merchantry in the province were listed as Orthodox. Here and elsewhere whole villages paid outward obeisance to the church but "secretly kept the old books." In Vladimir province the Old Believers dramatically increased their conversions among the merchantry in the 1860s, with the open support of elders of the edinoverie.[21] The ambiguities of religious belief among the merchantry were given perhaps their most profound and simplest expression in this curious exchange in Dostoevsky's The Idiot between Prince Myshkin and Rogozhin (whose name derives suggestively from Rogozhsk) about the latter's merchant father: "He was an Old Believer was he?" the prince asked, and Rogozhin answered, "No, he went to church but it's quite true that he used to say that the old faith was nearer the truth."

Even the adaptation of European ways by some Orthodox and Old Believer merchant families did not break down this cultural affinity; rather, as it had in the Slavophil nobles, it tended to produce a more passionate defense of what remained Russian in them. During the 1840s a series of economic changes expanded the internal market and

20. R. Gohstand, "The Shaping of Moscow by 19th Century Trade," in Hamm, City, pp. 164–65.
21. Meshcherskii, Ocherki, 1:174–75.

brought it into more direct contact and competition with the world market: the completion of the Moscow–St. Petersburg railroad, the end to the prohibition of the export of English textile machinery, the growth of Russia's export trade in grain, and the firm establishment of a domestic textile sector in the central industrial provinces. These opportunities and the challenge of foreign competition spurred a small number of Moscow merchant families to break with the tradition of family schooling. Tutors were hired to teach foreign languages, especially German, to their sons, some of whom were then sent on to gymnasia and then placed in the Moscow offices of foreign firms to acquire practical experience. In exceptional cases, when the family firm engaged in the export trade, the sons were sent abroad to perfect their training, acquire a veneer of European manners, and make business contacts. In the same families daughters were instructed in music and French, with the aim of securing suitable marriages in equally wealthy and ambitious merchant families or in the nobility. In one recorded case a merchant reached beyond the family circle to encourage literacy among his own workers, a charitable but sound business investment in the style of Robert Owen.[22]

It was inevitable that in some cases, and it is impossible to say how many, the traditional fears of the merchants were justified; excursions into the new worlds of alien cultures and abstract learning lured their sons away from the family business and into the free professions. In the absence of reliable statistics the impression remains that this occurred with far less frequency among merchant than it did among noble families, but in the two decades before the Crimean War the offspring of at least a dozen leading merchant families crossed over into a variety of noncommercial occupations, ranging from medicine and law to the creative arts.[23]

Yet the break with the merchant milieu was rarely complete, and for the first time a narrow and shaky connection was made between a handful of merchant families and the world of the intelligentsia. Thus, the merchants could find in the teachings of the Slavophils that blend of cultural stability and economic enterprise that matched their own

22. Vishniakov, *Svedeniia*, pt. 3, pp. 38, 117; Krestovnikov, *Semeinaia*, 1:56–57, 76; Shchukin, "Iz vospominanii," pt. 3, p. 544; ibid., pt. 2, pp. 101–2; Botkina, *Tret'iakov*, pp. 16–19, 30; "T. S. Prokhorov," *RBS*, 15:99–100; Akademiia nauk, *Istoriia Moskvy*, 3:461.

23. Among the most famous crossovers into the liberal professions were F. A. Koni, writer and journalist, father of the great jurist A. F. Koni; Anton and Nikolai Rubinshtein, musicians and founders of the St. Petersburg and Moscow conservatories, respectively; A. I. Kirpichnikov, the literary historian; I. F. Balandin, a physician; A. I. Selivanov, an ethnographer and librarian; and N. A. Polevoi, journalist, editor, and historian. Their biographies can be found in *RBS*.

ambitions and aspirations. Moreover, among those merchants who adopted a European life-style the external "presentation of self," as Erving Goffman puts it, masked a real internal life which had not undergone any change.[24] One common expression of this state of mind was the merchants' custom of fitting out a set of rooms in the finest European style for "state occasions," as Mackenzie Wallace calls them. Used exclusively for receiving important guests, these rooms were not to be lived in at all. The merchant and his family inhabited small shabby rooms in the back or on the ground floor of the house. As a general rule the ostentatious public life of the rich merchants was not permitted to corrupt the interior family life.[25]

Perhaps even more important, a growing number of merchants' sons used their newly acquired European values to become better businessmen without renouncing their cultural identity. The most striking examples occurred in Old Believer merchant families, where the stigma of Europeanization might be thought to have been totally incompatible with the faith. According to Prince Meshcherskii, that astute but by no means sympathetic observer of commercial and industrial life in the provinces, the very same Old Believers who were "secret but powerful protectors of the fanatics of Guslits [in Moscow province] sent their sons to be educated in Bremen or Liverpool" with unexpected results. "These sons returned to the family nest the faith of their fathers unshaken and brought back with them from England together with a superb knowledge of how to run a factory another conviction: relying on the Quakers and Dissenters in general, they said, 'Why can't people like us with our own religious beliefs not enjoy freedom at home.'"[26] This was a common view among the most powerful Europeanized Old Believer families who later played an outstanding role in the political life of the country, the Guchkovs, Morozovs, Riabushinskiis, Konovalovs, and others.

Cultural affinities should not gloss over important nuances of opinion that differentiated, for example, the hostility of the Old Believers and Slavophils toward Peter the Great and all his works from the

24. The Western reception rooms served, in Goffman's words, as "the setting" of "a social front." While expressing what he also calls "a discrepancy between appearance and overall reality," the front seems to me less a deception in this case and more of an explanation by the merchant that he recognized the proper style for the wealthy but preferred to dwell in his own comfortable quarters, even if they were dingy and dirty. See Goffman, *Presentation*, pp. 22–29 and 42–45.
25. Wallace, *Russia*, 1:237 ff. These observations are based upon Wallace's trip to Russia in 1877. Lest this be interpreted as the misguided view of a foreigner, Dostoevsky makes the same point in his brilliant scene in *Brothers Karamazov* between Dmitri and the merchant Samsonov. I am grateful to Gary Morson for this reference.
26. Meshcherskii, *Ocherki*, 1:119.

traditional merchants' sullen but muted distrust of government officials. But what they shared in both their cultural values and entrepreneurial roles did begin to distinguish them from the rest of Russian
society. Their mutual attraction and their subsequent success in business and politics may be clarified by an interpretation of their deviant
role in Russian society based upon two insights of Robert Merton:
(1) there are "varying rates and types of deviant behaviour" and
(2) "deviant behavior may be more adaptive than the old for realization of [society's] primary goals."[27] As to the first point, both the
entrepreneurial prowess and the cultural values of the Old Believer
peasant-cum-merchant were equally deviant. The Slavophil entrepreneurs exhibited a greater degree of deviant behavior in their entrepreneurial activities than their cultural values. The merchant entrepreneurs remained culturally orthodox, at least on the surface, and
deviant only in their entrepreneurial activities. With respect to the
second point, all three groups sought to protect Russia against foreign
domination—surely a primary goal of society as a whole—but they
perceived that the best method of achieving this aim was to adopt a
form of economic behavior and a political stance that deviated from
the routine and cautious attitudes of the majority of the merchantry.

These disparate elements of Old Russian culture and entrepreneurial zeal blended to produce a powerful vision of Russia made
strong from below, and not from above, by popular rather than bureaucratic forces, based in Moscow not St. Petersburg, against the
West not with it. To this amalgam the Slavophil noble industrialists
and the Old Believer merchants contributed an attitude of independence, at times virtually of defiance toward the government, while
avoiding that sense of alienation from the nation that doggedly pursued the radical intelligentsia. Under their guidance the xenophobia
and ethnocentrism of the old merchantry edged closer to modern
Great Russian nationalism.

Institutional Foundations: Legal and Social Changes

Before this process could be carried any further, however, profound
structural changes had to take place in Russian society. Under the
crushing weight of the Nicholaen system legal politics was impossible.
It required the shock of military defeat and the energetic intervention
of the state to clear away the obstacles that blocked the further evolu-

27. Merton, "Social Structure and Anomie: Continuities," *Social Theory*, pp. 211,
236–37.

tion of Russian society toward new forms of consciousness and organization. In the wake of the Crimean debacle the new tsar, Alexander II, moved quickly to relax the harsh police and censorship controls that had stifled civic life during the previous reign. Although the government opposed any mention of emancipating the serfs for fear of inciting peasant disorders, it perceived the value of allowing a public discussion of other economic questions. The government needed to restore confidence, stimulate investment, and revive overseas trade. The first railroad network, the revision of the tariff, the creation of new credit facilities, the employment of a large free labor force—all raised the larger issue of who would decide the pace and purpose of Russia's industrialization. The state was on the verge of bankruptcy and could not, as it had in the past, shoulder the burden of recovery. Never before in Russian history had such ample opportunities existed for an open and serious discussion of economic development.

A second structural change, the emancipation of the serfs, had the unexpected effect of bolstering the prestige and increasing the size of the merchant soslovie. Carried out by bureaucratic methods over the opposition of the nobles, the emancipation severely damaged the social and economic position of the dominant noble soslovie. The net result was to reduce the effectiveness of the social sanctions that the nobility could impose on the other sosloviia and to remove the liberated peasant entrepreneur from the protection of the landlord. Henceforth, both the nobles and the peasants were forced to compete with the merchants on equal legal and economic terms. Noble families engaged in commerce and industry gave greater prominence to their entrepreneurial role than to their social status, which, once diminished by the loss of the exclusive privilege of owning serfs, no longer offered any concrete economic advantages. Peasant merchants no longer had to lay out important capital to purchase their freedom. For them membership in the merchant guilds was now an accessible and affordable road to upward mobility. Not surprisingly, then, between 1852 and 1871 the merchant soslovie grew rapidly, more than doubling its size in Moscow.[28] In prestige and numbers the merchant soslovie reached new heights.

28. The increase is all the more astonishing because in 1863 the third guild was abolished. The exact figures are as follows:

	1852	1871
Merchants	13,943	29,222
Honored citizens	1,682	7,117

Compiled from data in Nifontov, "Formirovanie," pp. 244–45. Relying on figures supplied by V. M. Bostandzhoglo, *Spravochnaia kniga o litsakh, poluchivshikh na 1873 g.*

A political awakening was not far behind. Both the social and structural changes that set the stage for the merchantry's genuine debut in Russian politics originated outside its soslovie and intruded upon it abruptly in the last grim days of the Crimean War. In 1855 a desperate financial situation impelled Prince A. F. Orlov, the president of the State Council and of the Committee of Ministers, to seek advice from unusual quarters—the millionaire tax farmer Kokorev. With the aid of M. P. Pogodin, Kokorev drafted a strong memorandum on reorganizing the gold-mining industry. Concluding their report on an unusually urgent note, the authors charged that in the past the government's failure to act quickly and decisively had deprived Russia of railroads and other means to fight a modern war in the Crimea. Russia could not afford another mistake of similar proportions, they warned. As if to confirm their worst fears, the minister of finance, P. F. Brok, consigned their project to oblivion by referring it to the Siberian governors for consideration.[29]

In the past such a rebuff would have sent the merchants scurrying back into their shells. But the Crimean defeat and the relaxation of censorship inspired a different response. A small number of merchants and plebeian intellectuals like Kokorev, Mamontov, and Pogodin were aroused by the contrast between the heroism of the armed forces in a losing cause and the bureaucratic mismanagement that led to defeat and financial disorder. They organized a great round of receptions in Moscow for the officers of the Black Sea Fleet, whose courage had won the admiration of all Russia.[30] Even a rigid bureaucrat like Governor-General Zakrevskii could hardly object to their patriotic initiative. What surprised and angered him was their attempt to convert the banquets into political forums, much like the French republicans under the Orleanist monarchy.

In his first speech, Kokorev tied the fate of the empire to "a general prosperity proceeding from the correct development of the productive forces of Russia." Encouraged by the enthusiastic public reception, he expanded his views at subsequent banquets to which he invited

---

kupecheskie svidetel'stva po 1-i i 2-i gil'diam v Moskve (Moscow, 1873), the work concludes that of the first-guild merchants in 1873 only 17.3 percent came from the "old Moscow merchantry," 29.2 percent entered the guild between 1801 and 1860, and the rest (more than half) joined after 1861.

29. Kokorev, *Ekonomicheskie*, pp. 142–46.

30. ORBL, f. 231 (Pogodin), carton 6, no. 9, Kokorev to Orlov (undated). The merchant needled the prince by concluding that Peter the Great and Napoleon were great administrators because "they acted with advice of the estates [soslovie], that is to say, fresh practical elements." He urged a reform of the Senate to include representatives of the provinces as in the old days and, above all, *"publicity"* for the ongoing discussion of economic questions.

representatives of the merchantry from the provinces. What emerged from these speeches was nothing less than a full-blown political program advocating free labor, moderate free trade, and construction of a network of railroads and steamships to stimulate Russian industry and develop capitalist relationships in the countryside. In a characteristic flourish he proposed that merchant tax farmers, himself included, pay their debt to the Russian people by redeeming serfs with the profits they earned from selling vodka to the peasants.[31] This was the merchants' moral equivalent to Aksakov's plea to the nobility to liquidate itself as a class by emancipating their serfs.

When Kokorev sought to stage an explicitly political banquet in honor of the approaching emancipation, Zakrevskii flew into a rage. In a secret memorandum he foolishly denounced Kokorev to Prince Orlov and also to Prince V. A. Dolgorukov, the head of the secret police (Third Section), for allegedly plotting with Pogodin at Mamontov's and for his contacts with the dangerous Aksakovs.[32] But the old slogans of fear no longer had the same effect. The new tsar, Alexander II, and his advisers perceived that the merchantry was vital to the economic recovery of the country. Foreign loans, too, were necessary, but they were not enough. Besides, Russia had to demonstrate to the Western European bankers that it was a safe investment. This required not only a stable political order but also strong evidence of economic vitality. Without the vigorous activity of the merchants, the government would be unable to stimulate exports, stabilize the ruble rate, and increase its revenue from tariffs and taxes. Kokorev and others like him had high protectors in the government, and his super-

---

31. Barsukov, *Zhizn'* 14:497. Moscow intellectuals ranging from Konstantin Aksakov to K. D. Kavelin were impressed by Kokorev's natural oratorical skill. Pogodin estimated that the dinners and balls cost Kokorev one hundred thousand rubles (ibid., pp. 517, 530–31).

32. Ibid., 15:487–96; ibid., 17:39–40. For additional reports on Kokorev's speeches see "Sovremennaia letopis," *RV* 5, bk. 2 (September 1856): 167–69 (at a banquet organized by Kokorev for the mayors and representatives of the merchant soslovie throughout Russia), and Kokorev, "Obed," pp. 203–12 (a banquet organized by literary and academic figures to celebrate the Nazimov Rescript). Kokorev's most important articles were "Vzgliad," pp. 29–64 (also published in the semiofficial organ of the Russian government in Belgium, *Le Nord*), and "Milliardy v tumane," *SPB vedomosti*, nos. 5, 6 (January 1859). On Zakrevskii's views see Nikitenko, *Dnevnik*, 2:11 (entry dated 31 January 1858), and especially "Liubopytnoe pokazanie," pp. 447–52, letters to Prince Dolgorukov, 28 August 1858, and to Prince Orlov, 6 February 1858 and 21 June 1859. For Kokorev's rejoinder to these revelations see his "Vospominaniia," pp. 154–63, in which he ridicules the idea of a plot. Up to the time of the banquet incident, Kokorev was a welcome guest at the governor-general's office and even bought his Moscow mansion. The break in their relations reveals a new boldness in a merchant's attitude toward authority.

patriotic outbursts could easily be overlooked in light of his proven value to the regime.

Under the stimulus of the legal and social reforms of the early 1860s the more enterprising and innovative elements within the merchantry were prepared to take a more active role in the economic, social, and even political life of the country. But the form of their activity was largely determined by the government's reluctance to dismantle the entire structure of the hierarchical society. The old soslovie organizations, which remained in place for the time being, were wholly inadequate for the task of stimulating economic enterprise. Yet the government still opposed the formation of nationwide organizations of any sort, and it prevented the emergence of a free, corporate business community. The problem of mobilizing talent and capital could only be solved outside the state through informal means. The entrepreneurial group was one such device, and it made its first appearance in the Moscow region.

The single most important and complicated problem in dealing with the Moscow entrepreneurial group is to determine its membership. Like any political group, this one resembled a set of concentric circles with a center of activists and secondary and tertiary layers of those less involved and less committed. These circles were not rigid; they expanded and contracted over time, reflecting the volatile nature of the individual personalities and the specific issues involved. Yet, to merit the name at all, the group had to display a degree of cohesion that can be measured by something more tangible than a historian's conviction that its members belonged together. Membership in this group has been inferred from participation in three collective endeavors: (1) participation in a newspaper or journal as either an editor, a contributor, or a financial backer; (2) administrative responsibility or investment in a business enterprise; and (3) involvement in or financial support of a public-service organization.

As table 4.1 shows, fourteen men (and their families) constituted the center, the most active section of the group. Judged by the frequency with which they participated in the endeavors mentioned above, they may be subdivided into an inner core—F. V. Chizhov, T. S. Morozov and family, Dmitri and Alexander Shipov and family, I. F. Mamontov and family, and V. A. Kokorev—and a primary layer —I. A. Liamin, K. T. Soldatenkov, I. S. Aksakov, I. K. Babst, A. I. Del'vig, P. M. Tret'iakov and family, and A. I. and G. I. Khludov and family. The fine distinction between the two subgroups is not solely a quantitative one, as the case of Liamin indicates, but also reflects subjective evaluation of the intensity of their involvement.

A dozen or so men and their families, somewhat less involved than those at the center, made up a second level of the group; these men merged almost imperceptibly with an outer layer of sixty-odd men who were associated only on occasion with the activists (see table 4.1). Even at their maximum size of one hundred they represented a tiny fraction of the seventeen thousand merchants officially enrolled in the guilds of Moscow province at mid-century. In the following analysis the fourteen activists and their families occupy the center stage, as befits their leading role in the group.

At first glance the activists and their families appear to be a curious assemblage. They lack many of the characteristics normally attributed to small groups—that is, common social origins, education, religion, and occupation. For this reason a study of their activities will focus on the basic traits for identifying an interest group outlined at the beginning of this chapter. The first two, their functional role and cultural values, will be grouped together in this chapter under the search for a new identity, and the second two, their program and the pattern of their personal interactions under the new style of politics, will be dealt with in the following chapter.

A Common Social Role: Entrepreneurial Careers

To begin with their common functional role in society, all the core members, plus Tret'iakov, the Khludovs, Liamin, Krestovnikov, and Soldatenkov in the primary layer, enjoyed varied and successful entrepreneurial careers in the 1850s. Many of them founded fortunes before the Crimean War. Del'vig, Babst, and Aksakov became active entrepreneurs only later, in the 1860s. Although of these three only Aksakov came to rely upon these activities as the main source of livelihood, all of them participated in joint enterprises with the group and regarded the Moscow entrepreneurs as the leading element in the economic development of Russia. With few exceptions the members of the Moscow group accumulated their capital as tax farmers, textile manufacturers, or both. In the first case, they acted as substitutes for state tax collectors in the absence of an efficient and honest provincial bureaucracy. From 1844 to 1856 tax farmers were astonishingly successful in increasing government revenues from the sale of alcohol by over 50 percent, while other major sources of revenue remained virtually static.[33] No wonder the vodka tax farmers perceived the private capitalist under the protection of the state as the

33. For the general problem of the government's inability to collect its own taxes see Starr, *Decentralization*, pp. 17–18, 34–44. For Kankrin's reluctant decision to reestablish

TABLE 4.1. *The Moscow Entrepreneurial Group: First Generation*

	The Core				
	Chizhov	T. S. Morozov	Dmitri Shipov	Alexander Shipov	I. F. Mamontov family
Press:					
Vestnik promyshlennosti	●	●	●	●	●
Aktsioner	●	●			
Moskva	●	●	●	●	
Pressure groups:					
Moscow Exchange Committee	●	●	●		●
Delegate to Merchant Assembly	●	●	●	●	
Slavic Benevolent Society	●	●	●	●	
Business Activities:					
Moscow Merchants' Bank	●	●			●
Merchants' Mutual Credit Society	●	●	●		●
Iaroslavl Railroad Company	●		●	●	●
Russian company to purchase Nikolaevskii Line	●		●		●
Moscow-Kursk Railroad Company	●	●			●
Tashkent Silk Company	●	●	●		●
Arkhangelsk-Murmansk Company	●	●			●
Joint-stock Company for Resettlement in Western Provinces	●	●	●		
Educational and Technical Organizations					
Society for the Diffusion of Technical Knowledge					●
Society for the Encouragement of Russian Industry and Trade		●			
Total	14	13	10	5	10

Primary Layer | **Secondary Layer**

Primary Layer							Secondary Layer								
K. T. Soldatenkov	I. S. Aksakov	I. K. Babst	A. I. Del'vig	A. I. and G. I. Khludov family	Krestovnikov family	P. M. and S. M. Tret'iakov	Maliutin family	Samarin family	Sukhotin family	M. A. Gorbov	V. Rukavishnikov	A. I. Koshelev	I. I. Chetverikov	Vishniakov family	A. V. and H. V. Lepeshkin family
8	7	7	6	6	8	6	5	5	3	5	5	4	3	3	4

First Generation of Moscow Entrepreneurs

*P. M. Tret'iakov. (Courtesy of
Helsinki University Library)*

S. M. Tret'iakov. (Courtesy of
Helsinki University Library)

G. I. Khludov. (Courtesy of Helsinki
University Library)

A. I. Khludov. (Courtesy of Helsinki
University Library)

P. M. Riabushinskii. (Courtesy of
Helsinki University Library)

ideal entrepreneurial role, combining large profits with freedom from bureaucratic interference.

In the case of the textile manufacturers, an expanding market protected by tariffs and based on free hired labor before the emancipation put a premium on technological innovation and close cooperation with the government. Under these conditions the merchant industrialists could compete successfully with the inefficient, labor-intensive, noble enterprises based upon serfdom and with foreign, especially British, imports. Thus, the more enterprising merchants understood the vital connection between new forms of business enterprise and the benevolent attitude of the state bureaucracy.

What distinguished the merchants of the Moscow group from the rest of the merchantry was a willingness to invest profits in joint-stock companies in fields outside their manufacturing specialties and to create their own economic infrastructure of banks, railroads, and technical schools. While still attached to some of the traditional social values of the old Moscow merchantry, they began to employ modern business techniques and to display a willingness to manage other people's money and to take risks with their own.

The vital center of the Moscow group, F. V. Chizhov, got involved in textile manufacturing quite by accident. Born into a cultured but poor noble family in Kostroma, he was educated in the physics-mathematics faculty of St. Petersburg University. Like a growing number of déclassé nobles in the 1830s, he chose a professional career as a teacher of higher mathematics. Then his health failed, and he was forced to resign. While traveling abroad, he became involved in the Southern Slav movement. Arrested upon his return, imprisoned, and then exiled from the two capitals, he was forced by economic necessity to earn a living. Ingeniously, he converted his theoretical interests in science (he had already written a monograph on steam engines) into a practical business venture. In 1849 he leased fifty desiatinas of land near Kiev from the Ministry of State Domains and plunged enthusias-

---

vodka tax farming in 1827 see Pintner, *Economic Policy*, pp. 76–81. The following figures are taken from ibid., p. 77.

Year	Direct Taxes and Rents	Alcohol Revenue	Customs Revenue	Total Ordinary Revenue
1844	163,506	200,718	111,611	651,595
1856	163,110	309,291	104,538	811,072

To be sure under this system the tax farmers themselves grew rich, and corruption was not eliminated but merely transferred from state officials to private entrepreneurs. For the entire question see Nol'de, *Piteinoe*.

QUEST FOR IDENTITY · 159

tically into silk manufacturing, which he had studied while in Italy. First he constructed a large factory for making silk cloth; next he founded a school for training peasants to work on his silk plantation. From the outset he displayed a genuine concern over the mental and moral state of the workers under his authority. This paternal interest was to become one of the hallmarks of the Moscow group. He also found time to write a monograph on silk breeding which went through several editions, and he contributed articles on the same subject to national newspapers. Impressed by his zeal and his results, the government supported the expansion of his enterprise with free land and small loans until 1857, when he was pardoned by the new tsar and allowed to go to Moscow. There he became editor of a new journal, *Vestnik promyshlennosti* (The Messenger of Industry), which was devoted to advancing Russia's industrial interests and was the first joint venture of the Moscow entrepreneurs. Over the next two decades, Chizhov took the lead in organizing other members of the group into half a dozen major enterprises, including the Moscow-Iaroslavl and Moscow-Kursk railroads, the Moscow Merchants' and Mutual Credit banks, the Arkhangelsk-Murmansk Company, and the Joint-Stock Company for Resettlement in the Western Provinces.[34]

That the Shipov brothers adopted entrepreneurial roles shows deeper social forces at work. Sons of a well-to-do family of service nobles, they also came from Kostroma, which explains, no doubt, their close friendship with Chizhov. Originally, the brothers were destined for military careers. However, an unusually rich and varied home education, supplemented for Alexander Pavlovich by a few terms at the Institute of Transportation Engineers, turned them away from the routine of army life in their mature years and toward public service and business enterprise.

The oldest brother, Sergei Pavlovich, may be said to have provided a role model for his younger brothers. He spent his youth fighting the French and reading voraciously in the literature of political economy —Ludvig Baumeister, Heinrich Storch, Adam Smith, and Jean Babtiste See. After the Napoleonic Wars he attended the lectures of the

---

34. For Chizhov's early entrepreneurial activities see ORBL, f. 332 (Chizhov), carton 78, no. 11, "Perepiska o ssude ot ministerstva gosudarstvennogo imushchestva dlia razvitiia shelkovodstvo v Kievskoi gubernii," pp. 1–2; "Spisok predpisaniia departamenta sel'skogo khoziaistva ministerstva gosudarstvennogo imushchestva . . . 9 aprelia, 1859," ibid., pp. 3–4; "Spisok s prestavleniia upravliaiushchego kievskogo palatogo gosudarstvennogo imushchestva . . . ot 21 aprelia, 1859"; ibid., carton 78, no. 17; "Ob uchilishche shelkovodstva . . . programma." The most complete biography of Chizhov is Cherokov, *Chizhov*, but it does not make use of all the correspondence of the Chizhov archive now in the ORBL.

noted German-Russian statistician, Karl German, at St. Petersburg University. As commander of the crack Semeonovskii Guards regiment, he proselytized his soldiers with his enthusiasm for manufacturing by ordering them to learn a trade. Soon his ranks comprised carpenters, lathe operators, blacksmiths, and shoemakers. Taking over the terribly disorganized Commissariat of the Department of the Army, he ran it like an efficient business enterprise, hired trained accountants, and introduced new bookkeeping procedures. He used money borrowed from the Loan Bank to convert his father's declining estate into a profit-making enterprise, rather than squander it, as was common among the profligate nobility of his time.[35] By becoming a "secret" vodka tax farmer, he amassed sufficient capital to enable his younger brothers Alexander and Dmitri to establish a machine factory in Kostroma, which went on to become the largest Russian-owned enterprise of its type before the Crimean War. Alexander and Dmitri also invested heavily in the textile industry of Nizhnyi-Novgorod province and founded one of the earliest and most successful chemical factories owned and operated by Russians.[36]

When Sergei became governor of Kazan, he continued looking for new entrepreneurial talent. He took under his protection a young, energetic, but rough-hewn merchant from a village in Shipov's home district of Soligalich in Kostroma province and launched him on one of the most successful tax-farming careers in Russian history. This was V. A. Kokorev, the legendary Old Believer millionaire.

The son of a salt merchant of the sect of Shore Dwellers, Kokorev had no formal education, but he was endowed with a native shrewdness and a fine oratorical gift. While still a boy, he taught himself to read and write, traded on his own, and in 1843 became an agent for a vodka tax farmer. Drawing on his experience, he wrote a memorandum on reorganizing the entire tax-farming system. This brought him to the attention of Shipov, who helped him obtain a concession in Orel province, where he tested his theories so successfully that his reforms were adopted by the government and incorporated into a law that lasted until the abolition of tax farming in Russia in 1861.

His ingenuity in promoting himself while improving the state finances opened the doors of the chancelleries in St. Petersburg. He became an unofficial adviser to the minister of finance, F. P. Vronchenko, and to the president of the Committee of Ministers and chairman of the State Council, Prince A. F. Orlov.[37] Subsequently, these contacts enabled him not only to further his own business ventures

35. S. P. Shipov, "Vospominaniia," pp. 144–202.
36. A. P. Shipov, *Khlopchatobumazhnaia*.
37. K. A. Skal'kovskii, *Nashi gosudarstvennye*, pp. 165–66, based mainly on Skal'kovskii's

but also to present the collective views of the Moscow entrepreneurs to the highest state officials.

Having amassed a fortune before the Crimean War, he was quick to take advantage of new economic opportunities following the conclusion of peace. By 1859 he was a founder and major shareholder in the Trans-Caspian Trading Company, the Black Sea Steamship Company (2,000 shares), the Volga-Don Railroad Company (4,000 shares), the White Sea Company (500 shares), the Caspian Steamship Company (500 shares), and the Selvenyi Company, which was engaged in the southern trade (2,800 shares).[38] To establish the first important provincial bank in Russia, the Volga-Kama Bank, Kokorev lined up support from his coreligionists in the Old Belief, Morozov, Soldatenkov, and Khludov. Earlier than anyone else in Russia, he recognized the value of oil as a means of cheap illumination. On the advice of the famous German chemist Justus von Liebig, he constructed a factory near Baku designed to distill a kerosenelike substance for lamps.

In all these undertakings, Kokorev continued to benefit from his excellent relations with high officials, from whom he obtained concessions, privileges, and, much later when he overextended himself, relief from the threat of bankruptcy.[39] Although Kokorev moved easily among the Westernized governing elite, he never abandoned his old-fashioned Russian dress and manner or his sectarian faith. These loyalties enabled him to provide a crucial link between nobles like Shipov and Chizhov, on the one hand, and merchants of the Old Belief like himself, on the other.

Among the latter were his cosectarians in the Shore Dwellers, the Morozov family. The founder of the Morozov family, Savva Vasil'evich, was a former serf who bought his own and his family's freedom in

---

personal recollections; ORBL, f. 231 (Pogodin), vol. 3, carton 6, no. 9, V. A. Kokorev to Prince Orlov.

38. ORBL, f. 231 (Pogodin), vol. 3, carton 6, no. 5, V. A. Kokorev, "Beseda s samim soboiu" (9 January 1859), p. 4.

39. K. A. Skal'kovskii, *Nashi gosudarstvennye*, pp. 169–72. Kokorev's lobbying influenced the viceroy of the Caucasus to exchange the oil tax farming system for an excise tax, which increased the flow of oil and benefited Kokorev's refining operations (TsGIA, f. 1639, op. 1, d. 87, "Zapiski Bakinskego gubernatora i otvet emu Kokoreva o deiatel'-nosti kerosinogo zavoda v Surazanakh" [1869], p. 108). Up to 1864 the Ministry of Finance supplied Kokorev's Trans-Caspian Trading Company with iron at factory prices in order to enable him to engage in favorable trade with Persia (ibid., d. 59, "Zapiski departamentu manufaktury i torgovli" [1861], pp. 4–5; ibid., "Pis'mo departamentu manufaktury i torgovli" [27 iiunia 1864]," pp. 9–10). For the government's help in bailing out Kokorev from his financial disasters see Gindin, *Gosudarstvennyi bank*, pp. 277–79, which, nevertheless, underestimates the risks and losses of the entrepreneurs in order to demonstrate their dependence on the state.

1820 with profits made from manufacturing silk cloth, a business which he founded in Moscow following the occupation and fire in 1812. By the time of his death in the 1850s he was the largest employer of workers in the cotton textile industry in Moscow province. All of his five sons founded their own concerns and dynasties. Timofei Savvich established the first Russian textile factory to employ advanced cotton-spinning machinery. Like his friend Kokorev, he began to diversify in the postemancipation period, moving into banking, railroads, and other new fields. He was the only merchant member of the Moscow group and one of the few Russian merchants in general to take part in meetings on technical education sponsored by the Russian Technological Society. He accomplished all this even though he could not write correct Russian orthography to the end of his days. Among the many economic and cultural advantages that he secured through his large family were several marriages that linked him to other big merchant families in the Moscow group, including the Mamontovs, the Krestovnikovs, and the Khludovs.[40]

When Ivan and Nikolai Mamontov arrived in Moscow, their exploits as vodka tax farmers had already gained them a fortune and won them the admiration of Kokorev. Gradually, Kokorev brought them into his enterprises and introduced them to Pogodin and the literary world around *Moskvitianin*. But the Mamontov family's large-scale investments in railroads and banking did not really begin until the late 1850s and early 1860s when Ivan Fedorovich and his son Savva became close friends with Chizhov and the Shipovs.[41]

The Khludov family was united with both the Morozovs and the Mamontovs by the marriages of Aleksei Ivanovich's two daughters. Together with his brother Gerasim, Aleksei inherited a commercial company from their father, a former state peasant of the Old Belief who settled in Moscow after the Napoleonic Wars and turned from trading cotton to manufacturing cotton cloth. Through the intermediary of their older brother Savelii, a friend of Ludwig Knoop,

---

40. Iuksimovich, *Manufakturnaia*, 1:1–17, is the most complete source for the Morozov family enterprises. See also, however, Isaev, *Rol'*, pp. 162, 197; Liashchenko, *Istoriia* 2:444; Bill, "Morozovs"; *ZIRTO* (1871), no. 1, pp. 25–27, 70–71.

41. Barsukov, *Zhizn'*, 14:177, 285, 573–74; ibid., 15:52, 54–57; Buryshkin, *Moskva*, p. 168. When Ivan Fedorovich died in 1869, Dmitri Shipov wrote Chizhov how saddened he was by the passing of "our good comrade I. F. Mamontov. I was genuinely fond of him and respected him, and always enjoyed the most straightforward business relations with him and the most cordial reception from him" (ORBL, f. 332, carton 61, no. 8, D. Shipov to Chizhov, 18 July 1869). Shipov extended the same friendship to Savva Ivanovich inviting him to become a partner in several railroad ventures, including the Iaroslavl-Kostroma and the Donets lines (ibid., carton 61, no. 9, D. Shipov to Chizhov, 5 April 1871[?]; ibid., no. 10, 27 January 1876).

they helped to found the Krenholm Plant near Narva, soon to become the largest and technically the most advanced cotton mill in Russia. Later, they established their own factories in Riazan province with a steam engine and seven thousand spindles. Aleksei Ivanovich enrolled his three sons in good secondary schools in St. Petersburg to prepare them for a more active role in expanding his operations overseas. In 1860 he sent one son, Ivan, as his trade representative to Bremen, England, and the United States. As a result of this trip the Khludovs opened an office in Liverpool, a bold and rare initiative for a Russian merchant in those days. All three sons were among the first Russian merchants to visit and trade directly with Central Asia when the American Civil War cut off their supply of cotton from the United States.[42]

Another marital tie linked the Mamontovs to the Tret'iakovs, who were one of the oldest, if not one of the wealthiest, Moscow merchant families. The Tret'iakov flax manufactures in Moscow province had a larger number of workers concentrated in factory production, as opposed to the putting-out system, than any other textile firm, with the exception of the Morozovs.[43] Among Russian merchants flax earned a reputation as a national product in contrast to what Kokorev called "American cotton." Despite their business success the Tret'iakovs invested less in other companies than any other members of the Moscow group, due in part to their all-consuming passion for collecting art, which after the 1860s demanded much of their time and money.

The Krestovnikov family were early innovators in the textile industry, being the first to introduce velveteen into Russia. They kept abreast of technological changes abroad by importing English specialists and cotton-spinning machinery in the 1840s. Faced with such adversity as the Crimean War or the American Civil War, they diversified their holdings, building a stearin factory and a tannery in Kazan with the latest industrial processes and equipment. By the 1860s their enterprises had branch offices in Moscow, Irbitsk, Astrakhan, Rostov, Odessa, Tashkent, and Baku, with agents in Paris, London, and Berlin.[44]

The four brothers of the younger generation raised in the 1840s were provided with foreign governesses and tutors in the expectation that a knowledge of French and German would enable them to ex-

---

42. Shul'tse-Gevernits, *Krupnoe*, p. 39; Isaev, *Rol'*, p. 220; Rozhkova, *Ekonomicheskie*, pp. 154–56.

43. Isaev, *Rol'*, p. 162. The Tret'iakovs also founded in 1866 the Great Kostroma Works, which housed under one roof a larger number of spindles than anywhere else in Europe (Iuksimovich, *Manufakturnaia*, 2:2).

44. Krestovnikov, *Semeinaia*, 1:35–42.

pand the family's overseas operations and continue to import the latest technology. But like so many aspiring merchant families, the Krestovnikovs got the worst kind of foreigner, and the boys took an active dislike to both French and German. Only one of them ever learned languages well, and only Nikolai ever finished gymnasium. The others left school after their father died because their mother believed, like a good merchant's widow, that practical work in the family firm was the best preparation for business. All the brothers plunged enthusiastically into commercial activity and traveled widely in Russia and abroad. In Moscow they were appalled by the obtuse attitudes of the local merchant society and decided to settle in Kazan. There, they virtually created the entire public social life of the city. They organized the merchants' club, founded the Kazan Exchange and the Society of Mutual Aid for Shop Assistants, and established Kazan's first privately printed newspaper, to which Nikolai contributed articles on various industrial questions. He also served on the city duma and was a trustee of the Volga-Kama Bank founded by Kokorev. When a branch of Shipov's Society for the Encouragement of Russian Industry and Trade opened in Kazan, Nikolai was elected president.[45] The Krestovnikovs were related to the old merchant family of the Alekseevs and business associates of two other representatives of the Moscow entrepreneurial group, the Maliutins and the Chetverikovs.[46]

Both Soldatenkov and Liamin began their business careers in textiles and shared a keen appreciation of innovative techniques. By the mid-1870s Soldatenkov helped refinance and reorganize two of the largest calico factories in Moscow, the Guibner Company and the Tsindel' Company, the latter in association with Liamin, A. I. Khludov, and Ludwig Knoop.[47]

Although the economic interests of the Moscow entrepreneurs defined their functional role, they did not automatically determine their political consciousness. Many tax farmers and textile manufacturers continued to regard themselves as businessmen concerned solely with making and enjoying profits, while others confined their public role to fulfilling their soslovie obligations by serving in the town administration. The group did not yet possess the social cohesion necessary to expand a functional role into a political one. That would happen only when they acquired a strong sense of social responsibility: that is,

45. Ibid., 2:50, 56–57, 80, 97–98.
46. Ibid., 3:6–10, 18, 36–37, 54.
47. Brandt, *Inostrannye*, pt. 3, p. 44; Shchukin, "Iz vospominanii," pt. 2, pp. 83, 91, 99–100. The Giubner investment was one of the rare occasions when one of the Moscow group cooperated with foreign capitalists (*25-letie*, p. 7).

when they perceived a direct connection between the promotion of their private interests and the general welfare. This leads directly to a consideration of the second major characteristic of the group—a set of values that developed autonomously but reinforced their entrepreneurial role.

Cultural Values: Economics and Great Russian Nationalism

The social origins and ethical beliefs of the Moscow entrepreneurial group can be summarized with almost mathematical precision: Peasants of the Old Belief plus Slavophil merchants added to Pan-Slavic nobles equaled Great Russian nationalist entrepreneurs. Behind this schema, of course, lay a complex historical process. One wing of the Moscow entrepreneurial group was composed of former peasants who, with the exception of the Mamontovs, also adhered to the Old Belief: Kokorev, the Morozovs, the Khludovs, and Soldatenkov. The other wing was made up of déclassé nobles like Chizhov, Del'vig, Aksakov, Babst, and the Shipovs. In the center stood representatives of old merchant families who were partially Europeanized, including the Tret'iakovs, Krestovnikovs, Chetverikovs, and Liamin.

The popular sources of Great Russian nationalism were rooted in the social experience and cultural values of these three elements. The Old Believer peasants perceived the bureaucratic state and the fossilized church as corruptions of alien forces. They struggled for both their freedom from serfdom imposed by the state and the preservation of the old books and ritual from persecution by the church. At the same time they strove to take Russian commerce and industry out of the hands of foreigners and ethnic groups. In a word they sought to restore their version of a free, pure, and vigorous pre-Petrine society.

Descendants of the old merchant families, who could trace their lineage back to the eighteenth century, had begun to taste the fruits of a European-style education. A knowledge of foreign languages and foreign travel broadened their intellectual horizons, but also alerted them to the dangers of Western economic competition. How perfectly the Slavophil view of the universe suited their psychological needs. Like the Slavophil intellectuals of a generation earlier, the merchants' Westernized education and their Russian awareness led them to idealize a pre-Petrine past.

The déclassé nobles provided the modern secular thrust to the new ideology. To them cultural identity and economic strength were not enough. Through their first-hand experience with the Slavic liberation movement in Europe, they understood that political organization and a forward-looking ideology were also necessary to arouse Russia and check the encroachment of the West. Pan-Slavism owed much to Western-style nationalism, but it was also something more, something greater. These three strands were drawn together by the activities of the Moscow entrepreneurs into a potent combination of cultural pride, economic competitiveness, and political imperialism.

The peasant Old Believer wing gave dramatic expression to its search for a new identity by its lavish patronage of Old Russian culture. They specialized in paintings by the "Russian school," old Slavic manuscripts, and other antiquities. It was a short step from collecting art to subsidizing artists, architects, writers, and musicians. This led in turn to their supporting a wide range of artistic and intellectual endeavors, of which only the most spectacular, such as the founding of the Moscow Art Theater by the Morozovs and Mamontovs or of the Tret'iakov Gallery by the Tret'iakov brothers, are generally known. These activities proved to be not only sound investments but a means of gaining social approval. By preserving and popularizing the half-forgotten Russian national heritage in the face of Western cultural imports, even as they challenged Western textiles with their own manufactures, they showed themselves to be better Russians than the Westernized bureaucrats in St. Petersburg.

As early as the 1840s, K. T. Soldatenkov began to assemble his legendary collection of paintings. His most active period of buying followed a trip that he made to Italy in 1872, accompanied by his favorite Russian painter, A. A. Ivanov, whom he commissioned to acquire the most outstanding example of national art. "My desire," he wrote at the time, "is to build a collection of only Russian artists." By this time Soldatenkov was already a member of the council of the Moscow School of Painting and Architecture, which, as the center of the realist movement, trained and supported a generation of Russian painters. His country estate at Kuntsevo had long been a center for intellectuals who shared his deep interest in uncovering the many layers of Old Russian culture, including the historian I. E. Zabelin, the lithographer A. A. Kozlov, H. Kh. Ketcher, the translator of Shakespeare whose work Soldatenkov published, and members of the famous family of merchant-collectors, the Shchukins.[48]

Soldatenkov also began publishing historical documents and monographs that lacked a commercial market in a public-spirited effort to preserve and spread the popular, nationalist elements in Russian culture. When, for example, the Imperial Russian Library needed funds to bring out critical editions of rare books and original manu-

48. Shchukin, "Iz vospominanii," pt. 2, p. 101.

scripts of the pre-Petrine era, Soldatenkov helped to defray the cost. He founded his own publishing house, and with the assistance of his friends M. S. Shchepkin, the famous actor, and his son, N. M. Shchepkin, the editor, he made available to the public large, inexpensive editions of the Russian romantic poets N. P. Ogarev (1856), A. I. Polezhaev (1857), and the forerunner of the narodnik realists, A. V. Kol'tsov (1856). These were followed by two important collections of folklore edited by one of the leading ethnographers of the time, A. N. Afanas'ev: *Narodnye russkie legendy* (Popular Russian Legends) in 1859 and *Narodnye skazki* (Popular Fairy Tales) in 1858–59. In 1858 he published the popular eyewitness account *Zapiski ob osade Sevastopole* (Notes on the Siege of Sevastopol) by N. V. Berg, one of the so-called young editors of Pogodin's Slavophil journal *Moskvitianin*.[49] In characteristically romantic fashion all of these works glorified the rich and heroic traditions of the common people of Russia.

In similar fashion, T. S. Morozov was drawn into the secular culture of Moscow through his patronage of the arts and publishing. Having assured his children of an excellent education, which he lacked, he supported their enthusiasms for Russian culture, even though this effort carried them away from the family business. One daughter, Anna, became the wife of the historian G. F. Karpov, whose work on seventeenth-century Russia emphasized the religio-moral strength of the people as the crucial element in the drive for unification of the Eastern Slavs. Morozov joined his son-in-law in managing a publishing house that printed numerous works in Russian history. Following Karpov's death, Anna Timofeevna became a patroness of the Moscow Society of History and Antiquities. One of Morozov's sons, Sergei, married into the nobility (the sister of A. V. Krivoshein, later deputy minister of finance), but remained true to the Old Russian traditions. He founded the Museum of Handicrafts in Moscow and, in general, tried to stimulate the traditional crafts in the face of the very industrial progress his father helped foster. Morozov's most famous son, Savva, was the great patron of the Moscow Art Theater and the friend of Stanislavskii and Nemirovich-Danchenko.[50]

The cultural activities of A. I. Khludov represent the most dramatic shift in allegiance from the Old Believer community to the cult of the Russian people. Already known in the 1860s as a collector of Old Russian books and manuscripts, Khludov abjured his faith, embraced edinoverie, and, together with his close friend N. I. Subbotin, professor at the Moscow Ecclesiastical Academy, formed in 1872 the Brother-

---

49. Grits, *Shchepkin*, pp. 574, 609; Barsukov, *Zhizn'*, 12:410–13.
50. Kliuchevskii, "Chtenie," pp. 41–45; Buryshkin, *Moskva*, pp. 114–18.

hood of the Metropolitan St. Peter, dedicated to winning over the schismatics. Khludov became treasurer of the organization, covered its deficits out of his own pocket for ten years, played host to its meetings in his house, and purchased a large, valuable collection of seventeenth-century polemical works on the Old Believers in order to support Subbotin's research and publication on the schism. Moreover, his important collection of books on the early history of the Czechs, which was described by Kollar, testifies to his interest in the Slavic movement. He bought his large Serbian collection from the well-known Pan-Slav A. F. Gil'ferding (Hilferding). Although he lacked any formal schooling, he gave his daughters an excellent European-style education, which enabled them to play important roles of their own as patronesses of the arts.[51]

Although the Old Believer collectors set the tone for the other merchants in the group, Pavel Mikhailovich Tret'iakov and Savva Mamontov soon eclipsed their mentors in the size and scale of their patronage. The founder of the largest private picture gallery of national art in Russia, Pavel Tret'iakov began collecting paintings of the Flemish school in imitation of the Hermitage. Within a few years, however, according to the great critic of the realist school V. V. Stasov, the collections of Soldatenkov, Khludov, and Kokorev "could not help but influence" Tret'iakov to shift his attention to Russian painters. His house in Moscow became a haven for them, especially for N. V. Nevrev, who pioneered a realistic portrayal of Russian peasant life. By the time Tret'iakov wrote his first will in 1860, he was determined to construct a national gallery for Russian art. Over the next thirty years he, Soldatenkov, and Savva Mamontov liberally supported the Peredvizhniki (Wanderers) and helped them to become the dominant group in the Russian art world. Pavel Tret'iakov exercised the same patriarchal authority in the role of patron as he did in that of merchant. His personal taste influenced the choice of subject and even the style of painters like Repin and Perov. He insisted that his famous portrait gallery include likenesses of Ivan Aksakov, Dostoevsky, and even Katkov, as well as Nekrasov and Tolstoy. The enormous size of his purchases—over 800,000 rubles—enabled him to help move the Peredvizhniki in a more nationalistic direction.[52]

His friendship with the Mamontov family, based on common busi-

51. V. S. Markov, "K istorii," pp. 51–53, 125, 184, 238; Popov, *Opisanie*, preface (no pagination; the list of works occupies 664 pages); Subbotin, *V pamiat'*, throughout; *Perepiska Tret'iakova*, p. 55.

52. Valkenier, *Russian*, pp. 65–67. For the important and convincing argument that the Peredvizhniki represented a Russian national school rather than a radical critique of Russian society see Valkenier, "Peredvizhniki," pp. 247–65.

ness and artistic interests, was consolidated by his marriage to Savva Ivanovich's sister Vera, who was perfectly suited by temperament and education to preside over the expanding artistic and musical salon of the Tret'iakov house.[53] One daughter of their marriage, Vera Pavlovna, married the great Russian pianist-pedagogue Alexander Siloti and left a vivid memoir of the Tret'iakov family's patronage of musicians. Pavel Tret'iakov's less famous brother Sergei was a leading patron of Russian national music and a founder and strong supporter of the Imperial Russian Musical Society, as well as a backer of Anton and Nikolai Rubinshtein, the founders of the St. Petersburg and Moscow conservatories, respectively, who also came from merchant families and were Sergei's boyhood friends.[54]

When, in 1870, Savva Mamontov acquired the old Aksakov estate of Abramtsovo and turned it into Russia's most famous artist colony, he performed, consciously or not, one of the great symbolic acts in the development of the Russian national movement. The manor house where Gogol read aloud *Dead Souls* and the Slavophils gathered now sheltered the new artistic and musical life of the Peredvizhniki and the Private Opera of Fedor Shaliapin. Combining matchless taste and generous spending, Mamontov deserves more credit than anyone else for restoring Moscow as the cultural center of Russia in the last quarter of the nineteenth century. In the arts, as in business, he championed private initiative against the bureaucratic domination of the Petersburg court and the Academy of Fine Arts. He perceived a vital spiritual connection between the industrial and the artistic life of Russia. Upon the completion of the Donets railroad, which he and the Shipovs financed, he commissioned V. M. Vasnetsov, then a young and virtually unknown artist, to decorate the main station with a triptych symbolizing through the imagery of Russian fairy tales the marriage of technology and popular national traditions.[55]

A. I. Mamontov is less well known as a patron than is his brother, but his support of the architect V. A. Gartman helped accomplish for architecture what Savva Ivanovich achieved for painting. Gartman (or Hartman) is famous in the West as the author of the paintings that inspired Mussorgsky to compose *Pictures at an Exhibition*. But he was also and primarily a leading representative of the movement in architecture to revive the Old Russian style by means of applying ornamental devices borrowed from Russian handicrafts to the decoration of buildings. He designed A. I. Mamontov's dacha, his printing house,

53. Botkina, *Tret'iakov*, pp. 24, 27, 36, 52–54; Stasov, "Tret'iakov," pp. 573, 581, 597–99.
54. Siloti, *V dome*, pp. 18–19, 83–87, 251–63.
55. V. S. Mamontov, *Vospominaniia*, p. 25; see also Polenova, *Abramtsevo*.

and the wooden National Theater in Moscow, which was much altered in its final form. On the advice of Tret'iakov, Savva Mamontov bought several of Gartman's models and donated them to the Museum of the Academy of Artists.[56] When Gartman planned the military wing of the Moscow Polytechnical Museum in ornate "pseudo-Russian" style, he was expressing in this fusing of Russian folk traditions and modern technology a viewpoint similar to that of Vasnetsov and other artists of the Peredvizhnik school who were subsidized by the Moscow entrepreneurs.

Thus, the Moscow entrepreneurs asserted their fundamental belief in the superiority of the spontaneous, popular, private, and national over the bureaucratic, aristocratic, and foreign elements in Russian life. They claimed to place industry at the service of culture and, where possible, culture at the service of industry. By showing the mutual dependence of economic development and national consciousness, they provided, at least from their point of view, an alternative to obscurantism and backwardness, on the one hand, and crass materialism and foreign domination, on the other.

The social movement of Old Believer peasants into the merchant soslovie was accompanied by a secularization of their faith in the form of a nativist culture. They carred with them those representatives of the older merchant families whose contacts with patronizing foreigners kindled their latent patriotism. Together, they embraced the Slavophils' belief that somehow Russia could industrialize without losing its soul to the West. Although Khomiakov and Koshelev had preached this doctrine in the 1840s and 1850s, their philosophical arguments had passed over the heads of the merchantry. A better education for some and the direct emotional and sensual attraction of Russian art for others aroused a handful of merchants to perceive the higher mission of their calling.

If art facilitated a spiritual reconciliation, politics aided a pragmatic integration of the Old Believer merchantry into Russian society. The first days of the reign of Alexander II showed signs of greater tolerance toward the Old Belief. The emancipation of the serfs reconciled all but the most extreme sects to the secular authority of the state. When the Polish revolt broke out in 1863, the wave of patriotic demonstrations that swept the country also enveloped the Old Believers. A "most devoted letter" to the tsar from the Preobrazhenskii community was a ringing declaration of Russian patriotism. It still drew the distinction between religious beliefs and national feelings—"We retain our ritual but we are thy loyal subjects"—but it was no longer

56. *RBS*, 4:242–43 (V. A. Gartman); Nivitskii, *Istoriia* 2:189; *Perepiska Tret'iakova*, pp. 38, 226.

simply a question of obedience—"We are devoted to thee, Tsar Liberator, with our hearts." The community offered to defend the motherland against "the enemy in Poland in revolt" and to sacrifice "all our possessions and our lives" for "thy throne and the Russian land."[57] From this point on, the main Old Believer communities were counted even by the police to be among the most steadfast defenders of the throne. Subsequent attempts by Polish agitators to arouse the Old Believer peasants in the traditionally rebellious provinces of the middle Volga by invoking the magical names of Peter III and Pugachov fell on deaf ears.[58] The way was open for the Old Believer merchants to merge with the Pan-Slavic movement.

It was precisely along this alternate path that the noble-intellectuals in the Moscow group were moving toward the same conclusion as the merchants. The larger national goals of the Russian people could be achieved only through the development of the country's economic resources. For Chizhov, the Shipovs, Del'vig, and Ivan Aksakov direct exposure to the Slavic liberation movement, rather than Old Russian culture, provided both the impetus and the justification for their entrepreneurial activities. Above all, it inspired them to seek practical ways for Russia to escape the political and economic domination imposed by the Germans and the Austrians on the Western and Southern Slavs and to rescue their enslaved brethren in the Balkans from the Turkish yoke.

Chizhov's interest in the Slavic lands was first kindled in 1843 during his travels in Istria, Dalmatia, and Montenegro. There, he later confessed, the popular enthusiasm for him as "a Russian brother" converted him to Slavophilism. In the next few years he supplied religious books and objects for worship to Dalmatian Slavs, traveled widely in the Balkans and Central Europe, and met many spokesmen for the Slavic cause from Hanka, Kollar, and Safarik in Prague to Mickiewicz in Paris and Ljudevit Gaj in Croatia. In Italy he met Gogol and the Russian painters there, especially A. A. Ivanov, who later became the favorite and the artistic adviser of Soldatenkov. Returning home, he eagerly joined the Slavophil circle and wrote extensively in their thick journals *Russkaia Beseda* (Russian Conversation) and *Moskovskii Sbornik* (Moscow Magazine).[59]

---

57. "Pol'skii matezh," p. 159.
58. Vysotskii, "Pol'skii bunt," p. 388.
59. "Vospominaniia Chizhova," pp. 243–48, 253–57. According to the editor this was probably an excerpt from the draft of answers given by Chizhov to the Third Section after his arrest in 1847 upon crossing the Russian frontier. As early as 1845, Chizhov had considered the possibility of returning to Russia and editing a journal devoted to combating Western materialist influences in Russia (I. Rozanov, "Iz perepiski," 105–42).

As editor and publicist his credo was a popular national industrialism with Pan-Slavic overtones. "Political economy, trade, and industry," he confided to his diary, opened "the real path to uplift the lower strata of the people. In these fields, according to my views, the merchants ought to step forth into public life, for the merchants are chosen from the people. The merchants are the primary basis of our historical life, that is, they are strictly Great Russian."[60] Among the many industrial enterprises that he championed, none took precedence over the great southern railroad linking Moscow to the Black Sea. Although he and the Moscow group lacked the capital to launch the venture, he repeatedly proclaimed in the press its strategic and political importance in preventing a repetition of the Crimean War and strengthening Russia's position in the Balkans. Throughout his life he strove in vain to interest the Moscow merchants in commercial ventures that would tie them to the future development of the Balkan Slavs and weaken the influence of the Catholic Poles. No one else in the Moscow group was as single-minded in his efforts to defend the economic heartland of Russia—the central industrial region—from the penetration of foreigners and ethnic minorities.[61]

Among the Shipovs, Sergei Pavlovich once again provided the model for his family's attitudes on the Slavic problem. During the Russo-Turkish War of 1828 he became deeply committed to the idea of the liberation of the Orthodox population from Turkish control. A veteran of the Polish revolt of 1831–32 and director of the government commission on internal, spiritual, and education affairs in the Kingdom of Poland in 1837, he strove to assimilate the Poles through a

Only in 1857 was this hope realized when Chizhov became editor of *Vestnik promyshlennosti*. Meanwhile, Chizhov wrote for the Slavophil press, including an article on the Russian artists whom the merchants were beginning to patronize, "O rabotakh russkikh khudozhnikov v Rime," *Moskovskii sbornik*, 1846. Still, Chizhov declined Koshelev's proposal that he become the editor of the last real Slavophil journal, *Russkaia beseda*, whose tendency would be "pure Russian and Orthodox," but he agreed to write regularly for it (ORBL, f. 332, carton 35, no. 29, A. I. Koshelev to Chizhov, 25 April, 24 May, 20 June, 23 July, 2 September 1856).

60. ORBL, f. 332, carton 2, no. 9, "Dnevnik" (entry 22 March 1857).

61. On the southern line see the series of his articles in *Aktsioner*, 17 and 24 August, 26 November, 7 and 21 December 1863, and later on the southwest line in *Den'*, 28 November, 5 and 12 December 1864, and 23 January 1865, in which he attacks the "yid-contractors" for causing poverty in the south. Chizhov tried to recruit Russian shareholders in a joint-stock company for the development of trade and industry in Dalmatia in which Bishop Strossmayer, the ardent champion of Yugoslavism, was the major shareholder (ORBL, f. 332, carton 79, no. 3, "Obrashchenie k russkim predprinimateliam," 1 October 1869). For the formation of the Society for the Resettlement of the Western Provinces see below chapter 5.

policy of enlightened russification.[62] His ideas were warmly endorsed by his younger brothers, who later became active in Slavic benevolent societies and supported movements for Slavic unity under the auspices of a powerful, industrialized Russian Empire.

The enfant terrible of the Pan-Slavic movement, Ivan Aksakov, made his first journey to the Slavic areas of Europe only in 1859 when he carried with him Khomiakov's "Address to the Serbs." But by then his association with the Slavic cause already had a long history. In 1849, much like Chizhov, he had been arrested for harboring subversive thoughts about the liberation of the Slavs.[63] Historians have rightly emphasized that he was primarily interested in a political solution by political means. But it should be added that ever since his work on the Ukrainian markets, he had appreciated the need for commerce and industry to supplement the military power of the empire. On a more personal level he also required merchant subsidies for his own journalistic ventures. Without the direct financial support of the merchants in the Moscow group he could never have published his Pan-Slavic message in the pages of *Den'* (Day), *Moskva*, and *Rus'*. Although he had greater reservations about becoming a businessman than did other noble members of the group, he turned his directorship of the Moscow Merchants' Society of Mutual Credit into powerful political capital. During the crisis of 1875–78 over the Eastern question, the main offices of the bank, under his initiative, became the center for fund raising and recruiting volunteers for the struggle in the Balkans against the Turks.[64]

Baron A. I. Del'vig shared many of the views of the Pan Slavists, even though he was born into a Lutheran, Baltic noble family, trained as an engineer, and employed in the ministerial bureaucracy. Here was a case of a convert to Orthodoxy who readily perceived Russia's attraction for the Western Slavs. During his army service in the Hungarian campaign of 1849, he was deeply moved by the warm reception that the Slovaks gave to their Russian "brothers." Subsequently, through his friendship with the Shipovs and his participation in

62. S. P. Shipov, "Vospominaniia," pp. 189–90; *RBS*, 23:297–98.
63. For a thoughtful study of Aksakov's painful and slow conversion to militant Pan-Slavism see Lukashevich, *Aksakov*, especially pp. 21–42, and also Riasanovsky, *Russia*, pp. 52–55.
64. "Incidentally," Aksakov wrote Chizhov, "the Mutual Credit Society has been turned into some kind of political center; here in my name and the name of the Slavonic Committees telegrams and letters are sent from the theater of the uprising, from the Slavic countries—volunteers for the rising are recruited and money is received on current accounts especially opened by me for this affair" (ORBL, f. 332, carton 15, no. 10, Aksakov to Chizhov, 26 May 1876).

Chaadaev's Moscow circle in 1852 he met several Slavophils, including Aksakov, and became very close to Chizhov.[65] Disappointed with the professional performance of his colleagues in the Ministry of Transportation, he was equally opposed to the influx of French engineers to build the first Russian railroad network. Throwing in his lot with the Moscow group, he assumed a role as their "inside man" in the chancelleries of St. Petersburg and furnished them with invaluable confidential information on railroad concessions and other industrial ventures. He was the director and one of the founders of the Moscow-Iaroslavl railroad.

Babst also came from the Baltic nobility, and his conversion to militant Slavophilism owed much to the same sources that influenced Del'vig. Having received an excellent early education from his father, who was a graduate of Gottingen, he went on to study at Riga gymnasium and Moscow University, where he concentrated on literature and history. Babst formulated his views on political economy under the influence of a leading figure in the German historical school, Wilhelm Roscher, whose work he translated into Russian. Intellectually, he was already disposed to accept the Slavophil interpretation that economic development reflected the peculiarities of a country's geography, history, and culture. Yet as late as 1857 he still believed that these very factors dictated an economic policy based upon large-scale export of agricultural produce and foreign loans. Called to Moscow University from Kazan, he soon became a frequent visitor at Pogodin's and the Slavophil salons. Chizhov invited him to coedit *Vestnik promyshlennosti*, and his Slavophil friends elected him to the Society of the Lovers of Russian Literature. Gradually, his economic views changed, and by the mid-sixties he was a determined defender of the Moscow merchants' industrial program, including high protective tariffs. His expert financial knowledge was a great asset to the group, arming them against the naive antiindustrial views of Pogodin and advancing their views among skeptical bureaucrats. His unique position as tutor to two successive heirs to the throne, Nikolai and Alexander Alexandrovich, enabled him to propagate the ideas of the Moscow group at the highest level of government.[66]

65. Del'vig, *Moi vospominaniia*, 2:207–8, 233–36, 288, 340–41, 345.

66. *RBS*, 2:387; Babst, *O nekotorykh*, comes very close to Kokorev's views; idem "Teoriia i praktika," *Ekonomicheskii ukazatel'*, no. 5 (1857): 108–15, in which he defended the merchants against the nobles' criticism that they were to blame for high grain prices and advocated a railroad system and gradual reduction of tariffs; idem, "Istoricheskii," ibid., pp. 94–142, a review of Roscher's *System der Volkswirtschaft*; idem, "Obozrenie promyshlennosti i torgovli v Rossii," *VP*, no. 10 (1860): 73–104, begins his shift away from faith in foreign loans and foreign technology; Barsukov, *Zhizn'*, 14:278; ibid., 15:315; ibid., 16:136, 213, 216, 489; ibid., 17:406, 414, 417, 437, 452; ibid., 18:11–12; ibid.,

The Slavic liberation movement, as an almost natural extension of Slavophilism, also touched the lives of some merchant members of the group. The Mamontov family had its interest in Pan-Slavism kindled by Pogodin. In 1841 he gave his son a letter of introduction and sent him to accompany Ivan and Nikolai Mamontov on a visit to the great Czech Pan-Slav Safarik in Prague. When Pogodin himself followed, the Austrian police interpreted the trips, which may have been innocent enough to begin with, as an international plot. They came to regard poor Safarik as "the leader of the Russo-Slovene party" which aimed at breaking up the Hapsburg Monarchy.[67] The Mamontovs quickly learned that cultural ties with the Slavic peoples were political dynamite. Given their practical turn of mind, they, like the rest of the Moscow entrepreneurial group, perceived that the success of Russia's mission as a leader of the Slavs would depend as much upon national economic power as upon cultural ties. The question was whether the government could be persuaded to accept this view.

In general the attitude of the Moscow entrepreneurial group toward secular authority was ambivalent. This is not surprising in light of the potential conflict between their patriotism and their dislike of the Petersburg bureaucracy. Most of them had suffered indignities at the hands of officials. Old Believers and sectarians, such as Kokorev and Soldatenkov, were frequently under police surveillance, while others, such as Chizhov and Aksakov, had been arrested before the Crimean War for their excessive zeal toward the Slavic cause. Members of the group figured prominently in the famous list of subversives compiled by Governor-General Zakrevskii in his report to the head of the Third Section, V. A. Dolgorukov. Of the twenty-eight names eleven were either members of the group, like Kokorev, Babst, I. F. Mamontov, Aksakov, and Soldatenkov, or their "agents" and clients, like P. S. Stepanov, N. F. Pavlov, M. S. Shchepkin, N. M. Shchepkin, N. Kh. Ketcher, and Osip Ger.[68] In the Shipov family,

21:1–2, 64; ORBL, f. 332, carton 16, no. 2, I. K. Babst to F. V. Chizhov, 3 March 1857, 19 November 1859, and undated [1860?]. For the debate with Pogodin see *Aktsioner*, 16 July, 4 August 1861.

67. Barsukov, *Zhizn'*, 6:393.

68. Ibid., 17:39–40. Kokorev was placed under police surveillance because he displayed a "provocative sign" on his house, supported needy students, and was rumored to be "a Red." Kokorev complained that surveillance ruined a man's credit and wondered how a man who invested all his capital in enterprises of national importance could be so characterized (ORBL, f. 231, vol. 3, carton 6, no. 5, pp. 1–3). Soldatenkov was secretly investigated by the Third Section because it was rumored that he and Shchepkin had sent articles to Herzen for publication in *Kolokol*. A thorough report on all members of Soldatenkov's circle revealed no evidence to corroborate the charge (Grits, *Shchepkin*, pp. 660–65).

Sergei narrowly escaped a brush with the law because he had been a member of the Union of Welfare in the 1820s. His nephew, Alexander Pavlovich's son, was not so lucky. In 1862 he was arrested and imprisoned for revolutionary activity. Because the Shipovs, like all members of the Moscow group, considered themselves loyal subjects, the government's arbitrariness and unfounded suspicions irritated them all the more. "I am personally known from my articles and brochures," wrote Alexander Shipov to the head of the Third Section in defense of his son, "as a man who follows the movement of progress as initiated by the government, but with a possibly conservative direction, and I could not lead my children into subversion."[69]

In their eyes the government was not only arbitrary in its actions but lax in protecting the interests of the people. The "stupidity," "conceit," and "ignorance" of "the army of pen-pushers," as Chizhov contemptuously called the bureaucrats, blocked any movement toward the improvement of Russian industry.[70] "What we need are [political] tactics," wrote Dmitri Shipov to Chizhov, "and we must take action skillfully against our internal enemies, who are almost as bad as the external ones."[71] The actions taken make it clear that the internal enemies were bureaucrats, especially those associated with the Ministry of Finance who tied economic development to cooperation with foreigners, ethnic minorities in the empire, Baltic Germans, Jews, Poles, Greeks, and Armenians.

Despite their dislike of bureaucrats the Moscow group firmly rejected any form of political opposition to autocracy. Sergei Shipov refused to join the Decembrists, and Chizhov condemned them.[72] Aksakov at his most ecstatic never challenged basic institutions of government. Merchants like Khludov, Liamin, Morozov, Mamontov, Tret'iakov, and Soldatenkov served faithfully in the town government in Moscow. Yet even they hesitated to rally behind the more radical Pan-Slavic petitions of their noble contemporaries, like Prince Cherkassky, Samarin, and Aksakov himself.[73] At most, they favored a

69. S. P. Shipov, "Vospominaniia," p. 163; Alekseev and Koz'min, *Politicheskie*, p. 103.

70. Chizhov, "Novopodiatnyi vopros ob unichtozhenii privilegii," *VP*, no. 9, pt. 2 (1861): 95–96. See also Genkin, "Obshchestvenno-politicheskaia," p. 98, which softens the strong antibureaucratic tone of *Vestnik promyshlennosti*.

71. ORBL, f. 332, carton 61, no. 6, Dmitri Shipov to Chizhov, undated [1857].

72. Ibid., carton 1, no. 1, "Dnevnik" (entry 22 August 1826), where Chizhov calls the Decembrists "scoundrels" and suggests that Nicholas I was merciful in hanging "only five" of them. S. P. Shipov, "Vospominaniia," p. 164, where Shipov reports his efforts to talk his friend Pestel out of a rebellion. Later in 1829 the Shipovs tried to get pardons for the exiled Decembrists (Kokorev, *Ekonomicheskie*, p. 8).

73. Naidenov, *Vospominaniia*, 2:17–18. The submissiveness of the merchants was graphically demonstrated by the humiliating resignation of Liamin as head of the Mos-

form of decentralization best expressed in the words of Sergei Shipov: "For the successful development of the productive forces of the people, its wealth and well being and even the power of the state itself, [it is desirable] to create governing institutions in such a way so that each region would have its administrative autonomy and would live its own life." Lest this be misinterpreted as a signal for ethnic diversity, Shipov quickly added that the ties to the center would be guaranteed by an all-Russian army, including recruits from all tribes and regions, an administrative elite of merit appointed from the center, the active diffusion of "the general spirit of Nationality" (narodnost), and government assistance in the industrial development of the entire empire.[74] All members of the group were willing, up to a point, to seek government support for their entrepreneurial activities in the form of direct subsidies, privileges, and concessions. The questions were, then, how to influence the government without challenging it and how to court power without submitting to it. The answers lay in their being able to define a broadly based political program and then get the government to carry it out.

---

cow duma following an insulting remark by Governor-General P. P. Durnovo concerning his sartorial appearance on an official visit (ibid., 2:33).
74. S. P. Shipov, O gosudarstvennom, pp. 3, 21–22.

CHAPTER 5

THE MOSCOW

ENTREPRENEURIAL GROUP:

THE NEW STYLE

OF POLITICS

The Moscow entrepreneurs believed that to overcome the backwardness that threatened Russia's vitality and independence, the economic development of the country had to be placed in the hands of the most enterprising, hard working, and loyal elements in the population—namely, themselves and their allies. First-hand experience with the working population had taught them that St. Petersburg was too remote from daily life and too immersed in routine and paperwork to respond directly and intelligently to the needs of the people. They were equally convinced that reliance on foreign skills and capital could turn Russia into a dependency of the West without a single shot having been fired. Their object was to avoid the twin dangers of bureaucratic paralysis and foreign control. Their political response was a combination of theoretical statements and practical activities. This is hardly surprising given the two equally strong tendencies among its members toward intellectual and business interests. So closely intertwined were their ideas and their joint ventures that it would be difficult and confusing to separate them at this point in the analysis. It seems appropriate, therefore, to show how their political program grew out of a network of personal communication, association, and interaction covering a broad spectrum of public life. This approach combines the third and fourth characteristics of the Moscow entrepreneurs as an interest group outlined in the preceding chapter.

The Network: A Subsidized Press

Restricted by the government's prohibition on the formation of formal political associations, clubs, and societies, members of the Moscow group exchanged ideas and organized for political action through a private network of personal correspondence and meetings and a variety of public ventures, such as sponsoring and publishing newspapers and pooling capital to launch joint enterprises. In mid-nineteenth-century Russia the idea that a newspaper could represent a well-defined economic interest group was still a new one. Alexander and Dmitri Shipov founded and financed *Vestnik promyshlennosti* (1858–61) and invited Chizhov to be its first editor. In the words of Dmitri Shipov, its primary goal was "the development of industry and consequently of the wealth of the people together with their enlightenment."[1] Chizhov sought to recruit a wide range of journalistic talent, including I. K. Babst, who accepted his invitation, and Kokorev, who did not, while the Shipovs attempted to round up financial backing from wealthy merchants.[2]

From the outset the paper adopted a strongly promerchant stance. In their articles Babst, Chizhov, and Alexander Shipov mapped out a program featuring the rapid expansion of credit for trade and industry, the development of a mass internal market, railroad construction by private companies, the domestic production of rails and rolling stock, and a revision of the moderate duties in the tariff of 1857. They insisted, moreover, on the right of the press to expose the shortcomings of industrial enterprises and bureaucratic agencies. Above all, they deplored the tendency of the St. Petersburg bankers, bureaucrats, and journalists to discriminate against the Russian merchants in favor of foreigners or state enterprises. They did not hide behind Aesopian language: "If the government does not make credit available to the merchantry in the Moscow branch of the Commercial Bank under more favorable circumstances," wrote Shipov, "then bankruptcies will become numerous and significant and our internal trade will be severely shaken." Chizhov wrote: "Those who accuse the industrial strata of the people of backwardness and muteness are the same who make every effort, prompted by bureaucratic conceit, bureaucratic ignorance, and bureaucratic pomposity, to lord over every-

1. ORBL, f. 332, carton 10, no. 74, Chizhov to A. P. and D. P. Shipov (undated [1857]); ibid., carton 61, no. 6, Dmitri Shipov to Chizhov, 7 December 1857. See also Owen, "Merchants," pp. 26–38.
2. Ibid., carton 16, no. 2, I. K. Babst to Chizhov, 3 March 1857; ibid., carton 33, no 19, V. A. Kokorev to Chizhov, 29 May 1858; ibid., carton 61, no. 6, Dmitri Shipov to Chizhov, 9 August 1859.

thing in a bureaucratic fashion and stifle everything living and not wrapped in a bureaucratic form."[3]

Vestnik promyshlennosti sponsored and defended the creation of the Society for the Assistance of the Development of National Industry as the first organization that would provide a moral basis for the business activities and the very social existence of the merchantry. In contrast to the social clubs, the bureaucratic manufacturing and trade councils, and the commercial exchange, this society would give the representatives of trade and industry a real voice in the economic affairs of the country.[4]

At the same time, Aksakov sought to involve the merchantry in another kind of politics. By launching his own newspaper, *Parus* (The Sail), he hoped to bring the Slavic cause out of the abstract, learned, and scientific realm into the popular arena, "to make it a question close to our merchantry and in general to literate simple people."[5]

The response to both journalistic ventures by the mass of the Moscow merchants was disappointingly slow and feeble. Aksakov's paper was shut down by the authorities after two issues, but his main complaint was leveled at his putative audience: "The merchants did not give a kopek to the Slavic cause," he wrote.[6] In 1860, after *Vestnik promyshlennosti* gave ample proof of its promerchant sentiments, a small number of Moscow merchants contributed directly to its support. Among the most prominent were T. S. Morozov, the Mamontovs, A. I. Khludov, I. A. Liamin, K. T. Soldatenkov, Maliutin, and V. Rukavishnikov.[7] The few differences that existed between the editors and backers over editorial policy and finances could not mask the importance of this unprecedented collaboration between merchants and intellectuals. The first concrete step had been taken in the formation of the Moscow entrepreneurial group.

Despite merchant subsidies, *Vestnik* was not a commercial success. Clearly, the majority of the Moscow merchants had not yet perceived the wider responsibilities of their social role. Subsequently, Babst left for St. Petersburg, where he still kept in touch, but Chizhov was left

---

3. Alexander Shipov, "Kuda i otchego ischezli u nas den'gi?" *VP*, no. 7 (1860): 71–72 and throughout; Chizhov, "Novopodiatnyi vopros," ibid., p. 96. See also I. K. Babst, "Obozrenie promyshlennosti i torgovli v Rossii," *VP*, no. 10 (1860): 73–104; idem, "Sovremennye nuzhdy nashego narodnogo khoziaistva," *VP*, no. 3 (1860):203–48; and Alexander Shipov, "Prepiatsviia i neudobstva nashei vnutrennei torgovli," *VP*, no. 9 (1861): 164–80.

4. "Obozrenie promyshlennosti i torgovli v Rossii," *VP*, no. 10 (1861):1–31.

5. *Aksakov v'ego pismakh*, 4:2, Aksakov to M. F. Raevskii, 22 June 1858.

6. Ibid., 4:18, Aksakov to Raevskii, 13 April 1859.

7. ORBL, f. 332, carton 37, no. 21, I. A. Liamin to Chizhov, 2 December 1862; Laverychev, "Russkie kapitalisty," p. 29.

by himself to edit *Aktsioner*, formerly the supplement to *Vestnik* and now funded by Morozov, Liamin, Khludov, Maliutin, and others.[8] It was rescued from collapse in 1863 when Aksakov offered to merge it with his recently established daily, *Den'*. Capitalizing on its founder's popularity and the "hurrah patriotism" of that time, this publication had almost eight thousand subscribers.[9] Once the excitement of the Polish uprising died down, however, subscriptions fell off, and in 1865 the paper closed.

Threatened by a tariff agreement between the German Confederation and Russia, the Moscow entrepreneurs felt keenly the need for a new press organ. With Chizhov again in the role of intermediary, Aksakov and the Moscow merchants signed an agreement in Morozov's house on 9 October 1866 which set the financial and editorial conditions for *Moskva*. Assured of the editorship, Aksakov promised to devote no less than two out of twenty-four columns in the paper to commercial and industrial affairs and to permit either Chizhov or Babst to write one editorial a week on economic problems. Once again, however, the irrepressible Aksakov offended several high officials and even some of his merchant backers. He could not be restrained from criticizing the government on two sensitive points: foreign policy and police powers. Meeting at Morozov's, members of the Moscow entrepreneurial group reluctantly reconfirmed Aksakov as editor, but he could not be saved from the aroused censorship.[10] Following three warnings, the government suppressed *Moskva* and quickly rejected Aksakov's brash attempt to revive the paper under the title *Moskvich*. Reduced to desperate financial straits, Aksakov received subsidies from Morozov and Liamin until they found him a job in the Moscow Merchants' Society of Mutual Credit, where Chizhov was president. Thus, the embattled Pan-Slavist was launched on a business career.[11]

During this time the Shipovs had been increasingly concerned over

8. ORBL, f. 332, carton 10, no. 43, Chizhov to Liamin, 4 January 1862.

9. Lemke, *Epokha*, p. 192; cf. *Russkaia periodicheskaia pechat'*, p. 414, which incorrectly gives a figure of over seven thousand "circulation."

10. ORBL, f. 332, carton 15, no. 5, Aksakov to Chizhov, 24 September 1866; *Aksakov v'ego pismakh*, 4:90–91, Aksakov to Raevskii, 13 October 1866; Laverychev, "Russkie kapitalisty," pp. 32–34.

11. TsGAOR, f. 722, op. 1, d. 514, "Zapiska iz dela po raportu Ministerstva Vnutrennykh Del o prekrashcheniia gazety Moskva," pp. 13–15. At this time, Aksakov was still suspicious that the Moscow merchants were willing to support him only so long as his paper could be of some use in advancing their views on the tariff revision, and he wanted Chizhov to obtain guarantees from them on financing, staffing, and even a month's vacation at half pay (ORBL, f. 322, carton 15, no. 5, Aksakov to Chizhov [undated (1868)]). On Aksakov's work in the bank see ibid., no. 7, Aksakov to Chizhov, 4 and 10 June, 23 December 1869, 4 March [1870].

Aksakov's rashness. In 1864 they had founded *Torgovyi sbornik*, which claimed, somewhat disingenously as it turned out, to be interested more in informing the public about current commercial and financial problems than in advancing a political platform or even a well-defined economic viewpoint.[12] During the brief hiatus between the closing of *Den'* and the agreement on *Moskva*, more than forty Moscow merchants, including Morozov and Liamin, publicly had declared Shipov's paper to be their official organ and promised the editor financial support.[13] When several years later the Shipov brothers sought to create a national organization to promote trade and industry, they offered to make *Torgovyi sbornik* its official organ.

All these experiments with a subsidized press shared a common problem: they had to strike a balance between the material interests of the merchants and the high moral tone of the intellectuals in the Moscow entrepreneurial group. By the late 1870s the problem became acute. Babst and Shipov had drifted out of journalism. Chizhov's death in 1877 had silenced the most able, influential, and sympathetic voice on the merchants' side. Even the unexpected drift of Katkov toward their position on some issues, such as the tariff, could not wholly compensate for these losses. Enjoying complete financial independence, Katkov needed no merchant subsidies and tolerated no interference with his personal editorial policies in *Moskovskie vedomosti*.[14] Moreover, his temperamental preference for the nobility as the bulwark of Russian society made him an unpredictable ally.

Meanwhile, Aksakov, more irascible than ever, carried on alone. In his short-lived paper *Rus'*, his economic writers, S. F. Sharapov and Talitskii generally hewed to a promerchant line. They praised vigorous Russian entrepreneurs, criticized both government and zemstvos

12. At least this is the way Shipov explained it when he offered to publish the paper as the organ of the Society for Assistance to Russian Industry and Trade (*TOSRPT*, "Izvlechenie iz zhurnalov obshchogo sobraniia," meeting 31 January 1868, pp. 9–10). In fact, however, the paper was not as objective as Shipov would have had his audience believe. See below, note 49.

13. Laverychev, "Russkie kapitalisty," p. 31, based on materials in the archives of the State Historical Museum, which were not open to me.

14. Long a champion of low tariffs as a means to encourage trade and increase government revenue, Katkov began to move to a protectionist position in the wake of Russia's humiliation at the Congress of Berlin. By 1879 his anti-German views had spread to economic questions, and he was beginning to advocate "the need for a national policy in our economic questions." From higher duties on metals and coal he finally accepted a general protectionist policy (Katkov, *Sobranie*, vol. 17, 8 February, 2 March, 12 and 20 April 1879, pp. 73–75, 176–78, 191–93; ibid., vol. 18, 13 July, 20 September 1880, pp. 387–88, 493–95). Significantly, Katkov developed his economic arguments from published material of D. P. Shipov, who doubtless represented for him the more dispassionate voice of a noble entrepreneur in contrast to the more vulgar merchantry.

for meddling in industry, and supported a policy of protectionism, easy credit, monetary inflation, and Great Russian nationalism of the center against the foreign and ethnic merchants on the periphery. Aksakov even published some of Witte's earliest articles on industrialization. But a right-wing populist tone crept in occasionally, revealing the ambivalence of the intelligentsia to large-scale, rapid industrialization that might drag Russia along a Western path.[15]

Indeed, Sharapov's subsequent career dramatized the dilemma of the merchants in their quest for a strong and persuasive defender in the press. In the 1890s, Sharapov slid into an increasingly obscurantist position. As the editor of *Russkii trud* (Russian Labor), his violent ravings against Jewish and foreign domination of large capitalist enterprises in Russia and his militant claims for a Russian path to economic development brought him dangerously close to rejecting industrialization altogether.[16] The attempt to isolate the pure Russian strain from the alien virus in capitalism was destined to create as many difficulties for the merchantry as the infection itself would have.

With Aksakov's death *Rus'* folded and the big merchants floundered; uncertain of their ground, they ended up subsidizing second-rate journalists like G. Vasiliev and Sharapov who had served under either Katkov or Aksakov but lacked their style and prestige. For a while they ended up publishing short-lived and blatantly apologetic papers like *Golos Moskvy* (1885–86) and *Russkoe delo* (1886–90).[17]

Other journals and papers that have all too frequently and carelessly been identified as "organs of the big bourgeoisie" were in fact mouthpieces for the liberal Slavophil nobles who refused to accept the narrowly self-interested demands of the merchantry.[18] In the

15. S. F. Sharapov, "Nasha noveishaia literatura ob ekonomicheskom sostoianii Rossii," *Rus'*, no. 20 (10 November 1883); idem, "Russkaia ekonomicheskaia programma," ibid., no. 24 (15 December 1883); Talitskii, "Vysokii kurs i vysokii protsent," ibid., no. 9 (5 and 12 January); "Differentsial'nye tamozhennye poshliny vnutri Rossii," ibid., no. 11 (14 September 1885); S. F. Sharapov, "Iz ekskursii k zapadnoi granitse," ibid., no. 21 (23 November 1885); S. Iu. Witte, "Ob promyshlennosti," ibid., no. 3 (19 January 1885).

16. For a good survey of Sharapov's late journalism and its relationship to the anti-Witte salon of K. F. Golovin see von Laue, *Witte*, pp. 276–87.

17. Seeking a successor to Aksakov, Morozov and Khludov preferred to hire one of the economic writers on *Moskovskie vedomosti* rather than rely on more unpredictable aid from Katkov himself, even though they were warned that this tactic might rebound against them, as in fact happened (ORBL, f. 120, carton 21, book 3, p. 180, N. Novosel'skii to M. N. Katkov, 5 February 1884). Sharapov was an extreme Pan-Slavist, without Aksakov's redeeming humanism. See especially Sharapov, *Dve zapiski*, a sharp attack on Witte with anti-Semitic overtones, and *Samoderzhaviia*, vintage Aksakov supporting the zemskii sobor in an autocratic state.

18. Laverychev, "Russkie kapitalisty," pp. 42–46, lumps together such diverse journals

pages of *Beseda* (1871–72) and especially *Russkaia mysl'*, writers like Koshelev, A. A. Isaev, V. A. Gol'tsev, and S. A. Iur'ev defended the handicraft industry against the pressures of the "big capitalists."[19] Throughout the 1880s the only paper that sought to bridge the gap between the merchantry and the rest of society was *Russkii kur'er*, which reputedly won a following among the younger merchants. But its editor, the wealthy champagne merchant N. A. Lanin, ran the paper in a highly idiosyncratic way and alienated his most talented writers, like Gol'tsev.[20]

A real successor to Chizhov's *Vestnik promyshlennosti* and Aksakov's *Rus'* emerged only in 1890 with the publication of *Russkoe obozrenie*, founded by the merchant D. I. Morozov and edited by Prince D. N. Tsertelev. With the help of merchant subsidies, Tsertelev was able to recruit an impressive, if mixed, band of contributors from his old schoolmates and their friends, men like the eminent religious philosophers Vladimir Solov'ev and V. V. Rozanov, the notorious renegade revolutionary-turned-mystic L. A. Tikhomirov, and Katkov's old comrade and future Black Hundred leader V. A. Gringmut. Clearly, this was another attempt to unite economically progressive merchants with

and newspapers as *Golos Moskvy, Russkoe delo, Beseda, Russkaia mysl'*, and *Russkii kur'er* as organs of "the big bourgeoisie," without making any attempt to distinguish among them.

19. The only article in *Beseda* which treats large-scale industry was Dmitri Shipov's brief "Mekhanicheskoe proizvodstvo v Rossi . . . ," no. 5, section 2 (1872):147–51. The rest of the articles on trade and manufacturing extol the virtues of the kustar. See especially, A. I. Ch-V.,"Melkaia promyshlennost' v sviaze s artel'nym nachalom i pozemel'noi obschinoi," no. 5 (1871): especially pp. 196–97; M. Bogoliubtsev, "Russkaia sel'skaia tekhnicheskaia promyshlennost'," no. 5, section 2 (1871):59–71; A. I. Koshelev, "Otvet na statiu N. Koliupanova 'Zametki o perelozhenii podushnoi podati,'" no. 3, section 2 (1871):1–5; N. Orlov, "Programma issledovaniia krest'ianskoi promyshlennosti v Rossii," no. 3, section 2 (1872):63–73. Much the same pattern shows up in the early years of the *Russkaia mysl'*, for example, the criticism of property qualifications for elections to the town duma as a device for turning over self-government to "big capitalists" ("Vnutrennoe obozrenie" [April 1880], pp. 34–35; A. A. Isaev, "K voprosu o kustarnoi promyshlennosti v Rossii" [September 1880], pp. 73–126; idem, "Promyshlennye arteli v Rossii" [January 1881], pp. 253–77; and V., "Nashi velikie ekonomicheskie voprosy" [May 1881], pp. 79–104). While both journals were outright Pan-Slavist, they opposed forcible russification preached by the idiosyncratic organ of N. A. Lanin, *Russkii kur'er*; see "Vnutrennoe obozrenie," *Russkaia mysl'* (July 1880), pp. 49–50. Contrary to Laverychev's implication, *Russkaia mysl'* was supported by only one merchant's widow and not "a number of liberal wealthy merchants." See *Pis'ma Pobedonostseva*, 2:253, letter of 1 November 1891.

20. Skovronskaia, *Byl*, pp. 324–25, 327–30, 333, 343. The author, one of the first successful women journalists in Russia, wrote for both Giliarov-Platonov's *Sovremmennye izvestiia* and Lanin's *Russkii kur'er*. In a passage characteristic of the journalist cum intellectual she deplored the "commercial spirit" prevailing in the offices of *Kur'er*, adding disdainfully, "One cannot treat journalists like factory workers" (ibid., p. 344).

politically reactionary intellectuals. But this time the basis for the collaboration rested exclusively upon common ideological grounds, and the important ingredient of joint entrepreneurial ventures, which had cemented an earlier alliance, was altogether missing. This kind of association may have flattered the amour propre of the big merchants but in the long run it proved sterile. For Morozov and his friends the real attraction here was the willingness of the intellectuals to patronize the Old Belief and to insult non-Russian ethnic groups engaged in trade and industry throughout the empire. In both instances the inspiration came from Aksakov, who was proudly adopted by the journal as its patron saint.

At its best, *Russkoe obozrenie* carried some brilliant philosophical discussions, like V. V. Rozanov's sensitive portrayal of the Old Believers, and much fine literary material, including A. A. Fet's "Vospominaniia" and the correspondence of Turgenev and Tolstoy.[21] But there was the other less savory side to the journal which also evoked the spirit of Aksakov. The journal championed the demands of Moscow's economic interests against all foreign and ethnic competitors along the periphery from the Pacific Maritime provinces to Persia and the Balkans. Its favorite targets were what was called "the Lodzist nest" and "the aggressive Jewish-German enemy." Anti-Semitic polemics reached a new low, culminating in such provocative notes as "the Jews are stronger than the law." There were also scurrilous attacks on the intelligentsia and denunciations of the gentry-dominated zemstvos for their tax policies and their attempts to divert monies to elementary public education from the general fund for building railroads—"one of the most important needs of all Russia."[22]

The journal even voiced support for the merchant soslovie as, for example, when S. T. Morozov's ringing speech at the Nizhnyi fair in 1893 prompted sarcastic rejoinders from the mass-circulation dailies. In rather grandiloquent terms, Morozov had thrown down the gaunt-

21. Rozanov's contributions were subsequently republished as "Psikhologiia russkogo raskola," in *Religiia*, where he made the crucial connection in the Aksakov style between the spiritual strength of the Old Belief and the power of the state, "the thoughtful side of the enlightenment" introduced by Peter the Great (ibid., pp. 24, 53–54).
22. "Ekonomicheskie zametki," *Russkoe obozrenie*, January 1893, pp. 458–59; "Ekonomicheskie zametki," ibid., February 1893, pp. 986–87, 990–91; A. Vladimirov, "Russkoe zemlevladenie v severozapadnom krae," ibid., August 1894, p. 815; Palitskii, "Novyi ustav gosudarstvennogo banka," ibid., July 1895, p. 256; S. Minutko, "Evreiskoe zemlevladenie v tsentre Rossii," ibid., September 1896, pp. 812–24; "Vnutrennoe obozrenie," ibid., December 1895, pp. 1028–35; A. Elishev, "Vnutrennoe obozrenie," ibid., September 1896, pp. 450–58; idem, "Vnutrennoe obozrenie," ibid., March 1897, pp. 525–35; Prince N. Shakhovskoi, "Evreiskie obkhody zakona v piteinoi torgovle," ibid., May 1897, pp. 301–26.

let to Europe, claimed a leading role for the merchantry in building a
great industrial country, and expressed its willingness to bear heavy
sacrifices for the general good. It was indicative of the merchantry's
status in the empire that *Russkoe obozrenie* could find only one paper,
Meshcherskii's reactionary *Grazhdanin*, that had given "a correct understanding of the speech." Almost everyone else, from the liberal
Russkie vedomosti to Suvorin's extreme right-wing *Novoe vremiia*, had
shown only disdain for Morozov's merchant insolence.[23]

By the end of the century the coalition showed signs of strain.
Solov'ev drifted off into crypto-Catholicism, and Rozanov changed
his mind about the Old Belief. At its moment of greatest solidarity
this combination of defiant spirits was simply too strong a brew for
the greater part of the Russian merchantry. Despite the initial support
of Pobedonostsev and the sympathies of the imperial family, the circulation of *Russkoe obozrenie* barely reached two thousand. The old dilemma remained unresolved. No one would take the politically active
merchants seriously if they published what was in effect a trade journal which merely defended their commercial industrial interests. But
any alliance with intellectuals was bound to be unstable and could all
too easily end up frightening the rest of the merchants by trying to
stampede them into taking a more militant stance than their traditional
loyalties would allow.

The Economic Program: Railroads

In the decade 1858–68 the Moscow entrepreneurial group used its
press to help popularize its program of economic development. At a
time when the government was making crucial decisions for the future of the economy the Moscow entrepreneurs advocated railroad
construction by private Russian capitalists, protective tariffs, inflationary monetary policy, easy credit, and a vigorous nationalistic foreign policy. Except for monetary policy most of their program was
ultimately adopted in one form or another by the government. Clearly,
their press did not accomplish this alone and unaided, but it did
perform one indispensable function. By bringing to an end the almost
total secrecy surrounding government decisions on economic matters,
these papers helped introduce public initiative into the political process. The most striking example of this emerges in an analysis of the
two decades of correspondence between Baron Del'vig and Chizhov.
Due to Chizhov's widespread reputation for honesty and accuracy, his

23. K. Krasil'nikov, "Ekonomicheskie zametki," ibid., September 1893, pp. 514–19.

articles on railroad concessions were carefully read by bureaucrats in the Ministry of Transportation and by members of the Council of Ministers. On several occasions they led to revisions in the statutes of newly founded railroad companies and to the acceptance or rejection of specific proposals. Building on this foundation, Chizhov and other members of the group began to link their own business activities to their political program. Once again, railroad construction is a good case in point.

The Moscow entrepreneurs sought to realize the railroad dreams of Khomiakov and Koshelev. They planned to make Moscow the hub of a railroad network controlled by Russians and linking the main productive regions, the strategic border points, and the national minority areas in order to strengthen the moral and military unity of the empire. Their first move was to weaken and then eliminate foreign control over the large network undertaken in 1857 by La Grande Société des chemins de fer russes. They were quick to take advantage of the government's second thoughts about having granted extensive privileges to the French-based company. Their carefully coordinated press campaign helped undermine the company's credit standing, depressed the price of its stock, and forced the foreign bankers to come to terms with the government's demands.[24]

Almost a decade later the Moscow entrepreneurs organized to prevent the state-owned Nikolaevskii Railroad from Moscow to St. Petersburg from falling into the hands of the despised Grande Société. Under the leadership of the Shipov brothers the Nizhnyi Novgorod zemstvo proposed joining with those of Moscow, Tver, and St. Petersburg to purchase the line. Liamin carried the Moscow duma with him, but the others held back. Then Kokorev, Mamontov, and Chizhov struggled to put together a "Russian Company," proposed Del'vig as its head, and recruited ninety merchant sponsors. Working under great pressure, they drafted a proposal and for the next six months petitioned and lobbied important bureaucrats in the capital.[25] They won over Minister of Justice K. I. Palen, Minister of State Domains A. A. Zelenyi, the powerful favorite of the tsar Count P. P. Shuvalov, and the tsarevich, Alexander Alexandrovich, who personally presented their proposals to the tsar, only to be scolded by his father for having been taken in by the "nonsense and *slander*" of "Kokorev and former tax farmers like him."[26] At the same time, Aksakov, in an

24. Rieber, "Formation," pp. 382–84.
25. ORBL, f. 332, carton 25, no. 5, Del'vig to Chizhov, 27 March, 6 May, 6 December 1867; ibid., carton 61, no. 7, Dmitri Shipov to Chizhov, 26 May, 31 December [1867].
26. Ibid., f. 332, carton 33, no. 20, Kokorev to Chizhov, 24 January 1868; TsGAOR, f. 677 (Alexander III), op. 1, d. 641, Alexander Alexandrovich to Alexander II, 26 Feb-

editorial, violently denounced the proposed sale of the line to foreigners. The government issued a second warning to *Moskva* for having made a "harsh judgment of the financial administration in Russia [which] cast an unfavorable shadow on its activities as if they were enveloped in an impenetrable mystery to the detriment of society and to the benefit of a few shrewd people who are better acquainted with the motives and intentions of the financial administration."[27]

The Moscow group counted too heavily on the appeal of its patriotic motives and paid too little attention to the financial considerations that were uppermost in the minds of both the tsar and his finance minister, M. Kh. Reitern.[28] Their offer was rejected, but they had gained a highly placed and powerful permanent ally in the person of Alexander Alexandrovich.

Meanwhile, Chizhov, Del'vig, the Mamontovs, and the Shipovs sought to prove that Russians could build railroads without a state guarantee as solidly and more cheaply than foreigners. They organized a company to construct the first stretch of a line from Moscow to Iaroslavl as far north as the Troitse-Sergeevskii monastery, so that railroads could carry pilgrims to one of Russia's most venerated shrines.[29] Here was irrefutable proof that technology could serve religion. Once completed, the railroad proved a great financial success. The founders, with the help of Kokorev, sought both to extend the line to Iaroslavl and also to obtain a state guarantee of minimum income. It required almost two years of continuous lobbying with countless visits to individual ministers—Reitern at Finance, P. P. Mel'nikov at Ways and Communications, D. M. Miliutin at War—and constant pressure on officials in the Department of Railroads to move the documents through the bureaucratic maze. Even these efforts might have been in vain had the group not succeeded in raising all the capital from domestic sources, including nineteen members of the Moscow group's center and their families: Del'vig, Chizhov, eight members of the Mamontov family, and nine of the Shipov family, including the four brothers, Alexander, Dmitri, Sergei, and Nicholas;

---

ruary 1868; ibid., d. 669, p. 37, Alexander II to Alexander Alexandrovich, 9/21 August 1868.

27. TsGAOR, f. 722, op. 1, d. 514, p. 13, "Zapiski," referring to editorial in *Moskva*, no. 73 (1867).

28. ORBL, f. 332, carton 73, no. 10, "Zapiska po imia Ministerstva M. Kh. Reiterna"; ibid., carton 25, no. 5, Del'vig to Chizhov, 27 December 1867.

29. Ibid., carton 24, no. 1, Del'vig to Chizhov, 27 January 1861; ibid., carton 38, nos. 1, 17, 18, numerous letters I. F. Mamontov to Chizhov; Del'vig, *Moi vospominaniia*, 3:29–35; *Zhurnal Ministerstva putei soobshcheniia*, book 3 (1863):136–37.

additional subscribers from the secondary layer included Gorbov, Samarin, and S. M. Sukhotin.[30]

Of all the lines radiating from Moscow the one that exercised the greatest fascination for the group was the southern railroad. For them it represented the promise that the Crimean defeat would never be repeated, that the Ukraine would be tied firmly to Great Russia and not to the Kingdom of Poland, and that the vast coal and iron resources of the Donets Basin would nourish the industries of the north. The enterprise seemed so vast, however, that even the government hesitated to undertake it. Still, as early as 1858 the intrepid Kokorev sought to provide a rail link between the Don and the Volga, where so many efforts to build a canal had failed, in order to improve communications between Moscow and the southern river system and thus to maintain a Russian naval presence in the Sea of Azov.[31] Although he initially invested a million rubles and then more as the enterprise faltered, he reaped no profits even after the line was completed. Undaunted, he endeavored to organize his friends among the Moscow group to undertake the construction of a Moscow-Sevastopol line.[32] Chizhov supported him strongly in the press and, when the attempt failed, continued to agitate for a southern line, even if it had to be built by the state. By publicizing its importance for the national interest, Chizhov indirectly helped the minister of transportation, P. P. Mel'nikov, win approval in 1864 for his proposal, which had been languishing in the bureaucracy for two years, to begin construction of the southern line at state expense.[33]

As if to confirm Chizhov's fears that further delays would jeopardize Russia's national interests, another group of entrepreneurs, including a Baltic-German nobleman, Ungern Sternberg, a Ukrainian landowning aristocrat, Prince Kochubei, and several Odessa merchants, petitioned the government for an extension of the experimental Odessa-Balta railroad, built by army labor under their supervision, to Kremenchug and Kharkov. The Moscow group was stung into action by the political ramifications of tying the most productive area

30. ORBL, f. 332, carton 38, no. 16, Mamontov to Chizhov, 4 May 1865, 12 April 1866; ibid., no. 17, 6 November 1867; ibid., no. 19, 30 July, 11 November 1868; ibid., carton 74, no. 6, "Spisok gg. aktsionerov obshchestva Moskovsko-Iaroslavskoi zheleznoi dorogi, imeiushchikh 50 i bolee aktsii."

31. Kokorev, "Vzgliad," pp. 46, 62; A. A. Skal'kovskii, Don, p. 106; Barsukov, Zhizn', 22:158–61.

32. ORBL, f. 332, carton 24, no. 3, Del'vig to Chizhov, 4 January 1863.

33. Chizhov's articles in Aktsioner, 26 January, 9 and 23 March 1863; Kislinskii, Nasha, 1:137–38.

of the Ukraine to Odessa, with its Greek, Jewish, and foreign merchant interests, before it was connected to Moscow by the southern line. With Del'vig supplying valuable inside information on ministerial politics, Chizhov and Shipov orchestrated a press and lobbying campaign which carried the struggle into the Committee of Ministers. There a majority supported their views only to be defeated by the tsar's decision to side with his minister of finance.[34]

Despite this setback the Moscow entrepreneurial group achieved its primary purpose by stimulating the first signs of real interest among other entrepreneurs in bidding on the southern extension of the state-built Moscow-Kursk railroad. Ironically, it was a Jewish capitalist, S. S. Poliakov, who won the bidding and succeeded in carrying out the rapid, if shoddy, construction of the section to Kharkov before the line from Odessa reached that city.[35] It required more time, experience, and capital before the Moscow group could bring part of this railroad under its direct control. In 1870, Chizhov, the Mamontovs, and Liamin were joined by T. S. Morozov, who was just as wealthy and energetic as Kokorev but also steadier. They obtained the concession of the Moscow-Kursk stretch by underbidding several Russian and foreign competitors. They had learned their lesson from the Nikolaevskii fiasco; careful planning and solid financing preceded their entry into the bureaucratic maze.[36]

Once the line to Iaroslavl was completed in 1870, the Moscow entrepreneurs, led by Chizhov, undertook its further extension to Vologda. This undertaking marked the debut of Savva Mamontov, who took the place of his father, Ivan Fedorovich, in the inner circle of the group.[37] At the same time, Chizhov began organizing the

34. This complex and prolonged fight will be dealt with in detail in a planned study on the politics of economic development in nineteenth-century Russia. The important sources include, ORBL, f. 332, carton 24, no. 5, Del'vig to Chizhov, 29 October, 2 November 1864; articles by Chizhov in *Den'*, no. 48, 28 November 1864 (The Kremenchug line represents "all Polish propaganda and all those sympathizing with it."); ibid., nos. 49, 50, 5 and 12 December 1864; ibid., no. 5, 30 January 1865 (Whatever the economic advantages of the railroad for Odessa, "this cannot justify the penetration of alien products into our state when railroads are still in their infancy."); ibid., no. 8, 20 February 1865 (One of the causes of poverty in the south is the absence of a means of getting peasant produce to markets, thus leaving them dependent on "yid-leaseholders."). These brief excerpts emphasize the characteristic xenophobic, anti-Semitic tone of many similar articles. Cf. Shipov's more restrained views in *Torgovyi sbornik*, 10 October 1864.

35. Kislinskii, *Nasha*, 1:245–51.

36. ORBL, f. 332, carton 2, no. 10, "Dnevnik," 25 January, 10 April, 21 May 1871, pp. 29, 33, 35.

37. Ibid., 30 October 1870, p. 21. Savva Mamontov also replaced his father as a director of the Kursk line (ibid., carton 2, no. 11, 14 May 1872, pp. 15–16).

Arkhangelsk-Murmansk Steamship Company and the Company for Northern Industry.[38] Thus, by the early 1870s the Moscow entrepreneurs had firm control over the main north-south axis of Russia's transportation system (Vologda to Kursk), with important enterprises scattered all along the way but centered in and around Moscow. The result was an effective political counterweight to the control by the Grande Société of the east-west axis from Nizhnyi to St. Petersburg and an alternative basis for economic development which emphasized the industrial growth of the center and south as opposed to reliance on the grain trade between the Volga and the Baltic ports.

Banking and Currency

For the entrepreneurs of the Moscow group a major obstacle to their program of railroad construction in particular and industrialization in general was the difficulty encountered by Russian entrepreneurs in raising sufficient capital to compete for concessions and contracts on equal terms with foreign capitalists and state engineers. Therefore, they favored an inflationary monetary policy and the rapid expansion of credit facilities for industrial and commercial loans. They deplored the efforts of the Ministry of Finance in 1862 to stabilize the ruble on the international market and to introduce convertability. This meant tight money and the predominance of foreign investors in financing Russia's industrialization. Kokorev argued that one of the government's major errors in this period was not to have printed paper currency to finance railroad construction. The Russian people had faith in their government, he insisted, and accepted the paper ruble with as much confidence as the silver ruble. Yet the government's frantic efforts to stabilize the ruble on the international market ultimately led to a 40 percent depreciation. Its borrowing abroad cost the treasury one third of its income in the quarter of a century following the emancipation of the serfs. Never short on imagination, Kokorev also proposed using the excise tax on vodka to create a railroad fund from domestic sources.[39]

Alexander Shipov denounced the government's concern over the ruble rate as a dangerous "fixation." Refuting German and English economists on the importance of convertability, he argued that in any case the fate of the value of the ruble on the international exchange

38. Ibid., carton 3, no. 5, "Dnevnik," 23 January 1877.
39. Ibid., f. 231, vol. 3, carton 6, no. 7, V. A. Kokorev, "Glavnye osnovaniia agenstva po piteinomu sboru i tovarishchestva dlia sooruzheniia russkoi seti zheleznykh dorog," 19 April 1862, pp. 1–4; Kokorev, *Ekonomicheskie*, pp. 72–74.

after the Crimean War was not the result of the enormous quantity of paper money in circulation. Instead, it was foreign travel by Russian aristocrats, lower tariffs, increased imports of manufactured and luxury goods, and lower interest on bank deposits that caused the flight of hard currency abroad. To expand its industry, he declared, Russia needed cheap money and easy credit.[40]

Although, as Kokorev noted, Chizhov was not in favor of the un-limited printing of assignats, his ideas on credit resembled those of his colleagues. In an ambitious scheme to float a large internal loan for railroad construction, Chizhov proposed that the government print one hundred to one hundred and fifty million fully guaranteed but non-interest-bearing notes, which would be issued to the public in the form of 5 percent loans on deposit of immovable property by a spe-cially created "people's railroad bank." Interest on the loans would be extended in the form of credits to private entrepreneurs in order to build railroads. Backed by property the notes would not fluctuate in value like assignats. Even though they might drive down the value of paper money, the depreciation would be less than that following a large foreign loan. The crucial difference, and here Chizhov echoed his friends, was that the profits from an internal loan went into the pockets of Russians, not foreigners.[41]

These schemes evoked no sympathy within the bureaucracy, where the Ministry of Finance kept a tight reign on monetary and banking policy. Even the statutes of the State Bank drafted in 1860 by Reitern and E. I. Lamanskii, subsequently the deputy director, placed strict limitations on the extension of credit by permitting discounting of promissory notes exclusively on commercial (commodity) operations. Although the bank occasionally ignored its own statutes to grant spe-cial loans to merchants, it also confined these, at least until 1875, solely to short-term commercial credit. The Moscow entrepreneurs established their own banks in order to obtain long-term credits for the textile industry as well as for trade.

In 1864, on the initiative of Kokorev and Liamin, a powerful com-mittee was organized to draft the statutes for a Moscow merchants' bank, including themselves, T. S. Morozov, P. M. Tret'iakov, S. P. Maliutin, and V. Rukavishnikov, with the close consultation of Chiz-

40. A. P. Shipov, *O sredstvakh*, pp. v, 12–15.
41. ORBL, f. 332, carton 4, no. 3, "Sredstva dlia provedeniia seti zheleznykh dorog v Ros-sii," undated draft [1865?]; see also Chizhov's article in *Den'*, no. 4, 23 January 1865. Aksakov's paper also carried two other series on the need for either an inflationary monetary policy—see A. I. Koshelev in ibid., nos. 13, 14, 28 March, 4 April 1865—or a policy of cheap credit though based upon a convertible currency—see Iu. Gagemeister, in ibid., nos. 30, 34, 36, 38, 39, 40, 24 July, 22 August, 4, 14, and 26 September, 3 Oc-tober 1864.

hov and Babst.[42] As a next step Kokorev, Liamin, and Chizhov rounded up over a hundred subscribers among large merchants. Then, Kokorev, V. A. Poletika, and A. I. Mamontov energetically lobbied in St. Petersburg to persuade Reitern and other key officials to approve the statutes and grant a substantial initial loan to the bank.[43] After two years of this sort of pressure the government agreed. But by this time almost half the original participants either had dropped out or had reduced their original pledge because, according to Babst, many merchants feared that the delay, which was not unusual in such matters, was an expression of the finance minister's displeasure. They feared "upsetting the authorities."[44] The old attitudes of servility toward authority still characterized the majority of the Moscow merchants.

The success of the Moscow Merchants' Bank and the almost inevitable clashes of personality that resulted from the competition for capital among the members of the council stimulated the formation of other banks. The most important one was the Moscow Merchants' Society of Mutual Credit. Founded in 1869 by many of the same people, including Morozov, Kokorev, Liamin, and Tret'iakov, but with the additional participation of the Mamontovs, K. T. Soldatenkov, and the Guchkovs, the bank elected Chizhov as head and Aksakov as a member of the council.[45] Like the Moscow Merchants' Bank, the Moscow Merchants' Society of Mutual Credit reflected the interests of its founders in its "family" form of organization, moderate speculative

42. ORBL, f. 332, carton 37, no. 21, Liamin to Chizhov, 13 June, 15 July 1864.

43. Ibid., carton 33, no. 20, Kokorev to Chizhov, 18 March, 20 May, 15 June 1866; several years later, when Kokorev was on the verge of bankruptcy again, he complained that the two years he spent on this project had cost him a great deal of money for which he had never asked compensation and he now expected the bank to help him (ibid., letter to Chizhov, 15 October 1868).

44. Gindin, "Moskovskie banki," Akademiia nauk, *Istoriia Moskvy*, 4:209, citing an anonymous article "Tret'e pis'mo o bankakh," *RV*, no. 195 (1873), which he attributes to Babst. To be sure, Babst was always critical of the Moscow merchants and may be exaggerating their caution. Kokorev, who can not be accused of caution, attributed the falling away of the original subscribers to a tight money situation (ORBL, f. 332, carton 33, no. 19, letter to Chizhov, 23 March 1865). In fact this was a period of rapid expansion in which free capital was quickly invested (Iakovlev, *Ekonomicheskie*, pp. 86–92.)

45. Naidenov, *Vospominaniia*, 2:110–12, complained that Morozov "was profoundly convinced that Chizhov could do no wrong" in running the bank and that Chizhov let in all his friends, including Aksakov, who "as an idealist was filled with lofty dreams and did not know what was going on around him." Aksakov was shrewder than Naidenov thought; even though he did not much care for banking, he carefully analyzed the statutes and reported periodically to Chizhov on the financial developments (ORBL, f. 332, carton 1, no. 7, especially letters 10 June 1869, 25 July 1870; ibid., carton 15, nos. 8, 9, 10, and 11 [to 1877]).

activities, and close relations with the Moscow branch of the State Bank.[46] On the other hand it took greater risks in extending credit to industrial enterprises, with unexpected and dramatic results for the history of Russian banking.

In 1873 the Moscow Merchants' Society of Mutual Credit, together with the Moscow Trading Bank and the Society for Commercial Credit, formed a syndicate to loan N. I. Putilov 1,400,000 rubles in order to expand his rail manufacturing plant and undertake improvements in the St. Petersburg port. For the Moscow entrepreneurs, Putilov enjoyed the reputation of being the first Russian to undertake the organization on a large scale of the manufacture of rails and to put into production a new type of steel-capped rail that he had invented. Orders from both private railroads and the state encouraged him to expand and in 1873 to form a joint-stock company in hopes of attracting foreign capital. But the world economic crisis forced him back on domestic resources. The Moscow syndicate accepted as security for their loan shares in the Putilov Society with a book value of four million metallic rubles and insisted on placing one of its representatives, Baron Del'vig, as its watchdog on the society's council. When the notes came due, Putilov was unable to pay. He tried to play off one bank against another and to get the Moscow Merchants' Society of Mutual Credit to accept his promissory note on the assurance that the government would place a large order with him for railroad cars. The government complied. The syndicate, now joined by Kokorev's Volga-Kama Bank, continued to carry Putilov's debts, despite growing evidence of mismanagement, which culminated in the strike of 1876. Finally, the following year, the real threat of Putilov's bankruptcy became clear. Its potentially devastating effect on the Volga-Kama Bank, the three Moscow banks, and individual Moscow merchants, who were also involved, forced Reitern to take the unprecedented and extralegal step of ordering the State Bank to pay all Putilov's debts and to take over the shares and property from the banks and extend new credits.[47]

For the first time under Reitern's ministry the state reversed its policy and took a major step toward directly financing Russian industry. The enthusiasm and recklessness of the Moscow entrepreneurs in

46. Ibid., carton 2, no. 11, "Dnevnik," 16 November 1873, p. 48.

47. Ibid., carton 26, no. 7, Del'vig to Chizhov, undated [November?], and 12, 16, 17, and 18 November 1873; ibid., carton 27, no. 1, Del'vig to Chizhov, 26 July 1874; ibid., no. 5, 22 April, 4 May 1876; ibid., no. 6, 28 June 1877; Gindin, *Gosudarstvennyi bank*, pp. 239–40, which does not use the Chizhov archive. On the creation of the Volga Kama Bank, the founders of which included Morozov, Soldatenkov, and Khludov, see K. A. Skal'kovskii, *Nashi gosudarstvennye*, p. 172, and ORBL, f. 332, carton 33, no. 20, Kokorev to Chizhov, 27 March, 23 June, 22 December 1869.

backing a Russian industrialist had moved a reluctant Ministry of Finance into direct subsidization of Russian industry, a policy from which there was no turning back. Although the statutes of the State Bank were revised only in 1894, to permit discounting of promissory notes having "commercial-industrial importance," 1877 marked the beginning of a policy of direct loans to industry, which in the following decade increased rapidly in number and scope.[48]

The Tariff

Unlike railroad building and banking, the tariff question posed for the Moscow entrepreneurs an immediate and serious threat to business interests. This forced them to develop new forms of organization in order to exert direct pressure on the Ministry of Finance. In the successive tariff revisions of 1850 and 1857 the protectionist system erected under Alexander I and Nicholas I was dismantled, to the consternation of the Moscow merchants. Therefore, when in 1864 a rumor spread that the Russian government had secretly come to a trade agreement that extended favorable terms to the German Customs Union (Zollverein), the Moscow entrepreneurs rallied to expose and denounce this "outrage." Alexander Shipov took the lead in calling a series of mass meetings of Nizhnyi merchants to attack the reported convention, alerting his Moscow friends, including Chizhov, to recruit supporters for his campaign and writing a series of articles in which he outlined a strong protectionist position.[49] Together with Liamin, then *starshina* of the Moscow Exchange Committee and a member of the Commercial Section of the Moscow Manufacturing and Commercial Council, he proposed to organize assemblies (*s'ezdy*) of factory owners on the German model, with the participation of members of the Commercial Section as private individuals.

In January 1864, under the auspices of the exchange committee, almost two hundred merchants met, with A. I. Khludov in the chair, and agreed to elect twenty delegates and twenty candidates as a permanent committee to lobby on the tariff question in St. Petersburg. Reflecting the growing anti-German sentiment among the merchants,

48. Gindin, *Gosudarstvennyi bank*, pp. 324–26, 341–43.
49. ORBL, f. 332, carton 61, no. 2, A. P. Shipov to Chizhov, 6 September 1864; Shipov's articles were reprinted as chapter four in *O sredstvakh*. Although the director of the Department of Foreign Trade of the Ministry of Finance, Prince D. A. Obolenskii, sympathized with the Moscow entrepreneurs, he found these criticisms so sharp that he implored Chizhov to intercede on behalf of the government in order to restrain Shipov from making further attacks of this nature (ORBL, f. 332, carton 43, no. 7, D. A. Obolenskii to Chizhov, 6 October 1864).

great care was taken in the elections to eliminate anyone with a German name, even if several generations of his ancestors had been born in Russia. Among the first twenty delegates were Chizhov, Babst, A. P. Shipov, T. S. Morozov, Liamin, and Soldatenkov; D. P. Shipov and A. I. Khludov were candidates. Individual members of the committee worked on separate sections of the German memorandum, gathered in weekly plenary sessions to consult with other entrepreneurs, and finally produced a thick volume entitled "Opinion of the Permanent Delegation of the Moscow Merchants' Assemblies." Copies were distributed to the minister of finance and other high officials and influential people in the capital.[50] Because of this unexpectedly vigorous response the German memorandum was shelved.

At the same time officials of the Ministry of Finance worked out a complete draft revision of the Russian tariff without consulting any merchant organization. They submitted it to the Exchange Society in the summer of 1867 on the eve of the Nizhnyi market—that is, when the merchants were most preoccupied with their business affairs—and requested comments by 15 September. When the merchants complied, the Ministry of Finance grudgingly agreed to allow three elected representatives of their assemblies to sit on the Tariff Commission in St. Petersburg. But there the overwhelming majority, composed of bureaucrats and non-Russian delegates from the periphery of the empire, favored sharp reductions in the tariff and regularly steamrollered the Moscow group.[51] The gloomy reports sent back to Moscow stirred a flurry of banquets and meetings in the Exchange building and at the Moscow Merchants' Club. Two declarations of the merchants' assembly brought to the attention of the Ministry of Finance the grave dangers to Russian industry of accepting the Tariff Commission's proposals and petitioned for permission to send a special delegation of elected representatives to the State Council to present further explanations of the proposed revision. In the pages of *Moskva*, Shipov openly attacked, by name, bureaucrats in the ministry. Aksakov dispatched a correspondent to cover the meetings. Based on inside

50. Naidenov, *Vospominaniia*, 2:65–68.
51. Representatives from merchant organizations outside Moscow included E. E. Brandt, president of the St. Petersburg Exchange Committee, "a dry German"; Jules Wertheim of the Warsaw Manufacturing Council, who knew no Russian and submitted his views in French; I. I. Hafferburg of the Riga Exchange Committee, a Baltic-German; I. G. Fronshtein of the Rostov section of the Commercial Council, a Jewish merchant; G. Khandzherli and F. Rogokanaki of the Taganorog section of the Commercial Council, both Greeks; N. Pfeifer of the Odessa section of the Commercial Council, a German; and a certain Gol'denberg, also from Odessa, whom Naidenov claims was paid an enormous sum from the Treasury to oppose the Moscow group (ibid., pp. 76–77).

information and supplemented by Babst's witty feature articles, his reports infuriated the bureaucrats, who found copies of the issues that ridiculed them at their assigned places around the conference table.[52]

Behind the scenes, Babst obtained direct access to Alexander Alexandrovich, a member of the commission. From March to September he bombarded him with a series of letters and memoranda which played upon the well-known prejudices of the heir. Alternately anti-English and anti-German (or, to be more precise, anti-Bismarck), Babst evoked a touching picture of the honest, plain Russian merchants defending themselves (and the interests of the hard-working Russian working man) against the accusations of sloth, greed, and selfishness heaped upon them by unfeeling bureaucrats. He coached Alexander Alexandrovich carefully on the intricacies of the textile tariffs, advised him to pay special attention to particular interventions by Moscow merchants, and gently prodded the indolent heir to attend all the meetings, even if he had to summon members to his own palace.[53]

Throughout their campaign the Moscow group concentrated on raising tariffs on textiles, chemicals, semifinished iron, and steel products, lowering them on machinery, and abolishing them on pig iron.[54] On almost every one of these issues they clashed with the groups on the periphery of the empire, the Ural iron masters, the Greek and Armenian merchants from Taganrog and Rostov, the Jewish and Greek merchants of Odessa, the Polish manufacturers of Warsaw and Lodz, the German merchants in Riga and St. Petersburg. In the long run they also lost on almost every issue. They gained some satisfaction from the conviction that had they not fought the results would have been even worse.[55] Even more important, they consolidated their

52. Shipov's articles in *Moskva* (nos. 112, 131) were reprinted in a pamphlet by the Mamontov Publishing Company as *Zamechaniia*. Shipov's own organ, *Torgovyi sbornik*, also defended the protectionist point of view in no. 45 (1866), and nos. 7, 13, and 14 (1867). For additional details on the organization of protectionist campaign see Naidenov, *Vospominaniia*, 2:78.

53. TsGAOR, f. 677, op. 1, d. 499, "Pis'ma i zapiski I. K. Babsta v. k. Aleksandru Aleksandrovichu," pp. 11, 17, 21, 30, 33–36, 43–45.

54. Sobolev, *Tamozhennaia*, especially pp. 232, 236, 248, 263, 270–75, 280, 295–96, and 299. Characteristically, Shipov defined these proposals, which clearly reflected the special interests of the Moscow group, in terms of the national interest: "In international trade relations of governments which are not equally developed there is no free trade. The principle of free trade in this case leads to the hegemony of one government over the other" (A. P. Shipov, *Otvet*, p. 22 [originally printed in *Nizhnyi-Novgorodskaia iarmachnaia spravochnaia listka*, another house organ of the Shipov enterprises]).

55. The tariff of 1868 reduced rates on all cotton yarns and most woolen fabrics; cotton cloth was substantially reduced. There were only slight changes on linen, and duties on

alliance with the heir and future tsar, Alexander Alexandrovich. It was only a matter of time before the trade and tariff policies supported by the Moscow group became the law of the land.

The across-the-board increases in tariffs by 30 to 50 percent in 1877 (as a result of the requirement that duties be paid in hard currency rather than the depreciated paper ruble) and by 10 percent in 1880 were motivated primarily by fiscal policies. But the first general revision under Alexander III in 1882 demonstrated clearly that pressured by strong protests by the Moscow group and other regional interests, the new minister of finance, N. Kh. Bunge, was obliged to compromise again and again by raising duties above his original proposals.[56] Though Bunge endeavored to follow Reitern's policies, he could no longer count on the automatic support of the tsar when the interest groups opposed him, even if he won over a majority of the State Council.[57] By 1885, the tariff rates were more the result of consultations with the burgeoning industrial and trading interests than they were a product of the chancellery of the Ministry of Finance.

---

silk and silk products were actually increased slightly. The rates on iron products (except sheet iron) were all reduced or maintained; those on sugar were left unchanged (Lodyzhenskii, *Istoriia*, pp. 281, 283–84, 288–90, 308). However, the original draft of the Ministry of Finance recommended a reduction on cotton from 3.50 rubles to 2.50. This figure was the main object of the Moscow merchants' criticism (A. P. Shipov, *Zamechaniia*, pp. 1–20). In the final draft the reduction was only 25 kopeks (Lodyzhenskii, *Istoriia*, p. 290). With the exception of A. Shipov (who operated a machine factory in Kostroma), the Moscow group opposed duties on imported machinery, and in this case, Reitern sided with them against the views of the technological society (Sobolev, *Tamozhennaia*, pp. 295–96).

56. For example, in the course of discussions in the State Council, but before a final vote, Bunge reversed his opposition to Morozov's recommendations for higher rates on yarn (Sobolev, *Tamozhennaia*, pp. 451 ff.). Sobolev otherwise accepts the notion that until the tariff of 1890 the private interests had little effect on setting tariff rates. By this time the Moscow group had picked up the support of Russia's most influential journalist, M. N. Katkov, who was converted to protectionism following the Congress of Berlin. See Laverychev, "Russkie kapitalisty," pp. 35–40.

57. In 1884, for example, Bunge, supported by a majority of 33 to 8 in the State Council, recommended the creation of a Russian-American society for the construction of commodity warehouses and grain elevators, despite the "dark and unfounded suspicions" expressed by the merchant experts at a joint session of the departments of Law and State Economy that approval could only turn the grain trade over to the Americans. Alexander III refused to approve the opinion of the majority. Similarly, in March 1883, Bunge, supported by a majority of 28 to 18 in the State Council, proposed to modify but not abolish the Caucasian transit trade, long a bugbear of the Moscow merchants. Alexander III endorsed the minority view, which recommended totally abolishing the trade (Polovtsov, *Dnevnik*, 1:121, 487, 495).

Professional Organizations and Town Government

In the meantime the tariff fight taught another valuable political lesson. What was needed in dealing with the professional bureaucracy was an equally professional interest group possessing a corporate, legal organization. But the differences among the Moscow entrepreneurs over the character and the membership of such a body produced several varieties of these. Each represented a different tendency within the group and appealed to a different membership pool outside it.

The Moscow entrepreneurs took the initiative in petitioning the government for the establishment of a Moscow exchange association in hopes of creating a proto-political organization that would encompass the merchant soslovie of the central provinces. At the outset it appeared as though they had taken a decisive step toward their goal. Although it would be an exaggeration to say that they controlled the association, they were well represented on the small executive committee during most of the seventies: T. S. Morozov was president from 1870 to 1876, and other members of the committee included Babst (1870, 1873, 1876), Chizhov (1870, 1873, 1876), Kokorev (1870), P. M. Tret'iakov (1870–80), D. P. Shipov (1873–76), and I. S. Aksakov (1879). In addition, five other Morozovs and three members of the Mamontov clan served repeatedly on the committee. During these years the executive committee and the general sessions reviewed a great many questions dealing with the economy but returned most frequently to the tariff and railroad construction to Siberia and Central Asia. The Moscow entrepreneurs also sought to turn the association into a kind of political caucus for the election of mayors of Moscow. Their greatest successes brought Tret'iakov, Alekseev, and Rukavishnikov to the office. Yet, despite their efforts, the Exchange Association never quite lived up to their expectations. By the eighties, the majority of the merchants hesitated to follow the bold lead of the entrepreneurs and gradually relapsed into the more familiar attitudes of caution and deference to the bureaucracy.

Along a different line, A. P. Shipov appealed to a broader alliance of merchants with other social elements that shared some of their economic aspirations. Proposing the formation of a society for the encouragement of Russian industry, Shipov invited the guests attending the first "tariff banquet" at the Moscow Merchants' Club to form "a society which would stand guard permanently over Russian industrial interests and profits in our trade with Europe, preventing foreigners from exploiting us exclusively for their own gain."[58] Although

58. *ZOSRPT*, Prilozhenie no. 1, "Rech' v-p. A. P. Shipova," p. 38.

Shipov intended to base the society in Moscow, he envisaged it as a national rather than a regional organization. Discouraged by a lack of enthusiasm among his Moscow associates and despite the disapproval of Chizhov, Shipov finally decided to shift the headquarters of the society to St. Petersburg. Once there, he strove to get the Moscow merchants either to form a branch of the society or at least to coordinate the activities of their organizations with the society so that "in this way there would be a highly useful alliance between Petersburg and Moscow in connection with the economic development of 'Rus' " (sic).[59] Chizhov never took an active part in its work but accepted his election as a member, expressed his admiration of Shipov's energy, and approved of the society's policies. The other members of the Moscow entrepreneurial group did not join. Nor did they form a local branch as Shipov wished until many years later. Their abstention may be interpreted as another sign of their deep suspicion of anything that came from the capital and reflected the powerful sense of social and economic regionalism that stamped the merchantry of the center.

Not surprisingly, then, the Society for the Encouragement of Russian Industry and Trade drew its membership from a wider geographical area and a different social base than did the Moscow organizations. In its first year it enrolled over five hundred men from sixty-five towns and cities. The most active and influential members represented diverse regions and occupations. Its membership included, for example, I. N. Sobolev, the president of the Kazan Exchange Committee; K. A. Skal'kovskii, a publicist and engineer from Odessa; V. A. Poletika, a Ukrainian engineer, industrialist, and publisher; N. I. Peregrebov, the head of the St. Petersburg city duma; M. K. Sidorov, a merchant from Arkhangelsk and an Arctic explorer; S. S. Loshkarev, a geographer and economist from St. Petersburg; D. P. Skuratov, a Moscow industrialist and economist; A. A. Krasil'nikov, the editor of *Ekonomist*; I. I. Glazunov, the St. Petersburg publisher; and the Shipov brothers, with their business interests in Nizhnyi Novgorod, Kostroma, and Moscow.[60] As this brief list suggests, the society attracted many more nobles and *raznochintsy* who had entered the liberal professions than merchants. For this reason they perceived their role primarily as educational and their audience as all classes of Russian society.

59. ORBL, f. 322, carton 61, no. 1, A. P. Shipov to Chizhov, [1867] undated in original and misdated 1857 in the cataloging.
60. For total membership see *TOSRPT*, pt. 1 (1872), "Otchet . . . v 1871," pp. 2–3. For membership of standing committees of the four sections see Obshchestva dlia sodeistviia russkoi promyshlennosti i torgovli, *Izvlechenii iz zhurnalov obshchei sobranii*, 31 January 1867, p. 5. The biographical details are taken from articles in *RBS*.

Their regional diversity and professional outlook spurred them to expand the society's activities to an all-Russian scale, to open lines of communication and cooperation with other professional societies, and to organize national congresses of commercial and industrial interests, such as those in St. Petersburg (1870), Moscow (1882), and Nizhnyi Novgorod (1896). Their boldest gambit was to elect as their second president Count N. P. Ignat'ev, the controversial Pan-Slavist and former minister of the interior. While provisional governor-general of Nizhnyi Novgorod, Ignat'ev had forged close ties with the local elite—including the Morozovs and the Shipovs—and strongly endorsed their petition to transform the fair committee into an autonomous organization.[61] What must be regarded as an effort to unite a bureaucratic right opposition with the Moscow entrepreneurial group faded when Ignat'ev's influence declined and the technical intelligentsia took over the society.

In the course of the first twenty-five years of its existence, the society investigated and reported on virtually every major question connected with the economic life of the country. Their concern with an even, well-balanced industrial advance throughout the empire left little room for narrow regional concerns. Their close working relations with the Russian Technological Society and the interests of their own members drawn from the technical intelligentsia sensitized them to the advantages of innovative industrial techniques and new forms of business organization.

Although the society shared several aims with the Moscow merchants and even more with the Moscow entrepreneurial group, it parted company with them on issues that transcended the interests of the Moscow region. In general, it found a common ground on the protective tariff, the construction of railroads to open the interior of the country, and expanded trade with the Caucasus and Central Asia. But it did not always agree on the rates for the tariff, the direction for the railroads, or the necessity for taking greater risks in foreign trade. More significantly, the society differed sharply with the Moscow merchants over the need for technical education by insisting that child labor be limited in order to encourage workers' children to attend schools and that factory owners employ Russian graduates of technical schools rather than import foreigners who might have an edge over the Russians in training and experience. It opposed monopolies, favored wide-ranging reforms of commercial law, and championed the development of several regions such as the far north that fell

61. Laverychev, *Krupnaia*, pp. 103–4.

outside the purview of merchants who were not associated with the Moscow entrepreneurial group.[62] If anything, then, the distance separating the technical intelligentsia in the society from the merchantry grew over time. At the last of the so-called all-Russian congresses of trade and industry organized by the society before the revolution of 1905, the merchants were conspicuous by their absence and the special reports by the engineer technologists took them to task for their indifference to the plight of the workers and to the application of technical know-how to production.[63]

From the outset, Shipov admitted that the society's campaign to spread industrial enlightenment was no easy task. As he put it, this was the result of "an insufficient appreciation of the great importance of our society [and] the [physical] separation of our activists scattered over the enormous length and breadth of our fatherland who make little effort to unite their disparate productive powers. The proverb 'Beyond the threshold of my hut I know nothing' still plays a large role in our lives; we do not sufficiently understand the important advantages of the strength developed from mutual ties and a single voice defending the common interests of Russia."[64]

Shipov's declaration can serve as both the epitaph for an aborted bourgeoisie and the battle cry of a new interest group. Measured against the criteria outlined in chapter 3, the society fits the definition. Its functional role was to promote technological progress through education and propaganda. Broadly patriotic and with a thin veneer of xenophobia, it nevertheless cherished and sought to emulate the industrial organization and business practices of Western and Central Europe. These values were embodied in a political program that was articulated in regular, periodic meetings of the society and in its official organs, first in *Torgovyi sbornik*, which then became its *Trudy* [Transactions]. Although it claimed all-empire status and boasted a number of branches or sections, the parent society in St. Petersburg became increasingly regional in membership and differed on numerous key issues with its affiliates, especially following the long-delayed creation in 1884 of a Moscow section.

The initiative and leadership for the Moscow section of the society

62. *TOSRPT*, pt. 22 (1893), section 2, pp. 8–68, gives a thorough summary of the society's activities over the first twenty-five years of its existence.

63. *Trudy vserossiiskogo s'ezda 1896*, vol. 3, pt. 5, "Uluchenie byta rabochikh," throughout. The single exception was the bland report of the Moscow Exchange Committee, which suggested the importance of helping the workers in case of disability or death (pp. 315–24); ibid., vol. 6, pt. 11, "Tekhnicheskoe obrazovanie," especially the article by N. N. Alianchikov, "V kakikh tekhnikakh nuzhdaetsia russkoi manufakturnoi promyshlennosti," pp. 107–19.

64. *ZOSRPT*, "Rech'," pp. 39–40.

came from the Moscow entrepreneurial group, primarily from T. S. Morozov, its first chairman, and N. K. Krestovnikov, who succeeded him. Reacting to the timid policies of the Exchange Association and the domination by St. Petersburg of the parent organization, the Moscow section advocated the economic and political supremacy of the center over the periphery. Their chief propagandist was the ubiquitous Sharapov, the permanent secretary of the Moscow section, whose shrill denunciation of the foreign and ethnic encirclement echoed dully in the society's Transactions. Sharapov's prime target was the textile and iron interests of Lodz, Moscow's great rival in the Kingdom of Poland, which he dramatically described as "a serious danger" to the industry of "the indigenous Great Russian center."[65]

This kind of open attack could not have been published in the society's official organ. But its appearance under the auspices of the Moscow section exposed the polite fiction of the society's reputedly all-Russian character. Carrying on the tradition of Chizhov and Aksakov, the Moscow section fought for prohibitive tariffs, an end to all transit rights and free ports, easy credit, and a railroad policy which favored Moscow by constructing local lines radiating from the central network and manipulating freight rates to discriminate against industrialists on the periphery. To this formidable list the Moscow section added a series of enlightened industrial policies, enunciated by Krestovnikov, ranging from improved commercial education to higher standards for manufactured goods.[66] The dream of Chizhov had been realized; the Moscow entrepreneurial group had found its organizational home. But to his surprise the merchantry (to say nothing of other social groups) did not move to join the organization. Wary of the connection with the Pan-Slavists, some took shelter in the safer and more respectable haven of Naidenov's Exchange Association, while most remained in the cocoon of their merchant society. In the mid-nineties the Moscow section was withering away.[67]

65. Sharapov, *Pochemu*, p. 15. For a more balanced view cf. *TOSRPT*, pt. 22 (1893), B. D. Belov, "Lodz i Sosnovitsy," pp. 1–68.
66. *TOSRPT*, pt. 16 (1886), pp. 278–85, 323–27; ibid., pt. 20 (1890), section 2, pp. 148–82; ibid., pt. 21 (1892), pp. 295–320; ibid., pt. 22 (1893), p. 44; ibid., section 3, pp. 444–54; ibid., pt. 23 (1895), section 1, pp. 75–77. Thereafter, mention of the Moscow section disappears, although articles by Sharapov continue to appear, e.g., his attack on foreign capital in ibid., pt. 25 (1900), pp. 273–95.
67. By this time textile merchants in Moscow who showed interest in technological improvement had already formed still another society of even more limited aims—the Society for the Assistance, Improvement, and Development of Industry, which, following the now-familiar pattern, held aloof from the organizations in St. Petersburg devoted to the same ends. See *Izvestiia Obshchestva dlia sodeistviia*. A sampling of articles was made from vol. 6, nos. 1–3, 5–8 (1902), and vol. 10 (1906). The leading figures in

The lack of a solid organizational center also hampered the Moscow entrepreneurs from dominating the political life of their own city, although they enjoyed several fleeting moments of success. Following the municipal reform of 1862 they took the initiative in organizing a political meeting at Soldatenkov's house to select a merchant candidate for mayor. Inexperienced and victimized by their competition for status, they handed out nominations like badges of honor to five men and assured themselves of a sound drubbing. That three of the five were from the Moscow entrepreneurial group—I. F. Mamontov, G. I. Khludov, and Liamin—testified to its high standing among the merchants.[68] But the merchants were unable to win over any nobles to their side. Even Aksakov broke ranks with his friends in demanding the election of a member of the nobility who was "not tied to the old urban traditions."[69]

As the group drew more closely together, Aksakov rallied behind its political aspirations. With his help as a speech writer, Liamin was elected in 1871 as the first merchant mayor of Moscow. The humiliating lesson of his forced resignation taught them to choose more wisely next time. Taking advantage of the government's electoral manipulations that disenfranchised so many of the intelligentsia in 1873, the Moscow entrepreneurs mounted a successful campaign to elect Sergei Tret'iakov, whose cultural prestige and social manners matched his solid merchant credentials. The new mayor drafted the first compre-

---

the organization were M. L. Losev, who had been educated at the St. Petersburg Technological Institute, A. I. Baranov, who had long been associated with the Morozovs in a cotton-spinning enterprise, A. I. Prokhorov, scion of one of the oldest Moscow merchant families, owners of the largest and most highly mechanized calico factory in Moscow, and S. P. Maliutin and the Morozovs, who were members of the Moscow entrepreneurial group. For eulogies of Baranov, Prokhorov, and Losev see ibid., vol. 10, no. 6 (1906), pp. 235–41, 270–72, and vol. 11, no. 11 (1912), pp. 613–19. That these figures were atypical of the Moscow merchantry hardly needs further proof, but even in their eulogies a strong note of criticism is sounded against the secret, sluggish behavior and the despotic labor policy of the majority of Russian factory owners.

68. Naidenov, *Vospominaniia*, 2:17–18. I. F. Mamontov subsequently withdrew his name, possibly under the influence of his old friend and political mentor Pogodin. For a good survey of change in the Moscow government, which, nevertheless, misinterprets the struggle between nobility and the merchantry, see B. V. Zlatoustovskii, "Gorodskoe samoupravlenie" Akademiia nauk, *Istoriia Moskvy*, 4:461–506.

69. *Den'*, 16 February 1863. In an editorial comment, Aksakov replied to a letter from "a Moscow meshchanin" advocating the election of a merchant that "it is . . . terribly important that the new mayor be a success and that he place the new city government on firm foundations. And since the election of a mayor from the merchantry would draw constantly on people—undoubtedly honorable—but whose primary distinction was wealth and not firmness and boldness of character, and scarcely capable of breaking with the old traditions of submissiveness and servility, it would be doubtful whether such a mayor from the merchantry could make a sudden sharp turn to the new."

hensive program of civic renovation, recruited Russian technical personnel for the town administration, and courageously proposed to cover the cost of extensive new public works by floating a large subscription loan. Together with Liamin and others in the group, he sought in vain to break down the isolation of the merchantry from the intelligentsia by endorsing electoral reform that would have given back the franchise to the landless nobles, mainly in the urban professions.

During Tret'iakov's second term the Near Eastern crisis delayed consideration of his ambitious plans, and the Russo-Turkish War siphoned off merchant capital and energies. With the return of peace, Tret'iakov faced growing opposition among the merchants to the increased financial burdens and risks necessary to modernize the city. His bold but expensive initiative in acquiring the Sokolniki woodland as a municipal park touched off a controversy that led to his resignation. Municipal improvements virtually came to a halt until 1885, when the tough and energetic N. A. Alekseev was elected mayor.

The most dynamic figure to come out of the merchantry between Timofei Morozov and Pavel Riabushinskii, the youthful Nikolai Alekseev embodied the hopes of the Moscow entrepreneurs for a leader of the younger generation. His family had been Great Russian peasants in Moscow province engaged in the handicraft production of gold thread. They accumulated enough capital to set up a factory in the Old Believer Rogozhskii district of Moscow. In its outward appearance a typical patriarchal enterprise, the Alekseev factory was distinguished by the extreme solicitude of the owner, S. A. Alekseev, for his workers, whom he had brought with him from the countryside. The high cost and rapid turnover of his silk fabric trimmed with gold thread enabled him to accumulate reserves of hard currency which he used to purchase steam filatures from Italy and to hire English workers. The latter, incidentally, adapted readily to the patriarchal pattern of living in the owner's house, where thirty sat at table every evening. When his grandson Nikolai took over the firm and mechanized it, the patriarchal relations ended.

Alekseev was educated at home, but spoke fluent French and German, knew some English, and acquired a great love for music. One of the founders of the Imperial Russian Musical Society and a close friend of Nikolai Rubinshtein, also a merchant's son, who established the Moscow Conservatory, Alekseev became a protégé of another patron of the society and the mayor of Moscow, Sergei Tret'iakov. Alekseev's family was related by blood, marriage, and business to the Chetverikovs. Together with his friend and brother-in-law Sergei Chetverikov, Alekseev expanded his commercial activities and formed the enormously successful Siberian Business Company.

Under Tret'iakov's watchful eye, Alekseev plunged eagerly into public service, first as a municipal sanitary trustee, then as a member of numerous city commissions, and finally as a delegate to the district and provincial zemstvos. As a vigorous trustee of many charitable and educational institutions, he gained widespread respect and was easily elected mayor of Moscow in 1885 at the remarkably young age of thirty-one. In 1889 he was reelected for a second term.[70] Charming, shrewd, and, when necessary, ruthless, he delighted his fellow merchants by his high-handed treatment of the nobility and his skillful manipulation of the meschane. Grudgingly, they accepted his strong leadership in carrying out many of the proposals that Tret'iakov and I. N. Mamontov had drafted years before. With the exception of street lighting and the municipal railroads, which had been turned over to private concessionaires, the remainder of the public-works projects carried out under Alekseev's administration were financed and built by the city itself. Alekseev got his merchant followers to agree to float loans to expand the city's modest water supply (1885–92), to begin in 1886 the enormous task of widening, straightening, and improving the paved streets, to construct the first underground sewer system (1887–88) and then expand it, and to put up municipal slaughterhouses in 1888.[71]

When, on the eve of his certain election to a third term, he was assassinated by a demented man, the merchants were thrown into confusion. Although the Moscow entrepreneurs subsequently got one more of their number elected as mayor, K. V. Rukavishnikov lacked the energy and vision of his predecessor.[72] Thereafter, the second generation of the group had to wait until the outbreak of World War I before they could launch another bid for control of the municipal government.

Imperialism

In defending their economic interests, it was only natural for the Moscow entrepreneurial group to be drawn deeper into Imperial Russian politics. The search for new markets and sources of raw

70. Chetverikov, *Bezvozvratno*, pp. 31, 83–88, 102–4; *Moskovskie vedomosti*, no. 70, 12 March 1893, Alekseev's obituary.
71. I. N. Mamontov, *Programma*, pp. 27–40; Golitsyn, "Moskva," p. 154; Rerberg, *Moskovskii*, pp. 19–29; Ivanov, *40 let*, pp. 8–13; Gorbunov, *Moskovskii*, pp. 67–70, 85–87.
72. Astrov, *Vospominaniia*, p. 250. Naidenov and his faction dismissed Rukavishnikov contemptuously as "ruka-Vishniakova," that is, "the hands of A. S. Vishniakov," a strong-minded member of the group who always preferred to work behind the scenes.

materials, accompanied by the construction of a railroad network radiating from the center, intensified their competition with foreigners and ethnic groups on the periphery. Here on the frontiers, just as on their home ground, the entrepreneurs of the Moscow group desired a strong national government to provide a protective screen behind which they could carry on their commercial activities with a better chance of competing successfully with the more technically advanced and experienced representatives of West European trade and industry. If at first the merchants in the group perceived foreign policy almost exclusively in terms of immediate profits, the intellectuals helped raise their sights to a broader view which encompassed the greater complexities of Russia's position as a great power. So the initial involvement in the Kingdom of Poland, the Caucasus, and Central Asia led gradually to a keener interest in the Balkans and East Central Europe.

Following the revolt of 1863 in Poland the Moscow group strongly endorsed repressive measures of russification, especially as they cut away the commercial and industrial privileges of the Polish and Jewish entrepreneurs in the area. Consequently, at the first signs of an official policy of reconciliation with the Poles, they sounded the alarm and organized to combat its economic effects. Aksakov warned that the appointment of General A. L. Potopov as governor-general would undermine the firm nationalist positions established by his predecessors. Most serious in his eyes was Potopov's renewed attempt to win over the Polish nobility by permitting them to buy and sell landed estates. Historical conditions had forced the Russian population, in his words, "to the bottom of the social ladder," and little had happened to change that situation. The Poles, "who tried for centuries to destroy the Russian nationality," still "held the power of landed property and education in their hands." Meanwhile, the Jews, "who held down the Russian agricultural population," also "controlled trade and industry." To break their stranglehold, Aksakov urged the creation of a peasants' bank in the western region.[73] Despairing of energetic government action, he and Chizhov planned and, with the rest of the Moscow group, launched a joint-stock company for settling a Russian agricultural population in the western provinces. Capitalized at one million rubles, its "immediate aim [was] to facilitate the transfer of estates in the Western region to individuals of Russian origin by purchasing land from Polish proprietors and selling it to Russians at very favorable conditions." The original list of subscribers included Babst,

---

73. Editorials in *Moskva*, 7 April, 6 and 10 August 1868, in Aksakov, *Sochineniia*, 3:491–92, 518, 522–27. See also the description of these reforms in Zaionchkovskii, *Provedenie*, pp. 385–88.

Liamin, Morozov, Soldatenkov, and Dmitri Shipov, as well as Aksakov and Chizhov.[74]

In the controversy within the bureaucracy between the advocates of a forward policy in the East and the supporters of a more cautious approach, the Moscow group naturally favored the former group. Because overt interference of private citizens in the formation of foreign policy was unthinkable, the Moscow group restricted its political activities to cooperating with the proconsuls of the East, like Prince A. I. Bariatinskii, viceroy of the Caucasus, General N. P. Ignat'ev, director of the Asiatic Department of the Ministry of Foreign Affairs, General M. G. Chernaev, the conqueror of Tashkent and commander of the Russian volunteers in Serbia, and General K. P. Kaufman, governor-general of Turkestan. As Bariatinskii's economic adviser, Kokorev helped to convince the viceroy to support a number of commercial ventures that would blunt British influence among Caucasian and Turkomen tribesmen and consolidate Russia's military position in the area. These included the establishment of Kokorev's Transcaucasian Steamship Company, a concession to Kokorev of Russia's first kerosene factory in the Caucasus, proposals to improve the water and rail connections between the Volga, Don, Caspian, and Sea of Azov, which benefited Kokorev's Volga-Don railroad, a proposed railroad from Tiflis to Russia, and efforts to revive the Transcaucasus transit trade (at this time Kokorev was still a moderate free trader).[75]

By the mid-1860s the Moscow group had begun directing its attention to Central Asia, which offered an alternative source of raw cotton at a time when American supplies had been cut off by the Union blockade of the Confederate States. Alexander Shipov, T. S. Morozov, and Chizhov organized a hero's welcome for General Chernaev in Moscow, despite the fact that the war minister, Miliutin, had recalled him from Central Asia for having exceeded his orders in storming Tashkent. "The Germans want to remove him," complained Shipov. "They stand for the foreign interests."[76] At the same time, the Moscow group pressed for a more active government policy in securing broader and safer trade relations with Central Asia and Mongolia. In

74. ORBL, f. 332, carton 79, no. 4, "Priglashenie vstupit' v tovarishechstvo," dated Moscow, January 1869.
75. Rozhkova, *Ekonomicheskie*, pp. 178, 185; Rieber, *Politics*, pp. 70–72; K. A. Skal'kovskii, *Nashi gosudarstvennye*, pp. 169–70.
76. ORBL, f. 332, carton 61, no. 2, A. Shipov to Chizhov, 5 January 1866. Aksakov also supported the expansion in one of his rare editorials on Central Asia in *Den'*, 4 August 1867; see Aksakov, *Sochineniia*, 7:107–11. Under the influence of Aksakov's fiery Pan-Slavic editorials, Chernaev saw himself in a new role as the liberator of the Balkan Slavs, and within a decade he was organizing Russian volunteers to fight the Turks. See Sumner, *Russia*, pp. 184–85.

the strongly worded "Memo on the Means of Developing Our Trade with Central Asia" to the Foreign Ministry, Alexander Shipov blamed the government's "cold-blooded neglect"—and not the alleged "short-sightedness, ignorance, or even incompetence" of the Russian merchants—for the fact that the bulk of trade with Central Asia was in the hands of local Muslim merchants. He recommended a series of measures to exclude Western European goods from those markets and improve conditions for Russian traders.[77]

Subsequently, the Moscow group established close working relations with Turkestan Governor-General Kaufman, who, like Bariatinskii, perceived the opportunities to consolidate and extend Russian influence through trade as well as force of arms. On his initiative two attempts were made, with the participation of the Moscow group, to set up trading companies in the area. The most important, the Moscow-Tashkent Company for the Aid of Russian Silk Manufacturing, counted among its founding members T. S. Morozov, Chizhov, Dmitri Shipov, A. N. and N. F. Mamontov, Liamin, and A. I. Khludov. Notifying Kaufman of the group's enthusiastic response to his proposals, Chizhov pointed out that the idea met "complete sympathy not so much in the hope for profit and brilliant success for the affair, . . . so much as in a warm love for Russia and consequently in the desire to assist it in every way." He explained that he and his associates were willing to take the considerable risk of investing in a remote and undeveloped region because of their great faith in Kaufman's achievements.[78]

Difficulties with the bureaucracy developed over the business practices of both companies. Contrary to the wishes of the founders, the Committee of Ministers insisted on publishing the Moscow-Tashkent Silk Company's accounts, which aroused the investors' fears that the apparent lack of success in that risky undertaking might damage their reputations and weaken public confidence in their other enterprises. Moreover, the Moscow group was unsuccessful in its efforts to convince the governor-general of the need for monopoly in the silk trade. In the long run, Kaufman, like so many other high officials, became disillusioned with what he regarded as the excessive timidity of Russian merchants.[79]

When Russian military expansion reached its territorial limits in Central Asia and the government renewed its economic rivalry with

77. Rozhkova, *Ekonomicheskie*, pp. 148–50, citing Foreign Ministry archives.
78. ORBL, f. 322, carton 10, no. 37, Chizhov to Kaufman, 1871. Chizhov alone responded by drafting a "declaration to Russian entrepreneurs" appealing for support, but the list he prepared for Russian stockholders remained blank (ibid., carton 79, no. 3, 1 October 1869).
79. Rozhkova, *Ekonomicheskie*, pp. 170–76.

the British in Persia, the Moscow entrepreneurs took the lead in opening new markets in the area. One of the first and most enterprising firms was the Tsindel' Association. Controlled by Soldatenkov, Khludov, Liamin, and Knoop, this company established in the 1880s a network of warehouses in Persia (as well as Sweden and China) in order to cut out the Tatar and Persian middlemen. They were followed by the A. Giubner Company, in which Soldatenkov and Shchukin were major shareholders. By the 1890s, Tret'iakov's partner Konshin, the Nikol'skaia Manufactures of T. S. Morozov, and the Bogorodsko-Glukhovskoe also built their own facilities in Persia.[80] These were the same merchants who had cheered the march of empire in this direction for the previous forty years. In 1890, Tret'iakov, together with Baron Korf and a scion of Khomiakov, the Slavophil prophet of railroads, proposed the construction of a railroad in Persia to connect with the Russian Transcaucasus line at Vladikavkaz. But these echoes of old dreams found resonance neither among the merchant organizations nor, for that matter, within the Ministry of Finance, which was ever fearful of overextending its resources and clashing with British economic interests.[81] Besides, there was always a question in the minds of the bureaucrats whether any more than a handful of Russian entrepreneurs would take full advantage of an opening to the south.

Clearly, the Moscow group was willing to take on occasion unusual commercial risks in order to give proof of its political vision. In return the entrepreneurs insisted on minimal guarantees for their investment from the financial bureaucracy and noninterference from the military bureaucracy. For their part the bureaucrats were perfectly happy to use the merchants to consolidate military expansion and promote political penetration, but expected them to forego a monopolistic position, which they associated with lack of initiative and stagnation, and to take high risks with their capital for patriotic reasons. It was another scene in the dialogue of the deaf that had characterized the relations between the merchants and representatives of the bureaucracy in the Russian borderlands since the early nineteenth century. The support of the Moscow group for a more vigorous, nationalistic, and anti-British foreign policy all along Russia's southern rim was to pay more tangible dividends in the Balkans.

When in 1867 the First Slavic Ethnographic Congress met in Moscow, followed by the organization of the Slavic benevolent committees, only the noble-intellectual wing of the Moscow group (Aksakov, Chizhov, and the Shipovs) showed any real interest in promoting Russia's

80. Semeniuk, "Bor'ba," pp. 107–8.
81. "Anglo-russkaia," pp. 35–48.

political interests in the Balkans.[82] For the merchants in the group the area offered little scope for their commercial activities, despite the efforts of Pan-Slavists like Pogodin to involve them in such ventures as the Dalmatian Trading Company.[83] At first they were prepared to endow a few charitable and educational activities, building a church in Prague or establishing fellowships for Bulgarian students. To be sure, they raised no serious objections to Aksakov's strongly Pan-Slavic editorial policy in *Moskva*, which they subsidized, but there was no risk there because since 1861 the government had been supplying Aksakov with confidential information on the Balkans.[84]

By the early 1870s in the wake of the Franco-Prussian War they perceived how heightened Russian patriotism might influence the government's economic policies and began to join the Moscow Slavic benevolent committees. Among the first thirty merchants to subscribe were Morozov, Liamin, Soldatenkov, and Tret'iakov. From that moment on a series of dramatic events hastened their complete conversion, yet in keeping with their traditional respect for authority they were careful not to outrun the government's tolerance for the unprecedented outburst of public enthusiasm for the Slavic cause that rapidly built to a climax early in 1877. Thus, despite the uprising in Bosnia and Aksakov's impassioned pleas, Liamin, Morozov, and Khludov resisted direct appeals for funds to equip and arm Russian volunteers for Serbia, even though Russians from all other social categories contributed men and money. Chernaev appeared too irresponsible, Serbia too remote, and the tsar indifferent. In the following year, after the Bulgarian massacres, when the governor-general of Moscow and then the imperial family demonstrated their sympathy with the Slavic cause, the merchants in the Moscow group became increasingly active in the volunteer work. Both as individuals and through the Moscow Exchange Committee, Morozov and Tret'iakov appealed to their fellow merchants for aid to the Bulgars. Once Aksakov, whom they trusted, finally concentrated in his office at the Moscow Merchants' Society of Mutual Credit the entire collection and distribution of funds for the Bulgars, money poured in—590,000 rubles in the three-month period from August to November 1876, in

82. ORBL, f. 332, carton 6, no. 10, "Rech' o slavianskom s'ezde 1867 goda (mai)," draft copy in Chizhov's hand. Aksakov's role is most fully discussed in Nikitin, "Slavianskie s'ezdy," pp. 16–92; Alexander and Dmitri Shipov were among the first dozen contributors to the Slavic committees (Nikitin, *Slavianskie komitety*, p. 40).

83. ORBL, f. 332, carton 4, no. 44, Pogodin to Chizhov, undated and 23 December 1869.

84. Nikitin, "Iuzhnoslavianskie," p. 102.

contrast to the modest amount collected up to that time.[85] The Moscow group also agreed to his request that the Moscow-Kursk line offer free transportation for volunteers moving south by rail to Odessa.[86] At the same time, Aksakov, Morozov, and Tret'iakov formed a committee of three to meet officially with War Minister D. A. Miliutin to work out "a plan of action for arming the Bulgarians."[87]

After Russia officially entered the war, the Slavic committees were

85. The authorities disagree on the extent of the merchants' financial contributions and personal involvement in the Slavic cause. Pokrovskii and Sumner accord them a major role, while Nikitin and MacKenzie minimize their importance (Pokrovskii, *Russkaia*, 4:253; Sumner, *Russia*, p. 188; Nikitin, *Slavianskie komitety*, 59–61, 64, 74, 77, 78–79, 274–75, 284, 311–13, and throughout; MacKenzie, *Serbs*, p. 120). The latter view is more convincing if the merchants are defined in class or soslovie terms. But then the contributions of the Moscow group grow in proportion. A crucial piece of evidence is Aksakov's claim that two-thirds of the contributions "came from our poor, overburdened ordinary people . . . ," and that "our wealthy citizens did not participate to any great extent." But Aksakov did not make it clear whether the two-thirds referred to the total sum of over 1.5 million rubles collected in the two capitals or just to the Moscow contributions of 742,328 rubles (Aksakov, *Sochineniia*, 1:226–30). Moreover, no other contemporary records exist to verify Aksakov's figures. By emphasizing the ethical value of the monetary donations because of the sacrifice involved on the part of poor people who gave to a cause which was remote from their own material interests, Aksakov sought to justify his belief in the moral unity of the Russian people. Under such circumstances it is possible that he exaggerated the contribution of the poor (indeed if there was any way of calculating this in the first place). Even if he did not and assuming he was referring to two-thirds of the Moscow figure, he has admitted that over 247,000 rubles were donated by the wealthy. Aksakov's correspondence with Chizhov makes it clear that it did not come from the old-fashioned soslovie organizations of the merchantry (ORBL, f. 332, carton 15, no. 10, Aksakov to Chizhov, 11 June 1876). He berates the merchants' administration (*uprava*) for having promised only 1000 rubles a year for the Slavic cause, while offering 7000 for the construction of an Orthodox church in the German watering spa of Ems in order to buy off Alexander II from punishing culprits in the collapse of the Commercial Loan Bank. The number of wealthy nobles in Moscow was relatively small compared to St. Petersburg, and the intelligentsia lacked the means. It seems logical to conclude that this sum came from a handful of wealthy merchants, including most of the Moscow group, who once again were in advance of their soslovie and were taking the lead in trying to raise funds in the Moscow Exchange Society and working with the government to equip the Bulgarians. Naidenov identified the leaders as Tret'iakov, T. S. Morozov, Aksenov, Sanin, and himself (*Vospominaniia*, 2:158). To obtain a complete picture of merchant support for the war it is necessary to add to this total the sum of almost one million rubles contributed by the Moscow merchants and exchange committees for families of Russian soldiers killed or wounded in action (*Materialy dlia istorii Moskovskogo kupechestva*, 10:85, "Zhurnal sobraniia vybornykh Moskovskogo kupecheskogo sosloviia," 20 October 1883).

86. ORBL, f. 332, carton 15, no. 11, Aksakov to Chizhov, 12 January [1877]. The Kursk-Kiev and Odessa railroads also agreed to provide free passage for volunteers.

87. Miliutin, *Dnevnik*, 2:108 (entry 31 October 1876). That the minister of war and three private citizens should meet in order to draft such a plan is an extraordinary testimony to the influence of the Moscow group, yet no treatment of the war mentions it.

shunted aside by official agencies. They fell apart altogether when the Treaty of Berlin discredited Aksakov's messianic visions. The rest of the Moscow group held to a more cautious course, preserving its patriotic image without exposing it to the accusation by the authorities that it was too zealous in pursuit of the chimera of Slavic liberation. Aksakov was useful and influential to them, but they were not willing to sacrifice their hard-won favorable relations with high officials for a political will-o'-the-wisp. They sought to influence, not to challenge or embarrass, the government. Once Aksakov, duly chastened by arrest and confinement to his estates, returned to the fold, they were delighted to finance another one of his papers, Rus', which continued to defend their business interests, while adhering to a more properly loyalist position on foreign policy in general and the Slavic question in particular.[88]

Religious Policies

The Moscow entrepreneurial group came closest to taking an oppositionist stance not in economic or foreign policy but in religious policy, not in liberating the Slavs but in liberating the Old Believers. As had occurred with other questions, enthusiasm for this cause varied within the group. If the merchant wing resisted complete submission to the Pan-Slavic ideal so dear to the hearts of the nobles, the situation was almost the reverse with respect to the Old Belief. But the key figure was, once again, Ivan Aksakov, who, more than anyone else in Russia, was responsible for turning the treatment of the Old Believers into a public issue. Although he never embraced their faith, his spirited and courageous defense of their religious and civil rights amply repaid the Old Believer merchants for their years of subsidizing his journalistic ventures.

Like the Slavophils before him, Aksakov perceived an organic link between the Old Belief and Russian national feelings. He also shared their concern over the declining vigor of the Orthodox Church and

88. A collection of Aksakov's articles in Rus' on the Slavic question may be found in his Sochineniia, 1:319–791. Tame compared with his work before 1878, they reflect his disillusionment with events in the Balkans. On the other hand, he became more outspokenly anti-German, which fit in better with the ideas of the Moscow group. He even tried his hand at articles on economic questions, including two significant pieces on railroads in the issues of 22 August 1881 and 17 July 1882, where he attacked those old enemies of the Moscow group, "the Jewish, Koenigsberg, and Berlin bankers" who were trying to buy up Russian railroads in the strategic western and southwestern provinces and the Grand Société for its reckless mismanagement of the Nikolaevskii line (ibid., 7:601–11, 643–54).

feared for its ability to withstand the mounting pressures of Roman Catholicism in the western provinces and atheism among the intelligentsia. What troubled Aksakov most was the unwillingness of the members of the hierarchy to accept freedom of conscience, an attitude that forced them to rely too heavily on the repressive power of the state and not enough on their own spiritual resources in the struggle for Russia's soul. He singled out church censorship and the persecution of the Old Believers for building private chapels as particularly reprehensible and came out flatly for religious toleration. Unless the faith could be tempered in controversy, he was convinced, it would wither. Already Russian religious life was characterized by what he called "our indolent love for our indolent faith." And without a vigorous faith there could be no strong sense of national identity.[89]

It was a question, then, of seeking the deeper currents of belief. "We the educated part of society," he wrote, "constantly forget that there is a popular milieu, in the strictest sense of the word, where the movement of religious ideas is constantly going on, [and] though it is stigmatized as coarse and ignorant, it testifies at least to the vitality of an interest in faith; where the schism and heresy exist, there are teachers and preachers who are not dozing off, but who, without the assistance of the press, unflaggingly expose to the people . . . every error, every wickedness of our church administration." The strength and richness of this subterranean faith flowed out of a pre-Petrine national tradition and spread by means of open debate. "More than ever freedom is necessary for the internal life of the church because only freedom can restore the authenticity of truth itself."[90]

He denied that toleration for the Old Believers involved any risk, any clear and present danger for the state. However, his attitude toward Roman Catholicism was altogether different. That church could not be permitted to act freely in the northwest provinces or even the Volga because "it has become the symbol of a political idea," openly hostile to the essence of the Russian national spirit. By contrast, even those sectarians whose beliefs made them potential opponents of the government should be left alone, in Aksakov's view, so long as they did not engage in illegal actions against the state. The practical implications of all this for his merchant friends were as explicit as he could make them. Conceding that toleration could never lead to the appointment of an Old Believer to a commission charged with the organization of the life of the Orthodox clergy, he added that "it would be entirely incorrect (and this happens in Russia) to deprive him of the

89. *Den'*, 18 September, 28 October 1865; *Moskva*, 1 and 2 August 1865; *Moskvich*, 18 January 1868.
90. *Den'*, 16 October 1865.

right to be not only a member but even president of some kind of industrial council or of an official institution which manages the sorts of interests where religious relationships are irrelevant."[91]

When Aksakov became caught up in the Pan-Slavic crusade of the 1870s, he shifted the basis for his moral regeneration of Russia from internal to external sources, but his disillusionment with the outcome of the Russo-Turkish War brought him back once again to the Old Believers. Picking up his arguments where he had left them, he now reproached the church for its excessive rigidity and legalism, which prevented many sectarians from reuniting with the church through the edinoverie. As far as he was concerned, the Orthodox and the schismatics were divided by ritual, not dogma, so that it seemed perfectly logical to propose that the church undertake a reexamination of the old books with the participation of the Old Believers in order to verify the corrections made in Nikon's time.[92] Not satisfied with this extraordinary suggestion, he threw open the pages of *Rus'* to a new generation of heterodox religious writers, who launched a serious theological reevaluation of the schism.

In part, Aksakov was motivated by a fear that the newly awakened interest of the liberals in the Old Believers as a persecuted minority might lure the schismatics into genuine political opposition.[93] Acting to forestall this frightening possibility, he published a series of articles by Vladimir Solov'ev which, while they did not justify the schism, placed much of the blame for it upon the stubborn zealots of the church and the "latinizing" inspiration of Nikon's reforms.[94]

But Solov'ev's attraction to Catholicism undermined his relations with Aksakov, and the latter found a replacement in Nikita Giliarov-Platonov. A one-time theologian and clever right-wing journalist, he was something of an economic theorist as well, which made him par-

---

91. *Moskva*, 9 August 1868.
92. *Rus'*, 26 September 1881.
93. Ibid., 5 December 1881.
94. Ibid., 2 October 1882; Solov'ev's articles are most conveniently found in his *Sochineniia*, vol. 3, "O dukhovnoi vlasti v Rossii" (1881), especially pp. 258–59, and "O raskole v russkom narode i obshchestve" (1882–83), pp. 245–85. Konstantin Mochulskii called the second article in the series, "O raskole . . . ," "one of the most remarkable products of Russian religious thought" (*Solov'ev*, pp. 136–37). Even though Solov'ev soon drifted away from Aksakov and plunged into an eight-year polemic with the Slavophils over his crypto-Catholic views, he deepened his appreciation of the spiritual qualities in the Old Belief. See particularly, "Velikii spor i khristianskaia politika" (1883), *Sochineniia*, 4:72–76; "Istoriia i budushchnost' teokratii" (1885–87), ibid., p. 330; and "Vizantizm i Rossiia," ibid., 7:321. The Old Believer merchants avidly followed his evolution toward their views. See Riabushinskii, *Staroobriadchestvo*, pp. 80–81, who also admired Solov'ev's profound insights into the Old Believer psychology in his "Tri razgovory."

ticularly suited for Aksakov's purposes. A priest's son whose family was close to the Khomiakovs, he obtained his degree in the faculty of creeds, heresies, and schisms of the Moscow Theological Academy, then entered state service, became a member of the Moscow Censorship Committee and traveled abroad on an official mission to study Jewish schools. Through his career he acquired the attitudes on the press, the Old Believers, and the Jews that logically led him into Aksakov's circle. In his articles on the schism published in *Rus'* he compared the Old Believers' mastery of religious literature with the intellectual poverty of the official theologians—and got himself fired from the Moscow Theological Academy for his pains.[95]

By transferring his religious views into political economy, Giliarov produced an apologia for capitalism that is almost unique in Russian literature and was eminently suited to justify the role of the Old Believer merchants and industrialists. The main point of his analysis was the overwhelming importance of "the psychological moral element" in production and exchange. Directly confronting Marx, Engels, and Lasalle, he argued that value had a purely subjective meaning, that capital not labor was the basic creative force, that wages deserved no more compensation than other factors, and that factory legislation was not useful because it did not guarantee quality, which was just as important as time in determining cost. By maintaining that the highest good in production was to nourish the spiritual, "for material wealth is not an autonomous good," he restated in a new way the old Slavophil position on capitalism and reflected accurately the deepest-held sentiments of the Old Believers on the nature of their economic activities.[96]

By helping to launch the partial rehabilitation of the Old Believers, at least in the eyes of one section of the public, Aksakov left a valuable legacy to the next generation of the Moscow entrepreneurial group, and indeed his influence carried right down to the revolution, and even beyond into the emigration. As the premier political theorist of the group he had forged the last link which joined Great Russian people to a national religious tradition and a national economic policy.

A Balance Sheet

By the early 1880s the first generation of the Moscow entrepreneurial group was beginning to fade from the scene, and it is an appropriate

95. Giliarov-Platonov, *Iz perezhitogo*, pp. 308–11; idem, "Logika raskola," *Rus'*, nos. 7, 8, 10 (17 and 24 August, 7 September 1885); Riabushinskii, *Staroobriadchestvo*, p. 74.
96. Giliarov-Platonov, *Osnovye*, a posthumous work, episodic and often confusing, but

point at which to evaluate their contributions. As their economic legacy they endowed the old Muscovite center with an economic infrastructure and a protected industrial base that enabled it to withstand the pressure of encirclement and to maintain a high return on investment. In the 1880s profits in the cotton-spinning industry reached a level of 60 percent of the capital invested.[97] Thanks also to the energy and resourcefulness of the Moscow entrepreneurs, an economic infrastructure of new banks, railroads, and technical schools sprang up in the center. The combination of abundant investment capital and regional development enabled the textile industry to maintain its competitive position by introducing new technology and constructing new plants. As late as 1908 textiles accounted for 26 percent of the value of finished goods produced in Russia and over three-quarters of this production was located in the central industrial region. The commanding position of Moscow in textiles was the main reason that the center remained a major manufacturing region, accounting for 36 percent of finished goods produced in the empire in 1914. Thus, one valuable contribution of the Moscow group was to keep a significant share of the private sector in the hands of Russian entrepreneurs, especially during the 1890s, when the influx of foreign capital and technicians reached its peak. From this economic base in the center the merchantry was able to defend its economic independence until it was sufficiently strong and self-confident to cooperate with foreign concerns on equal terms. By steadily accumulating capital in their own banks, the entrepreneurs were in a position by 1908 to take a more active part in controlling industries and exploiting foreign investment and technology for their own ends.[98]

The group's political legacy was a new relationship between the government and the merchantry which was to have fateful consequences for the future of Russian society. By its vigorous lobbying and propaganda the Moscow group demonstrated conclusively that native Russian capitalists could organize to defend their interests and thus influence the course of economic development. To achieve their goals within the frame of the autocracy they tolerated much of the vague and ambivalent attitude toward state authority that was deeply

the essence of which is neatly summarized in the preface by Professor I. T. Tarasov, pp. v–x.

97. Livshits, *Razmeshchenie*, p. 149. In this connection it is significant that as late as 1900 the branch of Russian industry in which foreign investment secured the smallest share of capital was the textile industry (Crihan, *Capital étranger*, p. 249). See also Laverychev, *Monopolisticheskii*, for the emergence of the central region by the first decade of the nineteenth century as the undisputed leader in textiles in the three-way competition with Lodz and St. Petersburg.

98. McKay, *Pioneers*, pp. 237–38, 384–85.

imbedded in the traditional outlook of the merchant soslovie. Direct participation in representative institutions was much less important to them than creating a partnership with the state that permitted them a wide latitude for their entrepreneurial activities yet provided them with strong defenses against powerful foreign and domestic rivals. Given the conditions of slow urban growth and foreign-ethnic encirclement, it was in their best interests to maintain this special relationship with the bureaucracy, which unfettered competition and representative institutions, even based on property qualification, would have destroyed. The original Moscow group demonstrated the effectiveness of limiting political action to areas where they were certain of maintaining a high degree of influence and control: the Ministry of Finance and their own enterprises, newspapers, and local commercial-industrial organizations. Only gradually and cautiously did they move into the dangerous waters of urban politics. By the end of the nineteenth century their elitist tactics had produced stunning results. The relatively backward Muscovite center not only maintained but expanded its role in the economic life of the country. The government blessed the marriage of economic and political (that is Great Russian) nationalism that the Moscow entrepreneurial group had fostered from its beginnings. If the bureaucracy was motivated by different concerns from those of the merchants, this in no way marred their celebration of success. The real dangers of these achievements lay hidden in the future, when revolution and the creation of a truly representative national parliament would drastically alter the political game and threaten the very survival of interest groups as they emerged under an autocratic form of government.

CHAPTER 6

ENTREPRENEURS

ON THE PERIPHERY

On the periphery of the empire industrialization intensified rather than diminished the social and economic differences that gave precedence to region, nationality, and soslovie above class. In the south and northwest heavy industry and banking underwent startling transformations during the great spurts in the 1890s and after the revolution of 1905. Under the pressure of rapid economic growth the regional characteristics that had long distinguished them from the center became more pronounced. From this new social and economic milieu sprang a type of entrepreneur radically different from that of the central industrial provinces. In education, career patterns, ethnic origins, and attitudes toward industrialization they represented, in many ways, the antithesis of the insular, Great Russian merchant-patriarch, clinging to the vestiges of the family firm.

The Southern Industrial Region

The relatively late development of the south as an industrial region must be traced to the abolition of serfdom and the construction of a railroad network. In the wake of emancipation the old possessional factories collapsed, releasing a supply of trained workers, and the state sold off its industries, opening the way to the expansion of privately owned capitalist enterprises. By the 1870s and 1880s the main trunk lines linking northern and southern Russia were supplemented by a network of east-west lines and local connecting spurs which facilitated access to the major sources of coal and iron ore in the Donets Basin.[1] The availability of new plowlands and seasonal as

1. By 1913 the southern metallurgical region together with the southwestern provinces enjoyed a much more favorable ratio of railroad tracks per square kilometer than any other region (Bakulev, *Razvitie*, pp. 122–23).

well as permanent work in the mines attracted a steady flow of migrants to the pits from the overcrowded central provinces and local villages. In the period 1863–85 southern Russia suddenly became the fastest-growing area in the European part of the empire. Between 1863 and 1914 the population of the four industrial provinces the Don Military, Tauride, Ekaterinoslav, and Kharkov grew in absolute numbers more than that of Siberia and at just about the same rate of increase.[2]

Although the investment opportunities possessed an intrinsic attraction, the new finance minister, Sergei Witte, made certain, through a vast promotional campaign, that they were brought to the attention of West Europeans in order to stimulate a massive influx of foreign capital. A ready supply of foreign engineers and entrepreneurs was supplemented by a growing number of Russian-trained engineers providing the necessary technical and managerial skills. Blended together, these elements made possible the rapid construction of a colossal modern mining and metallurgical industry. The mutual relationship of the coal and iron industry and their joint reliance on an extensive railroad network produced an integrated economic system unlike that of any other region of the empire. Their interdependence emerged clearly from their pattern of growth. In the decade 1889–99 the extraction of fossil fuels for use in metallurgical factories increased eleven times, and by 1903 over 70 percent of the Don coal and anthracite was consumed in the south—most of it by railroads and metallurgical factories.[3] Sometime after 1905 coal replaced grain as the leading item of freight (by tonnage) on the Russian railroads.

The character and distribution of industrial enterprises strongly influenced the pattern of settlement and the urban profile of the south. By the end of the century the Donets Basin was one of the most highly industrialized subregions in the empire on the basis of three crucial measurements: the percentage of nonagricultural population in towns, the percentage of the commercial-industrial population engaged in industrial activity, and the turnover in rubles per capita. At the same time, the industrial population was more widely scattered in smaller towns than it was in the other major industrial regions (see table 6.1).[4] There were no large established urban centers where the industrialists could be absorbed into preexisting social and cultural structures. Kharkov and Ekaterinoslav, on the periphery of the area,

2. Rashin, *Naselenie*, pp. 44, 69. For a thorough analysis of the growth of the working-class population in the south see idem, *Formirovanie*, pp. 443–47.
3. Shpolianskii, *Monopolii*, pp. 25–26.
4. V. Semenov-Tian-Shanskii, "Gorod i derevnia v Evropeiskoi Rossii," *ZIRTO* (1910), vol. 10, pt. 2, pp. 178–79.

TABLE 6.1. *Industrial Subregions of the Russian Empire*

Regional and Subregional Type	Towns with Percentage of Urban Population in Each Category				Percentage of Nonagricultural Population in Towns	Percentage of Industrial and Commercial Population in Industrial Activity	Turnover Rubles per Capita
	A	B	C	D			
PriBaltic	60	14	11	51	59	35	404
Moscow	39	8	14	23	49	43	208
Donets	—	—	17	41	60	80	317
Polish metallurgical	—	—	32	31	60	81	248
Ural	—	—	18	29	43	46	99

Note: A—towns averaging 1,150,000 inhabitants; B—towns averaging 194,000 inhabitants; C—towns averaging 50,000 inhabitants; D—percentage of urban population in region.

had some mitigating effect on the life-style of the southern industrialist, but neither was in any way comparable to Moscow or St. Petersburg and rather resembled the position of Lodz in the Polish metallurgical region. The result was a kind of rough-and-ready, boom-town atmosphere which had no parallel anywhere else in the empire. If these elements were unusual or unique when considered separately, their combination in the south produced an industrial environment that demanded a wholly new spirit of entrepreneurship.[5]

The Southern Entrepreneurial Group

It required a very special blend of talent and energy to organize the extraction of coal and iron in the Donbas and manage the large complex freight system of the southwestern railroad network. It was necessary to deal with a wide range of economic decisions and treat with political institutions at several levels, ranging from local zemstvos to central ministries. In the course of establishing a combined mining and metallurgical enterprise, a single individual might be expected to give a preliminary evaluation of the economic potential of a project, design and construct a new plant, supervise the transfer of modern Western technology, and, finally, manage the completed enterprise. The proper mix of such entrepreneurial, technical, and managerial skills could be found only in a trained polytechnical engineer.[6] In Russia in the 1870s and 1880s those were still in short supply, and during these years they suffered from a dubious reputation.

Until the 1860s engineers in Russia had been trained along narrowly professional lines mainly to fill low-paid routine jobs in a ministry or department of the central bureaucracy. Then, following the reorganization of Russian industry after the emancipation, it suddenly became possible for them to make a great deal of money very quickly. The proliferation of private railroad companies made high fees and windfall profits on investments easily available to those who shared inside knowledge. Every railroad scandal or stock speculation appeared to involve engineers as well as merchants. Public attitudes hardened against them, and the word *engineer* became synonymous with *money-grubber*.[7] They themselves often lacked confidence in their

5. For a good analysis of the three different types of foreign entrepreneurs and their basic strategy see McKay, *Pioneers*, pp. 70–71 and chap. 3, throughout.
6. Green, "Industrialization," chap. 5.
7. Fenin, *Vospominaniia*, pp. 39–40.

own technical training, regarding the education at the Institute of Transportation Engineers as "dry bureaucratic formalism."[8]

In mining operations a strong bias against Russian engineers existed because the director of the Mining Institute in St. Petersburg preferred to recommend Germans even though their qualifications were often inferior.[9] Many French and Belgian investors in southern Russia had little respect for Russian engineers as late as the 1890s and early years of the twentieth century and recruited their own countrymen with high salaries and other benefits.[10] Soon the Russian-trained engineers found themselves outnumbered by foreign engineer-managers, mainly graduates from the *les grandes écoles* where polytechnical education had been taught for almost a century. There was never a question, however, of the French altogether replacing the Russian engineers, whose knowledge of local conditions was indispensable for the smooth operation of the enterprises. Moreover, by this time the professional character of the Russian engineers had undergone a striking change with the increased regulation and repurchase by the government of private railroads and the introduction of reforms in higher technical education.

The educational reforms of the 1860s had a profound and, to this day, largely unappreciated effect upon higher technical schools and, in particular, upon the two institutions that were destined to graduate the leading engineer-technologists in the last half century of the empire—and beyond—the St. Petersburg technological and the mining institutes. The transformation of the curriculum and, in the case of the Mining Institute, the liberation from military control and discipline made possible the introduction of a broader range of subjects and the hiring of a distinguished faculty.[11] By the mid-1870s and early 1880s steps had been taken to promote real polytechnical education at the higher institutes. The initiatives came mainly from southerners, all practical men and members of the Russian Technological Society, who understood the need for a more comprehensive and better-integrated program of training and employment for engineers. In the St. Petersburg Technological Institute the driving force was I. A.

8. Liubimov, "Iz zhizni," pp. 95–96. The author was subsequently an engineer on the Kursk-Kharkov-Azov line. See Witte, *Vospominaniia*, 1:87–88, 127, 199. For a more measured but equally telling criticism see D. Volkov, "Ot redaktora," *Inzhener* I, no. 1 (1882).

9. Auerbakh, "Vospominaniia," 138:451–52.

10. Lauwick, *L'Industrie*, pp. 178–80, 304–6.

11. *Kratkii ocherk o tekhnologicheskom institute*, pp. 60–67, 82–85; Loranskii, *Kratkii ocherk gornogo vedomstva*, pp. 86–90.

Vyshnegradskii, whose innovative work as director served as the basis for his subsequent reorganization of Russian technical education.[12]

The leaders of reform in the Mining Institute were N. A. Kulibin, a major figure in the training of a whole generation of mining engineers, and K. A. Skal'kovskii, the most successful propagandist for mining education in late-Imperial Russia. Both men were expert mining engineers and graduates of the institute, with extensive experience in Russia and abroad; Vyshnegradskii and Witte appointed them successive directors of the Mining Department of the Ministry of Finance. Under Kulibin's leadership all Russian metallurgical factories were brought under the authority of the department, and a geological committee was formed to undertake the first systematic mapping of Russia's subsoil. Skal'kovskii, whose father had been one of the first boosters of southern development, devoted his entire life to advancing the southern mining and metallurgical industry. During his brief four-year service as director he not only modernized the Mining Institute and created a new administrative division for the southern fields but he also drafted the basic legislation for the extractive industries of Russia, including laws regulating its relations with government and workers, which survived almost unchanged to the end of the empire.[13] These men personified the new spirit of Russian engineering, with its breadth of interests, self-confidence, and impatience with both the myth of foreign technical superiority and the reality of Russia's economic backwardness. And they transmitted these values to their students.

Among the new generation of engineers graduating from the higher schools, there was a tendency to regard the Moscow textile merchants and the southern noble industrialists as crusty holdovers from a bygone era. By contrast, they regarded themselves as the vanguard of a modern industrialization and sought fresh fields in which to exercise their talents; nowhere did the vistas appear more attractive than in the south.[14] In fact, their perceptions were solidly grounded. Whatever the enthusiasms of the Moscow entrepreneurs for technical education, the majority of the textile merchants showed little interest in hiring graduates of the higher schools. A questionnaire submitted in 1876 to graduates of the Technological Institute ranked the cotton textiles of the central provinces fifth (and last) among major employ-

12. ORBL, f. 169, carton 43, no. 23, Ivan Alek. Vyshnegradskii, "O preobrazovanii vyshikh spetsial'nykh uchebnykh zavedenii, marta 1879,"; *Tekhnologicheskii institut*, 2:22–28; A. Borodin, "I. A. Vyshnegradskii," *Inzhener*, November 1895, pp. 1–6.
13. Loranskii, *Kratkii ocherk gornogo vedomstva*, pp. 104–6; *BE*, 3:37, 59:172.
14. Fenin, *Vospominaniia*, p. 40.

ers of their talents.[15] In the Urals the metallurgical entrepreneurs were still, for the most part, the former noble owners of possessional factories, clinging to their outmoded technology and authoritarian management with the help of a government-subsidized financial structure.[16] The Kingdom of Poland had a surplus of trained engineers, and most of the German-owned concerns brought in their own technical personnel from the Reich. Although the southern noble industrialists were the first to employ large numbers of Russian-trained engineers, especially in the sugar-beet industry, by the 1890s they were no longer able to maintain control over their mining properties. The big landowners who exploited the subsoil of their own properties, men like I. G. Ilovaiskii, G. V. Depreradovich, Ia. I. Drevitskii, P. A. Karpov, V. N. Rutchenko, P. P. Rykovskii, and M. Shcherbatov, had begun to rent to Jewish merchants after the emancipation. Later, many sold out to the big foreign capitalists, who could afford to bring in the latest technology and hire the engineering specialists to apply it.[17]

Besides their polytechnical training, the engineers who worked in the south were distinguished by their heterogeneous ethnic background. Many of the leading engineers who came from non-Russian families were Polish, but there was a sprinkling of Jews, Germans, and Ukrainians as well. A long tradition of admiring Western Europe predisposed them to cooperate closely with foreign investors and rapidly adopt modern business organization and methods. On the negative side what proved a source of strength in the south became a drawback at the all-Russian level to the long-range political aspirations of the engineers.

Necessity as much as choice dictated the entry of the Poles into the field. The institutions of higher education in Poland regularly produced more graduates than the region could absorb. The revolt of 1863 cast a shadow over the loyalty of Poles in state service, closing off careers normally open to them outside the kingdom. Consequently,

15. *Kratkii ocherk o tekhnologicheskom institute*, pp. 121–22.
16. Gindin, "Pravitel'stvennaia podderzhka," pp. 120–62.
17. Rubin, "Rabochii," pp. 4–5, 11. Exactly how much real investment foreign capitalists provided remains unclear. Contemporary opponents of Witte's policy like Sharapov and P. V. Ol' appear to have exaggerated it, though von Laue accepts Ol's figures at face value (*Witte*, pp. 287–88). McKay supplies a valuable corrective, revising the figures downward in his *Pioneers*, pp. 25–31. Fred Carstensen is even more strongly revisionist, pointing out that in some cases, like the French acquisition of Huta Bankova, the foreign capitalists paid the former owners in shares, not cash (Carstensen, "Numbers and Reality," pp. 275–84). It is important to remember, however, that a large part of Russian opinion ranging from extreme left to extreme right accepted the picture of massive foreign investments and influence in Russian industry.

increasing numbers of Polish students enrolled in higher Russian technical schools. In 1881, on the eve of the great industrial spurt, about 20 percent of the student body at the Technological Institute, the Mining Institute, and the Institute of Transportation Engineers were Poles, who formed a tightly knit group that spoke only their own language and rarely to Russians at all.[18] But the relative decline of the Polish mining and metallurgical industry in this period threatened to create a large surplus of unemployed Polish technicians. The dramatic expansion of the coal and iron industries of the south offered them a brilliant opportunity. By virtue of their polytechnical training in Warsaw, Riga, and St. Petersburg they were perfectly suited to meet the growing and specific needs of southern industry. Moreover, foreign capitalists in the Ukraine, especially the French and Belgians, regarded them with great sympathy, not only for their technical skills but also for their "Western" cultural outlook and their ability, at the same time, to deal with local problems involving peasant labor, gentry landlords, and government officials. An impressive group, they monopolized the key positions in the south (as well as the Urals) and went on to become leading figures in the industrial life of independent Poland after World War I. Wherever they went, they preserved their subculture and sought to recruit only Poles to serve under them.[19] Although they were loyal Russian subjects, they remained partisans of autonomy for Poland. Although their sympathies were not made public until 1905, their advocacy of economic decentralization and regional integration of the Ukraine was always suspect on political grounds in the eyes of Great Russian nationalists. Old fears of closer ties between Poland and the Ukraine than between the Ukraine and Moscow were never far below the surface of Russian life.

Beginning as technical specialists, these engineers often became owners of the means of production. The most enterprising among the first wave of Russian-trained engineers who came south in the 1870s and 1880s quickly established themselves in competition with foreign engineers as managers of some of the biggest firms in the Donbas. With that base they gradually obtained a share in the ownership of the enterprises. As one Russian engineer recalled years later, the "smart" metallurgical engineers soon moved out of the factories into the mining areas, where profits were much larger and, for the Poles, at least, contacts were easier with the foreign capitalists.[20] Thus,

18. Bieniearzóna, "Polska," p. 287; Jaros "Polacy," pp. 506–8; Pavlov, *Vospominaniia*, p. 64.

19. Jaros, "Polacy," p. 509, Fenin, *Vospominaniia*, pp. 120, 122, 128, 131, Pavlov, *Vospominaniia*, pp. 65, 240, 224–48, 283–84.

20. Pavlov, *Vospominaniia*, pp. 283–84.

a new division was opened up within the engineering profession. The old distinctions had been based on the source of employment, either the state or private enterprise. While this distinction continued to exist, engineers in private enterprise in the south were further subdivided into two socioeconomic categories, the engineer-capitalist and the engineer-technician. The tensions between these two types showed up most clearly in attitudes toward the workers, as the revolution of 1905 would illustrate once again.

Because of the social and economic milieu in which they worked, it is more difficult to sort out layers within the southern entrepreneurial group, as these engineer-capitalists shall henceforth be called, than it was in their Moscow counterparts. They were all leaders of the Association of Southern Coal and Steel Producers, which became the most powerful lobbying organization for industry in the south. But not all members of the association can be identified as members of the group. During its early history, in particular, small independent owners and engineer-technicians in the organization strongly disagreed with the leadership and its policies. Most of the southern entrepreneurs were managers or directors of big firms with heavy foreign investments. They took the initiative in forming the big coal and metallurgical trusts at the turn of the century and subsequently became the key figures in the Permanent Advisory Office of Metallurgists, with its headquarters in St. Petersburg, and in the council of the Association of the Representatives of Trade and Industry. Even though several of them were elected to the State Council, their collective influence weakened after 1908 when the Petersburg investment banks began to take over their firms. But they remained in important positions, including the Special Council on Defense in World War I, right down to the revolution of 1917.

The core of the group was composed of V. V. Zhukovskii, I. I. Iasiukovich (Jasiukowicz), and A. A. Vol'skii (Polish); A. A. Auerbakh and N. F. von Ditmar (German); L. G. Rabinovich (Jewish); F. E. Enakiev (Ukrainian); and N. S. Avdakov (Russian). One of the pioneers in the investigation and exploitation of coal reserves in Russia, A. A. Auerbakh, the son of a Russified German doctor, graduated from the Mining Institute in 1863 and continued his research as a professor of mineralogy in the institute, where he was the first Russian to employ the microscopic method in analyzing minerals. Having completed his dissertation, he plunged into practical work as a consultant for foreign firms, first English in central Russia and then French in the south at the Rutchenko Mines. As a founder of the Association of Southern Coal and Steel Producers, a prominent member of the Russian Technological Society, and a frequent contributor to *Gornyi zhurnal* [Mining journal], he led the campaign to bring to an end the traditional state policy of exercising control over mining and railroad construction by means of subsidies and bounties. Equally distrustful of hidebound state engineers, remote foreign capitalists, and irresponsible Russian entrepreneurs, he was one of the first to outline a comprehensive program of industrialization for the south. He envisaged combining government measures to facilitate the immigration of workers and the organization of enterprises and markets with foreign capital to finance the operation, but all under the direction and control of Russian-trained engineer-managers employed by private firms competing for the concessions. As a representative of the older generation of engineer-entrepreneurs, he never became the director of a large coal-mining or metallurgical enterprise, although he founded the first mercury factory in Russia in the Donets Basin. To the end of his life he conserved an idealistic vision of classless cooperation between workers and engineers like himself, a vision realized in his own life by a vigorous program of constructing individual cottages for the families of workers, housing that was immeasurably superior to the dismal barracks that dotted the industrial landscape in most of the empire.[21]

Among the Poles, Iasiukovich's career offers a particularly brilliant example of the typical pattern. Born in Kovno and graduated from the Vilna gymnasium, he completed his studies at the St. Petersburg Technological Institute. First employed on a privately owned railroad, he moved into industry in 1874 and became the main engineer and later director at the Nevskii Steam Engine Plant. After joining the Putilov Works as director for four years, Iasiukovich went south in 1888 to become manager and, in 1903, managing director of the South Russian Dniepr Metallurgical Company, the largest firm in the southern iron and steel industry. Highly regarded by his French and Belgian employers as a man "whose competence, administration, and strength of direction are without equal in Russia," Iasiukovich employed a carefully chosen staff composed entirely of Polish engineers. Because his authority over the enterprise was "absolute," his colleagues called him "the Dalai Lama." An early supporter of trusts for southern Russian metallurgy, he was a driving force behind several syndicates, including the gigantic Prodamet. He occupied executive positions in the three most important public pressure organizations for Russian heavy industry, the Association of Southern Coal and Steel Producers, the Permanent Advisory Office of the Metallurgical

21. Auerbakh, "Vospominaniia," 138:451–52, 140:557–60; *BE* 4:483; *ZIRTO* (1876), vol. 10, no. 1, pp. 21–26, 41–44.

Industrialists, and the Association of the Representatives of Trade and Industry.[22]

Another Pole, Zhukovskii, embodied the tradition of romantic realism that accepted Russia's political hegemony in Eastern Europe but upheld the cultural and technical superiority of the Poles. Although he was trained as an engineer, his real talents lay in the areas of administration and public finance, where he consciously adopted as his model Prince Drutskii-Liubetskii, the finance minister of the Kingdom of Poland, whose contribution to the industrialization of that region has already been noted. Zhukovskii, too, dreamed of persuading the imperial bureaucracy to base its financial structure on the experience of Poland. As a leader in the establishment of both the Permanent Advisory Office and the Association of the Representatives of Trade and Industry, and even more influentially as a member of the Polish Kolo in the state duma and a key figure on the finance committee, he sought to apply Drutskii-Liubetskii's plans point by point. Shortly after the outbreak of World War I, Zhukovskii was positively carried away by his "romantic inclinations." He advocated the annexation by Russia of Koenigsburg and Danzig so that "Poland" could gain access to the Baltic Sea.[23]

Avdakov's career was even more spectacular, but the very fact that he was the only Russian at the top of the group must have worked in his favor, especially in his numerous elections as head of public pressure groups, where someone of Polish or Jewish extraction would have been vulnerable to criticism from nationalist circles. A graduate of the Mining Institute, he enrolled in state service, but then immediately took a position in the south with the privately owned Rutchenko Coal Company when it was acquired by the Société Générale in 1873 and remained with the firm for the next forty years, rising to the post of commercial director. Together with merchant V. F. Golubev he organized the Briansk Iron Works Company, the only major steel producer in Russia to be built without foreign capital. In 1911 this company bought out Avdakov's former employer, Rutchenko Coal.

From 1879, Avdakov served on every government commission and conference dealing with problems of southern railroads, coal mining,

22. *PT*, no. 17 (1 December 1913): 174–75; Pavlov, *Vospominaniia*, p. 281; McKay, *Pioneers*, p. 306. Another prominent Pole, A. A. Vol'skii, was also trained as an engineer, employed in private industry, and served as an active member of the same three public organizations.
23. V. Sharyi, "Pamiati V. V. Zhukovskogo," *PT*, nos. 36–37 (17 September 1916): 194; St. Zverev, "Mysli V. V. Zhukovskogo o promyshlennom kredite," ibid., pp. 198–99; SH. "V. V. Zhukovskii o russkikh finansakh," ibid., pp. 200–201; I. I. Levin, "Pamiati V. V. Zhukovskogo," ibid., p. 194.

and commercial tariffs. On critical issues he favored close cooperation with the bureaucracy and was less disposed than his Polish colleagues to take the initiative in launching purely industrial solutions to economic problems. A long-time president of the Association of Southern Coal and Steel Producers, he also was a founder and president of Produgol, the coal syndicate, a prominent figure in Prodamet, the metallurgical syndicate, and chairman of the Association of Trade and Industry. He helped to organize the Kharkov Iron and Coal Exchange, and he founded the Ekaterinoslav Mining Institute. He was elected as an Octobrist to the State Council to represent the commercial and industrial interests and there displayed all the diffidence toward the government that might have been expected of him.[24]

When World War I broke out, he worked to create the kind of intimate cooperation between industry and government that he had always favored, first as a member of the Special Council on Defense and then as the president of the Central War Industries Committee. But here, just before he died, he ran into the open opposition of the Moscow entrepreneurs over the critical question of whether the government or industry would really run the war effort.[25]

L. G. Rabinovich, another graduate of the Mining Institute who then acquired extensive experience in the coal and ore mines of the south, had, according to one of his friends and colleagues, "a rare combination of fine skills in both the technical-administrative and the financial-commercial area," enabling him to fulfill the dual role of the manager and the promoter of newly created or reorganized industrial undertakings. A cofounder of the Irmino Coal Company, he was closely associated with Etienne Manziarly, one of the shrewdest and possibly the most unscrupulous of the foreign promoters in the area. Among Rabinovich's more impressive achievements was his financial reconstruction of the Grushevskii Anthracite Company belonging to the big Stakheev firm. A long-time member of the executive of the Association of Southern Coal and Steel Producers, he represented the organization in St. Petersburg. Although, like the Poles, he considered himself "a Russian person," he joined the Kadet party, most probably because of its position on the Jewish question, and was elected to the second duma. Unlike most of his colleagues, he remained in Russia after the revolution, making his peace with the Bolsheviks and occu-

24. Ibid., no. 12 (14 June 1913): 545–46; ibid., no. 22. (19 September 1915): 305–6; ibid., no. 23 (26 September 1915). For an example of his cautious attitude toward the formation of a southern metallurgical trust which contrasted vividly with Iasiukovich's stand see *Trudy*, 27 SGIR, *stenograficheskii otchet*, 3:150, 156, 159–61.
25. Diakin, *Russkaia burzhuaziia*, pp. 7–6; *Trudy pervogo s'ezda*, pp. 3, 152.

pying a prominent post in Donugol until he was arrested and tried in the Shakhty Affair.[26]

Von Ditmar represented yet another social and ethnic strand in the heterogenous southern group. His father was a Russified German, and his mother came from a Russian noble family. That young von Ditmar decided to enter the Mining Institute after having passed through an elite cadet corps in Moscow was a sure sign of the rising prestige of engineers in Russia. After graduating, he never engaged in practical work in the mines, although he owned and managed a small factory in Kharkov, where he lived. A good administrator and a master of statistical detail, he built a successful career out of lengthy service as a permanent officer in the Association of Southern Coal and Steel Producers, beginning as a member of the association's statistical bureau, where he was Avdakov's right-hand man, and rising to the posts of secretary and president in 1907. In this capacity he sat on the council of the Association of the Representatives of Trade and Industry. Like Avdakov, he was elected to the State Council from the trade and industry curia, but showed his distrust of the parties by remaining unaffiliated with any of them.

Von Ditmar's effectiveness as a spokesman for the coal and steel industry derived largely from his dispassionate manner and his overwhelming command of precise information on the state of the economy. But he was by no means uncritical of the backwardness of Russian society. As a deputy to the Kharkov town duma, he ridiculed the somnolent atmosphere enveloping the city fathers, a state from which, he declared, they could only be aroused "by the horn of a German bugler playing in the streets of Kharkov."[27] He showed even less patience with the zemstvos. At the thirtieth congress of the association, he launched a devastating attack on the gentry-landlord dominance of local government, submitting a massively documented case against the unfairly high tax burden imposed upon the mining industry of southern Russia.[28]

To a far greater degree than those of their counterparts in Moscow and even Petersburg, the attitudes and values of these entrepreneurs amounted to a distinctive business culture.[29] Their devotion to technological improvement and corporate management supplied an autonomous, self-generating energy much like that associated with entre-

26. Fenin, *Vospominaniia*, pp. 129–31.
27. Ibid., pp. 140–43, provides the biographical details.
28. Fomin, *Istoriia s'ezdov*, pp. 54–60.
29. The following section owes a great deal to the suggestive analysis of Cochran, "Proprietary and Managerial Enterprise," in *Social Change*, pp. 97–111.

preneurs in Western Europe and the United States, whose industrial experience, incidentally, they were fond of holding up as an example to be followed. The Moscow entrepreneurs still struggled to free themselves from the old merchant milieu; the St. Petersburg entrepreneurs were closely intertwined with the bureaucracy; German and Jewish entrepreneurs in the former Kingdom of Poland battled old-fashioned noble values; and in the Urals the archaic forms of the "possessional industry" held sway. In the south, however, the prevalence of the managerial over the proprietary type of capitalist deeply affected the entrepreneurs' relations with the state and with other social groups as well.

In the course of performing their functions the southern entrepreneurs inevitably compared their own levels of efficiency and achievement in administering large-scale organizations and resolving conflicts involving other social institutions with the record of the bureaucracy. The startling contrast between the real concentration of authority in the corporation and the unresolved divisions among the governmental departments did not escape their critical eyes.

Yet they could not hope that their example would influence a large part of society to emulate their values and role. At the national level economic regionalism and cultural differentiation blocked the penetration of new modes of behavior among merchants and entrepreneurs; the few exceptions to that pattern were limited to the small metallurgical industries of Moscow and the Baltic littoral. Even at the regional level, where their impact was greatest, the southern entrepreneurs encountered opposition to the new industrialism, first from the merchants in the port cities and then, in a more obstructive form, from the landowning gentry, who attacked their monopolies.

Denied the opportunities for easy acceptance of their social roles through emulation, they also lacked the kind of informal but effective influence through personal contact with government officials that the Moscow entrepreneurial group enjoyed in its halcyon days of the 1860s and 1870s and that the St. Petersburg entrepreneurs were to obtain in the period after the 1905 revolution. Moreover, unlike the Moscow merchants, they could not appeal to some higher justification, because of their close identification with foreign capital and their ethnic heterogeneity. They had no sympathy with the Ukrainian national movement, whose adherents regarded the southern entrepreneurs either with indifference or, as in the case of the Radical party, with open hostility.[30]

30. Reshetar, *Ukrainian Revolution*, pp. 22–25. The incompatibility of the Ukrainian national movement and the southern entrepreneurs on the labor question also emerges clearly if unintentionally from Lavrov, *Rabochee dvizhenie*, pp. 38–40, 51–52.

Relations between the southern entrepreneurs and the non-Ukrainian professional intelligentsia in the region were no better. Neither the technological institute in Kiev nor that in Kharkov provided trained personnel or ideological support for them. The former, as we have seen, was an appendage of the sugar-beet and southwest railroad interests, and the latter, as we shall see, was in principle a critic of unregulated industry.

All this meant that to win the support for their ideas the southern entrepreneurs were obliged to put their own organizational skills to work in politics. They had already demonstrated that they were more willing than the other entrepreneurial groups to have their men run for election, and they were more successful in putting their members in the duma and particularly the State Council, which was the most effective public forum for the voice of trade and industry in Russia. But they also needed to display a high degree of internal cohesiveness and collective action over a wide range of issues and to condition the bureaucracy to receive a steady stream of detailed, documented, and persuasive policy recommendations. In brief, they needed a modern lobbying organization to match their modern industrial organization. Given these requirements, it is not surprising that the Association of Southern Coal and Steel Producers emerged as the best-organized and most permanent industrial interest group in the empire.

The Association of Southern Coal and Steel Producers

At first the association gave the appearance of being little more than a local branch of the Russian Technological Society with its mix of professional engineers, government officials, and industrialists gathered together in a sort of debating society. But it rapidly took on the distinctive coloration of a representative organization of big industry. As early as the eighth congress, V. V. Zhukovskii characterized the participation of the smaller firms as "unnatural and, consequently harmful for the future success of the coal industry in general" and proposed a property qualification for membership. At the twelfth congress a uniquely weighted voting system was introduced, based upon productivity of the mines, and in 1904 membership was limited to enterprises that paid dues. As a result, although membership increased sharply from the mid-1890s from an average of about 90 in the previous two decades to a peak of 325 in 1904, voting rights were limited to a much smaller number: in 1907 only 55 out of 313 participants.[31] Mean-

31. Livshin, "'Predstavitel'nye' organizatsii," p. 104.

while the budget increased from 158 rubles in 1874 to 340,000 rubles in 1904. A permanent bureaucracy emerged with the establishment of a council in the mid-1880s, the addition of a statistical bureau in 1897, and the formation of a full-time secretariat and permanent executive. "The patriarchal customs of the past," said von Ditmar, the secretary, have no place in "a huge organization like ours."[32] The association enlarged its scope of activities by organizing a workers' insurance section and a mutual credit society. In 1902, on its initiative, the Kharkov Coal and Iron Exchange was founded in order to broaden the financial base of the association. After having vainly petitioned the government over the years for more and better technical schools in the region, the association realized that its only recourse was to build one of its own, the Ekaterinoslav Higher Mining School.[33] On the basis of this imposing infrastructure the association promoted an integrated economic policy.

For over forty years it undertook a systematic and thorough investigation of every aspect of the economic life of the south and made public its findings through the stenographic reports of the congresses and the special reports of its commissions. On the basis of this work the association organized a strong lobby on issues ranging from tariffs to zemstvo reforms. At the same time its leaders served on most of the important government commissions dealing with the economy as it affected the south and often undertook personal negotiations of a more informal sort with high-ranking bureaucrats, who faithfully attended the association's meetings. Through the history of the association it is possible to track the awakening political consciousness of the southern entrepreneurs and their efforts to exercise a decisive influence on both the government and the other entrepreneurial groups in the struggle over the economic development of the empire.

The founders of the association represented the first generation of coal producers in the south: mining engineers like A. A. Auerbakh and P. N. Gorlov, the director of the South Russian Coal Company, owned by the Jewish entrepreneur S. S. Poliakov and subsequently controlled by the Banque Internationale de Paris; the Ukrainian landowner I. G. Ilovaiskii, the owner of the Makeevka Mines, subsequently controlled by the Société Générale; and the Jewish entrepreneur A. V. Sheierman, the founder of the Shcherbonovka Mine, later purchased by a French firm, the South Russian Rock Salt and Coal Company.[34] From the outset the coal interests predominated, occupying six out of the eight places on the council, but by the turn of the

32. *Trudy*, 27 SGIR, 3:254.
33. Fomin, *Istoriia s'ezdov*, pp. 11–17.
34. Auerbakh, "Vospominaniia," 138:458–61.

century the metallurgical interests assumed a more active political role on the all-imperial scale. During the same period the leadership passed almost entirely into the hands of the southern entrepreneurial group. But it is clear enough from their political activities that the Avdakovs, Iasiukovichs, Rabinovichs, and von Ditmars were more than employees of foreign firms. They became a political force in their own right and more often than not used the economic power of enterprises controlled by foreign capital to further their own careers. They moved far beyond a narrow concern with profit and loss of individual enterprises to an interest in the future economic and political development of the region and the empire as a whole.

The southern entrepreneurs displayed toward their workers a concern which was hierarchical rather than paternalistic. That is, the workers were perceived as contractual employees rather than as "members of the family," as they were in Moscow. The shortage of labor and the need to attract immigrants to the region obliged the southern entrepreneurs to create decent living conditions, work out a reliable system of legally binding contracts between employees and employers, and initiate a system of social services in advance of the government. Of the last the most significant was the Society for Aid to Families of Miners, a fund subscribed to entirely by the employers to compensate for loss of life and health in mine-related accidents and disease. In the twenty years between 1884 and 1904 the fund absorbed by far the largest share of the annual budget of the association, amounting to approximately one-third of its total expenditures for the period.[35]

The central problem for the southern entrepreneurs was protection against foreign competition. Without that, no improvements in organization, technology, or marketing could overcome the headstart of West European manufacturing industries. The south was even more exposed geographically than the center to the penetration of foreign coal—either English through the Black Sea ports or German over the land frontier between Silesia and the Kingdom of Poland. Beginning with the second congress the association showered the government with petitions for higher duties on coal and iron. No sooner had they secured one set of concessions than they redoubled their demands for

35. Fomin, *Istoriia s'ezdov*, pp. 20–21, 26–27. The association also drafted plans for a mutual insurance fund for large-scale mine disasters and established a medical consultative staff in Kharkov (ibid., pp. 34–35). For a different evaluation, which, however, does not deny altogether the innovative elements in labor relations, see Laverychev, *Tsarizm*, pp. 59–60, 85–86, 101. The records of the association are conspicuous for the absence of attacks on the factory inspection system, which aroused so much hostility among the Moscow merchants.

further increases and promises to maintain the new rates over prolonged periods. This process continued well into the twentieth century, but the big and decisive battle was fought in 1883–84 when the government recognized in principle the right of protection for the southern coal and metals industries. The debate ranged the southern entrepreneurial group (and the Kharkov Exchange) with the Moscow entrepreneurial group (and the Moscow merchant organizations as well) against the merchants on the periphery, especially the commercial interests in the big ports of the Black and Baltic seas, like St. Petersburg, Reval, Riga, Libau, and Odessa, as well as manufacturers in the Kingdom of Poland and the Ukraine. The Polish metallurgical group (but not the Warsaw Committee of Manufacturers) opposed higher tariffs on the overland route, for this would increase their payments for Silesian coal, and the sugar-beet factories of the Kiev region, supported by the southwestern railroads, rejected the proposal as too costly and even ruinous. In both cases the lack of connecting rail lines meant that even with higher duties on foreign coal the Donets coal still was not competitive. At the same time the Moscow merchants perceived the long-term benefits of weakening the foreign influence and strengthening their own ties with the burgeoning south, particularly since they controlled the Moscow-Kursk line (T. Morozov and associates) and the Donets Coal line (S. Mamontov), which could only benefit from increased coal shipments to the north.[36]

In a stunning reversal of its long-standing policy the government came down on the side of the southern entrepreneurs, imposing the first significant duties on coal entering from the Black Sea, in order to correct "the abnormal situation" of allowing foreign coal to dominate the markets of Russia's southern ports. An overwhelming majority of the State Council accepted Finance Minister Bunge's argument that the southern coal producers had given proof of their competitive worth and their capacity to fill Russia's domestic needs for coal. Admittedly, the rates were below the figure set by the Association of Southern Coal and Steel Producers, and the Petersburg bureaucrats appeared to be more impressed by the financial advantages to be won from reducing foreign payments than by the opportunities to develop

36. TsGIA, f. 1152, no. 203, "O poshline na kammenyi ugol', 1884," pp. 1–5. In a separate memorandum, Vyshnegradskii, then president of the southwestern railroad society, argued against the tariff increases, fearing their impact on the grain and sugar trade (which still provided the bulk of rail deliveries). He favored lowering railroad tariffs for long hauls and coordinating the state and private railroad schedules (ibid., "Po voprosu o poshline na kammenyi ugol'," pp. 186–89). Once Vyshnegradskii became finance minister, he abandoned this position, which represented special pleading for the private lines, and adopted a protective attitude toward southern coal and iron interests.

a powerful domestic industrial base. Nevertheless, whatever course the government may have followed in the absence of petitions from the association, it is clear enough in this case that it responded directly to the appeals from the southern coal interests and accepted many if not all of their arguments about the industry's capacity for survival and growth.[37]

Another strong petition by the association two years later initiated another round of consultations, which culminated in another increase in coal duties. Although the new rate still did not match the association's demand of 1882, its application enabled Donets coal to compete in the Odessa market and dramatically reduced foreign imports within a year from 15 to 2.5 million poods. To be sure, English coal recovered part of its share in the market and the struggle continued, but Donets coal had won its opening to the sea.[38]

The association also took the initiative in proposing stiff increases in the tariff on imported pig iron as a necessary step toward building a metallurgical industry in the south. Petitions drafted and circulated by the seventh and eighth congresses brought a sympathetic response from the associations of iron producers in the Urals and the Kingdom of Poland, which were newly created and had adopted the organization and tactics of their southern colleagues. As we have seen, the Moscow merchants swung into line behind them, although for their own reasons. Within the government the two strongest adherents of the association's views were Kulibin and Skal'kovskii, the chief and deputy chief of the Mining Department, who represented the Ministry of Finance at early intradepartmental discussions. It was they who insisted on immediate application of the protective duties in all frontiers except for the Baltic coast, where they suggested a gradual increase. The discussions within the bureaucracy revealed clearly that the compelling arguments in favor of the tariff had their origin in the petition of the southern coal owners.[39] Indeed, the final draft law came very close to meeting all their demands: the imposition of a fifteen-gold-kopek duty in three stages over an eighteen-month period on all imported unfinished iron (pig iron and bar iron) across all land and sea frontiers for a fixed time of twelve years.[40]

37. TsGIA, f. 1152, op. 10, d. 203, "Zhurnal soveta v soedinennykh departamentov gosudarstvennoi ekonomii i zakonov," pp. 371–76.
38. Fomin, Istoriia s'ezdov, pp. 70–73.
39. TsGIA, f. 1152, op. 10, d. 203, pp. 220–22; ibid., "Zhurnal gosudarstvennogo soveta, iiunia 1884," pp. 389–99.
40. On three key issues—the level of rates, the durations of the transitional period and of the fixed time—the law went beyond the initial proposals of the minister of finance (ibid., pp. 377 and 402–4).

In 1887 the tariff was raised to twenty-five gold kopeks per pood, with startling results. At the twenty-second congress of the association (1897) it was reported that the tariff and the construction of the first Ekaterinoslav line were the principal factors in the great spurt of industrial capacity over the previous ten years: that is, the increase in the number of blast furnaces from two to seventeen and the construction of twelve new metallurgical factories, fourteen finishing and steel plants, fifteen machine-construction and mechanical factories, seventeen other factories, and ten additional coal enterprises. The puddling of iron shot up from 2.87 to 39 million poods.[41]

The struggle against the foreigners had been won, and a modern heavy industrial base in Russia had been created. But its future was not yet assured. Many questions remained, including its ability to dominate the domestic market against regional competitors, its capacity for expansion and diversification of production, and its resilience in industrial crises. In all of these the association faced the delicate task of balancing the power and interests of the state against those of private enterprise.

The vital questions here were how to obtain governmental assistance without giving up control and how to preserve competition without surrendering to cannibalism. Railroad construction and rate setting was a case in point. The absence of an adequate rail network in the Donets Basin was generally recognized in the 1870s by both bureaucrats and coal producers as the major obstacle to the large-scale exploitation of mineral resources in the area. The notion of a systematic and rational plan for building a rail network in the region fell victim to the bureaucratic rivalry between the Ministry of Transportation, which favored state construction, and the Ministry of Finance, which demanded and obtained private construction with state guarantees. Bidding on individual lines and subsequent conflicts among the rival entrepreneurs proved highly disruptive to coal production and even pitted one firm against another over the question of where the first line would be built. In one instance, Auerbakh, representing the French interests, accused Gorlov, representing Poliakov, of sacrificing regional development for private gain. When Mamontov finally obtained the concession over Poliakov for the first northern Donets coal line, after some highly irregular bidding practices, the Kursk-Kharkov-Azov line, owned by Poliakov, simply refused to transship the coal carried in the cars of its rival to the markets. Meanwhile, representatives of the Kharkov-Nikolaevsk line bluntly refused to at-

41. Fomin, *Istoriia s'ezdov*, p. 74.

tend the congress of coal-mine owners, despite an order from the minister of transportation.[42]

Under conditions in which the government was unable to control or coordinate the railroad development necessary for the exploitation of the south, it was no wonder that the mining engineers showed contempt for their colleagues in state employment and for the private entrepreneurs as well. Undaunted, however, the association repeated at its annual congresses the proposals for railroad networks, buttressed with massive statistical data, until two decades later most of the original plan submitted by Gorlov became a reality. In a number of cases, particularly in the first and second Ekaterinoslav lines, the association's accurate surveys and profitability studies persuaded the government to undertake the traces recommended by their reports.[43]

Besides the construction of a southern railroad network a uniform and favorable rate policy was essential to the coal owners in the expansion of their internal market. But the Ministry of Transportation had adopted a differential tariff, which set higher rates for long hauls than for short hauls, in order to help keep the private lines solvent. Not until the government began to repurchase the private lines and only after Witte came to office with his strong ideas on uniform rates did the association get the results it sought. In response to its petition in 1895 a special commission of the Department of Railroads in the Ministry of Finance convened, with the participation of all the interested parties, and decided on substantial reductions for coal deliveries over long distances and specifically to the Black Sea ports.[44] The cuts were so drastic that the rates fell below the average real costs of transportation, providing what amounted to a state subsidy for long-distance coal deliveries. Within a short time a flood of Donets coal overwhelmed the old Moscow coal and peat industry, reducing its production even more rapidly than before. Renewed demands by the association led to a further reduction of rates in 1897, thereby opening up the Baltic and Central Asian markets to Donets coal.[45]

Even as the association strove to expand its potential market for

42. Auerbakh, "Vospominaniia," 138:455–56; Kislinskii, Nasha, 2:180–81, 216–17, 230–31; Tekhnicheskii listok 2, no. 2 (15 January 1879): 11–12.

43. Fomin, Istoriia s'ezdov, pp. 127–47; and Trudy, 25 SGIR, Doklad soveta no. 14, "O postroike novykh zheleznykhdorogov . . . ," pp. 6, 16.

44. Fomin, Istoriia s'ezdov, pp. 98–103. In 1883 the association finally succeeded in arranging private agreements with the Moscow-Kursk and Kursk-Azov lines for the cheaper transportation of coal to Moscow, where the local industries were eager to support the development of a national industry, especially if it did not cost them any more than imported English coal.

45. Solov'eva, Zheleznodorozhnyi, pp. 175–77.

coal and iron, it had to confront the twin dangers of periodic overproduction and falling prices, which were the hallmarks of industrializing societies. They responded, in much the same way that their European and American counterparts had, by seeking to regulate and manipulate the operations of the free market. As early as 1878, Auerbakh led the first attempt to form a joint-stock company for controlling the sale of coal on commission. More ambitious efforts followed in the 1880s and 1890s when the association's members conspired through informal agreements reached at the annual congresses to set production levels by assigning quotas, apportioning rolling stock, and fixing prices. These actions touched off an artificial "coal crisis," which scandalized the public and irritated the government. At the same time, under Avdakov's leadership, a special commission at the twentieth congress initiated the organization of an expert syndicate to emulate the West European practice of dumping competitively priced coal on foreign markets while maintaining higher domestic prices.[46]

A comparison of the enthusiastic reception given by the association to these proposals with the sullen resistance of the Moscow textile merchants to similar ideas advanced by members of the Moscow entrepreneurial group serves to underline again the distinct differences in the industrial mentality between the two regions. The contrast is even sharper when one considers the structural similarities between textiles and coal that hampered monopolistic practices: that is, the relatively low level of concentration and the ease with which new enterprises could be established. Moreover, the coal owners ran the risk of antagonizing the government, which had adopted an anti-monopolistic position in the 1890s. On several occasions it dispatched special investigative commissions to the south to verify the growing number of complaints against the association's activities.

The situation changed dramatically when the industrial crisis at the turn of the century laid bare the economic paradox buried in the foundations of the metallurgical industry. In southern Russia one of the world's most technologically advanced and highly integrated industrial complexes confronted a poor and underdeveloped market situation. The peasantry was impoverished. The few firms that had their own retail outlets reported modest sales. The merchant middlemen were not interested in selling iron products that yielded low profit margins. Industry was reluctant to extend credits to the zemstvos because they feared mounting debts and large peasant arrears. The gentry landowners retained their preference for English agricultural

46. Potolov, "Iz istorii," pp. 6–9, 13–14, 16–22. Even before this Avdakov boasted that the coal industry in the south had already achieved the organizational forms of Western Europe (*Trudy*, 27 SGIR, 2:527).

machinery, and the town administrations displayed an equally strong bias against Russian-made iron products. The state orders were insufficient to match the industry's productive capacity.[47] The most painless solution for the metallurgists was the formation of some kind of industrial combination, which would have the added advantage of expanding their influence over the economic life of the region and the empire as a whole.

The debut of a metallurgical trust coincided with an unexpected combination of threats to Witte's policy of industrialization. The beginning of the industrial crises of 1900–1903 struck Russia at the very time when public attacks against foreign investments were winning recruits within the government. The Moscow merchants had turned against the south, decrying high prices and alien influences. The exchange committee, abetted by Sharapov's paper *Russkii trud* and other voices of the radical nationalist press, found willing accomplices among Witte's high-ranking enemies Grand Duke Alexander Mikhailovich and M. N. Murev'ev, the foreign minister, who warned the tsar that "entire large regions of our country will fall into economic dependence on foreigners."[48] Soon after Witte defended himself in public and before the tsar against these accusations, he had to begin casting about for some way to prevent an exodus of foreign capital frightened by a new and more serious danger of an industrial slump. The notion of organized economic cooperation among competing firms was already being revived cautiously by the metallurgical interests.[49] But the first concrete proposal came from the Société Générale in Paris, owner of the Makeevka Steel Company. The Ministry of Finance followed this up in the pages of its official journal, *Vestnik finansov*, urging upon the metallurgical industry a policy of self-help through syndicates.[50]

The next step was the most delicate one of all. For Paris to have taken the lead at this point would have been politically unacceptable, even if it had been possible to satisfy the competing interests at a thousand miles distance. But it was no less difficult for the Russian government to force the foreign-owned metallurgical enterprises into an arrangement that would, in all probability, set artifically higher prices on the Russian market. What was required was an intermediary who could negotiate with both the French-Belgian capitalists and St.

47. *Trudy*, 27 SGIR, 3:152–55, 193–96.
48. Iu. V. Solov'ev, "Protivorechiia," pp. 385–86, and Gindin, "Ob osnovakh," p. 204 and throughout.
49. *Trudy*, PSKZh, 1900.
50. Crisp, "French Investment," p. 175; Gindin, "Politika," p. 103. These two emphasize the initiatives of the French and Russian governments, respectively.

Petersburg on behalf of the foreign-owned and Russian metallurgical enterprises. That role fell to the Association of Southern Coal and Steel Producers, whose leaders were eminently suited by training and experience to harmonize the different interests.

The complex organization of the first and most powerful pre-revolutionary syndicates, the Society for the Sale of Products of the Russian Metallurgical Industry (better known as Prodamet) was hammered out at the twenty-seventh congress of the Association of Southern Coal and Steel Producers. According to the statutes approved by the government the following year, Prodamet was simply a joint-stock company for marketing manufactured goods, but secret agreements among the participants revealed its basically monopolistic character.[51] From the outset Prodamet comprised thirty enterprises which accounted for 88 percent of the total production of assorted iron, 82 percent of ordinary iron, and 74 percent of wheels and axles.[52]

The election of Iasiukovich as its first president was a sure sign that the participants endorsed a combative policy aimed at bringing the entire metallurgical industry of the south into the fold. Iasiukovich was a partisan of free competition between the new trust and the independent companies for the state orders of rails, which since 1899 had been apportioned by the Ministry of Finance to favored firms at fixed and profitable prices. What is not clear, and perhaps never will be, was the extent to which Iasiukovich was acting merely as the agent of the Paris banking interests who controlled his company.

The South Dniepr Metallurgical Company already enjoyed a place among the six companies that were guaranteed state orders. But its share accounted for only 26 percent of its production, while the Russo-Belgian and Hughes enterprises, which had refused to join Prodamet, depended so heavily on these orders that their loss would have meant financial ruin.[53] By bringing pressure on the privileged enterprises through open competition, Prodamet would have ensured a more equitable distribution of government orders, but this would not necessarily have increased the profits of South Dniepr, even though it might have introduced greater market stability in the long run. But in the short run it would have meant a terrific struggle. Some leaders of the association, like Avdakov, sought to avoid this by relying upon the government to organize the syndicate and reallocate the state orders.[54]

51. *Trudy*, 27 SGIR, 3:141–90; Liashchenko, "Kontragentskie," throughout.
52. Crisp, "French Investment," p. 176.
53. *Trudy*, 27 SGIR, 3:177–79. According to the figures supplied by Goujon, state orders accounted for 56 percent and 81 percent, respectively, of the production of Russo-Belgian and Hughes enterprises.
54. Ibid., pp. 156–57. This was also the position of the French, who were themselves too

For Iasiukovich, however, free competition signified a greater independence from the St. Petersburg bureaucracy, which would then lose the leverage provided by the right to assign rail orders to certain firms arbitrarily. Freedom of action for Prodamet vis-à-vis the government would probably have been advantageous to those French investors whose companies were in financial difficulty, and their support for such a stand is not surprising. But South Dniepr was not one of these. Therefore, it is reasonable to suppose that something more than profit and loss was at stake here for Iasiukovich and his colleagues —that is, the creation of a powerful and independent trust which would act as a new political force in Russia, one concerned with issues that transcended the concerns of the Paris bankers.

Such an application of their newly acquired economic power by the southern entrepreneurs is a subject that properly belongs to the period after 1905. But it is appropriate at this point to outline in skeletal form the interlocking linkages between the big companies—and between them and their leading representatives, the major monopolies, the lobbying and interest-group organizations, and the big banks as they developed during the first decade of the twentieth century (see figure 6.1). Even in this schematic form it is an eloquent testimony to the ambition and enterprise of the southern entrepreneurs.

The Northwestern Industrial Region

St. Petersburg and the Baltic provinces made up the third major region of the empire where distinctive social and economic features exerted a powerful influence on the social structures and mentality of the local merchants and entrepreneurs. The region was favored in possessing the highest degree of urbanization and concentration of industry in the country; a tradition of technical innovation and pioneering in wholly new branches of manufacturing; a heavy reliance on both direct government support and foreign trade and investment; and an incomparable ability to adapt its major economic activities to the challenge of domestic and foreign competition. Whereas Moscow remained dominated by locally financed textiles and the south by internationally financed metallurgy, St. Petersburg and the Baltic ports periodically diversified their industries and reorganized their investment structures.

The scale, variety, and flexibility of economic activities in the north-

---

divided to force the Russian government to accept their views. See the good discussion on this in Crisp, "French Investment," pp. 180–81.

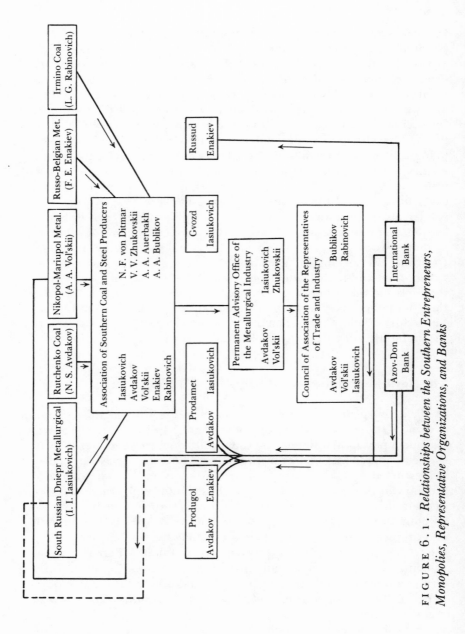

FIGURE 6.1. *Relationships between the Southern Entrepreneurs,
Monopolies, Representative Organizations, and Banks*

west produced a social picture in this region that was even more complex than that in the center and south. Particularly in St. Petersburg, a gap between the interests and attitudes of the merchants and those of industrialists opened up in the 1890s and remained even under the revolutionary pressures of 1905. Subsequently, there arose yet a third group, called the financial oligarchy, which set its sights on controlling the economy of the entire country, thus further dividing the capitalist world of St. Petersburg, the northwestern region, and the empire as a whole. Meanwhile, along the outer perimeter of the city a ring of huge modern factories created an industrial milieu for the emergence of a skilled, well-disciplined, and highly conscious workers' movement. A seemingly inexhaustible supply of peasant labor in the hinterland added its own volatile elements to the growing social tensions.

An artificial creation to begin with, geographically exposed on the outer reaches of a vast inland empire, St. Petersburg in the industrial age had to look to Western Europe for much of its capital and rely on the long, slender Russian railroad network for its labor supply and raw materials. (A similar situation prevailed in the Baltic ports of Riga and Tallin.) These elements together created a potentially explosive social amalgam, one in which those who had the most to lose—the merchants, industrialists, and bankers—were the most deeply divided and isolated in their efforts to defend their self-interests.

In the northwestern region the cities of St. Petersburg, Riga, and Tallin responded to the changing economic demands made upon them in a flexible and adaptive manner. This distinctive style was in large part responsible for the great variety and high concentration of their industrial development. St. Petersburg witnessed a relative and absolute decline in its dominant foreign-trade position following the 1860s, when the construction of the railroads linked the grain-surplus-producing provinces with the Black Sea and other Baltic ports. Soon after, the city lost its big lead in the mechanization of the metallurgical and textile industries to the south and center, respectively. But the region as a whole continued to maintain its edge over the center in labor productivity in all finishing industries and more than held its own in the overall production of machinery (see table 6.2).[55] This was accomplished with the assistance of foreign investment and economies of scale. At the same time, the most enterprising capitalists began to introduce new industries such as chemical (rubber) and electrical at an advanced level of technology that matched that of contemporary Western and Central Europe.

55. Adapted from Livshits, *Razmeshchenie*, tables 37, 40, pp. 200 and 205.

TABLE 6.2. *Labor Productivity for 1912 (in percentages)*

Region	Finishing Industries			Machine Construction		
	Number of Enterprises	Value	Workers	Number of Enterprises	Value	Workers
Central	20.8	35.9	42.6	16.8	31.4	27.5
Northwest	7.2	11.8	9.9	9.0	23.8	20.2
Northwest and Baltic	12.5	18.6	16.4	16.4	35.4	29.9

In these highly mechanized giant enterprises a disciplined industrial proletariat emerged in the 1890s. As early as 1894, for example, the Putilov Works employed 6000 workers making steamship parts and railroad and industrial machinery. With the French supplying three-quarters of its capital and the imperial government bailing it out of debt, the enterprise grew by leaps and bounds. In 1901 the number of employed workers reached well over 12,000. Similarly, in Tallin, the government decided to establish its major Baltic naval base, with the assistance of French and British capital. In the Russo-Baltic Shipyard and Mechanical Factory the number of workers jumped from 2763 in 1894 to 6868 in 1904.

The general level of concentration of workers in St. Petersburg province continued to increase until the eve of the revolution, when 140 factories, each employing more than 500 workers, accounted for three-quarters of the region's total industrial labor force. This percentage had already been reached by 1895 in the metallurgical, textile, and food industries. By contrast, in Moscow in 1910 just under 50 percent of the total industrial labor force was employed in factories of over 500 workers.[56] The high degree of concentration in St. Petersburg was accompanied by a rapid rise in literacy among industrial workers, from 38 percent in 1862 to 63 percent in 1897 (as compared, for example, to 23 percent in Moscow in 1881 and 56 percent in 1902). Further evidence of the maturity of the labor force comes from the fact that the provinces of St. Petersburg and Vilna led the rest of the country in the percentage of industrial workers engaged in year-round employment.[57]

This combination of literacy and permanence in a concentrated working population ignited in 1896–97 in the two greatest strikes the empire had ever known, forcing the government and the industrialists

56. Rashin, *Formirovanie*, pp. 106–10.
57. Ibid., pp. 565, 587, 591, 597.

to make important concessions.[58] Thus it was that the St. Petersburg industrialists were the first in Russia to be confronted by a militant, modern working-class movement. Reacting hastily, they organized themselves into the first genuine employers' union in the empire, the St. Petersburg Society for the Assistance, Improvement, and Development of Factory Industry (subsequently named the St. Petersburg Society of Factory and Mill Owners). From that point on, they were more hostile to the workers and more intransigent on labor legislation than any other entrepreneurial group.

Heavy industry working on state contracts dominated the northwest. This created a market situation that allowed little room for a close or beneficial relationship between the industrial entrepreneurs and the merchants. Unlike in Moscow, where the owners of large textile mills were also leading members of the Exchange Committee, in St. Petersburg the industrialists and merchants had separate identities and had little to do with one another either in business or society. Among the seventy-eight electors and candidates of the St. Petersburg Exchange in 1903, only one, E. L. Nobel, also belonged to the St. Petersburg Society for the Assistance, Improvement, and Development of Factory Industry. None of the founders or prominent members of the society, again with the sole exception of Nobel, held any elective position on the exchange. It is doubtful whether any were even members. Neither organization was to bridge the gap between them even under the revolutionary pressures in 1905.[59]

The extraordinary influence exercised by foreign capital in the northwest may be gauged from the fact that this region absorbed 20 percent of all foreign investment in Russia. St. Petersburg industry alone accounted for almost 50 percent of all foreign capital invested in Russian factories producing finished metal goods and machinery, 27 percent of foreign investments in Russian textiles, and 25 percent of their interests in the chemical industries. The largest factories in the empire producing electrical equipment and transformers were the St. Petersburg factories of the German firm of Siemens, Schuckert, and Decca. Also founded by foreign capital, the largest rubber concerns, the Russian-American Rubber Plant in the capital and Provodnik in Riga, employed over 12,500 workers in 1908. In Tallin the Schneider-Creusot Works provided almost 20 percent of the capital for the Russo-Baltic Shipyard and Mechanical Factory. The other two giant shipbuilding companies, Bekker and Noblessner (Nobel and

58. Pipes, *Social Democrats*, chap. 6.
59. Timofeev, *Istoriïa*, appendices 1, 2, 6, and 7; Obshchestvo zavodchikov i fabrikantov, *Otchet za 1897–1906 gg*, p. 16.

Lessner), were founded by joint ventures of Franco-Russian and German-Swedish-Russian capital, respectively.[60]

The highly developed banking system of St. Petersburg provided another opening for the penetration of foreign capital. Because of the dominant position of the State Bank and the Treasury in the financial life of the country, as well as the opportunities for foreign investors, St. Petersburg remained the money center for the empire throughout the second half of the nineteenth century. In the 1890s a banking boom in the city led to the establishment of a series of private banks. The founders were from professional banking families, not industrialists as in the central industrial provinces, the Caucasus, and the Kingdom of Poland. Most of them were from German or Jewish families, like I. E. Ginsburg, Vincken and Company, Leon Rozental, and S. Gvaier, with an occasional Russian like V. Ia. Oblonskii. At this time large amounts of foreign capital—first German and then French —were entering the banking system. The Diskonto Gesellschaft in Berlin founded the St. Petersburg Discount and Loan Bank and, together with several other German banks, set up the St. Petersburg International Commercial Bank. The Deutsche Bank and the Wiener Bankverein were the major founders of the Russian Bank for Foreign Trade, while French banking interests established the Russian Trade and Industry Bank.[61] By 1900 these Petersburg banks ranked seventh, third, fourth, and eleventh, respectively, out of forty-three banks in the empire.

The period after the revolution of 1905 witnessed a phenomenal expansion of the Petersburg investment firms. As central emission banks with a wide network of regional branches, they engaged in large-scale financing of heavy industry and formed the core of a virtual banking monopoly. Only the Moscow banks, sustained by the local merchants, and the Warsaw Commercial and the Riga Commercial banks, relying on German capital, were able to maintain some semblance of autonomy from the Petersburg giants.[62] From this commanding position the Petersburg bankers absorbed or replaced the industrialists of the capital and the south as the leaders of economic development in the country. But this is to anticipate, for the conflict that split the Russian merchantry in 1905 preceded the triumph of the financial oligarchy in St. Petersburg.

This concentration of industry and influx of foreign capital could

60. Akademiia nauk, *Ocherki istorii Leningrada*, 2:89–121; Akademiia nauk Estonskoi, *Istoriia Estonskoi*, 2:535–36; Akademiia nauk Latvishskoi, *Istoriia Latvishskoi*, 2:397–79; Livshits, *Razmeshchenie*, pp. 204–95, 831–32.
61. Akademiia nauk, *Ocherki istorii Leningrada*, 2:159–62.
62. Gindin and Shepelev, "Bankovskie," pp. 22, 55.

take place only in a cosmopolitan environment that was conducive to new ideas and practices. The large-scale accumulation of capital necessitated the formation of joint-stock companies at the expense of family firms. The application of new technology demanded rapid changes in traditional patterns of work. St. Petersburg and the Baltic ports enjoyed a long history of commercial contact with Europe, and foreign merchants living in the city conducted their business either without becoming Russian citizens or, if they did, without changing their essentially European life-styles and outlook. In the Baltic provinces the ethnic Germans continued to dominate the merchant soslovie and to control the town dumas. In St. Petersburg Russians made up the overwhelming majority of the merchantry, but this should not obscure the prominent position of many non-Russians among the leaders of the commercial and industrial organizations (see table 6.3).[63] The policy of the Finance Ministry from Reitern to Witte was to attract foreign capital and resist attempts by ultranationalistic cliques inside and outside the bureaucracy to weaken the social and economic position of these ethnic groups among the merchantry.

Despite its ethnic mix and foreign ties the entire northwest depended too heavily upon the all-Russian market to contemplate regional autonomy. Besides, in the Baltic towns the ethnic Germans found their best defense against the mounting demands of Lettish and Estonian merchants lay in appealing to the idea of a united Russia. On the other hand, the Petersburg and Baltic industrialists and merchants were precluded from competing with Moscow for leadership of a "national bourgeoisie" by virtue of their foreign origin and connections. Their ties to German capital, in particular, proved a formidable obstacle after 1907 and a positive embarrassment after 1914 to their assuming a prominent political role outside their own region. On cultural matters they could not hope to challenge the dominant position of the imperial court and the nobility who set the tone for the artistic, literary, and academic life of the capital. They edited no newspapers, presided over no salons, sponsored no theaters, built no museums; in a word, they offered no alternative to the established social order. Thus, the great wealth and economic influence of the northwestern entrepreneurs had little resonance within the political system and even less effect upon the cultural values and beliefs of society.

63. Calculated from *PVP*, 49:114, 21:208, 19:210, 38:232.

TABLE 6.3. *Ethnic Composition of Merchants in the Northwest in 1897 (by percentage)*

Province	Russian	German	Jews	Lithuanian-Latvian	Estonians	Poles
Kurland	8	71	16	5	—	—
Estland	17	63	3	—	16	—
Lifland	18	58	12.5	11	—	.05
St. Petersburg	85	11	4	—	—	—

The St. Petersburg Entrepreneurial Group

The general features of Petersburg industry are more easily drawn than the individual characteristics of its entrepreneurs. With few exceptions biographical information on them is practically nonexistent. Even a collective portrait is bound to have more blank spots than sharply defined figures. More is known about the Nobel family than about any other, yet in some ways this family was the least typical of the original group. Robert and Ludwig Nobel, founders of the dynasty, were Swedish entrepreneurs who threw their energies into an ambitious expansion of the oil industry in Baku at a time when Russian entrepreneurs drew back from the great risks. They introduced the latest American techniques of exploitation, established chemical laboratories, perfected the transportation of oil on railroad cars, tankers, and pipelines, and built storage tanks in the oil fields. Ludwig's son, Emil, a Russian subject, built up the family holdings into an international cartel that by the 1890s was powerful enough to deal on an equal footing with the Rothschilds and John D. Rockefeller.[64]

In the course of this campaign, the Nobel family followed the strategy that had proved so successful for the southern entrepreneurs. They eliminated the small local firms from the regional interest-group organization, the Association of Baku Oil Producers, by raising the property qualifications for membership. The only difference was that the Nobels entered the Caucasus from the outside, subordinated the regional economy to St. Petersburg, and thus forestalled the emergence of a distinctive regional entrepreneurial group in the area. Their policies foreshadowed those of the St. Petersburg financial oligarchy in the south a generation later. From the 1880s, when oil prices began to reflect their control, the merchants of Moscow and the Upper Volga, especially Nizhnyi Novgorod and Kazan, joined forces with local firms like that of Shibaev, the Old Believer friend of Savva

64. Brandt, *Inostrannye kapital*, 3:268–75. Fursenko, *Neftianye*, is the best treatment; see especially pp. 22–28, 73–76, 140–50, 160–61.

Morozov, in a long struggle to weaken the monopoly. The merchant exchanges claimed that the syndicate was setting artificially high domestic prices and taking over river transportation along the entire Volga at the expense of the central industrial region.[65] The traditional economic rivalry between St. Petersburg and Moscow assumed a new dimension.

For the time being, no one else in St. Petersburg could match the range and scale of Nobel's operations. Indeed, few entrepreneurs of the first generation survived long enough to try. Like Nobel, other members of the first generation of St. Petersburg entrepreneurs, including N. I. Putilov, P. M. Obukhov, Mark MacPherson, Thomson, R. K. Galli, V. P. Vargunin, and V. I. Butz came from foreign or noble backgrounds and also founded and managed their own enterprises. But most of them ran into financial difficulties, despite lucrative government contracts, and lost control to foreign interests or to the Naval Ministry. N. I. Putilov, by origin a nobleman, by training an engineer, and by occupation an official in the Naval Ministry, bought out an unsuccessful mechanical and iron works in St. Petersburg and rapidly converted it into the biggest Russian producer of rails. He accumulated an enormous fortune by virtue of his legendary energy, his day-to-day attention to detail in his factory, his cultivation of government officials, and his recruitment of the best technicians and the most pliant peasant-laborers.

However, he overreached himself on a heroic scale as well and ended by selling most of his share in the enterprise to foreign banking interests. Like Putilov, the founders of two other big Petersburg concerns, Thomson and Obukhov, were forced to sell out under financial pressure, in their case to the Naval Ministry. Only MacPherson, an English mechanic, was astute enough to dispose of his plant while it was still making a profit. In this way the government obtained the Russo-Baltic Iron-Working and Mechanical Society, the Obukhovskii Plant, and the Nevskii Shipbuilding Plant, but the first generation of Petersburg entrepreneurs was sadly depleted.[66]

In addition to their entrepreneurial activities, the members of the first generation were also heavily involved in a variety of informational, educational, and propagandistic activities centered on the Russian Technological Society, of which many of them were founders. At its meetings they rubbed shoulders with industrialists from other regions and professional intelligentsia from the technical schools and

65. *Monopolisticheskii kapital: Dokumenty*, pp. 53–56, 150–52, 323–31, 337–38, 351–52, 372–76.
66. Stoplianskii, *Zhizn' i byt*, pp. 162–65, 167, 172; Mitel'man, Glebov, and Ul'ianskii, *Istoriia*, pp. 11–13, 17–18.

university, as well as a sprinkling of journalists. The presence of high-ranking bureaucrats insured them easy access to policymakers. However, after the textile strikes of 1896–97 revealed the strength and militancy of the labor movement, a genteel debating society like the Russian Technological Society could no longer meet the dramatically altered needs of the St. Petersburg entrepreneurs. Led by representatives of the big textile, chemical, and mechanical enterprises, the entrepreneurs founded in 1897 the Society for the Assistance, Improvement, and Development of Factory Industry along more narrowly occupational lines. Originally comprising 98 firms employing 54,535 workers, it expanded over the following ten years to encompass 167 firms employing 109,340 workers. During that time the predominant element and leadership passed from textiles to the newer mechanical industries. They represented the second generation of St. Petersburg entrepreneurs.

The major figures in this group were professional managers, trained at the St. Petersburg Technological Institute and experienced in several branches of industry, including S. P. Glezmer, the chairman of the society, an engineer of Polish extraction, and M. M. Tripolitov, the deputy chairman, who had experience in the sugar-beet and paper industries and later served as a nonparty member of the State Council. Other prominent members included G. I. Vege of the Kinovievskii-Ul'tramarinovyi Factory, John Johnson of the Novo-Sampson'evskii Manufacturing Company, D. A. Naratov of the Putilov Works, P. A. Bartmer representing the Ludwig Nobel Company, A. Z. Mazing of the Nauman Box Factory, V. I. Voronin of the Voronin, Liutch, and Chesher Joint-Stock Company, B. A. Efron, N. N. Klimenko of the Northern Glass Company, and Ia. P. Beliaev, the St. Petersburg timber king.[67]

The activities of the society provide the most reliable guide to an understanding of their collective mentality. From its very first meetings the society sought to exercise its influence on government legislation using the same tactics that had won such an impressive reputation for the Russian Technological Society among the bureaucracy. The society's guiding principle was quite the reverse of that of the Moscow entrepreneurs. Not agitation but information was their weapon. They took great pains to amass all the pertinent data on an issue and then prepare a careful draft proposal. To a much greater degree than either the Moscow or southern entrepreneurs, they were preoccupied with labor legislation as a means of controlling the restless working class. One of the earliest successes was helping to draft the new rules

67. TsGIA, f. 150, op. 1, d. 484, pp. 6–7; *Golos Moskvy*, no. 151 (3 July 1909).

for working conditions that were incorporated into the laws of 2 June 1897. The following year the society began to participate on a regular basis in the Ministry of Finance's discussions on the railroad tariffs. From then on, it was routinely consulted on all pending legislation dealing with industry.[68] Most of these questions were technical until the revival of the strike movement in 1902–3 brought to the surface once more the delicate question of whether or not the workers should be permitted some form of elected representation. There was some sentiment among state factory managers and a few private owners that it was better to deal with a few "responsible" workers in a controlled situation than have to face the entire unorganized work force in potentially explosive mass meetings. The Obolenskii Committee of the Ministry of Finance concurred. The strictly subordinate and hierarchical nature of its proposal was revealed by the designation of the worker representative as a *starosta*, with all the patriarchal peasant overtones of village elder. Even so, the St. Petersburg society was horrified by the idea and "categorically opposed [the institution] of starosta" as well as any organization of the workers which, in its view, "stands in direct contradiction to the basic conditions of industrial life." It rejected as "incorrect" the very reasoning that two years later it was to accept, namely, that in the event of disorders it was less dangerous to deal with organized workers than with an inchoate mass.[69] Once again the peculiar logic of the St. Petersburg entrepreneurs set them at odds with Moscow.

Few issues provide a more reliable gauge of class consciousness than attitudes toward a presumptive class antagonist. The St. Petersburg and the Moscow entrepreneurs held widely divergent views of the situation of the worker. While Petersburg spoke of the need "to avoid isolating the factory workers from the rest of the population by all possible means," Moscow retorted that "a separate class of factory workers already exists in Russia." While Petersburg desired to integrate the workers' mutual aid societies with local government, Moscow dismissed the zemstvos and town dumas as "entirely unsuitable for the aims of mutual aid." In sum, the differences between them were ironically the very opposite of those which they stated in public. In St. Petersburg, where factory workers were in fact closer to a West European proletariat, the entrepreneurs opposed any form of workers' organization as the first step in a stampede toward militant international trade unionism. In Moscow, where the factory workers retained more real ties with the countryside and closer personal identity with

68. Obshchestvo zavodchikov i fabrikantov, *Otchet za 1897–1906 gg.*; *PSZRI*, 3rd ser., 2 June 1897, nos. 14231, 14232.
69. St.-Peterburgskoe obshchestvo, *Otchet za 1903*, pp. 1–3 and appendix.

the peasant soslovie, the entrepreneurs accepted the starosta as a patriarchal institution rooted in "the national culture" and offering no threat to the traditional factory order.[70] Despite the defection of Moscow, the St. Petersburg society lobbied vigorously for defeat, then for postponement, and, when all else failed, for a voluntary system of starosta, which was finally accepted by the government. Introduced in St. Petersburg in a few medium and smaller firms, the institution never won widespread acceptance although most of the thirty or forty enterprises that adopted it were in Moscow.

In a similar though less successful campaign the society opposed a second piece of legislation in Witte's belated program of labor reform, the law on accident insurance. For ten years the Ministry of Finance had advocated it and for ten years the St. Petersburg industrialists had fought it. When Witte finally forced it through the State Council in June 1903, the St. Petersburg society reacted sharply, despite the fact that the law was a much watered down version of Witte's original draft. In their criticism, the industrialists resorted to the specious argument that to extend benefits to factory workers, who numbered only two million, while denying them to agricultural workers, who numbered eighty million, was "not only unjust but dangerous." Once again they petitioned for a year's postponement in executing the law, bemoaning the cost to them of fifteen million rubles a year.[71]

Their experiences with both bills confirmed the industrialists in their sense of isolation from their presumptive social allies. The bureaucrats in the Ministry of Finance, with Witte at their head, had given up trying to shame them into reforms and sought instead to emulate Central European labor legislation. The landed nobles who dominated the State Council were disinterested in protecting the authority of the factory owners. Despite the society's partial success in winning support for agitation against reform from the Association of Southern Coal and Steel Producers, they lamented the "mutual alienation from, . . . indifference to, and distrust for any general understanding [among industrialists], even if it is clearly useful to every one" which, in turn, prevented them from uniting "into a single class organization."[72]

In local government the Petersburg entrepreneurs felt themselves victimized by the landed nobility, despite their common social and ethnic origins. Like the Moscow and southern entrepreneurs, they complained bitterly about the discriminatory tax rates and excessive property valuations levied on industry by the provincial zemstvo. But

70. *Zakonodatel'nye materialy*, pp. 18–24, 27–29.
71. St.-Peterburgskoe obshchestvo, *Otchet za 1903*, pp. 4–5.
72. Obshchestvo zavodchikov i fabrikantov, *Otchet za 1897–1906 gg.*, pp. 1–2.

unlike their fellow industrialists in Moscow, they could not even hold their own in the city duma. As a result they watched helplessly as lucrative contracts for public works were awarded to outside firms in Reval, Riga, Helsingfors, and even Moscow.[73] Their lack of experience in city politics and their social isolation were to relegate them to an even more modest role in the momentous events of 1905 and beyond than that of their colleagues in Moscow, whom they affected to disdain.

73. St.-Peterburgskoe obshchestvo, *Otchet za 1904*, pp. 27–30, 37–38.

PART 3

MERCHANTS AND

ENTREPRENEURS IN WAR

AND REVOLUTION

CHAPTER 7

MOSCOW MERCHANTS

AND ENTREPRENEURS

IN 1905

In 1905 the pressure of revolution broke down many of the barriers to change within the merchant soslovie. Most historians argue that, as a result, the merchantry realized that its class interest was best served by accepting the leadership of the zemstvos and professional unions within the constitutional movement. But the relationship between cause and effect here has been assumed rather than proven. To be sure, it is unthinkable that any social group could have emerged from the events of 1905 with its traditional outlook and values intact. Even though the tsarist regime weathered the storm, the attacks upon it were more prolonged, violent, and widespread than those of the successful revolution of February 1917. No major city or region remained untouched by the disorders. Moreover, the long-standing bars to public organizations and meetings disappeared and censorship practically vanished, encouraging a burst of political activity that swept up every element in the population, from one end of the country to the other. In this feverish atmosphere the merchantry could hardly remain as before, isolated from the rest of society, deeply divided within itself, and in its overwhelming majority profoundly attached to a soslovie mentality.

It is also true that the great reforms and the industrial spurt of the 1890s had prepared the ground for the emergence of a bourgeoisie. Three major regional entrepreneurial groups had demonstrated the value for industry of organization, lobbying, and propaganda outside the narrow confines of soslovie. With the growth of heavy industry in other regions, smaller organizations had emerged in the old Kingdom of Poland, the Caucasus, and even the backward Urals.

Moreover, the merchantry as a whole could no longer be considered by the end of the century an undifferentiated, inert mass. The exchange committees of Moscow, St. Petersburg, Kiev, and Nizhnyi had shed the most extreme forms of passivity as early as the 1860s and 1870s. They had sought and obtained a consultative role within the government on a range of economic questions. When invited, and occasionally on their own initiative, they had raised their voices against the ministerial bureaucrats on issues, such as tariffs and railroads, that touched their immediate economic interests. Although they had never moved beyond the limits set by the bureaucratic rules, which they had no share in defining, there was a good chance that this would change if the authority of the bureaucracy were challenged and reduced by a series of external shocks like those administered by the revolution of 1905. After all, the merchantry's loyalty to the tsar had always been tempered by its hostility to his bureaucratic servants. Because officials were everywhere under attack in 1905, the temptation for the merchantry to join in was very great.

Up to this time the active elements among the entrepreneurs and merchants had won their concessions by working behind the closed doors of the chancelleries and government commissions. But in 1905 the politics of oligarchy appeared doomed before the wave of disorders and the demands for a popularly elected government. Clearly, the entrepreneurs and merchants would have preferred that Russia's political institutions copy the France of 1830 rather than that of 1848, but a restricted franchise based upon property qualifications or even a consultative duma would still have required them to enter the arena of mass politics and explore the possibilities of new alliances and alignments with other defenders of social stability. For at the national level the stakes were much higher than they were in the town dumas and zemstvos, where merchant passivity was notorious, and the prospect of facing a unified working-class movement suddenly became a terrifying reality for them.

The revolution was a strong prod toward merchant unity, but countervailing factors, which may be all too easily overlooked if only because their effects were subtle, indirect, and largely negative in 1905, were also important and even proved decisive in the long run. For the merchants and entrepreneurs to organize at the imperial level and draft a political program with a broad appeal among propertied groups, they had to surmount the ethnic and regional differences that had crippled their collective action in the past. Somehow they had to overcome the latent hostility toward commerce that pervaded much of the landowning gentry and the professional intelligentsia. Finally, they had to shake off their own contemptuous indifference to the meshchanstvo, for without a mass base in the cities they could never hope to fashion an effective bourgeois policy.

The following three chapters will explore the dynamic interplay between these two social processes. The revolutionary upheaval squeezed together various social groups that may be said to constitute an ideal type of bourgeoisie defined as both an economic and a ruling class. Resistance to those pressures emanated from within those same social groups, particularly the merchantry, whose social evolution continued to bear the deep imprint of traditional values and institutional forms. This in turn placed additional strain upon the existing fault lines that separated the entrepreneurial groups and the merchantry into different strata: namely, (1) between the center and the periphery, (2) between the Moscow entrepreneurs and the exchange leadership, and (3) between entrepreneurial groups and the mass of merchants on the periphery. Henceforth, the historical narrative takes its shape from these divisions and how they were formed by conflicting loyalties between sosloviia, regions, and ethnic groups.

The Merchantry, Police Socialism, and Bloody Sunday

In the early years of the twentieth century, even before the outbreak of the Russo-Japanese War, the socioeconomic crisis that had slowly been building did not spare the Great Russian merchantry in the central industrial provinces. The textile industry was already suffering from the effects of a prolonged depression when a wholly unexpected danger threatened them from a most unlikely source: the police. With the connivance and support of highly placed figures in the court and central bureaucracy, the notorious Sergei Zubatov sought to forestall political and possible revolutionary activities against the government by endorsing the economic demands of the workers against their employers. In the beginning, Zubatov won support among Jewish workers in Minsk and Odessa, where the labor movement was already well developed. But Moscow was a different story. To be sure, the idea of incorporating the workers peaceably into the traditional social order appealed to right-wing intellectuals like Gringmut and Tikhomirov, who had been at one time subsidized apologists for the Moscow merchantry. Zubatov's plans also picked up support among a group of Moscow University professors who favored the rapid expansion of Russian capitalism, men like I. Kh. Ozerov, A. A. Manuilov, and A. E. Vorms, who subsequently formed the nucleus of a Moscow entrepreneurial brain trust. Like Zubatov, they believed that the industrialists lacked vision. Hoping to raise the cultural level of the workers, they cooperated with the police in an educational program sponsored by the local branch of the Russian Technological Society.[1]

The Moscow merchants and entrepreneurs at first restrained whatever uneasy feelings Zubatov's zealous activities may have caused them. But then his organizations pushed forward economic demands and unleashed a strike. The response from the Moscow capitalists was neither unified nor coordinated. The Zubatov organizations drew their early strength from among skilled workers in small enterprises, such as tobacco, perfume, woodworking, confectionary, and button factories, where the cowed owners were willing to accept, albeit grudgingly, this curious form of police protection racket. Most foreign owners also complied, even the "Prussians" Karl Veichelt and Gustav List in large metals, the cloth merchant and calico manufacturer Emil Tsindel', and the Swiss ribbon magnate Heinrich Hanshin, for they had good reason to avoid trouble with the Moscow governor-general and the minister of the interior, who stood behind Zubatov. But almost all the textile manufacturers, including S. T. Morozov and S. I. Chetverikov, rallied the merchants on the Moscow section of the Council of Trade and Industry behind their campaign to check Zubatov's activities and send a delegation to Witte to register their formal protest. Another defiant response was made by the Association of Silk Manufacturers, with Jules Goujon at its head, who represented the owners of the factories being struck. Goujon sought protection from the French ambassador on the well-founded assumption that this was worth more than a protest by the Russian minister of finance.[2]

Rebuffed by the big Moscow merchants, Zubatov left for St. Petersburg, where, sheltered by his high protector, Minister of the Interior Pleve, he made inroads among skilled workers, particularly at the Putilov Plant. The director, S. I. Smirnov, helped Zubatov's St. Petersburg Mutual Aid Society with money and moral support, perceiving in it a useful counterweight to the growing threat of Father Gapon's Assembly of Russian Factory Workers, which was not under direct police control and therefore far more unpredictable.[3] It quickly turned out that Zubatovism was an ephemeral social phenomenon. Its importance here lies in the mixed and confused reaction that this bizarre experiment elicited among merchants and entrepreneurs both along the periphery and in the center of the empire. The phenome-

1. Schneiderman, *Zubatov*, pp. 106–13, 161–63; *Osvobozhdenie*, no. 8 (2 October 1902).
2. Schneiderman, *Zubatov*, pp. 146–55; Bukhbinder, "Zubatovshchina," pp. 104–6, 120–31, and *Spravochnaia kniga*, pp. 13, 14, and 28.
3. Sablinsky, *Bloody Sunday*, pp. 144–46.

non itself and the divided response were a preview of the events of 1905.

For the merchants and entrepreneurs the sinister implications of the Zubatov movement lay in the willingness of government officials to deflect the workers' discontent from themselves to the factory owners. Pleve, the driving force behind Zubatov, was also apparently prepared to reach an accommodation with the landed nobility—and for a fleeting moment even with its liberal zemstvo wing—at the expense of the industrial interests, thus raising the old specter of encirclement. As it had in the past, the government seemed to favor the two groups standing at opposite ends of the social hierarchy over the merchant soslovie, which was boxed in the middle. As if these grievances were not enough, the merchants viewed Pleve as the architect of a foreign policy that had plunged Russia into war with Japan, imposed further strains upon the sagging economy, sharpened the strike movement, and led to a national humiliation. For the merchantry, who had supported Russia's expansion in the East as an economic necessity and a civilizing mission, the insult was equal to the injury.

Thus the merchants had good reason to add their voices to the mounting chorus of protest against government policies, even before the events of 9 January 1905, "Bloody Sunday," when troops fired on a large crowd of unarmed demonstrators and killed about a thousand of them. This act horrified and revolted people at every level of Russian society. Consequently, historians have concluded that the opposition to the government was at this point unanimous and that the "big bourgeoisie" were now forced to acknowledge the need for liberal constitutional reforms as the common denominator of national unity. A closer look at the behavior of the merchantry, however, casts some real doubts about just how far it was prepared to move beyond a defense of the narrow perimeter of its soslovie.

As the first shock waves of Bloody Sunday penetrated Russian society, the official merchant organizations remained silent. Then just before the tsar issued the so-called Bulygin rescript promising to convoke a consultative assembly, "the trade and industry soslovie of the internal region gathered at the Moscow Exchange" submitted "a most humble petition" to the throne. Proclaiming their "limitless devotion" to "the autocratic power [which] alone makes possible the preservation of the power and unity of Russia and its future prosperity," the merchants expressed their hopes and belief that "the memory of all the painful recent past will disappear."[4] The petition included not a

---

4. *Pravo*, no. 8 (26 February 1905): col. 588, published together with a letter of appreciation from the tsar.

word on civil rights or the new era. It was vintage "south-side" servility. Although it was not the only voice of the Great Russian merchantry to be heard in those days, it represented the overwhelming majority of the soslovie in the central provinces.

At a significantly earlier date, three weeks before, a group of big factory and mill owners of Moscow and the Moscow region, numbering about two hundred, had endorsed a more forceful and contentious statement, which squarely placed the blame for the disorders on "the absence in Russia of a firm law and the ubiquitous and stultifying tutelage of the bureaucracy." Among their specific demands contained in the nine-point memorandum, four dealt with matters of general interest to the whole population and in rather vague terms: equality of all before the law, inviolability of person and home, universal compulsory elementary education, and freedom of speech and the press (though here the curious justification given was that it was "the only possible way of achieving the best results for the constant growth of industry, of clarifying the workers' needs and interests and of improving the living standards of the workers"). A fifth point took up the desirability of the "participation of all classes of the population including workers and industrialists in working out legislative norms and in discussing the budget because this latter is a powerful lever in the hands of the government for resolving the industrial questions of the country." However, the only legislative model referred to in the text of the memorandum suggests that the industrialists were not thinking of a parliamentary government: "From time immemorial the Russian people discussed their affairs openly and freely in the squares, in meetings of the zemskii dumas [and] the zemskii sobor while gradually their inherent rights were taken away and the population was enserfed. The existing volost assemblies are a survival of the past freedoms belonging to the people." Even after thirty-five years of experience in the all-class Moscow city duma, the merchant-industrialists could do no better than summon up the ghosts of representation by hierarchical groups in the pre-Petrine period!

The final four points made it clear that the major concern of the Moscow merchant-industrialists was to get the government out of the factories. Here vague aspirations yielded to concrete proposals. What they really meant by strict application of the law becomes clear in their attack on "the ruling bureaucracy" for having dreamed up the pernicious idea of introducing "illegal and unlawful" organizations of workers under the leadership of "members of the secret police [okhrana] in both capitals and the gendarmes in the provinces." "This administrative guardianship of the bureaucracy over the workers led to a complete demoralization of the working masses, to dissension among the workers themselves, and to the aggravation of relations between them and the factory owners." While admitting the existence of economic difficulties, the merchant-industrialists insisted that the underlying cause for the wave of strikes sweeping the country was the workers' demand for political rights. These could best be advanced, they claimed, by allowing the workers to organize freely in "unions and any other kind of society for mutual aid and the defense of their interests [and] the right separately and collectively to refuse to work." To be sure, the factor owners also would enjoy "freedom to establish work rules, wages, set prices, hire, and select salaried office employees. . . . Under conditions of legal equality of all sides in the agreements the possible misunderstandings with the workers would be settled by peaceful and legal means."[5]

The rhetoric of workers' rights and legal equality could not conceal the real object of these proposals, which was to dismantle the entire structure of social legislation, including the factory inspectors, built up by the government over the previous twenty-five years.[6] Were the government to stand down from its role as intermediary, the merchant-industrialists could face the workers in an absolutely free labor market where they were convinced, and for good reason, they would prevail. They knew full well that the Russian worker had "not broken his ties with life in the villages in the majority of cases." This factor alone would have made permanent union membership difficult and discouraged the solidarity necessary in long strikes, but the merchant-industrialists further insisted that striking workers not be allowed to interfere with strikebreaking tactics, for this too was part of the freedom of labor.[7] Still, for all their narrow material interests and lack of a broader social vision, this group of industrialists had taken a bolder political stance than that of the soslovie organization. This difference foreshadowed a widening rift within the Moscow region between the

---

5. Ibid., nos. 4–5 (5 February 1905): cols., 260–66. The memorandum was presented to a gathering of over two hundred industrialists, who "greeted it with enthusiasm." Similar views were expressed in a subsequent meeting of industrialists from the central industrial region. The conservative leaders of the exchange committee, G. A. Krestovnikov and V. A. Naidenov, did not sign it (ibid., no. 8 [26 February 1905]: cols. 588–93).
6. When the factory owners found that they could not block the introduction of factory inspection and other government regulatory legislation, they worked assiduously to bring the inspectors and other police agents within their enterprises under their control, but the government persisted in seeking new ways to circumvent these blandishments in their efforts to influence the administration of new factories. For a thorough review of this muted struggle see Ozerov, *Politika*, pp. 25, 43–55, 98–100, 177.
7. *Pravo*, nos. 4–5 (5 February 1905): col. 265.

leadership of the Moscow Exchange Committee and a second generation of Moscow entrepreneurs over the role of the merchantry in the
new political life of the country.

The Moscow Exchange Society Splits

On the eve of World War I the Moscow Exchange Society constituted
a formidable array of enterprises drawn from a membership of 35
joint-stock banks and insurance companies and 173 commercial and
industrial firms. High property qualifications limited the individual
membership to about five hundred families. The leadership of the
society represented an even more restricted economic elite. According to the exchange statute of 1898 the members of the hundred-man
assembly of electors, whose main function was to elect the exchange
committee and the special commissions, were required to be guild
merchants engaged in trading with other towns. Almost all the electors were Great Russians, even though they constituted barely 60
percent of the first-guild merchants in 1892, as shown in table 7.1.[8]
The Jewish and foreign merchants were excluded from the exchange
leadership, and only a very few merchants from other ethnic groups
served as electors or on special committees. The Great Russian Moscow merchants paid a high price for their monopoly of privilege
and authority in their soslovie organization. At least one-third of the
wealthiest merchants in the city were unwilling to support them in
public ventures such as elections to the town dumas and also, after
1905, a national organization and elections to the state duma.

In the day-to-day business and administration of the exchange,
trading merchants, rather than industrialists, set the slow pace, quiet
tone, and informal style. Traders in securities were active on the floor,
but the textile merchants arrived mainly to see friends and hear the
news. Most of their business deals took place outside the exchange.
Even serious matters like bankruptcy proceedings were conducted
over a glass of tea while creditors decided whether to elect one of
their number as administrator or liquidate the enterprise. No one
thought of discussing politics in the strict sense of the word.[9]

8. Calculated from *Spravochnaia kniga na 1892*, pp. 7–55; *Torgovye doma 1–i gil'dii*,
pp. 3–13. The only public activity in which the Jewish and foreign merchants took part
was as wardens in the commercial courts, which did not involve making policy or
advising the government. Of the eighty-seven merchants from non-Russian ethnic
backgrounds (excluding Jews) I found only three who served as electors of the merchant assembly. Similarly, no Jewish or foreign merchants and only three from ethnic
groups served on the quasi-official Council of Trade and Manufactures.
9. Buryshkin, *Moskva*, pp. 233–39, 246–47.

TABLE 7.1. *Ethnic Composition of First-Guild Moscow Merchants*

	Great Russians	Jews	Foreigners	Ethnic Groups	Total
Individual membership	436	129	92	87	740
Full partnerships	82	10	20	12	124
Partnerships in trust	24	3	13	8	48
Totals	542	142	125	107	912

As Soviet historians from Liashchenko to Gindin have established, several features set the Moscow merchant elite apart from the rest of the country. Because the Moscow merchants depended less on the government for state contracts and direct subsidies, they were freer from bureaucratic controls. They required only the protection of tariffs to guarantee large profits and sufficient liquid capital to prevent their domination by large banks and foreign capital. But this relative independence from external influence came at a high price. Whereas merchants in other regions showed themselves open to industrial organization and technological innovation, the Moscow merchants continued to exhibit a marked degree of social conservatism and economic backwardness. However, the conclusion that the tension between these contradictory elements created a Moscow bourgeoisie that, according to Liashchenko, "played the leading role" in the development of capitalism in the empire or, in the words of Gindin, "became the public and political leader of Russian national capital" is open to question.[10]

10. Liashchenko rests his case in *Istoriia* upon two arguments: a misleading interpretation of statistics for industrial production and number of workers by region, p. 431, and the weak syllogism that because the Russian proletariat led the revolution, it represented the most advanced sector of world socialism and thus the Russian merchantry or bourgeoisie must have represented the most advanced sector of world capitalism. Nevertheless, Liashchenko's discussion of the Moscow industrial world on the eve of the war remains the basis for all subsequent treatments. The survey that follows, pp. 477–518, on economic developments in each of the national areas is equally good, even though it helps to undermine his Russo-centric thesis. As for Gindin's argument that the Moscow bourgeoisie was "the most conscious of all the politically inert groups taken as a whole of the imperial Russian bourgeoisie," it too reflects an overriding concern with political issues. In his view the heavy industrialists and big bankers of the periphery constituted a financial oligarchy and represented the most advanced form of monopoly capitalism in the empire, but their intimate involvement with the government and foreign capitalists deprived them of a leading political role in the empire. Along with the feudal survivals in the countryside, this split in the bourgeoisie differ-

From the 1880s until 1915 the presidency of the Moscow Exchange Committee was held by two men, V. A. Naidenov and G. A. Krestovnikov. Both vigorously defended the position achieved by the Moscow merchants in the era of the great reforms, but they also refused steadfastly to seek a wider political role for their soslovie outside the central industrial region. Like the bulk of the merchants who elected them to a total of nine uncontested terms of office, they were satisfied with minimal adjustments to the reforms of the 1860s and 1870s. They accepted the exchange committee as a permanent and more effective instrument than the old merchant society for consultation and negotiation with the bureaucracy on economic matters that touched their pocketbooks. For them the symbol of the transformed merchant status was the ceremonial visit made to the exchange by every new minister of finance within weeks of his appointment in order to hear an address by Naidenov or Krestovnikov and to give them, in return, a reassuring speech. The strong ties that both men enjoyed with the first generation of the Moscow entrepreneurial group were put to a severe test in 1905, when the unprecedented political crisis challenged the political style of oligarchic interest groups throughout the empire.

Naidenov had been an early associate of the Moscow entrepreneurs as a member of the administrative boards of the Merchants' Bank and the Mutual Credit Society, as well as a participant in the Moscow Industrial Commercial Company (Tovarishchestvo) to market cotton in Central Asia. He succeeded to the presidency of these banks at a time when their main activities of discounting promissory notes and lending solely for commercial purposes no longer answered the economic needs of a rapidly industrializing country. Much like his business style, Naidenov's cultural interests were closely bound by his soslovie and region. Together with the historian I. E. Zabelin, he induced the Moscow Merchant Society to begin a massive collection of its historical sources. The venture blossomed into a multivolume work containing data drawn from the ten census revisions of the population from the time of Peter the Great to 1857 and supplementary volumes on the history of the merchant soslovie in the seventeenth and late

entiated Russian from Western capitalism, creating, in Gindin's restatement of Lenin, an "Octobrist capitalism" so rent with its own internal contradictions that it was unable either to subordinate the tsarist state apparatus to its own interests or to hold power for very long by itself when it had the opportunity in 1917 (Gindin, "Russkaia burzhauziia," pp. 43–48, 58–60). In my view the chief shortcomings of Gindin's otherwise brilliant analysis lie, first, in attributing to the Moscow bourgeoisie as a whole the political consciousness that belonged only to a small number of activists whom I have called the Moscow entrepreneurial group and, second, in minimizing the profound ethnic divisions in Russian society which intensified the regional economic conflicts that he has done so much to illuminate.

eighteenth centuries. He also published at his own expense several volumes of foreigners' impressions of Moscow and finally a lavish limited edition of photographs of all the churches in Moscow.[11] Yet, as we have seen, he resisted efforts by men like Rukavishnikov and Vishniakov to carry on the work of Alekseev in the city duma, and despite his long friendship with the Riabushinskii family he opposed their even more ambitious political plans in 1905.

His successor as president, G. A. Krestovnikov, gave the appearance of being the modern merchant par excellence. A nephew of the Krestovnikovs who were active in the Moscow entrepreneurial group, Grigory Alexandrovich received a first-rate education in the physical-mathematical faculty of Moscow University and coauthored a number of works on organic chemistry in Russian and German scholarly periodicals. His interest in applied science led him to become one of the founders of the Moscow section of the Russian Technological Society. A vigorous entrepreneur in his own right, Krestovnikov inherited his family's large candle factory and personally supervised the organization of purchasing mutton tallow in Siberia, which no doubt led to his close business friendship with Chetverikov. He helped to found the Society of the Moscow Mechanical Factories and became the director of the Ivan Garelin Manufacturing Works. Krestovnikov married one of the daughters of T. S. Morozov.

Yet, for all these personal and entrepreneurial ties with what would become the second generation of the Moscow entrepreneurial group, he remained aloof from their political ambitions. It is not clear why this was so, but his association with high-ranking state bureaucrats like Witte and Vyshnegradskii may have had something to do with it. He served, for example, as a member of the governing board of the Moscow-Kursk line after it had been repurchased from the Moscow merchants by the government in the early 1890s. In any case, Krestovnikov, like Naidenov, fulfilled an unwritten bargain with St. Petersburg to help keep the civic peace in return for high protective duties and other advantages which guaranteed their phenomenal profits. Even during the tumultuous days of 1905, when both men felt obliged to remind the government in no uncertain terms of its side of the

11. Buryshkin, *Moskva*, pp. 129–34; Gindin, *Russkie kommercheskie*, pp. 48–62. The first nine volumes of *Materialy dlia istorii Moskovskogo kupechestva* provide only minimal biographical information, and none at all on property holding, so that its usefulness as a historical source is extremely limited. Volume 10, subtitled *Obshchestvennye prigovory* (Moscow, 1910), contains summaries of the discussions of the electors of the Moscow merchant soslovie. During the revolution of 1905, Naidenov's collaborator, Zabelin, turned violently to the extreme right, mounting scurrilous attacks against the intelligentsia from the pages of Suvorin's Black Hundred journal *Novoe vremiia* (Rubinshtein, "Zabelin," p. 74).

bargain, they kept their own part and continued to do so right up to the end of the empire. High officials came to trust Krestovnikov to such a degree that they twice considered him seriously for the post of minister of trade and industry.[12]

To be sure, there were limits to the exchange committee's cooperation with the government, as their initial reaction to Bloody Sunday demonstrated. Krestovnikov drew the line even more clearly when he skillfully maneuvered against the government's modest program of labor legislation, a rational if belated attempt to emulate the social paternalism of Imperial Germany. In appointing a commission to examine the government's proposals, Minister of Finance V. N. Kokovtsov attributed the strike movement to the depressed socioeconomic conditions of the workers and not to the deprivation of their political rights. Among industrialists on the periphery there was a sharp outcry against the government's blackmail of the employers with the threat of more strikes.[13] But Krestovnikov, who insisted upon representation on the commission for the commercial-industrial interests, avoided a head-on clash with the government, preferring delaying tactics, as was his custom. Dismissing Kokovtsov's agenda as incomplete, he ingenuously proposed that given the plans to convene a consultative duma the commission ought to consider its work preparatory rather than legislative. The great naval defeat of Tsushima offered him a convenient pretext for claiming that under the tragic circumstances it was impossible to continue the deliberations. This move effectively wrecked the commission and stranded the labor legislation.[14]

At the same time, however, the exchange leadership also demonstrated the limits of its opposition to the government. Throughout the summer of 1905, Naidenov and Krestovnikov struggled hard to prevent the merchantry from becoming associated in any way with the overt political attempts to weaken the power of the autocratic state. As early as January 1905, Naidenov wrote to the deputy minister of the interior that the declaration of the Moscow duma urging the government to allow peaceful strikes and to recognize the right of workers to organize into unions "cannot be taken as the opinion of the industrial soslovie." He blocked attempts to convoke an all-Russian conference of exchange committees and hampered efforts to

12. Buryshkin, *Moskva*, pp. 179–85; Witte, *Vospominaniia*, 3:167–68, 358, 517; Kislinskii, *Nasha*, 139–43; *Golos Moskvy*, no. 153 (3 July 1908), and no. 207 (10 September 1909); G. A. Krestovnikov, "Salo, stearin i mylo," in Kovalevskii, *Rossiia*, pp. 379–83; Gurko, *Figures and Features*, p. 556.

13. TsGIA, f. 150, op. 1, d. 484, pp. 89–92.

14. Romanov, *Rabochii vopros*, pp. 201–3, 235–37, 241.

organize an all-Russian organization of industrial and commercial representatives.[15]

Only reluctantly did Naidenov play host to the first two conferences of the representatives of industry of various regions convened in Moscow in March and July 1905. By the time of the second conference he and Krestovnikov had become frightened that rather than continue as a union to defend the purely economic interests of the industrialists, the organization was becoming an overt political force. At that point their attempt to check the slide toward a confrontation with the autocracy undermined the quest for class unity and opened up a new split within the ranks of the merchants and industrialists. Of the twenty-three participating organizations in the second conference, only the Moscow Exchange Committee voted in favor of the government's position that the duma should be a consultative rather than a legislative organ. The other merchant organizations of the Great Russian center—the exchange committees of Elets, Kazan, and Kostroma and the Ivanovo-Vosnesensk Committee of Trade and Industry—abstained, declined to vote, or were absent, all variations on the old theme of political confusion among the merchantry. Hopelessly outnumbered, Naidenov scurried off to the governor-general of Moscow, where he obtained authority to ban further discussion of political questions at the conference. He then forced the recalcitrant delegates to leave the premises of the Moscow Exchange Committee, an action interpreted by the incensed majority as a rude violation of traditional hospitality which, they concluded, in a model of understatement, "could hardly enhance the importance of the Moscow Exchange Committee in the milieu of Russian Trade and Industry."[16]

It soon became obvious that the breach was deep and permanent. In a joint declaration justifying their decision to quit the conference, the Moscow and Elets exchange committees and the Ivanovo-Vosnesensk Committee of Trade and Industry stated that "between them and the majority of the members of the conference there had appeared radical differences of views and convictions on basic questions of the future political structure of Russia."[17] By hewing to the government's line the Moscow Exchange leadership bears much of the responsibility for destroying the best and possibly the only chance to have organized the merchantry of the empire as a unified political

15. Chermenskii, *Burzhuaziia*, pp. 81–88; Sef, *Burzhuaziia*, pp. 53–65.
16. TsGIA f. 150, op. 1, d. 373, pp. 50–52.
17. Ibid., p. 53. The signatories included Krestovnikov, V. S. Barshev, A. I. Vagurin, A. L. Losev, N. N. Prokhorov, V. G. Saposhnikov, I. K. Polivakov, A. Petrov (president of the Elets Exhange), N. Burykin, and Sergei Polushin.

force. Subsequently, the October Manifesto, which promised a legislative duma, confirmed the bankruptcy of Moscow's position.

By this time the merchantry was once again so deeply divided along the traditional lines that half a dozen parties sprang up to compete for their small number of votes. Faced by the challenge of universal suffrage, the Moscow Exchange Committee was psychologically and politically unprepared to create and lead a mass party. For too long it had patronized the meshchanstvo and held itself aloof from the petty peasant capitalists, and it lacked any electoral base beyond its own soslovie in the central industrial region. The organization, platform, and fate of its hastily assembled Trade and Industry party made this abundantly clear.

Short lived and impotent, the Trade and Industry party left hardly a trace upon the history of the period, but an analysis of its failure demonstrates the extent to which the Moscow merchants remained isolated from the rest of the country. Although the Manifesto of August 6, creating the consultative Bulygin duma, also promulgated an electoral law, the members of the Moscow Exchange Committee made no move to organize themselves for the forthcoming campaign. However, their passivity may be attributed to the complex and indirect method of election rather than to their political inertia.

The government had yielded to pressures for popular representation in characteristic fashion by turning back to the traditional system of dividing the population into rigid social categories. A complete reversion to the old soslovie system was out of the question, but the bureaucrats adhered to its principles as faithfully as possible. Taking as their model the zemstvo regulations of 1864 and the town statutes of 1870, they created four electoral curia—one for landowners, another for peasants, and two for the urban populations of the empire (one for the provincial towns and one for the twenty-six largest cities). Their intention in this last division was, no doubt, to reduce the influence of the urban intelligentsia over the more conservative small towns, where the local merchants and gentry predominated. In addition, the urban curia were further constrained in their choices by the establishment of high property qualifications and a two-stage indirect voting procedure that left the final selection of deputies to local assemblies of electors. This scheme eliminated most of the meshchanstvo and a good part of the urban professional class, encouraged the old-style oligarchic politics of the towns, and weakened the opportunities for political parties. Nothing seemed better suited to the interests of the merchantry, who now had only to shake off their deference to the nobility in public life.

The Merchantry and the Elections to the First Duma

Before the merchantry had a chance to test its strength under the favorable conditions of a restricted franchise, the government was forced to give way again. The success of the general strike in October and the Moscow rising in December convinced Witte to revise the electoral law, against the expressed wishes of the Moscow merchants, in order to broaden the electorate. The revision collapsed the two urban curia into one (and a worker's curia was added) and based suffrage upon reduced property qualifications that admitted anyone who owned a commercial or industrial establishment, paid a professional tax, rented an apartment, or received a salary or pension from the state for at least one year.[18]

Even before the text of the revised electoral law was published, the October Manifesto made it clear that an enlarged franchise would sweep away the oligarchs unless they were willing to shed their old habits and plunge into the rough and tumble of mass politics. On 8 November the Moscow Exchange Committee, led by the newly elected Krestovnikov, responded by founding the Trade and Industry party. Proclaiming its opposition to "the extreme socialist and revolutionary parties," it pledged full support to the government in introducing the principles of the October Manifesto under the rule of law, in maintaining the integrity of Russia, and in regulating by law the freedoms granted by the tsar to the Russian people. On the agrarian question the party rejected obligatory expropriation, except in "extreme and exceptional cases." But it favored enlarging peasant landholding with the assistance of the Peasant Bank and breaking up the commune— an idea close to Krestovnikov's heart since the days of his business dealings in Siberia. What distinguished its program from that of the Union of 17 October, which later absorbed most of its members, was its industrial program and, in particular, its unequivocal stand against the eight-hour day or any legal limitations upon the work time of male laborers and its plea for the development of Russia's vast natural resources.[19]

Once having stated its principles, the exchange committee seemed not to know what else to do, except to reject any form of political cooperation with like-minded elements in St. Petersburg. The political vacuum at the top of the party was filled by V. S. Barshev, a well-educated industrialist experienced in zemstvo politics who came from

---

18. For the electoral laws see *PSZRI*, 3rd series, 6 August 1905, no. 26662, and 11 December 1905, no. 27029.

19. Ivanovich, *Rossiiskie partii*, pp. 75–92.

a distinguished family of criminologists—scarcely a typical Moscow merchant. Under his guidance the party set up local committees in nineteen provinces, all within the Great Russian core and Siberia, and formed a voting bloc wherever possible with other parties and groups on the right, especially with the Union of 17 October.

Despite his efforts, however, the party suffered a crushing and humiliating defeat in the elections to the first duma. Only two of its candidates were returned, and the party failed to win a single urban contest, including those in Moscow. Barshev himself was elected in Moscow province along with A. I. Mukhlynin, a merchant from Perm who also had received a university education and had served in the Perm provincial zemstvo. Prince G. G. Gagarin, who won in Moscow province with the joint endorsement of the Octobrists and the Trade and Industry bloc, bore little resemblance to the kind of candidate envisaged by the Moscow Exchange Committee: he was a very large landowner, a graduate of the St. Petersburg University law faculty, a marshal of the nobility, and court chamberlain (*kamerger*).[20]

If the Moscow merchants organized into the Trade and Industry party made a dismal showing on their home grounds, the Great Russian merchantry scarcely fared any better throughout the empire. Out of approximately five hundred deputies to the first duma, only nine or ten can be identified positively as Great Russian merchants, and even this small group gave no evidence of any political cohesion other than the fact that none of them were socialists. The ten boasted six different political affiliations: two Kadets, one from the Party of Democratic Reform, which was closely associated with the Kadets, two from the Trade and Industry party, one Moderate Progressive, one nonparty progressive, one nonparty monarchist, and two Octobrists.[21]

20. These and all subsequent biographical data on members of the first duma have been compiled from *Albom*, which was based on articles in the contemporary Russian press and autobiographical information furnished by the majority of the deputies. These entries have been checked against two other sources: Boiovich, *Chleny*, and *Pervaia duma*. In almost every case *Albom* has proven to be the most complete and accurate. The list of members in *Gosudarstvennaia duma, Ukazatel'*, first session, pp. 3–33, does not indicate party affiliation. Because of the general lack of reliable information and the uncertainty of many of the deputies themselves about their party affiliations, political labels in the first duma must be treated with caution. Even the total number of deputies is in dispute; the *Ukazatel'* lists 496 deputies (pp. 3–17); *Russkii kalendar*, ed. A. V. Suvorin (St. Petersburg, 1906), pp. 642–56, 658, and 1907 p. 633 set the figure at 508. *Albom* contains data on 492 deputies.

21. The doubtful case is Anton Kaetanovich Demianovich from Bessarabia, who was very possibly Moldavian. The two merchants who were Kadets were M. G. Komissarov from Vladimir, who had a law degree from Moscow University, and S. I. Kolokolnikov from Tobolsk, a graduate of the Moscow Commercial Academy, suggesting once more the moderating influence of higher education on traditional merchant attitudes (*Albom*).

The periphery of the empire sent seven additional merchants to the first duma, all of whom were non-Russian and none of whom belonged to a party or group that supported "Russia one and indivisible." A Jewish, a German, and two Muslim merchants joined the Kadet party, two other Muslims enrolled in the Peoples Muslim party, and one Polish merchant was a member of the Polish National Democratic party. Without exception, their demands for autonomy took precedence over solidarity with the merchantry as a soslovie or as an emerging bourgeois class.[22] The empire might have been well on its way to becoming a single market, but the economic transformation had not yet broken down the primary bonds of political loyalty along ethnoterritorial lines. The Russian merchants' fears of ethnic encirclement remained even through the era of widespread change brought by industrialization and political liberalization.

The most promising source outside the merchant soslovie for recruits to the Trade and Industry party should have been the trading peasants. This group had long since ceased to be an active rival of the merchantry and had served, instead, as a reservoir of potential members, particularly in the central industrial region. With the growth of capitalist relations in the countryside, the trading peasants had been drawn into closer commercial contact with the merchants in the local fairs and, increasingly, in the big towns.[23] Yet the election returns for the first duma strongly suggest that the Russian kulak was not yet prepared to trade in his soslovie mentality for a new class consciousness.

Thirty-one peasant deputies to the first duma mentioned their involvement in some form of trade, yet none of them associated himself with the Trade and Industry party or any of the other three parties established by merchants in Moscow and St. Petersburg. Of this total, six declared themselves to be Kadets without reservations, two wavered between the Kadets and the Trudoviks (Laborites), another ran as a member of the People's Muslim party but affiliated with the Kadets, and still another identified himself as "moderate progressive nonparty" but was known as a Kadet at the local level. In addition, three trading peasants were Trudoviks, one belonged to the Latvian Group, another called himself a social democrat, and fourteen, the

22. One of the two Kadets, Makhmet-tagi-Aliev, an Azerbaizhani from Baku, announced that on the issue of separatism he stood to the left of the Kadets. His stand is all the more surprising in light of his having been a landowner and a former official in the Ministry of Finance, both emblems of conservatives in the rest of the empire (ibid.).
23. The percentage of merchant capital provided by trading peasants enrolled in both guilds in the central industrial region rose steadily from 1865, when it constituted 4.9 percent, to 1898, when it reached 21.8 percent of the total (Gavlin, "Rol' tsentra," p. 342).

largest single bloc, indicated that they were "nonparty." Among these last, four stated a preference for the Kadets as a party and three others simply noted that they were conservative or monarchist. Finally, only four of the thirty-one peasants openly announced membership in parties of the right—that is, those whose programs opposed obligatory expropriation of the land—including two Octobrists and one each from the Party of Lawful Order and the Progressive party. Even if we add to these four the three peasant "conservatives" or "monarchists" (which does not necessarily mean that they were opposed to expropriation), the results show that less than one-quarter of the trading peasants were unequivocal defenders of the inviolability of private property.[24]

The major obstacle to a political alliance of urban merchants and trading peasants was the survival of precapitalist economic forms in the countryside. Although the kulak was a petty capitalist, his profits derived as much from his exploitation of the peasant commune—by selling vodka, granting loans, and even controlling repartition—as from his commercial operations on the open market. When Krestovnikov publicly endorsed the Stolypin reforms, his supporters deplored the fact that the kulak showed little inclination to leave the commune where he could "take advantage of his economic domination over the mass of its members to manage the communal affairs at his own discretion."[25]

Still another potential source of electoral support for the Trade and Industry party was the merchants' shop assistants (*kupecheskie prikazchiki*), who often appeared to be an organic part of the patriarchal family firm. But the very quasi-feudal character of their dependence had given rise to resentment and opposition as the relative advantages of contractual labor relationships became clear to them. Organizing their own congresses in Nizhnyi in 1896 and in Moscow in 1898, they complained that their relationships with the merchants were completely unregulated and open to the worst abuses. In Tambov, Samara, and Tula the merchants went so far as to forbid their shop assistants to join mutual aid societies, on pain of dismissal.[26] Not

24. *Albom*, throughout. Sir Bernard Pares pointed out that "the designation 'non-party' meant something very special to the peasants. . . . It meant trying to get land for the peasants in whatever was the likeliest way to be permanently successful" (*Memoirs*, p. 53).

25. *Golos Moskvy*, nos. 251 and 292 (31 October, 17 December 1908). See also ibid., no. 284 (7 December 1908), for a critique of additional remnants of the soslovie system which prevented the coalescence of economic classes. For a subsequent analysis of kulak domination of the commune see Chernyshev, *Obshchina*, pp. xii–xiii.

26. Prokopovich, *K rabochemu*, pp. 14–18.

surprisingly then, in 1905 individual societies of shop assistants in Ekaterinoslav and Samara declared themselves on the side of "the laboring masses" and protested against their "lack of rights in the face of the unrestrained arbitrariness of their masters."[27] From St. Petersburg, Odessa, and Irkutsk came horror stories of the shop assistants' plight. When the merchants made no attempt to alleviate these grievances, they lost any claim on the loyalties of their shop assistants outside the work place.[28]

The merchants had also been unable to win the confidence of the professional intelligentsia. Since the turn of the century organized opposition to the merchants had been building up within the Moscow section of the Russian Technological Society. Founded on the collaboration between the professional intelligentsia and merchants interested in technical education, such as G. A. Krestovnikov, V. A. Bakhrushin, M. L. Losev, S. I. Prokhorov, and S. I. Liamin, the society gradually had begun to take a keener interest in social questions that reflected on the harsh management of factories, and merchant membership had dropped off. Under the leadership of the eminent Jewish jurist V. G. Vilents and with cooperation of several prominent physicians, the sanitary section of the society had exposed the unhealthy living and working conditions of the Moscow proletariat.[29] Criticism of factory owners had spread to other areas, including technical education, which, under the sponsorship of the society's permanent committee, was almost completely in the hands of the technical specialists and educators by 1904.[30] Defense of the workers' interests continued

27. *Pravo*, no. 14 (10 April 1905): cols. 1108–9, and no. 38 (1 October 1905): col. 3257.
28. *Torgovo-promyshlennaia gazeta*, no. 218 (28 September 1905). At a tumultuous meeting of the Kursk merchants to debate "the shop assistant question," the timid supporters of setting limits—any limits—on the workday were intimidated by their opponents, whose excuse was the need to check immoral behavior spawned by leisure (ibid., no. 140 [25 June 1905]).
29. For the original membership lists in which the professional intelligentsia predominated over the merchantry by something like ten to one see *ZIRTO*, Moskovskii otdel (1885–86), no. 3, pp. 11–24; ibid. (1887–88), nos. 6–10, supplement, pp. 1–17. One of the earliest pieces of evidence concerning a clash between the two groups is A. Polozhaev, "O merakh dlia sodeistviia russkoi promyshlennosti v sanitarno-tekhnicheskom otnoshenii," ibid. (1896), nos. 6–10, especially pp. 55–56, 63–72. The criticism intensified in the period 1900–1904. See especially I. Gornostaev, "Deti rabochikh i gorodskogo popechitel'stva o bednykh v Moskve," ibid. (1900), nos. 1–2, pp. 1–56; A. V. Polozhaev, "Vzaimodeistvie tekhniki i meditsiny po okhrane khitrogo rynka ili opiat' slabye paliativy," ibid. (1903), nos. 6–8, pp. 99–104, which interestingly cites Gorky's *Lower Depths* as an accurate portrayal of working-class living conditions; and especially a series of articles commemorating Vilents in ibid. (1904), no. 1, pp. 1–30.
30. "Zhurnal zasedaniia postoiannoi komissiia po tekhnicheskim obrazovanii Moskovskogo otdela, 20 oktiabria 1904," ibid. (1904), no. 10, pp. 669–74. Of its eight mem-

to preoccupy the society even after the revolution of 1905 and despite the reactionary atmosphere.[31]

As activists in the formation of professional unions on the eve of the revolution, these doctors, lawyers, engineers, and men like them joined the Kadet party. It was not surprising then that at the founding congress, the Kadet leader, Paul Miliukov, touched a sympathetic chord among them when he declared the party to be "an uncompromising foe of [both] bureaucratic centralization and manchesterism." Attacking the "narrow class interests of the Russian agrarians and industrialists," he concluded: "Our party will never stand guard over these interests."[32] In the long run this turned out to be not quite true, but the undercurrent of hostility to the "real bourgeoisie," as the Kadets called them, ran deep in 1905 throughout the party as a whole and left a permanent mark on the left wing.[33]

The antibourgeois theme rapidly picked up impressive strength within the Moscow section of the Kadets. A. A. Chuprov, the acknowledged leader of the Moscow school of political economy, an enormously influential professor at the university, and a belated convert to Marxist revisionism, interpreted Miliukov's remarks to mean that the party could more easily accommodate socialists of a moderate persuasion than capitalists of almost any type. Surely, he argued, there was no room for accommodation with "the patriarchal landlords and industrialists" or with the champions of "free contractual relationships between owners and workers." Chuprov had come round to the position held by his former opponents, the legal Marxists, that the full development of capitalism in Russia meant democratization of education, encouragement of municipal socialism, the establishment of a "constitutional regime" in the factories, and the organization of consumer societies. In a word, capitalism in Russia was not only a civilizing force, as Struve had put it, but the training ground for the "planning and allocation of resources."[34] Whereas the socialist left in Russia had deprived the "bourgeois" of a leading political role in the "bourgeois-

---

bers only one, P. O. Sliozberg, was a factory owner. See also A. A. Didrikil, "Itogi zemskoi deiatel'nosti v oblasti narodnogo obrazovaniia dannym Iaroslavskoi vystavki severnogo kraia 1903 g.," ibid. (1903), nos. 6–8, pp. 80–98; N. Bychkov, "Rabochie po gorodskoi sluzhby v Moskve," ibid. (1904), no. 3, pp. 193–215; and S. Listov, "K voprosu o polozhenii sluzhashchikh v torgovykh zavedeniiakh," ibid. (1904), no. 3, pp. 326–69.

31. "K proektam o strakhovanii rabochikh, vnesennym v gosudarstvennuiu dumu," ibid. (1911), no. 6, pp. 195–222.

32. *Russkie vedomosti*, no. 268 (6 November 1905).

33. For the period 1907–17 see Rosenberg, *Liberals*.

34. *Pravo*, nos. 45–46 (20 November 1905): cols. 3664–74.

democratic revolution," the democratic center sought to exclude him from an economic role in the higher stage of capitalism.

The utter rout of the Trade and Industry and other merchant-inspired parties cannot, then, be attributed solely to the revolutionary situation, although the persistent social cleavages widened under the seismic pressures of 1905. After all, the government was doing everything in its power to counterbalance the general shift to the left. The voters were under massive pressure to elect supporters of the status quo. By mid-1906 the majority of the Russian provinces were subject to some form of martial law. The minister of the interior had instructed his representatives in the countryside, the *zemskie nachalniki*, to interfere in the selection by the electoral assemblies of any "untrustworthy" candidates and had instructed officials to remove any elector "who deceived the peasants with unrealizable hopes of the gratuitous distribution of private lands."[35] Moreover, the extreme left boycotted the elections, and the extreme right had scarcely organized itself. Circumstances clearly favored the center parties and the men of property. But it was the Kadets who benefited, and they were not sympathetic to either the merchants or the interests of commerce and industry.

Not only did the Moscow merchants fail to break out of their isolation in the elections, but they learned no useful lessons from their bitter experience. At the first congress of the Trade and Industry party, the leadership stubbornly resisted appeals from the rank and file to broaden their social base. The speeches from the floor sounded a plaintive note—soon to disappear from Russian political life—which suggested the dimensions of the lost opportunities. They were the voices of the little people who by dint of energy, ruthlessness, or plain good luck had managed to lift themselves above the mass. In other societies they might have been called the petty bourgeoisie—the landowning peasants, the shop assistants, the tradesmen—but in Russia they were segregated by the walls of their soslovie. Cut off from one another and lacking a common class consciousness, they sought protection from the rich and the powerful. "How can we dependent people protect ourselves against the arbitrariness of our employers?" asked a shop assistant from Penza. He explained that only 100 out of 750 of his occupational group in Penza had joined the party because it refused to take a stand on limiting working hours.[36]

35. Maslov, *Agrarnyi*, 2:270–75.
36. "Pervyi s'ezd torgovo-promyshlennoi partii," p. 15 (speech of G. I. Krivosheev). A similar speech followed by N. S. Savost'ianov, who represented the shop assistants of St. Petersburg (ibid., p. 16).

From the ranks of the poor tradesmen came the request to include at least the word *meshchanstvo* in the party platform in order to prove that this was not exclusively a party of capitalists. They also begged the congress to establish a savings bank for deferred payments (*emerital'naia kassa*) with capital raised from a small duty on commercial certificates. And they asked what could be done for the inhabitants of the old coachmen's suburbs (*iamskaia sloboda*) who had been enrolled in the meshchanstvo after the emancipation, thereby losing their land. Soon after, they lost their occupation as well, when railroads replaced the horse and carriage.[37] Who, one delegate asked, would represent their interests?

The peasants who attended, and it may be safely assumed that they were kulaks, presented a long list of requests for better schools, state credit, an end to the vodka monopoly, and, inevitably, the call for more land. A peasant from Kaluga province pleaded with the congress to forgive the peasants their evil deeds in 1906, for they had been punished; the fault lay not with them but with the revolutionaries who misled them; "help them as you would younger brothers," he concluded. Whether calculated or not, it was a moving speech, but neither natural eloquence nor humble petitions changed the mind of the big merchants. Barshev made it clear at the outset that the party stood foursquare "against violation of the principle of private property." Krestovnikov brushed aside the meshchanstvo's claims as either irrelevant or too complicated to be resolved in the party's platform. Their colleagues reproached the shop assistants for complaining of bad treatment, something that occurred only "in Biblical times," not in Russia.[38]

If the merchants were indifferent to their social inferiors, they were openly hostile to their closest neighbors in the middle ranges of Russian society. They caricatured the professional intellgentsia as fuzzy-minded theoreticians, denounced Miliukov as an opportunist, assailed the Kadets for being "more dangerous" than the Socialist Revolutionaries, and tarred them with the brush of anti-semitism and polonophobia.[39] Just as strongly rejecting the monarchist right, the leadership

37. Ibid., pp. 22 (speech of Zhitkov, Briansk) and 17 (speech of Goldubenkov, Spassk in Riazan province).

38. Ibid., pp. 13 (Barshev's speech), 24 (Kgaevskii's speech), and 26 (Krestovnikov's speech). Only V. P. Riabushinskii made an effort to bridge the gap by calling for a coalition of "those who create value"—peasants, landowners, workers, bankers, brokers, engineers, and traders—against "those suspicious of labor"—the intelligentsia organized into the Kadet and Social Democratic parties, but this "bourgeois" idea found no echo in the congress (ibid., pp. 22–23 [Riabushinskii's speech]).

39. Ibid., pp. 5 (protocol), 12 (Barshev's speech), 16 (Gerasimov's speech), 20 (Krestovnikov's speech), and 21 (Ivaniushenkov's speech).

of the Trade and Industry party claimed that there was no contradiction between an autocratic tsar and a constitutional order. But this explanation did not silence outcries from the floor that the peasantry needed reassurance that the party was "not against the tsar."[40] For Barshev and Krestovnikov the only acceptable political allies were the Octobrists and the Party of Rightful Order, both dominated by the landed gentry, and the Moderate Progressives, led by the Moscow entrepreneurs.[41] Deference to the gentry and regional loyalty retained their grip on the merchantry's political mentality.

The lackluster performance of the congress and the patriarchal posture of its leaders spelled ruin for the party. During the sessions of the first duma the realignment of political parties deprived the Trade and Industry party of its only official deputies. In the provinces the party withered away. It is doubtful whether the leaders of the exchange committee had ever given it much of a chance to begin with. Perceiving little scope for their talents in the lower house of Russia's new parliament, Krestovnikov and his colleagues resisted further efforts to drag them into electoral politics at that level. They coldly rejected a carefully prepared attempt by the Guchkov brothers to win their financial backing for a new big party of the right, which would compete in elections to the second duma.[42] A more restricted field of political action better suited their style.

The exchange leaders had no reason to think that the chances were any better for organizing the merchants as an economic interest group. Krestovnikov had never cherished any illusions about the merchants' isolation from and indifference to all forms of public life, but their divided reaction to the powerful manifestation of working-class unity deepened his pessimism. "The unity of our industrialists proceeds very sluggishly," he commented in 1908, "and only in those cases where the strikes and workers movement hurt their pocketbooks do they begin to speak of unity." He deprecated the employers' unions like the St. Petersburg and Moscow associations of factory and mill

40. Ibid., pp. 14 (Barshev's speech), 16 (Svishchov's speech), and 26 (Krestovnikov's speech).
41. Ibid., pp. 14 (Barshev's speech) and 21 (Krestovnikov's speech); explaining away the Octobrist indifference to trade and industry as a function of honest ignorance and social distance rather than hostility, Krestovnikov revealed that he had helped draft the Octobrist platform.
42. "Things went unbelievably sour," A. I. Guchkov wrote of his encounter with representatives of the Trade and Industry party. "The thick-skinned propertied classes sent me into a positive rage" (Chermenskii, Burzhuaziia, p. 335). This was despite the fact that his brother N. I. Guchkov, who was a mayor of Moscow, had sponsored the meeting and the family firm had been a fixture in the merchant community for over one hundred years.

owners because their regional and industry-specific limitations prevented them from launching collective actions, such as a national lockout, in defense of their material interests.[43] Consequently, his view of both politics and social action remained firmly oligarchic, in line with the well-established traditions of the Moscow Exchange Committee.

During the long decade between the revolutions, Krestovnikov occupied influential positions in three "corporatist-soslovie" institutions —the exchange committee itself, the State Council, and the Association of the Representatives of Trade and Industry—where he defended with remarkable consistency the interests of trade and industry in general and those of the Moscow merchants in particular. Aside from the exchange committee, Krestovnikov was less concerned about either the legitimacy of these institutions and their wider political role than about the relative autonomy and weight granted to his constituency within them. He had no objection to the corporatist character of the State Council as the upper house of the parliament, but he wanted the trade and industry groups to have thirty instead of the scant twelve representatives that they were assigned. He did not oppose the creation of an all-Russian association of representative organizations from trade and industry, but as soon as it became evident that Moscow could not dominate it, he insisted that it be decentralized and federalist.

His association with the Union of 17 October was largely formal, despite his membership in the party's central committee. In his confidential memorandum of June 1911 to all exchange committees he urged that "every effort be made to elect to the Fourth Duma representatives the largest possible number of people who either are directly involved in commercial-industrial activities or at least understand the significance of the development of trade and industry in the country."[44] Krestovnikov was perfectly aware that this description did not fit the majority of Octobrists. Yet at the same time he consistently opposed any kind of binding political organization or faction of the commercial-industrial deputies within the duma and State Council, for this would mean surrendering the autonomous position of the Moscow interests. As for his program, it skillfully combined the vague rhetoric of industrialism with specific proposals to defend the merchantry against the traditional enemies who surrounded them.

Krestovnikov's reputation among merchants as the statesman of trade and industry rested in part upon his careful choice of both the occasions and the themes of his infrequent public pronouncements. At the very time when the first duma solemnly convened in St. Peters-

43. *Golos Moskvy*, no. 2 (3 January 1908).
44. As cited in Avrekh, *Stolypin*, p. 233.

burg, Krestovnikov preferred a more familiar forum—the exchange committee—from which to lecture the newly appointed minister of trade and industry, I. P. Shipov, who was making his obligatory ceremonial visit to "the first capital city" of the empire. Acting as though he thought it was now "the Horde" which sent and Moscow which received, Krestovnikov outlined for the minister an economic program which mirrored far more accurately the basic aims of the Moscow merchantry than it did the policies of the Trade and Industry party. Over the following decade he pursued the same themes in the State Council, to which he was elected in 1907 and again in 1912 as a representative of trade and industry, and at congresses of the Association of Trade and Industry, where he represented the Moscow Exchange Committee.

His first theme was the defense of the merchantry against discriminatory taxes. Decrying the popular tendency to exaggerate merchants' profits, he warned that the small enterprises would be most heavily hit by the business tax and higher railroad rates. He rejected the proposal by the zemstvos to level a property tax on trade and industry and form a general zemstvo fund from the proceeds. It was unthinkable to him that "the industry of the Moscow region would support the zemstvos of Ufa and the Crimea [Tauride province]." He dismissed all other schemes to tax various forms of business practice as sadly lacking in the most elementary understanding of commerce and industry, a constant refrain of the merchantry as a whole in its increasingly bitter complaints about the policies of the bureaucracy, the duma, and the elective local government.[45]

A second theme sounded by Krestovnikov was the danger of foreign encirclement, which took two forms: the existence of a free port in the Far East and the control of the big metallurgical trusts in southern Russia by foreign capitalists.[46] His hostility toward German pressure from the West took longer to mature. On the eve of the war, however, the Moscow Exchange Committee was in the forefront of the

45. *PT*, no. 8 (15 April 1906): 486, 488; ibid., no. 5 (1 March 1908): 270–81, where he denounced plans to tax interest on debts exceeding 8 percent and to tax promissory notes which were challenged and not fully redeemed, and taxes on loans; and ibid., no. 6 (15 March 1910): 394–401, opposing a tax on freight transfers from railroad stations to towns. The theme is repeated in his speech welcoming Shipov's successor, V. I. Timiriazev, to the exchange (ibid., no. 7 [1 April 1909]: 405–8).

46. Ibid., no. 8 (15 April 1906): 489, where a rare racist remark slipped into the public record: "Only by closing the free port, by allowing the Russian population and not the Chinese, Japanese, and people of every color to conduct commerce there and use the region for their interests will it be possible to retain this region for Russia" (ibid., no. 3 [1 February 1909]: 165–67, expressing fears of Japanese colonization). See also ibid., no. 20 (15 October 1909): 400.

battle to renegotiate the Russo-German trade treaty on different terms from those prepared by the Ministry of Finance. Nothing less than "national independence" was at stake here.[47] Once the war broke out, the exchange committee spearheaded the drive to confiscate German and Austro-Hungarian industrial properties. To justify the violation of private property rights, it published the results of a questionnaire that it had circulated throughout the empire which demonstrated the "domination" of German capital over Russian industry.[48]

A third theme, alluded to frequently but never fully developed, was the need for a rational program for economic growth that would increase the purchasing power of the peasantry and stimulate the exploitation of Russia's natural resources.[49] When pressed for specific plans and priorities, Krestovnikov declared that those decisions could only be made by the government. His one concrete proposal—for universal elementary education—was hardly controversial.

Yet a fourth theme was the labor question, which Krestovnikov hesitated to broach in public. But behind the scenes in the deliberations of the Ostrogorskii Commission in 1908 he worked hard to block obligatory workers' insurance, if for no other reason than that it would cost the owners money. Incidentally, here was yet another issue where he parted company with the southern metallurgical interests.[50]

These four themes had a wide, if diffuse, resonance among many, if not all, merchants in the empire. The common elements that endowed them with broad appeal was their defensive tone and passive attitude toward the problems facing the merchantry. However, even when combined, they do not add up to much of a national policy. Krestovnikov's intellectual rationale was barren and devoid of any broad appeal outside a restricted circle of exchange merchants in the central industrial provinces. With the exception of fleeting references to the need for obligatory elementary education and a fair judicial system, he passed in silence over the important social questions of the day. Only complete insensitivity to the real state of affairs in the country could have led him to conclude that "no small share of the disturbances which we have lived through in the course of recent times, can be attributed, of course not directly, to this unjust [income]

47. Roosa, "Association," pp. 621–23 and chap. 19.
48. *Doklad komissii.* The St. Petersburg banks protested against the effect of this campaign on the influx of foreign capital, but when the government began to liquidate the German firms, the Petersburg banks did better than their Moscow rivals in getting control of them (Diakin, "Pervaia mirovaia voina," pp. 231–38). For the general problem of merchant opposition to the trusts see Gefter, "Bor'ba," pp. 124–48.
49. *PT*, no. 8 (15 April 1908): 485–87; ibid., no. 7 (1 April 1909): pp. 405–7; *Russkie vedomosti*, 8 June 1911.
50. Avrekh, *Stolypin*, pp. 181–84.

tax" on salaried employees. Small wonder then that representatives of political parties to the right and left of the Trade and Industry party and social groups above and below the Moscow merchantry regarded them with disdain. The only mistake of those who condemned their "narrow class interest" was that those interests did not yet deserve to be called those of a class.

The Reemergence of the Moscow Entrepreneurial Group

In the summer of 1905 a small band detached itself from the leadership of the Moscow Exchange Committee and demanded that the merchantry claim their historical birthright as the political leaders of a modern industrial Russia. The crisis of 1904–5, like that of the Crimean War, infused the Moscow entrepreneurial group with a new sense of urgency and stimulated a flurry of organized political activity. Since the 1890s a new inner core of leaders had emerged embodying the same traditions and drawn from many of the same families as their predecessors. A. I. Konovalov, the Riabushinskii brothers, and the Morozov clan were united by Old Believer ties. S. N. Tret'iakov, A. S. Vishniakov, and S. I. Chetverikov represented the old merchant families who despised the Petersburg bureaucracy, patronized Great Russian culture, and supported Slavic causes. They were joined together by a network of intermarriages, personal friendships, patronage activities, and joint business enterprises (see table 7.2).

As an economic elite, they dominated the textile industry of the center and from this profitable source drew the bulk of their income. But they also continued to invest in a few powerful banks and insurance and trading companies. Their railroad stocks had been bought up by the government, and they did not, for the most part, move into the machinery industry, where Russians of German descent maintained a strong hold.

A more dramatic change took place in their patronage activities. Here, they accomplished an aesthetic transformation from the old Slavic to the avant-garde with a Russian flavor. They bid fair to establish new standards for the cultural life of the country. In a symbolic challenge to the social prominence of the gentry, Riabushinskii, Morozov, and Konovalov moved out of the south side and built splendid mansions on prominent sites in the center of the city. Finally, in response to the revolution of 1905 their political views rapidly advanced to the point where they boldly claimed a leading role in running the country. In general, all their activities were characterized by a remarkable degree of cohesion and consistency in an era (1905–17)

TABLE 7.2. *The Second Generation of Moscow Entrepreneurs*

	Core					Primary Layer				
	Riabushinskiis	Konovalov	Morozovs	S. N. Tret'iakov	Chetverikov	Vishniakov	S. A. Smirnov	P. A. Buryshkin	M. N. Bardygin	Bakhrushins
July Bureau (Moscow faction)	●	●	●		●	●				●
Moderate Progressive party (1906)	●	●	●		●		●			
Protest of the 66 Progressive party (1912)	●	●	●	●	●	●		●		
Moscow War Industries Committee	●	(●)*		●		●	●			
Bank of Moscow	●	●	●	●						●
Moscow Merchants' Mutual Credit Society	●			●		●				
All-Russian Mutual Insurance Union	●	●	●	●					●	●
Utro Rossii	●	●	●	●	●		●	●	●	
Total	9	8	7	6	5	4	3	3	3	2

*Deputy chairman of Central War Industries Committee.

when personal and party loyalties were more honored in the breach than in the observance. In a word, they acquired the proper trappings of a full-fledged bourgeois elite. All they lacked—and ultimately it proved to be a decisive weakness—was a following.

The patriarchal founder of the Konovalov dynasty fits into the now-familiar pattern of an Old Believer serf entrepreneur who moved from Kostroma into the Moscow area following the Napoleonic campaign of 1812, utilized his contacts with coreligionists to build a textile empire, purchased his freedom, and became a leader in introducing new technology into the cotton-spinning industry.[51] His most famous grandson, Alexander Ivanovich, born in 1870, acquired only a minimal secondary education before entering the family business. Largely self-educated in economics, he rose quickly in the Moscow Exchange Committee, where, as deputy president, he presided over a special commission which drafted a plan for organizing commercial-industrial chambers of commerce. Although it never became law, parts of it served as the basis for important industrial legislation. He was also closely associated with S. N. Tret'iakov and N. D. Morozov in the cotton-spinning commission of the exchange, which he headed. As president of the All-Russian Mutual Insurance Union, his colleagues were Tret'iakov, P. P. Riabushinskii, E. V. Morozov, A. A. Bakhrushin, M. N. Bardygin, and S. V. Krestovnikov. Deeply concerned over the low level of technical education in Russia, he joined the Moscow Society for the Spread of Technical Education and closely supported the efforts of its president, A. S. Vishniakov, in founding the Moscow Commercial Institute. Although he left the Old Believer church, he converted to edinoverie like Guchkov and other sectarians who wished to keep the old books and rites. A cultured man and an accomplished musician, he studied with the well-known pianist-pedagogue Alexander Siloti, who was the husband of S. N. Tret'iakov's aunt, and later became a patron of Rachmaninoff.[52]

However, Konovalov found his real métier in politics. Aside from a brief period of recuperation from tuberculosis, he continually stood in the forefront of the Moscow entrepreneurial group's political action, as a deputy to the state duma, as a founder of the Moscow Progressive party, as a member of the Central War Industries Committee, and finally as minister of trade and industry in the first and the last coalitions of the Provisional Government. In almost every one of those activities, Konovalov was associated with the Riabushinskii family, until he clashed with Pavel Pavlovich for leadership of the group in the last mayoralty election in Moscow under the old regime.

The Riabushinskiis suffered from police persecution more than most Old Believer families in the Nicholaen period, yet they managed to rise from obscurity to one of the wealthiest and most tightly knit textile dynasties by the beginning of the twentieth century.[53] As early as 1874, Pavel and Vasili Mikhailovich Riabushinskii joined forces

51. A good survey of the family's rise and its connections with the Old Belief is West, "Moscow Progressists," pp. 38–52.

52. *Tovarishchestvo Konovalova*, pp. 7, 14–16, 23–26; Sovet s'ezdov, *Fabrichno-zavodskie*, p. 8; Buryshkin, *Moskva*, pp. 250–51; Bertenssen and Leyda, *Rachmaninoff*, p. 478.

53. The most complete account of the early history of the Riabushinskii family is Portal,

Three Generations of Konovalovs

A. P. Konovalov. (Courtesy of Helsinki University Library)

*I. A. Konovalov. (Courtesy of
Helsinki University Library)*

A. I. Konovalov. (Courtesy of Helsinki University Library)

with members of the first generation of the Moscow entrepreneurial group, T. S. Morozov, N. K. Krestovnikov, the Tret'iakovs, and Konshin, in establishing the first company to buy and sell Central Asian cotton at the Nizhnyi Novgorod fair. Together with the Morozovs and Krestovnikovs, P. M. Riabushinskii was also a member of the administrative board of the Moscow Commercial Bank.[54]

Pavel Mikhailovich made certain that his eight sons benefited from a solid, practical education. Five of the brothers finished the Moscow Practical Academy of Commercial Science and three graduated from *real* schools in Moscow. As a result, only one son, Vladimir Pavlovich, was tempted to break away from his father's control. He seriously studied philosophy at Heidelburg before returning to the family firm. The entire family, however, was determined to leave its mark on Russian society not just as businessmen but as cultural leaders. It is clear from their patronage activities that they consciously strove to challenge the dominant neoclassical style and taste of the St. Petersburg nobility by championing the new architecture and decorative effects of Art Nouveau as part of a neo-Russian revival. They gave a number of important commissions to one of Russia's most innovative young architects, F. O. Shekhtel', a brilliant exponent of Art Nouveau, who became president of the Moscow Architecture Society from 1908 to 1922 and was one of the first in Russia to explore the possibilities of iron, glass, and reinforced-concrete technology. Shekhtel' constructed all the main edifices for the Riabushinskii family and their business enterprises—the stunning Riabushinskii mansion on Malaia Nikitskaia (1900), the Moscow Bank in Birzhevaia Square (1904), and the printing house of the paper *Utro Rossii* in Strastnoi Passage (1907). With the family's support he was commissioned to build the new Moscow station for the Iaroslavl railroad, the pride and joy of Chizhov and the first generation of the Moscow entrepreneurs, in a style combining neo-Russian and Art Nouveau. He also constructed the trading house of the Moscow Merchant Society and even designed an Old Believer church for the Riabushinskii family.

Leading the way in the visual arts, brother Nikolai assembled a fine collection of French Postimpressionists and Russian moderns, and edited and financed one of those brilliant universal art journals at the turn of the century, *Zolotoe Runo* [The golden fleece]. In its pages he advocated a new acquisitions policy for the Tret'iakov Gallery which would focus on contemporary Russian artists, who were beginning to

---

"Industriels," pp. 5–46. For the later period see also West, "Moscow Progressists," pp. 57–64.

54. Semeniuk, "Bor'ba," pp. 124; Courtais, *Manuel*, pp. 413, 698.

Second Generation of Moscow Entrepreneurs

*P. P. Riabushinskii. (Courtesy of
Helsinki University Library)*

*V. P. Riabushinskii. (Courtesy of
Helsinki University Library)*

lay the foundations for the modern movement in Russia. In his own fashion he was carrying on the work begun by Mamontov at the Abramtsovo art colony, challenging the accepted standards not only of the Imperial Academy but of all traditional European art criticism.

In the business world the three most active entrepreneurs in the family, Pavel, Vladimir, and Mikhail, turned their creative energies to bolstering the economic power of Moscow. Adopting as their motto the "Napoleonic quadrant" of intelligence, talent, personality, and will, they transformed the failing Alekseev Bank in Kharkov into the Bank of Moscow. With the participation of the Konovalovs, Morozovs, and Tret'iakovs they built it into the first truly industrial investment bank in the city.[55]

After 1908 the Riabushinskiis finally broke out of their traditional attachment to textiles and launched a series of enterprises for exporting flax, timbering, manufacturing automobiles, and, during the war, producing armaments. In their attempts to corner the flax market they joined forces with Tret'iakov, who proved to be a sticky collaborator even though the Riabushinskiis made him a member of their Bank of Moscow and chairman of the Russian Flax Company. Personal rivalries continued to dog the cooperative efforts of the Moscow entrepreneurs.

The Riabushinskiis recognized that "the error of the Moscow banks from the beginning consisted in their excessive caution leading them to concentrate all their activities in Moscow." They now felt strong enough to take on the St. Petersburg banks. In a series of bold but ultimately unsuccessful initiatives, they tried to buy a controlling interest in one of the big Petersburg banking houses. Unless they could fight the capital with its own weapons, they feared that "the Germans and the Jews" would take over all of Russian industry and run it for their own interests. And the government seemed incapable or unwilling to help the Moscow patriots.[56] Still, it must be admitted that for all their Napoleonic bluster the Riabushinskiis clung to their old business methods, their "prudent merchant economies," as Gindin put it, which differed in scale and risk not only from the methods of the St. Peters-

55. Riabushinskii, "Kupechestvo," pp. 172–79, 184–88; Kirichenko, *Moskva pamiatniki*, plates 116–21, 194–98; Belyi, *Mezhdu dvukh* 1:245–48; idem, *Nachalo*, pp. 108, 160; Gerstein, "Shekhtel," *Macmillan Encyclopedia*; *Zolotoe Runo*, no. 5 (1907): 18–19; Gray, *Great Experiment*, pp. 69–73.

56. "Dokumenty po istorii monopolisticheskogo kapitalizma v Rossii," Akademiia nauk, *Materialy po istorii*, 6:606–8, 615–20, 642–45, 629–31. The document, reproduced in full here, is a memo by M. P. Riabushinskii, "Tsel' nashei raboty," written in November 1916. The introduction is by I. F. Gindin. For a detailed commentary see Lavigne, "Le Plan," pp. 90–104. For the Riabushinskiis' entrepreneurial activities in automobile manufacturing see Voronkova, "Stroitel'stvo," pp. 149–50.

burg entrepreneurs but also from those of such daring newcomers to the Moscow scene as Vtorov (a Siberian manufacturer) and Stakheev (a Volga grain merchant), who engaged in dramatic speculation and stock raids reminiscent of the American robber barons.[57]

In addition to their regional patriotism, the semiclandestine nature of the family's early business activity and its deviant religious life reinforced the Riabushinskii's hostility to the state bureaucracy. Beginning even before the revolution of 1905 and continuing unabated to 1917, the Riabushinskiis openly identified their oppositionist sentiments with a sturdy defense of the Old Belief against government persecution. The centerpiece of their organizational efforts was the Belokrinitskii community, the largest, wealthiest, and most disciplined of the popovtsy sects.[58] Following the October Manifesto, Riabushinskii in Moscow, D. V. Sirotkin in Nizhnyi Novgorod, and other leaders fought off attempts by the extreme right and left to exploit the Old Believer discontent for their own ends. First they supported the liberation movement and strove to rally the Old Believer masses behind an electoral program for the state duma. Then, they sought to build a permanent legal organization around annual congresses and an executive committee, bring to the surface their underground press with the publication of *Staroobriadets* in Nizhnyi and *Narodnaia gazeta* (with its supplement *Golos Staroobriadchestva*) in Moscow, and finally organize the countryside by calling an all-Russian congress of peasant Old Believers in Moscow. But outside the area of religious toleration the Old Belief proved no more unified in outlook or prepared for political action than the merchantry.[59] Despite repeated disappointments on this score throughout the period between the revolutions, Riabushinskii donated generously to Old Believer causes and worked tirelessly to overcome the internal splits in order to instill a sense of common purpose among all sectarians.

57. Gindin, "O nekotorykh osobennostiakh," pp. 63–64.

58. Bonch-Bruevich, "Staroobriadchestvo i samoderzhavie," *Izbrannye*, 1:90–102, who in his report to the second congress of the RSDLP in London (1902) summarized the first two clandestine Old Believer congresses organized by Riabushinskii on the basis of hectographed documents anonymously sent to his editorial offices of *Zhizn'*. According to the Soviet historian V. F. Milovidov, the Belokrinitskii community claimed almost 800,000 adherents with seventeen bishops and in Rogozhskii alone a capital of three million rubles (*Staroobriadchestvo*, pp. 72–73).

59. Melgunov, *Staroobriadchestvo*, pp. 4–5, 9–22, 27–31. Vserossiiskii s'ezd krest'ianstaroobriadtsev, *Materialy*, was devoted primarily to refuting Tolstoyan "communism" and organizing the collection and distribution of books, icons, candles, and other religious objects. On the other hand, Riabushinskii's public criticism of the government's treatment of the Old Believers at a dinner in honor of Finance Minister V. N. Kokovtsov caused a scandal in the Moscow Exchange Society (Kokovtsov, *Iz moego*, 2:56).

Although those initiatives proved unsuccessful, the brothers Pavel and Vladimir launched a personal crusade to rescue the Old Belief from secrecy and obscurity and place it at the center of Russian social and cultural life. Defining its appeal in very broad terms, they championed the idea of an organic link between the "zealous religious feelings" of the Old Belief and an intense patriotic attachment to Great Russia. In the tradition of the Moscow entrepreneurial group they identified the merchantry with the peasantry on one side of the great schism in Russian culture which opened up under Peter the Great between "the muzhik" and "the barin."

> The well-read, wealthy merchant–Old Believer with a beard and in a Russian floor-length robe, a talented industrialist, the boss of hundreds, sometimes thousands of men of the working people, and at the same time a connoisseur of old Russian art, an archaeologist, a collector of icons, books, manuscripts which delve into historical and economic questions, fond of his business but filled with spiritual concerns, such a man was a *muzhik*— But a petty chancery clerk, clean shaven, in a Western jacket, having grabbed hold of some kind of higher education, in essence little cultivated, often a bribe-taker, though not by necessity, criticizing and condemning in secret everyone who stands above him, profoundly contemptuous of the peasant, one of the forerunners of the coming Russian intelligentsia, he is already a *barin*.[60]

In a daring and brilliant piece of historical sleight of hand, the Riabushinskiis sought to complete the process begun by the Denisov brothers and carried forward by Chizhov and Kokorev. They aimed to transform a religious dispute into a cultural and political one and to convert the Russian merchantry from an embattled and despised minority into the saviour of the empire. Following another trail blazed by Chizhov, Pavel Riabushinskii founded a newspaper, *Utro Rossii*, with the express purpose of defending the merchantry against its enemies and seeking to raise its collective consciousness.

Riabushinskii's debut in the world of journalism was marked by two false starts due to his lack of experience and his unwillingness to allow intellectuals to guide him. His *Narodnaia gazeta* and *Utro*, both edited by Old Believer business associates, were banned by the police shortly after their appearance "in view of harmful tendencies" and "a sharp,

---

60. Riabushinskii, *Staroobriadchestvo*, pp. 23–24, 38. See also Kirillov, *Pravda*, pp. 377–87.

at times insolent tone approaching extreme lack of respect for the supreme power and abuse of the Orthodox Church."

Applying his "Napoleonic maxims," Riabushinskii called up reserves from the intellectuals who attended his economic discussions, spread the financial burden among a larger circle of his friends, and launched *Utro Rossii*, the most successful of the mass dailies ever sustained by Russian merchants. Only moderating slightly his "insolent tone"—the paper was heavily fined and lost editors like inexperienced first lieutenants on the battlefield—he built up its circulation to forty thousand in 1913, making it the second largest Moscow newspaper. He handpicked the editorial board, recruiting his brother Vladimir, his associate S. N. Tret'iakov, and two younger representatives of merchant families, S. A. Smirnov and P. A. Buryshkin.

One of their main concerns was to awaken within the merchantry a pride in its Great Russian essence, its "muzhik blood." In a set of metaphors common to many right-wing movements in Europe, they juxtaposed the primitive vigor of their social milieu with the enfeebled old elites. Russia had only to choose, they argued, between the nobility and "the bourgeoisie," by which it was clear they meant themselves. In the first flush of their class messianism they read out of the bourgeoisie both the landowning nobles and the bulk of the Moscow merchantry, who, under Krestovnikov's leadership, had joined the Union of 17 October.[61]

They also sought to link a militant bourgeois class consciousness to an aggressive foreign policy in the Balkans and at the Straits. During the Balkan Wars of 1912–13, their Pan-Slavic rhetoric far surpassed that of the extreme right and foreshadowed the subsequent stand of Miliukov, Struve, and Guchkov during World War I.[62] At long last, thanks to the Riabushinskiis, the merchant wing of the Moscow entrepreneurial group gained sufficient self-confidence to proclaim its message to the world in a language that the merchantry might understand.

A third member of the inner core of the group, S. N. Tret'iakov, was almost as active as Pavel Riabushinskii, but more unstable in per-

61. Bokhanov, "Iz istorii," pp. 266–73. The main contributors were V. P. and P. P. Riabushinskii, A. I. Konovalov, N. D. Morozov, S. I. Chetverikov, S. N. Tret'iakov, D. V. Sirotkin, G. M. Mark, P. A. Buryshkin, A. G. Karpov, A. I. Kuznetsov, and M. N. Bardygin; see also Berlin, *Russkaia*, pp. 292–94; Riabushinskii, "Kupechestvo," p. 186; Avrekh, *Stolypin*, pp. 294–95.

62. During the entire crisis of the last phase of the Balkan Wars, almost every editorial in *Utro Rossii* promoted a forward policy for Russia and the Slavic cause in the Balkans. Characteristically, the paper also sought to discredit the Polish and Ukrainian nationalist revival as harmful to the Slavic (read Great Russian) cause in general. See *Utro Rossii*, no. 274 (28 November 1912).

sonality and politics. The only competent grandson of Sergei Mikhailo-vich, he ran the big family flax business in Kostroma and managed its large Moscow properties almost single-handedly. His marriage to Na-talia Savichna Mamontova enlarged his fortunes and enhanced his standing in the merchant community, even though the union was ultimately an unhappy one. A patron of the arts, Sergei Nikolaevich brilliantly carried on the tradition of his forebears as a trustee of the council of the Tret'iakov Gallery and a generous supporter of the Moscow Conservatory. An active participant in several industrial or-ganizations, he was permanent president of the All-Russian Society of Flax Manufacturers. He served for a time as an elector to the town duma and occupied an influential position in the Moscow Exchange Society, where he showed greater tact than Riabushinskii in his rela-tions with Krestovnikov. Still, he served on the editorial board of the controversial *Utro Rossii* and became one of the founders of the Mos-cow Progressive party. During the war he was one of Pavel Riabushin-skii's deputies on the board of the Moscow War Industries Committee and played a central role in the organization of the textile industry for supplying uniforms for the army. But in all his activities his neuras-thenic behavior and notorious unreliability made him an unpredict-able collaborator.[63]

The Chetverikovs, like the Tret'iakovs, proudly traced their family lineage to the eighteenth-century Moscow merchantry. Their long-standing ties to the Alekseevs through marriage and business flow-ered in several joint ventures, including a factory manufacturing silk fabric ornamented with gold thread, which maintained its patriarchal structure until Nikolai Alekseev, later mayor of Moscow, introduced machinery. The education and cultural life of Sergei Chetverikov followed the pattern of many other members of the Moscow entre-preneurial group. A graduate of a Moscow *real* school, he received his commercial training from a German who ran the St. Petersburg branch of the family firm, though his real love was music. One of the original subscribers of the Moscow Musical Society, he first became acquainted with the Tret'iakovs as a young visitor to their musical evenings. Like the Riabushinskiis, he consciously adopted "Napoleonic tactics" as the model for his business activities. In this spirit he carried out one of the most spectacular transfers in modern Russian business history by moving the famous Alekseev merino sheep farm in the North Caucasus to new grazing grounds near Minusinsk in Siberia. Simultaneously, he developed the big copper mines in the vicinity. His active thirty-year service in the Moscow provincial zemstvo, highly unusual in itself for a merchant, won him the respect and friendship

63. Buryshkin, *Moskva*, pp. 247–49.

of its gentry leaders, D. N. Shipov and N. A. Astrov.

A champion of labor reform, he introduced the nine-hour day into his enterprises as early as 1881. After 1905 he sponsored a workers' society for mutual aid and self-education. As a member of the Bunge Commission and head of the labor commission of the Moscow Exchange in 1905, he led unsuccessful attempts to have his practices generally adopted, and he opposed the introduction of martial law to break the October strike. For all these reasons, no doubt, his enterprises remained untouched by labor violence throughout the year of revolution. Regarding Naidenov as "an extreme reactionary" and Krestovnikov as "more than conservative," he stood in the forefront of the Progressive party. His last service to his colleagues was to help free Konovalov and Tret'iakov from Bolshevik jails and organize their flight from Russia. Although the Chetverikovs were Orthodox, the family maintained "the strictest possible observation of the rituals of religious life," which drew them close to the "zealous feelings" that Riabushinskii extolled as the link between the merchants who remained in the official church and those of the Old Belief.[64]

At least three of the four branches of the Morozov family continued to maintain their ties to the Old Belief, support generously the development of Russian national art activities, and nourish the spirit of patriotic opposition that had long characterized the inner core of the Moscow entrepreneurial group. In one case, that of the legendary Savva Timofeevich, the failure to resolve the profound contradictions in his deviant social role led to tragic consequences. Made in the image of his father, who was a man of enormous energy and foresight, Savva Timofeevich managed his own enterprises, headed the Nizhnyi Exchange Committee and also devoted years of service to the Moscow provincial zemstvo, first as a member of the commission of the economic section for aid to kustar industries and then as founder and benefactor of the Moscow Handicrafts (*Kustar*) Museum.[65] Married to a former worker in his own factory, he was a close friend of Gorky's and a contributor to revolutionary parties. He experienced the revolution of 1905 as a civil war within his own psyche and committed suicide in France.[66] Here, no doubt, was the model for the "repen-

64. Chetverikov, *Bezvozvratno*, pp. 5, 20–21, 41–46, 54, 64–70, 83–85, 102–4; N. Astrov, "Pamiati S. I. Chetverikov," *Poslednye novosti*, 26 December 1929; *Golos Moskvy*, no. 134 (10 June 1907). At least one of his sons benefited from his father's enlightened views on education, reform, and entrepreneurship to become a leading scientific researcher and organizer in the early years of the Soviet regime. See Adams, "The Founding," pp. 23–39.

65. *Golos Moskvy*, no. 153 (3 July 1908).

66. For different insights into Morozov's character see Gorky, *Literaturnye*, pp. 335–64; Nemirovich-Danchenko, *My Life*, pp. 130–35; and Stanislavskii, *Moia zhizn'*, 385–89.

The Commercial World

The market in the Kitai Gorod, Moscow, 1898. (Courtesy of Library of Congress)

The great Jewish and Tatar market, Moscow, around 1900. (Courtesy of Library of Congress)

The fair at Nizhnyi Novgorod, 1898. (Courtesy of Library of Congress)

The cloth market at Nizhnyi Novgorod, 1902. (Courtesy of Library of Congress)

Tatar merchants at the Nizhnyi Novgorod fair. (Courtesy of Library of Congress)

A fleet of grain barges on the Volga, around 1900. (Courtesy of Library of Congress)

Wheat for export in Odessa, 1898. (Courtesy of Library of Congress)

The salon of the merchant Butin in Nerchinsk, Siberia, near the Chinese frontier in the 1870s. (Courtesy of Library of Congress)

tant merchant" of whom the Mensheviks dreamed. The rest of the Morozovs, however, were made of sterner stuff.

By the end of the century the clan had intermarried with many of the big textile families in the central region and penetrated most of the large-scale cultural, intellectual, and charitable institutions of Moscow. Among the most active figures in the Moscow entrepreneurial group were the brothers Nikolai and Ivan Davydovich of the Bogorodsko-Glukhovskaia enterprise, whose successful defense of the family firm against the stock raid of a powerful St. Petersburg bank was hailed by Riabushinskii. Nikolai, "a combination of traditional Old Believer rigidity and profound, Western, specifically English culture," had studied industrial technology in England and played an active role in the exchange committee, where he championed higher commercial standards. Although less active in public affairs than his brother, who became a deputy in the state duma, he was a powerful influence behind the scenes and a founder of the Moscow Progressive party.[67]

The Abramovich branch of the family also combined entrepreneurial zeal with social service and patronage of letters and arts. Abram Abramovich, who managed the Tver Manufacturing Plant, married his first cousin Varvara Alekseevna Khludova and raised a family in the Riabushinskii style. One of their sons, Nikolai, became a pilot and early leader in Russia's aviation industry.[68] Following Abram's death, his widow married the editor of *Russkie vedomosti*, V. M. Sobolevskii, thus opening the pages of that influential organ to the activities of the Moscow entrepreneurial group. Like other wives of Morozovs, she vigorously supported social causes, having been among other things one of the principal founders of the Prechistenka evening courses for workers in Moscow.

Perhaps even more famous in her day, Margarita Kirillovna, another Morozov wife of the Abramovich branch, patronized Scriabin, sponsored a religious-philosophical salon which attracted such eminent figures as Prince S. N. Trubetskoi, and facilitated political cooperation between members of the Moscow entrepreneurial group and the Slavophil zemtsy.[69]

On particular issues the inner core of the group could rally another fifty or sixty Moscow merchants, but its effective membership had shrunk since the first generation of the 1860s and 1870s. Meanwhile

67. Buryshkin, *Moskva*, pp. 120–21, 251–52; Sef, *Burzhuaziia*, p. 67; Akademiia nauk, *Materialy po istorii*, 6:630.

68. *Russkie vedomosti*, nos. 1 and 36 (1 January, 11 February 1911).

69. Buryshkin, *Moskva*, pp. 124–25; Miliukov, *Vospominaniia*, 1:271–72; Nemirovich-Danchenko, *My Life*, p. 200.

the central political dilemma that had always faced the Moscow entrepreneurial group became more acute: how to break out of the social
isolation that weakened its claim to represent the emerging elite of
industrializing Russia in an era of mass politics.

It is clear from their public pronouncements that they were not
certain themselves who or what they represented. In their more ex-
pansive moods, they called themselves leaders of the bourgeoisie, but
more often they referred to themselves simply as merchants or even
representatives of the merchant soslovie. Similarly, their attempts to
organize or to find the proper forum for their political activities revealed other nagging uncertainties about their strength and their
appeal, and consequently whether they should play the role of popular leaders or oligarchs. To a large extent, then, their history in this
period is one of abortive, ephemeral, and broken alliances with other
social forces who were wrestling with the same problem.

The Quest for Unity in 1905

From the eve of one revolution to the eve of another the Moscow
entrepreneurs sought repeatedly to unify the merchantry and then to
bridge the gap separating the merchant soslovie from the liberal gentry and professional intelligentsia. Driving toward the first goal, they
clashed with the leadership of the exchange committee, without, however, convincing regional groups in Petersburg and the south that
they were worthy partners in an all-Russian organization. Their second goal proved just as elusive. They found themselves stretched to
the breaking point between the two wings of the Liberation Movement and forced to relinquish their hold first on one side and then on
the other.

Their initial step toward unity was to win agreement within the
Moscow Exchange Committee for the creation of a special commission
on the labor question which, under the chairmanship of Chetverikov,
whose enlightened views on the working day were well-known, was
authorized to hammer out a common view among factory owners in
response to the demands of the strikers. Of the commission's twenty-
one members the Moscow entrepreneurial group probably numbered
eight, including Chetverikov, Konovalov, P. P. Riabushinskii, S. T.,
I. A., and I. D. Morozov, S. N. Mamontov, and V. A. Gorbunov.

From the outset it was clear that the idea of "unity of the factory
owners of the inner [central] region" was acceptable to the majority
only on a decentralized, industry-specific basis. Similarly, the recognition of workers' rights to organize and strike was burdened with

reservations. S. T. Morozov and Riabushinskii insisted on the need to discuss the organization of the workers immediately following the discussion of the owners' organization "in order not to produce a bad impression on the workers" and also "because it was unfair not to do so." Encountering fierce opposition, they fell back on a compromise formula which resolved, in principle, "to recognize the organization of the factory worker as desirable."

Compared with the program of the Liberation Movement, it was a very cautious stand, but at the time it represented a sharp departure from the traditional position of the Moscow merchantry. On the other hand, efforts to support a reduction of the working day were beaten down, despite the intervention of Chetverikov and Mamontov, who assured the skeptics that the experience of their factories had shown that the reduction in the working day had no appreciable effect on productivity and had actually improved the quality of work as a direct consequence of the increase in the energy of the workers.[70] Differences within the labor commission were papered over when the government hastily assembled the so-called Kokovtsov Commission to settle the strikes. Unity against bureaucratic interference was easier to obtain than unity in favor of labor legislation. But this was scarcely the direction in which the Moscow entrepreneurs sought to lead.

Their second initiative was to persuade the exchange leadership to summon representatives of the major industrial and commercial organizations to meet in Moscow in March under the chairmanship of S. T. Morozov to discuss plans for defending their common interests. By its very name, the Congress of Representatives of Industry of Various Regions of the Empire symbolized the deep differences that undermined all subsequent efforts to unite the merchantry. Representatives of the south, the Kingdom of Poland, and the Krestovnikov faction in Moscow simply wanted to turn the organization into an antiworkers union. Not surprisingly, the major opposition to any kind of centralized organization of merchants came from the Moscow Exchange Committee leadership. The best that could be salvaged was a memorandum to Minister of the Interior A. G. Bulygin which requested separate representation for the industrial interests in the consultative duma because the zemstvos and dumas were not "competent to express the needs of industry in the different regions of the Russian empire."[71] Thus, the merchants admitted that differences be-

70. TsGIA, f. 150, op. 1, d. 484, pp. 40–41. The main spokesman against the shorter day was V. S. Barshev, a close associate of Krestovnikov and with him a cofounder of the Trade and Industry party. For Chetverikov's conciliatory speech on the workers' question to the Polytechnic Museum see Laverychev, *Tsarizm*, p. 254.

71. *Pravo*, no. 12 (27 March 1905): col. 914.

tween the industrial and agricultural interests blocked that road to class cooperation as well.

The Moscow entrepreneurs had not yet given up all hope of bringing about a greater degree of unity among the merchants. In May the Nizhnyi Novgorod Exchange Committee called upon the Moscow Exchange Committee to convoke representatives of all the exchange committees in the empire. It was clear enough that this maneuver was again inspired by the Morozovs, whose influence among merchants in Nizhnyi Novgorod had been paramount since the days of *Volgar*. The exchange committee in the big market town was really dominated by the Moscow merchants, and it frequently met in Moscow under Savva Timofeevich's chairmanship.[72]

Once again, however, Naidenov rebuffed them, splitting the Moscow Exchange Committee into two factions and paralyzing its political initiatives. In July, Naidenov's disruption of the second congress of the representatives of industry led to a realignment of forces within the ranks of the merchantry as a whole. Driven from the premises of the exchange, a small group of Moscow merchants, including the core of the Moscow entrepreneurs—the Riabushinskiis, Chetverikov, N. D. Morozov, Konovalov, and Vishniakov—joined with representatives of heavy industrialists from St. Petersburg and the periphery to continue their deliberations on the Bulygin duma in a session held at Pavel Riabushinskii's Moscow mansion.

No longer constrained by the need to placate the leadership of the Moscow Exchange Committee, they adopted a strongly worded resolution calling for sweeping political reforms. They took care "to apportion no blame" for the disorders. But, they declared, since the government could no longer guarantee the protection of private property, the representatives of trade and industry were obliged to unite on a political program to restore order and promote the peaceful development of the country's civic and economic life. They defined the "basic condition" for the reconstruction of Russian society as the equality of all under law, freedom of speech, conscience, association, and the press, the right to strike and form unions, the protection of property, and the inviolability of persons and property.

Rejecting the idea of a consultative duma, they endorsed a bicameral legislative duma, the lower house of which was to be elected by universal, direct, and secret manhood suffrage. (Extending the vote to women was considered "impossible" due to the prevailing opinion in the countryside on the subordinate role of women in the household.) Accepting three "tails" of the "four-tailed formula" of the

72. Buryshkin, *Moskva*, pp. 258–59.

Liberation Movement—"universal, direct, and secret"—they could not support "equal" suffrage. Their resolution proposed to offset the enormous numerical advantage of the peasantry by granting the towns overrepresentation through smaller electoral districts. The upper house, representing the regions and corporate institutions, would have its composition and suffrage determined by the lower house. As if to dispel any lingering vestige of humble, supplicatory merchant petitions of the past, the document ended by warning that a consultative duma would not "lead to the reestablishment of a stable and tranquil life" and any delay in implementing fundamental reforms would be "ruinous for Russia as well as for trade and industry."[73] The rump session then elected an executive—the July Bureau, as it became known—to carry on the work of informing their organizations of the results and bringing about formal unification in an all-Russian association of trade and industry.[74]

Elsewhere in Moscow the exchange committee met in an altogether different mood, under the leadership of Naidenov and Krestovnikov, and endorsed the government's offer of a consultative duma as the official position of the Exchange Society and implicitly of the Moscow merchantry as a whole. Reacting swiftly the dissident Moscow merchants held another private meeting at I. A. Morozov's mansion and drafted a vigorous disclaimer, which was signed by thirty-nine individuals. In an open letter the leaders of this faction restated their opposition to a purely consultative duma and to the resolution passed by what they called "the majority of a small gathering of members of the Moscow Exchange Committee." They further justified their call for "a real legislative assembly" by the need to meet the bureaucrats "on an equal footing." The letter was signed by S. Chetverikov, P. Riabushinskii, I. A. Morozov, Alek. Vishniakov, P. P. Solov'ev, V. Alekseev, P. Voronin, I. A. Prigovkin, A. V. Got'e, R. Shen, I. A. Poliakov, A. Shamskii, V. Bakhrushin, A. V. Iokish, and Petr Botkin.[75] The second generation of the Moscow entrepreneurial group had emerged as the potential nucleus of a new political movement.

The next question was whether the Moscow entrepreneurs could realize this potential by securing an alliance with the zemstvo constitutionalists who shared their political outlook while simultaneously strengthening their ties through the July Bureau with the regional entrepreneurial groups. Surely there was no lack of willingness or initiative on their part to do both. As early as November 1904 they had sought to establish contact with the burgeoning Liberation Movement. S. T. Morozov and Vladimir Riabushinskii had led a small group of like-minded Moscow merchants into the first zemstvo congress, where they had supported the liberal program embodied in the Eleven Theses, which was adopted by the majority. Meanwhile, Pavel Riabushinskii, I. A. Morozov, and V. A. Bakhrushin had introduced similar proposals on the floor of the Moscow town duma. It was only natural, then, that in July 1905 the rump session meeting at Riabushinskii's should have taken up as the first order of business its relations with the second zemstvo congress meeting at that very moment in Moscow. Nor was it surprising that they should have sent a small delegation bearing greetings to the zemstvo delegates "as brothers-in-arms on the field of seeking ways of reestablishing order in Russia by peaceful means." Therefore, it came as all the more of a shock that they were turned away at the door on the flimsy excuse that only "written" communications would be received by the congress.[76] There was worse to come.

In the subsequent discussions of the zemstvo congress on the advisability of forming a political party, the delegates virtually ignored the existence of the merchants and industrialists. Only Miliukov made an oblique and contemptuous reference to them, when he warned against an opening to the right which would only mean that "our future party could not be democratic, for democracy defines a social-economic program, and with respect to those relations the social elements on the right are hopeless."[77]

The tenacious, if often unspoken, prejudice among the Russian educated public against big merchants and industrialists also undermined the efforts of the Moscow entrepreneurs to draw closer to the small but distinguished group of "Slavophil" zemstvo members who constituted the conservative wing of the Liberation Movement. This was an even more devastating setback than the rejection by members of the professional intelligentsia, like Miliukov. It came at the hands of enlightened landlord capitalists, men like D. N. Shipov, M. A. Stakhovich, P. A. Geiden, N. A. Khomiakov, and S. N. Trubetskoi, whose ethnoreligious patriotism, entrepreneurial activities, and personal ties with Morozov and Chetverikov made them the spiritual

---

76. TsGIA, f. 150, op. 1, d. 373, p. 53. The furious merchants requested that the zemstvo bureau consider that "this visit had not taken place." But the story got into the papers anyway in rather garbled form, thus further poisoning the atmosphere.

77. *Osvobozhdenie* (28 July 1905), appended to no. 78/79, p. 5.

descendants of the noble wing of the first generation of Moscow entrepreneurs. Even the evolution of their political views in 1905 ran closely parallel to that of the Moscow entrepreneurs. Both groups, for example, accepted the need for civil liberties and a popular legislature.

What drove a wedge between them and the second generation of Moscow entrepreneurs was the terrible combined effect upon the agrarian economy of the famine of 1891 and Witte's tariff and trade policies. In their words, this led "to a colossal disturbance in the balance between the processing and the agricultural industries to the advantage of the former and the ruin of the latter." In the name of restoring the balance the Slavophil zemtsy proposed a program which at two points struck at the very heart of the merchantry's vital interests: lowering duties on agricultural machinery and pig iron and transferring the major share of the tax burden from the land to industry in the form of a graduated income tax.

They launched their agitation from every forum within reach, beginning with the provincial zemstvo assemblies in 1890, continuing with the All-Russian Congress on Agriculture in 1895, and culminating in Witte's committees on the needs of the agricultural economy in 1902–3. They broadcast their views in the pages of the Transactions of the Imperial Free Economic Society, which they controlled, and Vestnik Evropy, which shared their position on liberalizing the tariff.[78] A strong defense of an alternative, gradualist form of capitalist development sprouting organically out of kustar manufacturing and flowering in a peasant-based internal market ran like a guiding thread through the deliberations of the Moscow provincial committee on the needs of agricultural industry in 1903.[79]

This powerful current defending the countryside against industrialization should be set against the much weaker trend of what is sometimes called "the embourgeoisment of the provincial gentry."[80] While it is true that the wealthiest landowners were moving into industry at the end of the nineteenth century, their numbers and influence were probably no greater than they had been in the immediate postreform period. As late as 1887, out of 508 enterprises owned by

---

78. B. Veselovskii, "Dvizhenie zemlevladel'tsev," in Martov, Obshchchestvennoe dvizhenie, 1:300–303.

79. Trudy mestnykh komitetov, "Moskovskaia guberniia," 23:9–11, 227–33, and also in the district (uezd) committees, see for example Dmitrievskii uezd, pp. 210–13, for a particularly sharp denunciation of the demoralizing effect of factory production on peasant stability, morality, and financial solvency.

80. Cf. Karelin, "Dvorianstvo," pp. 165–67. But the author correctly presents abundant evidence demonstrating the juridical and economic cleavages within the gentry even though he finally returns to the orthodox position that it was the dominant class (ibid., pp. 92, 114–15).

the nobility in Moscow, more than three-quarters hired fewer than 11 workers and only .6 percent employed more than 100. The nobility's enterprises accounted for only 6 percent of the turnover values of the goods produced in the city.[81] On basic economic issues the gentry opposition in the zemstvos, whether Slavophil or constitutionalist, stood much closer to the old populists and even the new Socialist Revolutionary zemtsy than it did to the merchants and industrialists.[82] Following a different road to capitalism carried the Slavophil zemtsy away from their natural political allies.

The suspicion remains, however, that there was something more to it than differences over purely economic questions. After all, entrepreneurs like Morozov and Chetverikov had proven their dedication to rural development in long years of zemstvo service. The Old Believer merchants, in particular, looked favorably upon keeping alive the kustar, if only because it guaranteed the material well-being of so many of their coreligionists in the provincial towns. More generally, the economic ties between the kustar and factory production were often more complementary than competitive, as M. I. Tugan-Baranovsky first demonstrated. By contrast, it was not so easy to span the social distance between the merchant and noble sosloviia. There remained a touch of the traditional aristocratic snobbery and intellectual disdain for the merchantry, however much individual personalities might have been exempted.

When the Liberation Movement broke up into separate political parties following the second congress, the Slavophil zemtsy preferred to enter the elections on their own. In the first duma a handful of deputies held aloof from the even small number of Moderate Progressives and formed their own Faction of Peaceful Renewal (Fraktsiia mirnogo obnovleniia). After the dissolution of the duma, its leaders toyed with the idea of forming a separate party, then settled for running a few candidates. On the eve of the elections to the second duma, Pavel Riabushinskii, Konovalov, Chetverikov, and Vishniakov declared for the mirnoobnovlentsy. But the incipient coalition was stillborn, the first of many to suffer a similar fate.[83]

The Slavophil zemtsy claimed that what distinguished their faction from the parties on their right and left was more tactical than programmatic, namely, an uncompromising commitment to strict constitutionalism and an aversion to compromise, or to what another age

81. *Torgovo-promyshlennye zavedeniia*, pp. 16, 48–52.
82. Simonova, "Zemsko-liberal'naia," pp. 164–74, 192, 196, 206–7, 211–12.
83. *Russkie vedomosti*, 26 October 1906. Cf. Pipes, *Struve*, pp. 179–80, who sees this as the beginning of "a coalescing of various liberal elements" rather than the first of many dead ends.

would call "dirty politics."[84] It is not difficult to detect traces here of the abstract moral tone so characteristic of the Slavophils when they were confronted with the harsh realities of life. The temptation then is great to see how easily it might also be found embedded in their attitudes toward certain forms of commerce and industry, as well as power, which appeared to lack a higher purpose. This speculation is inspired as much as anything by the need to explain why over the following decade they continued to grope cautiously toward some kind of understanding with the Moscow entrepreneurial group, yet at the last minute they recoiled from taking the final step toward providing a natural home, in the form of a genuine bourgeois party, for the many unhappy adherents of the jerry-built and crumbling coalitions to their left and right.

The Moscow entrepreneurial group was no more successful in cementing its ties with the heavy industrialists from St. Petersburg and the periphery. The July Bureau struggled vainly to resolve the long-standing regional differences between the merchants in order to present a united front for the duma elections. Its deliberations over the summer and fall produced a program that reflected the generally liberal attitudes of its members on constitutional issues and civil rights, but passed in silence over the irreconcilable dispute on national autonomy and left the question of factory work rules to local agreements between employers and employees.[85] If the national problem was bound to block cooperation between the Moscow entrepreneurs and the Poles, regional economic rivalries linked to foreign investments jeopardized close relations with Petersburg and the south. In the early years of the twentieth century competition between St. Petersburg and Moscow intensified in textiles, where Petersburg maintained its qualitative and technological leadership, while Moscow kept its costs low by drawing on its great reservoir of cheap peasant labor. Different sources of raw cotton—St. Petersburg importing from abroad and Moscow obtaining its supplies from Central Asia—set them at odds over the tariff question. Even before 1905 the Petersburg banks were beginning to undermine Moscow's control over Central Asian sources by extending credit to local entrepreneurs.[86]

Within Moscow itself the events of 1905 brought home to the industrialists outside textiles the harsh truth that their interests were not represented by either the exchange or the informal group of the

84. Trubetskoi, *Partiia*, pp. 4–6.
85. *Torgovo-promyshlennaia gazeta*, no. 226 (24 October 1905). For a detailed analysis of the St. Petersburg entrepreneurs see chapter 8.
86. Akademiia nauk, *Istoriia Moskvy*, 5:213–14; Laverychev, "Moskovskie fabrikanty," pp. 63 ff.

Moscow entrepreneurs. In 1907 they founded their own Moscow Society of Factory and Mill Owners, made up primarily of metallurgical firms but also including printing, perfume, and confectionary establishments. The most distinctive and suggestive social characteristic of the membership was the non-Russian names of all of its founders— Jules Goujon, N. G. List, S. V. Hopper, K. L. Hantert, and I. V. Nabgolts. They defined themselves as an employers' union, but through Goujon, who was a member of the Association of Southern Coal and Steel Producers and of the monopoly Prodamet, they associated themselves more with the industrial interests of the south than with those of the Moscow region.[87]

As the prospects for an all-Russian industrial organization collapsed, the Moscow entrepreneurs founded their own Moderate Progressive party, which, like its Moscow rival, the Trade and Industry party, had a short and unhappy life. Yet its program is important for what it tells about social and economic cleavages in the Russian Empire. And although the Moderate Progressive party had little success and soon became moribund, it was later resurrected in another form: its leaders and its program were incorporated into the Progressive Bloc and later the Provisional Government. In contrast to the Trade and Industry party, the Moderate Progressive party addressed itself to a broad range of issues in a precise and forthright fashion.

Its seventeen-point statute of organization had all the earmarks of a modern political party. Endorsing the four-point slogan of universal, direct, equal, and secret elections, the party also supported a civil-rights program much like that of the Kadets. Only in its intensive discussion of religious freedom, where it is tempting to see the hand of the Riabushinskiis, can a slight distinction be made. Its agrarian program also resembled that of the Kadets, but on two vital issues they parted company—the national and the labor questions. The Moderate Progressives stood for a "unified integral and indivisible Russian government," conceding only the need for local self-government. Workers were to have the right to strike and to organize in trade unions; labor by women and children was to be limited; and obligatory workers' insurance covering illness, accidents, and professional disability at the expense of the enterprise and state insurance for old age and disability were to be enacted. But factory inspection was to be independent—that is, not under state control—and mixed

87. *Golos Moskvy*, no. 134 (10 June 1907); *Trudy*, 27 SGIR, 3:177–78. The society changed its name in 1909 to the Society of Factory and Mill Owners of the Moscow Industrial Region and published its own *Doklady* and *Biuleteny* in order to coordinate employers' actions against both the workers and the factory inspectors (Lur'e, *Organizatsiia*, pp. 177–78).

commissions of workers and owners were to resolve their own differences, thus eliminating the bureaucracy from the factory. The Moderate Progressives could not bring themselves to approve the eight-hour day, but instead offered to negotiate a working year in order to average out the time lost by the large number of holidays in the Orthodox calendar.[88] The labor plank may not have matched that of the Kadets, but it was a vast improvement over the platforms of the Trade and Industry party and Union of 17 October.

At first, the Moderate Progressives made a substantial effort to expand their organization throughout the central industrial region, but the violent strikes following the October Manifesto threw its leaders into a panic and drove them into a series of improvised measures to defend their property against the workers. Chetverikov converted the labor commission of the Moscow Exchange Committee into a strike-breaking organization, though he opposed Naidenov's appeal to the governor-general to declare martial law. Later, he boasted that his workers left his plant unscarred, and he rewarded them with a profit-sharing plan. Konovalov, I. A. Morozov, and the Riabushinskiis signed a joint appeal denouncing the extreme socialist and revolutionary parties and called for the creation of an electoral front against them. Chetverikov and V. P. Riabushinskii even joined the Moscow Central Committee of the Union of 17 October.[89]

Clearly, the Moscow entrepreneurs were now more frightened by the workers than by the government, and they rapidly shifted to a counterrevolutionary position. What is less clear is whether even in this state of fear and confusion they were really prepared to move beyond this negative unity, to abandon their autonomous position and submit to the authority of their rivals in a unified political movement of the bourgeoisie. To the extent that they, together with other merchants, appealed for the assistance of the government to restore order, they behaved as members of a capitalist propertied class faced by a workers' revolution. This is hardly surprising. More unexpected was the failure of the propertied elements, when threatened with destruction, to organize themselves into a coherent political force or even to maintain a working alliance for more than a few months beyond the December uprising of the workers in Moscow.

In the elections to the first duma and throughout its abbreviated session the Moscow entrepreneurs clung to their own political identity, despite their association with both the Trade and Industry party and the Union of 17 October. It should be kept in mind that in a frag-

88. *Polnyi sbornik*, pp. 76–80.

89. Chetverikov, *Bezvozvratno*, p. 46; Chermenskii, *Burzhuaziia*, pp. 180–81, 191–92; Sef, *Burzhuaziia*, p. 95.

mented society like Russia, which elected its first national parliament in a period of political upheaval, membership in political parties was bound to be a tentative, often ephemeral affiliation, a quality as characteristic of the right as of the left. Party discipline hardly existed, and personalities were as important as programs. The Union of 17 October was, from the outset, a loose coalition, held together by little else than the fear of social revolution. Many of the merchants who sought refuge under its electoral banner remained officially members of other parties. Once the duma began its deliberations, there was much switching of party labels and the Octobrists lost half of their original strength.

The Moderate Progressive party was among those which quickly cut their ties to the Union of 17 October, even though the election could not have encouraged its ambitions: none of its leaders were returned and only two trading peasants won seats in its name.[90] The Moscow entrepreneurs simply recognized that there was no room for them in a political organization dominated by gentry landowners who displayed indifference to their industrial interests. The break with the Octobrists came over Alexander Guchkov's decision to approve Prime Minister Stolypin's harsh repressive measures against the peasant disorders. Rejecting the terror of the right as well as that of the left, Konovalov, Pavel Riabushinskii, and Chetverikov quit the party at the same time as Shipov and other mirnoobnovlentsy.

Yet finding a congenial political home proved a difficult matter. The Moscow entrepreneurs could not accept the leadership of the Kadets, who challenged the constitutional settlement of October and who championed the eight-hour day. Swallowing their pride they took part in a series of meetings in September and October 1906 with representatives of the Slavophil zemtsy, who had once before rejected their proffered friendship, in order to form a Party of Peaceful Renewal. Their aim was to detach elements from the left-wing Octobrists and the right-wing Kadets and to attract small, but influential, nonparty groupings. The membership drive failed, and the party never materialized.

A more modest attempt followed to create a joint editorial committee for the newspaper *Slovo* as the nucleus for a future party. Although the board had representatives from the left-wing Octobrists, the right-wing Kadets, and the mirnoobnovlentsy, no merchants were included. The experiment was not a success, and a third effort to accomplish the same purpose within a Slavic committee also collapsed.[91]

90. *Albom*; they were from Vologda and Perm. For an analysis of party changes see Sidel'nikov, *Obrazovanie*, pp. 192–94.
91. D. N. Shipov, *Vospominaniia*, pp. 514–15, 524–27.

In one year the Moscow entrepreneurs had joined three political groupings, the Octobrists, the Moderate Progressive party, and the Party of Peaceful Renewal, in a vain search for a right-center coalition. Over the next six years they made several more abortive attempts to lay the foundations for a genuine bourgeois party in Russia. In the meantime the representation of the merchantry in the duma remained insignificant. In the second duma three factory owners and eleven kuptsy were returned. In the third duma only seven "business men" won seats.[92]

The Moscow entrepreneurs were not easily discouraged. They resorted to local politics again. Together with other "progressive" elements among the gentry landowners, like Shipov, and the intelligentsia, like Astrov, they supported the Kadet candidacy of the merchant M. V. Chelnokov against the Octobrist Nikolai Guchkov, Alexander's brother, for mayor of Moscow. They lost, but they would return to the fight again.[93]

By the end of 1908 it had become clear to the Moscow entrepreneurs that a great deal more groundwork had to be done before they could expect to forge the kind of political alliance that they envisaged. Above all, they had to overcome the residual suspicion that all merchants were motivated solely by economic self-interest, a view harbored even by those gentry and members of the intelligentsia who appeared to be most sympathetic to the idea of launching a strong, stable, and united Russia on the path to rapid industrialization. The Vekhi affair provided a perfect opportunity for the Moscow entrepreneurial group to restore the lines between itself and the self-declared renegade intelligentsia, who embraced its vision of a dynamic, nationalistic capitalism accompanied by a spiritual revival of the Great Russian people.[94]

From 1909 to 1912, Konovalov and Pavel Riabushinskii played host to a series of economic discussions which brought their merchant friends together with luminaries like P. B. Struve and S. N. Bulgakov of the Vekhi group, professional economists I. M. Gol'dshtein, I. Kh. Ozerov, and S. V. Lur'e, Moscow University professors M. M. Kovalevskii, S. A. Kotliarevskii, and G. N. Trubetskoi, and A. A. Manuilov, the university rector. These contacts blossomed briefly into an intel-

92. Walsh, "Composition," pp. 113–14. The second duma also included eight cattle breeders from Central Asia and seventeen "torgovtsy." In the third duma the social identity of the businessmen was even more vague: two "bankers," two "capitalists," and three "industrialists."

93. D. N. Shipov, Vospominaniia, pp. 544–49.

94. Vekhi, especially the contribution of A. S. Izgoev, pp. 119–23. See also Zimmerman, "Political Views," pp. 307–27.

lectual collaboration in the pages of Riabushinskii's *Utro Rossii* and the symposium *Velikaia Rossiia*, brought out by Riabushinskii's publishing house. The general thrust of these joint ventures expanded the earlier views of Chizhov and his generation that Russia's political power and its economic development were inseparable and that the future of both lay in expansion to the south, control of the Black Sea, and penetration of the Balkans, the Middle East, and the Far East.

Although none of the contributors was prepared to go so far as to recommend that the merchantry take over the leadership of the country, all agreed that both the bureaucracy and the intelligentsia had failed to provide the moral and material means for Russia's defense against its external enemies. Their appeal for an "Industrie-staat" and a Great Russian national identity transcending both official nationality and all-Russian cosmopolitanism echoed the demands first made by the Moscow entrepreneurs over half a century before.[95]

Yet, despite their vows, the marriage of these two groups was never celebrated, let alone consummated. They appeared to be divided less by tactical differences than by social distance. The professional economists I. Kh. Ozerov and I. M. Gol'dshtein, who were long-time champions of rapid industrialization in Russia, urged Russia to adopt "an industrial character" in the style of German and American entrepreneurs. What worried them was the Russian industrialists, their lack of initiative, their ignorance of the domestic market, their dishonest practices. Similar doubts lay behind their opposition to "the mania of high protectionism" which they claimed led to the enrichment of a handful of great industrial magnates and the impoverishment of the mass of consumers.[96] The distinguished sociologist Maxim Kovalevskii blamed the narrow class interests of the industrialists for the terrible hardships imposed on the proletariat and the unfair distribution of the tax burden in the countryside.[97]

Of them all, P. B. Struve was the closest to the Moscow entrepreneurs. As the Soviet historian A. Ia. Avrekh has rightly observed, Struve had more in common with Riabushinskii than with Miliukov.

95. Riabushinskii, *Velikaia Rossiia*. See in particular the preface to volume 1 by V. P. Riabushinskii; G. N. Trubetskoi, "Rossiia kak velikaia derzhava," p. 121; L. M. Bolkhovitnikov, "Kolonizatory dal'nogo vostoka," pp. 217–36; the preface to volume 2 by Riabushinskii, pp. 5–6; S. A. Kotliarevskii, "Russkaia vneshnaia politika i natsional'nye zadachi," pp. 57, 63–65; L. N. Iasnopol'skii, "Finansy Rossii i ikh podgotovlennost' k voine," pp. 99, 105, 110–12, 122; P. B. Struve, "Ekonomicheskaia problema 'velikoi Rossii.'"

96. Ozerov, *Itogi*, pp. 61 ff.; idem, *Problèmes*, pp. 21–29, 44–48. See also his *Nuzhdy rabochogo klassa* and *Bol'shie goroda*; Gol'dshtein, *Sindikaty* and *Voina*, especially pp. 59–63.

97. M. M. Kovalevskii, *Ekonomicheskoe*, pp. 91–96, 118–26, 129.

One wonders, then, why he never joined them, and why he continued to edit his own paper, *Russkaia mysl'*, and officially remain a member of the Kadet party even after the creation of the Progressive party by a coalition of Moscow entrepreneurs, defecting left-wing Octobrists, and right-wing Kadets. Struve nurtured the greatest admiration for large-scale capitalism as a civilizing force and as a necessity for a great power. For him the budgetary policies of Minister of Finance Kokovtsov were too passive and the liberals' protection of kustar too slow as methods of industrializing Russia. He warmly endorsed the views of the Association of the Representatives of Trade and Industry on the need for investments in heavy industry and public education combined with his own prerequisite of a constitutional order. Still, "the question of the economic rebirth of Russia is above all," he wrote, "a question of creating the new economic man."

The signs of the appearance of such a man were, according to Struve, encouraging. Perhaps impressed by his recent contacts with the Moscow entrepreneurial group, he portrayed the Russian capitalists themselves in a positive light for the first time: they could no longer be intimidated by the bureaucrats; their organizations showed indications of "a liberal spirit" surprising in a "milieu so recently terrified by the revolution and the police."[98] But the sticking point remained for Struve the moral dilemma of sanctifying the profit motive. "The practical economic promoter of this process [production] . . . cannot think of himself only as the representative of a group or class interest . . . [because] at the heart of this interest lies a certain service to society, the accomplishment of a certain function in having creative significance for the society as a whole."[99]

What Struve meant by "creative significance" emerged most clearly in his postrevolutionary tribute to Ivan Aksakov, who, he wrote, "was not afraid to enter the economic life of his country and his native city of Moscow as a practical man." This was no accident, to Struve's way of thinking, because it corresponded to Askakov's profound conviction that an indissoluble link existed between the spiritual and material cultures of the country. It as his form of "social service."[100] It might be added that in 1909 there was no one to take Aksakov's place, not even Struve, who, like other intellectual apologists for capitalism, was really afraid or disdainful of plunging into the hurly-burly of the

---

98. Struve, "Ekonomicheskii programmy i 'neestestvennyi' rezhim," in *Patriotica*, pp. 157–59, 161–63. See also, idem, *Torgovaia politika*, pp. 30–31, where Struve makes it clear that he is talking about the "industrial bourgeoisie" and not the trading merchants.

99. Struve, "Intelligentsia i narodnoe khozaistvo," in *Patriotica*, pp. 364–65.

100. Struve, "Aksakovy i Aksakov," *Russkaia mysl'*, June–August 1923, p. 353.

business world. Moreover, they were not forced to do so, because by this time professional journalism had become a paying proposition. Instead, as a weak substitute, Struve proposed that "the zemstvo itself should become the entrepreneur" in the countryside where the handicraft artels were unequal to the task and the merchants were simply inert.[101] These sentiments, long shared by the Slavophil zemtsy, were spreading throughout the provincial zemstvos. The foundations were being laid for the fierce rivalry that broke out between the zemstvos and the trading merchants over the control of food supply during World War I.[102] Nothing could have been better calculated to wreck hopes for binding together the two elements in Russian society most essential to the formation of a middle class.

The Moscow entrepreneurs emerged with a different message from the economic discussions at Riabushinskii's mansion. It appeared to them that the intellectuals involved expected some kind of earnest money from the merchants in the form of a social commitment as the basis for a real partnership. The entrepreneurs were determined to prove their worth by defending academic freedom, a cause which could not in any way be linked to their "narrow economic interests." Intoxicated by their own rhetoric in *Utro Rossii*, they took a boldly anti-government stand in the Manuilov affair, which involved the resignation of the rector of the Moscow University and one of the mainstays of their discussion group, following the arbitrary dismissal of three of his professors by the Ministry of Education. Led by Konovalov, Riabushinskii, Chetverikov, and N. D. Morozov, sixty-six merchants signed a public declaration which criticized bureaucratic influence in higher education, without, however, excusing the student disorders that had triggered the incident.[103]

One effect of their demonstration was to enrage the extreme right. The Black Hundred press savagely turned against the Moscow entrepreneurs, vilifying them as "the biggest Jewish muck" and accusing them of having both sold out to the intelligentsia and abdicated the traditions of their fathers, who may have been "coarse" but had performed useful functions for Russia. The "dandified" sons, who sponsored decadent journals and posed as aristocratic gentlemen, could

101. Struve, *Ekonomiia promyshlennosti*, pp. 158–59.
102. Glavnoe upravlenie zemleustroistva i zemledelia, *Obzor*, pp. 18–21. For the struggle over the food supply see below, chapter. 9.
103. *Russkie vedomosti*, 11 February 1911. Their action brought a sharp rebuke from Krestovnikov in the Octobrist organ *Golos Moskvy* accusing them of arrogating the role of merchant leadership. The Moscow entrepreneurs defended themselves but damaged their cause by acknowledging Krestovnikov's formal leadership of the Moscow merchant community (ibid., 13 February 1911). The entire episode smacked of merchant paternalism.

not even maintain control over Russian markets in the face of German and Jewish intrigues.[104] Whatever influence the Moscow entrepreneurial group hoped to exercise among rabid nationalists and anti-Semites vanished in this vicious denunciation.

A second and more important consequence of the Manuilov affair was to clear the way for the last experiment in centrist coalition politics before the outbreak of the war. The formation of the Progressive party and a few isolated, if much publicized, electoral successes at the local and national level gave contemporaries the impression that the elusive political unity of the "bourgeoisie" was at hand. Beginning in 1911 the Moscow entrepreneurs began to participate in a series of conferences with left-wing Octobrists, right-wing Kadets, and mirnoobnovlentsy aimed at creating a bloc of "progressive" candidates for elections to local government organs and the fourth duma in 1912.

In the discussions over a platform it proved easier to reach a consensus on the need to defend the October Manifesto than on concrete economic problems. For example, when Kadets Manuilov and Ozerov proposed making tariff concessions to German industry on the eve of negotiations for a new trade treaty, Riabushinskii was infuriated. His newspaper accused the economists of endangering Russia's entire economic policy by their defense of the agricultural interests. Riabushinskii used the occasion to condemn his erstwhile collaborators in the economic discussions as "too theoretical and imprecise" and "tainted with noble-landlord sympathies."[105] By May he was accusing the entire Kadet party of being riddled with Utopian fantasies of "state socialism." How could they attack the government for mismanaging the country, he asked, and then urge that same government to take over more and more of the economy from private hands?[106]

His polemics with the Kadets were far from "feigned," as one Soviet historian has suggested. They expressed long-standing and deep-seated differences over the nature and pace of Russia's industrialization. As for the Octobrists to the right of the progressives, Riabushinskii and his friends had already written them off as allies for much the same reason. Without distinguishing among the various factions, Riabushinskii categorized the party as gentry-ridden, with a "feudal cast," and lacking "any correct understanding of the interests of Russian industry."[107] He was equally contemptuous of the representa-

104. *Novoe vremiia*, 13 and 17 February 1911.

105. *Utro Rossii*, nos. 55, 97 (7 March, and 1 May 1912), where Tugan-Baranovskii is also taken to task for the same errors.

106. Ibid., no. 118 (28 May 1912).

107. Ibid., no. 69 (10 February 1910). See ibid., no. 56 (8 March 1912), for a sharp attack on the St. Petersburg United Nobility for their proposal on joint noble-peasant cooperatives.

tives of trade and industry in the State Council, like Tripolitov and Timiriazev, who, he said, were even afraid to appear at the meeting: of the Association of the Representatives of Russian Trade and Industry because they were unable to defend their parliamentary record as "presumed" spokesmen for the interests that elected them.[108]

Even as the Moscow entrepreneurs jointly approved a common slate of progressive candidates for the elections, Riabushinskii aggressively pressed his demand that the merchants have the leading role in Russia's political future. At the same time he sought to expand his own mass base by agitating the Old Believers to shift their political loyalties to the left. This wave of "merchant messianism," as one historian has called it, crested at the jubilee celebration of the Konovalov firm when Riabushinskii rapturously proclaimed the replacement of the nobility by the merchantry as the leading class in Russia.[109]

In the national elections the progressives won forty-one seats. But their most spectacular successes were in Moscow and Kostroma, a stronghold of the Old Belief and the economic base of the Moscow entrepreneurs since the days of Chizhov, Kokorev, and the Shipovs. Konovalov was returned by Kostroma, and Alexander Guchkov was defeated in Moscow by M. V. Chelnokov, a right-wing Kadet from a merchant family. In the wake of these victories the Progressive party was founded. At its first congress the delegates approved a program calling for the abolition of the state of siege, the introduction of representatives from the towns into the State Council, freedom of religion, the abolition of the soslovie principle, and the political responsibility of the ministry to the representatives of the people. Lenin was sufficiently impressed to dub the party "the national liberals" of Russia: that is, a party of "the 'real' capitalist bourgeoisie such as we see in Germany" as distinct from the demogogic Kadets and gentry-ridden Octobrists.[110] In fact, the Progressive party proved to be something less than this.

The Progressive duma faction was a mixed bag of undistinguished individuals lacking party discipline and organization. Only one of them was an industrialist. The elections had led to a split in the Octobrist party, but the center under Guchkov would not join the Progres-

---

108. Ibid., no. 105 (13 February 1912). Riabushinskii even scolded the merchants, or at least those in the Association of Commercial and Agricultural Exchanges, for their childish opposition to speculation in grain futures (ibid., no. 98 [2 May 1912]).

109. West, "Moscow Progressists," pp. 333–35.

110. Lenin, *Collected Works*, 16:218–19. Lenin perceived the different social strata within the new party—the big merchants, moderate gentry, zemtsy, and nationalistic intellectuals—but assumed a sufficient degree of cohesion among these disparate elements to ensure them a "certain 'future'" in Russia." This vague if tantalizing formulation has become the subject of much historical exegesis in the Soviet Union.

sives. Most of the left-wing Kadets also followed their party leader, Paul Miliukov, in resisting the Progressives' siren call of unity. Years later, Buryshkin, who had been in the center of the movement, recalled that "outside the limits of the duma the Progressive party scarcely existed."[111] This was perhaps an exaggeration, but the party's central committee rarely met and had no control over the duma faction.

Meanwhile, Riabushinskii and Konovalov redoubled their efforts to expand their political base in Moscow and take over the Progressives from the inside. The opening move in their campaign was to help form an electoral bloc of Progressives in order to contest the city duma elections of 1912. Their prime objective was to unseat Nikolai Guchkov as mayor. But although the Progressives won a majority of the seats, an analysis of the elections reveals the weakness and fragility of their coalition at the very center of their political power base.

The voting behavior of the electors was characterized by a low turnout, blurred party lines, and a reluctance to replace incumbents with "new men." In five out of the six city election districts only one-third to one-half of the enfranchised electors cast ballots. The single exception was the small fifth district, where 90 percent voted in a fiercely contested personal struggle over the reelection of the Progressive leader N. I. Astrov. Bearing in mind that there were fewer than two thousand eligible voters in each district (and under five hundred in the fifth), then the degree of political apathy is even more striking.[112]

It is difficult to avoid the conclusion that a majority of the propertied and educated elite of Moscow perceived very little difference between the candidates, or else considered the outcome unimportant for their own interests. Indeed, with a few individual exceptions like Astrov and Nikolai Guchkov the ideological lines were not clearly drawn. Candidates of the two major factions—the Progressives and the moderate rights—were most often elected on a joint slate drawn up by one side or the other or else by the independent association of leaseholders, which often tipped the balance. This often annoyed Riabushinskii and his friends, who attributed the outcome, ironically, to "the influence of the merchantry." But other times they too ad-

111. Buryshkin, *Moskva*, pp. 281–83. See also West, "Moscow Progressists," pp. 409–11.
112. The following analysis is based on the reporting of *Utro Rossii* during the election period from 25 November to 21 December 1912. Each of the six districts held its election on a separate day. According to the complex rules for voting, at least two-thirds of the full membership of 160 deputies had to be elected so that the duma could function. In this election the first round of balloting yielded only 98 deputies, so a second round had to be organized (*Utro Rossii*, no 281 [6 December 1912]).

mitted that some of the candidates from the moderate right were very valuable to the duma because of their experience and specialized knowledge.[113]

This was fair-minded but not conducive to sustaining a fighting political spirit. Consequently, the electors tended to vote for the incumbent, whatever their political affiliation. This attitude shifted only during the second round of voting, after the most prominent duma deputies had been reelected. By party affiliation, the final tally showed seventy-seven Progressive deputies, with seven alternates, and sixty-nine moderate rights, with five alternates. By another standard, equally important as it turned out, the results were significantly different: seventy-seven incumbents and sixty-nine newcomers were returned.[114]

The reaction of the Progressive leaders to this "victory" was scarcely jubilant. At their first postelection caucus they called upon Guchkov to run again as mayor. This was the man that they had organized to drive out of office. They had planned to replace him with G. E. L'vov, who, though "not a Muscovite and a prince," as *Utro Rossii* put it, was preferable to the scion of an old Moscow merchant family infected by a "a noble-bureaucratic outlook."[115] When the final returns were in, however, the Progressives backed off; they claimed that they could not run their own man, because "with the present relation of forces in the new duma [it] was recognized as undesirable." And this with a majority of votes!

It soon became clear that the Progressives lacked unity as well as self-confidence. A minority of them, led by the Kadets, rejected an accommodation with Guchkov and advocated the election of either L'vov or Chelnokov.[116] Guchkov obligingly saved the Progressives from an open split by declining to run, as he had promised, unless he was the sole candidate. The Progressives pulled themselves together and backed L'vov, but the imperial government refused to confirm his election for political reasons. The conservative Moscow merchants now found themselves dragged into the very sort of confrontation with the authorities which they had always feared and avoided. On the other hand, the Moscow entrepreneurs were delighted with an issue which strengthened their ties to the professional intelligentsia. They might not have noticed that this was once more the result of obtuseness in St. Petersburg rather than their own cleverness. The

113. Ibid., nos. 274, 275 (28, 29 November 1912).
114. Ibid., no. 294 (21 December 1912).
115. Ibid., no. 288 (14 December 1912).
116. Ibid., nos. 299, 300 (29, 30 December 1912).

stalemate dragged on for a year until Kokovtsov persuaded Nicholas II to confirm Chelnokov as a compromise candidate acceptable to all factions in Moscow. While it is true that in the end the Progressives won something, the election and its aftermath held out little hope that they were either willing or able to challenge the power of the autocracy.

In the Moscow Exchange Committee itself the Moscow entrepreneurs gradually undermined Krestovnikov's position. As early as 1910, Konovalov was elected his deputy. Two years later, Riabushinskii replaced him and Tret'iakov and A. I. Kuznetsov were added to the executive committee. This growing influence of the Moscow entrepreneurs was due in part to the changing character of the organization. Its membership continued to decline from 500 in 1905 to 379 in 1910.[117] Like the Association of Southern Coal and Steel Producers, the exchange committee gradually evolved into a "big business" organization. As the small and medium-sized merchants dropped away, the committee shed its traditionally cautious views. The Moscow entrepreneurs drew more support from the big industrial firms for their policy of standing up to the bureaucracy. For example, after Riabushinskii made his provocative speech at Konovalov's jubilee, Goujon wrote him an enthusiastic letter of support.[118] Other members of the Moscow Society of Factory and Mill Owners, like Poplavskii, also came over to Riabushinskii's side.

In the executive committee as in the city duma elections the Progressives' gains were won by a very small shift of votes in a very small constituency. On the national scale, even in an era of limited suffrage, their political influence was still insignificant and would remain so until they could broaden their appeal dramatically. Yet the opportunities for cooperation were limited. Every setback produced fresh recriminations among the prospective allies. Few leaders were willing or able to break out of the ineffectual pattern of narrow and informal political agreements.

Among the Moscow entrepreneurs, Konovalov understood better than anyone the need to transform the Progressive coalition into a unified opposition movement. On the eve of the war he made two abortive efforts in this direction. His first one in the duma was aimed at coordinating the parliamentary activities of the right center (Octo-

117. Moskovskii birzhevyi komitet, *Otchet za 1910*, p. 2; idem, *Otchet za 1913*, p. 3. Riabushinskii was already a member of the executive committee in 1910. The Moscow entrepreneurs dominated the powerful cotton committee; Vishniakov was head of the Banking committee; and Riabushinskii was head of the timber committee (idem, *Otchet za 1910*, pp. 3–5).
118. Cited in Laverychev, *Po tu storonu*, pp. 80–81.

The Architecture of Merchant Moscow

The Tret'iakov gallery, designed by V. M. Vasnetsov, 1900–1905.
(Courtesy of Stephen Perloff)

Pavel Riabushinskii's mansion, designed by F. O. Shekhtel', 1900.
(Courtesy of Stephen Perloff)

The Riabushinskii mansion, main staircase. (Courtesy of Stephen Perloff)

The printing house of Utro Rossii, *designed by F. O. Shekhtel'.*
(Courtesy of Stephen Perloff)

brists, Progressives, and Kadets). But it collapsed because the right wing of the Octobrists, representing the most conservative gentry in the old zemstvo constitutional movement, refused to participate.[119]

In his second and bolder effort, Konovalov proposed a grand coalition between the duma opposition and the revolutionary parties, including both the Bolsheviks and Socialist Revolutionaries. But this veiled effort to check the mounting wave of strikes and disorders in the countryside had even less chance of success, for the social gulf had been rapidly widening for a generation. His initiative led to the formation of an information bureau which included himself, Nikolai Morozov, and Riabushinskii, together with several Mensheviks, a non-party socialist, and a Bolshevik. Clearly, the left was interested in obtaining money for their depleted party treasuries from the wealthy merchants. Apparently, the Moscow entrepreneurs were gambling that they could employ the agitation of the dissatisfied elements to bring pressure against the government for political concessions before the popular movement turned into a full-fledged revolution. In other words they were replaying the Kadets' game of ten years earlier. Neither side got what it wanted, and the dubious experiment came to an end when the Progressive deputies voted in the duma to support a government motion expelling the Social Democrat and Trudovik deputies for having obstructed discussion on the budget.[120]

In the meantime, on the floor of the duma, Konovalov sought to correct the impressions left by Krestovnikov and other deputies in the State Council representing the corporate interests of trade and industry that the merchants were a narrow-minded and hidebound soslovie. In sharp contrast to Krestovnikov, Konovalov insisted upon the direct connection between the resolution of economic problems and the emergence of "specific norms of political order" which would guarantee freedom of personal initiative and "the independent activities" of the population.[121] He proposed a radical overhauling of outmoded rules and attitudes which hampered economic growth ranging from joint-stock legislation, patent, and commercial law to reorganization of the Ministry of Trade and Industry, labor legislation, and the removal of rules discriminating against Jewish merchants. He even extolled the vital role of foreign capital in Russian industrialization.[122] But all Konovalov's activities dissipated in the air of unreality that

119. *Otchet TsK soiuz 17 ogo oktiabria*, p. 7.
120. For the Bolshevik contacts see Volodarskaia, *Lenin i partiia*, pp. 36–39. See also Hosking, *Russian Constitutional*, pp. 95–96; Haimson, "Social Stability," pp. 4–8, and Laverychev, *Po tu storonu*, pp. 103–7.
121. *PT*, no. 11 (131) (1 June 1913): 499.
122. Ibid., no. 13 (133) (1 July 1913): 4–12.

surrounded them, for he represented nothing in Russian society except for a small group of ambitious Moscow merchants. Moreover, to a certain extent, Konovalov and his friends must share the blame for their isolated position.

An internal malaise sapped the political strength of the Moscow entrepreneurs and repelled their natural allies among the landed gentry and intelligentsia. Molded by the patriarchal authority that they wielded in family and factory alike, they lacked the flexibility and tactical skills needed to excel in public life and parliamentary maneuvering. Their political philosophy placed too much emphasis on the force of personality and psychological factors. Their own business experience taught them to admire the bold and selfless individual creators of value and to scorn the "envious" and the "disorderly" mass as inferior social types. Their hero image of Napoleon was fused with that of the Old Russian saints. They were obsessed with a peculiar form of "aristocratism," the need to "conserve and develop the hereditary strength of the merchantry" in order to pass on the primordial energy of their forebears and prevent its dilution by other sosloviia like the nobility above and the meshchanstvo below.[123]

Yet they shied away from public office. Not until 1912 did they put forth a single successful, or even viable, candidate for the duma, and not until 1917 did they run one of their own men for mayor of Moscow. Their appeals for mass support, whether to Old Believers, workers, or meshchane, were too often couched in condescending or paternalistic language. They welcomed signs of social democratic revisionism among the workers, but with the exception of Konovalov, they did not know how to exploit it.[124] Perhaps most damaging of all, they found it difficult to work closely with one another in the glare of publicity when their paternalistic authority was on the line.

Lacking the qualities necessary to lead a mass movement, the Moscow entrepreneurs were not politically impotent. Like their predecessors, they were masters of informal, behind-the-scenes dealings where they could bring to bear personal influence on high officials in order to defend their own economic interests. Although they publicly disdained the oligarchic style of politics, in private they made it their own. The outbreak of World War I gave them their best, if last, chance to prove that their real power in the country could not be measured in votes.

123. Riabushinskii, "Sud'ba," pp. 44–45, 51; Utro Rossii, no. 256 (6 November 1912); Chetverikov, Bezvozvratno, pp. 5, 37.
124. Utro Rossii, no. 260 (12 November 1912).

CHAPTER 8

ON THE PERIPHERY

IN 1905

Throughout 1905 the entrepreneurial groups on the periphery of the empire struggled to contain the revolutionary eruptions without giving up any of their economic privileges or organizational autonomy. They immediately took the initiative in defending the interests of the capitalists in their regions, while the merchant exchanges remained generally quiescent. Better organized than the Moscow entrepreneurial group, they were also less fettered by ties to traditional merchant communities. But their advantages rapidly became liabilities when larger political issues assumed greater importance because they were reluctant to break out of their narrow professional membership to rally broader strata of the population. Even more than the Moscow entrepreneurs, they felt the lack of a potential mass base.

As competition mounted among interest groups for the national political leadership over trade and industry the Petersburg and southern groups were handicapped by their ethnic heterogeneity and their close identification with foreign capital, making them particularly vulnerable to the double edge of the revolution. Rising social antagonisms threatened their control at the enterprise level, while national antagonisms frustrated their political unity against the common enemy. The revolution taught them lessons that were different from those it taught Moscow. If the Moscow entrepreneurs saw salvation in some form of political alliance, those on the periphery sought theirs in economic combinations. Their paths occasionally crossed, but never merged.

The Southern Entrepreneurs Bid for Political Leadership in 1905

When the strike movement engulfed the mines and factories of the Donets, the southern entrepreneurs were well prepared to deal with it, and success emboldened them to claim a wider role in the reconstruction of the empire. The strikes were particularly violent in the south, and the entrepreneurs felt compelled to appeal to the government for large-scale military forces to protect their properties. But the members of the Association of Southern Coal and Steel Producers resisted all efforts to convert it into primarily an antiworkers organization. Quite the contrary, the southern entrepreneurs concentrated their energies on forging an empire-wide representative organization of trade and industry in order to influence directly the overall economic development of the country.

The chosen instrument of their ambitions was the Permanent Advisory Office of the Metallurgical Industrialists. Originally founded by the Ural metallurgists in the years from 1888 to 1892, the Permanent Advisory Office soon represented forty-four firms and comprised 77 percent of the productive output of the Russian ferrous-metal industry. Until 1904 the organization was dominated by the conservative Ural group and was confined mainly to preparing useful information for the industry and the government.[1] When Prodamet undertook to force the Ural manufacturers into the syndicate, it rapidly moved to take control as well of the advisory office.[2] By the spring of 1905, Prodamet dominated the office's executive, with the Association of Southern Coal and Steel Producers occupying six out of twelve seats; Zhukovskii, of the Polish Mining and Factory Owners, Vol'skii, of the Nikopol-Mariupol Metallurgical Company, Avadkov, of the Kharkov Coal and Iron Exchange, Enakiev, of the Russo-Belgian Metallurgical Company, Iasiukovich, of the South Russian Dniepr Metallurgical Company, and von Ditmar, the president of the association. Five additional members of Prodamet represented the Baltic and northwestern group (S. A. Erdeli and M. P. Norpe), Moscow (Goujon), and the Urals (V. I. Kotliarevskii and N. N. Kutler). As former associates of Witte who had become disillusioned with his policies, Kotliarevskii and Kutler had excellent contacts within the government and a good knowledge of the Urals, where they had helped to manage the state enterprises. This formidable coalition of metallurgical interests took advantage of the revolutionary situation to assert its claim for political leadership over trade and industry.

Like other proto-political groups in 1905, its first step was to berate the government publicly for its arbitrary and erroneous economic policies. They painted a devastating picture of "the backwardness of the law-making process" in Russia. "The absence of a government

1. *Trudy*, PsKZh, 1900, pp. 1–5. These proceedings were often devoted wholly to lengthy reports on the state of industry in the rest of Europe.
2. Shpolianskii, *Monopolii*, pp. 77–78.

policy, the interdepartmental struggles, and the timidity of the government's ideas" had paralyzed the implementation of reform. Legislation of vital importance to economic growth, such as the reform of joint-stock companies, the passport system, and promissory notes, had been bottled up in the bureaucracy for periods of thirty, forty-five, and fifty years, respectively. Laws already on the books to assist industry were undermined by secret instructions. The Urals suffered especially from the continued existence of an archaic "possessional structure" and the persecution of the Old Believers and sectarians. The metallurgists deplored the neglect of the workers as "one of the greatest evils of our life." To correct these general abuses the advisory office called for equality before the law, freedom of the press and speech, and the right of workers to form unions and to strike so long as they did not resort to violence. Specifically, the advisory office endorsed the ten-hour day, or even less in dangerous industries. It regretted the "absence of a domestic market" and called for "economic freedom." It also claimed the same right to organize freely for themselves and demanded the participation of both workers and owners in the state legislative process.[3] Increasingly concerned over the extent of the strike movement, the advisory office drafted a special declaration on the labor question which emphasized the common political interests of owners and workers in the face of police socialism and administrative arbitrariness.[4]

In its broad outlines and in its specific concerns with Old Believers and workers, the program aligned the advisory office with the Moscow entrepreneurial group and laid the foundations for the creation of the July Bureau. But at the same time its very moderation on social questions was destined to irritate and then antagonize the St. Petersburg entrepreneurs, who took a harsher line on the workers and the national-religious question. Whatever the implications of their stand for domestic politics, there is no evidence that the southern entrepreneurs were acting as representatives of foreign capital. On the contrary, their independence from external influences emerges clearly from the record of their political activities during the revolution of 1905 and its aftermath.

Once the Moscow merchants showed themselves unwilling or incapable of leading an empire-wide political movement in the summer of 1905, the Permanent Advisory Office seized the initiative, calling for a second conference of representatives of trade and industry for the specific purpose of organizing a political party to contest the duma

3. *Pravo*, no. 9 (6 March 1905): cols. 672–74.
4. Ibid., no. 12 (27 March 1905): col. 919.

elections. It authorized a five-man bureau, composed of M. F. Norpe, A. A. Vol'skii, V. K. Kovalevskii, F. E. Enakiev, and A. A. Bobrinskii (the sugar magnate), to draft a program, which was quickly adopted by a general assembly of the organization as the basis for the Moscow congress. Its guiding principle was the restoration of order so that economic life could recover.

The insertion of two critical social issues challenged the basic interests of the Petersburg entrepreneurs. The first was "the rational protection of Russian labor from the foreign yoke," that is, the maintenance of a high protective tariff. The second was the decentralization of state authority and "the division of the country into a series of self-governing regions under the general guidance of the central power." The advisory office outflanked the more conservative leadership of the St. Petersburg Society of Factory and Mill owners by convening an ad hoc meeting of industrialists in the capital. It convinced them to send plenipotentiaries to Moscow in order to negotiate an agenda for the second conference of trade and industry.[5] The temporary ascendancy of the advisory office was confirmed by the choice of the five-man drafting committee (with the substitution of A. N. Ratkev-Rozhkov of the Urals for Bobrinskii) as the plenipotentiaries. The St. Petersburg society was unrepresented. This made for smoother sailing in Moscow, but proved harmful to unity in the long run.

Euphoria pervaded the planning session in Moscow. Agreement was reached for a second conference of trade and industry (the unnecessarily restrictive modifiers "of various regions" having been dropped) that would assume a "primarily political" character. But success rested on a faulty assumption. The political base of the undertaking was much narrower than it appeared. The driving force behind the organization of a bourgeois political party was the Moscow entrepreneurs, who were still dragging along a reluctant Moscow Exchange leadership, and "the Petersburg delegation," as the five plenipotentiaries were misleadingly called, who also claimed to speak for a much wider constitutency than they really represented. The illusion was maintained when the plenipotentiaries returned to St. Petersburg and persuaded a second ad hoc meeting of industrialists to endorse their work and to elect a strong delegation to the conference, including, this time, some leading representatives of industry within the capital, Johnson, Nobel, Shreder, Beliaev, and Voronin, as well as Norpe and Vege of the advisory office.[6]

The second conference held in Moscow was, as we have seen,

5. Chermenskii, *Burzhuaziia*, p. 80.
6. TsGIA, f. 150, op. 1, d. 373, pp. 39, 50.

wrecked by the Moscow Exchange leadership. But a semblance of unity was retained with the creation of the July Bureau, which, on the surface, appeared to comprise the most active elements in Moscow and St. Petersburg and the metallurgists of the south and the Urals. It, too, was only a mirage, however, which vanished when the St. Petersburg entrepreneurs began to awaken to the full implications of the program, which they had approved, as it turned out, much too uncritically.[7]

As the prospects for a single party of trade and industry faded, the Permanent Advisory Office made one last attempt to convince the St. Petersburg entrepreneurs of the need to recognize regional autonomy before acknowledging that the fissiparous tendencies were too strong. Then they reluctantly formed their own splinter party. The Progressive Industrialists party was scarcely founded before it expired, leaving nothing else but a program to mark its existence.

The advisory office perceived more quickly than most other groups of trade and industry the futility of competing for power through elections to the duma. Instead, it resolved "to convert itself into a nonpolitical organization for the promotion of its economic interests" on an all-Russian scale. While the other groups expended their energies on electoral politics, the office drafted a charter for a Union of Commercial-Industrial Enterprises of the Russian Empire.

It soon became evident that the organizers had not abandoned politics at all but smuggled it under a different guise into the strong, centralized structure of the union, which they proposed and, presumably, intended to control. Such, at least, was the conclusion of the regional delegates from Moscow, the Kingdom of Poland, the Baltic provinces, and the Urals who opposed the plan and wrote into the charter the principle of autonomy for member organizations and a weak executive authority composed of representatives from every region and every type of representative organization of trade and industry. Even then the exchange committees hung back from joining until the government gave its approval to the organization, placed it "under the direction of the Ministry of Trade and Industry," and denied it permission to use the designation "empire-wide" (*obshcheimperskie*).[8]

The name of the new organization, the Association of the Representatives of Trade and Industry, reflected its decentralized structure. Still, it was the single most important achievement of the entrepreneurs to come out of the revolution of 1905. With a membership, in

7. For the opposition of the St. Petersburg Society of Factory and Mill Owners to the July Bureau see below, chapter 7.
8. Livshin,"'Predstavitel'nye' organizatsii," pp. 108–9; Roosa, "Association," 1:69–70, 73–87.

1914, of over three hundred organizations of trade and industry, it maintained a permanent council of thirty-six, held annual congresses, published an expensive, slick magazine, and claimed to speak with one voice for the interests of its constituents. Yet, from the outset, it was more imposing in appearance than in reality. The deception was due in part to its having been the product of a three-way compromise. The government finally permitted an all-Russian representative organization—even if it withheld the name—but prevented the emergence of an autonomous social or political force in the Russian business community. The merchant exchanges obtained a larger forum from which to proclaim their grievances without having to surrender their particularism, but the southern entrepreneurs salvaged only the blueprints of the mighty structure that they had envisaged, and they immediately set about to build what they wanted from the bottom up. Even though the association was a confederation of interest groups, the entrepreneurs were determined to transform it by the simple device of proving themselves to be its most active and hard-working members.

The real work of the Association of the Representatives of Russian Trade and Industry was carried on by only a few figures, of whom Avdakov, Zhukovskii, and Vol'skii were the most prominent.[9] Vol'skii was editor in chief of the association's official organ, *Promyshlennost' i torgovlia*, and the South Russian Dniepr Metallurgical Company (with Iasiukovich as director) was by far the largest contributor among the member organizations to the journal's upkeep. The southern entrepreneurs consciously sought to improve their control over the association by seeking and obtaining a larger representation of the Association of Southern Coal and Steel Producers on the executive council.[10] For all that, they were unable to get the association to endorse their specific policy recommendations and often had to be satisfied with vague statements of general principles in both the pages of

9. Roosa, "Association," 1:114–20, 133–43, who, however, follows Gushka, *Predstavitel'nye*, p. 136, in identifying these men as representatives of "the third element" so dear to the hearts of the Mensheviks. The point is, however, that they were not simple technicians but entrepreneurs and administrators with a material stake in private enterprise.

10. *Trudy 4-ogo ocherednogo s'ezda predstavitelei promyshlennosti i torgovli, 10, 11, 12, 13, noiabria 1909* (St. Petersburg, 1910), appendixes 1 and 2 (no pagination). Out of the total contributions of 19,389 rubles, South Russian Dniepr supplied 4,000. The millionaire G. M. Mark was the largest contributor with 10,000. By contrast the only Moscow contributor was the Merchant Bank with 500 rubles. As for membership dues, only four organizations were assessed the top figure of 5,000 rubles: the Association of Southern Coal Mine Owners, the Moscow Exchange Committee, the Association of Representatives of Insurance Companies, and the Baku Oil Industrialists (ibid., appendix 3).

the official journal and in the reports of the annual congresses. Yet they never renounced their own grandiose vision of a modern, industrialized Russian empire modeled after their development of the south. Occasionally, their enthusiasm broke through the bland collective pronouncements of the association and illuminated the main features of their industrialization policy.

Assuming that their views have a common source, it is possible to construct from them a model of a mixed economy in which a balance is struck between central planning and rational expectations, on the one hand, and managerial decentralization and profit incentives, on the other. In the scheme of the southern entrepreneurs the bearer of progress was the master of technical knowledge. There was not a single economic problem, from increasing crop yields to lowering freight costs in Russian harbors, that could not be solved by the proper application of technology.[11] The forces of inertia were state socialism and the soslovie system. Together they created "an atmosphere [in the state duma] on economic questions [which] is a combination of the intelligentsia's hostility to any kind of productive activity with a thick stream of peasant hostility to any other form of economy except following behind a plow."[12]

Although they were industrializers par excellence, they were convinced that agriculture had been sorely neglected and, indeed, that there had been a whole series of unbalanced investments in one or another sector of the economy. A case in point, in their eyes, was the bias favoring railroads over inland waterways, which had caused bottlenecks and irrational use of resources and had resulted in Witte's "unsystemmatic system."[13]

Because of the government's enormous role in the economic life of the country, the annual state budget, they declared, was an inadequate foundation for planning; five- or even ten-year projections were nec-

11. Vol'skii, *Osnovy*, pp. 12–30.
12. Sovet s'ezdov predstavitelei promyshlennosti i torgovli, *Promyshlennost' i torgovlia*, p. 5. The analysis also deplores "the sharp ideological conflict of agricultural and commercial industrial interests" which sprang from the preponderance of the peasant and gentry landlord sosloviia in the duma (ibid., pp. 7–8). This document was drafted for the Association of the Representatives of Trade and Industry by Zhukovskii and here as elsewhere bears the stamp of his viewpoint. Similarly, Vol'skii criticized "the Russian intelligentsia who with very few exceptions, having been raised in the school of state socialism, were not used to thinking in terms of practical questions of economic life," and praised Konovalov for having organized the economic discussions which he viewed as "a turning point in Russian economic thought" ("Ekonomicheskofinansovaia politika Rossiia, doklad A. A. Vol'skogo," *Trudy 4-ogo ocherednogo s'ezda predstavitelei promyshlennosti i torgovli*, pp. 1–2).
13. Vol'skii, *Proizvoditel'nye sily*, pp. 23–24.

essary, especially in transportation and forestry. Furthermore, they called on the government to abandon its policing functions in the economy, to confine its active intervention to certain aspects of the economic infrastructure, and, above all, to encourage and cultivate the spirit of enterprise. The initiative in setting up and running mines and manufacturing industries should be left in the hands of private enterprise, they said, and toward this end new laws should sweep away the outmoded legislation in order to regularize the formation of joint-stock companies and give individual initiative full reign.[14]

The leitmotiv of regionalism even carried Zhukovskii to recommend "rational decentralization" of the entire financial system, with an end to creating "strong local centers of social activity and economic initiative."[15] The southern entrepreneurs took pains to make a distinction between their policy of attracting foreign capital and the dangers of foreign commercial domination, warning, on the eve of the war, against the German and Japanese penetration of Russian markets beyond the frontiers and within the empire itself.[16]

In its comprehensive and integrated character alone the developmental policy of the southern entrepreneurs was superior to anything that the government or other regional groups could offer. Beyond this, they took into account the historic evolution of the Russian economy and sought to transform its peculiarities into sources of strength. But their appeal was undermined and their influence dissipated by the economic competition within their ranks and powerful political enemies at their own back door.

The Southern Entrepreneurs and the Metallurgical Cartel

Nothing illustrates more vividly the socioeconomic contradictions that crippled the southern entrepreneurial group as a potential political force in Russia than the struggle over the formation of a metallurgical cartel in 1908. Reacting to a sharp cut in state rail orders, nine major companies, of which eight were in southern Russia, endeavored to

14. I. Glivits, "Politiko-ekonomicheskie vzgliady V. V. Zhukovskogo," PT, no. 42 (22 October 1916): 306–9; Avdakov's speech to the State Council recommending the transfer of the Ural mining and metallurgical complex from state to private hands (ibid., no. 11 [1 June 1909]: 644–46).

15. Shch, "V. V. Zhukovskii o russkikh finansakh," ibid., nos. 36–37 (17 September 1916): 201.

16. The fear of encirclement was one of the few issues where the southern group and the Moscow merchants saw eye to eye. See, for example, the speeches to the State Council of Krestovnikov and Avdakov opposing a free port in the Far East (PT, no. 3 [1 February 1909]: 165–69). For a thorough survey of the problem see Joffe, "Cotton," chap. 5.

form a vertical trust to be called the Joint-Stock Company of Metallurgical Factories, Mines, and Pits. It strove to settle some of the internal rivalries between Prodamet and Produgol, on the one hand, and within Prodamet, on the other. In a short time it succeeded in pooling 82–85 percent of the pig iron industry and 90 percent of the semifinished iron products industry in the region and almost 65 percent of the pig iron industry and 50 percent of the semifinished products industry in the empire.[17]

The projected trust represented such a formidable array of productive power that it roused the frightened landowners of the south, and they rallied the Octobrist party to block its approval by the government. Within the boundaries of the Ukraine the conflict had all the earmarks of a class struggle, but as other interests were pulled in, the lines of class solidarity blurred. It soon became evident that the southern entrepreneurial group could not win over Moscow and the Urals. Support collapsed within what they considered to be their own camp. The social conflict that had been threatening for so long now seemed imminent.

The seeds of division between the southern entrepreneurs and the capitalist agrarian interests in Russia had been sown in the 1890s when the Imperial Free Economic Society began to speak out against the high tariff on agricultural machinery and pig iron and the coal famine, which they attributed to the artificial restraint of trade by the big southern producers. In the backwash of the famine of 1891 they perceived these tactics of the industrialists as a direct threat to the recovery of the peasant economy and an obstacle to the mechanization and rationalization of their own capitalist enterprises.[18] The tariff and taxation issues that had split the agrarian and industrial interests of the center also prevented a capitalist coalition in the south on the eve of the revolution of 1905. Almost immediately afterward, the conflict between the two groups grew sharper as the southern entrepreneurs refined their monopolistic control over the production of iron and steel. The formation of the metallurgical cartel in 1908 touched off a new phase in the struggle.

17. Liashchenko, *Istoriia*, 2:298–300, for the struggle between the rival French interests and Shpolianskii, *Monopolii*, pp. 100–109, for the internal struggles within Prodamet.
18. "Vsepoddanneishee khodataistvo imperatorskogo vol'nogo ekonomicheskogo obshchestva o ponizhenii tamozhennogo poshlin no kamennyi ugol', zhelez/nuiu rudu, chugun, stal', zhelezo i izdeliia iz nikh," *TIVEO* (1897), no. 6, pp. 125–27; A. A. Radtsig, "O poshlinakh na zhelezo v Rossii i posledstviiakh ego dorogovizny," ibid. (1897), no. 2, pp. 202–10; "O ponizhenii poshlin na chugun. Beseda v obshchem sobranii imperatorskogo vol'nogo ekonomicheskogo obshchestva," ibid. (1898), no. 2, pp. 65–78; A. A. Radtsig, "O kamennougol'noi promyshlennosti i merakh udeshevlenii uglia i drugogo topliva v Rossii," ibid., (1900), no. 1, pp. 50–61.

Under the energetic leadership of P. V. Kamenskii, an Octobrist deputy from Kharkov in the third duma, a well-organized antitrust campaign took shape. Turning up the dark side of American business practices, Kamenskii and his colleagues warned that trusts in Russia would raise prices, rather than cut production costs, and facilitate industrial manipulation of local government and the press. Kamenskii cleverly recruited allies both among engineers, like V. I. Arandarenko, of Kharkov Coal and Iron, whose company was outside the trust, and within the council of the Association of Ural Coal and Steel Producers, who urged expansion of the domestic market through increased production of iron utensils and tools for the peasantry instead of relying upon declining state orders and the highly competitive export market.[19]

Iasiukovich struck back fiercely, not only defending the formation of a metallurgical trust on economic grounds, but attributing to its opponents motives of social and ethnic antagonism. He denounced the Octobrist memo as "unworthy of a serious political party" and condemned what he called a tendency in Russian society "to look at economic phenomena exclusively from the point of view of the consumer, not only regarding the questions of labor and productivity with suspicion but, whenever new economic advances appear, believing willingly any cock and bull story spread by the press or in private conversations by the parasites of our economic infirmity"—a clear slap at the gentry landlords who controlled the Octobrist party. He was equally contemptuous of those who attributed the trusts to "nothing more than a 'Polish intrigue.' "[20]

But Kamenskii sought to avoid the charge of being antiindustrial and appealed instead to that form of popular industrialism which had its roots planted firmly in both the Slavophil right and the populist left. Neither the influence of the southern entrepreneurs in the Association of the Representatives of Trade and Industry nor their editorial control of its journal guaranteed them immunity from criticism on this score. Krestovnikov was quick to pick up the antiforeign line in the campaign.[21] Meanwhile, Kamenskii, together with Guchkov, rounded up signatures from 111 duma deputies on a petition to the president of the Council of Ministers, P. A. Stolypin, and obtained from him a written promise by the government to reject the application of the Joint-Stock Company of Metallurgical Factories, Mines,

19. Kamenskii, *Znachenie*, pp. 1–10, 30–38, 45.
20. (I. I. Iasiukovich), "Tresti i finansy russkikh zheleznykh predpriatii," PT, no. 8 (15-April 1908): 473–79.
21. "Minister torgovli i promyshlennosti v moskovskoi birzhy: rech' G. A. Krestovnikova," ibid., p. 489.

and Pits and to declare its opposition in principle to all industrial combinations with monopolistic tendencies.[22] This did not mean the abolition of existing monopolies or the end of attempts to form new ones. But it did set definite limits upon their scope and, consequently, upon the aspirations of the southern entrepreneurs to direct the industrial life of Russia.

A balance had been reached in the relationship between the southern entrepreneurs and the government. On the one hand, the government was willing to permit and, indeed, protect a limited monopoly by the coal and steel interests of the south. During the prewar years, the government continued to place state orders with the largest firms, maintain and extend the protective tariff on raw materials and semifinished goods, grant loans, whether guaranteed or not, block the importation of tariff-free agricultural machinery, and, finally, reduce the production of state factories in the nonmilitary area.[23] On the other hand, the government discouraged industrial combinations which it regarded as too powerful and threatened to place its orders abroad if the trusts pushed their prices too high.[24] In announcing the creation of a commission on trusts and syndicates, the Ministry of Finance made it quite clear that the government sought some way to balance the advantages of maintaining a high level of industrial technology with the disadvantages of price fixing.[25]

A continuing aim of the post-Witte industrial policy of the Ministry of Finance was to protect—in the south and in the center—a vigorous regional economy without allowing it to dominate the whole. By helping to erect and maintain defenses against domestic criticism as well as foreign competition, the government guaranteed market stability in bad times and high profits in periods of economic expansion. This created the appearance of "hothouse capitalism," which the populists and their Socialist-Revolutionary successors denounced so passionately. Whether, as they claimed, the industrial economy would have collapsed if the protective measures had been abolished is a moot point. It was, after all, an era of state protection of industry throughout Europe and America. Beyond this, it may be argued that in Russia the largest and most modern enterprises in textiles and metallurgy could have survived all but the most drastic elimination of state assistance and could continue to compete successfully for a portion of the domestic and foreign markets. In any case, the government as a whole, and not just the Ministry of Finance, was not prepared to abandon its

22. Kamenskii, *Znachenie*, appendix 1, pp. 73–75; ibid., appendix 2, pp. 75–76.
23. A good summary of this policy can be found in Gefter, "Tsarizm," pp. 94–99.
24. Shpolianskii, *Monopolii*, pp. 117–18.
25. *Torgovo-promyshlennaia gazeta*, no. 145 (26 June 1910).

industrial potential which assured Russia a place among the great powers.

At the same time, however, it was sensitive to the danger of political hegemony by the economic interests. This policy of keeping the regional economies strong but separate was maintained at a high social cost. Not only was the bulk of the laboring population impoverished, but the capitalists remained disunited and dissatisfied with bureaucratic interference in the economy; this was the price they had to pay for protection. Ironically, the government, and particularly the Ministry of Finance, failed to perceive the situation in this light. Instead, it kept up a drumfire of criticism against the southern metallurgists and the Moscow textile owners for ignoring the internal and external markets open to them. In one case it attributed their slackness to excessive reliance on state orders and in the other to merchant inertia.[26] By constantly reminding the public of the sins of the big capitalists, the government nourished the antibourgeois sentiments that had taken root in every section of Russian society.

Another important aim of the Ministry of Finance in the same period was to divert the flow of foreign capital away from direct investment in the south and into the St. Petersburg investment banks. Through its close ties with the leading banks the ministry was able to offer foreign capital the powerful inducement of participation in state credit and factory orders almost without risk. The ministry thereby obtained greater control over investment decisions and at the same time assured the Russian banks greater profits from their financial operations.[27] This policy increased the dependence of the southern entrepreneurs on state-supported financial institutions and deprived them of whatever leverage the direct foreign investment afforded them in negotiating with the ministry. Yet it also increased the government's commitment to maintain the profitability of the industry even if it meant accepting artificial limitations on the market.

In sum, the southern entrepreneurial group, like that in Moscow, had achieved a position of great economic power within its region, but it was unable to convert it into political power. The southern entrepreneurs failed to expand their narrow social base, and their

26. Ibid., nos. 146, 177, 210, and 237 (27 June, 6 August, 3, 18 September, 21 October 1910). The unwillingness of the government to do anything about the self-imposed production levels of Prodamet was dramatically revealed on the eve of the war when the Council of Ministers admitted "the inadmissability of state influence on the industry for the purpose of speeding up an accommodation to demand" (cited in Gefter, "Tsarizm," p. 126).

27. For the strengthened position of Russian banks and money market vis à vis those abroad see Gindin, *Kommercheskie banki*, pp. 195 ff.

favorable attitude toward the nationalities and their monopolistic practices proved insuperable obstacles to alliance with either the Moscow or the St. Petersburg entrepreneurs. Their newly established financial ties with the big banks could not compensate for these weaknesses, for the banking oligarchy was, if anything, more vulnerable than they were to the external shocks of war and revolution which overtook them all.

The St. Petersburg Enterpreneurs Organize

Following Bloody Sunday, St. Petersburg bore the brunt of the strikes. Throughout the industrial depression and the Russo-Japanese War pressures had been building up under the influence of two powerful, antithetical movements—the social-democratic organizations and Father Gapon's Assembly of Russian Factory Workers. Drawing upon these conflicting sources, the workers made demands that could only be met by political as well as economic changes.

This involved the owners and the government in a controversy over who should be the first to make concessions. The St. Petersburg Society for the Assistance, Improvement, and Development of Factory Industry, which had recently changed its name to the St. Petersburg Society of Factory and Mill Owners to emphasize its real character, promptly denounced the workers' demands as "unrealizable" and "nonsensical." The director of the Putilov Works announced that Russian workers lived no less well than English workers.[28] The government's reaction was different, even though the state factories were as hard hit as private industry. Witte's distraught successor, Kokovstov, expressed the government's willingness to draft new labor legislation, pleaded for more time, and appealed to the private entrepreneurs to make immediate concessions.

When the owners continued adamant in their refusal, Kokovstov reproached them for "not wishing to understand the needs and interests of the workers."[29] Stung into action, the St. Petersburg industrialists publicly defended themselves, immediately setting themselves apart from the entrepreneurs of the center and south. They ignored the questions of civil and political rights, which were on everyone else's lips, and even skirted the issue of bureaucratic interference in the life of the factory, which occupied such a prominent place in the public petitions of other interest groups. In their view the disorders

28. Petrov, *Progressivnaia partiia*, pp. 19–20.
29. TsGIA, f. 150, op. 1, d. 484, p. 5.

stemmed far more from the conditions of backwardness prevailing in Russian industry, particularly the low cultural level of the workers. The labor question, they warned, could not be resolved in isolation from the general crisis without increasing the workers' demands. They concluded that immediate and partial concessions such as those suggested by the minister of finance could not restore calm and order.[30]

While other groups came out flatly for the rights of workers to organize in unions and to strike, the St. Petersburg society was evasive. Ignoring the issue of unions, the owners ingenuously proposed to have the issue of improved working conditions taken up by existing public organizations, such as the town dumas or zemstvos, "in order not to isolate the workers artificially." The repetitious euphemism "isolating the worker" meant, of course, allowing the formation of autonomous labor unions. As if this were not clear enough, the society insisted that the purpose of organizing the workers should be to avoid increasing the causes of conflict between workers and employers, an interpretation which scarcely favored a class-based organization.

What the members of the society had in mind, then, was allowing the workers to participate in administering mutual insurance societies, with the state assuming the burden of financial support. This measure, they hastened to add, "should not be confused with participation in the administration of the factory which was absolutely forbidden under any conditions." Beyond this, they recognized, "in principle," the right of the workers to meet and submit collective declarations, "but in view of the low level of industrial development of the workers, [at present] this can hardly be considered opportune." They also hedged the right to strike with similar restrictions. Their general attitude toward the workers found its most complete expression in their dire prediction that "once the right to organize is granted in any form whatsoever, there is no way to limit the full development of such an organization to its logical end—general unification within the country and organic links with the international organization of workers."[31]

In reviewing the major obstacles to improving the workers' conditions, the society enumerated four points, three of which touched upon the cultural and social impoverishment of the workers themselves: their low level of literacy, their immaturity and ignorance, and their ties to the countryside (which, on the other hand, made them somehow "superior" to the proletariat of Western countries). Faintly discernible behind this muddle of self-interested ideas is the notion

30. Ibid. The memo dated 31 January 1905 was published in *Pravo*, no. 6 (13 February 1905): cols. 840–44, and signed by almost one hundred representatives of the largest enterprises in the city.
31. TsGIA, f. 150, op. 1, d. 484, p. 3.

that Russia was still in the early stages of industrialization, whereas the workers were demanding rights that could only be earned by long years of apprenticeship to the industrialized world.

Opposed to any concession that could lead to what it repeatedly called "limitless new demands," the St. Petersburg society thrust upon the government full responsibility for improving the state of the economy, without making it clear just how this was to be done. Thus, while the rest of the country claimed that the problem was political and not economic, the St. Petersburg entrepreneurs argued that the problem was indeed economic, but had nothing to do with them as individual capitalists. For all their international ties, their sophisticated business techniques, and their technological awareness, their social attitudes were more benighted than the Moscow merchant-entrepreneurs they affected to despise. Or, to put it another way, their entire outlook reflected the mentality of the European industrialist in the colonies.[32]

Despite the government's promise to summon a consultative duma, the St. Petersburg entrepreneurs remained hypnotized by the strike movement. When they finally reached out for support to industrialists in the rest of the country, they found none. At the first conference of representatives of industry of various regions, which met in Moscow in March 1905, the St. Petersburg society pressed hard for acceptance of a comprehensive strike program as the main business of the organization. But delegates from the Kingdom of Poland and the south refused to go along. The badly divided Moscow delegation took no firm stand; they displayed greater interest in defining a political position on the composition of the Bulygin duma. On this issue too, as we have seen, agreement was elusive, and only a weak compromise enabled representatives from the conference to petition the government to guarantee a place for industrialists in the consultative duma. Hoping for something different, the St. Petersburg delegates met separately to sign a convention that vigorously denounced the strike movement and categorically refused to make any concessions to the workers.[33] Once back in St. Petersburg, they obtained additional signatures to the convention from sixty-seven factories, but their exclusive reliance on local support signified their isolation from the rest of the country and guaranteed their failure.

The government supplied them with the best opportunity to extricate themselves when it summoned representatives of trade and industry to participate in the deliberations of the Kokovtsov Commis-

32. I owe this felicitous analogy to Leopold Haimson.
33. Sef, *Burzhuaziia*, pp. 17–19, 26–31; Chermenskii, *Burzhuaziia*, pp. 71–74; Laverychev, *Tsarizm*, pp. 183–84.

sion. Under pressure from the strike movement, officials of the Ministry of Finance drafted four legislative projects limiting the working day to ten hours, abolishing the punitive articles of the criminal code on strikes and termination of contracts, providing medical assistance for workers at the expense of the owners, and introducing comprehensive workers' insurance, with the cost to be shared equally by workers and owners.

The hasty and radical nature of some of the provisions must have frightened all the industrialists, but only the St. Petersburg society took it upon themselves to subject each and every draft law to a systematic and shattering attack. They denounced the entire package of legislation as more extreme than anything in the advanced industrial countries of the West. But the other representatives joined with them only to endorse the society's proposal to transfer industrial contracts from the criminal to the civil code.[34] Beyond this, the most the industrialists could all agree upon was that the government was, as usual, going about things the wrong way.

Krestovnikov's clever ploy to adjourn the commission nicely sidestepped the issues that divided them, and their final joint statement captured the same spirit. In it the St. Petersburg entrepreneurs acknowledged, however reluctantly, that the word *union* was disarmed in this statement: "First and foremost it is necessary to raise the question of the freedom of unions in connection with the general question for all Russia of the inviolability of the individual and the home."[35] It was scarcely a call to arms for civil rights. Unsupported by solidarity against the workers, this opposition to the government's pressure failed to last much beyond the early meetings of the ill-fated July Bureau.

The slim prospects for interregional cooperation among the industrialists dissipated in the late summer as the full implications of the July Bureau's work became clear to the St. Petersburg society. It came as something of a shock, for example, when the Ministry of Finance strongly reprimanded them for having sponsored the two irregular (and possibly illegal) ad hoc meetings of industrialists. Giving proof of its political subservience, the society quickly responded that the delegates to the Moscow conference attended as individuals and did not

---

34. Romanov, *Rabochii vopros*, pp. 52–62, for the memorandum of 12 May which spells out in general terms the society's position; ibid., pp. 72–92, 99–109, 174–93, for separate memoranda and alternative draft laws of the society on the length of the work day, medical assistance, and strikes, respectively; and ibid., pp. 232–35, for the conclusions of a private session of the representatives of industry on the punitive articles.
35. Ibid., p. 63.

represent the society, even though they were recognized as such in the official protocols.

This was the prelude to a gradual disengagement from the planning activities of the July Bureau. Under the firm leadership of M. P. Tripolitov, who had not attended the Moscow congress, although he had been elected to it in absentia, and did not approve of the July Bureau, the society expressed its growing misgivings over the prospects of cooperating with alien social and ethnic groups. Reports that the union of towns and zemstvos was reconsidering its snub of the industrialists and might be willing to form an electoral bloc were discounted by members of the society, who underscored the irreconcilable differences between them on economic policy. As for the nationalities, there was no question of the society's accepting religious toleration for the Jews or political autonomy for other ethnic groups on the borderlands. Wary of any concessions to labor, the council of the St. Petersburg society opposed including any mention of a guarantee for worker representation in the duma in the body of its own electoral statement, agreeing only to mention such a possibility in the preface. This would refute newspaper reports that the society was hostile to the idea, the council reasoned, without requiring a flat public denial.[36] Thus the society matched caution with hypocrisy.

As labor disturbances reached a new peak in the October general strike, the Permanent Advisory Office made one last attempt to check the disintegrating united front of industry and dissuade the St. Petersburg society from forming its own political splinter group. At a dramatic meeting held on the very day of the October Manifesto, the society heard members of the July Bureau, Vol'skii, Zhukovskii, and Kavos, warn them that internal disunity among industrialists and isolation from the mass of voters could only lead to disaster. Kavos and Vol'skii urged an alliance with all urban-industrial elements including not only engineers and clerical help but workers as well. Claiming that the interests of the workers and owners were drawing closer, Vol'skii pointed to the negotiated settlement of the Baku crisis as proof that the class struggle could be peacefully resolved. Just as unacceptable for the St. Petersburg society was Vol'skii's final rebuke that "the indivisibility of Russia and the failure of the [society's] electoral program to mention the right of the use of local languages constituted the weak side of the program." Zhukovskii seconded him "from the point of view of the Kingdom of Poland," adding that the industrialists of the kingdom could not unite with the party of the St. Petersburg industri-

36. TsGIA, f. 150, op. 1, d. 50, pp. 134–35.

alists, "since there the alignments are completely different based on another kind of guiding principle."[37]

The reaction of the St. Petersburg society was swift and decisive. Its electoral bureau refused to invite any representatives of either the July Bureau or the Permanent Advisory Office—"Messrs Vol'skii, Kavos, and Zhukovskii in particular"—to a conference of commercial and industrial representatives to discuss plans for political action in the new circumstances created by the October Manifesto.[38] Moreover, the society made final preparations for the formation of its own political party, despite the formidable obstacles posed by the introduction of universal manhood suffrage by the October Manifesto.

Members of the society were aware of the serious difficulties of electing any of their own people to a consultative duma. But they counted on the appeal of a vaguely worded program and "the conservative elements of the merchantry and home owners in Petersburg." Tripolitov also believed that the electors would "sooner vote for men of experience and reason than for *belletristy* [fiction writers]."[39] But not to have perceived that the October Manifesto had radically transformed the situation testified to their utter lack of political realism. In fact, the council of the society was incapable of reacting at all to the Manifesto. One faction, including Tripolitov, Efron, and Beliaev, was willing at least to endorse the Manifesto, but others demanded a set of repressive measures, in addition. By a vote of seven to six the council decided to refrain from taking any public stand at all, a further sign of the society's own internal divisions. It was also an ironic, if unintentional, comment on Witte's advice; barely a week earlier he had urged the industrialists to take every possible measure to assure the election of strong supporters of industry to the duma because "it was impossible to count on such a defense from the side of the government."[40]

As the society wrestled with the problem of its own uncertain identity, it found no easier the task of winning adherents from the wider community of St. Petersburg merchants and industrialists. Addressing a select audience at a political rally, Tripolitov attempted to frighten the property owners with demogogic invocations of class war and claims that the workers' movement was "inseparably linked to socialism, . . . the natural enemy of the fundamental values of modern civi-

37. Ibid., f. 150, op. 1, d. 266, pp. 98–99. A handwritten marginal comment at this point reads, "only full autonomy—that is the slogan of all Poland." Whether or not these were Zhukovskii's exact words, omitted from the official record for political reasons and later restored, they represented his real sentiments on the matter.
38. Ibid., p. 109.
39. Ibid., f. 150, op. 1, d. 50, p. 133.
40. Ibid., pp. 142–43.

lization." He exaggerated the high level of workers' organization to the point where he spoke of push-button strikes. In contrast, he deplored the weak forces of trade and industry, "scattered like raindrops." Rejecting out of hand both the Social Democrats and the Kadets, he also ridiculed as "naive" those who dreamed of restoring the old patriarchal relations with the worker. Yet his declaration that trade and industry should have its own party rang hollow, if only because he had done his share in making that impossible. His call for the creation of a political club to support the party came as a depressing anticlimax.

Among those whom Tripolitov failed to convince were a number of influential spokesmen for different segments of the commercial and industrial community. A. A. Auerbakh, from the south, and M. M. Fedorov, the St. Petersburg editor of the semiofficial *Torgovo-promyshlennaia gazeta*, dismissed the chances of launching a separate party based on the defense of narrow economic interests. Most of Tripolitov's audience favored alignment with one of the moderate parties, either the Octobrists or the Kadets. Even his own colleagues in the society wavered. Brofman predicted a "cruel fiasco." N. N. Klimenko concurred, admitting that it was futile to identify a party as capitalistic when the majority of people were not. But Tripolitov brushed aside Auerbakh and Fedorov as "outsiders" and scoffed at his colleagues' notions of making peace with the workers.[41] He was determined to preserve the separate political identity of the society, even if it meant "a cruel fiasco" in the election. The Progressive Economic party was to be the political arm of the St. Petersburg society.

An air of unreality surrounded the party's preparations for the duma elections. It took all the correct measures: creating a formal party apparatus, drafting a platform, and publishing a daily. But the apparatus was manned by the same people who served on the council of the society. The press organ was shut down by its own sponsors, who found it too radical. The membership rolls of the party were largely filled by the technical and clerical personnel who were employed in the large factories and brought under pressure to sign up.[42]

The platform was, at best, vague and, at worst, downright misleading. It was designed by and for members of the society, but clumsily disguised to imply otherwise. In tone and emphasis it revealed substantial differences with the Moscow Moderate Progressives on its left and, to a lesser degree, with the Octobrists on its right. Its endorse-

41. Ibid., f. 150, op. 1, d. 266, pp. 169–74, 190–99, 222–31.
42. Sef, *Burzhuaziia*, pp. 89–90; Reikhardt, "Partinnye gruppirovki," pp. 24–25; Chermenskii, *Burzhuaziia*, p. 189.

ment of "Russia, united and indivisible" was not tempered by any concession to autonomous local government; its statement of civil rights was brief, almost perfunctory. Its agricultural plank placed greater emphasis on diminishing the commune than on transferring land to the peasants. Less space was devoted to advancing workers' rights than to condemning factory inspection. The main thrust of its economic policy was to eliminate government competition with private industry in almost every field, including military supplies. At the same time it demanded protective tariffs and state development of the economic infrastructure.[43] As critics on the left pointed out, its advocacy of civil and political rights was virtually vitiated by the party's warning that "it did not foresee an early realization of the hopes expressed" in the platform.[44] The document reeked of deceit.

The party's newspaper, *Novyi put'* (later renamed *Perelom*), marched to the same discordant tune. The society had no trouble raising funds —the Russo-American Company set the pace by offering fifteen thousand rubles—and made plans for a circulation of sixty thousand. Although the council of the society favored an independent paper, the leader of the Octobrists and mayor of the city, M. V. Krasovskii, persuaded it to form a joint editorial committee of five members from the society and three Octobrists, Krasovskii himself as the editor, A. A. Stolypin, and Tarasov.[45] Sixty-eight firms purchased shares in the enterprise.

The collaboration proved unsuccessful. Octobrists like Krasovskii were always willing to concede something to the workers, for they had no direct interest in the factories. They stood firm against changes in the countryside. After the terrifying December uprising in Moscow, disgruntled shareholders in the new venture, like Efron, declared that "to be further to the left in order to calm the workers is not the way; in the future we will publish for the good of the workers and ourselves."

On the very eve of the elections it was decided to change the name and the character of the paper. The search for a reputable editor "inspired by the proper spirit" led them to N. A. Demchinskii, a

43. *Polnyi sbornik*, pp. 83–86. The principal differences between the Progressive Economic party and the Octobrists lay in the area of labor and economic policy. The Octobrists favored regulating relations with the workers at the local level and placing more emphasis on state aid in developing agriculture, forestry, mineral deposits, and railroads (ibid., pp. 100–102). The interests being served here were clearly those of the capitalist landowner and the merchant engaged in trade or small-scale manufacturing employing peasants and artisans rather than a skilled industrial labor force.

44. Petrov, *Progressivnaia partiia*, p. 2.

45. TsGIA, f. 150, op. 1, d. 50, pp. 152, 158–59, 161.

talented but utterly unscrupulous opportunist, constantly in debt, who had tried his hand as an engineer, lawyer, weather forecaster, and journalist for half a dozen papers of the right, left, and center. Under his erratic direction *Perelom*'s circulation never went above thirteen thousand, and its policies failed to satisfy the industrialists, who finally liquidated the whole venture.[46] Predictably, the St. Petersburg entrepreneurs were no more able than those in Moscow or the south to present their case to the public in general political terms that might have an appeal beyond their own narrow professional interests.

Even before the duma elections their sporadic attempts to form electoral coalitions left unresolved problems, and internal weaknesses encouraged defections from its ranks. As early as November 1905, Tripolitov agreed to join a bloc of constitutional-monarchist parties which shared the principles of resolving the social question by evolutionary means and opposing a constituent assembly. But almost at once disputes broke out. The Progressive Economic party accused one of its partners in the coalition, the Party of Rightful Order, of dispatching their agents to factories, where "[they] did not employ political ideas but, wishing to acquire influence over the working masses, resorted to blackmail," presented ultimatums to factory owners, and threatened them with strikes.[47] Right-wing professionals and nobles were not above playing a demogogic role in inciting workers against factory owners in order to improve their own electoral chances.

In the meantime, the Petersburg merchants refused to acknowledge the political leadership of the Petersburg entrepreneurs and announced the formation of the All-Russian Commercial and Industrial Union, which was not all-Russian and scarcely industrial. Its leader, the timber king Beliaev, was, it is true, an active member of the council of the St. Petersburg society, but when forced to choose, he sided with the merchants, where he really belonged. The Commercial and Industrial Union routinely endorsed the October Manifesto and the "united and indivisible empire." It struck a more original tone by expressing a vague and sentimental belief in "the economic friendship of the commercial industrial classes [sic] and their employees." This was a clear bid to distinguish themselves from the social relations that prevailed in the factories: in short, to deny the existence of a class struggle between the big merchants and their clerks and shop assistants. But what set them off most distinctly from the Progressive Economic party was their insistence on "the struggle against all forms

46. Sef, *Burzhuaziia*, pp. 90–91; Reikhardt, "Partinnye gruppirovki," p. 26; Witte, *Vospominaniia*, 1:147–52, 526.
47. TsGIA, f. 150, op.1, d. 50, p. 163.

of illegitimate trade." This oblique remonstrance against monopolies took concrete form in the first and only issue of the union's party organ, which launched a quasi-populist polemic against the state supported sugar norms, the oil syndicate, and credit privileges extended exclusively to landowners by the Nobles Bank.[48]

The St. Petersburg entrepreneurs had even less success in rallying the technical and professional intelligentsia to their cause. If the merchants rejected their prescribed class role on patriarchal grounds, the technical and professional intelligentsia rejected it on radical-democratic grounds. Of all the social fractures in 1905, the break between the technical intelligentsia and the factory owners was the most surprising. It disrupted a long and fruitful relationship which had grown up within the Russian Technological Society. Even after the owners formed a separate organization in 1897, the St. Petersburg Society for the Assistance, Improvement, and Development of Factory Industry, they continued to attend meetings of the society, and Tripolitov even became editor of its official organ. Unlike the Moscow entrepreneurs, who struggled to find a common forum with the intelligentsia of their city, the St. Petersburg entrepreneurs had one ready-made. But behind the facade of a common interest in industrialization, differences had cropped up over fundamental political and social issues. It required only a crisis of the magnitude of 1905 to provoke an open rift and drive the technical intelligentsia to the left.

As early as 5 December 1904 a meeting of several hundred technical specialists in St. Petersburg laid the groundwork for the Union of Engineers and Technicians, which soon became one of the most vigorous and outspoken advocates of reform in the Union of Unions. Under the presidency of the distinguished professor of mechanics at the St. Petersburg Technological Institute, V. I. Kirpichev, the assembly proclaimed as its guiding principle the indissoluble connection between personal liberty, technological proficiency, and economic development. Its bold program of extensive civil and political rights, including a plank on popular control over the budget, set it on a collision course with the St. Petersburg society. Describing itself as "standing between the working masses, capital, and the government," the union defined its main task as judging "the social action of the leaders of industry." In concrete terms it censored those engineers who consorted with the industrialists by compiling a list of "'unreliable' workers." Their frontal assault on the main defenses of the industrialists spread from the liberal electro-technical section throughout the entire Russian Technological Society.

48. *Polnyi sbornik*, pp. 91–92; *Vestnik vserossiiskogo torgovopromyshlennogo soiuza* (1905), no. 1, p. 9.

In a public declaration the society associated itself with the aims of the union and called for a resolution of the labor problem by a congress of workers and employers meeting under a guarantee of free speech. Following Bloody Sunday a proposal to create a special commission of the society to pursue this goal won quick approval "among outstanding Russian economists, jurists, physicians, and leaders in technical education." Meanwhile, the union criticized the efforts of government and industry to break up workers' solidarity by treating the strikers in every factory as a separate case. They regarded the Shidlovskii Commission, appointed by the tsar to investigate workers' discontent, as a bureaucratic nightmare, and when its worker representatives were arrested, they issued "a sharp protest." As the disorders mounted in the spring, the engineers reaffirmed their close ties to the workers and organized collections and canteens for the unemployed and their families.[49]

Declarations of solidarity with the St. Petersburg engineers rapidly poured in from other regions. The response was very strong in the southwestern region from the former colleagues and students of Kirpichev, who had been director of both the Kharkov and Kiev polytechnical institutes before he returned in 1903 to St. Petersburg. But this was not the work of one man or a small group, for the movement spread throughout the whole western part of the empire. Although in the southwest the political tenor was the same, the emphasis there was on the need for "a rational solution of many questions which are supremely important for the successful development of engineering activities in other areas of governmental life."[50] By this was meant the regulation of a broad range of public services at the local level. The first signs can be detected here of a technocratic movement among Russian engineers which, over the following decade, gained momentum and emerged full-blown in the crisis of world war.

As part of their "rational solution" to the country's social problems, the engineers adopted a more radical position on the nationalities question than had any of the so-called bourgeois parties, including the Kadets. At the first all-Russian congress of engineers, meeting in the capital, the Russian delegation recognized the right of every nation in the empire to self-determination and unanimously endorsed the demands of their Polish and Lithuanian colleagues for full regional autonomy, including the establishment of a legislative *sejm* in

49. *Pravo*, no. 11 (20 March 1905): cols. 833–40; ibid., no. 14 (10 April 1905): col. 1112. By this time the St. Petersburg bureau of the union counted 687 members.
50. Ibid., no. 11 (20 March 1905): cols. 841–44.

Warsaw. In their labor platform, also adopted at the congress, they proposed a progressive reduction in the work day to eight hours, a full thirty-six-hour weekend, unemployment insurance funded by employees and employers, and a host of restrictions on child labor, woman labor, and night work. In addition, they favored establishing conciliation boards with equal representation from workers and employers and extending the protection of labor legislation to all forms of hired work. Denouncing the police control over industry, they advocated workers' committees as an integral part of the factory management.[51] While falling short of being a socialist document, the platform had all the earmarks of an "antibourgeois" manifesto. The breadth and depth of its opposition to the existing conditions belies the sociological stereotype of the supine engineer, apolitical and narrowly professional in outlook.

A full explanation of this extraordinary outburst of civic responsibility and ethical concerns would require a separate treatment of the rise of the engineering profession in Russia. To be sure, the revolutionary conditions of 1905 drove most social groups to the left. For the engineers, however, sympathy with the workers had a longer tradition. From the beginning, technical education in Russia showed strong ethical and social concerns.[52] By the 1860s and 1870s the professional engineering schools were hotbeds of political radicalism.[53] Even in the relatively quiet years of the 1880s the schools were not immune to the penetration of democratic and socialist ideas, the rise of student organizations, and the outbreak of serious demonstrations, all of which intensified in the 1890s.[54] Throughout the period, the Russian Technological Society served as a forum for the debate over the broader nature of technical education and provided a meeting place for engineers and other members of the liberal professions interested in the issue. Thus, leading engineers were exposed to a rich fare of social issues even before a purely professional organization of their own had been created.

51. Ibid., no. 17 (1 May 1905): cols. 1394–95; ibid., no. 20 (22 May 1905): cols. 1670–71. The congress comprised the St. Petersburg bureau, seventy-one delegates from provincial organizations, and twenty-two from the Kingdom of Poland, representing all together three thousand engineers. This figure probably amounted to one-third of the total engineers in the empire.

52. For some preliminary assessments of the influence of St. Simonian views see Rieber, "Formation," pp. 377–78.

53. ORBL, f. 69, carton 43, no. 23, I. A. Vyshnegradskii, "O preobrazovanii vyshikh uchebnykh zavedenii—zapiska o sviazi so studenticheskimi volneniami, marta 1879," pp. 1–3; Evnevich, *Kratkii ocherk o tekhnologicheskom institute*, pp. 102–8.

54. Leikina-Svirskaia, *Intelligentsia*, pp. 282 ff.

For all the importance of this intellectual preparation, however, the conditions at the work place appeared to be decisive in determining the social attitudes of the engineers.[55] The graduates of the higher technical schools sometimes found themselves sharing with the workers a strong resentment against the dominant place occupied by foreigners among the supervisory personnel in the large factories.[56] Beyond this, and even more important, a crucial distinction evolved between those engineers who became managers and directors in metallurgical and mining enterprises, especially in the south, as we have seen, and those who either entered the academic world, like Kirpichev, or those who remained factory specialists, like M. A. Pavlov. A close identification with the interests of the owners converted engineer-managers into defenders of the existing order. Opposition among academic engineers was linked to their theoretical analysis of the role of technical education and specialists in economic development which they regarded as insufficient. At the opposite extreme, in the most practical experience at the plant level, the engineers were exposed to the harsh Russian factory order. As their public statements in 1905 make clear, their sympathy with the workers was reinforced by their resentment over the authoritarian, as opposed to the rational-efficient, management of the factory and the arbitrary interference of the police. Once again, the peculiar configurations of social evolution in Russia precluded the identification of interests between engineers and industrialists which became a predictable feature of Western capitalist societies.

The attitude of the legal profession toward the industrialists was less clear-cut, but lawyers also deviated from the accepted norm and displayed little enthusiasm for a rigid defense of the absolute property rights of the factory owners. *Pravo*, the semiofficial voice of the legal profession in St. Petersburg and a leading organ of the Kadet party, took the industrialists to task for their attempt to emasculate the right to strike by imposing upon workers the responsibility for all damages, loss of production, and deterioration or breakage of machinery incurred during work stoppages. The very notion of a calm and pacific strike was a contradiction in terms, wrote O. Buzhanskii, for "such is the aim of the strike—to break up the normal order." That strikes could be used by employers as an excuse to break contracts was a view for which he found no precedent in the West European legal systems that normally served as the touchstone for the

55. See, for example, Tits, *Ocherk*.
56. Pavlov, *Vospominaniia*, pp. 70, 283.

social attitudes of the Russian industrialist. Buzhanskii also rejected the idea of company unions for the simple reason that the dependence of workers on owners was already too great.[57]

It is difficult to estimate how widely shared these opinions were among jurists. But there is a tantalizing passage in the memoirs of the well-known Petersburg lawyer and leader of the right wing of the Kadets V. A. Maklakov that recalls that in the summer of 1905 the Union of Lawyers called for a debate within the organization on the nature of "the capitalist structure" and, in the same breath, brandished Proudhon's watchword, "Property is Theft."[58] Out of this milieu came the legal defenders of the striking workers in the spectacular labor trials of the following decade. Taken altogether, the antibourgeois attitudes among members of the legal profession and the technical intelligentsia completed the social and political isolation of the St. Petersburg entrepreneurs and dashed their electoral hopes.

In the elections for the first duma candidates of the Progressive Economic party and other members of the squabbling Rightist bloc were swamped by the Kadets by a margin of more than two to one within St. Petersburg. Only 6 of the 147 electors chosen by popular vote in the city represented the commercial and industrial milieu, a grim reminder, if any was needed, that the merchants and industrialists carried little appeal outside their own ranks. The Progressive Economic party limped on for another year but did not field any candidates in the elections to the second duma. Most of its leading members drifted in and out of the Octobrist party, but only Klimenko rose to prominence there. After complaining that the revised electoral law of 1907 guaranteed the worker at least six seats in the duma but none at all for the industrialists, the party expired.[59] When Tripolitov was finally elected to the State Council as a representative of trade and industry, he expressed his complete disillusionment with party politics by running as an independent. The St. Petersburg society as a whole retreated from politics. Yet even in the role of an employer's association pure and simple, the society displayed a remarkable incapacity for unified action and a benighted attitude toward labor reform.

On May Day 1912, the large-scale workers' demonstration which

---

57. *Pravo*, no. 37 (18 September 1905): cols. 3024–25. Provincial legal organizations like the Kazan Juridical Society had passed resolutions insisting the reform of labor legislation be carried out "in the interests of the laboring classes" (ibid., no. 19 (14 May 1905): col. 1593).

58. Maklakov, *Iz vospominaniia*, pp. 324–25. Among this group were the left-wing Kadets M. Mandelshtam and M. S. Margulies, the Polish Social Democrat M. Iu. Kozlovskii, and the Bolshevik V. P. Antonov-Saratovskii.

59. Reikhardt, "Partinnye gruppirovki," pp. 32–34.

signaled a new militant phase in the labor movement, threw the St. Petersburg entrepreneurs into disarray. They split into three factions over how to deal with the workers: some advocated severe penalties for demonstrators, including a lockout; others favored fines and dismissal of social democratic workers; and a third group was reluctant to take any repressive measure. The Ministry of Trade and Industry, under S. I. Timashev and his deputy, V. P. Litvinov-Falinskii, head of the industry section, advised a group of owners led by Tripolitov not to fine the workers, for fear of touching off widespread disorders, but even under government pressure the society could not agree. Despite an advisory vote that took a hard line, three-quarters of the member enterprises did not fine their workers. Infuriated by the society's public stance, Timashev refused to consider its request for assistance in ending a new wave of strikes touched off by the attempt of some plants to levy fines, and he blamed the industrialists for the impasse.[60] In a final attempt to impose discipline upon its members, the society adopted a twelve-point antistrike convention which laid down strict rules for a common policy against striking workers and provided for fines and legal action in the event of noncompliance.[61] But this was all in vain: the agreement remained a dead letter. The society as a whole never again imposed a fine system for May Day.[62]

In the meantime the society conducted a running battle with Timashev over his campaign to get a comprehensive workers' medical insurance program—promised since 1907—passed into law. In the State Council, Tripolitov led the attack against the plan to have the factory owners shoulder a good portion of the contribution and complained that the legislation was being forced down their throats by bureaucratic pressure.[63] In the important field of labor legislation, then, there is little evidence to suggest, as Soviet historians have done, that the government was either "subordinated" to heavy industry or "combined" with it in an equal partnership to manage the industrial life of the country.

60. Dmitriev, "Pervoe maia," pp. 70–73.

61. *Rabochee dvizhenie v Petrograde*, pp. 58–60, for the texts of convention and guarantees.

62. Dmitriev, "Pervoe maia," pp. 74–77.

63. Gosudarstvennyi sovet, *Stenograficheskii otchet*, session 7, sitting 53 (18 April 1912), cols. 3406–14; ibid., sitting 55 (21 April 1912), cols. 3525–38. These speeches give a revealing picture of Tripolitov's views of the workers. Running like a guiding thread throughout them is a profound contempt for the absence of labor discipline among Russian workers and the fear that the hospital benefits of four months would be exploited by the workers limitlessly (ibid., sitting 55, col. 3537). In this case he was strongly supported by Krestovnikov. The owners ended up being assessed 40 percent and the workers 60 percent of costs (*PSZRI*, 3rd ser., 23 June 1912, no. 37446).

The narrow and inflexible view of the St. Petersburg society not only certified the political bankruptcy of the St. Petersburg entrepreneurs but also irreparably damaged the chances for genuine social and economic integration of the major representative organizations of the merchants, on the one hand, and the industrialists, on the other. The St. Petersburg entrepreneurs bear much of the responsibility for restoring to life in a new institutional setting the traditional separation of Russian economic life into discrete commercial and industrial sectors. By their arrogant behavior, Tripolitov and his friends confirmed the long-standing suspicions of the Petersburg merchants that organizational unity within the capitalist world could only be achieved at the expense of subordinating merchant to industrial interests. It was not surprising, then, that in the revolution the St. Petersburg Exchange joined and often led the opposition that undercut efforts to form a single commercial and industrial organization.

Entrepreneurs Versus Merchants

The revolutionary period witnessed two major attempts to establish a unified class organization for trade and industry, one launched by the government and the other by heavy industrialists in the advisory office. In both cases merchants of the St. Petersburg Exchange played the spoiler's role. The long resistance of the Ministry of Finance to any form of an all-Russian organization began to crumble in 1903 when the economic crisis demonstrated to Witte the advantages of letting a single authoritative voice speak for the commercial and industrial interests. His first step was to seek agreement among the existing exchange committees to broaden their competence in order to include heavy industry, to open their membership to small traders, and to clarify their relations with the town dumas. Encouraged by the response of the merchants, the ministry began to draft legislation for new elective institutions for the "trade and industry class," but soon discovered that despite its pressures for reform, neither the exchange committees nor the merchant societies "fully represented the interests of [that] class."[64] In the midst of the revolution, therefore, it proposed another solution: chambers of commerce based upon the German model with the participation and supervision of ministerial bureaucrats. The advantage of building such a completely new organization was that trade and industry would enter as equal partners. But the plan inevitably meant a substantial reduction in the importance of the

64. *Golos Moskvy*, no. 205 (4 September 1908).

exchange committees and an increase in the centralizing role of the bureaucracy.

Predictably, the response was not enthusiastic. Only a few exchanges on the periphery, like Libau, Reval, and Odessa, responded favorably, reasoning, no doubt, that as the dominant organizations in those regions they could easily transfer their control to the chambers of commerce. The great majority of exchanges opposed the idea. Some, like St. Petersburg, Riga, and Samara, dismissed the proposals as too theoretical, bureaucratic, and harmful to the wholesale trade. Clearly, the fear here was that industry would quickly dominate the chambers. Others, like Kherson and Astrakhan, suggested that the same ends could be achieved through existing organizations, that is, the exchange committees.[65] The ministry persisted, submitting fresh drafts in 1907 and 1909, but it then ran into the stubborn opposition of the Moscow Exchange Committee, which raised a host of formal objections which masked its own concern over the impending dilution of its influence in the new organs. No sooner did the ministry meet the demands of one committee than it antagonized another.[66] Unable to win the approval of the exchanges, the government shelved the project, where it remained when the war broke out.

The merchants also resisted the blandishments of the industrialists to draw them into a unified and autonomous association of trade and industry. As we have seen, the heavy industrialists grouped in the advisory bureau and led by Norpe and Vol'skii strove to salvage something from the wreckage of 1905 by forming a nonpolitical union of trade and industry. But the merchants from the St. Petersburg Exchange boycotted the founding congress of the Association of the Representatives of Trade and Industry, where the industrialists had the upper hand. Once they made their stand public, merchant exchanges all over Russia—except for Moscow—immediately rallied behind them. Together, they organized their own congress to form the rival all-Russian Association of the Representatives of Commercial and Agricultural Exchanges, where the merchants predominated.

While the merchants were able to maintain their traditional forms of regional organization in the face of pressures from state and industry, they were unable to translate them to the national level. To be

65. Ibid., no. 207 (6 September 1908). Kherson also feared the effect of locating the southern regional chamber in Odessa, which was its traditional commercial rival.
66. *Trudy 4-ogo ocherednogo s'ezda predstavitelei promyshlennosti i torgovli*, pp. 5–10. For example, von Ditmar, representing the Southern Coal and Steel Producers, favored obligatory membership in the chambers and payment of contributions on the model of his own organization as the only guarantee of effectiveness. But it was this very obligatory character that most exchanges, including Moscow, most feared.

sure, the Association of the Representatives of Commercial and Agricultural Exchanges, like the entrepreneurial organizations, perceived as its main function the defense of its members' immediate economic interests. But the almost exclusively merchant character of the eighty participating exchange committees guaranteed that its activities would skirt the major social and economic problems of the time. A representative selection of topics drawn from the third congress in 1908 reveals a narrow, if natural, preoccupation with government assistance in facilitating the wholesale trade, particularly in grain, timber, and cattle.[67] But despite the annual congresses and the flood of resolutions, the association lacked a mass base. The traditional problem of inertia among the merchantry came to the surface again.

A survey of the exchanges conducted by the editors of *Golos Moskvy* turned up a widespread pattern of apathy and ineffectiveness. The records of the Omsk Exchange Committee lamented that although it frequently called meetings to discuss questions of direct interest to the merchants, such as labor legislation and freight rates on railroads, "unfortunately all of these sessions were poorly attended." More surprisingly, in Kherson "the exchange as a major factor in our organization de facto does not exist." In the course of one year not a single commercial transaction was registered in the exchange, and although the merchants promptly paid their dues, they conducted their business elsewhere. Expressing a deep sense of frustration, the Omsk Exchange Committee concluded that "this would not have been tolerated in the time of Peter the Great." But when "self-help and professional organization" were on everyone's tongue and "with the present cultural level of our merchantry, such a phenomenon is utterly incomprehensible." Regrettably, the editors concluded that the desire for unity among the trade and industry class had not penetrated deeply and is "confined to a small group of the most enlightened and energetic representatives of the Russian merchantry."[68] Thus, instead of responding to the revolutionary dangers as might have been expected by forging the all-class unity that had eluded them for so long, the merchants and entrepreneurs raised new barriers to cooperation between them. Many merchants avoided taking any national responsibilities, effectively retreating into their shells to await the next storm.

It was doubly ironic that the split between the merchants and entrepreneurs occurred when and how it did. First, no sooner had the government finally begun to recognize the need for an all-Russian

67. "Tretii vserossiiskii s'ezd predstavitelei birzhevoi torgovli i sel'skogo khoziaistva," *PT*, no. 4 (15 February 1908): 271–73. See also Livshin, "'Predstavitel'nye' organizatsii," p. 110; Lur'e *Organizatsiia*, p. 64.

68. *Golos Moskvy*, no. 189 (15 August 1908).

organization of trade and industry than the merchants and industrialists, who had long favored such action, began moving in a different direction. So the government ended up approving two all-Russian organizations, neither one of which served as an effective spokesman for its constituency. Second, the split at the national level disrupted regional trade and industry organizations, like the Moscow Exchange Committee, which had already achieved a high degree of unity between merchants and industrialists and led to the formation of splinter groups along occupational lines.

Up to this time the Moscow Exchange Committee had exemplified the fusion of merchant and industrial capital. This was exceptional in Russia, but followed the classic pattern of the rest of Europe, where there had been a natural evolution of one into the other. But the pull of extremes accelerated by the revolution divided the loyalties of both groups and disrupted their unity. In their relations with the external world, the exchange members hesitated between joining the Association of the Representatives of Commercial and Agricultural Exchanges or the Association of the Representatives of Trade and Industry. They ended up entering both without giving either their full allegiance.

In the exchange committee itself there were disquieting signs that the leaders of Moscow's metallurgical industry—with their ties to Prodamet and their reliance on foreign capital and government contracts —were feeling more and more out of place. This was why, in 1907, they founded their own employer's union, the Moscow Society of Factory and Mill Owners. Men with such names as Jules Goujon, N. G. List, S. V. Hopper, K. L. Hantert, and I. V. Nabgolts could hardly have been altogether comfortable in that bastion of Great Russian nationalism, the Moscow Exchange Committee, nor could they remain insensible to the rising tide of Germanophobia which after 1907 made little distinction between citizenship and ethnic origin.[69] Meanwhile, in St. Petersburg the tensions among economic interest groups and among ethnic groups intensified as a new center of entrepreneurial activity emerged outside the circles of heavy industry and the merchant exchanges and rapidly overshadowed both of them.

69. Ibid., no. 134 (10 June 1907), announced that the member firms employed 23,000 workers in metallurgy, 7,000 in printing, 4,500 in confection, and 2,000 in perfumes. There were, to be sure, Russian members like Iu. I. Poplavskii, who perhaps for the very reason of his name was secretary of the executive committee and a frequent spokesman for the organization.

The Emergence of the Petersburg Financial Oligarchy

In St. Petersburg the political gap left by the persistent inability of merchants and entrepreneurs to resolve their differences or to assume national leadership within their own constituency was filled by the rising economic power of the big banks. Their spectacular growth and monopolistic control over whole sectors of Russian industry accelerated after 1905 and reached a peak on the eve of the war. In the middle of this period there was also a tremendous surge of financial activity on the St. Petersburg Exchange, but this did not create a rival for the banks in managing the flow of Russian investment capital. As Gindin has shown, the speculative fever on the exchange was more of an illusion than a source of real economic power.[70] Stocks were bought by short-term investors from the provinces, and the exchange remained a limited market for industrial securities. The placement of long-term industrial capital remained firmly in the hands of the giant Petersburg banks.

In the short period between 1900 and 1913 the big Petersburg investment firms took over the top five places in the imperial banking system; they were the Russo-Asiatic Bank, the Petersburg International Bank, the Russian Bank for Foreign Trade, the Azov-Don Bank, and the Russian Trade and Industry Bank. Meanwhile the largest commercial banks, the Volga-Kama Bank and the Moscow Merchants' Bank, slipped from first and second to sixth and eighth places, respectively. The Siberian Trade Bank, with headquarters in St. Petersburg, rose from fourteenth to seventh. Over the same time span the six leading banks increased their share of the total outstanding liabilities of the banking system from 46.6 to 55.3 percent.[71]

In addition to these giants there were several smaller emission banks, including the Moscow United Bank, the St. Petersburg Discount and Loan Bank, and the St. Petersburg Private Bank, which also financed large industrial enterprises. With the Petersburg group setting the pace, these eleven joint-stock banks developed a three-pronged investment policy which secured them a dominant role in Russia's economic growth during the last prerevolutionary decade.[72] First, they moved into heavy industry, primarily machines, metallurgy, transportation, and oil. Second, they obtained a virtual monopoly over the wholesale trade in sugar, oil, and, in competition with the Moscow textile industry, cotton and flax from Central Asia.[73] Third,

70. Gindin, *Kommercheskie banki*, pp. 174–76.
71. Gindin and Shepelev, "Bankovskie," pp. 21, 55.
72. Ibid., pp. 22–23.
73. For details on the latter point see Laverychev, "Moskovskie fabrikanty," pp. 64–67.

they played a large role in the growth of the domestic money market, signaling a dramatic shift in investment sources away from state and foreign capital, which predominated in the 1880s and 1890s, to native Russian capital.[74] Altogether, the eleven leading banks controlled 468 enterprises, representing slightly more than 50 percent of all the joint-stock capital invested in the country. In heavy industry the figure was even higher, around 60 percent.[75]

Beyond concentrating great economic power in their hands, the banks knotted stronger ties than ever before with the government. Ever since the establishment of the State Bank in 1860 successive ministers of finance had pursued a vigorous policy of creating and supporting joint-stock banks. Witte spared no effort to rescue floundering banks during the crisis of 1900, and Kokovtsov pumped massive infusions of state funds into the banks after 1910 in order to maintain the expansion of Russian industry.[76] After 1905 the St. Petersburg banks reciprocated by placing state loans, paying short-term treasury obligations, and floating railroad loans.[77] At the same time the sharing of personnel between the bureaucracy and the largest banks became a distinctive feature of the Russian banking system. From their posts in the upper echelons of the administration former banking officials could help the banks obtain large state contracts, especially in armaments and munitions, for those enterprises that they had brought under their financial control. As a result of these combinations a small group of bankers who would chart their own course for Russia's economic development emerged. They represented a new type of Petersburg entrepreneur, one that exemplified the so-called coalescence (*srashchivanie*) between finance capital and the government which one influential group of Soviet historians has perceived as the dominant characteristic of Russian monopoly capitalism as a whole on the eve of war and revolution.[78]

74. For example, in the period from 1904 to 1913 the joint-stock banks placed more than twice the sum of industrial securities in Russia as abroad. See Komiteta s'ezdov predstavitelei aktsionernykh bankov, *O zhelatel'nykh*, p. 42.

75. Gindin and Shepelev, "Bankovskie," p. 44. For individual branches of industry see ibid., table 3, pp. 58–61, which shows that the greatest concentration of capital from these banks was to be found in industries on the cutting edge of technology, e.g., rubber, 99 percent of total capital invested; electricity, 90 percent; and heavy machinery, 99 percent.

76. Gindin, *Kommercheskie banki*, pp. 192–96.

77. Sidorov, *Finansovoe*, p. 181.

78. The model was systematically developed by the "Sidorov School" as an alternative to the interpretation that the government was "subordinated" to finance capital. The conflicting theories, which have a central importance in Soviet historiography on the revolution, may be explored in Akademiia nauk, *Ob osobennostiakh*, and Tarnovskii, *Sovetskaia istoriografiia*.

The core of this financial oligarchy was composed of men who, for the most part, had been protégés of Witte and held the top posts in the Ministry of Finance from his ascendancy right down to the revolution of 1917. Following their retirement from state service, they simply moved into the executive leadership of the eight largest Petersburg banks. From 1905 to 1917 they exercised almost equal authority within both the ministry and the leading investment banks in the country. This blend of wealth and power gave them a degree of control over the economic life of the country which, up to that time, had eluded both the government and the entrepreneurial groups.

There were a number of remarkably striking parallels in the careers of four of the dominant figures in the four largest Petersburg banks: A. I. Putilov, president of the administration of the Russo-Asiatic Bank (1910–17), A. I. Vyshnegradskii, director and head of the Petersburg International Bank (1906–17), M. M. Fedorov, president of the council of the Azov-Don Bank (1907–11), and V. I. Timiriazev, president of the council of the Russian Bank for Foreign Trade. All four graduated from St. Petersburg University and entered government service, Putilov and Vyshnegradskii in 1893 as protégés of Witte in the credit chancellery of the Ministry of Finance, Fedorov and Timiriazev earlier but also in the Ministry of Finance, where Fedorov served under Witte as the editor of the official organs *Vestnik finansov promyshlennosti i torgovli* (from 1891) and *Torgovo-promyshlennaia gazeta* (1893–97). Putilov rose to become deputy minister in 1904–5 and director of the Russo-Chinese Bank; Fedorov was named director of the commercial section in 1903; Timiriazev became deputy minister of finance in 1902 and then the first minister of commerce and industry in 1905.

Soon after the revolution of 1905 they retired from state service to devote themselves to private banking and investment. (Timiriazev briefly returned to his ministerial post in 1909.) Putilov was president of the gigantic metallurgical works that bore his father's name and a major stockholder in forty industrial concerns, including the largest oil, metallurgical, electrical, mining, and railroad companies. Vyshnegradskii was president of the Sormovo complex of metal factories, a member of the administration of the Russo-Chinese Bank, and a stockholder in many of the same companies that his close friend Putilov owned stock in. As the real power in the Russian-Asiatic Bank and the International Bank they created a series of trusts in machine production (Sormovo-Kolomenskoe group), steamships, and railroads (the Black Sea and Baltic groups). Fedorov was active primarily in mining and railroad companies. As the leading figure in the Azov-Don Bank, he fostered cooperation with the International Bank in several large-scale undertakings of metallurgical companies in the south which tied both banks closely to Prodamet. On the eve of the war the Azov-Don Bank and the International Bank gave important support to Produgol and then named a member of the administration of the Azov-Don Bank as its president. Timiriazev took the lead in expanding commercial relations with Germany based on contacts that he had made there while representing the ministry as a commercial agent. Elected to the State Council, he was also president of the Association of the Representatives of Trade and Industry.[79]

A similar career pattern characterized two leading figures in the banks that ranked fifth and sixth in 1914, the Volga-Kama Bank and the Russian Bank for Trade and Industry. P. O. Bark also began his government service as one of Witte's men in the chancellery of the credit department of the Finance Ministry, moving over in 1895 to the State Bank, where he occupied a number of high posts, including that of chief of the St. Petersburg office. A member of the administration of the state-run Russo-Chinese Bank and president of the Discount and Loan Bank of Persia, he became director of the Volga-Kama Bank in 1907–11, resigning only to accept an appointment as deputy minister of trade and industry. Bark was the last minister of finance of the imperial government and held that post throughout the war.[80]

E. D. Maksimov, a more complex and unusual figure in this gallery, was a quasi populist in his younger days. He taught school, worked as

79. The data for careers have been taken from the short biographies in the index of names for Akademiia nauk, *Materialy po istorii*, vol. 6; Witte, *Vospominaniia*, 1:143–44, 228, 3:208, 236–67; Gindin and Shepelev, "Bankovskie," pp. 21–22; "V. I. Timiriazev" and "M. M. Fedorov," in *BE*, 82:884 and 4D (supplement), p. 789. Administrators in these three banks who had served in the Ministry of Finance included: (1) from the Russo-Asiatic Bank, the director from 1910 to 1911, I. M. Kon, formerly an inspector of the Russo-Chinese Bank (1909) and subsequently director of the Russian Bank for Trade and Industry (1912–15); president of the council from 1914 to 1915, A. V. Konshin, formerly in the administration from 1910 to 1914; P. A. Bok, formerly director of the Russo-Chinese Bank and also director of the Petersburg Railroad Car Construction Company; from the International Bank, the president from 1901 to 1917, S. S. Khrulev, formerly the representative of the Ministry of Finance to the Land Bank; member of the administration from 1912 to 1917, Rakusa-Sushchevskii, an official in the Ministry of Finance from 1892 to 1897 and also a member of the Russian Bank for Trade and Industry; (3) from the Azov-Don Bank, member of the administration from 1907 to 1917, D. I. Darmolatov, a former tax inspector of the St. Petersburg Fiscal Board under the Ministry of Finance; (4) from the Private Commercial Bank, president of the administration, L. F. Davydov, vice-director and then director of the credit chancellery of the Ministry of Finance (1906–13).

80. Witte, *Vospominaniia*, 1:144; Gurko, *Figures and Features*, pp. 541, 680–81, who disputes Witte's claim that he was responsible for having Bark appointed minister of finance.

a statistician in zemstvo organization, and contributed articles on elementary education and statistics to a number of thick journals. He received an appointment as tax inspector in the Caucasus and served under Witte, but his strong attachment to local self-government set him at odds with his chief, and he shifted to the Ministry of Interior, where he continued to work until 1905 in the economic department on questions dealing with the famine and other social issues. Suddenly resigning in 1905, he assumed the presidency of the Russian Bank for Trade and Industry, which he held until 1917. The paradox of a conscience-stricken member of the intelligentsia becoming the head of one of Russia's largest banks is partially offset by Maksimov's continued devotion to social causes as the director of the charitable society Social Aid and as editor of the journal *Vestnik kustarnoi promyshlennosti*.[81]

The financial oligarchy aimed at carrying out Witte's general policies of economic growth, but sought both greater balance between the agricultural and industrial sectors and between foreign and domestic capital and a closer coordination between the financial and budgetary policies of the Ministry of Finance and the investment decisions of private capital. The three key elements in their program concerned foreign investment, control of monopolies, and foreign trade.

Their first concern was to keep a constant flow of foreign capital but to channel it through the Petersburg banks, where it could be invested in the most rationally productive way for the country at large. A good indication of their success is the steady rise in foreign investment during the decade 1904–13 even though its share in joint-stock company securities declined relative to domestic capital.[82] As bureaucrats, the members of the financial oligarchy had a long history of defending foreign investment against domestic critics.[83] As bankers, they continued to encourage its placement in Russia, even when its source was Germany. For example, the International Bank attracted German capital by investing heavily in the electrical industry, where the main enterprises in Russia were branches of German concerns.[84] The Foreign Trade Bank, under Timiriazev's leadership, had very close ties with German commercial companies.[85] That Petersburg

81. Akademiia nauk, *Materialy po istorii*, vol. 5, index; *BE*, 3D (supplement), pp. 127–28. Maksimov was not altogether unique, for well-known publicist and critic of Witte I. Kh. Ozerov also became a member of the administration of the Russo-Asiatic Bank.

82. Gindin, *Kommercheskie banki*, p. 171.

83. See for example, M. M. Fedorov, "Pis'ma o russkoi promyshlennosti i inostrannykh kapitalakh," *REO*, no. 12 (1898):1–22.

84. Sheplev and Gindin, "Bankovskie," p. 22.

85. Timiriazev, *Torgovlia*. Witte, who cannot be accused of anti-German sentiments, thought Timiriazev was overeager in his attempts to negotiate a trade agreement with Germany (Witte, *Vospominaniia*, 1:77).

banks were particularly hospitable to German capital was demonstrated during the war when they strongly protested that the Senate's decision giving the government the right to confiscate enemy property would be a crushing blow to foreign investment.[86] Unlike the southern entrepreneurs, who played the antiforeign line when it suited their purposes, the financial oligarchy studiously avoided any such phrase-mongering because they understood the immense damage that it could do to their interests. But however straightforward their neutral stance on the source and aims of foreign capital, it exposed them to charges of unpatriotic conduct during the war when their profits continued to rise but their political capital fell sharply.

A second area of major concern to the financial oligarchy was the monopolies in which they had become deeply involved on the eve of the war. Both the Azov-Don Bank and the St. Petersburg International Bank were strong supporters of Prodamet. In 1911–12, the Azov-Don Bank, together with the Trade and Industry Bank and the Siberian Bank, undertook a vast reorganization and modernization of the Ural enterprises that had participated in Prodamet. The same three banks maintained significant control over two large trusts manufacturing for railroads and steamship lines, Prodvagon and Prodparavoz. Just before the war the Azov-Don and International banks began to support Produgol with massive investments.[87] The International Bank successfully challenged the Franco-Belgian monopoly, Naval, by creating the Russian Shipbuilding Society (Russud) and organizing a syndicate of six banks to finance the construction of warships for the Ministry of the Navy.[88]

These extensive commitments meant that the financial oligarchy was included in the criticism against the monopolies that had spread from the press and the duma into the top level of the government, the Council of Ministers. There, the close ties between the banks and key ministers served the entrepreneurs well. The leader of the anti-monopolists was S. V. Rukhlov, an extreme rightist, who from the moment he became minister of transportation in 1909 sought to curb the power of Produgol by awarding large coal contracts from the state-owned railroads to firms not participating in the syndicate.[89] His efforts to weaken Prodamet were less successful, due in part to complex economic factors but also to the opposition of Kokovtsov, the chairman of the Council of Ministers and minister of finance, and S. I.

86. Diakin, "Pervaia miroviaia voina," p. 233.
87. Gindin and Shepelev, "Bankovskie," pp. 21–22.
88. Shatsillo, "Formirovanie," pp. 35–50.
89. Gindin, "Politika," pp. 107–9; Shpolianskii, *Monopolii*, pp. 114–18; Liashchenko, *Istoriia*, 2:340.

Timashev, the minister of trade and industry. In the Witte tradition, Kokovtsov defended monopolies as a necessity in an age of ruthless international competition. Without their organizational skills, he stated, heavy industry in Russia would be destroyed by foreign competitors.[90] Similarly, Timashev argued in the Council of Ministers that controlled production under the aegis of monopolies was a hedge against unbridled expansion in boom periods, which would lead to overproduction, depression, and widespread misery.

When Kokovtsov was replaced by I. L. Goremykin, Rukhlov was free to move against Prodamet and reorganize the entire system of state orders, even though the war had just broken out and despite the protests of Timashev and a collective petition by the Petersburg banks connected to Prodamet.[91] Meanwhile, another of the right-wing clique, Minister of Justice I. G. Shcheglovitov, was organizing a judicial inquiry into Produgol and, through the Kharkov procurator's office, beginning a major law suit accusing the syndicate of illegal activities. The timing of this fresh assault on the monopolies was hardly accidental, and it is tempting to see the outlines here of a large-scale, coordinated campaign of the right to smash the power of the monopolies. This thrust was parried, reportedly, by the diplomatic intervention of France and Belgium, but the discreet encouragement and support of the monopoly by the Ministry of Finance should not be disregarded.[92]

Thus, on the eve of the war the coalescence between the financial oligarchy and the government was limited, for the most part, to the ministries of Finance and Trade and Industry. The interministerial conflict spurred by the growing ascendancy of the antimonopolistic and, to a degree, antibourgeois right wing foreshadowed serious problems for the big industrialists. In retrospect, it also points up the fragmentation of the bureaucracy and underlines the difficulty of arriving at any simple formula for the relationship between industry and government in Russia.

The effect of the revolution of 1905 on the three major entrepreneurial groups was, paradoxically, to increase the political awareness and organizational activity of each but also to diminish the prospects for the unity of all. This is neither to deny that the entrepreneurs shared common material interests nor to claim that they were unaware of them. But it is one thing to perceive common class interests and another to act upon them. The particular interests of each group,

90. *Gosudarstvennaia Duma, Stenograficheskii otchet*, 4th ser., pt. 2 (10 May 1913), pp. 942–43.

91. Gindin, "Politika," p. 114.

92. Gaister, "Produgol," pp. 119–48.

which were based upon regional, cultural, and national differences, proved irreconcilable with their larger class interests. Ironically, the Great Russian nationalist capitalists resented the contributions of the ethnic and foreign entrepreneurs to economic development though this was the very thing making possible a Great Russia. Moreover, the defense of class interests by the entrepreneurial groups took several different forms. The entrepreneurial groups (and the merchants as well) could not agree over who was more to blame for their difficulties, the government or the workers, and they were unwilling to challenge either on fundamental issues. They shrank both from organizing to take power and, except in St. Petersburg, from declaring a class war on the workers. In this sense 1905 *was* a dress rehersal for 1917.

In twentieth-century Russia presumptive economic leadership of the country did not lead to political or social hegemony. The government continued to fight harder to keep the capitalists out of power than the latter did to gain a share in it. In the social arena only one side—the workers—behaved predictably like a class. On the very eve of the war the eighth annual congress of the Association of the Representatives of Trade and Industry confirmed its persistent refusal to recognize the fundamental political and social issues facing entrepreneurs and merchants in the empire. Their major grievance against the government was the encroachment of the state on private industry and the "peculiar 'national' [Great Russian] policy which threatens to hold back the development of domestic industry by . . . establishing artificial limitations which plunge Russia into greater dependence on foreign industry." Concerning the massive outbreak of strikes and disorders, the association sang the old refrain: "The disquieting mood is increased by the rising workers' movement which is fed, in significant measure, by factors lying outside the sphere of action of trade and industry, . . . in part as a consequence of political factors."[93] In a word, neither the conquest of political power nor the closing of ranks against the workers was an acceptable course of action for the most powerful representatives of the commercial and industrial capitalists of Russia. It may not have been a feasible one either.

93. "Vos'moi ocherednoi s'ezd predstavitelei promyshlennosti i torgovli," *PT*, no. 10 (15 May 1914): 527, 531.

CHAPTER 9

SOCIAL FRAGMENTATION

World War I offered the merchants and entrepreneurs an unparalleled opportunity to wrest control of the empire's industrial and commercial life from the bureaucracy. As the prospects for a quick victory by either side faded, economic policy assumed equal importance with military strategy in determining the outcome of the fighting, and the representative institutions of Russian society began to demand a share in organizing and running the war effort. The bureaucracy responded characteristically by resisting those efforts, while failing to coordinate or centralize its own policies, and the outcome was disastrous. Having lost control over the production and distribution of war material and food, the monarchy collapsed in February 1917.

By then the administration was so completely discredited and its opposition so widespread that the revolution appeared to be the direct outcome of the struggle over the conduct of the war. Contemporaries and historians alike saw it as the culmination of the long duel between government and society and as the destruction of the feudal autocracy by the bourgeois-democratic revolution. The difficulty with this view is that it underestimates the disunity within the putative bourgeoisie before and after the revolution and creates a false impression concerning the origin and capabilities of the Provisional Government. For this reason alone, the social conflict within Russia during the war deserves more attention than it has received, particularly with respect to the role of the merchantry and the entrepreneurial groups, who have been miscast as the rising bourgeoisie.

The principal issues that divided Russian society had nothing to do with war aims. Disputes erupted over the questions of who would make the crucial economic decisions and whether a constitutional change would be necessary in order to win the war. The main lines of the social divisions are familiar: the center against the periphery, the merchantry and entrepreneurs against the zemstvo and professional intelligentsia. Moreover, the fissiparous tendencies within each of these elements multiplied as the war dragged on. A few individuals made noteworthy attempts to overcome these splits; Konovalov stands out here. But as they had in the prewar period, the near misses far and away outnumbered the successes. Russia never had an equivalent of the Burgfrieden or the Union sacrée. Its absence signified something more than the impotence of the autocracy. It was symptomatic of an impending social disintegration in a society so badly fragmented that the propertied and intellectual elites could not unify around a common program of action even when faced with mortal danger.

Conflict among the Entrepreneurial Groups

After a slow start the Moscow entrepreneurial group emerged as the most vigorous proponent of handing over the wartime economy to private enterprise. Their proposals to mobilize industry brought them into direct conflict with the southern entrepreneurs and the Petrograd financial oligarchy, as well as the government bureaucrats. This split among the entrepreneurial groups ran through both established representative organizations, like the Association of the Representatives of Trade and Industry, and the new wartime agencies, like the special councils and the war industries committees. The issues ranged from the allocation of resources to cooperation with organized labor.

The first skirmish occurred in May 1915 when the Moscow entrepreneurial group attempted to take control of the Association of the Representatives of Trade and Industry away from the southern entrepreneurs. Avdakov and Zhukovskii had been maneuvering behind the scenes since the war began to have their organization admitted to the inner councils making economic policy. But the government was unwilling to cooperate with representatives of trade and industry until threatened by military collapse. It then agreed to permit a meeting of the association, but with the proviso that debates be limited "purely to business" and avoid politics. The southern entrepreneurs complied willingly but A. I. Konovalov wrecked their efforts when he took the chair and allowed Pavel Riabushinskii, who had just returned from the front, to deliver one of his characteristically fire-eating speeches that blended patriotic sentiments and political demands. Only the moderating influence of Zhukovskii checked the conference's slide toward making an open break with the government.[1]

At this time, too, the staggering Russian defeat in Galicia shook

1. Shakhovskoi, *Sic transit*, pp. 96–98.

public confidence. To bolster its sagging position, the government finally accepted Avdakov's advice and appointed a joint committee of industrialists and bureaucrats, the Special Council for the Discussion and Coordination of Measures Directed toward the Regular Supply to the Army of Munitions and Other Material during the Present War. This was much the lesser of two evils in light of what Riabushinskii had advocated.

By the careful wording of the title of the new organization the bureaucracy intended to limit its functions as strictly as possible. The restricted membership confirmed this determination. The first chairman was the notoriously incompetent minister of war, V. A. Sukhomlinov. Bureaucrats from the ministries of war and navy composed half of the council membership. The three original representatives of trade and industry—A. I. Putilov, A. I. Vyshnegradskii, and V. P. Litvinov-Falinskii—came from the Petersburg financial oligarchy. So did most of the dozen who were subsequently co-opted: Ia. I. Utin, president of the St. Petersburg Discount and Loan Bank, V. I. Timiriazev, former minister of trade and president of the council of the Russian Bank for Foreign Trade, A. P. Meshcherskii, member of the council of the International Bank and director of the Kolomenskoe Plant, K. P. Fedorov, of the Trade and Industry Bank, and others. Moscow was not represented at all. Four duma members, all Octobrists, made up the third grouping in the council.[2] In composition and purpose it bore a strong resemblance to the old manufacturing and commercial councils established by Nicholas I.

During the earliest deliberations of the council the financial oligarchy won several important advantages. First, they brushed aside the suggestion that Russia emulate the German wartime mobilization of industry with the disingenuous argument that Russian law forbade "combinations of entrepreneurial unions into syndicates." This tactic effectively froze out the Moscow group. Second, they obtained further loans and concessions for the Petrograd and Baltic defense factories, which they owned. Finally, they blocked a move by the military to increase bureaucratic surveillance and interference in plant management.[3] These decisions established precedents that protected the interests of the financial oligarchy when the composition of the council changed. Behind the scenes a three-way struggle was shaping up between the bureaucrats, the duma members, and the representatives

2. *ZHOS*, vol. 1: 1 (session 14 May) and 13 (session 23 May). The duma members were M. V. Rodzianko, A. D. Protopopov, I. I. Dmitriukov, and N. V. Savich. Sukhomlinov was soon succeeded by General A. A. Polivanov as minister of war.

3. Ibid., pp. 7–10 (session 18 May), 14–15, 16, 18 (session 23 May), 27–28 (session 27 May).

of the entrepreneurial groups which even the dry official minutes could not conceal.[4]

Disagreements multiplied. After the duma reconvened in June, it passed a reorganization plan creating four separate councils for defense, commerce, agriculture, and transportation. Although each council was still subordinated to the appropriate ministry, the new representation gave rough parity to the three groupings, and this balance produced a stalemate. Shifting alignments among and within the three groupings prevented any one of them from gaining the upper hand, but also destroyed any hope for a clear, consistent, and coordinated policy. For example, a quarrel over the proper site for its reassembly fatally delayed the evacuation of the General Electric Plant from Riga to Moscow. A coalition of industrialists and members of the Progressive party thwarted a proposal to sequestrate the Putilov Plant on proven grounds of mismanagement, irresponsibility, and indebtedness. This prompted a characteristic outburst from Kadet A. I. Shingarev: "The government is beginning to lose its way, selling out to the plutocracy."[5]

On a related matter, only the presentation of overwhelming evidence of scandalous behavior convinced the council on defense to discharge the director of the Kolomenskoe Plant, A. P. Meshcherskii, one of the original members of the council. In a running battle with the majority, Minister of Transportation S. V. Rukhlov, a notorious right-wing nationalist tacitly supported by Moscow, insisted on reassigning all defense orders to factories in the center and south nearer the sources of fuel and the major rail networks.[6] Proposals multiplied for the creation of a still "higher organization of defense," but to the end of the empire the special council of defense clung to its precarious position. It did not, however, go unchallenged.

No sooner had the special council convened for the first time than the Moscow entrepreneurial group moved to diminish its influence. Riabushinskii and his friends proposed to replace this "company union" with an all-Russian central organization. Freed from bureau-

4. Almost from the outset Rodzianko sought to draw in the zemstvo organizations. In a countermove the St. Petersburg group was obliged to petition for more industrialists, even though this meant opening the door to their Moscow rivals (ibid., pp. 23 [session of 27 May] and 35 [session of 1 June]).

5. Ibid., p. 430 (session 18 November); see also pp. 135 (session 31 July), 377–80 (session 28 October), 400–401 (session 7 November). The final vote was fifteen for and sixteen against sequestration, capping a debate in which the traditionally strong antiindustrialist bias of the landowning gentry (largely Octobrists), the professional intelligentsia (mainly Kadets), and the government bureaucrats comes through with remarkable clarity (ibid., pp. 427–33).

6. Ibid., p. 475 (session 5 December), 74 (session 24 June).

cratic controls and similar in structure to the Union of Towns, it would have had the right to assign state orders to individual factories, exercise control over filling them, supply enterprises with raw materials and labor, and transport munitions.[7] The representatives of the St. Petersburg financial oligarchy feared jeopardizing their special relationship with the bureaucracy and opposed the idea. Riabushinskii prevailed only after he had rallied to his side the local exchanges and representatives of smaller merchant organizations, who were delighted with his plan to establish regional war industries committees that would guarantee their autonomy from the major centers of Petrograd and Moscow. Within the council of the Association of the Representatives of Trade and Industry a compromise was reached whereby the war industries committees were created, but their functions were limited to supervising the conversion of civilian to military production. They were to be placed under the general supervision of the council of the association, and Avdakov was elected the first president of the Central War Industries Committee.[8] It seemed a hollow victory for the Moscow entrepreneurs.

Having lost the first battle for control at the top, the Moscow entrepreneurs fell back on their regional base in order to mount a new campaign. They quickly took charge of the Moscow War Industries Committee: Pavel Riabushinskii was elected president, and S. N. Tret'iakov and S. A. Smirnov were appointed his deputies. Their tactic was to weaken the special councils by diluting their memberships with delegates from the local war industries committees and by obtaining a leading role in organizing war production. When the president of the duma, Rodzianko, advised accommodation with the government rather than confrontation, he was ignored. Instead, Riabushinskii attacked the reigning chaos and confusion.

One theme soon came to dominate all the rest: if Russia was to win the war it would have to return to the real heart of its strength—Moscow. Early in the war, Riabushinskii had warned of the price that the country was paying for having ignored that truism. "Moscow has always been in favor of having defense factories transferred from the West, from the periphery to the center. No one listened, however, and here are the results: Libau has been taken, now Riga is being evacuated." Still, the government refused to order the industrial ma-

7. *Utro Rossii*, no. 143 (26 May 1915).
8. Diakin, *Russkaia burzhuaziia*. The first two delegates from the Central War Industries Committee to the Special Council on Defense were V. V. Zhukovskii and Baron G. Kh. Maidel, a Petrograd industrialist and Vol'skii's successor as editor of *Promyshlennost' i torgovlia* (*ZHOS* 1:45 [session of 6 June]). They were hardly the sort of independent representatives whom Riabushinskii must have had in mind.

chinery of these towns dismantled and sent east. The Moscow War Industries Committee kept up a drumfire of criticism against the bureaucracy for blocking the rapid evacuation of vitally needed arms plants. At the same time, Riabushinskii's press organs conducted a vitriolic campaign against Jewish, German, and Ukrainian cultural rights on the periphery in the name of Great Russian chauvinism of the center linked with the true national spirit of the Old Belief.[9] The implications of these criticisms were clear: the defense of the country was being sacrificed, as it had been in the past, to non-Russian regional interests.[10]

The smoldering rivalry between Moscow and the other entrepreneurial groups flared up at the first two congresses of the representatives of the war industries committees. Sensing this time had come, Riabushinskii sought to discredit the leadership of the council of the Association of the Representatives of Trade and Industry, dominated by the southern entrepreneurs and the financial oligarchy. Lashing out at what he called "the deadening atmosphere and German influence of St. Petersburg," he demanded an openly political role for the war industries committees. He called for the creation of a separate ministry of supply, representing "the public elements," and insisted on increasing Moscow's representation to make it the largest regional group on the Central War Industries Committee. Avdakov and Zhukovskii weakly defended themselves, claiming that "the aim of the war industries committees is strictly business." Refuting the accusation that the council sought to concentrate power in its hands, Avdakov plaintively concluded: "We only did what the government called on us to do." This is precisely what enraged the Moscow group, and they pressed their attack into 1917.[11]

9. *Utro Rossii*, nos 272, 273, 274, 307 (5, 6, 7 November, 2 December 1914); *Staroobriadcheskaia mysl'*, no. 1 (January 1915): 79–83, which specifically attacked Russian citizens with German names; ibid., no. 2 (February 1915): 124–30; ibid., no. 3 (April 1915): 321–24, a report on the Old Believer Cultural Educational Society in Moscow advocating driving out the "German spirit" and replacing it with the Russian national spirit, which was equated with the Old Belief.

10. "Zapiska moskovskogo okhrannogo otdeleniia o torzhestvennom otkrytii voenno-promyshlennogo komiteta," in Grave, *Burzhuaziia*, pp. 8–9; "Oblastnoi voenno-promyshlennyi komitet severo-zapadnogo kraia," *IMV-PK*, no. 14 (January 1916): 27–30, which, however, complained about the obstacles to reestablishing factories owned by Jews in new locations because of unnecessarily restrictive laws.

11. *Trudy pervogo s'ezda voenno-promsyhlennykh komitetov*, pp. 3, 17–18, 32–37, 152, 238–39. Later von Ditmar joined the chorus pleading for a cessation of attacks on the government and urging constructive cooperation (*Izvestiia tsentral'nogo voenno-promsyhlennogo komiteta*, 24 August 1915, p. 23). See also Tret'iakov's devastating attack on the Special Council for Defense and the ministries in "Vtoroi vserossiiskii s'ezd voenno-promyshlennykh komitetov. Stenograficheskii otchet," in *IMV-PK*, nos. 17–18

The conflict escalated in the elections to the State Council when the Moscow group, including Riabushinskii and Guchkov, defeated Avdakov and Zhukovskii for the seats allotted to trade and industry.[12] Soon after this Avdakov died. The Moscow entrepreneurs campaigned to fill his place as president of the Association of the Representatives of Trade and Industry with Konovalov and to turn the organization into a political instrument. To fail in this, Riabushinskii declared, would be to forfeit the unity of the bourgeoisie as a class.[13] But the organization was too deeply split, and the rival candidacies of Krestovnikov, Zhukovskii, von Ditmar, and Konovalov paralyzed it. Without a prominent successor to Avdakov the association became moribund.[14]

The Moscow entrepreneurs proved more successful in electing A. I. Guchkov to succeed Avdakov as chairman of the Central War Industries Committee. Ever since November 1913, Guchkov had been drifting toward a more uncompromising oppositionist stance. Throughout his parliamentary career two issues had marked his growing disaffection: toleration for the Old Believers and modernization of the army.[15] With the decline and disintegration of the Union of 17 October in the fourth duma, he was irresistibly drawn to those other champions of Russia's spiritual and military renascence, who sprang from the same tradition that he did—the Moscow entrepreneurial group. By 1915 he had returned, like the prodigal son, to his home—the Old Believer, textile merchant families of Moscow. In his new role as chairman of the Central War Industries Committee, he hammered at the government to funnel its defense orders through his agency, rather than allow individual state departments like Central Artillery and Army Supply to place their orders directly with the factories. A significant shift in this direction would have virtually required the government to guarantee the supply of all the necessary raw materials, manpower, and capital to those enterprises designated by the war industries committees. This would have meant nothing less than a large-scale recapitalization of heavy industry. With Guchkov and Konovalov leading the central committee and Riabushinskii holding sway in Moscow,

---

(March 1916): 28, and Zhukovskii's counterattack on mismanagement and excessive pessimism in the committee (ibid., pp. 34, 44).

12. *Russkie vedomosti*, no. 180 (5 August 1915).

13. *Utro Rossii*, nos. 197, 210 (22 August, 4 September 1915).

14. Diakin, *Russkaia burzhuaziia*, pp. 147–50.

15. Pinchuk, *Octobrists*, pp. 67–80, 87–92, 189–91. As early as 1911, Guchkov cooperated with the Moscow textile owners to demand higher duties against American cotton as a reprisal for American pressure to alleviate the plight of the Russian Jews (ibid., pp. 171–72). See also Hutchinson, "Octobrists," pp. 220–37.

such a transformation would have led to the ascendancy of the center over the periphery in the future development of Russian history.[16]

Guchkov and Konovalov also employed the Central War Industries Committee as a conduit to the working class. In this way they sought to strengthen their bargaining power with the autocracy and to check the anarchistic tendencies that flourished among the mass of workers who were deprived of any "responsible organization."[17] The formation of workers' sections attached to the war industries committees brought Guchkov and Konovalov into close contact with representatives of the defensist elements of the socialist left. To many observers this represented the kind of alliance between the radical bourgeoisie and the workers which had given rise to a bourgeois-democratic revolution in other places and at other times. It is quite possible that this is exactly what Guchkov and Konovalov contemplated. It was certainly what the Mensheviks envisaged when they spoke of "repentant merchants," who would be forced by the mounting pressure from below to assume revolutionary roles. And it was precisely the linkage that Lenin had in mind when he condemned the petty bourgeois instincts of the Menshevik and Socialist-Revolutionary defensists. It was from the outset a shaky coalition. Each of the protagonists— workers and industrialists—sought to use the other for its own ends, and they were deeply suspicious of one another. The merchants and entrepreneurs disagreed among themselves over the necessity and extent of cooperation with the workers. The government was able to exploit these differences to keep the opposition divided and off balance.

There were, by February 1917, a total of fifty-eight war industries committees with workers' sections; the most active of these were the Central War Industries Committee and the three local committees of Petrograd, Moscow, and Kiev. The establishment of the first three of these was clearly the work of Guchkov and Konovalov. The Petrograd committee operated in the shadow of the central committee. In Moscow the creation of a workers' section aroused the ire of the Society of

---

16. The actual contribution of the war industries committees to supplying the army is a matter of dispute. Shigalin, *Podgotovka*, and Rudoi, *Gosudarstvennyi kapitalizm*, give a generally positive estimate of their work while Pogrebinskii, "Voenno-promyshlennye komitety," p. 167, argues that no more than 50 percent of the orders received by the war industries committees were actually filled and that this amounted to only 2–3 percent of the total value of defense orders. Sidorov, *Ekonomicheskoe*, pp. 191–212, takes an intermediate position.

17. "K istorii 'rabochei gruppy,'" pp. 49–84. For a discussion of these contacts see Katkov, *Russia 1917*, pp. 16–22.

Factory and Mill Owners and even disturbed other members of the Moscow Entrepreneurial Group, especially Riabushinskii and, to a lesser extent, Tret'iakov, who opposed autonomous sections for workers and strove to organize mixed "sections." Later, under pressure from Konovalov, Tret'iakov abandoned his opposition. In Kiev the initiative for workers' sections belonged to the millionaire sugar-beet industrialist M. I. Tereshchenko, who was bound to Guchkov and Konovalov by personal, Masonic, and political ties. The nucleus of the last coalition in the Provisional Government was taking shape around a few entrepreneurs who hoped for a patriotic alliance with the workers. But the majority of merchants and entrepreneurs in the war industries committees feared the radical implications of this cooperation. They resisted efforts by the workers' sections to obtain substantial labor reforms and to advance political slogans. When the workers resorted to strikes in early 1916, the government countered with repressive measures. By the summer the police had broken up numbers of workers' sections in the provinces and even made arrests in Moscow under the indifferent gaze of the merchant and entrepreneur members of the committees.[18]

Meanwhile, in Petrograd, the Central War Industries Committee broadened its authority. It intervened in disputes between the workers and employers which were brought to their attention by the workers' section, often supported the workers' demands for higher wages, and urged the government to relax or abolish its repressive measures. Guchkov strongly endorsed a proposal for setting up conciliation boards which was favored by the workers' section. Here, he ran into resistance from the Special Council on Defense and the minister of trade and industry, V. N. Shakhovskoi, both representing the interests of the Petrograd entrepreneurs.[19] His subsequent attempt to set up temporary boards on his own initiative collapsed when, as a sign of their total opposition to the idea, the Petrograd Society of Factory and Mill Owners refused to send delegates.[20] Already displeased by their loss of influence in the council of the Association of the Representatives of Trade and Industry, the Petrograd entrepreneurs were outraged by Guchkov's and Konovalov's opening to the left. Instinctively, they swerved sharply to the right. The financial oligarchy was equally

18. P. P. Riabushinskii, "O rabochem otdele," *IMV-PK*, nos. 13–14 (January 1916): 1–2; see also ibid., pp. 48–51, for Tret'iakov's speech; "Pechatnaia zapiska departamenta politsii ot nachala marta 1916 goda o rabochikh gruppakh pri voenno-promyshlennikh komitetakh," in Fleer, *Rabochee dvizhenie*, pp. 281–83; Siegelbaum, "The War Industries Committees," pp. 241–42, 248, 262.

19. *ZHOS*, 1:485–86 (session 12 December 1915); Shakhovskoi, *Sic transit*, pp. 99–104.

20. "K istorii 'rabochei gruppy,'" pp. 51–59.

unhappy over the decline of their influence in the special councils and the rise of the war industries committees. Together, the two Petrograd interest groups joined forces in yet another organization to defend their regional interests.

Despite its name, the Association of the Representatives of the Metal-Finishing Industry was a Petrograd operation from beginning to end. To be sure, the ubiquitous figures of Goujon from Moscow and von Ditmar from the south made their obligatory appearance, but neither one was elected to the twenty-seven-man executive council of the new organization.[21] The real leaders were Meshcherskii, Putilov, Vyshnegradskii, and—a rising star—A. D. Protopopov, the deputy chairman of the duma, future minister of the interior, and one of the grave-diggers of the monarchy, who served as the president and political brains of the association.

To justify the creation in wartime of yet another representative organ of trade and industry its founders cited the shortcomings of the official policies. According to Meshcherskii, the special councils had fallen upon evil days ever since their reorganization had admitted representatives of the duma, the zemstvos, and Moscow. There were "very few real industrialists" left. In the "tense atmosphere" now prevailing, he continued, fear of denunciation and anonymous accusations against the management of the Putilov, Nevskii, and Kolomenskoe works made work impossible. Putilov lamented that the council of the Association of the Representatives of Trade and Industry was also weak, without influence, and "completely swallowed up" by the war industries committees. The Petrograd interests had been eliminated from both these organizations.[22]

The subsequent debate over membership revealed a deep suspicion of the metallurgical enterprises in the south, whose interests, in the words of one delegate, were "diametrically opposed" to those of the metal-working industry. The association turned against both the bureaucracy and the Moscow entrepreneurs. On the one hand, they denounced the government's policy of sequestration and intervention in private industry. On the other hand, they challenged the authority of the Central War Industries Committee and condemned its flirtation with the workers.[23]

21. *Trudy 1-go s'ezda predstavitelei metalloobrabatyvaiushchei promyshlennosti*, pp. 32, 103. Goujon urged the assembly to put up a fight for the leadership of the council of the Association of the Representatives of Trade and Industry rather than go its own way. Presumably, he thought his own voice would carry farther in a national than in a regional and predominantly Petersburg organization.

22. Ibid., pp. 24–30 (Meshcherskii's speech), 39–40 (Putilov's speech), 78–79 (Savin's speech), 85–87 (Putilov's and Tokarskii's speeches).

23. Ibid., pp. 44–49.

As the labor question intensified in the fall of 1916, the Association of the Representatives of the Metal-Finishing Industries mounted a political campaign to rally its members against the workers and to elect a bloc of delegates to the duma.[24] The breach with the Moscow group was completed when Protopopov was unexpectedly appointed minister of the interior through the influence of Rasputin.[25] The division between the entrepreneurial groups had come over two fundamental issues—relations with the government and with the workers. It made a mockery of any further appeals to the unity of the trade and industry class.

There may be objections that this description merely characterizes a struggle among rival elites competing for the leadership of a class that required only a strong hand to shape its program and define its sphere of action. The evidence points in another direction, however, toward the collapse of social cohesion among the entrepreneurs as part of a general disintegration of all social forces in Russia. Among the entrepreneurial organizations the same lament could be heard from all sides: there was no program, no leadership, no unity. Gradually, each group withdrew behind its own defenses and castigated all the rest. As the crisis sharpened, it became more and more difficult to arouse sustained activity at any level. Even when a political consciousness was most fully developed and the stakes were highest, a growing sense of helplessness set in. Absenteeism at the meetings of the Central War Industries Committee reached a peak when out of a membership of 140 to 150 only 30 to 35 showed up, and of these, 16 were representatives from the workers' section.[26] The attempts of the Moscow entrepreneurial group to form a union of the trade and industry class comparable to the Union of Zemstvos and the Union of Towns met a similar fate. Out of 120 invited for this purpose to meet at Tret'iakov's mansion, only 25 or 30 attended, and "the majority came to listen, avoiding any expression of their own ideas on unity."[27]

24. *Padenie*, 6:60–61, 472.

25. *Utro Rossii*, (16 September 1915), opposed the appointment of Protopopov. His entrance into the government was accompanied by appointments of some of his St. Petersburg friends like A. S. Putilov to the chancellery of the Council of Ministers.

26. *Trudy vtorogo s'ezda voenno-promyshlennykh komitetov*, pp. 35–36.

27. "Donesenie nachal'nika moskovskogo okhrannogo otdeleniia direktoru departamenta politsii ob organizatsii kooperativnogo i rabochego soiuzov," and idem, ". . . o chastnykh sobraniiakh torgovtsev i promyshlennikov, 16/IV/1916," in Grave, *Burzhuaziia*, pp. 97, 99.

Dissension within the Merchantry

Another ominous sign of social disintegration was the dissension within the merchantry itself. Early in the war the Moscow entrepreneurial group antagonized the rest of the merchantry in the countryside and the big cities by its arrogant and authoritarian behavior. Quarrels broke out over the assignment and control of state orders to factories and the grain supply. Through their undercover agents the police were well informed about these problems. According to reports from the St. Petersburg Okhrana, "the greatest discontent is being created in society by the [War Industries] Committee's activity aimed exclusively at the defense and support of big industry at the obvious expense of the middle and small."[28] The petty merchants retaliated by withdrawing from the war industries committees and working through their local organizations. One of these, the Petrograd Committee of Medium Industry, established separate sections for rolled steel, metal, leather, and other products and made direct contact with the Petrograd town committee in order to solicit orders from the army. To the dismay of the Moscow entrepreneurs, the Ministry of Trade and Industry promptly sent an official delegation to the committee. Here was a splendid opportunity to whittle down the ambitions of Guchkov and his friends by playing the small and medium against the big merchants. The Moscow entrepreneurs had seen the danger coming long before, but they had done nothing to avert it.[29] This time-honored tactic of the bureaucracy worked once again. Despite the decline of the guilds and the weakness of the soslovie system, the government was still able to exploit the traditional differences in wealth and regional loyalty which fragmented the merchantry and entrepreneurs.

A three-way economic struggle now ensued between the capitals and the provinces and within the cities. The Central War Industries Committee constantly harassed the Petrograd medium merchant industrialists by blocking deliveries to their factories. The Petrograd town committee, "under pressure from the Central War Industries Committee," then retreated from its cooperation with the medium industrialists and forced them to appeal directly to the government agencies. The same high-handed methods characterized the Central War Industries Committee's relations with the provincial committees:

28. Grave, *K istorii*, pp. 262–63.
29. When the Committee of Medium and Small Industry held its first congress in 1910, it had already displayed such marked hostility to the big merchants that *Utro Rossii* accused it of being a tool of the bureaucracy *Utro Rossii*, nos. 10, 161, 165 (9 February, 7, 10 June 1910).

Nizhnyi, Orel, Saratov, and Kursk all reported blatant cases of discrimination against them.[30] The medium and small merchant traders also resented the attempts of Guchkov and Konovalov to organize the shop assistants and clerks. "It is bad enough that the War Industries Committee got into a mess with the workers and now cannot disentangle itself," declared I. D. Sytin, the editor of *Russkoe slovo*. As for this latest adventure, he added, "No, it is too dangerous; they are going much too far."[31]

Meanwhile, the provincial exchange committees revolted against "the hegemony of the Moscow merchantry" and insisted on presenting their own candidates for election to the State Council.[32] The unhappiness with Moscow showed up again at the congress of representatives of the exchange committees in 1916 when the Siberian delegates led the opposition to proposed intervention by the Moscow War Industries Committee in organizing grain shipments.[33] In the provincial backwoods of Russian life the local merchants turned against any kind of control by organizations at the center which claimed to represent their interests. War industries committees had appeared in many provincial towns that had no war industries, and these had nothing to do except flaunt their patriotic sentiments. The view of one Soviet historian that the provincial committees signified a rise in political consciousness and were a "representative organ of the Russian bourgeoisie" is belied by reports from a wide range of sources on the mood of the merchantry in the provinces. A conference of provincial governors in 1916 concluded on a note that should ring familiar to the reader of these pages: "The merchant element in the town administrations is entirely absorbed by personal interests [and] regards public affairs with an indifferent and inert attitude, passing up no opportunity to make a profit."[34] Hoarding and speculation were, to many observers, the major preoccupation of the provincial merchants. At the Nizhnyi Novgorod fair speculation had become a mass phenomenon, Struve lamented, "an all-Russian disgrace bearing the stamp of the all-Russian merchantry."[35]

30. "Donesenie nachal'nika moskovskogo okhrannogo otdeleniia o vzaimootnosheniiakh tsentral'nogo voenno-promyshlennogo komiteta s organizatsiami srednei i melkoi promyshlennosti, 16/XII/1915," in Grave, *Burzhuaziia*, pp. 16–18.
31. "Donesenie . . . o chastnykh sobraniiakh torgovtsev i promyshlennikov, 16/IV/1916," ibid., p. 100.
32. *Russkie vedomosti*, no. 153 (4 July 1915).
33. *Russkie vedomosti*, no. 96 (27 April 1916).
34. "Soveshchanie gubernatorov," pp. 162–63; *Birzhevye vedomosti*, 8, 29 July 1916; *Russkie vedomosti*, no. 66 (21 March 1915); ibid., nos. 195, 198 (24, 27 August 1916). Cf. Pogrebinskii, "Voenno-promyshlennye komitety," p. 177.
35. *Birzhevye vedomosti*, 29 July 1916. See also ibid., 8 July 1916.

Actually, the situation in the countryside was more complex than the governors or the press made out. The merchants themselves could not agree on what was to be done about the drastic decline in the grain trade. Once again their ranks divided along economic lines hardened by growing urban-rural tensions. Yet these differences could not surface as long as the old regime lasted, and their traces are hard to uncover in contemporary accounts. Fortunately for the historian, the February revolution ended all restrictions on public meetings and made possible the gathering of over eight hundred merchant representatives at the first congress of the All-Russian Association of Trade and Industry, where they felt free to air their views. No longer fearful of police repression, they were not as yet intimidated by the outbreak of mass agrarian disturbances. It is as good a sample as exists of merchant attitudes during the war years and illuminates not only the dispute over the grain trade but also a whole range of controversies that sapped their unity at this critical juncture.

The first congress followed months of hard organizational work by Riabushinskii, Tret'iakov, and Konovalov. They harangued the merchant exchanges of the Great Russian center to rally around the Moscow entrepreneurial group as a counterweight to the Association of the Representatives of Trade and Industry, which was dominated by the Petrograd and southern entrepreneurial groups.[36] Riabushinskii made no secret of this. In the pages of his newspaper he wrote, "Up to this time there has been not only no influential, but in general no unified organ of the all-Russian trade and industry class." He contemptuously dismissed the Association of the Representatives of Trade and Industry as an "industrial bureaucracy."[37]

Although the association sent a token representation to the congress, the large majority of delegates represented the trading exchanges of the Great Russian center, with Moscow in the lead. The presidium of the congress, elected from a prearranged list, reflected this supremacy: Riabushinskii, Tret'iakov, S. A. Smirnov, D. V. Sirotkin (an Old Believer merchant from Nizhnyi and an administrator of Riabushinskii's bank) from Moscow, and (not without protests from the floor) N. N. Kutler and M. M. Fedorov from Petrograd.[38] While

36. "Donesenie nachal'nika moskovskogo okhrannogo otdela direktoru departamenta politsii ob organizatsii kooperativnogo i rabochego soiuza," and idem, ". . . o chastnykh sobraniiakh torgovtsev i promyshlennikov, 16/IV/1916," in Grave, *Burzhuaziia*, pp. 97, 99; *PVT-PS*, pp. 3–11; Laverychev, "Vserossiiskii soiuz," pp. 35–38.
37. *Utro Rossii*, no. 32 (1 February 1917).
38. *PVT-PS*, pp. 20–21. Riabushinskii claimed that the choice of Kutler and Fedorov expressed the interregional character of the congress, but surely there was more to it than that. Both men were members of the administration of the Azov-Don Bank, which

Riabushinskii presided over the congress, his closest associates chaired the key subcommittees: Smirnov on the political question, Sirotkin on the food supply question, Tret'iakov on the organizational question, and A. A. Bublikov, a Progressive deputy, on the transport question. The fuel supply subcommittee was chaired by von Ditmar, the only representative of the southern entrepreneurs, but this was logical considering his expert knowledge. At the conclusion of its deliberations the congress elected a permanent council of Riabushinskii, Tret'iakov, A. A. Skorokhodov (from the Omsk Exchange Committee), Sirotkin, Smirnov, Iu. I. Poplavskii (of the Moscow Society of Factory and Mill Owners), and A. A. Petrov (of the Moscow Exchange Committee), thus altogether excluding Petrograd and the south.[39]

Although the Moscow entrepreneurs controlled the congress, they could not prevent frank and often acrimonious debates which ripped apart the image of the unified "trade and industry class" so carefully cultivated by Riabushinskii. The center of the merchantry's concerns and disagreements was the grain supply question. Although almost all the speakers blamed the tsarist government's policy of fixed grain prices and requisitioning for the food crisis, they divided into several factions over the proper solution.

Representatives from provincial exchanges like Feodosia (Tauride province), Kharkov, Karachev (Orel province), Siberia, Borovichi (Novgorod province), and Mtsensk (Riazan province) agitated for a return to free trade, excepting only purchases for the army at fixed prices. For the most part they were the small and medium merchants, whose business had been badly hurt by the severe curtailment of the middleman's functions in the controlled market. They had witnessed first hand the peasant hoarding, the piles of surplus grain accumulating at the railroad stations, and the helplessness of the government inspectors. Their sympathies lay with the peasants, who were caught between state-fixed grain prices and the rapid inflation of the prices of manufactured goods on the free market.

These views were not shared by the representatives of the big grain exchanges in the cities, particularly those from the Kalashnikov Exchange in Petrograd, who rejected both a state monopoly and free

---

had recently sought to "go over to the attack on the Moscow enterprises," as Riabushinskii put it, but Morozov had "paralyzed their efforts." At the same time, Riabushinskii was seeking an alliance with one of the big Petrograd banks. What would have been more logical than to negotiate with Azov-Don, having already proven Moscow's right to be considered as an equal? See M. P. Riabushinskii, "Tsel'," Akademiia nauk, *Materialy po istorii*, 6:630.

39. *PVT-PS*, p. 236. Von Ditmar left the congress before it had even voted on the resolution drafted by his subcommittee.

trade in favor of a complex set of regulations aimed at putting the grain trade in the hands of the large wholesale dealers. To them a real shortage of grain existed. The peasant soldiers were consuming more than they had when they were civilians, and the transportation system was in ruins. The cities were feeling the pressures from consumers. A few delegates hinted darkly at pogroms against grain dealers.

Sensing the dangers of mass discontent but disagreeing as to its source, the two groups could not always mask their mutual hostility. For example, a member of the subcommittee on food supply, Petrov, touched a raw nerve when he asked the assembly to vote either "for free trade or for a series of measures of a purely socialist character." When the cries of protest died down, a small majority voted for a return to free trade.[40] But the bitterness remained. At the plenary session the minority leveled recriminations against excessive profits by grain speculators, further inciting the congress.

Behind the scenes a compromise resolution was worked out. On the one hand, this resolution endorsed the abolition of the state monopoly over the grain trade and the reestablishment of free trade under the auspices of the merchant organizations, which would also take responsibility for regulating all commercial profits in order to avoid unnecessary price increases on necessities. On the other hand, taking cognizance of the disorganization of transport and the small reserves, the resolution recognized the need both to postpone the implementation of these decisions until the next harvest and to increase present levels of fixed prices.[41]

The behavior of the Moscow delegates suggests they were engaged in a transparent piece of demagoguery. They courted the provincial merchants by clamoring for "free trade in a free country," and they posed as the responsible leaders of a governing class. Whatever their motives, the outcome was politically disastrous. The compromise could not but diminish the congress in the eyes of the new government because it encouraged the hoarders and speculators to hold back their reserves in anticipation of a reversion to free trade and high prices in the fall. If the merchantry could not chart a resolute course through these familiar waters, then it could little expect to win the respect of the other social groups without which a center coalition was doomed.

The two major political questions debated by the congress also aroused strong, contrary emotions, although the form that the debate took was peculiar to the merchantry. The first of these was the ques-

40. Ibid., pp. 70–101.
41. Ibid., pp. 183–211, 230–33.

tion of whether the Constituent Assembly should meet in Moscow or Petrograd. The choice of a site for the Constituent Assembly was a decision of great symbolic importance for the merchantry. In the past, two fundamental ideologies had competed for supremacy in the Russian state—the cosmopolitan and multinational, represented by Petrograd, and the Great Russian and xenophobic, represented by Moscow. Now the revolution would legitimate one of those principles.

The organizers of the congress left no doubt that Moscow was, as Smirnov put it, "the symbol of the unity of Russia." In the words of Sirotkin, the choice between "bureaucratic Petrograd and national Moscow" was really no choice at all.[42] In an eloquent defense of Petrograd, Jewish leather merchant S. I. Khoronzhitskii pleaded for a spirit embracing "all nationalities and all citizens." But he was interrupted and cut short by shouts from the floor. The rest of the Petrograd delegates were intimidated into silence.[43]

It is not difficult to detect in these exchanges the overtones of anti-semitism and the echoes of the old struggle between the center and the periphery. The debate over the site of the Constituent Assembly spilled over into the nationalities question. The majority endorsed "Russia's unity" and denounced any form of national autonomy. In this context, once again, the attempts of the Jewish delegates to clarify the meaning of "equality" as opposed to "equal rights" provoked the congress to shout down the speakers.[44]

The other major political question to which the congress addressed itself was the question of whether it should direct its organizational activities toward consolidating class solidarity or toward forming a political party. The Moscow entrepreneurial group regarded the congress as its final victory in the long struggle to overcome the ambivalence within the merchantry. The entrepreneurs referred to

42. Ibid., pp. 153 (Sirotkin's speech), 164–65 (Riabushinksii's speech), and 165–66 (Smirnov's speech). A similar view was expressed by Poplavskii, who had returned to the fold after February (ibid., pp. 129–30). Especially noteworthy for its tone was Sirotkin's earlier speech in which he compared "the new Moscow" of Riabushinskii and Tret'iakov to "the old Moscow" of Krestovnikov linked to Petrograd, all in a folksy patriarchal style strongly evocative of traditional Old Believer tales (ibid., p. 29).

43. Ibid., pp. 130–33 (Khoronzhitskii's speech). When Baron Maidel of the Association of the Representatives of Trade and Industry and editor of *Promyshlennost' i torgovlia* attempted to intervene at this point, he was ruled out of order by Riabushinskii.

44. Ibid., pp. 10 (Riabushinskii's speech), 61 (Gudkov's speech), 47 (A. Ia. Akimov-Petrets's speech), 153 (Sirotkin's speech), and 162 (A. I. Rotner's speech and the unsuccessful attempt of Khoronzhitskii to speak). The Siberian delegate Skorokhodov insisted on another distinction, that between autonomy, which he rejected, and self-government for the eastern periphery—Siberia, Central Asia, and the Caucasus—which had never been permitted zemstvos, and this position was fully acceptable to the congress (ibid., pp. 30, 139, 154–55 [speeches of A. A. Skorokhodov]).

themselves as an economic class whose political awareness had grown dramatically since 1905. Here, the War Industries Committee had played, in the words of Smirnov, "an enormous educational role." The leadership extolled—and exaggerated—what Riabushinskii called "the active part which the trade and industry class through its representatives took in the preparatory work of the [revolutionary] movement." But they admitted the need for class unity and agreed that it should take the form of a professional union rather than a political party. As Riabushinskii made clear, their aim was to catch up with the other social classes, the workers and the professional intelligentsia, which already possessed their own unions. Without a union of its own, the merchantry had not been able to make its voice heard. To reach beyond the organizational form of a union, to strive for the formation of a political party, was out of the question, Riabushinskii declared, given the variety of political views represented by the congress. The crucial role for the merchantry was, in his view, to take charge of "the organization of the economic life of the country." In a political system based upon universal suffrage its main goal would be unattainable unless it was recognized as its corporate right.[45] Without such social defenses either the Germans would enslave the merchants or else the "dark masses" in Russia would swallow them.[46]

What he envisaged, then, was a society in which all the large interest groups would organize themselves around their social roles and occupational functions. In its general outline the plan resembled a twentieth-century version of the Petrine corporate state, but without the mediating authority of the autocrat. As a device to avoid the class struggle it was not original with Moscow entrepreneurs. It appeared throughout Europe in many manifestations during periods of great twentieth-century social crisis. But in the Russian case, the inspiration came more from the theory and practice of the soslovie system than from a conservative intellectual tradition.

To many of the delegates, the principle of all-class unity was a pipe dream and the class struggle a frightening reality. They knew neither whether to seek allies nor, if so, where to find them. No issue produced so much confused rhetoric. Still, it is possible to identify four "tendencies" ("factions" would be a misleading term here).

By far the largest number of speakers who stated a preference on the social question appealed for closer ties with the peasantry. The

45. Ibid., pp. 3–11 (Riabushinskii's speech) and 36–37 (Smirnov's speech).
46. At this point the Moscow entrepreneurs still expressed greater fears about the economic imperialism of the Germans, or even their French allies, in the postwar period than about a social revolution (ibid., p. 13 [Riabushinskii's speech], 24 [Tret'iakov's speech], and 37 [Smirnov's speech]).

precise nature of this relationship, however, was more difficult for them to define. The representatives of one tendency expressed a willingness to sacrifice even the principle of inviolability of private property in order to forge a close alliance with the peasantry, although they ignored the question of whom this alliance would be directed against.[47] M. A. Tokarskii, a small factory owner in Novgorod province, spoke for those of the second tendency when he declared that concessions to the peasantry were scarcely necessary, since "the peasantry as a whole is [already] petty bourgeois" as a result of accumulating wartime profits. Therefore, it was important to strengthen the defense of property in the countryside and to shore up the dwindling authority of the Provisional Government.[48] A representative of a third tendency, M. M. Fedorov, advised the delegates to avoid taking any stand on the agrarian question: "It is not our affair, and it will be settled without us." This position appeared to reassure a number of delegates who were concerned lest any strong approval for the peasants' demands might compromise the economic and social status quo, which they were determined to defend with or without class allies.[49]

One wonders why the merchants experienced such difficulty in placing the peasantry in social perspective. Some of their confusion appears to stem from uncertainty about their own social role. This dilemma suggests a similar pattern of evolution for both groups in the social space between caste and class. Perhaps the merchants perceived in the flux of the countryside the outlines of a drama made familiar to them by their own unfinished quest for self-identity. If the outcome for the merchants was still uncertain, then it must have been even more problematic for the peasants. It was becoming ever more difficult to ascertain where the lines of social stratification would be drawn in the future.

A fourth tendency, more pronounced among the urban merchants, was to extend a fraternal hand to the workers, an attitude which came close to denying the class struggle. Among the proponents of this view were numbered the foremost political personalities at the congress, including Smirnov and Bublikov, though Riabushinskii remained cool to the idea. But any passionate defense of workers' rights was bound to elicit a hostile reception from the congress.[50]

47. Ibid., pp. 51 (Ravkin[d]'s speech), 63–64 (Belkin's speech), 136 (Ratkin's speech), and 148 (Tseitlin's speech).
48. Ibid., p. 56 (Tokarskii's speech).
49. Ibid., pp. 60 (Fedorov's speech, 71 (Goloborodko's speech), 72 (Vorms's speech), and 140 (Bogachev's speech).
50. Ibid., pp. 36 (Smirnov's speech), 145 (Bublikov's speech), 17 (Riabushinskii's

Confronted with this welter of conflicting opinions, many of which were only half-formulated, Tret'iakov, the chairman of the subcommittee on organization, admitted his frustration: there would be no statutes for an all-Russian union of trade and industry. Although he recommended the creation of a network of local organizations, capped by a council of thirty, he conceded that his subcommittee looked forward in the near future to "a more systematic organization of the trade and industry class"[51]

Similarly, the political resolution reflected the hopeless deadlock of the delegates over the future relations of the new organization with other social groups. It recommended that all the great social problems be resolved by means of gradual systematic legislation based on the satisfaction of legitimate interests of various classes in compliance with the general good.[52] On this indecisive note the congress ended.

Union Manquée in the Duma and Zemgor

As the Moscow entrepreneurs failed to unite the merchantry and other entrepreneurial groups behind them, they drifted even farther from the landed gentry and the professional intelligentsia. The gap widened despite their attempt to launch one final assault on the crumbling barriers of the system that had for so long prevented Russia's transformation into a genuine class society. This wartime episode in Russia's social fragmentation also has a mournfully familiar ring. The same alternating process of attraction and repulsion took place simultaneously at several levels within the body politic. It began at the top with the formation and disintegration of the Progressive bloc in the duma, spread into the half-hearted cooperation and open conflicts among the representative organizations of the joint committee of the Union of Zemstvos and the Union of Towns (*zemgor*) and war industries committees, and ended in the collapse of the Provisional Government.

Within the duma in 1915 the opportunities had never been better

---

speech), 62 (Bishliager's speech), 67 (Khoronzhitskii's speech), 156 (Matov's speech), and 31 (Mikheev's speech, which caused an uproar).

51. Ibid., pp. 170–79, 232–34 (Tret'iakov's speeches).

52. Ibid., pp. 167–69. The remainder of the resolution supported the Provisional Government, the war effort, the establishment of political and civil liberty and the calling of a Constituent Assembly (without, however, even stipulating a suitable date) by universal, direct suffrage and propositional representation in the big cities and areas of mixed populations. But with the exception of the last provision there was hardly anyone in Russia who could not have subscribed to these aspirations.

for cooperation and unity of action among the centrist factions that represented those social elements that normally make up the middle class—the landowning capitalists, merchants, entrepreneurs, and members of the free professions. The prewar political alignments were in flux. The Octobrist and Kadet parties were in various states of disarray and close to dissolution. The Progressives were eager for an opening to the right and left. Disillusionment or outright revulsion with the government's mismanagement of the war gave a new sense of urgency to the movement for political reform, which included groups as diverse as the moderate nationalists and the Kadets. Together, they still commanded an impressive following on the floor of the duma, in the press, in local government, and among the representative organs of trade and industry. On the surface their differences appeared tactical and not irreconcilable. If one looks no deeper than this, then their failure to build a strong coalition determined to take power into its hands remains something of a mystery.

At bottom, the union manquée of the centrist forces reflected the underlying instability and fragmentation of social groups in Russia. Time and again during the critical war years individuals who claimed to represent these groups attempted to join together in some kind of political alliance. Their successes were few and fleeting. The cracks in the social structure were too wide to be papered over with announcements of new organizations, joint platforms, or working coalitions. The leaders could not carry their constituents with them. The agreements made by the Konovalovs, Guchkovs, Riabushinskiis, and Tereshchenkos, as well as by the professional intelligentsia, had almost no binding force beyond these individuals and their immediate followers. This was true of the relationships among the progressive factions both in the duma and in the war industries committees.

The origins of the Progressive bloc in the duma were as varied and numerous as the groups represented within it.[53] Its program was comprehensive but disjointed, its leadership distinguished but indecisive, and its legislative record mediocre.[54] Although its members

53. According to one of its members, V. I. Gurko, the "power behind the formation of the bloc" was A. V. Krivoshein, the minister of agriculture (Gurko, *Figures and Features*, p. 571). Miliukov accepts, with all due modesty, the designation of "author of the bloc" in his *Vospominaniia*, 2:206–7. The police attributed the initiative to Konovalov and I. N. Efremov, the leader of the Progressive fraction. "Donesenie obrazovanii 'progressivnogo bloka,' 13/VIII/1915," in Grave, *Burzhuazii*, pp. 26–29. Secondary authorities follow one or another of these interpretations, but it appears likely that initiatives from all three sources developed independently and simultaneously.

54. The activities of the bloc are treated in a number of works, most comprehensively in Diakin, *Russkaia burzhuaziia*, 94 ff., 200–207, 288, 300–304. See also Chermenskii, *IV-aia gosudarstvennaia duma*, 96–105, 270–71; Laverychev, *Po tu storonu*, pp. 24–28,

agreed on the need for effective and responsible government, they could not agree on what form it should take. On this crucial issue the real debate took place not among the duma deputies but within the local representative organizations. At that level social and political loyalties were drawn along lines other than those of class or party.

On the issue of responsible government the Moscow entrepreneurial group sought to radicalize the local government organizations and, when they resisted, to impose upon them a closer political unity than that that existed in the loose duma coalition of progressives. At a small meeting at Riabushinskii's on 4 August, the host and his friends tried to persuade M. G. Chelnokov, the mayor of Moscow and a right-wing Kadet, to endorse their proposal that "public elements" take "full executive and legislative power into their hands." This slogan signified a radical departure from the position that the centrist parties had maintained ever since the fiasco of the Kadet declaration at Helsingfors in 1907. What it suggested was the willingness to use militant tactics to force concessions from the autocracy, despite the great risks involved. Not surprisingly, then, Chelnokov demurred politely and in the privacy of his own circle characterized the group as "ignorant [*serye*] merchants."[55]

As preparations were under way for a larger meeting of the representative organizations to be held at Konovalov's, Riabushinskii attempted to force the hand of Chelnokov and the reluctant city duma delegates by publishing in the pages of his newspaper a list—soon to become famous—of cabinet members from the Progressive bloc in a rumored "government of defense."[56] When the so-called Konovalov Congress met, Chelnokov once again found himself outnumbered and under pressure to form a network of coalition committees representing the zemgor and the war industries committees in order to propagate the program of the Progressive bloc and to adopt a joint resolution calling for a government "responsible to the duma." But the mayor and the city duma representatives refused to nominate delegates to the coalition committee because of what the police re-

---

110–12; Riha, "Miliukov," pp. 16–24; and Hamm, "Liberal Politics," pp. 453–68. With the exception of Riha all these authors agree to a greater or lesser extent on the weakness of the bloc.

55. "Donesenie nachal'nika moskovskogo okhrannogo otdeleniia direktoru deistvii politsii o soveshchanii u P. P. Riabushinskogo, 4/VIII/1915" in Grave, *Burzhuaziia*, p. 11. This is a revealing statement because Chelnokov, himself, came out of the Moscow merchant milieu, a point given prominence by Miliukov, who considered him a political ally but, one judges from the tone of the memoir, a social inferior (Miliukov, *Vospominaniia*, 2:273).

56. *Utro Rossii*, no. 222 (13 August 1915).

ports termed "insufficient faith in the personality of Konovalov, whose demagogic appeal had frightened the industrialists." They also insisted upon a different formula for the resolution, calling only for a "government enjoying the confidence of the people."[57]

From then on the prospects rapidly dimmed for any close political cooperation among members of the Progressive bloc. Within the month the Moscow entrepreneurs resigned from the Special Council on Defense, and Riabushinskii demanded that the Union of Zemstvos and the Union of Towns disband as a gesture of solidarity in protest against the government's restrictions on the representative organizations. But Kadet A. I. Shingarev, speaking for the Moscow duma, rejected the suggestion and criticized the resignations as signs of "a failure of nerve."[58] Further disagreements broke out over whether or not to use the workers' sections and the representatives of the Allied governments as leverage to extract political concessions from the tsar. Bitterness grew apace until Konovalov savagely attacked the Kadets for "inertness, dogmatism, academism, and isolation from democracy," while Miliukov warned that "to encourage the activists of anarchist revolution in the name of the struggle with the government would be to risk all the political achievements conquered in 1905."[59]

The split and paralysis of the Progressive bloc has been attributed by one Soviet historian to "the bourgeoisie having insufficient confidence in itself," but this formula begs the question of whether the elements making up the bloc displayed sufficient cohesion at any level to deserve the class epithet.[60] Moreover, "a failure of nerve" applies only to the right-wing Kadets, notably Miliukov, who shrank before the risk of reaching for power. It fails altogether to explain why the bloc was utterly incapable of passing any of its reformist legislative program.

57. "Zapiska moskovskogo okhrannogo otdeleniia po obshchestvennuiu dvizheniiu, no. 108, o chastnom soveshchanii glasnykh moskovskoi gosudarstvennoi dumy . . . , 19/VII/1915," and "Pamiatnaia kniga moskovskogo okhrannogo otdeleniia po obshchestvenniu dvizheniiu v g. Moskve s l iiunia po l oktiabria 1915 g.," in Grave, Burzhuaziia, pp. 23, 35. There is a curious slip here on the part of the normally well-informed police agent "Blondie" when he calls the opponents of Konovalov's interest in the workers group "industrialists." They were rather the professional intelligentsia who dominated the Moscow city duma.
58. "Donesenie nachal'nika moskovskogo okhrannogo otdeleniia direktoru departamenta politsii o 4-m ob'edinennom soveshchanii predstavitelei obshchezemskogo i obshchegorodskogo soiuza i moskovskogo voenno-promyshlennogo komiteta, 8/XII/1915," in Grave, Burzhuaziia, p. 15.
59. ". . . o soveshchaniiakh u A. I. Konovalova, 12/X/1916" and ". . . ob oktiabrskoi konferentsii partii K-D, 2/XI/1916," in ibid., pp. 141–42, 148.
60. Chermenskii, IV-aia gosudarstvennaia duma, p. 201.

If a rigid class analysis does not serve well here, neither does an interpretation along traditional party lines offer much insight into the collapse of the bloc. The Progressives, who had stood to the right of the Kadets in the prewar dumas, were shifting to a more radical stance on the crucial issue of the political order, even as some of them, like Smirnov, were joining the Kadet party. Moreover, the Kadets themselves were divided over the question of how much pressure should be brought to bear on the tsar in order to create a new government. A left wing, including N. V. Nekrasov, N. A. Astrov, and M. Mandelshtam, took a hard line and drew closer to the Moscow Progressives. They shared an aversion to the Petrograd atmosphere, which bred a spirit of caution and compromise with the government, and they found a common field of action in the war industries committees, where Nekrasov, in particular, worked tirelessly to foster the workers' section.[61]

Thus, the bankruptcy of the Progressive bloc and the Kadet party must be described in other terms. Paul Miliukov was astute enough to discern in these events some of the psychological and social currents that were pulling his quondam allies and old friends into new combinations. Still, even he did not fully grasp the enormous implications of his observations and integrate them into a broader pattern of historical explanation.

Returning from a visit to Moscow in late 1916, Miliukov reported to his duma colleagues that the oppositionist mood of Moscow had become absolute intransigence toward Petrograd. In addition to this renewed outburst of an old regional rivalry, Miliukov noted the curious realignment of forces within Moscow centered in the Moscow War Industries Committee and expressed in the militant alliance between merchants and workers. "Frankly," he reflected, "it is strange to hear the conclusions on this matter [of opposition to the regime] issuing from such a milieu as the Old Believers." What bewildered Miliukov was the close contacts between "the patriarchal south side circles of the Rogozhskii and Preobrazhenskii sections" and the Social Democrats, whose influence, in his opinion, had been confined up to this point to "narrow circles of workers and intelligentsia." He could not see that these two groups had anything in common and concluded: "This sounds like a joke, but the idea of this joke is too serious for the government."[62]

61. Even in Petrograd there were Kadet defectors from Miliukov's line like M. M. Margulies, who also centered his political activities in the Central War Industries Committee, where he became deputy chairman.
62. Grave, *Burzhuaziia*, p. 143. As a historian, Miliukov had misjudged the oppositionist

Subsequently, in his memoirs, Miliukov alluded to still another curious association of his political opponents, including Nekrasov, Konovalov, Tereshchenko, and Kerenskii, who were joined together by "a personal bond, not purely political but of a politico-moral character," the exact nature of which he did not recognize until long after the revolution. As it turns out, Miliukov was referring to their membership in the Masonic Order, a murky subject which has been explored but not entirely clarified by several historians of the revolution.[63] The point that Miliukov continued to miss was that Freemasonry, like the Old Belief, was one of those "politico-moral" associations that were gradually exercising a stronger pull on individuals than were larger groupings of class, bloc, or party. As Leopold Haimson has shown, society as a whole was moving to the left. But it was also coming apart at the seams: the greater the resistance of the autocracy to compromise, the greater the disunity among the organized opposition. This was felt particularly in the social center of Russian life, where there had never been any real community of interests to begin with.[64]

It was even more difficult for the entrepreneurial groups and merchants to cooperate with the landed and professional interests in the zemgor than it had been in the duma. The war exacerbated their differences over organizing and managing industrial production and the grain trade. At the local level the war industries committees and the zemstvos not only resisted fusion with one another but competed for influence in the wartime economy. At the same time each group

---

potential conserved within the Old Believer faith, believing that by the early nineteenth century both the priestist and priestless wings of the schism had returned to the position of submission and formalism which characterized the Russian church as a whole (Miliukov, *Ocherki*, 2:89–93). He was not alone in this belief, for the police, among others, shared it: "With particular regret," reported the Moscow okhrana, "it is necessary to note that the decline in the prestige of the supreme power, the most extreme insults against feelings of loyalty to the person of the monarch can be observed in that milieu where those feelings were formerly especially strong—precisely among the Moscow Old Believers and patriarchal merchantry"("Sovdka moskovskogo okhrannogo otdela o 'nastroenii obshchestva' na 29 fevraliia 1916 g.," in Grave, *Burzhuaziia*, p. 78). The parallel here with attitudes toward the peasant commune before 1905 by officials and "Westernizer" intelligentsia suggests once again that the enormous social distances separating the sosloviia of Russian society led to profound errors of judgment and, even more seriously, political confusion.

63. Miliukov, *Vospominaniia*, 2:330–33. On the role of Freemasonry see Radkey, *Agrarian Foes*, pp. 160, 274, and 303, for a restrained and balanced evaluation; Haimson, "Social Stability." pp. 13–16. Katkov, *Russia 1917*, gives masonry a very prominent role in the preparation of the overthrow of the monarchy and the formation of the Provisional Government.

64. For suggestive comments on the same phenomenon on the left see Radkey, *Agrarian Foes*, throughout, but particularly pp. 64–66 and chapter 4.

struggled to maintain its own cohesion against the factionalism within its ranks that threatened to discredit it in the eyes of the public and the government. The economic struggle did not have an appreciable effect on the production of war material, which was still largely in the hands of the government agencies and state factories, but it did lead to a serious disruption of the food and fuel supply and contributed further to the process of social fragmentation.

The major problem remaining was that the representatives of the gentry landowners and the professional intelligentsia in the zemgor refused to recognize the merchants and entrepreneurs as equal partners in their public mission unless and until the "trade and industry class," as they called it, could organize itself in the same way as the Union of Towns and the Union of Zemstvos. There was ample proof by this time that this is one thing that the trade and industry class was incapable of doing.

The zemgor would not accept as a substitute the claims of the Moscow entrepreneurs to represent that class. Dissatisfied with the special councils, which were dominated by the Petrograd financial oligarchy, and rebuffed by the zemgor, the Moscow entrepreneurial group threw all its energies into the war industries committees, making it abundantly clear that this was exclusively their terrain. At the first congress of the Central War Industries Committee, Riabushinskii dismissed the zemstvo leaders as "a particular circle of people" who had no right to criticize the war industries committees for being "an interested party"—the intelligentsia's code phrase for the selfish material concerns of the merchants. Opposing the participation of any nonindustrialists on the committees, Riabushinskii boasted that "a consciousness has been born precisely among us [merchants], and perhaps it is a broader consciousness than among many others in Russia."[65]

By this time the zemgor had already taken the first preliminary steps toward supplying the army by creating its own technical sections.[66] Following the rebuff by the congress of the war industries committees, the zemgor decided to establish its own Committee to

---

65. *Trudy pervogo s'ezda voenno-promyshlennykh komitetov*, pp. 32–37, 144. Not surprisingly, one of the rare exceptions to the rule of separate organizations for merchants and professional intelligentsia appeared in Kiev where the war industries committee and zemgor agreed to fuse under the chairmanship of the governor-general, Bobrinskii. A joint fund of two and one half million rubles was established with the provincial zemstvo contributing 500,000 and two big sugar-beet industrialists, L. I. Brodsky and M. I. Tereshchenko, paying a million apiece (*Russkie vedomosti*, no. 157 [9 July 1915]).

66. F. A. Danilov, "Organizatsii tekhnicheskoi pomoshchi v sviazi s voinoi," *Vestnik inzhenerov*, no. 1 (1915): 74–75.

Supply the Army, with full powers to deal with the military authorities, accept orders, distribute them among town and zemstvo administrations, and construct its own factories in order to produce war material for the front.[67] This decision placed the zemgor in direct competition with the war industries committees, as well as with the special councils, in supplying the army. It also signaled the growing influence within the zemgor committee of the so-called third element, that is, the technical specialists—economists and engineers—who favored central planning and identified themselves with the left, particularly the Mensheviks.

Under the pressure of war the loose coalition of economic interests which composed the zemstvo movement began to separate into its constituent parts. Among them the gentry landlords and the technical specialists had appeared an unlikely combination in the first place. Traditionally, to be sure, they had shared a suspicion of "uninformed bureaucrats" and "self-interested merchants," but they had supported different roads to economic development. The gentry landlords, often seconded by the professional intelligentsia that had no technical training, favored local initiatives and the kustar industry as the basis for balanced growth. The technical specialists extolled central planning and technical innovation. Paradoxically, their diametrically opposed positions in a country that was undergoing a particularly intensive phase of uneven economic development had enabled them to coexist, at least in the short run, and to join against the common enemy, which occupied the middle ground between them. In any event, the zemgor had provided a protective covering for the public activities of the technical specialists until they were prepared to bid openly for the economic leadership of the country. When that time came, they found themselves face to face with their close social relations, the southern entrepreneurs.

The technical specialists had social and educational backgrounds that were similar to those of the southern entrepreneurs, and the fundamental difference in their attitudes and values could be attributed to their contrasting economic situations and occupational roles. The latter, who were likely to be engineers who ran mining and metallurgical industries as managers or directors and often held shares in their companies, were inclined to perceive the world in terms of their own and their firms' material interests. The former, often engineers employed in the academic world, by the zemstvos, or even by industrial firms in the capacity of technical advisers, took a more detached view. To put it another way, their sense of social identity

67. *Russkie vedomosti*, no. 160 (12 July 1915); Grave, *K istorii*, p. 43.

derived from their special form of mental activity, their technical knowledge, which alone gave them status in society. They were neither simply technicians, in the narrow meaning of serving "whatever strata happens to be in power," nor were they full-fledged technocrats, aspiring to political power. They represented a variation of what Robert Merton has called "the unattached intellectual." Without in any sense being alienated, nonetheless, they were "not expected to utilize their specialized knowledge for shaping the policy of the bureaucracy."[68] But their clientele was a public far more statist in structure and conception than that normally found in Western, if not Central European, societies. As did most social groups in Russia after 1905, they grew increasingly ambivalent toward state power. Their attitudes were a strange mix of patriotic sentiments and abstract admiration for central authority combined with disillusionment and despair over the arbitrariness and weakness of the tsarist autocracy.

Many of the technical specialists had attended the same state schools that the southern entrepreneurs had attended, but after graduation their paths diverged sharply. The technical specialists taught in the leading universities and higher technical schools and formed their own organizations, the Polytechnical Society in Moscow (1891) and the Society of Technologists in St. Petersburg (1894). During the revolution of 1905 they stood for liberal political reforms and against bureaucratic rigidity. As we have seen, they insisted on their intermediate position between capital and labor, sponsored an all-Russian congress of technologists, and sought to organize local unions of engineers.[69] Like many professional unions, these were quiescent during the post-1905 reaction, but the Moscow, Petersburg, and Kharkov branches were galvanized into action by the disruptive effects of the war upon their specialized fields. This time they aimed less at liberalizing the regime than at rationalizing its operations. Among their foremost spokesmen were professors K. V. Kirsh and P. I. Novgorodtsev of Moscow University, V. I. Grinevetskii, a professor of engineering and director of the Moscow Technical School, V. G. Groman, the Menshevik economist and zemstvo employee who later became famous as the head of the supply committee of the Provisional Government and a leading figure in Gosplan during the 1920s.

68. Merton, *Social Theory*, pp. 265–68.
69. See above, chap 7. Among the best-known leaders were Professor V. L. Kirpichev, the first director of the Kharkov Technological Institute, Professor N. A. Beleliubskii of the Institute of Transportation Engineers and the Mining Institute, a world-famous specialist on bridge building, and Professor A. S. Lomshakov of the St. Petersburg Polytechnic Institute, who was to play a prominent part in the central offices of the Special Council for Fuel Supply in 1915.

Grinevetskii had been one of the first to recognize the importance of mobilizing the economy for a long war in case Russia was cut off from Western sources of strategic materials. Reviewing the needs of the wartime economy, he argued that authority for the overall coordination of Russian industry ought to be placed in the hands of the technical specialists because "of the two other groups [involved] the first, the government departments, lacks practical experience, technical knowledge, breadth of view, and initiative and the second, the industrialists, lacks a disinterested point of view—and, perforce, sufficient breadth as well." Grinevetskii doubted that the industrialists and the government could "be free from their inertia in political economy and their primitive way of formulating questions" in order to act quickly and decisively.[70]

As the head of the zemgor's technical sections, Grinevetskii attempted, with the help of Groman, to put these ideas into practice. Both men were convinced that the key to success was their monopoly of technical information, and Groman took the lead in organizing economic-statistical bureaus within separate sections for each branch of the economy. Together, they would make the necessary theoretical analyses and submit practical recommendations for legislation. In other words they would serve as "a sort of technicians' clearing house" for regularizing the economic life of the empire.[71]

The cutting edge of the proposed technical transformation of Russian industry was to be the introduction of the Taylor system of scientific management into the defense plants. According to its strongest Russian advocates, the system, as it worked in the United States, "eliminated antagonism between workers and employers," as well as sharply increasing production. In Russia technical personnel organized into a planning bureau would "gradually expand [their] activities throughout the entire factory," thus becoming the ultimate arbiter and rationalizer of the manufacturing process.[72]

Not satisfied with their subordinate role in the zemgor and con-

70. V. I. Grinevetskii, "Tekhniko-obshchestvennye zadachi v sfer promyshlennosti i tekhniki v sviazi s voinoi," *Vestnik inzhenerov*, no. 1 (1915): 13, 54.

71. *Russkie vedomosti*, no. 166 (19 July 1915).

72. I. M. Bezrozvannyi, "Vvedenie printsipov sistemy nauchnago upravleniia v zavodskoe predpriiatie," *Vestnik inzhenerov*, no. 20 (15 October 1915): 933–35. The author published similar articles in *Tekhnicheskii vestnik*, May 1915, and *Volzhskii tekhnicheskii vestnik*, January, February, March, and May 1915. Among the foremost innovators of scientific management in the south was the Polish-born, Russian-trained engineer Karol Adamiecki, who devised his own theory of the harmonogram while employed at the Huta Bankora smelting works and as technical director of the rolling mills in Ekaterinoslav. He first described his results to a congress of Russian engineers in 1903 and published them in *Przeglad techniczy*, nos. 17–20 (1909). See L. Urwick, *Golden Book*, pp. 107–8.

vinced of the need for greater coordination, the technical specialists held the first congress of technical representatives in 1915. They established a permanent Bureau of Unified Technical Organizations in Moscow and combined the regional bureaus of the technical sections to form the Committee of War Technical Assistance.[73] Their aim was to strengthen and centralize the activities of the specialists, but its real effect was to create still another representative organization which claimed a share in running the war economy. This brought the specialists into a head-on clash with the merchants and entrepreneurial groups over the production and marketing of the basic necessities of life.

From the first days of the war the merchantry expressed grave misgivings over the government's decision to organize the purchase of grain for the army with the help of the zemstvos, thus bypassing the wholesale grain dealers. Quite reasonably, they pointed out that the zemstvo "was ill-equipped and in no way suited for the complex business of making massive purchases of grain brought to the bazaars in small lots and [then] putting together large lots of grain of corresponding quality." Twenty years of hard experience, including the disastrous collapse of the Kiev agricultural export society, had demonstrated to them that the zemstvos could not compete with the merchantry in the wholesale trade: as one merchant spokesman declared, "It was impossible to ignore the economic law of the correct division of labor."[74] But it was all to no avail—and there were worse things in store for the merchants.

In the summer of 1915 the Union of Towns flung down the gauntlet: "In wartime free trade and private initiative cannot guarantee the supply of foodstuffs to the country."[75] In October the government introduced fixed grain prices and requisitioning, both of which were strongly supported by the zemgor and just as strongly opposed by the merchantry. Then, at the congress of commercial exchanges, zemstvo representatives further infuriated the merchants by denouncing speculation and requesting the transfer of all meat purchases to the local and provisional zemstvos.[76] Under pressure from the zemstvos to reduce the cost of prime necessities, the Ministry of Agriculture lowered grain prices in the late summer. The merchants held Groman

---

73. "Protokol komiteta voenno-tekhicheskoi pomoshchi," *Vestnik inzhenerov*, no. 11 (August 1916): 545–47.

74. G. A. Rokhovich, "Snabzhenie armii prodovol'stviem," *PT*, no. 17 (1 September 1914): 203–6.

75. Grave, *K istorii*, p. 43.

76. *Russkie vedomosti*, no. 96 (27 April 1916). See also ibid., nos. 195, 198 (24, 27 August 1916), for additional zemstvo criticism of high food prices.

responsible for this measure, which they attacked as "antipeasant" (read antikulak), a heavy blow to the grain trade and a dangerous step toward socialism. They denounced Groman himself as "a utopian" who blamed the merchants for having ruined the system of grain deliveries. Their worst suspicions about him appeared to be confirmed when the February revolution raised Groman and other technical specialists to positions of prominence, where they became powerful advocates of a statist economy.[77]

At the first congress of the All-Russian Association of Trade and Industry a delegate from the Petrograd Grain Exchange, in an emotional speech, lifted the curtain on the social antagonism underlying the problem of the food supply: "Our intelligentsia has always been against the merchantry. It considered it some kind of parasite which, so to speak, lived unjustly [naprasno]. It was unwilling to recognize the important role of trade. The intelligentsia has now come to power. It brings with it ideas of state socialism. These ideas can ruin Russia."[78] Although the merchant delegates warmly acknowledged the Provisional Government's political legitimacy, they denounced its economic policy. The fundamental differences over economic organization that had long divided the merchantry from the professional and technical intelligentsia could not be resolved easily, if at all, by a change in the political structure.

The food supply was the major but not the only source of social conflict within the representative organizations. On numerous occasions the Union of Towns blamed the high cost of cotton cloth on the fact that the agencies entrusted with controlling prices were in the hands of the big manufacturers.[79] Right up to the end of the old regime the Union of Towns kept up a drumfire of criticism against "the big textile merchants" whose "collusion with the government" gave them a monopolistic position in supplying the army with cloth.[80] At the same time the zemstvos fought a losing battle to obtain a share of military orders for the kustar industries, which they had so assiduously protected against big industry over the preceding three decades.[81]

77. PVT-PS, pp. 88, 102–3, 183. Some of the same delegates had supported Groman at the congress of commercial exchanges when he championed the public organizations against the tsarist government. But the Petrograd Exchange opposed his plan for a unified food committee, foreseeing that the merchants would be swallowed up by the zemstvo representatives (Russkie vedomosti, no. 96 [27 April 1916]).

78. PVT-PS, p. 86.

79. Russkie vedomosti, no. 152 (12 July 1915).

80. M. Buniatian, "Normirovochnaia politika v khlopchatobumazhskoi promyshlennosti," Vserossiiskii soiuz gorodov, Polozhenie.

81. Russkie vedomosti, no. 170 (24 July 1915).

In the leather industry the zemgor, protecting the kustar manufacturers, and the All-Russian Society of Leather Manufacturers, representing the big merchants, engaged in a fierce tug-of-war over control of the production and supply of boots, harness, and other vitally needed supplies for the army. Characteristically, the government departments favored first one side and then the other, more concerned with keeping the political balance than with rationalizing production.[82]

The scarcity of industrial fuel led to the most serious conflicts between the technical specialists, acting in an increasingly independent capacity, and the southern entrepreneurial group. The fuel crisis affected every industrial region and all aspects of the national economy, yet its solution was left to local bodies. When the duma created the Special Council for Fuel Supply as one of the four central organs of the economic mobilization, it delegated most of its authority to regional councils made up of industrialists, government officials, zemstvo men, and university professors. From the outset the mine owners dominated the special council and the regional councils in the south, but the technical specialists took firm hold of the Moscow council, where, under the benevolent leadership of the economist P. I. Novgorodtsev, the technical section became the nucleus for national planning.[83]

The head of that section, K. V. Kirsh, an engineer, had already predicted a shortfall in coal production for 1915 of twelve hundred poods (over one-third of Russia's peacetime production), and he argued that on the basis of past performance private industry in the Donets Basin would be capable of closing the gap only "under the pressure of state authority invested with broad and sufficient power." He proposed the creation of a central technical council, staffed by specialists, which would draft and implement a rational plan for the use of all fuels, based upon a complex and flexible formula involving delivery costs, quality of fuel, and local supplies, so that "the industrialists could have faith in each separate case."[84] Pursuing this proposal throughout 1916, Kirsh worked steadily to expand the power of the Moscow council and to impose an external authority over the Donets coal industry.[85]

---

82. Laverychev, "Is istorii regulirovaniia," especially pp. 220–26.
83. Novgorodtsev, "Universities and Higher Technical Schools," in *Russian Schools* pp. 184–87, and Zagorsky, *State Control*, pp. 124–25, which in general, however, tend to minimize conflicts within the war effort.
84. K. V. Kirsh, "K voprosu o snabzhenii russkoi promyshlennosti toplivoi," *Vesnik inzhenerov*, no. 16 (15 August 1915): 746–48.
85. Ibid., no. 21 (January 1916): 115–16; ibid., no. 13 (February 1916): 145–49; ibid., no. 15 (August 1916): 513–14, and no. 24 (December 1916): 789–94.

Despite resistance by the southern entrepreneurial group the special council, under the growing influence of its technical personnel, finally established in late 1916 the Central Committee for the Trade of Hard Mineral Fuels of the Donets Basin (Tsentrougol), which superseded the regional council and established national priorities for coal deliveries. The move was denounced by the coal owners as "a frightening economic experiment."[86] From this point on, the major preoccupation of the southern entrepreneurs was to reverse the centralizing trend and to return not only the coal industry but the railroad system as well to the authority of the regional councils.[87] Similarly, the Moscow entrepreneurs took sharp exception to the statist planning of the technical intelligentsia. In a public debate, Chetverikov and N. D. Morozov rejected Grinevetskii and Novgorodtsev's fuel-allocation plan as a waste of time and urged instead a reduction in supplies to Petrograd.[88]

In drawing up a final balance sheet for the Russian war effort, it is not possible to determine exactly how the responsibility for the economic collapse should be shared among the zemgor, merchantry, entrepreneurial groups, and technical specialists. But as demonstrated here, their attempts at unity in an endeavor that was vital to their own survival could never overcome the shortsightedness and self-interest of the groups involved. Their hesitant steps toward political unity were no more successful. Above them an intransigent and hostile regime toyed with notions of a coup d'état. Below them a restive working class joined the strike movement in growing numbers. The divided centrist groups reacted in a series of obscure and ineffective plots and intrigues, which were greatly exaggerated by their proponents after power came to them. They soon showed themselves no more capable of holding on to that power than they had been of seizing it in the first place.[89]

86. "Protokol ugolnogo otdeleniia tsentral'nogo voenno-promyshlennogo komiteta 24 oktiabria 1916 g.," *Vestnik inzhenerov*, no. 4 (February 1917): 127–28. For a general discussion of the opposition of the coal and iron interests to Tsentrougol see Sidorov, *Ekonomicheskoe*, pp. 552–64.

87. Such was the major thrust of the fuel resolution drafted by von Ditmar and the transportation resolution drafted by Bublikov at the first All-Russian Trade and Industry Congress (*PVT-PS*, pp. 197, 212–14, 232–33).

88. *Utro Rossii*, no. 73 (2 February 1917).

89. Throughout the brief life of the Provisional Government the professional intelligentsia and the leading elements within the Kadet party maintained an attitude of contemptuous aloofness toward the merchantry and the Moscow entrepreneurs. It did not even help very much that Konovalov joined the Kadets and that Tret'iakov and Buryshkin ran under the party's label for the municipal duma. For while Miliukov grudgingly admitted the need for a coalition with representatives of "the genuine big bourgeoisie of the trade and industry class," he could not help sneering at the "motley

Political Impotence from March to November

Very soon after February 1917 the merchants and entrepreneurs discovered, to their dismay, that the so-called bourgeois revolution had not been made with them in mind. Their uneasiness grew apace until the July Days, when a crackdown on the Bolshevik organizations aroused their hopes for a strong and stable regime. Within a month their optimism was gone, replaced by a sense of desperation. The fleeting appearance of a few entrepreneurs like Konovalov and his Moscow friends in the coalition governments did little to console them. The February revolution had swept away their defenses against the working class, and they were incapable of rebuilding them alone. The problems that had kept them weak and divided for so long could not be solved by a handful of well-meaning decrees. The change in regime did not break down their social isolation. Even the imminent danger of a workers' revolution could not reconcile the merchants and entrepreneurs with the professional intelligentsia. The war had inflamed latent social antagonisms, which undermined the structure of the Provisional Government. The subsequent instability and collapse must be attributed to more than weak leadership and party factionalism. At a deeper level the government succumbed because it rested upon incompatible social groups. It turned out to be not a class government at all, but a sterile hybrid.

From the first "days of freedom" the merchants and entrepreneurs were at odds with the new government over the same two fundamental problems that had tormented them under the old regime: labor relations and state intervention in commerce and industry. The first press conference of Konovalov as minister of trade and industry was not at all reassuring for the merchants and entrepreneurs. To be sure, he had already taken steps to eliminate all restrictions on the formation of joint-stock companies and had promised to "the commercial class" assistance in simplifying and reorganizing commercial law. But reviving his pet project to form chambers of commerce was certain to meet an indifferent response from the merchants. More ominously,

---

group of Progressives" such as Efremov and Buryshkin, who belonged to "the new party of radical democrats unknown to anyone" (Miliukov, *Istoriia*, vol. 1, pt. 3, pp. 22–26). Cf. Laverychev, *Po tu storonu*, pp. 40–41 and throughout, who lends greater weight to the contacts between bourgeois groups. Rosenberg demonstrates more correctly, it seems to me, their ephemeral nature (*Liberals*, pp. 122–23, 156, 161–65, 191–92, 210, 116–17, 227, 251, 273). Aside from the "repentant Moscow merchants" the only other entrepreneurs who joined the Kadets were the Jews like L. G. Rabinovich of the southern entrepreneurs or those associated with the Azov-Don Bank, which was dominated by Jewish financiers like B. A. Kamenka.

he placed great emphasis on the government's centralization and rationalization of the war economy: democratizing the special councils, establishing special on-the-spot committees to control production in the Donets and Ural areas, concentrating all authority over coal distribution in state hands, and annulling all private contracts. Most frightening of all was his warm endorsement of a new Ministry of Labor, whose staff, he thought, "ought to be nominated by representatives of the socialist groups and parties."[90] Konovalov's ambition and his skillful cultivation of the workers' groups in the war industries committees had gained him a ministerial portfolio. But his proposals evoked no sympathetic response among his own social group and soon appeared much too moderate in the eyes of the workers and the rest of the government.

Rather quickly after this the economic policy of the Provisional Government began to draw more and more of its inspiration from the technical intelligentsia, who occupied key positions in the economic bureaucracy of the Provisional Government and pressed for greater care in planning and stricter controls. Among the more prominent were engineers associated with the leftist electrical section of the Russian Technological Society and academic centers like the Petrograd and Moscow polytechnical institutes, many of whom later became the so-called bourgeois specialists in the first decade of the Soviet regime: P. I. Pal'chinskii, president of the Special Council on Defense; Professor N. N. Savvin, deputy president of the Economic Council (created in the summer 1917 as an advisory body) and deputy minister of trade and industry; professors L. S. Tal' and V. M. Speranskii of the Petrograd Polytechnical Institute; and Kirpichnikov and Grinevetskii, both on the Factory Conference of the Moscow Region.[91] They proposed that capital and labor be granted full freedom to organize and bargain collectively but that the state reserve the right to intervene if necessary as an impartial arbiter.[92] Particularly in wartime the state

90. "Soobshchenie gaz. Vestnik Vremennogo Pravitel'stva o besede ministra torgovli i promyshlennosti A. I. Konovalov s predstaviteliami pechati 29 marta 1917," in EPR, 1:216–18, no. 89.

91. Pal'chinskii and others in this group were tried in 1930 by the Soviet government as leaders of the so-called Industrial party. Another of the main defendants, L. K. Ramzin, had been a student of Kirsh and Grinevetskii. For their Soviet careers see Bailes, Technology, pp. 96 ff, and Smolinski, "Grinevetskii," pp. 100–15.

92. Professors V. D. Kirpichnikov and Grinevetskii were in the forefront of the group proposing courts of arbitration. Arandarenko and N. Guchkov sought to oppose them and to resort instead to closing down the Moscow Metal Factory as a way of bringing the workers to heel ("Iz zhurnala no. 116 zasedaniia zavodskogo soveshchaniia Moskovskogo raiona o polozhenii na Moskovskom metallicheskom zavode . . . 3 iiunia 1917," and "Ob'iavlenie pravleniia Tovarishchestva Moskovskogo metallicheskogo zavoda . . . 22 iiunia 1917," EPR, 1:437–38, 445, nos. 235, 238).

would be obliged to regulate vital sectors of the economy like fuel. They advocated no outright socialist measures, such as nationalization, but strongly recommended government allocation of resources and the compulsory formation of trusts for defense production.[93]

But it was easier to articulate these guidelines than to apply them in the chaos of 1917. Almost at once interministerial disagreements broke out in a way reminiscent of the old regime. The Ministry of Trade and Industry, headed and staffed mainly by Progressives or Kadets, tended to favor the interests of the owners, while the Ministry of Labor, created in May and headed and staffed mainly by Mensheviks, inclined toward the workers. Not surprisingly, the merchants and entrepreneurs were not all happy with the latter, but neither were they enchanted with the former. Like the government, they agreed in principle on the nature of the capitalist regime, but they remained divided over the means to achieve it. Increasingly, they were squeezed between government pressures, on one side, and workers' demands, on the other.

In the period from February to July the merchants and entrepreneurs were on the defensive, forced to make a series of uncoordinated concessions to the workers, disillusioned by the Provisional Government, and paralyzed by their own disunity. With the collapse of the old regime, representatives of three hundred Petrograd enterprises announced a startling reversal in their long-standing policies by endorsing the eight-hour work day without a corresponding reduction in wages in order "to guarantee the full spiritual development of the working class" and to facilitate "self-education and the creation of a professional organization." With equal unanimity the delegates accepted the once-despised starosta system, offered time and a half for overtime, and proposed the establishment of conciliation boards with equal representation for owners and workers.[94] Undoubtedly, the entrepreneurs were reacting to the pressure of revolutionary events in the capital and counting on their technological edge to compensate for the projected decline in productivity, but whatever their motives, their unilateral action stunned the Moscow and southern entrepreneurs and aggravated regional tensions.[95] The Petrograd entrepre-

93. "Pis'mo predsedatelia tsentral'nogo komiteta po vostanovleniiu i podderzhaniiu normal'nogo khoda rabot v promyshlennykh predpriatiiakh . . . 30 maia 1917" and "Protokol chastnogo soveshchaniia pri Ministerstve torgovli i promyshlennosti . . . 1 iiulia 1917 g.," ibid., 1:180–81, 274–77, nos. 71 and 125.

94. "Tsirkuliarnoe pis'mo no. 247 Vremennogo komiteta petrogradskogo obshchestva zavodchikov i fabrikantov . . . 14 marta 1917," ibid., 1:511–12, no. 296.

95. "Iz zhurnala zasedaniia Moskovskogo torgovo-promyshlennogo komiteta . . . 17 marta 1917," and "Informatsionnoe pis'mo upravleniia 'Prodameta' . . . 20 marta 1917," ibid., 1:160–61, 513, nos. 64 and 297.

neurs soon regretted their hasty decision, but the damage to unity was done.[96]

Meanwhile, in the south the entrepreneurs slowly retreated, granting an eight-hour day and higher wages, in the face of growing worker militancy. These concessions were accompanied by desperate appeals to the Provisional Government. Complaining that the wage increases were swallowing up all the liquid assets of their enterprises and that undisciplined workers were terrorizing management, the entrepreneurs all over the country raised the specter of economic catastrophe unless the government saved them. As they had done so often before, they called on the Treasury to help them cover the wage increases spurred by the inflationary spiral. They regarded with horror the proposals emanating from the socialist ministers that they dig into their profits from the early years of the war to cover current costs and demanded that the Provisional Government announce its unshakable support for a capitalist system.[97] Thus, in the midst of the rapidly deteriorating economic situation, with production slumping, labor discipline disappearing, and supplies running low, the merchants and entrepreneurs resorted to their traditional dependence on government aid and displayed a reluctance to act for themselves. Officials in the Ministry of Trade and Industry admitted that "the energy of the trade and industry class which is so necessary for saving the country is extremely enfeebled." It was ironic that such opinions came from the same members of the professional intelligentsia who had long held the merchants and entrepreneurs at arm's length.[98]

In early June, however, another abortive attempt was made to create "a single, powerful, authoritative all-Russian trade and industry organization." Despite the urgency of their task it required two months for representative organizations to hammer out an agreement to create the Main Committee of Unified Industry. However, the new organization could not bring Riabushinskii's Moscow-based association

96. "Dokladnaia zapiska Petrogradskogo obshchestva zavodchikov i fabrikantov . . . 9 maia 1917," and "Dokladnaia zapiska Soiuza promyshlennykh predpriatii Petrograda po mekhanicheskoi obrabotke dereva . . . 4 maia 1917," ibid., 1:165, 514, nos. 67 and 298.

97. "Tsirkuliarnoe pis'mo no. 6 Sovet s'ezdov predstavitelei metalloobrabatyvaiushchei promyshlennosti . . . 6 aprelia 1917"; "Zhurnal no. 21 zasedaniia Sovet s'ezdov gornopromyshlennikov Urala . . . 13 maia 1917"; Deklaratsiia konferentsii promyshlennikov iuga Rossii . . . 27 maia 1917"; "Proekt pravitelstvennoi deklaratsii po voprosam ekonomicheskoi politiki, 8 iiunia 1917," ibid., 1:61, 169–70, 173–78, 225–27, nos. 65, 68, 70, 93.

98. "Dokladnaia zapiska vremenno upravliaiushchego Ministrom torgovli i promyshlennosti, V. A. Stepanova . . . 8 iiunia 1917," ibid., 1:221–23, no. 92.

under its wing.[99] In fact the All-Russian Association of Trade and Industry continued to act as a sounding board for the Moscow entrepreneurial group.

In May, Tret'iakov had announced a membership in the association of over five hundred merchant organizations, but the overwhelming majority of these were commercial exchanges in the Great Russian center. The banks and heavy industry of Petrograd and the south left the organization. To balance these losses the "economic seminars" were resurrected and given a more permanent organization in the political section of the association. For the last time the elusive coalition of merchants and intellectuals made its appearance. Riabushinskii, Smirnov, Tret'iakov, and Chetverikov joined with old associates like Lur'e, Kotliarevskii, and a brilliant new recruit, Nicholas Berdiaev. To broaden their mass base the Riabushinskii brothers and Sirotkin formed a committee for the Old Believers within the political section and urged greater political participation upon the Old Believer congress of the Belokrinitskii persuasion. However, all this frenetic political activity rapidly dissipated. In the provinces merchant support for the association dwindled. The more conservative elements among the Old Believers stiffened their resistance to Riabushinskii's blatantly political appeals, and the intellectuals sought in vain to temper the excessive Great Russian chauvinism of their allies.[100]

At the second congress of the All-Russian Association of Trade and Industry, Riabushinskii appeared disheartened and confused. His high hopes for the Provisional Government had faded: "For all intents and purposes the state power does not recognize [the trade and industry class]," he lamented, "and in many cases hinders its work in newly created organizations of all sorts of names which either exclude its representatives or permit them to participate in such insignificant numbers that they can have no influence on affairs." He plaintively reminded the left that the "recent revolution was a bourgeois revolution" and the government ought "to think and act in a bourgeois fashion." It was outrageous, he added, that the Economic Council meeting in Petrograd closed its doors to representatives of

99. "Rezoliutsiia konferentsii predstavitelei torgovo-promyshlennykh organizatsii ... 1–2 iiunia 1917," ibid., 1:181–83, no. 72.

100. *Utro Rossii*, no. 299 (26 October 1916); ibid., nos. 106, 118 (3, 17 May 1917); Laverychev, "Vserossiiskii soiuz," pp. 4–42. In his memoirs Berdiaev preferred to remain silent about his association with the "big bourgeoisie," declaring somewhat ingenuously: "When the February revolution flared up, I found myself a complete stranger. I was above all revolted by the way in which some members of the revolutionary intelligentsia were intent on making a career in the Provisional Government" (*Dream and Reality*, p. 219).

the association. He hinted darkly at the need for private armies in the spirit of another merchant, the legendary butcher Minin, at another "time of troubles" in the seventeenth century, but he ended on a note of resignation.[101]

In the period from the end of July to the Kornilov coup the entrepreneurs, if not the merchantry, showed signs of taking the offensive against the workers. But they discovered that the government, invigorated by its successful suppression of the Bolshevik party, was more determined than ever to set its own course. All the entrepreneurial groups outside of Moscow interpreted the aftermath of the July Days as a new beginning. They revived their flagging enthusiasm for the Provisional Government and admitted freely that they could not run their enterprises on "prerevolutionary principles." Recognizing as a fait accompli the new balance between capital and labor, they expected, in return, that the laws that established this balance would be vigorously enforced. Above all, they insisted that the government get the local soviets out of industrial life. "Give us good politics," declared von Ditmar, "and we will give you good economics in the Don Basin." As for the future, the entrepreneurs wanted to make certain that all legislation touching industry would be discussed with them before it became law. The recent decrees on strikes and workers' accident insurance had too many flaws, to their way of thinking. Moreover, they wanted the price of coal raised, the eight-hour day substituted for the de facto six hours, transport restored, and the new taxes on profits drastically revised downwards.[102] However, hostility in the south toward the factory committees and resistance to further wage demands foreshadowed more drastic action. The entrepreneurs' first appeals for martial law and their clandestine contacts with Cossack forces were the prelude to overt counterrevolution.[103]

The Provisional Government was as eager as the entrepreneurs to repress the disorders and increase productivity in the defense plants. From its point of view, however, the owners were often as much to blame for the chaotic conditions as the workers. P. I. Pal'chinskii, the deputy minister of trade and industry and himself an entrepreneur, berated the owners because they "had not displayed sufficient determination in the struggle with reigning disorganization and had not taken any decisive measures of opposition to the illegal demands of

101. "Rech' P. P. Riabushinskogo pri otkrytii Vserossiiskogo torgovo-promyshlennogo s'ezda . . . 3 avgusta 1917," *EPR*, 1:196–201, no. 80.
102. "Tsirkuliarnoe pis'mo soveta Soiuza ob'edinennoi promyshlennosti . . . 22 iiulia 1917," and "Dokladnaia zapiska Soveta s'ezda gornopromyshlennikov iuga . . . 2 avgusta 1917," ibid., 1:189, 192–95, nos. 77, 79.
103. Volobuev, *Proletariat*, pp. 248–50.

the workers." He urged the entrepreneurs to "organize themselves, taking an example from the workers, for only in this case was a practical correlation of forces possible."[104] Yet this advice, as it had been so often before, was ignored.

In the meantime the government pressed ahead with its plans to bring the fuel and defense industries under its direct control. A state trade monopoly over Donets fuel was approved in mid-July, when it was obvious that the southern entrepreneurs absolutely refused to create a large-scale industrial syndicate along the lines laid down in Germany.[105] The final stage in the struggle over the control of industry followed the attempted coup d'état of General Kornilov.

By mid-August both merchants and entrepreneurs were clamoring for a show of military force in order to stem the erosion of labor discipline and the increased personal attacks on managers and service personnel. Under the leadership of the Petrograd financial oligarchy, including Putilov, Vyshnegradskii, Kutler, and Meshcherskii, together with the irrepressible Alexander Guchkov, who never could resist the lure of a military solution, the Society for the Economic Regeneration of Russia was founded with the express purpose of financing Kornilov. But Riabushinskii and his All-Russian Association of Trade and Industry kept aloof. Although they demanded military measures against the workers, they refused to join the plot and threw in their lot with Kerenskii.[106] For their loyalty they were rewarded with three portfolios in the last coalition of the Provisional Government, Konovalov as deputy prime minister and minister of trade and industry, Tret'iakov as president of the Economic Council, and Smirnov as state controller.[107] While it is difficult to say for certain just what or whom they represented by this time in light of their complete break with Petrograd and their distant relations with the south, it was surely not Russia's "trade and industry class," still less the bourgeoisie. Perhaps it was little more than themselves.

In its last phase the Provisional Government was torn by internal feuds between the Moscow entrepreneurs and the Mensheviks. Consequently, irreconcilable contradictions marked its dealings with capi-

---

104. "Iz zhurnala no. 179 zasedaniia Osobogo soveshchaniia po oborone . . . 19 iiulia, 1917," *EPR*, 1:231, no. 296.

105. "Pis'mo Soiuza predstavitelei metallurgicheskoi i zhelezodeiatel'noi promyshlennosti . . . 7 iiulia 1917," ibid., 1:186, 590, no. 75 and footnote 126.

106. *Poslednye novosti*, 30 September 1936, 20, 29 January 1937; Laverychev "Russkie monopolisty," pp. 32–41.

107. Laverychev, "Vserossiiskii soiuz," pp. 48–50; Miliukov, *Istoriia*, vol. 1, pt. 3, pp. 24–30; and Buryshkin, *Moskva*, pp. 342–45, who although a member of the group paints a devastating picture of his colleagues' hunger for portfolios.

tal and labor. After Kornilov's defeat a flood of reports from the provinces on the general breakdown of relations between capital and labor inundated the government. Each side in the struggle resorted more and more frequently to its most fearful weapon. The workers seized the managers and began to dismantle the factories; the owners ordered the factories closed and the workers thrown out into the streets.[108] Mensheviks in the Ministry of Labor, supported by representatives of the general staff, blamed the owners for sabotaging the war effort and recommended sequestration. In one case an order to sequestrate was brought against the Likinskaia Textile Works, which was owned by a member of the government, the new state controller, the former prolabor member of the Moscow War Industries Committee, a protégé of Riabushinskii—S. A. Smirnov.[109]

Officials from the Ministry of Trade and Industry strove to balance these actions with strong denunciations of worker terrorism. This sparked a fierce controversy. The Economic Council, over which Tret'iakov presided, split over the use of Cossack detachments to repress disorders in the south. In the Special Council on Defense representatives from the Ministry of Trade Representatives from the Ministry of Labor demanded and finally obtained approval for the dispatch of a military commissar armed with dictatorial powers to the Donets Basin.[110] Konovalov, who countersigned the decree, also warned a delegation from the Urals that the government could raise fixed prices on metals only by a fraction in order to meet the increased wage demands of the workers. The industrialists would have to make up the rest out of their own pockets.[111] This was the extent of bourgeois solidarity on the eve of the October Revolution.

108. "Predstavlenie Glavnogo ekonomicheskogo komiteta . . . 23 sentiabria 1917,"*EPR*, 1:420–21, no. 222.
109. "Tovarishchestvo Likinskoi manufaktury," ibid., 1:450–60, nos. 244–55. Less surprising was a similar recommendation for Meshcherskii's Sormovo firm, "Sormovskii zavod," ibid., 1:476–85, nos. 264–70.
110. "Iz zhurnala no. 196 zasedaniia Osobogo soveshchaniia po oborone . . . 23 sentiabria 1917," and "Postanovlenie Vremennogo pravitel'stva . . . 13 oktiabria 1917," ibid., 1:562-63, 234–36, nos. 337 and 98.
111. "Zhurnal no. 47 zasedaniia Soveta s'ezda gornopromyshlennikov Urala . . . 21 oktiabria 1917," ibid., 1:543, no. 320.

PART 4

CONCLUSION

CHAPTER 10

BETWEEN CASTE

AND CLASS

On the eve of the revolutions of 1917 the middle ranks of Russian society were rapidly breaking up into smaller and smaller fragments. This process had been under way since the emancipation, but its beginnings can be traced to an even earlier period in Russian history. During the two centuries between Peter's reforms and the end of the empire, social change had taken an irregular course. The merchantry, in particular, had not followed an ascending, linear progression from caste to middle class. The mere ownership of the means of production in a burgeoning capitalist society had been insufficient by itself to create a full-blown bourgeoisie. Over the course of two centuries no common social or political consciousness had emerged to bind together the merchants and entrepreneurial groups into a cohesive class striving for power and cultural supremacy. In the absence of a clear ideology, a unified organization, and a strong will, the divided merchants and entrepreneurs had not been able to rally around them the mass of small producers—the meshchanstvo and trading peasants—or even their economic dependents—the clerks and shop assistants. The very narrowness of their outlook had cut them off from the professional intelligentsia, including large numbers of engineers and technical personnel who had been deeply involved in the same productive process. It was this general aspect of Russia's peculiar social evolution that the populists seized upon as proof of the artificial nature of Russian capitalism and the unique quality of Russia's social structure.

But Russia was not a static society. By the turn of the century industrialization had weathered its transplanting from "the hothouse" to natural soil. If the "Asiatic mode of production" had ever existed there, it had been undermined in the eighteenth century and smashed in the nineteenth. Indigenous capitalists contributed as much to the great industrial spurt as did foreign entrepreneurs and the state.

Economic differentiation had penetrated the countryside, and economic conflicts between workers and owners exhibited many features of the class struggle. Marxists seized upon this aspect of Russia's peculiar social evolution as proof of Russia's conformity to the West European model of socioeconomic development.

Both the populists and the Marxists constructed such a convincing case that the two positions have remained unreconciled to the present, and each continues to enroll partisans. But the contradiction between them is more apparent than real if one admits that there is a great deal of social space between the immobility of caste and the dynamism of class—and if one admits that there is no historical imperative to force an outright choice between them. In Russia social groups that normally composed the bourgeoisie in Western Europe moved into this space separately without giving any indication of joining together or moving forward at some future time. How they got there and why they could not get out has been one of the main themes of this book.

Over two centuries of socioeconomic change in Imperial Russia one characteristic was remarkably persistent: the fragmentation and isolation of social groups. In Muscovite Russia a bewildering variety of duties, obligations, and privileges was attached to different elements of the population. Peter the Great tried his best in the little time allowed him after the Great Northern War to impose a new corporate structure upon Russian society, but his system of service classes was never fully realized and its built-in social mobility was subverted by the nobility. Catherine failed to endow the system with truly representative institutions of self-government. Nicholas made it more rigid at a time when economic growth required that it be more flexible. Thus, sosloviia in Russia lacked the essential ingredients for the development of corporate rights and self-consciousness. Unlike Western Europe, Russia had not properly laid the foundations upon which to construct a genuine class society.

When the government finally acknowledged in 1861 that the soslovie system was bankrupt, it could not or would not abolish the sosloviia themselves. Theoretically, an all-class principle underlay the reforms of justice, local government, education, and the military draft. In reality, the new institutions were tainted by the residue of soslovie mentalities. The government preserved legal and status distinctions among the population for purposes of taxation, local government, the administration of justice, census taking, and, perhaps most important of all in its subtle way, the awarding of honors and decorations. Although the sense of social hierarchy was no longer so rigid as before, it was just as pervasive. It may be argued that the implications of social differences became more obvious as opportunities for social intercourse among the sosloviia increased in the postreform period. In any case, legal equality of the population remained as incomplete and inconsistent at the end of the nineteenth century as corporate rights and self-government had been in the earlier period.

The impact of bureaucratic centralization and the great industrial spurt in the 1890s failed to sweep away the remnants of the soslovie system. In fact, the attempt by the government, with the support of powerful elements in society, to preserve the traditional social structure while promoting modern administrative and economic policies created serious tensions within the country. The bureaucracy and the intelligentsia bear much of the responsibility for this anomalous situation. They believed that capitalism had to be tamed before it could be unleashed. Suspicion of any uncontrolled social process was deep seated in Russian political culture. Beginning with the Marxists, part of the intelligentsia finally accepted the coming of capitalism to Russia, but they, and many of the liberals as well, scorned the capitalists for their lack of social conscience. The bureaucrats feared that a free market and joint-stock companies would spawn autonomous social organizations and promote financial speculation and lead inevitably to political opposition and social instability. For these reasons the government piled up fresh obstacles to the formation of class consciousness among capitalists from different sosloviia and regions by limiting private associations and prohibiting all-Russian organizations. Even such a partisan of dynamic capitalism as Count Witte endorsed these controls.[1] What Russia needed to enforce these restrictions was a strong and unified government, and that was sorely lacking.

Economic and social policies varied from reign to reign and from minister to minister, and bureaucratic infighting often crippled those that were adopted. Of all the government departments the Ministry of Finance and, later, the Ministry of Trade and Industry were most sympathetic to the needs of the merchants and entrepreneurs. Yet even they insisted on close surveillance and imposed strict controls over the whole range of economic activity, from railroad concessions to stock market regulations. Official ministerial representatives were prominent at the meetings of the representative associations of trade

1. In his long memo to the tsar on autocracy and the zemstvo he concluded an introductory attack on autonomous self-government institutions by stating: "But I do not have in mind and do not consider dangerous for the autocracy the activity of various kinds of corporations, societies, sosloviia, or professional unions which enter as separate units into the general structure of the state system and fulfill some administrative functions with respect to their members but manage their own affairs without dealing with either general state problems or the entire population of a given locality" (*Samoderzhavie*, p. 8).

and industry and chaired the manufacturing and commercial councils. For all their sympathy they could not rid themselves of their conviction that the merchants were benighted and inert. Right down to the end of the empire the financial bureaucracy berated the merchants for their failure to organize, expand their markets, and compete with foreigners.

Other ministries were even more contemptuous of or openly hostile toward the merchants and entrepreneurs. The Ministry of Transportation, staffed by professional engineers, scorned private enterprise and favored a state-built and state-operated railroad system (except for a brief period in the 1870s). The ministries of Internal Affairs and Justice blamed the capitalists as much as the workers for strikes and disorders and devised dangerous schemes to patronize the working class in classical *Polizeistaat* fashion. The Ministry of Agriculture, a stronghold of the landholding nobility, sought to protect handicrafts and cottage industries against big merchants and manufacturers. In the absence of true ministerial government the fragmentation of the bureaucracy matched that of the merchants and entrepreneurs, with tragic consequences for all.[2]

No social group in the empire suffered a greater loss of identity and vitality in this unsystematic system than the merchantry. But its unhappy condition was not solely the work or responsibility of the state. Like other enfeebled sosloviia, but more pathetically, the merchantry failed to generate the intellectual vigor and collective action necessary to carry out its own emancipation and transformation. The explanations here are more complex.

The merchantry underwent many legal and administrative changes in the two centuries of its existence, but it also retained much of its traditional character. There was a greater turnover in the merchant population than in any other group, yet the newcomers did not effectively challenge the old ways. Mainly peasants, they tended to reinforce the patriarchal family customs and cautious business practices. The main exceptions were the Old Believers. In their case a deviant social position stimulated political awareness and economic enterprise. Nobles who joined the guilds after the 1880s showed no inclination to alter its structure.

Besides its customary behavior and outlook the merchantry was characterized by internal differences in wealth, status, and rank. Membership in the first guild, the distinction of honored citizen, titles like commercial counsellor, decorations and orders, choice elective offices

2. For a preliminary analysis of bureaucratic fragmentation see Rieber, "Bureaucratic Politics," pp. 399–413.

—all were the tangible signs of the pervostateinye merchants. Their lordly manner and high-handed treatment of lesser merchants were rarely balanced by qualities of leadership and independence toward their social superiors, the nobles and officials. This one-sided arrogance contributed to their lack of a popular following. Alekseev and Konovalov were rare exceptions.

A second kind of split in the ranks of the merchantry was cultural. By the end of the empire it was possible to distinguish three roughly defined horizontal strata among the merchants. Those who made up the largest layer, which included the mass of the merchantry, accommodated themselves as little as possible to the demands of a modern capitalist economy and, after 1905, a parliamentary government. They were very slow to shake off what Clifford Geertz has called "the nonrational pressures of institutional custom."[3] Living mainly in the provincial towns of western and central Russia and throughout Siberia, but also to be found in the largest cities, these merchants were primarily engaged in retail trade, owned a shop or small factory, and belonged to the second guild. Wealth was not, however, an exact criterion. This layer also included first-guild merchants in the wholesale trade, mainly grain, timber, and leather goods. Resisting the adoption of foreign dress, formal schooling, and modern business practices, they clung to their patriarchal attitudes, their extended-family firms, their bazaar mentality, and their antiintellectual bias. They traded at the fairs or in one of the large urban markets, avoided the commercial exchanges, and conducted business in their shops or warehouses. They took little interest in secondary or higher education for their sons and daughters and even less in politics. Standing in awe of the tsar-batiushka, they despised his officials. Deference to the nobility marked both their social life generally and their attitudes toward local governmental politics, except on occasion in Moscow. In 1905 their timid foray into national politics brought them little but humiliation. Thereafter, they constituted the bulk of the nonvoters in the second curia for the duma elections, forming the inert mass described by the provincial governors in 1916. At the turn of the century they numbered under a quarter of a million.[4]

Merchants whose traditional lifestyle and values had undergone some important modifications during the previous half century, made up a second, much thinner layer. These men adopted European dress, gave their children formal schooling, traveled abroad, showed great interest in technological innovation, and carried out their commercial operations on the floors of the exchanges. Mainly first-guild merchants

3. Geertz, *Peddlars and Princes*, pp. 138–39.
4. *PVP* 1:160–63.

and honored citizens, they engaged in wholesale and foreign trade, light industry, and commercial banking. Vigorous defenders of merchant rights, they participated in government commissions and ran for office in the town dumas and, less frequently, in the provincial zemstvos. After 1905 they tended to vote Octobrist, but they also gave support to the smaller parties of the center and, if they were members of national minorities that had no parties of their own, to the Kadets. But they retained their faith in the family firm, conceding to the need for greater capital only in the formation of partnerships. Residing in the merchant districts of the large towns and cities, they posed no challenge to the social domination of the nobility. On the contrary, eager for decorations and rank, they still aspired to noble status or at least to that of honored citizen. Before 1905 they were steadfastly loyal to the tsar and externally respectful of all state authority, while remaining suspicious of bureaucratic interference in business and asking only to be consulted on matters touching their material interests. Their number can be estimated by adding up the total membership in the exchanges of the main towns of Moscow, St. Petersburg, Odessa, Nizhnyi, Kiev, and Warsaw, which was about two thousand.

The top stratum comprised the merchant members of the various entrepreneurial groups. Most of these were in Moscow, but a few resided in Petersburg and Kiev, like Beliaev and Tereshchenko. Strong supporters of the guilds and the commercial exchanges, they were proud of their status as merchants and scorned the scramble for ennoblement, though not the title of honored citizen or other civic distinctions. Fiercely nationalistic, they eagerly patronized Russian culture in whatever form it took, from the realism of the Peredvizhniki to the avant-garde journals the *World of Art* and the *Golden Fleece*. But beyond this they had also taken on the complex social roles of a modern industrial world. They were bankers and industrialists as well as traders. Having accumulated most of their capital in traditional economic activities like textiles, vodka, timber, and sugar beets, they invested in a wide variety of enterprises, including banks, railroads, newspapers, publishing houses, and foreign trade. They adopted new technologies and up-to-date business methods, opened new markets, and endowed technical schools, expositions, and museums, although they tried to maintain patriarchal or at least fraternal relations with their workers. In a word, they sought to russify industrialization, to avoid the horrors of mass secular culture and class conflict which they saw in the West. Of course, they meant to do all this without diminishing their profits or control over their enterprises.

This small group of merchants boldly plunged into mass politics. At times, they reached out to the professional intelligentsia, the rest of the merchantry, the Old Believer peasants, and, in 1916, even to the workers. While they criticized the bureaucracy openly, they remained nominally loyal to the monarchy. Their conversion to democratic institutions and civil rights came too late and was too shallow. Politically naive and elitist and personally contentious, they could not bridge the deep social cleavages within their soslovie or their region, to say nothing of the country at large. By the end of the empire they had fallen to quarreling among themselves. They numbered no more than one hundred families.

Cutting through these layers were vertical divisions based upon ethnic and regional loyalties. The vertical divisions in Imperial Russian society sliced more deeply through the merchantry than through any other soslovie. The ethnic encirclement of the Great Russian merchantry outlived the coming of the transportation revolution and finance capitalism, the decline of the fairs, and the creation of an all-Russian market. With it flourished various forms of anti-Semitism, polonophobia, and xenophobia, even though Russians frequently employed foreigners as agents, technicians, or managers in their enterprises. On the eve of the war it appeared to many merchants that German economic penetration was tightening the bands of ethnic encirclement. But the non-Russian merchants on the periphery were too closely tied to foreign trade and foreign capital to share these sentiments. Thus, it is small wonder that they were reluctant to join with the Great Russians in any strong empire-wide economic or political organization.

During times of crises, such as 1905 and 1917, merchants on the periphery associated themselves with local autonomist or national movements. In the former Kingdom of Poland, along the Tatar Volga, and in Central Asia, groups supported national parties in the duma. Jewish, Ukrainian, Baltic-German, and Armenian merchants confronted a more difficult choice. On the one hand, all of them resisted extreme russification. On the other hand, they equally opposed autonomous movements led by moderate socialist parties like the Bund, the Ukrainian Socialist Federalist party, and the Dashnaks. For the Baltic-Germans the enemy was the national movements of the Estonians, Latvians, and Lithuanians. The embattled merchants of this second group were the true advocates of a *Rossiiskaia imperiia*, a term which lacks a good English equivalent but comes close to the idea of cultural autonomy, which was favored more by the Kadets than by any other political party in Russia.

These vertical differences did not signify a complete absence of common aims among the merchantry. In areas like taxation, relations with bureaucratic agencies, and zemstvos, there was generally much agreement. But strong disagreements persisted over the tariff, railroad rates, trusts, and the labor question. It has been customary to mask these differences and to ignore the ethnic conflicts by calling each segment of the merchantry or, more loosely, of the trade and industry class a national bourgeoisie. But to add an ethnic or regional modifier like Tatar, Jewish, German, Ukrainian, Armenian, or Russian (to say nothing of Muscovite or Petersburg) to the term *bourgeoisie* simply deprives it of all meaning as a category of historical analysis. In such disguises bourgeoisie is at best an occupational description and at worst an utter confusion.

If the merchantry as a whole can be identified by reference to soslovie and ethnic composition, entrepreneurial interest groups must be defined by social role and economic region. The distinction between the two was not absolute: the Moscow entrepreneurial group, for example, was virtually synonymous with the top layer of the merchantry. But the members of the second generation of the Moscow entrepreneurs were the only genuine merchants to dominate an entrepreneurial group.

The other main entrepreneurial interest groups—the southern entrepreneurs, the Petersburg group, and the financial oligarchy—were made up of individuals from varied social backgrounds, mainly nobility who had cut their ties to the land and raznochintsy in the professions. Culturally, they were worlds apart from the merchantry—even from those in the Moscow entrepreneurial group. Their ethnic origins were mixed, with Russian, Jewish, German, and Polish predominating. In education, appearance, and manner they were thoroughly Europeanized. They resembled the merchants on the periphery in that they felt most comfortable in a cosmopolitan empire where ethnic nationalism was subordinated to loyalty to the tsar and the state. Although they were usually directors and managers of joint-stock enterprises, rather than the outright owners, they held stock and had a material stake in those firms. In many cases their investments were large and well distributed among the biggest banks, railroads, and industrial complexes in the empire.

They shared with the Moscow entrepreneurs the particular characteristics outlined in chapter 4 and subsequently elaborated. To repeat these in somewhat different form, they occupied a new set of social roles free from the attachment to soslovie and characterized by technological innovation, economic risk taking, and political activism. As the leaders of the great industrial spurt in their regions, they perceived the necessity of constructing a solid economic infrastructure by establishing technical schools and credit and transportation facilities. They produced for a national market but organized on a regional basis. They sought to influence the government through propaganda, petitions, membership in official commissions, and personal influence in the corridors of power. Strongly opposed to bureaucratic interference in the work place as socially disruptive, they relied heavily on government loans, contracts, and protective tariffs for their economic well-being. This contradiction nourished an ambivalent attitude toward authority, stronger in Moscow perhaps but keenly felt in the south and northwest as well. Thus, their uncertain stand in 1905 and 1917 reflected more their interest in obtaining a free hand in their factories than in winning civil and political rights.

Their relationships with each other alternated between abortive attempts at alliances and bids by individual groups for hegemony over the others. After 1905 the southern entrepreneurs conspired to control the Permanent Advisory Office and then the Association of the Representatives of Trade and Industry. The financial oligarchy worked more obliquely through the trusts and then briefly and unsuccessfully through the special councils early in the war. Moscow, too, waited until the war to hatch its schemes in the war industries committees and the Congress of Trade and Industry. If they joined the same all-Russian organizations or sent delegates to the same congresses, it was mainly to prevent their rivals from claiming to represent "all-Russia." It was impossible for them to join in supporting a single political party. The Moscow entrepreneurs were mainly Progressives, the Petersburg entrepreneurs and financial oligarchy voted Octobrist, and the southern entrepreneurs scattered their support from the Kadets to the Polish Kolo.

It is significant that the members of entrepreneurial groups never referred to themselves as a bourgeoisie or a middle class, except for Riabushinskii, who was himself not consistent on this point. At most, they called themselves the trade and industry class. It is hard to avoid the conclusion that this was no quirk of language but a conscious choice. Like the merchants, the entrepreneurs knew full well that the idea of a bourgeoisie, no less than its existence, in Russia was extremely unpopular among officials, intellectuals, and the laboring masses of workers and peasants. The neutral occupational definition that they adopted could only be much safer.

By West European standards the entrepreneurs most nearly resembled a fully developed class in their economic interest, organization, and ideology, but each group remained a general staff without an army. Not by any stretch of the imagination can their small numbers be equated with the dimensions of a socioeconomic class, even when compared to Russia's underdeveloped urban population. Nor can they be regarded as merely the highest stratum of their class—an haute bourgeoisie. There are two compelling reasons why not. First, they may have dominated the economic life of their regions, but they did not achieve an equivalent degree of social preeminence. Despite their wealth and status they played an insignificant role in setting the norms of social behavior—the ethical and moral standards, the cultural values, the life-style—that must be expected of the top stratum of a class, even one *in statu ascendi*. Second, they made no significant contribution to the political orientation of the country; they neither produced important changes in its institutional life or its code of civic responsibility nor effected innovations on matters of economic policy. In a word, they did not stand at the summit of a hierarchical structure serving as a reference group for the aspirations of the social strata below them.

Even after the destruction of the old regime gave them a place in the Provisional Government the entrepreneurial groups did not coalesce into a ruling class. They expected, it appears, that in an open society their economic power would automatically confer upon them the respect and authority that they had vainly demanded in a closed one. They can hardly be blamed for thinking so because the European experience pointed in that direction and they had no other to guide them.

Social isolation as much as social division condemned both the merchantry and the entrepreneurial groups to languish between caste and class. In Russia the business and professional worlds enjoyed no close relationship. In other societies the lawyers, doctors, journalists, teachers, and engineers gave the bourgeoisie much of its ethical legitimacy and cultural panache. Their Russian counterparts displayed skepticism or hostility toward what they called "the narrow economic interests." They drew their ethical and political models from a tradition in Russia that went much deeper than the theories linking private property, free competition, and individual liberty. Even those like Struve and Ozerov who made a fetish of capitalism as a civilizing force could not quite stomach the Russian merchant-capitalists. To be sure the professional intelligentsia was not composed only of socialists or revolutionaries. But even the moderates perceived themselves as the bearers of liberal and humanistic values against the ruthless pretensions of the traders and the factory owners. In every attempt to bridge the gap the results hardly justified the effort. The quest for a center party in 1905, the economic debates in 1909–12, the Progressive party in 1912, the war industries committees and the Progressive bloc in 1915–16—all ended in mutual frustration and recrimination. In a long history of failures, the first and last coalitions of the Provisional Government were simply the most spectacular examples.

The merchants and entrepreneurs also cut themselves off from their potential "class reserves." The uncompromising, patriarchal attitudes of the merchantry toward their shop assistants, clerks, petty traders, and meshchane were repaid with mistrust and fear. In city government the successes of Alekseev in forging a coalition among these elements appear almost unique. It was not so much a case of missed opportunities for the merchants as of political inertia and intellectual bankruptcy. Except for the Moscow group the entrepreneurial groups showed little inclination to get involved in urban affairs. At the national level they withdrew from mass politics to a safer refuge in the State Council, rather than appeal to a broader electorate. In the countryside the kulaks went their own way, seeing no reason to surrender their profitable monopoly of capitalism in the commune to the vagaries of a free market dominated by wholesale merchants or to the structures of a controlled one run by big bankers and industrialists.

If class identity means anything, it means consciousness of one's class enemy. In Russia the merchants and entrepreneurial groups held on to the myth of nonantagonistic social relations between owners and workers far beyond the point at which reasonable doubts might have been expected to set in. Most of the merchants, the Moscow entrepreneurs, and some of the southern group fostered patriarchal ties with the workers long after those relations were outmoded. As we have seen, the same spirit animated their attempts to distinguish themselves from a Western bourgeoisie. Their social myopia stemmed from their confused self-perceptions and their belief in Russia's uniqueness. The St. Petersburg entrepreneurs shook off this self-perception, but only at the cost of isolating themselves from the other entrepreneurs. The government did not help matters by arbitrarily intervening in the relations between the owners and workers. This often obscured the naked economic character of the conflict. To be sure, near unanimity prevailed among the employers over such issues as the length of the working day, factory discipline, and strikebreaking. But there were disagreements over equally important questions, such as the workers' right to organize and participate in government commissions, boards of conciliation, and the war industries committees.

Only during periods of violent mass assaults upon their property did they abandon their illusions and grope toward unity of action. Yet even when confronted with imminent loss of control over the productive forces the capitalists exhibited little evidence of real class solidarity. They did not organize themselves on a national basis to deal with either the government or the workers on the labor question. In 1917 their confusion in the face of mass strikes, falling production, and a chaotic supply system contrasted sharply with the energy of the technical intelligentsia, though that, too, proved insufficient to check the slide toward ruin. They could not even agree on who should save them at the end, Kornilov and the army or Kerenskii and democracy. The denouement resembled less a two-sided class conflict as portrayed in the classical version of the end of the bourgeois epoch and more a multifaceted struggle waged on several levels by social groups strung out along the theoretical spectrum between caste and class. It is unlikely that this process of social fragmentation would have been reversed if the war and revolution had not happened when they did. As the government gained the means to regulate the economy, it lost the unity of purpose to apply them. As the economy grew more sophisticated, entrepreneurial interest groups proliferated. As Great Russian nationalism sharpened, ethnic loyalties became stronger.

It might be well to stop here, but another, broader conclusion may be in order. Social fragmentation and political disunity were not phenomena unique to the merchantry and the entrepreneurial groups. Recent studies have shown that the political parties were in various stages of factionalism and disintegration on the eve of the war, a process which accelerated right down to the revolution and beyond.[5] Much less has been done on the condition of the large social formations like the peasantry, nobility, and meshchanstvo. Yet even here the evidence suggests that as the old soslovie boundaries were breaking down, they were not being replaced by clear lines of class demarcation.[6]

The nobles, for example, had no common economic interest. The main concern of landlords after 1907 was to defend themselves against the industrial monopolies and the skupshchiki (middlemen) who had ceased to be independent but who had become agents of big commercial banks and exchanges. In both cases the noble landlords found themselves facing noble industrialists, particularly in the Urals but also in the Donbass, and noble bankers, especially in St. Petersburg, who were taking over the wholesale grain trade from the local merchants. At the sixth congress of the United Nobility in 1910 a special report recommended a unified noble organization modeled on the Association of the Representatives of Trade and Industry to defend the economic position of the noble soslovie. But the delegates voted it

---

5. Pinchuk, *Octobrists*; Rosenberg, *Liberals*; Radkey, *Agrarian Foes*; Rabinowitch, *Prelude to Revolution* and *The Bolsheviks Take Power*; Haimson, *Mensheviks*; Edelman, *Gentry Politics*.

6. On regional differences among the peasantry see Vinogradof, "The Russian Peasants and the Elections of the Fourth State Duma," in Haimson, ed., *Politics of Rural Russia*, pp. 219–27. See also Haimson's conclusion in ibid., pp. 263–95, on both the nobility and peasantry.

down on the grounds that they were too divided by economic and regional interests to join a single organization.[7]

Yet the noble capitalists, divided as they were among themselves, were unwilling to join with the merchants to create a powerful political or economic organization in defense of their joint interests. Like the merchantry, they were split by the contradiction between a hierarchical social structure buttressed by law, custom, and tradition and a dynamic economic process that rewarded mobility, initiative, and technical skills. It is conceivable, then, that in Russia, behind the facade of industrialization, bureaucratization, and social reform—that is, of modernization—another less visible process of social disintegration was taking place.

7. Anfimov, *Krupnoe pomeshchichie*, pp. 285–88, 303–12. For the struggle in the Urals between the noble-dominated zemstvo and the noble-controlled mining syndicate, Krovlia, see Viatkin, *Gornozavodskii Ural*, pp. 197–204, 217–20.

SELECTED BIBLIOGRAPHY

Archival Sources

Fundamental'naia biblioteka obshchestvennykh nauk v Moskve (FBON)
Rossiia. Manufakturnyi sovet. Moskovskoe otdelenie. Zhurnaly zasedanii
za 1829, 1833, 1843, 1846, 1858, 1864, 1868, and 1869.
Otdel rukopisei gosudarstvennoi biblioteki im. Lenina v Moskve (ORBL)
fond 231, Pogodin archive
fond 169, Miliutin archive
fond 332, Chizhov archive
Tsentral'nyi gosudarstvennyi istoricheskii arkhiv SSSR v Leningrade (TsGIA)
fond 150, Society of St. Petersburg Factory and Mill Owners archive
fond 1152, Department of Economy of the State Council
fond 1639, Kokorev archive
Tsentral'nyi gosudarstvennyi arkhiv oktiabrskoi revoliutsii v Moskve
(TsGAOR)
fond 672, Nicholas I archive
fond 677, Alexander III archive
fond 678, Alexander II archive

Newspapers and Journals

Aksioner
Beseda
Biblioteka dlia chteniia
Birzhevye vedomosti
Den'
Ekonom
Ekonomicheskii ukazatel'
Golos Moskvy
Gornyi inzhener
Inzhener
Khristianskoe chteniia
Moskovskii nabliudatel'
Moskovskii sbornik
Moskovskie vedomosti
Moskva

Moskvich
Moskvitianin
Novoe vremiia
Osvobozhdeniie
Poslednye novosti
Pravo
Promyshlennost' i torgovlia
Rech'
Rus'
Russkaia beseda
Russkaia mysl'
Russkii vestnik
Russkoe ekonomicheskoe obozrenie
Russkoe obozrenie
Staroobriadcheskaia mysl'

Tekhnicheskii listok	*Zapiski imperatorskogo russkogo*
Torgovyi sbornik	*tekhnologicheskogo obshchestva*
Vestnik Evropy	*Zapiski Moskovskogo otdela im-*
Vestnik inzhenerov	*peratorskogo russkogo tekhnologiches-*
Vestnik vserossiiskogo torgovo-	*kogo obshchestva*
promyshlennogo soiuza	*Zhurnal Ministerstva putei soobshcheniia*
Voskhod	*Zolotoe Runo*

Published Documents, Proceedings, Reports, and Collections

Akademiia nauk SSSR, Institut istorii. *Ekonomicheskoe polozhenie Rossii nakanune velikoi oktiabr'skoi sotsialisticheskoi revoliutsii. Dokumenty i materialy.* 2 vols. Moscow-Leningrad, 1957.

———. *Materialy po istorii SSSR.* Vol. 6. Moscow, 1959.

———. *Zhurnaly osobogo soveshchaniia dlia obsuzhendiia i ob'edineniia meropriatii po oborone gosudarstva, 1915–1918.* Vol. 1. Moscow, 1975.

Alekseev, V. P., and V. P. Koz'min, eds. *Politicheskie protsesy 60-kh gg.* Moscow-Petrograd, 1923.

Albom portretov chlenov gosudarstvennoi dumy. Moscow, 1906.

Androssov, V. P. *Statisticheskaia zapiska o Moskve.* Moscow, 1832.

"Anglo-russkaia konkurentsiia v Persii 1890–1906 gg." *Krasnyi arkhiv* 1 (1933).

Anopov, I. A. *Opyt' sistematicheskogo obozreniia materialov sovremennogo sostoianiia srednogo i nizshego tekhnicheskogo i remeslennogo obrazovaniia v Rossii.* Vol. 3, St. Petersburg, 1889.

A. N. Ostrovskii v russkoi kritike. Moscow, 1953.

Bakmeister, Ludvig. *Topograficheskiia izvestiia sluzhashchiia dlia polnago geograficheskago opisaniia Rossiiskoi imperii.* 4 parts. St. Petersburg, 1771–73.

Blagotvoritel'nost' v Rossii. 3 vols. St. Petersburg, 1901–3.

Boiovich, M. M. *Chleny gosudarstvennoi dumy: portrety i biografii, pervyi sozyv,* Moscow, 1905.

Bukhbinder, N. A. "Zubatovshchina v Moskve (neizdannyi material)," *Katorga i ssylka,* no. 1 (1925).

Courtais, fils, Alphonse, ed. *Manuel des fonds publics et des sociétés par actions.* Paris, 1878.

Dmitriev, N. "Pervoe maia i peterburgskoe obshchestvo zavodchikov i fabrikantov." *Krasnaia letopis',* no. 2 (1926).

Doklad komissii po vyiasneniiu mer bor'by s germanskim i avstro-vengerskim vliianiem v oblasti torgovli i promyshlennosti. Moscow, 1915.

Fabriki i zavody v St. Petersburge v 1863 gode. St. Petersburg, 1863.

Fleer, M. G., ed. *Rabochee dvizhenie v gody voiny.* Moscow, 1925.

Glavnoe upravlenie zemleustroistva i zemledelie, Otdel sel'skokhoziaistvennoi ekonomii i sel'skokhoziaistvennoi statistiki. *Obzor deiatel'nosti zemstv po kustarnoi promyshlennosti.* St. Petersburg, 1913.

Gosudarstvennaia duma, chetvertyi sozyv. *Stenograficheskii otchet.* St. Petersburg, 1912–14.

———. pervyi sozyv. *Ukazatel' k stenograficheskim otchetam.* St. Petersburg, 1906.

Gosudarstvennyi sovet. *Stenograficheskii otchet.* St. Petersburg, 1906–17.

Grave, B. B. *Burzhuaziia nakanune fevral'skoi revoliutsii.* Moscow-Leningrad, 1927.

Ivanovich, I. *Rossiiskie partii, soiuzy i ligi.* St. Petersburg, 1905.
Izvestiia Moskovskogo voenno-promyshlennogo komiteta. Moscow, 1915–16.
Izvestiia Obshchestva dlia sodeistviia, uluchsheniia i razvitiia manufakturnoi pro-myshlennosti. 10 vols. Moscow, 1889–1906.
Izvestiia tsentral'nogo voenno-promyshlennogo komiteta za 1915–1916 gg. St. Petersburg, 1915–16.
Izvlecheniia iz zhurnalov obshchikh sobranii i komiteta Obshchestva dlia sodeistvii russkoi promyshlennosti i torgovli. 4 vols. St. Petersburg, 1867–70.
Kelsiev, V. *Sbornik pravitel'stvennykh svedenii o raskol'nikakh.* 2 vols. London, 1860–61.
"K istorii 'rabochei gruppy' pri tsentral'nom voenno-promyshlennom komitete." *Krasnyi arkhiv* 67 (1933).
Keppen, P. I. *Deviataia reviziia: Issledovanie o chisle zhitelei v Rossii v 1851.* St. Petersburg, 1857.
Komiteta s'ezdov predstavitelei aktsionernykh bankov. *O zhelatel'nykh iz-meneniiakh v postanovke aktsionerno-bankovogo dela Rossii.* Petrograd, 1917.
Krasnyi-Admoni, G. Ia., ed. *Materialy dlia istorii antievreiskikh pogromov v Rossii.* 2 vols. Petrograd-Moscow, 1923.
"Liubopytnoe pokazanie o nekotorykh predstaviteliakh moskovskogo ob-razovannogo obshchesvta v nachale proshlogo tsarstvovaniia." *Russkii arkhiv* 23 (1885).
Materialy dlia istorii Moskovskogo kupechestva. 13 vols. Moscow, 1887.
Materialy po peresmotru tarifov na perevozku sakharnykh gruzov po vsei seti rossiiskikh zheleznykh dorog v 1904–1905 gg. St. Petersburg, 1904.
Ministerstvo finansov, Departament manufaktur i vnutrennei torgovli. *Obzor razlichnykh otraslei manufakturnoi promyshlennosti Rossii.* St. Petersburg, 1863.
Ministerstvo narodnogo prosveshcheniia. *Vsepoddaneishii otchet za 1912.* Pet-rograd, 1915.
Ministerstvo torgovli i promyshlennosti. *Torgovlia i promyshlennost' evropeiskoi Rossii po raionam v 1900.* 12 vols. St. Petersburg, 1900–1911.
Ministerstvo vnutrennykh del, Khoziaistvennyi departament. *Materialy ot-nosiashchiesia do novogo obshchestvennogo ustroistva v gorodakh imperii.* Vol. 5. St. Petersburg, 1879.
Monopolisticheskii kapital v neftianoi promyshlennosti Rossi, 1883–1914: Dokumenty i materialy. Moscow-Leningrad, 1961.
Moskovskii birzhevyi komitet. *Otchety o deiatel'nosti Moskovskogo birzhevogo komiteta za 1910, 1914 goda.* Moscow, 1911, 1914.
Nebolsin, G. P. *Statisticheskoe obozrenie vneshnei torgovli Rossii.* 2 vols. St. Petersburg, 1850.
Obshchestvo zavodchikov i fabrikantov 1906-i god. *Otchet za desiat' let 1897–1906 gg.* St. Petersburg, 1907.
Ocherk deiatel'nosti Moskovskogo obshchestva vzaimnogo kredita za dvadtsatipiatiletie (1869–1894). Moscow, 1895.
Otchet TsK soiuza 17-ogo oktiabria o ego deiatel'nosti s 1 sentiabria 1912 goda po oktiabr' 1913. Moscow, 1913.
Pervyi vserossiiskii s'ezd torgovo-promyshlennoi partii 1906 god. Moscow 1906.
Pervyi vserossiiskii torgovo-promyshlennyi s'ezd v Moskve, 19–22 marta 1917 goda. *Stenograficheskii otchet i rezoliutsii.* Moscow, 1918.
Polnoe sobranie zakonov Rossiiskoi imperii. 3 series. St. Petersburg, 1825–1916.
Polnyi sbornik platform vsekh russkikh politicheskikh partii. 2nd ed. St. Petersburg, 1906.

"Pol'skii matezh 1863 goda." *Russkii arkhiv* 27, pt. 2 (1889).
Protokoly pervogo s'ezda partii sotsialistov-revoliutsionerov. N.p., 1906.
Rabochee dvizhenie v Petrograde v 1912–1917 gg.: Dokumenty i materialy. Leningrad, 1958.
Romanov, B. A., ed. *Rabochii vopros v komissii V. N. Kokovtsova*. Moscow, 1926.
Russkaia periodicheskaia pechat', 1702–1894 gg. Moscow, 1959.
Russkii kalendar. Edited by A. V. Suvorin. St. Petersburg, 1906.
St-Peterburgskoe obshchestvo dlia sodeistviia, uluchsheniia i razvitiia fabrichnozavodskoi promyshlennosti, *Otchety za 1903, 1904*. St. Petersburg, 1903, 1904.
Sbornik imperatorskogo russkogo istoricheskogo obshchestva. 148 vols. St. Petersburg, 1867–1916.
"Soveshchanie gubernatorov 1916 godu," *Krasnyi arkhiv* 33 (1929).
Sovet s'ezdov predstavitelei metalloobrabatyvaiushchei promyshlennosti. *Trudy I s'ezda*. Petrograd, 1916.
Sovet s'ezdov predstavitelei promyshlennosti i torgovli. *Fabrichno-zavodskie predpriiatiia Rossiiskoi imperii (iskliuchaia Finlandiiu)*. 2nd ed. St. Petersburg, 1913.
Sovet s'ezdov predstavitelei promyshlennosti i torgovli. *Promyshlennost' i torgovlia v zakonodatel'nykh uchrezhdeniiakh*. St. Petersburg, 1912.
Spisok vospitannikov okonchishikh kurs v Moskovskom kommercheskom uchilishche za 100 let (1804–1904). Moscow, 1904.
Spravochnaia kniga o litsakh poluchivshikh na 1892 kupecheskie svidetel'stva po 1 i 2 gil'diiam v Moskve. Moscow, 1893.
Stenogrammy soveshchaniia o polozhenii metallurgicheskoi i mashinostroitel'noi promyshlennosti. St. Petersburg, 1908.
Svod zakonov rossiiskoi imperii (editions 1832, 1899, 1903, 1914).
Tekhnologicheskii institut, sto let, 1828–1928. Leningrad, 1928.
Timiriazev, D. A. *Statisticheskii atlas glavneishikh otraslei fabrichnozavodskoi promyshlennosti Evropeiskoi Rossii s poimennym spiskom fabrik i zavadov, I*. St. Petersburg, 1869.
Tits, B. N. *Ocherk istorii postoianoi komissii po tekhnicheskomu obrazovaniiu pri imperatorskom russkom tekhnicheskom Obshchestve s ee osnovaniia v 1868 godu do 1-go ianvaria 1889 g*. St. Petersburg, 1889.
Torgovo-promyshlennye zavedeniia g. Moskvy v 1885–1890 gg. Moscow, 1892.
Torgovye doma 1-i gil'dii otkrytie v obraze polnogo tovarishchestva i torgovye doma 1-i gil'dii otkrytie v obraze tovarishchestva na vere. Moscow, 1893.
Tovarishchestvo manufaktur Ivana Konovalova s synom. Moscow, 1892.
Trudy imperatorskogo volnogo ekonomicheskogo Obshchestva. St. Petersburg, 1890–1908.
Trudy mestnykh komitetov o nuzhdakh sel'skokhoziaistvennoi promyshlennosti. St. Petersburg, 1903.
Trudy Obshchestva dlia sodeistviia russkoi promyshlennosti i torgovli. 22 vols. St. Petersburg, 1872–93.
Trudy pervogo s'ezda predstavitelei voenno-promyshlennykh komitetov, 25–27 iiunia 1915 g. Petrograd, 1915.
Trudy s'ezdov predstavitelei promyshlennosti i torgovli. 8 vols. St. Petersburg, 1907–14.
Trudy vysochaishie utverzhdennoi postoiannoi soveshchatel'noi kontory zheleznozavodchikov za 1900 god. St. Petersburg, 1900.

Trudy vysochaishie uchrezhdennogo vserossiiskogo torgovo-promyshlennogo s'ezda 1896 g. v Nizhnom Novgorode. 6 vols. St. Petersburg, 1897.
Trudy 25, 27, 33 s'ezdov gornopromyshlennikov iuga Rossii. Kharkov, 1900, 1902, 1909.
Tsentral'nyi statisticheskii komitet Ministerstva vnutrennykh del. *Pervaia vseobshchaia perepis' naseleniia Rossiiskoi imperii.* 79 vols. St. Petersburg, 1903–5.
Tsentrarkhiv. *Rabochii vopros v komissii V. N. Kokoktsova.* Moscow, 1926.
Vserossiiskii s'ezd krest'ianstaroobriadtsev. *Materialy po voprosam zemelnomu i krestianskomu.* Moscow, 1906.
Vserossiiskii soiuz gorodov: glavnyi komitet. Ekonomicheskii otdel. *Polozhenie tekstil'noi promyshlennosti.* Pt. 1. Moscow, 1917.
Vysotskii, N. G. "Pol'skii bunt i staroobriadtsy." *Russkaia starina* 154 (1913).
Zakonodatel'nye materialy k zakonu o starostakh v promyshlennykh predpriiatiakh. Stuttgart, 1903.
Zhurnal godogo obshchego sobraniia Obshchestva dlia sodeistviia russkoi promyshlennosti i torgovli 7 aprelia 1871 g. St. Petersburg, 1871.
Zhurnaly Moskovskoi gorodskoi dumy za 1890–1901. Moscow, 1890–1901.

Memoirs, Diaries, Letters, and Contemporary Accounts

Aksakov, Ivan. *Ivan Sergeevich Aksakov v ego pis'makh.* 4 vols. Moscow–St. Petersburg, 1888–92.
———. *Sochineniia.* 7 vols. Moscow, 1886–87.
Astrov, N. I. *Vospominaniia,* Paris, 1940.
Auerbakh, A. A. "Vospominaniia o nachale razvitiia kamennougol'noi promyshlennosti v Rossii." *Russkaia starina* 138, 140 (1909).
Babst, I. K. "Istoricheskii metod politicheskoi ekonomii." *Russkii vestnik,* no. 3 (1856).
———. *O nekotorykh usloviiakh sposobstvuiushchikh umnozheniiu narodnogo kapitala.* Kazan, 1856.
Baer, K. M. *Aftobiografiia.* Leningrad, 1950.
Barsukov, Nikolai. *Zhizn' i trudy M.P. Pogodina.* 22 vols. St. Petersburg, 1888–1910.
Bartenev, P. I., ed. *Arkhiva kniazia Vorontsova.* Moscow, 1871.
Belinskii. V. G. *Polnoe sobranie sochinenie.* Vol. 9. Moscow, 1953.
Belousov, Ivan. *Ushedshaia Moskva.* Moscow, 1927.
Belyi, Andrei. *Mezhdu dvukh revoliutsii.* 2 vols. Leningrad, 1934.
———. *Nachalo veka.* Moscow, 1933.
Berdyaev, Nicholas. *Dream and Reality: An Essay in Autobiography.* New York, 1950.
Bertenssen, Sergei, and Jay Leyda. *Sergei Rachmaninoff.* New York, 1956.
Bilbasov, V. A., ed. *Arkhiv grafov Mordvinovykh.* Vols. 1–10. St. Petersburg, 1901–3.
Bolotov, A. I. *Zapiski.* St. Petersburg, 1873.
Botkina, A. P. *Pavel Mikhailovich Tret'iakov v zhizni i iskusstve.* Moscow, 1951.
Bunge, N. *Znachenie promyshlennykh tovarishchestv i usloviia ikh rasprostraneniia.* St. Petersburg, 1857.
Chekhov, A. P. *Sobranie sochineniia.* 12 vols. Moscow, 1960–64.

Chernov, Viktor. *Rozhdenie revoliutsionnoi Rossii (Fevral'skaia revoliutsiia)*. Paris, Prague, New York, 1934.

Chetverikov, Sergei. *Bezvozvratno ushedshaia Rossiia*. Berlin, n.d.

Chicherin, B. N. *Vospominaniia Borisa Nikolaevicha Chicherina: Zemstvo i Moskovskaia Duma*. Moscow, 1934.

Chizhov, F. V. "Vospominaniia F. V. Chizhova," *Istoricheskii vestnik*, no. 3 (1883).

Dan, F. I. *Proiskhozhdenie bolshevizma*. New York, 1948.

Del'vig, Baron A. I. *Moi vospominaniia*. 5 vols. St. Petersburg, 1913.

Dolinskii, V. L. *V zashchitu Moskovskoi dumy novago ustava napadok 'Russkikh Vedomostei' ili zaimy kak istochnik dokhoda i khoziaistva*. Moscow, 1877.

Dvadtsatiletie kievskoi birzhi, 1869–1894. Kiev, 1895.

Fenin, A. *Vospominaniia inzhenera k istorii obshchestvennogo i khoziaistvennogo razvitiia Rossii (1882–1906)*. Prague, 1938.

Finn-Enotaevskii, A. *Sovremennoe khoziaistvo Rossii 1890–1910*. St. Petersburg, 1911.

fon [von] Ditmar, N. *Zadachi promyshlennosti v sviazi s voiny*. Kharkov, 1915.

Giliarov-Platonov, N. P. *Iz perezhitogo. Avtobiograficheskie vospominaniia*. Moscow, 1886.

———. *Osnovye nachala ekonomii*. Moscow, 1889.

Gol'dshtein, I. M. *Sindikaty i tresty i sovremennaia ekonomicheskaia politika*. Moscow, 1912.

———. *Voina, germanskie sindikaty, russkii eksport i nashi torgovye dogovory*. Moscow, 1915.

Gorky, Maxim. *Literaturnye portrety*. Moscow, 1959.

Grigor'ev, A. A. *Sochineniia, I*. St. Petersburg, 1876.

Gromyko, N. N. "K kharakteristike sotsial'noi psikhologii Sibirskogo kupechestva XVIII v." *Istoriia SSSR*, no. 3 (1971).

Gurko, A. L. *Nashi vybory voobshche i Moskovskie gorodskie v osobennosti*. Moscow, 1889.

Gurko, V. I. *Figures and Features of the Past*. Stanford, 1939.

Gushka, A. O. [Kogan]. *Predstavitel'nye organizatsii torgovo-promyshlennogo klassa v Rossii*. St. Petersburg, 1912.

Ianzhul, I. I. "Iz vospominanii i perepiski fabrichnogo inspektora." *Russkaia starina* 140 (1909), 141–44 (1910), 145 (1911), 146 (1912).

"Iz vospominanii E.I. Lamanskogo, 1840–1890." *Russkaia starina* 161 (1915).

Kamenskii, P. V. *Znachenie torgovopromyshlennykh trestov na zapad i u nas*. Moscow, 1909.

Kasperovich, G. *Zheleznodeiatel'naia promyshlennost' v Rossii za poslednye desiatiletie 1903–1912*. St. Petersburg, 1913.

Katkov, M. N. *Sobranie peredevykh statei Moskovskikh vedomostei, 1883–1887*. Moscow, 1897–98.

Khomiakov, A. S. *Polnoe sobranie sochineniia*. Vol. 3. Moscow, 1900.

Kniazhin, V. *Apollon Aleksandrovich Grigor'ev: materialy dlia biografii*. Petrograd, 1917.

Kokorev, V. A. *Ekonomicheskie provaly po vospominaniiam s 1837 goda*. St. Petersburg, 1887.

———. "Istoricheskii metod politicheskoi ekonomii." *Russkii vestnik*, no. 3 (1856).

———. "Obed 28–go dekabria." *Russkii vestnik*, no. 5 (1856).

———. "Vospominaniia dalnoproshedshego." *Russkii vestnik*. no. 23, pt. 3 (1885).

———. "Vzgliad russkogo na evropeiskuiu torgovliu." *Russkii vestnik*, no. 14 (1858).

Kokovtsov, V. N. *Iz moego proshlogo: vospominaniia, 1903–1919.* 2 vols. Paris, 1933.

Koni, A. F. *Izbrannye proizvedeniia.* Moscow, 1956.

Kovalevskii, M. M. *Ekonomicheskii stroi Rossii.* St. Petersburg, 1889.

Kovalevskii, V. I., ed. *Rossiia v kontse XIX veka.* St. Petersburg, 1900.

Krestovnikov, N. K. *O neobkhodimosti izdaniia osobykh zakonov otnositel'no tor-govykh komissionerov i agentov.* Moscow, 1888.

———. *Posrednicheskie uchrezhdeniia mezhdu kapitalom i predprinimatel'skoiu deiatel'nostiu v promyshlennosti.* Moscow, 1896.

———. *Semeinaia khronika Krestovnikovykh (pis'ma i vospominaniia).* 3 parts. Moscow, 1903–4.

———. *Znachenie kommercheskogo obrazovaniia i sredstva k ego rasprostraneniiu.* Moscow, 1895.

Lenin, V. I. *Collected Works.* 45 vols. Moscow, 1960–70.

Leskov, Andrei. *Zhizn' Nikolaia Leskova po ego lichnym semeinym i nesemeinym zapisiam i pamiatiam.* Moscow, 1954.

Leskov, N. *Izbrannoe.* Moscow, 1954.

Maklakov, V. A. *Iz vospominaniia.* New York, 1954.

Mamonotov, I N. *Programma deiatel'nosti Moskovskogo gorodskogo obshchestven-nogo upravleniia v 1885–88 g.* Moscow, 1885.

Mamontov, V. S. *Vospominaniia o russkikh khudozhnikakh.* Moscow, 1950.

Martov, Iu. *Obshchestvennye i umstvennye techeniia v Rossii.* Moscow, Leningrad, 1924.

Maslov, P. *Agrarnyi vopros v Rossii.* 2 vols. St. Petersburg, 1905–8.

Melnikov, P. I. "Iz rasskazov i zapisok Sapelkina." *Russkii vestnik*, 54 (1864).

Meshcherskii, Prince V. P. *Ocherki nyneshnei obshchestvennoi zhizni Rossii: Pis'ma iz srednykh Veliko-Russkikh gubernii.* 2 vols. St. Petersburg, 1868.

Miliukov, P. N. *Vospominaniia.* 2 vols. New York, 1955.

Miliutin, D. A. *Dnevnik.* Edited by P. A. Zaionchkovskii. 4 vols. Moscow, 1947–50.

Naidenov, Nikolai. *Vospominaniia o vidennom, slyshannom i ispytannom.* Moscow, 1905.

Nemirovich-Danchenko, V. *My Life in the Russian Theater.* London, 1968.

Nikitenko, A. V. *Dnevnik.* 2 vols. Leningrad, 1955.

Ozerov, I. Kh. *Bol'shie goroda: ikh zadachi i sredstva upravleniia.* Moscow, 1906.

———. *Itogi ekonomicheskogo razvitiia XIX veka.* St. Petersburg, 1902.

———. *Nuzhdy rabochego klassa v Rossii.* Moscow, 1905.

———. *Politika po rabochemu voprosu za poslednie gody.* Moscow, 1905.

———. *Problèmes economiques et financiers de la Russie moderne.* Lausanne, 1916.

Pavlov, M. A. *Vospominaniia metallurga.* Moscow, 1945.

Padenie tsarskogo rezhima. Edited by P. E. Shchegolev. 7 vols. Leningrad-Moscow, 1924–26.

Perepiska P. M. Tret'iakova i V. V. Stasova, 1874–1897. Moscow, 1949.

Petrov, M. *Progressivnaia ekonomicheskaia partiia organizatsiia i partiia peter-burgskikh fabrikantov i zavodchikov.* St. Petersburg, 1906.

Pis'ma Pobedonostseva k Aleksandru III. Vol. 2. Moscow, 1925–26.

Plekhanov, G. V. *Sochineniia.* Edited by D. Riazanov. 2nd ed. 24 vols. Moscow, 1923–27.

Polenova, N. K. *Abramtsevo: Vospominaniia.* Moscow, 1922.

Polevoi, K. P. *Zapiski o zhizni i sochineniakh N. A. Polevogo*. Vol. 1. St. Petersburg, 1860.

Polovtsov, A. A. *Dnevnik*. Edited by P. A. Zaionchkovskii. 2 vols. Moscow, 1966.

Popov, A. I., comp. *Opisanie rukopisei i katalog knig tserkovnoi pechati biblioteka A. I. Khludova*. Moscow, 1872.

Prokopovich, S. N. *K rabochemu voprosu v Rossii*. St. Petersburg, 1905.

Riabushinskii, V. P. "Kupechestvo moskovskoe." *Den' russkogo rebenka*. April 1951.

————. *Staroobriadchestvo i russkoe religioznoe chuvstvo*. Joinville le Pont, 1936.

————. "Sud'ba russkogo khoziaina." *Russkii kolokol*, no. 3 (1928).

————, ed. *Velikaia Rossiia: Sbornik statei po voennym i obshchestvennym voprosam*. 2 vols. Moscow, 1911.

Rozanov, I. "Iz perepiski N. M. Iazykova s F. V. Chizhovym, 1843–1845." In *Literaturnoe nasledstvo*. Vols. 19–20. Moscow, 1935.

Rozanov, V. V. *Religiia i kul'tura: Sbornik statei*. St. Petersburg, 1899.

Rybnikov, I. N. "Rossiiskoe kupechestvo na obed u imperatora Nikolaia Pavlovicha." *Russkii arkhiv* 29 (1891).

Saltykov-Shchedrin, M. E. *Sobranie sochinenii*. 20 vols. Moscow, 1965–77.

Samarin, Iu. F. *Sochineniia*. Vol. 7. Moscow, 1889.

Semenov, A. *Izuchenie istoricheskogo svedeniia o rossiiskoi vneshnoi torgovlia i promyshlennosti*. St. Petersburg, 1859.

Sergei Ivanovich Mal'tsov i Mal'tsovskoe promyshlennotorgovoe tovarishchestvo. St. Petersburg, 1880.

Shakhovskoi, Kniaz Vsevolod. *Sic transit gloria mundi*. Paris, 1952.

Sharapov, S. F. *Dve zapiski o russkikh finansakh*. Berlin, 1901.

————. *Pochemu Lodz' i Sosnovitsy pobuzhdaiut Moskvu*. Moscow, 1886.

————. *Samoderzhaviia i samoupravlenie*. Moscow, 1903.

Shchepkin, M. P. *Obshchestvennoe khoziaistvo goroda Moskvy v 1863–1887 godakh*. Vol. 1. Moscow, 1888.

Shipov, A. P. *Khlopchatobumazhnaia promyshlennost' i vazhnost' ee znacheniia v Rossii*. Moscow, 1857.

————. *O sredstvakh k ustraneniiu nashikh ekonomicheskikh i finansovykh zatrudeniia*. St. Petersburg, 1866.

————. *Otvet g. Lamanskomu*. Moscow, 1865.

————. *Zamechaniia na "Materialy po peresmotru tarifa."* Moscow, 1867.

Shipov, D. N. *Vospominaniia i dumy o perezhitom*. Moscow, 1918.

Shipov, S. P. *O gosudarstvennom ustroistve v Rossii*. Moscow, 1870.

————. "Vospominaniia S. P. Shipova." *Russkii arckhiv* 16 (1878).

Siloti, V. P. *V dome Tret'iakova*. New York, 1954.

Skal'kovskii, A. A. *Don i Volga*. Odessa, 1858.

————. *Zapiski o torgovykh i promyshlennykh silakh Odessy*. St. Petersburg, 1865.

Skal'kovskii, K. A. *Nashi gosudarstvennye i obshchestvennye deiateli*. St. Petersburg, 1891.

Skovronskaia, M. S. *Byl i dumy*. Moscow, 1900.

Sliozberg, G. B. *Dela minuvshikh dnei: Zapiski russkogo evreii*. Paris, 1933.

Slonov, I. A. *Iz zhizni torgovoi Moskvy: Pol veka nazad*. Moscow, 1914.

Solov'ev, V. S. *Sobranie sochinenii*. Vol. 3. St. Petersburg, n.d.

Stanislavskii, K. N. *Moia zhizn'*. Moscow, 1934.

Stasov, V. V. "Pavel Mikhailovich Tret'iakov i ego gallereia." *Russkaia starina* 80 (1893).

Struve, P. B. *Ekonomiia promyshlennosti*. St. Petersburg, 1909.
————. *Patriotica: sbornik statei za piat' let (1905–1910)*. St. Petersburg, 1911.
————. *Torgovaia politika Rossiia*. St. Petersburg, 1913.
Subbotin, N. I. "Epizod iz istorii Moskovskogo rogozhskogo kladbishcha." *Khristianskoe chtenie*, no. 19 (1887).
————. *V pamiat' ob A.I. Khludova*. Moscow, 1882.
Timiriazev, V. I. *Torgovlia Rossii s Germaniei s 1887 po 1901 dannym germanskoi imperskoi statistiki*. St. Petersburg, 1903.
Trubetskoi, Kn. E. N. *Partiia "mirnogo obnovleniia."* Moscow, 1906.
Valuev, P. A. *Dnevnik*. Edited by P. A. Zaionchkovskii. 2 vols. Moscow, 1961.
Vekhi: Sbornik statei o russkoi intelligentsia. Moscow, 1909.
Vermel, Shmuel. "The Expulsion from Moscow: Impressions and Memories" (in Hebrew). *Heavar*, no. 18 (1971).
Vishniakov, N. P. *Svedeniia o kupecheskom rode Vyshniakovykh (1762–1847)*. 2 vols. Moscow, 1905.
Vol'skii, A. A. *Osnovy torgovo-promyshlennoi politiki Rossii*. St. Petersburg, 1908.
————. *Proizvoditel'nye sily i ekonomichesko-finansovaia politika Rossii. Doklad gornogo inzhenera A. A. Vol'skogo soveshchatel'noi kontory zheleznozavodchikov*. St. Petersburg, 1912.
V. V. [V. P. Vorontsov]. *Sud'ba kapitalizma v Rossii*. St. Petersburg, 1882.
Witte, S. Iu. *Samoderzhavie i zemstvo*. Stuttgart, 1903.
————. *Vospominaniia*. 3 vols. Moscow, 1960.

Secondary Sources

Adams, Mark B. "The Founding of Population Genetics: Contributions of the Chetverikov School, 1924–1934." *Journal of the History of Biology*, no. 1 (1968).
Akademiia nauk Estonskoi SSR. *Istoriia Estonskoi SSR*. Vol. 2. Tallin, 1966.
Akademiia nauk Latvishskoi SSR. *Istoriia Latvishskoi SSR*. Vol. 2. Riga, 1954.
Akademiia nauk SSSR, Institut istorii. *Istoriia Moskvy*. Vols. 3, 4. Moscow, 1954–55.
————. Leningradskoe otdelenie. *Iz istorii imperializma v Rossii*. Leningrad, 1959.
————. *Ob osobennostiakh imperializma v Rossii*. Moscow, 1963.
————. *Ocherki istorii Leningrada*. Vol. 2. Moscow-Leningrad, 1957.
————. *Pervaia mirovaia voina, 1914–1918*. Moscow, 1968.
Anfimov, A. M. *Krupnoe pomeshchich'e khoziaistvo evropeiskoi Rossii*. Moscow, 1969.
Andreev, V. V. *Raskol i ego znachenie v narodnoi russkoi istorii*. St. Petersburg, 1870.
Apollova, N. G. "Kazakhstan." In *Ocherki istorii SSSR, Rossiia vo vtoroi polovine XVIII v*. Moscow, 1956.
Avrekh, A. Ia. *Stolypin i tret'ia duma*. Moscow, 1968.
Baburin, D. M. *Ocherki po istorii manufaktur-kollegii*. Moscow, 1939.
Bailes, Kendall E. *Technology and Society under Lenin and Stalin: Origins of the Soviet Technical Intelligentsia, 1917–1941*. Princeton, 1978.
Bakulev, G. D. *Razvitie ugol'noi promyshlennosti Donetskogo baseina*. Moscow, 1955.
Balabanov, M. *Ocherki po istorii rabochego klassa v Rossii*. 2 vols. Moscow, 1925.

Baron, Salo W. *The Russian Jews under Tsars and Soviets*. 2nd ed. New York, 1976.

Baron, Samuel, "The Fate of the Gosti in the Reign of Peter the Great." *Cahiers du monde russe et soviétique* 14, no. 4 (1973).

_____. *Plekhanov: The Father of Russian Marxism*. Stanford, 1963.

Bennett, Helju Aulik. "Chiny, Ordena, and Officialdom." In *Russian Officialdom: The Bureaucratization of Russian Society from the Seventeenth to the Twentieth Century*, edited by Walter M. Pintner and Don Karl Rowney. Chapel Hill, 1980.

Bennigsen, Alexandre. "The Muslims of European Russia and the Caucasus." In *Russia in Asia*, edited by Wayne Vucinich. Stanford, 1972.

Berlin, P. A. *Russkaia burzhuiia v staroe i novoe vremiia*. Moscow, 1922.

Bernadskii, V. N. "Ocherki iz istorii klassovoi bor'by i obshchestvenno-politicheskoi mysli Rossii v tretei-chetverti XVIII veka." Leningradskii gosudarstvennyi pedagogicheskii institut im. Gertsena. *Uchenye zapiski*, vol. 229 (1962).

Bieniearzona, Janina. "Polska kadra technicza w Rosji na przelomie xix i xx w." *Zeszyty Naukowe Akademii Ekonomicznej w Krakowie*, no. 70 (1974).

Bill, Valentine. *The Forgotten Class*. New York, 1959.

_____. "The Morozovs," *Russian Review* 14, no. 2 (1955).

Blackwell, William L. *The Beginnings of Russian Industrialization, 1800–1860*. Princeton, 1968.

_____. "The Old Believers and the Rise of Private Industrial Enterprise in Early Nineteenth Century Moscow." *Slavic Review* 14, no. 3 (1965).

Blanc, Simone. "A propos de la politique économique de Pierre le Grand." *Cahiers du monde russe et soviétique* 1 (1962).

Bokhanov, A. N. "Iz istorii burzhuaznoi pechati, 1906–1912 gg." *Istoricheskie zapiski* 97 (1976).

Bonch-Bruevich, V. D. *Izbrannye sochineniia*. Vol. 1. Moscow, 1959.

Borovoi, S. Ia. *Kredit i banki Rossii*. Moscow, 1958.

Bovykin, V. I. *Zarozhdenie finansovogo kapitala v Rossii*. Moscow, 1967.

Brandt, B. F. *Inostrannye kapitaly: Ikh vliianie na ekonomicheskoe razvitie strany*. Vol. 3. St. Petersburg, 1901.

Bruford, W. H. *Chekov and His Russia*. London, 1948.

Buryshkin, P. A. *Moskva kupecheskaia*. New York, 1954.

Carstensen, Fred V. "Numbers and Reality: A Critique of Foreign Investment in Russia." In *La Position internationale de la France*, edited by M. Levy Leboyer. Paris, 1977.

Chermenskii, E. D. *Burzhuaziia i tsarizm v pervoi russkoi revoliutsii*. Moscow, 1970.

_____. *IV-aia Gosudarstvennaia duma i sverzhenie tsarizma v Rossii*. Moscow, 1976.

Cherniavsky, Michael. "The Old Believers and the New Religion," *Slavic Review* 25, no. 1 (1966).

Chernyshev, I. V. *Obshchina posle 9 noiabria 1906 g*. Petrograd, 1917.

Cherokov, Arkadyi. *Fedor Vasil'evich Chizhov i ego sviazi s N. V. Gogolem*. Moscow, 1902.

Christoff, Peter. "A. S. Khomyakov on the Agricultural and Industrial Problem in Russia." In *Essays in Russian History*, edited by A. D. Ferguson. Hamdon, Conn., 1964.

Chulkov, N. "Moskovskoe kupechestvo XVIII–XIX vv." *Russkii arkhiv* 45, pt. 3 (1907).

Confino, Michel. *Domaines et seigneurs en Russie vers la fin du XVIIIe siècle*. Paris, 1963.

Crihan, Anton. *Le Capital étranger en Russie*. Paris, 1934.

Crisp, Olga. "French Investment and Influence in Russian Industry, 1894–1914." In *Studies in the Russian Economy Before 1914*. New York, 1976.

Crummey, Robert O. *The Old Believers and the World of Antichrist: The Vyg Community and the Russian State, 1694–1855*. Madison, 1970.

Diakin, V. S. "Pervaia mirovaia voina i meropriiatiia po likvidatsii tak nazyvaemogo nemetskogo zasil'ia." In Akademiia nauk, *Pervaia mirovaia voina, 1914–1918*. Moscow, 1968.

————. *Russkaia burzhuaziia i tsarizm v gody pervoi mirovoi voiny, 1914–1917*. Leningrad, 1967.

Ditiatin, I. I. *Ustroistvo i upravlenie gorodov Rossii*. 2 vols. *Goroda Rossii v XVIII stoletie*. St. Petersburg, 1875. *Gorodskoe samoupravlenie v Rossii v nastoiashchem stoletie (do 1870 goda)*. Iaroslavl, 1877.

Druzhinin, N. M. *Gosudarstvennye krest'iane i reforma P. D. Kiseleva*. Vol. 1. Moscow, 1946.

————. "Razlozhenie feodal'no-krepostnicheskoi sistemy v izobrazhenii M. N. Pokrovskogo." In Akademiia nauk, *Protiv istoricheskoi kontseptsii M. N. Pokrovskogo*. Vol. 1. Moscow-Leningrad, 1939.

Dudzinskaia, E. A. "Burzhuaznye tendentsii v teorii i praktike slavianofilov." *Voprosy istorii*, no. 1 (1972).

25-letie Tovarishchestva sitsennabivnoi manufaktury 'E. Tsindel' v Moskve, 1874–1899), istorikostatisticheskii ocherk. Moscow, 1899.

Edelman, Robert. *Gentry Politics on the Eve of the Russian Revolution, The Nationalist Party*. New Brunswick, 1980.

Edlitskii, Ezhi "Gosudarstvennaia promyshlennost' v tsarstve Pol'skom v XIX v." In *Genezis kapitalizma v promyshlennosti*. Moscow, 1963.

Eventov, L. Ia. *Inostrannye kapitaly v russkoi promyshlennosti*. Moscow-Leningrad, 1931.

Fadeev, A. V. *Rossiia i Kavkaz pervoi treti XIX v*. Moscow, 1960.

Fanger, Donald. "The Peasant in Literature." In *The Peasant in Nineteenth Century Russia*, edited by Wayne Vucinich. Stanford, 1968.

Fedorov, V. A. *Pomeshchich'ie krest'iane tsentral'nogo-promyshlennogo raiona Rossii kontsa XVIII–pervoi polovina XIX v*. Moscow, 1974.

Firsov, N. N. *Russkie torgovo-promyshlennye kompanii v pervuiu polovinu XVIII stoletiia*. Kazan, 1896.

Fomin, P. I. *Istoriia s'ezdov gornopromyshlennikov iuga Rossii*. Kharkov, 1908.

Freeze, Gregory. *The Russian Levites*, Cambridge, Mass., 1977.

Fursenko, A. A. *Neftianye tresty i mirovaia politika 1880–e–1918 g*. Moscow-Leningrad, 1965.

Gaisonovich, A. E. *K. F. Vol'f i uchenie o razvitii organizmov*. Moscow, 1961.

Gaister, A., ed. "Produgol (k voprosu o finansovomkapitale v Rossii)." *Krasnyi arkhiv* 18 (1926).

Gasking, Elizabeth. *Investigations into Generation, 1651–1828*. London, 1967.

Gately, Michael O. "The Development of the Russian Textile Industry in the Pre-Revolutionary Years, 1861–1913." Ph.D. dissertation, University of Kansas, 1969.

Gavlin, M. L. "Rol' tsentra i okrain Rossiiskoi imperii v formirovanii krupnoi moskovskoi burzhuazii v poreformennyi period." *Istoricheskie zapiski* 92 (1973).

————. "Sotsial'nyi sostav krupnoi moskovskoi burzhuazii vo vtoroi polovine XIX v." In Akademiia nauk, Institut istorii, *Problemy otechestvennoi istorii*. Vol. 1. Moscow, 1973.

Gefter, M. Ia. "Bor'ba vokrug sozdaniia metallurgicheskoi tresta v Rossii v nachale XX v." *Istoricheskie zapiski* 48 (1954).

Genkin, L. B. "Obshchestvenno-politicheskaia programma russkoi burzhuazii v gody pervoi revoliutsionnoi situatsii (1859–1861 gg.): Po materialam zhurnala 'Vestnik Promyshlennosti,' " In *Problemy sotsial'no ekonomicheskoi istorii Rossii*. Moscow, 1971.

Gerschenkron, Alexander. *Economic Backwardness in Historical Perspective*. New York, 1962.

————. *Europe in the Russian Mirror*. Cambridge, 1970.

Gerstein, Linda. "Fedor Shekhtel." In *Macmillan Encyclopedia of Architects*, forthcoming.

Getzler, Israel. *Martov: A Political Biography of a Russian Social Democrat*. Cambridge, 1967.

Gindin, I. F. *Gosudarstvennyi bank i ekonomicheskaia politika tsarskogo pravitel'stva, 1861–1892*. Moscow, 1960.

————. "Moskovskie banki v period imperializma." *Istoricheskie zapiski* 58 (1956).

————. "Ob osnovakh ekonomicheskoi politiki tsarskogo pravitel'stva v kontse XIX–nachale XX v." In Akademiia nauk, *Materialy po istorii SSSR*. Vol. 6. Moscow, 1959.

————. "O nekotorykh osobennostiakh ekonomicheskoi i sotsial'noi struktury rossiiskogo kapitalizma v nachale XX v." *Istoriia SSSR*, no. 3 (1966).

————. "Politika tsarskogo pravitel'stva v otnoshenii promyshlennykh monopolii." In Akademiia nauk, Institut istorii, *Ob osobennostiakh imperializma v Rossii*. Moscow, 1963.

————. "Pravitel'stvennaia podderzhka ural'skikh magnatov vo vtoroi polovine XIX–nachale XX v." *Istoricheskie zapiski* 82 (1968).

————. "Russkaia burzhuaziia v period kapitalizma: Ee razvitie i osobennosti." *Istoriia SSSR*, nos. 2, 3 (1962).

————. *Russkie kommercheskie banki*. Moscow, 1948.

————, and L. E. Shepelev. "Bankovskie monopolii v Rossii nakanune velikoi oktiabr'skoi revoliutsii." *Istoricheskie zapiski* 66 (1960).

Gol'dovskii, O. "Evrei v Moskve." *Byloe* 9 (1907).

Golikova, N. B. "Rostovshchichestvo v Rossii nachala XVIII v. i ego nekotorye osobennosti." In *Problemy genezisa kapitalizma*. Moscow, 1970.

Golitsyn, V. "Moskva v semidesiatykh godakh." *Golos minuvshago* 5–12 (1919).

Gorbunov, D. G. *Moskovskie gorodskie boini*. Moscow, 1913.

Grave, B. B. *K istorii klassovoi bor'by v Rossii v gody imperialisticheskoi voiny, iiul' 1914–fevral' 1917: Proletariat i burzhuaziia*. Moscow-Leningrad, 1926.

Gray, Camilla. *The Great Experiment: Russian Art, 1863–1922*. London, 1962.

Green, Donald Webb. "Industrialization and the Engineering Ascendency: A Comparative Study of American and Russian Engineering Elites, 1870–1940." Ph.D. dissertation, University of California, Berkeley, 1972.

Gregorian, Vartan. "The Impact of Russia on the Armenians and Armenia." In *Russia and Asia*, edited by Wayne Vucinich. Stanford, 1972.

Grits, T. S. *M. S. Shchepkin: Letopis', zhizn' i tvorchestva*. Moscow, 1966.

Haimson, Leopold. "The Problem of Social Stability in Urban Russia, 1905–1917." *Slavic Review* 23, no. 4 (1964), 24, no. 1 (1965).

_____, ed. *The Mensheviks from the Revolution of 1917 to the Second World War.* Chicago, 1974.

_____. *The Politics of Rural Russia.* Bloomington, 1979.

Hamm, Michael F., ed. *The City in Russian History.* Lexington, Ky., 1976.

_____. "Liberal Politics in Wartime Russia: An Analysis of the Progressive Bloc." *Slavic Review* 33, no. 3 (1974).

Hellie, Richard. *Enserfment and Military Change in Muscovy.* Chicago, 1971.

Hilchen, Henryk. *Historya drogi zeleznej Warszawsko-Wiedénskiej, 1835–1843–1898: Przyczynek do historyi kolejnictwa w Królestwie Polskiem.* Warsaw, 1912.

Hittle, J. Michael. *The Service City, State and Townsmen in Russia, 1600–1800.* Cambridge, Mass., 1979.

Hosking, Geoffrey. *The Russian Constitutional Experiment.* Cambridge, 1973.

Hutchinson, J. F. "The Octobrists and the Future of Imperial Russia as a Great Power." *Slavic and East European Review* 50, no. 119 (April 1972).

Iakovlev, A. F. *Ekonomicheskie krizisy v Rossii.* Moscow, 1955.

Iakovtsevskii, V. N. *Kupecheskii kapital v feodal'no-krepostnicheskoi Rossii.* Moscow, 1953.

Iasman, Z. D. "Voznikovenie sel'skokhoziaistvennogo mashinostroeniia v krepostnoi Rossii." *Voprosy istorii,* no. 3 (1972).

Iatsunskii, V. K. "Rol' Peterburga v promyshlennom razvitii dorevoliutsionnoi Rossii." *Voprosy istorii,* no. 9 (1954).

Ilovaiskii, D. "Novgorodskaia guberniia sto let tomu nazad: Iz biografii grafa Ia. E. Siversa." *Russkii vestnik* 55–56 (1865).

Isaev, G. S. *Rol' tekstil'noi promyshlennosti v genezise i razvitii kapitalizma v Rossii.* Leningrad, 1970.

Iuditskii, A. D. "Evreiskaia burzhuaziia i evreiskie rabochie v tekstil'noi promyshlennosti pervoi poloviny XIX v." *Istoricheskii sbornik,* no. 4 (1935).

Iuksimovich, Ch. M. *Manufakturnaia promyshlennost' v proshlom i nastoiashchem.* Vol. 1. Moscow, 1915.

Ivanov, E. M. *40 let deiatel'nosti Moskovskoi sanitarnoi organizatsii, 1883–1925.* Moscow, 1925.

Ivanov, L. M. "O soslovno-klassovoi strukture gorodov kapitalisticheskoi Rossii." In *Problemy sotsial'noekonomicheskoi istorii Rossii.* Moscow, 1971.

Ivanova, N. A., and V. V. Shelokhaev. "Torgovye sluzhashchie v revoliutsii 1905–1907 gg." *Istoricheskie zapiski* 101 (1978).

Jaros, Jerzy. "Polacy w Leningradzkim instytucie gorniczym." *Kwartalnik historii nauki i techniki* 17, no. 3 (1973).

Jedlicki, Jerzy. *Nieudana proba Kapitalistycznej Industrializacji: Analiza pastwowego gospodarstwa przemyslego w Krolestwie Polskim XIX wieku.* Warsaw, 1964.

Joffe, Muriel. "The Cotton Manufacturers in the Central Industrial Region, 1880s to 1914." Ph.D. dissertation, University of Pennsylvania, 1981.

Kabanov, P. I. *Amurskii vopros.* Blagoveshchensk, 1959.

Kabuzan, V. M. *Narodonaselenie Rossii v XVIII–pervoi polovine XIX v.* Moscow, 1963.

Kafengauz, B. B. *Istoriia khoziaistva Demidovykh v XVIII–XIX vv.* Vol. 1. Moscow, 1949.

_____. "Kupecheskie memuary." In *Trudy Obshchestva izucheniia moskovskoi gubernii.* Vol. 1. Moscow, 1928.

Kafengauz, L. B. *Sindikaty v russkoi zheleznoi promyshlennosti.* Moscow, 1910.

Kahan, Arcadius. "Continuity in Economic Activity and Policy During the

Post-Petrine Period in Russia." *Journal of Economic History* 25, no. 1 (1965).
————. "The Costs of 'Westernization': The Gentry and the Russian Economy in the Eighteenth Century." *Slavic Review* 25, no. 1 (1966).
————. "Entrepreneurship in the Early Development of Iron Manufacturing in Russia." *Economic Development and Cultural Change* 10, no. 1 (1962).
————. "Government Policies and the Industrialization of Russia." *Journal of Economic History* 27, no. 4 (1967).
Kaminka, A. I. *Aktsionernye kompanii.* St. Petersburg, 1902.
Kamosko, L. V. "Izmeneniia soslovnogo sostava uchashchikhsiia srednei i vyshei shkoly Rossii (30–80–e gody XIX v.)." *Voprosy istorii,* no. 10 (1970).
Karelin, A. P. "Dvorianstvo i torgovo-promyshlennoe predprinimatel'stvo v poreformennoi Rossii (1861–1904 gg.)." *Istoricheskie zapiski* 102 (1978).
————. "Dvorianstvo v prereformennoi Rossii." *Istoricheskie zapiski* 87 (1971).
Karma, O. O. "Ocherk razvitiia manufakturnoi stadii promyshlennosti v Estonii." In *Genezis kapitalizma v promyshlennosti.* Moscow, 1963.
Karnovich, E. P. *Zamechatel'nye bogatstva chastnykh lits v Rossii.* St. Petersburg, 1885.
Kassis, Zh. *Polozhenie russkoi torgovli i sostoianie shelkovodstva v Sirii.* Kiev, 1913.
Katkov, George. *Russia 1917: The February Revolution.* New York, 1967.
Keep, J. H. L. *The Rise of Social Democracy in Russia.* Oxford, 1963.
Khlostov, I. P. *Don v epokhu kapitalizma, 60-e-seredina 90-x godov XIX veka.* Rostov, 1962.
Khromov, P. A. *Ekonomicheskoe razvitie Rossii v XIX–XX vekakh, 1800–1917.* Moscow, 1950.
Kirchner, Walther. *Commercial Relations between Russia and Europe, 1400–1800.* Bloomington, 1966.
Kirichenko, E. *Moskva, pamiatniki arkhitektury, 1830–1922.* Moscow, 1977.
Kirillov, I. A. *Pravda staroi very.* Moscow, 1916.
Kislinskii, N. A. *Nasha zheleznodorozhnaia politika.* Vol. 1. St. Petersburg, 1902.
Kitanina, T. M. *Khlebnaia torgovlia Rossii, 1875–1914 gg.* Leningrad, 1978.
Kizevetter, A. A. *Posadskaia obshchina v XVIII st.* Moscow, 1903.
Kliuchevskii, V. O. "Chtenie o G. F. Karpove v chrezvychainom zasedanii imp. obshchestva istorii i drevnostei rossiiskikh pri Moskovskom universitete 18 noiabria 1890 g." *Chteniia Obshchestva istorii i drevnostei rossiiskikh* 1 (1892).
————. "Dva vospitaniia." *Ocherki i rechi.* Moscow, n.d.
————. *Istoriia soslovii v Rossii.* 3rd ed. Petrograd, 1918.
Klochkov, M. V. *Ocherki pravitel'stvennoi deiatel'nosti vremeni Pavla I.* Petrograd, 1916.
Klokman, Iu. P. *Sotsial'no-ekonomicheskaia istoriia russkogo goroda vtoraia polovina XVIII veka.* Moscow, 1967.
Knabe, Bernd. "Die Struktur der russischen Posadgemeinden und der Katalog der Beschwerden und Forderungen der Kaufmannschaft (1762–1767)." *Forschungen zur Osteuropäischen Geschichte.* Vol. 22. Berlin, 1975.
Kniapina, N. S. *Politika russkogo samoderzhaviia v oblasti promyshlennosti.* Moscow, 1968.
Kohut, Zenon. "The Abolition of Ukrainian Autonomy." Ph.D. dissertation, University of Pennsylvania, 1975.
Korf, Baron S. A. *Dvorianstvo i ego soslovnoe upravlenie za stoletie 1762–1855 godov.* St. Petersburg, 1906.

Korsak, A. *O formakh promyshlennosti voobshche i o znachenii domashnego proiz-vodstva v zapadnoi Evropy i Rossii.* Moscow, 1861.
Koshelev, A. I. *Golos iz zemstva.* Vol. 1. Moscow, 1869.
Kozmin, M. I. *Ocherki ekonomicheskoi istorii Litvi 1860–1900.* Riga, 1972.
Kratkii istoricheskii ocherk o S-Peterburgskom prakticheskom tekhnologicheskom institute, 1828–1878. St. Petersburg, 1878.
Krestinin, Vasil'ii. *Kratkaia istoriia o gorode Arkhangel'skom.* St. Petersburg, 1792.
Lappo-Danilevskii, A. S. "Russkie promyshlennye i torgovlie kompanii." *Zhurnal ministerstva narodnogo prosveshcheniia* 320, 321 (December 1898, February 1899).
Lauwick, M. *L'Industrie dans la Russie meridionale, sa situation, sa avenir.* Brussels, 1907.
Laverychev, V. Ia. "Iz istorii gosudarstvennogo regulirovaniia voennoi ekonomiki Rossii v gody pervoi mirovoi voiny (1914–fevral' 1917)." In Akademiia nauk, Institut istorii, *Pervaia mirovaia voina, 1914–1918.* Moscow, 1968.
_____. *Krupnaia burzhuaziia v poreformennoi Rossii, 1861–1900.* Moscow, 1974.
_____. *Monopolisticheskii kapital v tekstil'noi promyshlennosti Rossii (1900–1917 gg.).* Moscow, 1963.
_____. "Moskovskie fabrikanty i sredneaziatskii khlopok." *Vestnik Moskovskogo universiteta (seriia istoriia)*, no. 1 (1970).
_____. *Po tu storonu barrikad: Iz istorii bor'by Moskovskoi burzhuazii s revoliutsii.* Moscow, 1967.
_____. "Russkie kapitalisty i periodicheskaia pechat' vtoroi poloviny XIX v." *Istoriia SSSR*, no. 1 (1972).
_____. "Russkie monopolisty i zagovor Kornilova." *Voprosy istorii*, no. 3 (1964).
_____. *Tsarizm i rabochii vopros v Rossii, 1861–1917.* Moscow, 1972.
_____. "Vserossiiskoi soiuz torgovli i promyshlennosti." *Istoricheskie zapiski*, no. 70 (1961).
Lavigne, M. L. "Le Plan de Mikhajl Rjabushinskij: Un project de concentration industrielle en 1916." *Cahiers du monde russe et soviétique* 5 (1964).
Lavrov, P. A. *Rabochee dvizhenie na Ukraine v 1913–1914 gg.* Kiev, 1957.
Leikina-Svirskaia, V. R. *Intelligentsiia v Rossii vo vtoroi polovine XIX veka.* Moscow, 1971.
Lemke, Mikhail. *Epokha tsenzurnykh reform (1859–1865 gg.).* St. Petersburg, 1904.
Levin, I. I. *Aktsionernye kommercheskie banki v Rossii, Petrograd.* Vol. 1. Petrograd, 1917.
_____. *Nasha sakharnaia promyshlennost'.* St. Petersburg, 1908.
Liashchenko, P. I. *Istoriia narodnogo khoziaistva SSSR.* 3rd ed. Vol. 2. Moscow, 1952.
_____. "Kontragentskie dogovory 'Prodameta' kak orudie monopolisticheskoi politiki." *Istoricheskie zapiski* 20 (1946).
Lincoln, W. Bruce. "N. A. Miliutin and the St. Petersburg Municipal Act of 1846: A Study in Reform under Nicholas I." *Slavic Review* 33, no. 1 (1974).
_____. "The Russian State and Its Cities: A Search for Effective Municipal Government." *Jarhbücher für Geschichte Osteuropas* 17, no. 4 (1969).
Liubomirov, P. G. *Ocherki po istorii russkoi promyshlennosti.* Moscow-Leningrad, 1947.

Livshin, Ia. I. "Predstavitel'nye organizatsii krupnoi burzhuazii v Rossii v kontse XIX–nachale XX vv." *Istoriia SSSR*, no. 2 (1959).

Livshits, R. S. *Razmeshchenie promyshlennosti v dorevoliutsionnoi Rossii*. Moscow, 1955.

Lodyzhenskii, K. *Istoriia russkogo tamozhennogo tarifa*. St. Petersburg, 1886.

Loranskii, A. M. *Kratkii istoricheskii ocherk administrativnykh uchrezhdenii gornogo vedomstva v Rossii, 1700–1900 gg.* St. Petersburg, 1900.

Lukashevich, Stephen. *Ivan Aksakov, 1823–1886: A Study in Russian Thought and Politics*. Cambridge, Mass., 1965.

Lur'e, E. S. *Organizatsiia i organizatsii torgovo-promyshlennykh interesov v Rossii*. St. Petersburg, 1913.

Luxemburg, Rosa. *The Industrial Development of Poland*. New York, 1977.

McKay, John. *Pioneers for Profit, Foreign Enterpreneurs and Russian Industrialization, 1885–1913*. Chicago, 1970.

MacKenzie, David. *The Serbs and Russian Pan-Slavism*. Ithaca, 1967.

Marek, P. "K istorii evreev v Moskve." *Voskhod* 3 (1893).

———. "Moskovskoe getto." *Voskhod* 9 (1895), 10 (1896).

Markov, V. S. "K istorii raskola-staroobriadchestva vtoroi poloviny XIX stoletiia: Perepiska prof. N.I. Subbotina." *Chteniia Obshchestva istorii i drevnostei rossiiskikh*, vol. 1 (1915).

Martov, L., P. Maslov, and A. Potresov. *Obshchestvennoe dvizhenie v Rossii v nachale XX-go veka*. 3 vols. St. Petersburg, 1909.

Melgunov, S. P. *Staroobriadchestvo i osvoboditel'noe dvizhenoe*. Moscow, 1906.

Mel'nik, L. G. *Promyshlennyi perevorot na Ukraine v 60-e nachale 90-x godov XIX stoletiia, (avtoreferat)*. Kiev, 1972.

Meyer, A. W. *Human Generation: Conclusions of Burdach, Dollinger and von Baer*. Stanford, 1956.

Mikulinskii, S. R. *Razvitiia obshchikh problem biologii v Rossii*. Moscow, 1961.

Miliukov, P. N. *Istoriia vtoroi russkoi revoliutsii*. 2 vols. Sofia, 1921.

———. *Ocherki po istorii russkoi kultury*. 3 vols. 4th ed. St. Petersburg, 1905.

Milovidov, V. F. *Staroobriadchestvo v proshlom i nastoiashchem*. Moscow, 1969.

Missalowa, Gryzelda. *Studia nad powstaniem lodzkiewego okregu przemyslowego, 1815–1870*. Vol. 3. Lodz, 1975.

Mitel'man, M., B. Glebov, and A. Ul'ianskii. *Istoriia putilovskogo zavoda, 1780–1917*. 2nd edition. Moscow-Leningrad, 1941.

Mochulskii, Konstantin. *Vladimir Solov'ev: Zhizn' i uchenie*. Paris, 1951.

Moskovskoe kupecheskoe sobranie. *Istoricheskii ocherk*. Moscow, 1914.

Naidenov, N. *Moskovskaia birzha, 1839–1889*. Moscow, 1889.

Nifontov, A. S. "Formirovanie klassov burzhuaznogo obshchestva v russkom gorode vtoroi poloviny XIX v." *Istoricheskie zapiski* 54 (1955).

Nikitin, S. A. "Iuzhnoslavianskie sviazi russkoi periodicheskoi pechati 60-x godov XIX veka." Akademiia nauk, Institut slavianovedenie, *Uchenye zapiski*, vol. 6 (1952).

———. *Slavianskie komitety v Rossii v 1858–1876 godakh*. Moscow, 1960.

———. "Slavianskie s'ezdy shestidesiatykh godov XIX veka." In *Slavianskii sbornik: Slavianskii vopros i russkoe obshchestvo v 1867–1878 godakh*. Moscow, 1948.

Nikolskii, N. M. *Istoriia russkoi tserkvi*. Moscow-Leningrad, 1931.

Nisselovich, L. N. *Obshchedostupnye ocherki po russkomu torgovomu pravu*. St. Petersburg, 1893.

Nol'de, Baron B. E. *Piteinoe delo i aktsiznaia sistema*. St. Petersburg, 1882–83.

Novgorodtsev, Paul J. "Universities and Higher Technical Schools." In

Russian Schools and Universities in the World War. New Haven, 1929.
Novitskii, A. P. *Istoriia russkogo iskusstva*. Vol. 2. Moscow, 1903.
Novitskii, K. A.*Sbornik birzhevikh ukazanenii i ustavov birzh rossiiskoi imperii*. St. Petersburg, 1877.
Ogloblin, A. P. (Ohloblyn). *Ocherki Ukrainskoi fabriki: Predkapitalysticheskaia fabrika*. Kiev, 1925.
Ogorodnikov, S. F. *Ocherk istorii goroda Arkhangel'ska v torgovo-promyshlennom otnoshenii*. St. Petersburg, 1890.
Ostapenko, S. "Kapitalizm na Ukraini." In *Chervony Shlakh*. Kharkiv, 1924.
Owen, Thomas G. "The Moscow Merchants and the Public Press, 1858–1868." *Jahrbücher für Geschichte Osteuropas* 23, no. 1 (1975).
Pares, Sir Bernard. *My Russian Memoirs*. London, 1931.
Patouillet, J. *Ostrovskii et son théâtre de moeurs russes*. Paris, 1912.
Pavlenko, N. I. *Istoriia metallurgii v Rossii XVIII veka: zavody i zavodovladel'tsy*. Moscow, 1962.
———. "Iz istorii sotsial'no-ekonomicheskikh trebovanii russkoi burzhuazii vo vtoroi polovine XVIII v." *Istoricheskie zapiski* 59 (1950).
———. "Odvorianivanie russkoi burzhuazii v XVIII v." *Istoriia SSSR*, no. 2 (1961).
Pervaia Rossiiskaia Gosudarstvennaia Duma. Edited by N. Pruzhanskii. St. Petersburg, 1906.
Pinchuk, Ben-Cion. *The Octobrists in the Third Duma, 1907–1912*. Seattle, 1974.
Pintner, Walter. *Russian Economic Policy under Nicholas I*. Ithaca, 1967.
Pipes, Richard. "Catherine II and the Jews." *Soviet Jewish Affairs* 5, no. 2, (1975).
———. *Russia under the Old Regime*. New York, 1974.
———. *Social Democrats and the St. Petersburg Labor Movement, 1885–1897*. Cambridge, Mass., 1963.
———. *Struve: Liberal on the Left, 1870–1905*. Cambridge, Mass., 1970.
Pogrebinskii, A. P. "Voenno-promyshlennye komitety." *Istoricheskie zapiski*, no. 11 (1941).
Pokrovskii, M. N. *Russkaia istoriia s drevneishikh vremen*. 4 vols. Moscow, 1934.
Pokrovskii, S. A. *Vneshnaia torgovlia i vneshnaia politika Rossii*. Moscow, 1947.
Polianskii, F. Ia. *Pervonachal'noe nakoplenie kapitala v Rossii*. Moscow, 1958.
Portal, Roger. "Aux origines d'une bourgeoisie industrielle." *Revue d'histoire moderne, et contemporaine*, no. 1 (1961).
———. "The Industrialization of Russia." In *The Cambridge Economic History of Europe*. Vol. 6, pt. 2. Cambridge, 1965.
———. "Industriels moscovites: Le secteur cotonnier." *Cahiers du monde russe et soviétique*, nos. 1–2 (1962).
———. *L'Oural au XVIIIe siècle*. Paris, 1950.
Pososhkov, I. *Kniga o skudosti i bogatstve*. Edited by B. B. Kafengauz. Moscow, 1937.
Potolov, S. I. "Iz istorii monopolizatsii ugol'noi promyshlennosti Donbassa v kontse XIX v." In Akademiia nauk, Institut istorii, Leningradskoe otdelenie, *Iz istorii imperializma v Rossii*. Leningrad, 1959.
Prugavin, A. S. *Staroobriadchestvo vo vtoroi polovine XIX veka*. Moscow, 1904.
Przhetslavskii, O. A. "Kniaz' Kseverii Drutskoi-Liubetskii." *Russkaia starina* 21 (1878).
Pyliaeva, M. I. *Staryi Peterburg: Rasskazy iz byloi zhizni stolitsy*. St. Petersburg, 1887.
Rabinowitch, Alexander. *The Bolsheviks Come to Power*. New York, 1978.

———. *Prelude to Revolution*. Bloomington, 1968.

Radkey, Oliver. *The Agrarian Foes of Bolshevism*. New York, 1958.

Raeff, Marc. "The Style of Russia's Imperial Policy and Prince G. A. Potmekin." In *Statesmen and Statecraft of the Modern West: Essays in Honor of Dwight E. Lee and H. Donaldson Jordan*. Barre, Mass., 1967.

Rashin, A. G. *Formirovanie rabochego klassa Rossii*. Moscow, 1958.

———. *Naselenie Rossii za 100 let (1811–1913 gg.)*. Moscow, 1956.

Reikhardt, V. V. "Partiinye gruppirovki i 'predstavitel'stvo interesov' krupnogo kapitala v 1905–1906 godakh." *Krasnaia letopis'*, no. 6 (old series, 39) (1930).

Rerberg, I. *Moskovskii vodoprovod: Istoricheskii ocherk ustroistva i razvitiia vodosnabzheniia g. Moskvy*. Moscow, 1892.

Reshetar, John S. *The Ukrainian Revolution, 1917–1920*. Princeton, 1952.

Riasanovsky, Nicholas V. *Russia and the West in the Teaching of the Slavophils*. Cambridge, Mass., 1952.

Rieber, A. J. "Bureaucratic Politics in Imperial Russia." *Social Science History* 4 (1978).

———. "The Formation of La Grande Société des chemins de fer russes." *Jahrbücher für Geschichte Osteuropas* 21, no. 3 (1973).

———. *The Politics of Autocracy: Letters of Alexander II to Prince A. I. Bariatinskii, 1857–1864*. Paris and The Hague, 1966.

Riha, Thomas. "Miliukov and the Progressive Bloc in 1915: A Study in Last Chance Politics." *Journal of Modern History* 32 (1960).

Roosa, Ruth. "The Association of Industry and Trade, 1906–1914." Ph.D. dissertation, Columbia University, 1967.

———. "Russian Industrialists and 'State Socialism,' 1906–17." *Soviet Studies* 23, no. 3 (1972).

Rosenberg, William G. *Liberals in the Russian Revolution*. Princeton, 1974.

Rosovsky, Henry. "The Serf Entrepreneur in Russia." *Explorations in Entrepreneurial History* 6 (1953).

Rozhkova, M. K. *Ekonomicheskie sviazi Rossii so Srednei Aziei, 40-60-e gody XIX veka*. Moscow, 1963.

Rubin, V. N. "Rabochii vopros na s'ezdakh gornopromyshlennikov iuga Rossii." Moskovskii gosudarstvennyi pedagogicheskii institut im. V. I. Lenina, *Uchenye zapiski. Nekotorye problemy klassovoi bor'by v period kapitalizma*. Moscow, 1966.

Rubinshtein, N. L. "Ivan Egorovich Zabelin: Istoricheskie vozzreniia i nauchnaia deiatel'nost' (1820–1908)." *Istoriia SSSR*, no. 1 (1965).

———. "Ulozhennaia komissiia 1754–1766 i ee proekt novogo ulozheniia i o sostoianii poddannykh voobshche." *Istoricheskie zapiski* 38 (1951).

Rudoi, Ia. *Gosudarstvennyi kapitalizm v Rossii v gody imperialisticheskoi voiny*. Moscow-Leningrad, 1927.

Russkii biograficheskii slovar'. 25 vols. St. Petersburg, 1896–1918.

Rutkowski, Jan. *Historia Gospodarcza Polski*. Vol. 2. Poznan, 1950.

Ryndziunskii, P. G. "Gil'deiskaia reforma Kankrina 1824 goda." *Istoricheskie zapiski*, no. 40 (1952).

———. *Gorodskoe grazhdanstvo doreformennoi Rossii*. Moscow, 1951.

———. "Gorodskoe naselenie." In *Ocherki ekonomicheskoi istorii Rossii pervoi polviny XIX veka*. Moscow, 1959.

———. "Staroobriadcheskaia organizatsiia v usloviiakh razvitiia promyshlennogo kapitalizma po primere istorii Moskovskoi obshchiny fedoseevstev v 40-kh godakh XIX v." *Voprosy istorii religii i ateizma*, no. 1 (1950).

Sablinsky, Walter. *The Road to Bloody Sunday.* Princeton, 1976.
Sakulin, P. N. *Iz istorii russkogo idealizma: Kniaz' V. F. Odoevskii.* 2 vols. Moscow, 1913.
Schapiro, Leonard. "The Vekhi Group and the Mystique of Revolution." *Slavic and East European Review* 34 (1955).
Schneiderman, Jeremiah. *Sergei Zubatov and Revolutionary Marxism.* Ithaca, 1976.
Sef, S. E. *Burzhuaziia v 1905 godu.* Moscow-Leningrad, 1926.
Seletskii, V. N. "Obrazovanie partii progressistov." *Vestnik Moskovskogo universiteta (seriia istoriia)*, no. 5 (1970).
Semeniuk, G. F. "Bor'ba moskovskoi tekstil'noi burzhuazii za rynki, sbyta i ekonomicheskaia politika tsarizma v kontse XIX veka." Moskovskii gosudarstvennyi pedagogicheskii institut im. V. I. Lenina, *Uchenye zapiski: Nekotorye voprosy istorii Moskvy i Moskovskoi gubernii v xix–xx vv.* Moscow, 1964.
Shatsillo, K. F. "Formirovanie finansogo kapitala v sude stroitel'noi promyshlennosti iuga Rossii." In Akademiia nauk, Institut istorii, Leningradskoe otdelenie, *Iz istorii imperializma v Rossii.* Leningrad, 1959.
———. *Russkii imperializm i razvitie flota nakanune pervoi mirovoi voiny (1906–1914 gg.).* Moscow, 1968.
Shcherbatov, Prince. *General Fel'dmarshal Kniaz' Paskevich, ego zhizn' i deiatel'nosti.* Vol. 5, *1832–1847.* St. Petersburg, 1896.
Shchukin, P. I. "Iz vospominaniia P. I. Shchukina." *Russkii arkhiv* 50 (1912).
Shepelev, L. E. *Aktsionernye kompanii v Rossii.* Leningrad, 1973.
———. "Iz istorii russkogo aktsionernogo zakonodatel'stva." In *Vnutrennaia politika tsarizma (seredina XVI–nachale XX v.).* Leningrad, 1967.
Shershenevich, G. F. *Kurs torgovogo prava.* Kazan, 1892.
Shigalin, G. *Podgotovka promyshlennosti k voine.* Moscow, 1928.
Shpolianskii, D. I. *Monopolii ugol'no-metallurgicheskoi promyshlennosti iuga Rossii v nachale XX veka.* Moscow, 1953.
Shugurov, M. F. "Istoriia evreev v Rossii." *Russkii arkhiv* 32, pt. 2 (1894).
Shul'tse-Gevernits, G. V. *Krupnoe proizvodstvo v Rossii.* Moscow, 1899.
Shuster, I. A. "Ekonomicheskaia bor'ba Moskvy s Lodz'iu." *Istoricheskie zapiski*, no. 5 (1939).
Sidel'nikov, S. M. *Obrazovanie i deiatel'nost' pervoi gosudarstvennoi dumy.* Moscow, 1962.
Sidorov, A. L. *Ekonomicheskoe polozhenie Rossii v gody pervoi mirovoi voiny.* Moscow, 1973.
———. *Finansovoe polozhenie Rossii v gody pervoi mirovoi voiny.* Moscow, 1960.
Siegelbaum, Lewis H. "Moscow Industrialists and the War-Industries Committees During World War I." *Russian History* 5, pt. 1 (1978).
———. "The War Industries Committees and the Politics of Industrial Mobilization in Russia, 1915–17." Ph.D. thesis, Oxford, 1975.
Simonova, M. S. "Zemsko-liberal'naia fronda (1902–1903 gg.)." *Istoricheskie zapiski* 89 (1973).
Slabchenko, M. *Orhanizatisya khozyaystva Ukrainy.* 3 vols. Kharkiv, 1925.
Sliozberg, G. B. *Baron G. O. Gintsburg, ego zhizn' i deiatel'nosti.* Paris, 1933.
Smetanin, S. I. "Formirovanie klassovoi struktury gorodskogo naseleniia Rossii." *Istoricheskie zapiski*, no. 12 (1978).
Smirnov, P. P. *Posadskie liudi i ikh klassovaia bor'ba.* Moscow-Leningrad, 1947–48.
Smolenski, Leon. "Grinevetskii and Soviet Industry." *Survey* 13 (April 1968).

Sobolev, M. N. *Tamozhennaia politika Rossii vo vtoroi polovine XIX veka.* Tomsk, 1911.

Solov'ev, Iu. B. *Samoderzhavie i dvorianstvo v kontse XIX veka.* Leningrad, 1973.

Solov'ev, Iu. V. "Protivorechiia v praviashchem lagere Rossii po voprosu ob inostrannykh kapitalakh v gody pervogo promyshlennogo pod'ema." Akademiia nauk, Institut istorii, Leningradskoe otdelenie, *Iz istorii imperializma v Rossii.* Moscow-Leningrad, 1959.

Solov'ev, S. M. *Istoriia Rossii s drevneishikh vremen.* 2nd ed. St. Petersburg, n.d.

Solov'eva, A. M. *Zheleznodorozhnyi transport Rossii vo vtoroi polovine XIX v.* Moscow, 1975.

Starr, S. Frederick. *Decentralization and Self-Government in Russia, 1830–1870.* Princeton, 1972.

Stoplianskii, P. N. *Zhizn' i byt peterburgskoi fabriki za 210 let ee sushchestvovaniia, 1704–1914.* Leningrad, 1925.

Storozhev, V. N. *Istoriia moskovskogo kupecheskogo obshchestva, 1863–1913.* 5 vols. Moscow, 1913–1916.

_____. *Voina i Moskovskoe kupechestvo.* Moscow, 1914.

Sumner, B. H. *Russia and the Balkans, 1870–1880.* London, 1937.

Suny, Ronald G. "Russian Rule and Caucasian Society in the First Half of the Nineteenth Century: The Georgian Nobility and the Armenian Bourgeoisie, 1801–1956." *Nationalities Papers* 7, no. 1 (spring 1979).

Tager, P. S. "Soslovnaia organizatsiia advokatury." In *Istoriia russkoi advokatury,* edited by M. N. Gerbet. Vol. 2. Moscow, 1914.

Tarnovskii, K. N. *Sovetskaia istoriografiia rossiiskogo imperializma.* Moscow, 1974.

Tartakovskii, A. G. "Naselenie Moskvy v period frantsuzskoi okkupatsii 1812 g." *Istoricheskie zapiski* 92 (1973).

Tatarinov, L. E. *Zhurnal "Moskovskii Telegraf" (1825–1834).* Moscow, 1959.

Timofeev, A. G. *Istoriia S-Peterburgskoi birzhi, 1703–1903.* St. Petersburg, 1903.

Tsitovich, P. P. *Uchebnik torgovogo prava.* Kiev, 1900.

Tugan-Baranovskii, M. *The Russian Factory in the Nineteenth Century.* Translated by A. and C. Levin. Homewood, 1970.

Urwick, L., ed. *The Golden Book of Management.* London, 1956.

Valkenier, Elizabeth Kridl. "The Peredvizhniki and the Spirit of the 1860's." *Russian Review* 34, no. 3 (1975).

_____. *Russian Realist Art.* Ann Arbor, 1977.

Vartanov, G. L. "Kupechestvo i torguiushchee krest'ianstvo tsentral'noi chasti evropeiskoi Rossii vo vtoroi polovine XVIII veka." Leningradskii gosudarstvennyi pedogogicheskii institut im. Gertsena, *Uchenye Zapiski,* vol. 229 (1962).

Vassor, A., and G. Naan, eds. *Istoriia Estonskoi SSR.* Vol. 1. Tallinn, 1961.

Veselovskii, B. B. *Istoriia zemstva za sorok let.* Vols. 1–3. St. Petersburg, 1909–11.

Viatkin, M. P. *Gornozavodskii Ural v 1900–1917 gg.* Moscow-Leningrad, 1965.

Voblyi, K. G. *Ocherki po istorii pol'skoi fabrichnoi promyshlennosti.* Vol. 1, *1765–1830.* Kiev, 1909.

_____. *Opyt' istorii sveklosakharnoi promyshlennosti SSSR.* Vol. 1. Moscow, 1928.

Volkov M. Ia. "Tamozhennaia reforma 1775, 1757." *Istoricheskie zapiski* 71 (1962).

Volobuev, P. V. *Proletariat i burzhuaziia Rossii v 1917 g.* Moscow, 1964.

Volodarskaia, A. M. *Lenin i partiia v gody revoliutsionogo krizisa, 1913–1914.* Moscow, 1960.

von Laue, Theodore. *Sergei Witte and the Industrialization of Russia*. New York, 1963.

Voronkova, S. V. "Stroitel'stvo avtomobil'nykh zavodov v Rossii (1914–1917)." *Istoricheskie zapiski* 75 (1965).

Vovchik, A. F. *Politika tsarizma po rabochemu voprosu v predrevoliutsionnyi period (1895–1904)*. Lvov, 1964.

Vydaiushchiesia uchenye Gornogo instituta. Sbornik statei posviashchennykh 175-letiiu Gornogo instituta. 2 vols. Leningrad, 1948, 1951.

Walkin, Jacob. "The Attitude of the Tsarist Government toward the Labor Problem." *American Slavic and East European Review* 13, no. 2 (1954).

Wallace, Sir Donald Mackenzie. *Russia*. 2 vols. London, 1905.

Walsh, Warren B. "The Composition of the Dumas." *Russian Review* 18, no. 2 (1949).

Welsh, D. J. "Satirical Themes in Eighteenth Century Russian Comedies." *Slavonic and East European Review* 42 (June 1964).

West, James L. "The Moscow Progressists: Russian Industrialists in Liberal Politics, 1905–1914." Ph.D. dissertation, Princeton University, 1974.

White, James D. "Moscow, Petersburg and the Russian Industrialists." *Soviet Studies* 24, no. 3 (1973).

Yaney, George. *The Systematization of Russian Government*. Urbana, 1973.

Zablotskii-Desiatovskii, A. P. *Graf P. D. Kiselev i ego vremia*. Vol. 4. St. Petersburg, 1882.

Zagorsky, S. O. *State Control of Industry in Russia During the War*. New Haven, 1928.

Zaionchkovskii, P. A. *Provedenie v zhizn' krest'ianskoi reformy 1861 g*. Moscow, 1958.

_____. *Rossiiskoe samoderzhavie v kontse XIX stoletie*. Moscow, 1970.

Zakharova, L. G. *Zemskaia kontrreforma 1890 g*. Moscow, 1968.

Zaklund, Georgi. *G. P. Kamenev (1772–1803): Opyt' imushchestvennoi kharakteristiki pervogo russkogo romantika*. Kazan, 1926.

Zelnik, Reginald. *Labor and Society in Tsarist Russia*. Vol. 1. Stanford, 1971.

Zenkovsky, Serge. "The Ideological World of the Denisov Brothers." *Harvard Slavic Studies* 3 (1957).

Zimmerman, Judith. "The Political Views of the Vekhi Authors." *Canadian and American Slavic Studies* 10, no. 3 (1976).

Zlotnikov, M. F. *Kontinental'naia blokada i Rossiia*. Moscow-Leningrad, 1966.

Works of a Theoretical and Comparative Nature

Anderson, Perry. *Lineages of the Absolutist State*. London, 1974.

Bottomore, T. B. *Classes in Modern Society*. New York, 1966.

Cochran, Thomas C. *Social Change in Industrial Society in 1972*. London, 1972.

Daumard, Adeline. *La Bourgeoisie parisienne de 1815 à 1848*. Paris, 1963.

Dumont, Louis. *Homo hierarchicus*. Paris, 1966.

Geertz, Clifford. *Peddlars and Princes*. Chicago, 1963.

Goffman, Erving. *The Presentation of Self in Everyday Life*. New York, 1959.

Kilby, Peter, ed. *Entrepreneurship and Economic Development*. New York, 1971.

Korkunov, N. M. *Russkoe gosudarstvennoe pravo*. St. Petersburg, 1914.

Kroeber, Alfred. "Caste." In *Encyclopedia of the Social Sciences*. Vol. 3. New York, 1932.

La Question de la "bourgeoisie" dans le monde hispanique au XIXe siècle: Colloque international. Bordeaux, 1973.

Lhomme, Jean. *La Grande Bourgeoisie au pouvoir, 1830–1880*. Paris, 1960.

Merton, Robert. *Social Theory and Social Structure*. New York, 1968.

Mörner, Magnus. *Race Mixture in the History of Latin America*. Boston, 1969.

Nisbet, Robert A. *Social Change and History: Aspects of Western Theory of Development*. New York, 1969.

Schumpeter, Joseph A. *The Theory of Economic Development*. Cambridge, Mass., 1934.

INDEX

with workers, 127–29, 261–66, 390, 395. *See also* Armenian merchantry; Baltic German merchantry; Bureaucracy, relations with merchantry; Central Asian merchantry; Exchange associations; Foreign merchants; Great Russian merchantry; Greek merchantry; Guilds; Intelligentsia, relations with merchantry; Jewish merchantry; Moscow entrepreneurial group; Old Believers; Polish merchantry; Soslovie; Tatar merchantry; Textiles

Merton, Robert, 148, 399

Meshchanstvo, xxiii, xxv, 14, 17, 30, 50, 51, 57, 84, 85, 88, 89, 96, 99, 101, 140, 261, 272, 280, 332, 415, 426

Meshcherskii, V. P., 25n, 28, 95, 147, 186

Meshcherskii, A. P.: member of St. Petersburg financial oligarchy, 374, 375, 381, 411

Metallurgical cartel, 340–45

Metalworking. *See* Factories; Kustar industries

Middle class. *See* Bourgeoisie

Mikhail Nikolaevich, Grand Duke, 69

Military supplies, manufacturing of. *See* Factories

Miliukov, P. N., 278, 280, 297, 312, 325, 394, 395, 404n

Miliutin, D. M., 188, 208, 212

Minerals: 37, 64–65, 116–17, 219–20, 222–43, 366, 367, 403–4; potash, 6; Salt, 6, 41, 64, 160; lead, 11; iron, 21, 37, 41, 64, 75, 117, 189, 220, 222–43, 341, 403, 404, 406; copper, 37, 41, 298; zinc, 64; steel works, 66, 75, 227–43, 343; alum, 118; gold, 150; oil, 161, 250–51, 364

Ministries: Interior, 95, 103, 368, 418; State Domains, 158; Transportation, 174, 187, 238, 239, 418; Foreign Affairs, 208; Education, 322; Trade and Industry, 331, 337, 359, 370, 383, 407, 408, 412, 417; Naval, 251, 369; Agriculture, 401, 418; Labor, 406, 407, 412; Justice, 418. *See also* Finance, Ministry of

Mirnoobnovlentsy. *See* Party of Peaceful Renewal

Moderate Progressives, 274, 314, 316, 317, 318, 319, 351

Monopolies: state, 6, 280, 387; industrial, 6, 114–15, 210, 227, 228, 230, 232, 240–43, 250–51, 316, 334–35, 354, 369–71. *See also* Prodamet; Prodarud; Prodparvoz; Produgol; Prodvagon

Morozov, A. A.: founder of Abramovich branch of family, entrepreneur and patron, 307

Morozov, D. I.: patron of *Russkoe obozrenie*, 184, 185

Morozov, E. V.: member of Moscow entrepreneurial group, 287

Morozov, I. A.: member of Moscow entrepreneurial group, 308, 311, 312, 317

Morozov, N. D.: member of Moscow entrepreneurial group, 287, 297n, 307, 310, 322, 331, 404

Morozov, Savva T.: patron, 167, 251, 299; member of Moscow entrepreneurial group, 310

Morozov, Sergei T., 185, 262; patron, 167; member of Moscow entrepreneurial group, 308, 309, 312, 314

Morozov, S. V.: founder of family, 161

Morozov, T. S., 108, 109, 115, 205; member of Moscow entrepreneurial group, 152, 175, 180–81, 182, 183n, 201, 212; textile manufacturer, 162, 210; patron, 167; railroad entrepreneur, 190, 236; banker, 192; member of pressure group, 203, 208, 211; related by marriage to Krestovnikovs, 269

Morozova, A. T.: patroness, 167

Morozova, M. K.: patroness, 307

Morozov family, 49, 114, 143, 147, 152, 161–62, 165, 166, 167, 199, 201, 204n, 285, 294, 299–308 passim, 310

Moscow Agricultural Society, 118

Moscow Architecture Society, 291

Moscow Art Theater, 166, 167

Moscow Censorship Committee, 216

Moscow Commercial School, 30, 36, 125, 287

Moscow Conservatory, 169, 205, 298

Moscow Council of Trade and Industry, 116

Moscow Ecclesiastical Academy, 167, 216

Moscow entrepreneurial group, xxv, 113–218, 285–332, 333, 335, 336, 337, 380, 384, 407, 411, 422, 424; membership, first generation, 153–65, 216–18,